BLOOD, TEARS,
and GLORY

BLOOD, TEARS, *and* GLORY

How Ohioans Won the Civil War

James H. Bissland

ORANGE FRAZER PRESS

WILMINGTON, OHIO

ISBN 978-1933197-05-0

Orange Frazer Press
P.O. Box 214, Wilmington, OH 45177
Telephone 1.800.852.9332 for price and shipping information.
www.orangefrazer.com

Cover design Kristen Schade *&* Chad DeBoard
Interior design & formatting Kristen Schade

Cover—Gen. William Tecumseh Sherman was just one of Ohio's contributions to Union leadership in the Civil War. His face was "the picture of grim-faced war," according to an aide to General-in-Chief Ulysses S. Grant, another Ohioan. The image above Sherman shows an attack made by his forces at Vicksburg on May 19, 1863.

page 8—Lincoln's most important leaders in the war, all from Ohio, were (clockwise, from upper left): General-in-Chief Ulysses S. Grant; Maj. Gen. William Tecumseh Sherman, who was Grant's commander of military operations in the Western Theater 1864-5; Maj. Gen. Philip H. Sheridan, Grant's cavalry commander, and Edwin M. Stanton, secretary of war.

Library of Congress Cataloging-in-Publication Data

Bissland, James.
  Blood, tears, and glory : how Ohioans won the Civil War / by James Hope Bissland.
     p. cm.
  Includes bibliographical references and index.
  ISBN 978-1-933197-05-0
  1. United States--History--Civil War, 1861-1865--Anecdotes. 2. United States--History--Civil War, 1861-1865--Biography--Anecdotes. 3. Ohio--History--Civil War, 1861-1865--Anecdotes. 4. Ohio--History--Civil War, 1861-1865--Biography--Anecdotes. 5. Soldiers--Ohio--Biography--Anecdotes. 6. Generals--United States--Biography--Anecdotes. I. Title.
  E655.B593 2007
  973.7092'2771--dc22
                                    2007023637

To my bright and beautiful children

Sarah   Betsy   Andrew   Daniel

Each of whom has given me far more

than they will ever know

 IT IS THE DEAD
NOT THE LIVING,
WHO MAKE THE LONGEST DEMANDS.
WE DIE FOREVER.

Antigone

❧ CONTENTS

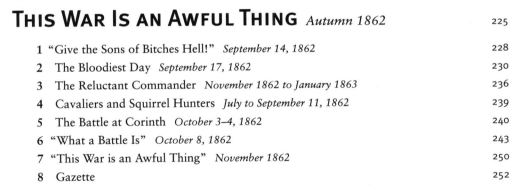

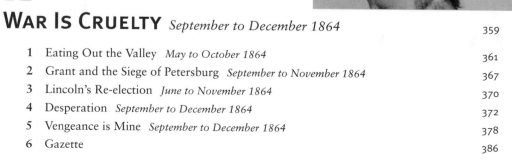

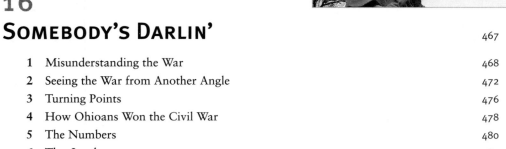

❧ FOREWORD

You may not realize how close this country came to destroying itself. Most Americans don't. I didn't, and I've been a student of American history much of my life. And yet, the America we think we know, the country for which we claim so much—superpower, world's best hope for democracy, sweet land of liberty, and all the rest—this remarkable country of ours with its promise of the American Dream for everyone could have died at the hands of its own people.

But it didn't. It didn't because the great Civil War threatening it turned out to be the most important event of the United States since the Constitution, instead of its last. It didn't because the war and its aftermath proved that, ultimately, the "mystic chords of memory" (in Lincoln's words) that hold us together are stronger than any force that tries to divide us.[1] It didn't because, in a struggle for the common good, ordinary people rose up to do extraordinary things, leaving their farms and offices, and shops and schoolrooms, and comfortable routines for lives of deprivation and danger, lives that sometimes ended all too soon.

And that made the men and women of the Civil War era one of our greatest generations. Tom Brokaw told us the Americans of World War II were "the Greatest Generation," as if there was only one. That's wrong. We've had more than one: the one Brokaw celebrated, of course, and, more than two centuries ago, the generation of Founding Fathers and their shirt-sleeved Minute Men (and remember the ladies!) who fought the world's greatest empire to a standstill and won our independence. And—not all that long ago, in the deep mystery of time—we had the generation of our ancestors who fought and won a terrible civil war. That they shed so much blood and so many tears to keep this one nation, indivisible, makes their generation one of the greatest. That they did it on behalf of liberty and justice for all makes it glorious as well.

—JAMES BISSLAND

Whatever Grant's failures in his previous life, when thrust by circumstance into the military sphere, he entered a realm in which his touch was complete.

INTRODUCTION

Sometimes it seemed as if the nation had split in half, the old sense
of common purpose gone, replaced by two countries with the same
name. One America, mostly quiet, rural, and sure of its goodness,
was proudly conservative and revered the values of the past. The other
America was more urban and industrialized, disputatious, and irreverent.
It considered itself progressive and looked to the future. The conservative
America was firmly rooted in the South, while the other America was
populated mostly by Northerners. After years of suspicion, fear, and
name-calling between the two Americas, the United States—united more
in name than fact—teetered on the edge of violence. It was April 1861.

IN the town of Galena, Illinois, in the spring of 1861 there lived a man
who had failed at almost everything except for one thing. Midway
through each day he would leave the leather goods store where he was a clerk
and tramp up a steep hillside to his small, rented house for a meal with his
family. Every night he would return to play with his four children and read
out loud to his wife, Julia. He spent little time elsewhere, had only a few
friends, and even after a year in Galena thought himself "a comparative
stranger."[1] He treasured his time at home, for his only real success in adult
life had been to marry the woman he loved and raise a family.

This was Ulysses S. Grant, a broad-chested, stolid man of few words and
no great height, reduced at age thirty-eight to what must have seemed his last,
best chance in life. Born and raised in southern Ohio, son of a tanner, he had
glumly attended West Point because his father willed it. In 1843 young Grant
began an army career with no enthusiasm. Stationed far from home, lonely,
and still a junior officer after eleven years of service, he drank to ease the pain
and in 1854 resigned, possibly to escape a court martial for drunkenness.[2]

Almost penniless, the civilian Grant rejoined his family near St. Louis,
Missouri, "to commence, at the age of thirty-two, a new struggle for our
support."[3] The struggle would last six years and be fruitless. Grant failed
at farming, could not make a go of selling real estate, and was passed over

for a position with the county government. Finally, he humbled himself
to ask his father for a job—signifying he couldn't support a family on his own.
In April 1860 Ulysses and Julia Grant and their four children left St. Louis and,
led by Ulysses wearing his old army coat and lugging the family's chairs, arrived
by steamboat in the northwestern Illinois town of Galena.

For the next year, ex-Captain Grant led the humdrum life of a clerk,
waiting for a partnership in a store managed by his two younger brothers
and owned by his absentee father, now living in Covington, Kentucky, across
the Ohio River from Cincinnati. Every day he trudged the steep hillsides
of Galena from home to store and back again. Occasionally he traveled the
surrounding territory on store business, finding the rising tensions between
North and South discussed wherever he went. Grant would listen quietly
and now and then speak, measuring out the words as if he were putting
money on the table, stopping exactly when he had spent enough.

One day someone said, "There's a great deal of bluster about these
Southerners, but I don't think there's much fight in them." Grant—who had
married a woman with Southern roots and knew a great deal about them—
replied concisely. Southerners liked to "bluster," he agreed, but he warned,
"[I]f they ever get at it, they will make a strong fight." One more thing:
"[E]ach side underestimates the other and overestimates itself."[4]

There was something about this quiet man that commanded respect,
but to his listeners he was no more than a clerk who had once been in the army.
In three years, he would command all of the nation's armies. In eight years
he would be president of the United States.

A year after Grant left the St. Louis area, a tall, lanky, talkative man with
red hair arrived in the city. He, too, had been born in Ohio and attended
West Point, graduating three years before Grant. Like Grant, he had become
an army captain, but then he married and left the service. His father had named
him Tecumseh in the hope that he would become a great warrior, but by April
1861 William Tecumseh Sherman's only battle was with boredom. Trained
to be a military officer, he now, at age forty-one, was running a horse-car line.

Sherman's civilian career had paid more than Grant's, but was just as filled
with roadblocks and dead-ends. He had managed the San Francisco branch
of a St. Louis bank until the bank gave up on it. A real estate law venture
in Kansas failed. Next, army friends helped Sherman win the job, in 1859,
of superintending the newly established Louisiana State Seminary and Military
Academy (today's Louisiana State University). But within a year and a half

Louisiana seceded from the Union, putting Sherman's loyalties to the test. Sherman liked Southerners and he liked his job, but he was a loyal Union man, so he resigned and returned north in March 1861.

On his way home, Sherman was introduced to the newly inaugurated president, Abraham Lincoln. A jocular remark by Lincoln offended the highly sensitive Sherman, a man as tightly wound and delicately balanced as a watch spring. He went huffing back to Lancaster, Ohio, to pick up his wife and five children, who, after more than a year, he still had not brought to Louisiana. The Sherman marriage was less serene than Grant's, for the tirelessly Catholic Eleanor (called "Ellen") Ewing Sherman had dedicated herself to bringing her husband into the faith, while he was just as dedicated to remaining unchurched.

Once again, friendship helped Sherman get a new job, this time as president of the Fifth Street Railroad in St. Louis. Except for the title, with salary to match, it wasn't much of a job; the horse-car line was already up and running smoothly. As Sherman remembered it, "[A]ll I had to do was to watch the economical administration of existing affairs."[5] And so, in April 1861, as Civil War loomed, the man with the name of a famous Indian warrior was not preparing for battle but making sure the horse cars kept plodding on their endless rounds. Eventually, his fame as a general would rival Grant's, and for years after the war he would have to fend off urgings to run for president.

IN the nation's capital, seven hundred miles from Galena and St. Louis, a third Ohio-born man was drumming his fingers and fuming during April 1861. Short, pudgy, myopic, and asthmatic, he was a brilliant lawyer known for his bad temper. Until Lincoln's inauguration, he had been the nation's attorney general. In the hapless Buchanan administration he had been the smartest man in the room. With the change of administrations from Buchanan's to Lincoln's, however, he had been returned to the sidelines.

The man was forty-six-year-old Edwin McMasters Stanton, a lifelong Democrat who did not fit the Democratic stereotype, for he was strongly pro-Union and thoroughly opposed to slavery. Faced with the prospect of the South seceding while a fractured Democratic administration argued with itself, Attorney General Stanton had been forced to choose among his loyalties. As the nation slipped into chaos while Buchanan dithered, Stanton had secretly begun subverting his own president.

Openly, Stanton worked to stiffen Buchanan's wobbly backbone in defense of the Union, but unbeknownst to the president he was passing inside information to the Republican opposition in Congress. When he could, Stanton also sabotaged efforts by disloyal Cabinet members to secretly divert the nation's military resources to the nascent Confederacy.

Now, in April 1861, Buchanan was gone, replaced on Inauguration Day the month before by Abraham Lincoln—and former Attorney General Stanton was growing angrier by the day. Contrary to Stanton's expectations, the new Republican president was making conciliatory noises toward the South. Expected to act decisively for the Union, Lincoln seemed to be temporizing, and that made Stanton even madder at Lincoln than he had been at Buchanan. "There is no settled principle or line of action," he complained of the new administration. "What but disgrace and disaster can happen?"[6] But Stanton's opportunity for a settled principle would come soon enough.

Stanton's irritability drew from a deep well of tragedy and loss, aggravated by severe asthma. While Stanton was living in Ohio, his fifteen-month-old daughter, Lucy, died in 1841, followed in less than three years by his beloved wife, Mary. Then, in 1846, Stanton's brother Darwin cut his own throat—"The blood spouted up to the ceiling," a doctor recalled.[7]

So many losses in so short a time changed Stanton's personality, replacing a hearty good humor with a brusque, even rude, intensity. He moved to Pittsburgh, lost himself in legal work, and turned into a ferocious litigator. Andrew Carnegie, then only a telegraph messenger boy, recalled Stanton was "ever deeply serious."[8] The Ohio-born lawyer re-married, this time to a much younger woman, Ellen Hutchison. A member of a prominent Pittsburgh family, Hutchinson matched Stanton in aloofness.

In 1856, the Stantons moved to Washington, where Stanton had a growing clientele. After solving some legal problems for the Buchanan government, Stanton was appointed attorney general in 1860. Until Lincoln's ascension to the presidency the next year, Stanton was the nation's top lawyer, recognized in high circles. But only a name, and little known at that, to most Americans.

So it was, on the eve of the Civil War, that Ulysses S. Grant in his old army coat silently trudged the hills of Galena while William Tecumseh Sherman idled in his St. Louis office, and Edwin McMasters Stanton smoldered in Washington. All had been born in Ohio within the span of a generation, but didn't know each other. Few outside their own circles knew them either, and, for that matter, with their depths unplumbed, they scarcely knew or understood themselves. They had been traveling bumpy roads from plain beginnings and, having been tested but little for greatness, seemed unlikely candidates for it.

And yet, by the end of the war, they could be called saviors of the nation, three of the four most important leaders who saved a threatened America and the promise it held out to everyone. All came from the region known then simply as "the West," which we know today as the Midwest. The fourth of these rescuers was Abraham Lincoln of Illinois, yet another obscure Midwesterner, a gawky rube ("I am, in height, six feet, four inches, nearly; lean in flesh"), and the man with the plainest beginning of all.[9]

Proof for all time that any boy can grow up to be president in this land of opportunity, the story of Lincoln's rise from rail-splitting poverty to national father figure, may be, as one historian has said, "the great American story."[10] But there are others.

Novelist Allan Gurganus calls his fellow Southerners "championship grudge-bearers," but points out, "True, we lost once, big-time. But our concession prize? The stories."[11] Take those tales—many romanticized, some bitter—that Southerners tell about the Civil War, add the fascination many of us have with Eastern battles like Gettysburg, and the examined result is this: we've missed some of the most important stories of the Civil War. Among them are true accounts of how the Civil War was decided mostly west, not east, of the Appalachians, how rough-hewn, hard-to-discipline "Westerners"—especially those from the sister states of Ohio, Indiana, and Illinois—did the fighting that made the difference, and how Western commanders finally had to go east to finish the war the Easterners couldn't.

To fight this war came the citizen-soldiers—in one Midwestern state alone, Ohio, 300,000 men, roughly one of every ten citizens, participated. Another 450,000 came from Ohio's sisters, Indiana and Illinois, meaning these three raw-boned, relatively young and still-developing states by themselves supplied a fourth of the Union's soldiers.[12] They came from every corner of their states and from every walk of life, putting down their law books and ledgers, pens and plows to become colonels and captains and sergeants and ordinary infantrymen for three or four years. They streamed off farms and out of offices, shops, and classrooms to wear uniforms for the first time in their lives and learn war the hardest, most dangerous way: on the battlefield. They encountered lives of hardship unimaginable by our modern high-tech, well-supplied military. The men of the Civil War ate gut-grinding food (and sometimes didn't even have that), drank bilious water, and frequently slept on the ground. They went unwashed for weeks, wore ragged, faded clothing, sometimes marched shoeless, and most of the time were infested with lice.

For all that, the privates were paid $13 a month, if they even got it on time. But they were sustained by wives and sweethearts and mothers and sisters and children and all those who nursed the sick and wounded or wrote the letters and packed the food parcels and held the soldiers in their hearts. And they were sustained by a great sense of purpose: this was a citizen's fight to save their country, a sacred cause that would take almost every ounce of energy the nation had. It was not war on the cheap.

The Unionists of the 1860s believed, first of all, that this was one nation, indivisible, a place unique in world history, illuminated by the Enlightenment, created by and for all the people, not just the privileged. For the South to reject that and deny, by their breaking away, what so many had worked and fought so hard to create was wrong. "The cause of America," Thomas Paine wrote in his commonsensical way more than 230 years ago, "is in a great measure the cause of a mankind," and a century and half before that, John Winthrop famously told us we were a city upon a hill.[13]

In their schools, political arenas, and cultural artifacts, the Americans of 1860 were endlessly reminded of the greatness of their forefathers and how they had made a land that was like no other, a beacon for the world. And, for the sake of all mankind, Unionists believed and the Confederates denied, the United States *had* to be defended.

There was something else, something that made that city upon a hill possible and kept its light shining. The generator of the American ideal, the wellspring of the American Dream, is the "equality promise" the Founding Fathers had made in the Declaration of Independence and of which Lincoln kept reminding everyone: All men are created equal, endowed with certain inalienable rights, among them life, liberty, and the pursuit of happiness. Burdened with inherited prejudices and occupied with their chores, most nineteenth-century Americans did not so much understand the equality promise as sense it, meaning in its most elemental terms, "I am a free man in the land of opportunity."

In time, though, with the help of the Railsplitter, Americans would come to understand the equality promise applied to others, and most immediately it meant this: slavery, human bondage, the owning of one human being by another, not only was inhumane, but also a denial of the promise of America, and it had to be ended.

In 1853 a Northern senator whose sentiments lay Southerly declared, in sneering tones, that the phrase "all men are created equal" was not a "self-evident truth," but "a self-evident lie." Rising to answer, Sen.

Benjamin F. Wade of Ohio thundered, "The great declaration cost our forefathers too dear to be lightly thrown away by their children."[14]

And it would not. We of the twenty-first century have been disappointed by too many leaders to quickly remember there was a time when millions of Americans volunteered not only to defend the nation but also, implicitly, to keep the equality promise. They risked their lives, their health, and their futures to protect the nation and the covenant it had made with them … and us. And that may be the greatest American story of all.

BLOOD, TEARS, *and* GLORY

How Ohioans Won
the Civil War

John Brown, leaving jail and on his way to be hanged, pauses to kiss a black child, according to this propaganda picture. (It never happened.)

1

THE BALL OPENS

December 1859 to mid-April 1861

Hard feelings between America's North and South had been building
for decades, but they broadened and deepened in the year and half before
the Civil War. However, the spark igniting the powder trail to war didn't come
from the old states of the industrializing North or the plantation country
of the South. It came from the West.

The America of the 1850s, the Northern states especially, was a chest-
thumping, knee-slapping, jim-dandy, sockdologer kind of a place, a place
where a man had the freedom and the elbow room to do what he wanted
and, if he had enough gumption, find a fortune under the earth or on the
land or over the seas. Old Europe could have its castles, kings, and queens.
America, the land of opportunity, the place where all men were created equal,
was raising things, making things, selling things. And right in the middle was
Ohio, its third largest state.

Growing furiously for much of the century, Ohio gushed wheat, corn,
and wool; had treasuries of coal, iron ore, and oil under its feet; was laced
together by the most railroad track of any state; and was raising new industries
like pups.[1] As they liked to say when railroads were still wondrous creations,
and the fastest things around, Ohioans were "going to beat the cars."

And most Ohioans, like most Americans, had been trying to act
as if nothing were wrong.

John Brown rode to his execution in a light delivery wagon, admiring the scenery along the way while seated on his own coffin.

JOHN BROWN'S BODY

December 2, 1859: one year, four months, and ten days before the outbreak of the Civil War ...

The old man, riding in a wagon with his arms bound at the elbows, sat on his coffin and admired the passing scenery.[2]

"This *is* a beautiful country," he said, fixing his hard eyes on the landscape of fertile fields and meadows, dotted with farmhouses, that melted away to the Blue Ridge Mountains of western Virginia.[3] It was a vista swathed in the unseasonably warm gauze of a hazy morning in early December 1859. "I never had the pleasure of seeing it before," added the man, who had spent much of his life on the plainer landscape of northeastern Ohio.[4]

Then John Brown's wagon and its armed escort arrived at the gallows that had been built for him in a field on the edge of Charles Town. For a moment, Brown stared intently at the scaffolding. He was a tall man with a prominent nose and forehead, his dark hair flecked with gray, his beard white. He stepped down from the wagon and strode briskly, almost eagerly, up the steps to where he would be hanged. "His movements & manner gave no evidence of his being either terrified or concerned," a watcher commented later.[5]

The scaffolding had been built on a small rise and was surrounded with a fence guarded by mounted men. Inside the fence were rows of Virginia militia and military cadets, arranged in a hollow square. The small number of carefully screened spectators included a thirty-year-old newspaperman from Cincinnati named Murat Halstead. Raised to be a farmer (and named for a French general named Murat), Halstead had decided he'd rather be a newsman and had become known throughout the West for his writing.[6] Outside newsmen weren't welcome at this strictly Southern event, but the enterprising Halstead had used prestigious letters of introduction to finagle admission.[7]

With anxiety similar to what Americans felt after the 9/11 attacks in 2001, Virginia officials had put law officers on heightened alert, were checking trains for suspicious passengers, and subjecting strangers to unusual scrutiny. Townspeople were told to stay home on the day of the execution.[8] Cavalry patrols scoured the surrounding countryside, "apparently anxiously looking for the anticipated rescue," Halstead wrote.[9] An obscure army officer named Robert E. Lee supervised the guarding of access routes to Charles Town.[10] All together, upwards of 1,500 men had been summoned from throughout Virginia to safeguard the execution.[11]

By his armed attacks on the institution of slavery—most recently, a fatally flawed raid at nearby Harpers Ferry—John Brown had aroused dangerous passions in America, especially in the South. In a rushed trial a month before, Brown had been found guilty of treason against the Commonwealth of Virginia (although Brown wasn't a citizen of Virginia), conspiring with slaves to rebel, and murder.[12] Fears of a violent attempt to free him were

The wagon in which John Brown rode to his death is in a museum in Charles Town, West Virginia, a few miles from Harpers Ferry.

well founded. Brown's friends had proposed the very thing, but the old man had a better idea. He had come to appreciate the power of martyrdom. "I am worth now infinitely more to die than to live," he said.[13]

Wearing, according to Halstead, a "battered black slouch hat, the rim turned up squarely in front … a baggy brown coat and trousers, and red carpet slippers over blue yarn socks," Brown waited calmly on the platform.[14] By now, the sun was high in the sky. The condemned man stood stiffly erect, staring ahead with the sun's fire lighting his face, as the jailer, John Avis, put the noose around his neck.[15] The rope had been made of cotton and contributed by cotton planters in a gesture they considered grandly symbolic.

Then Avis covered Brown's head with a white hood, taking extra time to fasten it with a pin when it flapped in the warm breeze. When the jailer asked Brown to "move ahead," the old man replied, "You will have to guide me." He refused the offer of a handkerchief to drop as a signal that he was ready, saying only, "Be quick."[16]

Among those present were a rising young actor named John Wilkes Booth and the "gaunt, severe figure" (in Halstead's words) of a professor from the Virginia Military Institute, a "stern man" named Thomas J. Jackson, later to become famous as "Stonewall."[17] Jackson commanded a contingent of V.M.I. cadets detailed for guard duty at the hanging. The smartly attired cadets wore specially purchased uniforms: gray trousers and scarlet shirts crisscrossed with white bandoliers.[18]

Joining the cadets to watch Brown die was an older man, a strange fellow who, out of fashion for his time, shaved his face but let his long white hair fall to his shoulders. He was a Virginian named Edmund Ruffin. Ruffin had acquired some prestige as an agricultural scientist and one of the Southern hotheads called "fire-eaters," so he had been allowed to don a cadet's uniform and share their view of the proceedings.

The nervous boy-soldiers ("bright boys" and "gay youths," reporter Halstead called them) were amused to have the sixty-five-year-old Ruffin in their ranks. He had chatted briefly with them to ease the tension. Then he turned his gaze to the man on the scaffolding, a man who stood for all Ruffin hated and who now was about to die.[19]

By Halstead's account, nearly eighteen long minutes passed with the only sounds the shuffling of the soldiers' feet and the orders barked by officers as they fine-tuned ranks for the sacramental moment. "The suspense was distressing," Halstead wrote, but "only Brown's hands betrayed any emotion: he was rubbing his thumbs hard but slowly on the inside of his forefingers, between the first and second joints."[20] Finally an officer shouted, "We are ready," and civilian officials left the platform, leaving Brown standing "as motionless as … a statue."[21]

As the crowd hushed, the sheriff used a hatchet to cut the rope holding the platform under Brown. With "a sharp twang of the rope [and] a creaking of the hinges of the trap door," the old man plummeted down, the rope halting him with a savage jerk that made his arms fly up from the elbows. "As he dropped, he turned sharply round and faced North," Halstead wrote.[22] The body shivered convulsively, then stopped and swung gently "like a pendulum" in the warm southern breeze.[23] John Wilkes Booth, a civilian who, like Edmund Ruffin, had wangled himself a uniform and a place in the ranks, suddenly paled, felt faint, and wished for a bracing drink of whiskey.[24]

In what some might call an omen, the pleasantly warm weather turned cold and snowy by the next morning. Hail fell in the region.[25] But even more ominous storm clouds were billowing the North and South, for, just as Brown had hoped, his death stirred a fury of emotions. A feeling of triumph at Brown's death swept the South. A Savannah newspaper exulted over the end of "the notorious horse thief, murderer, insurrectionist and traitor." It insisted that "thousands of white-cravated necks in New England and the Northern States" deserved the same fate.[26] Booth, his equilibrium restored, thought abolitionists like Brown were "the *only* traitors in the land," but he also told his sister, "He was a brave old man."[27] However, Southerners

On a warm, hazy morning in December 1859, John Brown died on a gallows in a field guarded by hundreds of Virginia militiamen and military cadets.

feared Brown's attack might only have been the first, with more to come. In months to come, their fears would grow into panic.

Northern opinion was mixed. Some Northerners dismissed Brown as insane and some—such as Democratic presidential hopeful Stephen A. Douglas—agreed that Brown deserved execution for his crimes. Abraham Lincoln admired Brown's "great courage" and "unselfishness," but could not excuse "violence, bloodshed, and treason."[28] But other Northerners, their sympathies aroused by Brown's courage in the face of death, were outraged. They fired salutes, tolled bells, and held meetings commemorating a man they now considered a martyr to the anti-slavery cause.

Many Ohioans paid tribute to Brown. In Hudson, where he had lived, and in other towns throughout the strongly anti-slavery Western Reserve region in northeastern Ohio, hundreds attended memorial services. In Cleveland, a banner was suspended over the street with Brown's words: "I cannot better serve the cause I love than to die for it."[29] An evening meeting called in Brown's memory attracted 1,500 persons to a Cleveland hall draped in black.[30]

There were individual protests. The *Cleveland Herald* reported that a Professor Kirtland had furled the national flag and entwined it with black crepe on the "liberty pole" in front of his house. On the pole was an inscription: "When our citizens are hanged for attempting to carry out the principles of the Declaration of Independence … it is meet that the people shall mourn."[31]

A church in Oberlin set aside the afternoon of Brown's execution as a time of public prayer to "implore for the family of this Christian Hero and Martyr; and for the enslaved, and for our nation, a speedy delivery from the withering curse of 'Slave Power.'"[32] The *Western Star* in Lebanon predicted history would "canonize" Brown.[33]

In Cincinnati, 1,500 German and African-American residents attended a memorial meeting to honor this "new saint."[34] The *Sandusky Register* called Brown's execution a "Sacrifice to the God of Slavery" and warned, "The better natures of mankind will somehow or other rise up in rebellion against this verdict."[35]

Elsewhere, an obscure poet named Walt Whitman—present at Brown's hanging only in his imagination—was forming lines that would become part of "Year of Meteors" in *Leaves of Grass*:

I would sing how an old man, tall, with white hair, mounted the scaffold in Virginia; (I was at hand—silent I stood, with teeth shut close—I watch'd;

I stood very near you, old man, when cool and indifferent, but trembling with age and your unheal'd wounds you mounted the scaffold).

TORCHLIGHT SEASON

Scarcely four months after John Brown's body had been laid to rest on his farm in upstate New York—a good Northern coffin having replaced the one of Southern manufacture—Democrats met in Charleston, South Carolina, to nominate a president.

They would fail, and this was one of the reasons: Southerners had hung the old Ohioan, but they hadn't killed him. His ghost, with its strange and piercing eyes, was roaming the streets of Charleston.[36] Old Brown's raid on Harpers Ferry in October 1859 had terrified the white rulers of the South, in their minds having come close to unleashing what they feared most: a slave rebellion in which blacks would rise up against their oppressors, slashing, burning, pillaging, raping—in short, paying back their white masters with the coin that had been paid them.

Plantations would burn, these Southerners imagined. Gentlemen would die. White women would be ravaged and miscegenation, hitherto a privilege reserved to white men for the black slave women they owned, would become general. The South would be laid waste, a way of life destroyed. Abolitionists—radical Northerners who wanted slavery wiped from the land—would gloat and say it was God's will, long overdue.[37]

And so, in April 1860, Democrats from throughout the thirty-four United States—the *barely* United States, some would say—converged on Charleston to decide who they would nominate for president in this fevered time and place. Slavery was the issue on everyone's mind. Pragmatic Northern Democrats, led by Illinois Sen. Stephen A. Douglas, believed the increasingly fractured Union could be saved by "popular sovereignty," meaning voters in each new state could decide for themselves whether to become a slave state or not.

The Douglas plan failed to placate frantic Southern Democrats who wanted something more than this insipid compromise. There should be *no* limits on slavery's expansion, they argued. Unless it could expand westward like the rest of the nation, they feared the institution was probably doomed as free states opposed to slavery gained seats in Congress.

Murat Halstead, the young Cincinnati newsman with sharp eyes, was there to watch it all. The convention's steamy days bubbled with conspiracies,

Loudly opinionated and a strong opponent of the Civil War, Ohio Congressman Clement L. Vallandigham never stopped attacking the Lincoln government.

rumors, and arguments, while the nights shook with the rowdyism of hard-drinking, tobacco-chewing delegates.[38] A convention hotel, he wrote, was "as lively as a molasses barrel with flies."[39]

Gliding behind the scenes and whispering in delegates' willing ears was a smooth-spoken defender of slavery from South Carolina named William Lowndes Yancey, a brilliant orator with the temperament of a water moccasin. Yancey had once joked that he had "a little nigger broiled every morning for breakfast and a roasted Union man for dinner."[40]

The Democrats had drawn a large delegation from Ohio, mostly Douglas men. Among them was a Dayton lawyer and U.S. Congressman with the elegant name of Clement Laird Vallandigham. Sturdily built, dark-complected but clean-shaven in an age of whiskers, the Congressman was hard-headed, politically ruthless, and loudly opinionated.

Vallandigham, a *New York Times* correspondent once acidly observed, was endowed with "a large mouth, rather more useful to the speechmaker than ornamental to the man."[41] No friend to blacks, "Val," as his friends called him, opposed abolitionism—but he also dreaded secession. He feared that abolition's noisy agitators, together with the Republican party's desire to limit slavery, would tear the country apart.

Now, as Northern Democratic delegates wrangled with their Southern counterparts, Vallandigham sensed his worst fears would come true. With eerie prescience he told friends at dinner one night that "if the Democratic party is dissevered in the … Convention, the result will be the disruption of the Union, and one of the bloodiest civil wars on record, the magnitude of which no man can estimate."[42]

The convention dragged on, with bitterness growing daily between the Northern and Southern delegates. It didn't help the mood of the Ohio delegation when, on the seventh day, "a great calamity" came upon them. Halstead reported, "Their private whiskey, of which they laid in a supply supposed to be equal to all emergencies, the nomination of Douglas included, gave out this morning. They attribute their good health which they have enjoyed to this article."[43]

As Vallandigham had feared, the nominating process collapsed, the Southern delegates walked out, and the Northern delegates gave up, planning to try again within a few weeks. June found the Democrats striving for unanimity in Baltimore. On the fourth day, part of the convention floor collapsed, sending the delegates scrambling for safety as "nimble as monkeys."[44] On the fifth day, the Southerners walked out again, this time

In his pre-war presidential campaign portrait, Abraham Lincoln's face reflects none of the suffering he would soon endure.

to nominate their own candidate. A splinter group of Democrats calling themselves the Constitutional Unionists nominated yet another candidate, meaning the Democrats would enter the election of 1860 with three different candidates.[45]

In the interval between the two Democratic conventions, Republicans convened in May in Chicago in a huge new hall they dubbed the Wigwam. The well-traveled Halstead was there to report events to readers back in Ohio. Sen. William H. Seward of New York, a strong opponent of slavery, was the heavy favorite, but waiting in the wings was a tall, craggy lawyer from Illinois named Abraham Lincoln. Lincoln had achieved a modest prominence for his 1858 debates with Sen. Douglas and for his well-received address the previous February at the Cooper Union, a New York college.

Northerners considered Lincoln a moderate on the divisive issue of slavery. Lincoln detested slavery, but his lawyerly mind told him that the Constitution had grandfathered slavery where it already existed. Lincoln was not unknown to Ohioans. During his one term in Congress (1847–49) he had become fast friends with Ohio's Sen. "Tom" Corwin and Rep. Joshua R. Giddings, and with them probably discussed the slavery issue. A decade later, on behalf of Republican candidates in the 1859 political campaigns, Lincoln had spoken in Columbus, Dayton, Hamilton, and Cincinnati. In Cincinnati, he said, "I think slavery is wrong, morally and politically. I desire that it should have no further spread in these United States."[46]

Lincoln was a cannier politician than his plain appearance and homespun background suggested. He had lined up, in advance, just enough delegates to the 1860 Republican convention to deny Seward a victory on the first ballot. He also had an enthusiastic team of clever political operatives working behind the scenes to crowd the hall with leather-lunged Lincoln enthusiasts.

When the name of Abraham Lincoln was placed in nomination by an Illinois delegate, it was seconded by Judge Columbus Delano of Mount Vernon, Ohio. The nomination triggered an uproar from the Lincoln supporters that Halstead claimed was "beyond description." The doughty journalist tried anyway, using terms familiar to his Ohio readers: "Imagine all the hogs ever slaughtered in Cincinnati giving their death squeals together, a score of big steam whistles going …, and you conceive something of the same nature. … [The] Lincoln boys … took deep breaths all around, and gave a concentrated shriek that was positively awful, [and] accompanied it with stamping that made every plank and pillar in the building quiver."[47]

Balloting began on the convention's third day. With each successive ballot, Seward's early lead shrank while Lincoln gained. After the third ballot, Halstead reported, former Congressman David K. Cartter from Cleveland, "a large man with bristling black hair [and a face] terribly marked with the smallpox," arose to speak: "I arise (eh), Mr. Chairman (eh), to announce the change of four votes of Ohio from Mr. Chase to Mr. Lincoln." With Lincoln nominated at last, thanks to Ohio's votes, the Wigwam erupted with a roar of approval loud enough to drown out cannons firing salutes outside the doors.

Their work done, Republican delegates scattered to their home states, brimming with a young party's energy and optimism. Facing long odds, Douglas—a powerful speaker some called "a steam-engine in britches" —defied tradition by going on the campaign trail. Lincoln stayed home, making no speeches and issuing no public statements, saying he had made his positions clear on earlier occasions. Other party leaders spoke in his place, delivering upwards of 50,000 speeches.[48]

The Republicans had a rousing campaign song ("Ain't you glad you joined the Republicans?"), a network of local Republican clubs, a meeting hall called a Wigwam in every major city, and a huge stock of campaign literature.

The torchlight parade was a favorite way to arouse the party faithful and impress voters in 1800s America. Through the autumn of 1860, Ohio streets echoed with the tramping of hundreds of men marching in serried ranks while carrying, above their heads, flaming oil lamps mounted on poles. Bands accompanied the processions and some of the marchers carried banners or pictures of their candidates. Republican ranks often were swelled by uniformed members of the "Wide-Awakes," a claque mostly of young,

In the 1860 presidential campaign, young men known as "Wide-Awakes" enlivened the night with noisy torchlight parades in support of Abraham Lincoln.

unmarried men who ratcheted up excitement at campaign events by their chanting, band music, and ensigns that featured a single staring eye.

On election evening Tuesday, November 6, partisans put away their torches and journalists briefly suspended their poisonous pens to gather at party headquarters for the results. In Toledo, Republicans congregated at their new brick Wigwam. Election returns arriving by telegraph were shouted out late into the evening. For those not attending the event, the Toledo's *Blade*—ordinarily an evening paper—promised an extra edition the next morning.

As soon as results showed Lincoln had been elected the sixteenth president of the United States, Toledo Republicans began planning a "jubilee" of celebration. Their young party had helped Lincoln win Ohio soundly. In an astounding voter turnout of 81.2 percent nationally, Lincoln fell short of a majority of popular votes.[49]

Southern voters almost universally ignored him, dividing their vote among the three Democratic candidates. But Lincoln's plurality of forty percent was more than any other single opponent and more than enough to capture a solid majority in the electoral college.

It would be four months until Lincoln was inaugurated on March 4, 1861, but the votes had barely been counted after his election when rumblings of discontent began rolling up from the South. Lincoln's victory worried the winners as well as the losers. This is "the beginning of the end," the *Toledo Blade,* a stoutly Republican paper, warned only three days after the election.[50]

Throughout the nation the atmosphere was crackling ominously. Coincidentally, Toledo's Republican "jubilee" of celebration had to be postponed because of bad weather. It was not a good omen, and worried citizens celebrated with diminished enthusiasm a few days later.[51]

THE REVOLUTION IS INITIATED

In less than four months after Lincoln's election, matters had come to this. At 4:30 in the morning on Friday, April 12, 1861, as dawn was beginning to soften the sky over the harbor at Charleston, South Carolina, a cannon ball crashed into the outside wall of Fort Sumter, a Federal stronghold built on a reef at the harbor's entrance. On the other side of that wall, separated from the missile by a scant twelve inches of material, was the curly-haired, mustachioed and slightly jowly head of one Abner Doubleday, who until that moment had been enjoying a few extra winks.

Doubleday, a New Yorker, was a captain of artillery in regular forces of the United States Army. Only a few minutes earlier he had been awakened

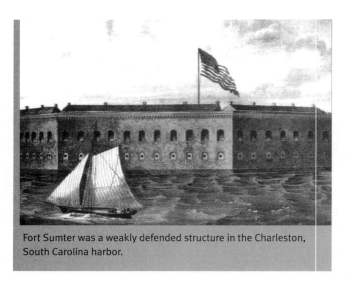
Fort Sumter was a weakly defended structure in the Charleston, South Carolina harbor.

by his commander, Maj. Robert Anderson. Anderson said the secessionists on the shore were going to start firing on the fort within an hour, but lack of light would prevent return fire until "after breakfast." Doubleday had gone back to sleep.

Then the cannon ball arrived "in very unpleasant proximity to my right ear," Doubleday later wrote. Taking his wake-up call seriously this time, Doubleday went down to breakfast. In the mess hall, he found the fort's handful of officers "calm, and even somewhat merry" as nineteen secessionist batteries pounded their fort in a continuous roar, shaking loose large patches of masonry.[52]

The captain later learned that the cannon ball may have been fired by the ubiquitous Edmund Ruffin, the Virginian who had witnessed John Brown's execution. A prominent agriculturist and secessionist firebrand, Ruffin had been given the honor of firing one of the first shots at Fort Sumter. Ruffin, Doubleday declared, "might almost be called the father of secession. This is the [shot] that probably came with Mr. Ruffin's compliments."

Although Doubleday seems to have laughed off Ruffin, he was genuinely angered that one of the Confederate officers directing fire at Fort Sumter was a former U.S. officer named Roswell S. Ripley. "Being a man of talent, and a skillful artillerist, he did us a great deal of harm," Doubleday wrote in some indignation.[53] Ripley, he said, had been born in Ohio.[54]*

After a paltry meal of pork and water, the men of Fort Sumter went up to the gun galleries, and, now that it was daylight, began returning fire. Captain Doubleday had the honor of firing the Union's first shot in reply, which uselessly bounced off the roof of a building on shore.

---

* Born in Worthington, Ohio, in 1823, Roswell S. Ripley had graduated from West Point in 1843 and served with distinction in the artillery during the Mexican-American War. He resigned his commission in 1853 while stationed in South Carolina but joined the Confederacy after secession, rising to the rank of brigadier general. The state of Ohio has placed a historical marker in front of his brick home, which remains today at 623 High Street in Worthington, used for offices.

Both sides kept up the firing for the rest of Friday, with pauses by the Federals to put out fires caused by shells hitting their barracks. No one on either side was killed. On shore, Mary Boykin Chesnut, the wife of a secessionist leader, complained that the sound of the guns reverberating throughout Charleston made meals impossible. Later, at tea, she and some Charleston ladies agreed, "God is on our side. Of course, He hates the Yankees."[55]

Major Anderson's little force maintained its resistance until early the next morning. With no serious casualties on either side, Anderson agreed on Saturday—about thirty-four hours after the bombardment began—to surrender the next day. His fortress was crumbling, his supplies were almost exhausted with no hope of re-supply, and his guns were having no effect on the shore batteries encircling him with fire.

Sumter was the final chord in the overture to war that had begun five months before with the election of Lincoln. On the day after the election, Charlestonians had raised their state's palmetto flag in a gesture of defiance. The Stars and Stripes disappeared. "The revolution of 1860 has been initiated," the *Charleston Mercury* shouted.[56]

President-elect Lincoln tried to reassure the South, saying he had no intention of interfering with slavery where it already existed. The assurances fell on deaf ears as Southern leaders, who had been working themselves into a frenzy ever since John Brown's raid on Harpers Ferry. They dismissed

Southern volunteers eager to strike a blow against their nation's government encircled Fort Sumter with artillery and pounded it until its tiny garrison surrendered.

Lincoln as a "black abolitionist," although Lincoln had called only for limiting slavery's expansion, not its abolition.

On December 20, 1860, the South Carolina Convention had unanimously voted a resolution declaring that "the union now subsisting between South Carolina and other States, under the name of "The United States of America," is hereby dissolved."[57] A befuddled President Buchanan did nothing. Next, South Carolina troops had seized the federal arsenal in Charleston. Within a few months—before Lincoln had even been inaugurated—Mississippi, Florida, Alabama, Georgia, Louisiana, and Texas also seceded, while lame-duck Buchanan waffled. The seven states formed the Confederate States of America, chose Mississippian Jefferson Davis as their president, and adopted a constitution guaranteeing the right of some people to own others.

Fort Sumter fell, and Virginia, Arkansas, North Carolina, and Tennessee joined the secession movement. Throughout the South, lightly defended federal forts and arsenals were seized by the rebellious Southerners. The "border states" of Missouri, Kentucky, Maryland, and Delaware, where slavery was legal but sentiment over secession sharply divided, would remain in the Union, however.

With his influence dwindling daily, the best President Buchanan could do was to temporize, duck, and weave, an exit strategy intended to hold what was left of the Union together until it became somebody else's problem. All the while, one member of his administration, Attorney General Edwin M. Stanton, was helping defend the Union by secretly passing intelligence to the Republicans in Congress.

During the winter of 1860–61, worried speculation about the nation's future took its place in Ohioans' daily conversations, along with crops, the weather, and local politics.

Just as the South's defiance had grown since Lincoln's election, so had anger in the North. War fever was breaking out all over. Shortly before the attack on Fort Sumter, the *Daily Toledo Blade* told its impatient readers, "No fighting yet. We have today any quantity of 'rumors of war,' but no 'war.' We know this announcement will disappoint some, but we can't help it."[58]

Still, public opinion on just what to do about the rebels—fight them to preserve the Union or let them go their way—was mixed. As Lincoln guessed it would, the attack on Sumter galvanized the North in favor of the Union like nothing else could have. John G. Nicolay, Lincoln's private secretary, later wrote that the president's "carefully matured purpose [was] to force the rebellion to put itself flagrantly and fatally in the wrong by attacking Fort Sumter."[59]

With the attack on Fort Sumter, the North exploded in righteous anger at the South, rallied around the flag, and declared itself united and ready to march to war. Northerners who hadn't been able to make up their minds about secession wavered no longer. Abraham Lincoln, the homely railsplitter and the country bumpkin from Illinois, had won the first round.

GLORY TO GOD!

Years later, Jacob Dolson Cox could still remember how the woman's scream pierced the solemnity of the Ohio Senate Chamber, which, because of rising tensions in the nation, happened to be even more solemn than usual.

It was a shrill cry of triumph—"Glory to God!"—and it came from a woman in the visitors' gallery, one Abby Kelley Foster from Massachusetts. Foster was a radical advocate of abolition, a feminist, and a bitter critic of the South, the kind of sharp-tongued agitator who got under the skin of conservatives. Probably she was on one of her lecture tours and had just dropped by the Ohio Senate to see if the distinguished gentlemen were doing anything interesting.

They were not, but midway through a droning discussion of routine matters, as Senator Cox was struggling to keep his mind on business, another senator rushed in from the lobby. Catching the chairman's eye, he exclaimed, "Mr. President, the telegraph announces that the secessionists are bombarding Fort Sumter!"[60] Mrs. Foster's scream rose out of her belief that only a war could end slavery.

It was Friday, April 12, 1861, and telegraph machines in cities across Ohio chattered with messages from Charleston, South Carolina: *"The ball is open. War is inaugurated. The batteries of Sullivan's Island, Morris's Island and other points were opened on Fort Sumter ... this morning."*[61]

The news trickled into Ohio unevenly. On the day the attack began, in a rolling mill in northeastern Ohio, an old man rushed in shouting, "They've fired on her! They've fired on her!"[62] In Cincinnati, the news was not posted on bulletin boards outside news offices until shortly before 9 p.m. Friday evening, but then it "spread like wildfire ... an hour had not elapsed before it had been carried by eager messengers to the outer wards, and soon every household was in possession of the startling intelligence."[63]

On the next day, a Saturday, Ohio's newspapers broke out their largest and boldest type, added a generous sprinkling of exclamation marks, and shrieked the news. In Columbus, the *Ohio State Journal* cried, "THE WAR BEGUN!! The Rebels Fire the First Shot!"[64] In Toledo, the *Blade* shouted, "THE ISSUE IS MADE UP! The blow is struck!"[65] The *Cleveland Morning Leader* front page carried the heading, 'THE WAR HAS BEGUN!!! FORT SUMTER ATTACKED YESTERDAY MORNING!'"[66]

Months of uncertainty had been resolved in favor of war. Editorialists, letter writers, and street-corner sages chorused, "The ball is open," a catchphrase signifying the beginning of something big. Editors loudly demanded that young men rally to the cause, doubters shut up and lay low, and Congressional leaders demanded that the "Government … assert its power, and make that power felt by the traitors, even if it necessary to lay every rebel city in ashes." Little guessing the horrors and discouragements that lay ahead, editorialists trumpeted the "thrill" and the "joy" news of war brought the citizenry. "Never before was there such a burst of enthusiasm and military fervor as now," proclaimed the *Cleveland Morning Leader.*[67] The *Leader* called it all "the great pulsation."[68]

Sweeping across Ohio, the news created a frenzy of patriotic excitement "bordering on delirium," as one observer put it.[69] Flags and bunting burst into bloom on public and private buildings throughout the state. In Toledo, the *Blade* reported "every pole in the city … now flaunts the glorious ensign."[70] When all flagpoles were filled, new ones were quickly erected. Cart men decorated their horses' heads with little flags. Men wore the Stars and Stripes as shirtfronts or wore stickpins decorated with the national flag. Women trimmed their bonnets with red, white, and blue ribbons.[71]

In Cincinnati, "thousands upon thousands" of citizens gathered around the newspaper offices of the *Commercial* and the *Gazette* waiting for dispatches to be read to them from a second-story window.[72] In Cleveland, the office of the *Morning Leader* "was besieged to a very late hour with anxious crowds."[73] The commotion by anxious news seekers assailing "our Sanctum," a Toledo editor complained, made it "next to impossible for us to do our duty to our readers."[74]

On Sunday in Columbus, churchgoers stopped to read the headlines outside newspaper offices.[75] By Monday, the martial music of fife and drum could be heard throughout Toledo and other cities and towns from morning until evening.[76] In Cincinnati, the public was asked not to "congregate at the telegraph office and besiege the operators for news."[77]

In every city and town, people with grave faces gathered on street corners to discuss events.[78] In Toledo, "the streets were filled with excited

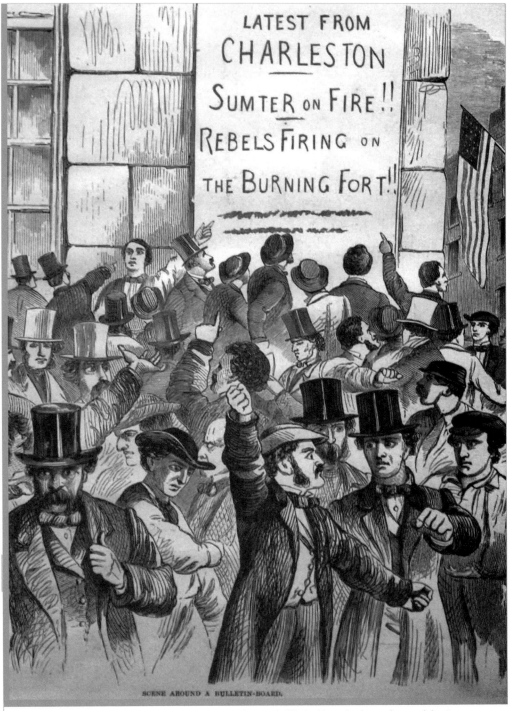

SCENE AROUND A BULLETIN-BOARD.

At news of the attack on Fort Sumter, city streets in the North filled with excited crowds promising to suppress the South's "traitors" and put down their rebellion.

and indignant crowds."[79] Stores did little business because customers and proprietors alike joined excited crowds on the streets.[80] In Elyria, members of a band were so giddy with excitement they and their neighbors across the street staged a mock Battle of Fort Sumter, using lengths of stove pipe in place of cannon. Then, "dressed in fantastic style," they commemorated the occasion by having a group picture taken.[81]

Lacking telegraph connections of their own, small towns sent emissaries to cities to gather the news. A Michigan man rode thirty miles to Toledo by horseback to get the latest information. Railroad handcars—propelled by men furiously pumping handles up and down—appeared in the city from outlying rail points.[82]

Throughout the state, public meetings were called and stirring speeches given by politicians and old soldiers. These assemblages followed a pattern that, for the modern reader, has a town-meeting kind of charm. Some official or other prominent citizen would organize a public assembly, at which he would appoint a committee to develop resolutions on the subject at hand.

After the committee had retired to do its work, the crowd would "call out" leading citizens to give impromptu speeches. A man so honored would clear his throat, modestly declare he had not come prepared to speak, but launch into a speech anyway. After several such speeches had been delivered, the committee would return with patriotic resolutions to propose to those assembled, who would shout their assent. All would go home reassured that they lived in a democracy in which their voices had been heard.

In Toledo, on the Monday evening after the Sumter attack, thousands gathered in Union Depot. Resolutions condemning the rebellion were approved by the crowd with a roar that "rolled over the assembly like a peal of thunder."[83] To accommodate the crowd, the railroad cleared the terminal's tracks and illuminated the speaker's platform with two locomotive headlights.[84]

Elsewhere in Ohio, citizens packed meetings in theaters, assembly halls, and wherever sufficient space could be found. In Springfield, the City Hall proved too small for the crowd and the meeting "was adjourned to Market Square."[85] In Cincinnati, a patriotic rally "packed" Catholic Institute Hall, with "hundreds" unable to get into the crowded hall.[86] Another, impromptu, meeting drew a crowd of "thousands" that gathered around the post office steps and filled connecting streets "for a considerable distance."[87]

Any citizen who seemed less than wholeheartedly for the Union cause was looked upon suspiciously. Anyone foolish enough to voice support for the Secessionists was apt to be harassed, accosted physically, or targeted for eggs. A Cleveland paper declared that "no man should be allowed to live in Ohio who is not for the Union first, last, and all the time."[88]

A Columbus paper warned that any Northerners who sympathized with the South "had better change their tune, and that speedily. None but traitors deserving the gibbet will be found sustaining the cause of the Southern rebels." The writer added words that would grow worn from repeated use: "Those who are not *for* the Stars and Stripes are *against* them."[89]

In Toledo one morning, an "ugly looking noose" was found attached to a lamp post with a placard, "Death to Traitors."[90]

In a way, it was a memorial to John Brown.

TO LEARN MORE:

The beautifully restored Ohio Senate Chamber, where Abby Foster Kelley shouted out in triumph, can be seen while touring the Statehouse, downtown Columbus. You can even sit on one of the sofas where Mrs. Kelley may have sat (only the upholstery has been replaced). Listen carefully and you may hear her exultant cry echoing yet. See **http://www.statehouse.state.oh.us/** or call **614-728-2695** for more information on one of the oldest working statehouses in the nation.

The wagon in which John Brown rode to his execution is in the Jefferson County Museum, 200 East Washington St., Charles Town (near Harpers Ferry) in West Virginia: **http://jeffctywvmuseum.org** or **304-725-8628**. Further afield, Fort Sumter is now a national monument in South Carolina, accessible by ferry: (**http://www.nps.gov/fosu/** or **843-883-3123**).

Ohio journalist Murat Halstead's eyewitness account of Brown's execution can be read online by going to **http://www.ohiohistory.org/resource/publicat**, then to the Ohio History OnlineArchive. Choose "Browse by Volume" and look up Volume 30, page 290. "The Life, Trial and Execution of Captain John Brown, 1859...compiled from official and authentic sources" is available online at **http://www.yale.edu/lawweb/avalon/treatise/john_brown/john_brown.htm**.

Two men with opposing purposes, the cold stare of John Brown (l) and glittering eyes of Edmund Ruffin were fixed on worlds only they could see.

2

I SAY, LET IT BE DONE

The Years of Growing Bitterness

In the last years before the Civil War, two angry old men—one a Northerner, the other a Southerner—roamed the American landscape, listening only to the gods and demons in their heads. One was John Brown, the white-bearded sometime-Ohioan whose travels would end on a gallows in December 1859. The other was Edmund Ruffin, the long-haired Virginia firebrand who had rushed to get a good view of Brown's last moments.

To know something about these men, mark their eyes. Brown's are like drills, his face glacial, his body tense. Here is an avenging angel on assignment from God to end slavery. Ruffin seems relaxed, deep into a thousand-yard stare, but there is something else going on with this man. His eyes are fixed on the dawning horizon of a land you and I cannot see, an agrarian paradise governed by a few wise and privileged men for whom human bondage is a righteous part of the natural order of things. The romanticized Old South transformed into a wondrous nation of its own. Utopia with slaves.

Two very different men, and yet, in the end, so much alike, each sowing dragon's teeth—one North, one South.

FLASHBACK: PARALLEL LIVES

With white hair flowing down to his shoulders, Edmund Ruffin looked like nothing so much as somebody's weird grandpa—the kind you'd lock in the attic, if only you could—and when he began to address a crowd with his drab, apologetic, sometimes stumbling speech, you'd think: this man is harmless.

You would be wrong. Edmund Ruffin's head was stuffed with resentments, suspicions, vituperation, and repugnant ideas about race and human rights. Those poisonous thoughts may have only stumbled from his lips but they rushed in corrosive streams through his writings in newspapers and journals. And they helped push the South into secession.

Born in 1794, son of one of the largest slave-holders in Virginia, Ruffin was a sickly, unpromising boy with spindly legs who wore his hair shoulder-length. Sent to the College of William and Mary, but suspended for drinking, he settled down on an inherited plantation, trying to make a go of its worn-out soils. After years of struggle, he discovered the fertilizer value of fossil shells.[1]

Continuing his experimentation, Ruffin became one of the most influential figures in Southern agriculture, and "the father of American soil science," according to a modern authority.[2] Periodically, he launched crusades for agricultural and political reforms, but almost as regularly he turned out to be his own worst enemy. His hot temper, bluntness, and self-righteous refusal to compromise on any issue angered opponents. It even alienated friends and supporters. When he had angered enough people, he would retreat to his plantation to brood in solitude.

In the early 1850s Ruffin emerged from one of his self-imposed exiles to launch a new crusade, this in defense of slavery. By now, the nation's long-running debate over it had turned partisans of the North and South into furious opponents, their rhetoric heated to the boiling point. A vocal minority in the North screamed to the heavens about the immorality of slavery. The South, egged on by its own orators, mounted extravagant arguments in its defense, among them, that slavery was a "positive good," sanctioned implicitly by the Bible. In a typical screed, Ruffin argued that God had intended blacks for slavery, making them "inferior in intellect to the white" but superior in obedience and endurance in tropical climates.[3]

With the grandiose passion that ruled his life, Ruffin—with unconscious irony—labeled Ohio and other Northern states "fanatical," bubbling with "treason & rebellion." He hoped *they* would secede.[4] Nothing in Ohio was much good anyway, Ruffin thought. On a trip through the state in 1860, he peered out the train window and "saw no neat, or apparently good farming in Ohio."[5] The free state clearly was inferior to its slave-holding neighbor, Kentucky. (Years earlier, Alexis de Tocqueville thought *Kentucky* offered the inferior appearance, and blamed it on slavery.[6]) Ruffin was "much disappointed in the size of the river Ohio" and annoyed "by the numerous mosquitoes" in the railroad car.[7]

Ears burning from denunciations by Northern abolitionists, Southerners listened gratefully to Ruffin and other agitators, but initially dismissed their prophets of secession as "fire-eaters," radicals outside the political mainstream. Ruffin never doubted he was right, of course. He was obsessive, combative, and rigid in his thinking, unable to compromise—the same qualities possessed by a certain Northern man with whom Ruffin would one day share a sunny day in December.

The man was John Brown.

Born to plain beginnings in Torrington, Connecticut, in 1800, John Brown was the second child of a threadbare tanner named Owen Brown.[8] In 1805 the Brown family moved to the alluring frontier of Ohio, newly minted as a state. The Browns settled in Hudson in one of the northeastern counties known collectively as the Western Reserve, a region popular with migrating New Englanders.

John Brown was a thin and somber child, belligerent and aggressive, a rough playmate. He grew into a lean, sinewy man of average height with a face chiseled from granite and all edges and angles, a down-turned mouth, and black hair he combed straight back. He was scrupulously honest, rigidly Puritanical, austere, intense, and almost totally lacking in humor. He also was impatient, imperious, and intolerant of others in small things. Brown's eyes were his most striking feature: they were steel-gray, intense, and angry looking.[9]

Young Brown's first business venture, a tannery in Ohio, failed. For the next two decades he restlessly moved from place to place, in and out of Ohio, ranging as far as Massachusetts, searching for his fortune and never finding it. He tried farming, sheep-raising, land speculation, dealing in cattle, and dealing in wool, but he harvested only debts, lawsuits, controversies, and hardship. He was his own worst enemy.

Like Ruffin, Brown held a life membership in the fraternity of those who are often wrong but never in doubt. He refused all counsel. A business acquaintance called him a victim of delusions. Others bluntly said he was well-intentioned but crazy. Brown's own attorney called him "peculiar in many of his notions."[10] He and Ruffin are nineteenth-century examples of what twentieth-century longshoreman-philosopher Eric Hoffer called the "true believer"—the absolutist who hears no voice but his own. The fanatic.

In northeastern Ohio, Brown grew up in a region boiling with antislavery sentiment. In 1837 he stood up at an abolitionists' meeting in Hudson, raised his right hand, and vowed to consecrate his life to the destruction of slavery.

John Brown's face was that of a belligerent, obsessive, crusader who was "often wrong but never in doubt."

He and his father worked as conductors on the Underground Railroad. Though many abolitionists did not believe in equality in all things for blacks, Brown did. In 1838 he shocked a church in Franklin Mills, Ohio, by inviting blacks, who had been forced to sit in the back, to join him in his pew.

While Edmund Ruffin was emerging from self-imposed exile in the early 1850s to champion the cause of slavery, events were conspiring to convert John Brown into its fulltime opponent. After suffering teeth-rattling business reverses in New York and New England, by 1854 Brown had turned to plain-dirt farming near Akron. That year Congress passed the Kansas-Nebraska Act, under which each of the two states could decide by popular vote whether to allow slavery or not.

The territory offered farmland for the taking and some Ohioans were infected with "Kansas fever." Five of John Brown's sons moved there and urged their father to join them. If enough anti-slavery "free-soilers" moved there, they pointed out, Kansas could be saved from the clutches of the slave-owners. Father John pondered all this and decided he heard God's voice calling him. In late summer 1855, he set out for Kansas in a one-horse wagon loaded with the usual household goods and farm tools, plus revolvers, rifles, broadswords, and explosives. After brooding about slavery's evils for years, Brown was about to become a full-time soldier of the Lord.

Arriving near the town of Osawatomie in eastern Kansas, Brown discovered that pro-slavery "Border Ruffians" from neighboring Missouri were invading Kansas, terrorizing settlers, and taking control of the territorial government by fraudulent voting. On May 21, 1856, the Border Ruffians boldly ransacked the antislavery stronghold of Lawrence, killing six people. At almost the same time, in the nation's capital, South Carolina Congressman Preston Brooks used a cane to beat anti-slavery Sen. Charles Sumner of Massachusetts almost to death for his outspokenness.

On news of the two events, John Brown and his sons "went crazy— crazy."[11] Muttering "something must be done," Brown led a small company of men, including some of his sons, along nearby Pottawatomie Creek on a spring night. Carrying broadswords, honed to razor sharpness, they moved from cabin to cabin, waking up the pro-slavery residents so they could slaughter them. Cutting off arms and splitting skulls with swift, slashing blows of their glistening blades, Brown's band hacked to death five strangers and two yelping bulldogs.

The murders made the former Ohioan a nationally known figure dubbed "Osawatomie Brown" or "Old Brown." The territory exploded into "Bleeding Kansas," notorious for the viciousness of its guerilla warfare. Brown vowed, "I will die fighting for this cause. There will be no more peace in this land until slavery is done for."[12] A little civil war occurred here as deadly bands of pro- and antislavery men, Brown's among them, roamed the landscape in pursuit of each other, killing, burning, and pillaging.

For the next three years, Brown eluded the authorities as he shuttled in and out of Kansas. Touching abolitionist bases in Ohio and elsewhere, he traveled as far as Boston to raise funds and recruits, returning to Kansas to stir that boiling pot. Riding rattling trains around New England and New York, Brown raised funds by lecturing in a word-of-God voice that held audiences spellbound. When he wasn't shaking strangers' hands with a firm grip and a burning gaze, he paced restlessly, hands clasped behind his back, looking neither left nor right, saying little, absorbed in distant thoughts.

Brown had an air of mystery about him and more than a suggestion of menace. A contemporary described him as "a sort of meteoric character, appearing very unexpectedly now at one place, and then at another … He seemed to be ever on the alert." His gaze was so penetrating that "[f]ew men could look him steadily in the eye more than a breath."[13]

Brown's passion impressed such worthies as Henry David Thoreau and Ralph Waldo Emerson (who called him "the rarest of heroes"). Not everyone was dazzled. Massachusetts businessman Amos Lawrence looked Brown over and decided he suffered a "monomania" on slavery. Another reform-minded Massachusetts businessman, John Murray Forbes, detected a "little touch of insanity" in Brown's "glittering, gray-blue eyes."[14] The manic grace notes dotting Brown's presentations made many listeners nervous, unwilling to open their pocketbooks very wide.

Nonetheless, Brown was able to organize a clandestine "Committee of Six," some notable financial backers—later known as the "Secret Six"— to whom he revealed part of his secret plan. Unlike many go-slow opponents of slavery, these prominent New Englanders, including two ministers, agreed with Brown that Southern intransigence meant only violent action—ultimately, perhaps, a civil war—could end slavery in the United States.

As he traveled across the North, Brown collected a small cadre of followers. In May 1858 he went to Chatham, Ontario, where he led a secret "constitutional convention" to organize a commonwealth in the Southern mountains, location undisclosed, for the slaves he expected to free. He returned briefly to Kansas and led a cross-border raid into Missouri in which a white settler was killed and eleven slaves freed. The raid panicked Missouri slaveholders the way a later Brown raid would panic the entire South. Brown safely delivered the slaves to their freedom in Canada, then headed east again.

After a final barnstorming tour of New England, Brown had decided by July 1859 that he had gathered the support he needed. It was time to move to the seat of war. He had already dispatched one of his followers to scout out Harpers Ferry, an arms-manufacturing town in northwestern Virginia. After saying goodbye to his wife, Mary, and their family at the farm in North Elba, New York, that they had acquired years before, Brown turned south.

First, however, Brown disclosed his scheme to Frederick Douglass, the famed ex-slave and abolitionist. Douglass, who knew the South from personal experience and had a cooler head than Brown, warned him that Harpers Ferry would prove "a trap of steel."[15] Brown, as usual, would hear no objections.

Elsewhere in Virginia, meanwhile, a lonely Edmund Ruffin languished in despondency, grumping to his diary how unhappy he was. Long a widower, he had suffered the unexpected deaths of three adult daughters and a daughter-in-law. Efforts by Ruffin and his fellow "fire-eaters" to persuade fellow Southerners to secede from the Union hadn't worked. By October 18, 1859,

Ruffin was sounding as if suicide was on his mind.

But the next day brought wonderful news: the notorious "Osawatomie Brown" had tried and failed to start a slave insurrection at Harpers Ferry. To Ruffin, that meant Southerners would finally realize how dangerous the abolitionists really were. *Now* they would understand what could happen if the Southern states remained yoked to the North and did not secede. The incident at Harpers Ferry was just what was "needed to stir the sluggish blood of the south," he gloated to his diary.[16]

Suddenly, Ruffin wanted to live.

FLASHBACK: OLD BROWN'S WAR

This is what happened in October 1859 to gladden Edmund Ruffin's heart. On a cold, drizzly, and moonless Sunday evening, while Ruffin was still brooding in eastern Virginia, a little procession moved down a mountain road in western Maryland. The only sounds in the clammy air were the clopping of horses' hooves, the creak of a wagon, and the shuffling of men's feet.

Driving the wagon was a lanky old man with a beard, hard eyes, and a tight mouth. In his wagon were tools, rifles, and pikes—six-foot-long poles, each with a nasty looking knife at one end. Marching solemnly behind, carrying rifles on their shoulders and trying to look soldierly, was his "Provisional Constitutional Army," eighteen men, most of them young. They were armed with pistols, knives, and Sharps breech-loading carbines.[17]

Wearing long gray shawls that made them look like ghosts moving through the mist, the men were following John Brown into war. For years, Brown had brooded over slavery, argued for the equality of blacks and whites, and felt the rage build until there was nothing left to do ... but to strike this blow. It was he who was driving the wagon.

A few miles ahead, tucked into a valley where the Shenandoah River flows into the Potomac River, lay their unsuspecting target, the town of Harpers Ferry, in what was then western Virginia and is now West Virginia. Located seventy miles north of Washington, D.C., Harpers Ferry was a crowded little factory town, a place where most of the men worked in a government armory or a private rifle works. Together the facilities produced ten thousand stands of arms a year for the United States government.

In his travels, Brown had recruited a motley fighting force of twenty-one men, three of them his sons. Among them were an intelligent and idealistic schoolteacher, an eccentric spiritualist from Canada, a runaway slave, a menacing hulk of a man who liked to sing, two free blacks (one of them a college student, the other his uncle), and, remarkably, two young Quakers who had overcome their pacifist upbringings to join Brown's war. Some of these men were veterans of guerilla warfare in Kansas; others had no military experience at all.

In addition to Brown, eight of his "soldiers" had an Ohio connection: sons Owen, Watson, and Oliver Brown had been born there, as had the schoolteacher, John Henry Kagi. The black college student, John A. Copeland, and his uncle, Lewis S. Leary, were from Oberlin. The Quaker brothers, Barclay and Edwin Coppoc, had been born in the anti-slavery hotbed of Salem, Ohio, although they had later moved to Springdale, Iowa.

In July, pretending to be "Isaac Smith," a cattle buyer from New York, John Brown had rented a dilapidated farm on a Maryland hillside only a few miles from Harpers Ferry. There he stockpiled his weapons, which included 950 pikes, 200 revolvers, and 198 Sharps carbines. He summoned his troops, and spent his days working out strategy, which did not, however, include much planning for the long range or for contingencies.[18] God would provide.

Holed up at the farm for weeks on end, Brown's little army grew itchier daily as their leader tried to read the portents and decide when to go into action. To blow off steam, the men would run about and scream during thunderstorms. Finally, a one-eyed mental defective named Francis Jackson Meriam showed up on October 15, bringing $700 in gold and a commitment to the cause. That, Brown decided, was a sign from God. The revolution would begin the next day.

Now on this cold, wet Sunday night in 1859, Brown was on his way to trigger a slave revolt he expected to sweep the Cotton Kingdom like wildfire and burn away the evil. First, his "army" would capture the stockpile of newly manufactured arms at Harpers Ferry and take hostages. Word would spread (in some way not explained in Brown's plan) to slaves in the surrounding region, who would surely rush to join him. Then, Brown and his black legions would march across the South, freeing more slaves as they went. They would settle in a mountain commonwealth, which Brown expected to create—somewhere.

That was Brown's grand strategy, and to support it he had only a few tactical moves in mind. Everything else was an act of faith, a war of choice governed by what Brown alone *hoped* would happen, not what *could* happen. Doubt and dissent were not allowed. This was a true believer at work.

Most of Brown's men marched to Harpers Ferry, but three stayed behind: Owen Brown, Barclay Coppoc, and the one-eyed Meriam. At a prearranged time they were to take guns and pikes to a schoolhouse on the Maryland side of the river and arm the slaves and any whites who came to join the revolution.

Brown's men moved easily into the sleeping town. They cut telegraph wires, posted sentinels at the bridges, and took over the armory, where thousands of arms were stored, and (several hundred yards away) the private rifle works where they were made.

They captured some watchmen and a few late-nighters still on the streets. Brown told his hostages, "I want to free all the negroes in this state. ... If the citizens interfere with me I must only burn the town and have blood."[19] He did not harm the hostages, however, and even sent out for their breakfasts from a nearby hotel.

The raiders set up headquarters in the brick fire-engine house just inside the gate to the armory's complex of buildings. A detachment sent by Brown returned from the countryside with ten bewildered slaves they had "liberated" and three more hostages, including Col. Lewis W. Washington, a great-grandnephew of the Father of His Country. Having quickly captured both the rifle works and armory with their millions of dollars in arms and munitions, Brown must have felt: so far, so good.

But things began to go awry. The raiders halted a train and, inexplicably, let it go, even though it was sure to carry an alarm down the track. In the darkness, a Harpers Ferry baggage handler was shot and killed by Brown's men. Irony of ironies: the victim turned out to be a free black and innocent bystander. Meanwhile, an alarm by word of mouth and ringing of church bells was spreading in the countryside around Harpers Ferry.

Instead of blacks rushing to his aid, Brown soon got a white population wild over what they thought was a long-feared slave insurrection. As the sun climbed into the sky Monday morning, townspeople, joined by farmers, opened fire on the raiders barricaded in the engine house and rifle works. Brown's men fired back, killing the town's popular mayor, further enraging the crowd. The streets seethed with a mob of furious white men armed with every weapon they could find, from axes to squirrel guns, shouting "Kill them! Kill them!" Heavy drinking gave the crowd liquid courage.

When some of Brown's men lost their nerve and tried to flee, they were shot down and their bodies used for target practice the rest of the day. One of Brown's outlying sentinels, Dangerfield Newby, was dropped by a long bolt fired from a rifle that cut his throat "literally from ear to ear."[20] Newby probably had the greatest personal stake in Brown's "war." A forty-eight-year-old free mulatto described as "quiet, sensible, and very unobtrusive,"

Newby had hoped to free his wife and seven children enslaved on a Virginia plantation.[21]

As he lay dead in the gutter, Newby's ears were sliced off as souvenirs. Later, hogs came to root on the body. In his pocket Newby carried a heart-wrenching letter from his wife, Harriet: "Oh dear Dangerfield, com this fall without fail monny or no Monny I want to see you so much that is the one bright hope I have before me."[22] Subsequently, Harriet Newby was sold to a Louisiana slave dealer and probably separated from her children.

Federal authorities in Washington panicked at reports from Harpers Ferry. President Buchanan dispatched three artillery companies, a company of Marines, and the U.S. 1st and 2nd Cavalry to suppress the "insurrection." He put a career army man named Robert E. Lee in charge.

With soldiers, militias, and angry citizens surrounding his stronghold and no slave insurrection in sight, Brown tried to negotiate safe passage out of Harpers Ferry. Colonel Lee refused to negotiate and early on Tuesday morning unleashed a surprise assault on the engine house. U.S. Marines battered down the doors and rushed in with fixed bayonets. Before Brown had a chance to fire, the Marine commander struck him repeatedly with a saber until the old man was unconscious.[23]

Brown's "war" was over within thirty-six hours, with ten of his men—including two of his sons—dead or mortally wounded. Four more were captured on the spot and two more a few days later in Pennsylvania. Five, among them Meriam, the Quaker Barclay Coppoc, and Brown's son Owen, escaped for good.

While Brown lay cut and bleeding on a pile of bedding on Tuesday afternoon, a crowd of reporters and officials, including Gov. Henry A. Wise of Virginia and Democratic Congressman Clement L. Vallandigham of Ohio, arrived to question him. Brown seemed undaunted, answering questions so fearlessly that even Governor Wise called him "the gamest man I ever saw."[24]

Vallandigham pressed the old man, trying to make him say that abolitionists in Ohio were behind the plot. Revealing little, Brown told the crowd gathered around him that he considered himself an instrument in the hands of God, his actions justified by the Golden Rule. When bystanders taunted him as fanatical and a robber, Brown snapped back that he considered *them* "fanatical" and "robbers" for their support of slavery.[25]

Brown and his "army" were taken to jail in nearby Charles Town. Fearing a rescue attempt or a lynching, authorities held a rushed trial beginning October 27. On October 31, a jury deliberated forty-five minutes to find

Under the command of Col. Robert E. Lee, U.S. Marines stormed the fire-engine house in which John Brown had fortified himself in Harpers Ferry.

Brown guilty of treason, conspiracy, and murder. He was sentenced to hang December 2. Brown's captured soldiers were to be hanged later. In court, Brown unleashed a five-minute burst of eloquence, concluding, "Now, if it is deemed necessary that I should forfeit my life for the furtherance of the ends of justice, and mingle my blood with the millions in this slave country whose rights are disregarded ... *I say let it be done.*"[26]

Brown's raid had been greeted with dismay across the North. Even anti-slavery newspapers called it the work of a madman. Lincoln admired Brown's selflessness, but told an audience that "no man, North or South, can approve of violence or crime."[27] A Cleveland newspaper commented, "Slavery drives John Brown to madness, and then hangs him for that insanity."[28] Some opinion turned in Brown's favor when the convicted man exhibited unfailing "coolness," meaning manly courage.

(Members of the "Secret Six" supporters of Brown panicked when letters implicating them were published. One went temporarily insane. Four— including Julia Ward Howe's husband—briefly left the country. Ultimately, none was prosecuted.)[29]

Brown won respect for his resoluteness at every turn, expressed in the many letters he wrote from jail, some of which were published in newspapers. They, and the friendly visitors he was allowed to have, told the world that Brown was a man at peace with his fate, willing to die for his convictions, nobly sacrificing

The fire-engine house in which John Brown made his last stand is preserved in the Harpers Ferry National Historical Park in West Virginia.

himself in the best romantic tradition. "Do not grieve on my account," he wrote.[30]

In the South, however, Brown's raid touched off a hysteria of fear and hatred that gripped the region until the Civil War's outbreak little more than a year later. Many Southerners assumed that Harpers Ferry foreshadowed a much larger assault by Northern abolitionists. Diabolical plots were imagined everywhere, leading to senseless violence. Anyone, black or white, including innocent Northerners traveling in the South, could be terrorized, tarred and feathered, or even lynched merely for arousing no more than suspicion. In town after town, vigilance committees were set up. Books were burned. Baseless but panicky rumors circulated that abolitionist agents were secretly at work across the South.

The firestorm was fed by the South's long, deep-seated fear of its own slaves, the apprehension that their white masters might someday reap the whirlwind they had sown. As imaginations ran amok, the South was suffused with (as one historian put it) "a feeling of tenseness which led Southerners to hang peddlers and piano tuners, and to see abolitionists swarming everywhere."[31] An Alabama paper repeated a common thought: "Who knows but what some deep-dyed villain … may be at this time tampering with our slaves, and furnishing them with arms and poisons to accomplish their hellish designs."[32] A Houston, Texas, newspaper claimed to have learned of the plotting of "a gigantic servile uprising" when, on cue, slaves would murder their owners and "the young and handsome women [would be] parceled out amongst these infamous scoundrels."[33]

As his execution neared, Brown became a candidate for martyrdom in the eyes of many Northerners while remaining a candidate for perdition in the eyes of many Southerners. He remained impressively calm. Brown's wife, Mary, who had endured his many absences and now faced the final one, visited him the day before the execution. Guards surrounded them, giving them no privacy. At first, the couple burst into tears, but then Brown repeatedly told Mary, "My dear, you must keep your sperrets up" ("sperrets" being Brown's pronunciation).[34]

Brown was hanged the next day as his wife waited at the hotel in Harpers Ferry. She accompanied her husband's body to New York City where a public viewing was held. Then she took the coffin to their North Elba farm for burial.[35] Meanwhile, Abraham Lincoln was declaring that "even though [Brown] agreed with us in thinking slavery wrong, that cannot excuse violence, bloodshed, and treason." He said he "believed the old man insane."[36]

After witnessing Brown's execution for "his atrocious crimes & worse intentions," Ruffin left Charles Town strangely touched. Brown's unflinching courage, his commitment to his cause, however much Ruffin opposed it, impressed the Southerner. Perhaps he felt a kinship with a fellow fanatic.[37]

But the experience also energized Ruffin. He obtained some of Brown's pikes and labeled them "Samples of the favors designed for us by our Northern Brethren," causing a stir wherever he carried one. He sent others to Southern governors and at least one governor mounted his on the wall of his office. Carrying a captured pike and a supply of pamphlets, Ruffin traveled throughout the South, preying on fears as he preached secession in his homely way. The crowds were listening now. Ruffin even wrote a novel, *Anticipations of the Future,* that predicted a civil war.

In November 1860, a year after Brown's execution, Ruffin harangued an audience in Charleston and knew that he, the fire-eater, was speaking to their hearts and minds at last. To cheers he declared, "I have thought and studied upon this question for years. It has been literally the one great idea of my life, the independence of the South."[38] Within weeks, South Carolina seceded from the Union, to be followed over the next few months by ten other Southern states—every one of them haunted by the spirit of John Brown.

An Iowa acquaintance of Brown's, Dr. George B. Gill, remembered how he had tried to talk the old man out of the raid. "You and your handful of men cannot cope with the whole South," Gill had said. Brown had calmly replied, "I tell you, doctor, it will be the beginning of the end of slavery."

Old Brown was right about that, and he was right about something else too. As he left his cell for the gallows, he pressed a piece of paper into the hand of one of the guards. On it he had written this prophecy: "I John Brown am now quite *certain* that the crimes of this *guilty, land: will* never be purged *away;* but with *blood.*"[39]

FLASHBACK: A RAILROAD UNDER THE GROUND

Long before John Brown thought of going south to free the slaves, thousands of the bravest and strongest were freeing themselves. Since the early 1800s, they had dared to run away from their Southern masters and make dangerous journeys north to places like Ohio, where they might be helped by a mysterious railroad with no trains and no track.

One of these stalwarts was a twenty-one-year-old Kentucky slave named Henry W. Bibb. Slogging through the snow near Cincinnati on a winter morning in January 1837, Bibb grew desperate as he fled north through Ohio, a fugitive in a strange land. It was bitterly cold, his shoes had worn through to his bare feet, and he knew no one in the area.

Faint, hungry, and lame, Bibb could see people eating breakfast inside their warm homes. The night before, he had twice knocked on doors to ask for admission to the fireside. Both times he was refused and now, having somehow survived the night, Bibb was feeling hopeless.

Then he saw a low cottage, its breakfast table "spread with all its bounties," and only a single woman in sight. Unable to bear his hunger any longer, he worked up his courage and went to the cottage door. He asked the woman if she would be good enough to sell him "sixpence worth of bread and meat."[40]

She cut off what he wanted and handed it to him. When he tried to hand her the money, she burst into tears, and, saying "never mind the money," turned away, gently bidding him to continue his journey.

The woman's generosity revived Bibb's body and soul. He forged ahead, using the North Star for guidance. Sustained by sources he never identified, but which probably were furnished by the Underground Railroad, he reached a hotel in Wood County in northwest Ohio after several days. There he worked as a cook for a few hours to earn his room and board. Then he walked a few more miles to Perrysburg, near Toledo, where he found a community that welcomed him like a brother. Like him, they were African Americans, many of them runaway slaves.[41]

Bibb had run away on Christmas Day 1836, crossing the Ohio River from Kentucky and making his way to the home in Cincinnati of a black man named Job Dundy. Dundy told him about Ohio's Underground Railroad and the abolitionists, neither of which Bibb knew about. Then Dundy had taken Bibb to an abolitionist who fed him and gave him directions to the next "station" on the way north to Canada, where the fugitive slave law of the United States could not reach him.

Bibb's story would unfold for years as he repeatedly returned south in futile efforts to rescue his wife and children. Repeatedly, he was recaptured and forced to escape again by way of Cincinnati. Finally, Bibb went to Canada and stayed, where—his wife apparently having left him—he married another woman. He dedicated his life to helping other runaway slaves. Later, he wrote and published his story, a book that went through several printings.[42]

Bibb was the son of a slave and, he believed, a white legislator in Kentucky. He was brought up there or, "more correctly speaking … I was *flogged up:* I received stripes without number," was starved, and denied adequate clothing.[43] As a child, Bibb served a woman named White. "She would often seat herself in a large rocking chair, with two pillows about her, and would make me rock her, and keep off the flies. She was too lazy to scratch her own head, and would often make me scratch and comb it for her, and keep off the flies. She would at other times lie on her bed, in warm weather, and make me fan her, while she slept, [and] scratch and rub her feet."[44]

Bibb's story tells us something about the Underground Railroad. Except for the woman who gave him food, Bibb never revealed how he was helped to reach Wood County from Cincinnati, a hard winter's journey by foot of more than 150 miles. Under the Fugitive Slave law, the Underground Railroad's work was illegal, so it was secretive and remains shadowy even today. The hardships Bibb endured in Ohio suggest the Underground Railroad was not quite the carefully organized system of legend, smoothly carrying passive black "passengers" north to freedom. It was an informal network of brave, like-minded men and women who persistently improvised without a blueprint.

The Underground Railroad wouldn't have existed but for the courage and ingenuity of the runaway blacks themselves. Despite the fevered imaginings of Southerners, the abolitionists had no network of secret agents. Most runaways had to find their own way out of their owners' clutches. Then they had to creep through a countryside teeming with suspicious slave owners and search parties using bloodhounds.

Using disguises or false identity papers, the fugitives traveled by foot and usually at night, hiding in the forest during the day. Even when they reached a "free" state, runaways could be pursued by slave-catchers. Many escapes, one historian has argued, were mostly unaided.[45]

Which is not to deny that the Underground Railroad was an important, noble conspiracy of high moral order, an admirable enterprise of both whites as well as blacks. It was, as historian Alfred Bushnell Hart wrote, "the unconstitutional but logical refusal of several thousand people to acknowledge that they owed any regard to slavery."[46] It was America's first great example of interracial cooperation and its first great resistance movement after the American Revolution. However, it couldn't have worked without the courage, energy, and initiative of the African Americans themselves.

Today, it is hard to go very far in Ohio without being shown a building said to have been an "Underground Railroad station," equipped with hiding places for runaways. Modern researchers have had trouble verifying the existence of all those hidey-holes.[47] Some claims may be suspect, the stories more folklore than history.[48] Even if the activity of the Underground Railroad has been exaggerated, however, it seems likely that thousands of runaway slaves got aid and comfort from Ohioans, black and white.

Much of what we think we know about the Underground Railroad comes from pioneering research by an Ohio State University professor named Wilbur Henry Siebert who joined the history faculty in 1891. The new professor soon realized that his young scholars' minds were prone to wander, but their attention could be recaptured with "a mysterious and romantic subject that was rich in adventure"—the Underground Railroad.

In those days, some OSU students had parents or grandparents with first-hand experience with the Underground Railroad, so Professor Siebert sent them questionnaires. Grouping the returns by Ohio county, he could see patterns pointing to "railroad lines" and "stations" used by fugitive slaves. Fascinated, Siebert used his summers to travel the state by horse and buggy, talking with old residents, visiting sites, and gathering memorabilia. Later, he branched out to other states.

Of the fourteen Northern states, from New England to Iowa, Ohio was "the great thoroughfare" to Canada for runaway slaves, according to Siebert. His maps show a spider's web of 2,800 to 3,000 miles of escape routes throughout Ohio, a network connecting thirteen ports of entry, on the state's

Ohio River border with Kentucky and western Virginia, to five embarkation points along Lake Erie. "Ohio was the foremost state in the abolition business, being peculiarly located for this purpose," Siebert asserted.[49]

Siebert identified 1,600 Underground Railroad "operators" in Ohio and estimated that at least forty thousand fugitives were aided in Ohio between 1830 and 1860. The total could be even larger, for Siebert believed Underground Railroad activity began in Ohio around 1815 and continued to 1865.

The most important ports of entry along the Ohio River were two Ohio communities: the city of Cincinnati and its little neighbor forty miles up the river, the town of Ripley. Each winter, after the Ohio River froze, Cincinnati abolitionists learned to expect "a stampede of fugitives from Kentucky," according to Siebert. Cincinnati had a community of free blacks who could help runaways, as well as a body of white sympathizers, among them the Quaker Levi Coffin, so dedicated to helping fugitive slaves that he was sometimes called the "President of the Underground Railroad."

In Ripley, a town that was a fraction of Cincinnati's size, were two of the most remarkable men in Ohio's early history. They were the Rev. John Rankin, a white Presbyterian minister, and John Parker, a free black man who was an iron molder. Allies who worked independently of each other, Rankin and Parker, and some other citizens of Ripley, helped thousands of fugitive slaves from Kentucky on the opposite shore of the Ohio River.

Born in Tennessee, Rankin came to Ripley in 1822, where, over a busy forty-four-year career in ministry, he would attack Ripley's "immorality," establish several new churches in nearby towns, write influential tracts on abolitionism and speak widely on the subject, and help found abolition societies. He and his wife, Jean ("who contributed greatly to my success"), would raise thirteen of their own children, plus an orphan. Apparently never resting, the Rankins and their older children defied the Fugitive Slave law to help hundreds of runaway slaves in their flight north.[50]

The Rankins' little brick house still sits on a hill overlooking the town and the river. They kept a light burning in their window as a beacon. Runaway slaves would cross the river and climb long steps to the Rankins, who would hide them in a root cellar or barn and care for them until they could be sent on their way north. The Rankins endured slave-hunters pounding on their door and sometimes had to brandish weapons to face them down. One of Rankin's sons estimated his family helped at least two thousand fugitives, "not losing one."[51]

The Rev. John Rankin House, where many escaped slaves were welcomed on their way to freedom, overlooks the Ohio River from a hill in Ripley.

The Rankins knew the Lyman Beecher family in Cincinnati, who also were Presbyterians, abolitionists, and volunteers for the Underground Railroad. Rankin told the Beechers how a mulatto slave woman from Kentucky named Eliza Harris and her baby, pursued by slave-catchers and their dogs, had fled across the frozen Ohio River, leaping from one ice floe to another. The Rankins sheltered Eliza and sent her north to Canada via the Underground Railroad.[52]

Eliza's story was the genesis, in 1853, of *Uncle Tom's Cabin,* by Harriet Beecher Stowe, a best-selling novel that connected Northerners emotionally to the plight of the slaves. Suddenly, the suffering of the slaves became more than a moral or legal issue. Now it was a compelling human story, and one that swept the country, arousing enormous sympathy for African Americans in bondage. Mrs. Stowe, who called herself "a little bit of a woman, about as thin and dry as a pinch of snuff," was invited to the White House. On bending down to shake her hand, tradition holds that President Lincoln said, "So this is the little woman who made this big war."[53]

Near the banks of the Ohio River lived an ex-slave named John Parker. Parker had bought his freedom in 1845 and settled in Ripley where he was able to practice his trade as a foundryman. Highly intelligent, Parker ran a successful business and was an inventor. For Parker, the worst part of slavery had been "the taking away from a human being the initiative, of thinking, of doing his own ways."[54]

Although few agents of the Underground Railroad ever entered slave territory, Parker rowed to the Kentucky shore about one night a week, sometimes going inland to help fugitives. "These long-distance travelers were usually people strong physically, as well as people of character, and were resourceful when confronted with trouble," he later said. Most needed "weeks to make the journey, sleeping under trees in the daytime and slowly picking their dangerous way at night."[55] Parker didn't dare to keep records of the slaves he helped, but it was at least several hundred and perhaps as many as two thousand.

On one occasion Parker and two runaways evaded slave-hunters by lying in three empty coffins and pulling the lids over themselves. Another time, Parker met two runaway girls on the Kentucky shore and noticed "one was short, the other tall, but both were unusually fat." That was because they had taken their mistress's clothing. One had on three dresses, the other four, and both were wearing "much underwear," as well as their owner's "tilter hoops."

Taking the girls on board, Parker recalled "they filled the boat to overflowing with hoop skirts." Probably gritting his teeth, Parker set out rowing for the Ohio shore but soon realized the party was being pursued. Reaching the other shore, "the tall girl with her hoop skirts drawn up about as high as her head went like a scared rabbit." Parker made the shorter girl take off all her dresses but one, but then, gentleman that he was, carried her dresses for her. The two girls' escape was successful.[56]

Parker met a man and his wife who wanted to escape slavery but would not leave their baby in the hands of their owners. The owners took the infant every night into their bedroom, where the man kept a candle burning and a pair of pistols

In Ripley, the house of an enterprising former slave named John Parker was a station on the Underground Railroad.

Eliza's escape across the ice floes, told in Harriet Beecher Stowe's novel, *Uncle Tom's Cabin*, was based on an event that occurred near Ripley.

beside the bed. Late one night, Parker crept into the bedroom on his hands and knees, seized the baby from the bed where the man and woman lay sleeping, and fled. With the angry owner in pursuit, Parker rowed the baby and its parents across the river and successfully hid them.[57]

In his autobiography, John Parker called Ripley "the real terminus of the Underground Railroad. ... It wielded more influence in the west than any other town, big or little. ... That the town deserved its reputation is shown by the fact [that] it was generally known throughout Kentucky as 'the hell hole of abolition.'"[58]

FLASHBACK: A BARGAIN WITH THE DEVIL

If there was a moment in American history of which it could be said, *here* civil war was foreordained and its bloodshed and misery made inevitable, it would have to be a hot day in the summer of 1787 in Philadelphia. Here, from the thirteen original states, several dozen delegates in wigs and knee breeches—scratching themselves and sweating in a stuffy room—arrived at a decision that would lead to civil war seventy-four years later. They produced our Constitution.

Praised as the "Miracle at Philadelphia" and "A Brilliant Solution" and justly regarded with reverence to this day, the Constitution was, nonetheless, an imperfect document.[59] It was imperfect because it was produced by politicians practicing what politicians do best: the art of the possible. It was a set of compromises, written according to the understandings of the day, which is why it has to be amended every now and then.

If they had not compromised with each other to produce a document that their states would ratify, these men faced the possibility the United States of America—a nation many had helped bring to birth—would dissolve in a bitter cloud of failure. The Articles of Confederation, under which the thirteen original states had first organized themselves, was the problem.

Riots and insurrections were breaking out like measles across the new nation. Under the weak central government established by the Articles, the new nation had no coherent foreign policy, was unable to levy taxes, and couldn't adequately defend itself from rebellions or attacks. Competition between states stifled commerce. Two popular insurrections—the Whiskey Rebellion and Shays' Rebellion—and a host of smaller uprisings by armed and angry farmer raised fears the nation was breaking apart. The United States was under siege from within and vulnerable to threats from without. Something better than the Articles was needed, and quickly.

Because federal law deemed slaves "property," armed and ruthless slave hunters pursued runaways into Northern states.

By this time, slavery had existed in the United States for about a century, largely in the South. Some delegates to the 1787 convention wanted to abolish it, calling it a "nefarious institution" and denying "the idea that there could be property in men."[60] However, Southern intransigence, led by South Carolina and Georgia, made clear that no document would be born if it included a ban on slavery.[61]

Abolitionist sentiment in Philadelphia's Independence Hall faltered in face of the urgent need to strengthen the government. The country was at risk of falling apart. The Founding Fathers settled for a document that did not mention slavery, and, by making certain allowances, grandfathered it. And so, as Johns Hopkins University political economist Francis Fukuyama put it, "The United States itself was born with the birth defect of slavery."[62]

Trying to put the best face on things, some abolitionists assumed that slavery would dwindle away of its own accord. It did not. A New England Yankee named Eli Whitney invented the cotton gin in 1793, enabling one man to do the work of fifty picking seeds from cotton lint. Suddenly, it was economically possible to raise and process huge crops of the fiber and make money ... so long as there were enough hands to cultivate and pick it. Textile mills sprang up in the North and Europe. Southerners came to call cotton their "king." Because so much field labor was needed, the slave population mushroomed, becoming a cornerstone not only of the Southern economy, but also of Southern life. At one time, there had been some opposition to slavery even in the South, but money talked and what it said was: keep the slaves. The opposition faded.

As slavery grew, so did opposition to it in the North. It became the issue that would not die. Again and again, government tried to paper over the problem: in 1820, with the Missouri Compromise's boundaries on slavery: then the Compromise of 1850, which further enabled the pursuit of fugitive slaves; followed by the Kansas-Nebraska Act of 1854 and "Bleeding Kansas;" capped off by the Dred Scott decision of 1857 in which the Supreme Court ruled blacks "had no rights which the white man was bound to respect."

Every effort to solve the slavery problem failed. Years of bitter argument over it drew a painful, red scar across the nation's face. By the 1850s, the atmosphere was explosive. Then came John Brown's raid on Harpers Ferry.

From the creation of the Constitution in 1787 to John Brown's raid in 1859, Ohio was a drum on which the nation's tensions could be heard beating. Here were heard some of the loudest voices against slavery as well as the shrill cries of racists defending it. Congress had banned slavery in the Northwest Territory, from which Ohio was formed, but it did nothing about racial ignorance. "Negrophobia" was rampant in Ohio and the N-word fell casually from the lips even of genteel Ohioans.

One year after achieving statehood in 1803, Ohio enacted "black laws" to discourage African Americans from coming to the state. Under the laws, which were enforced unevenly and arbitrarily, free blacks had to furnish "certificates of freedom," register, and pay fees to settle in Ohio. They could not vote or testify in court. "Black codes" in Indiana and Illinois also punished blacks for being black.

Blacks fleeing the South caused Ohio Gov. Allen Trimble to worry in 1827 about a "rapid increase" in immigration by "this unfortunate and degraded race."[63] In 1829, race riots erupted in Cincinnati. Many blacks fled the city, while others remained behind to fight, at one point using a cannon to drive back a white mob. On the border between free and slave states, Cincinnati would see racial clashes again and again. Tensions there have continued into the twenty-first century.

And yet, co-existing uneasily with the Midwestern racists were many anti-slavery people. They were noisy and persistent enough to turn Ohio into the western capital of the anti-slavery movement. In 1815 in St. Clairsville, a Quaker named Benjamin Lundy formed the first antislavery society west of the Appalachians.

In 1817—fourteen years before William Lloyd Garrison, an Easterner, produced his famous anti-slavery journal *The Liberator*—a Quaker preacher named Charles Osborn began publishing an anti-slavery newspaper, *The Philanthropist,* in Mount Pleasant, Ohio. It was said to be the nation's first anti-slavery newspaper. Founded in 1835 in northern Ohio, Oberlin College was one of the first American institutions of higher learning to enroll blacks and the first to admit women. In the same year, an eastern Quaker named Augustus Wattles established a community for blacks at Carthagena in Mercer County, which is on the Indiana border west of Lima, Ohio. Black farmers and tradesmen thrived there.

Anti-slavery sentiment was so widespread in Ohio that by the late 1830s more than two hundred local anti-slavery societies had sprung up. (In reaction, some *anti*-anti-slavery groups appeared.) The anti-slavery group in Portage County boasted nine hundred members and claimed to be the largest in the nation.[64] Salem, Ohio, was home to many Quakers and a center of anti-slavery activities. It hosted conventions and was the headquarters of the *Anti-Slavery Bugle,* published from 1845 to 1861.

Two of the most outspoken abolitionists in Congress were Ohio's Joshua Giddings, who served in the House from 1838 to 1859, and Benjamin F. Wade, in the Senate from 1850 to 1868. Giddings and Wade came from that watershed of anti-slavery sentiment, Ashtabula County in the Western Reserve region of northeast Ohio. In his private law practice in Cincinnati, Salmon P. Chase did so much pro bono legal work for fugitive slaves in Ohio that critics derided him as "the Attorney General for Runaway Negroes."[65] Chase carried his anti-slavery sentiments to the Ohio governorship from 1856 to 1860.

In 1854, an anti-slavery society meeting in Salem was hurriedly adjourned so members could take advantage of a legal loophole and pluck a slave child from her master, who was passing through town by train.[66] Some escapes ended tragically. In 1856, a party of seventeen Kentucky slaves escaped to Cincinnati, pursued by slave hunters. Nine of the runaways escaped, but when eight others, including Margaret Garner and her children, were cornered, the mother slashed the throat of one of her daughters to prevent her capture.

A memorable series of events occurred in 1858 and 1859 involving Oberlin. Progressive from the start, the northern Ohio college and its town became a hub of abolition sentiment. In September 1858 a U.S. deputy marshal seized a fugitive slave, named John Price, who had been living in Oberlin, and took him to nearby Wellington to be sent south by train. A crowd of men from Oberlin and Wellington overpowered the marshal and freed Price.

The "Oberlin-Wellington Rescuers" were indicted, but only two were sentenced, and only to short terms. The rest were freed under a plea agreement. By this time, John Price had long since escaped to Canada and the rescuers claimed a moral victory. By a three-to-two vote in 1859, however, the Ohio Supreme Court turned down the rescuers' appeal, ruling it couldn't nullify the hated federal Fugitive Slave law.

The decision was a blow to the rescuers, but, for the moment, the court's ruling averted a showdown between federal and state authority. But only for the moment. Prophesying better than it knew, the *Cleveland Morning Leader* asserted that the "struggle between Freedom and Slavery, Liberty and Despotism is but begun. The past is full of encouragement, the Future of promise, for 'Revolutions never go backward.'"[67]

Within two years, the *Morning Leader*'s prophecy would be fulfilled. The sins of "this guilty land" were going to "be purged away ... with blood."

A GRAND ADVENTURE

The Civil War began as a grand adventure, with fine speeches, bands oom-pah-pahing, girls in pretty frocks waving goodbye to their brave soldier boys, and huzzahs everywhere for the Grand Old Flag, sure to wave once more over one nation, truly indivisible. The nation was intoxicated with war, fevered by excitement; much later, an American war correspondent named Chris Hedges would explain this universal and eternal kind of mass thrilling: "*War is a force that gives us meaning,*" he wrote.

Although the Union would achieve victory in the end, the war to win it would penetrate people's lives far more deeply and painfully than they could have ever imagined. It would reach into every hamlet, town, and city in Ohio, touch everyone and, for many, change things forever.

It was a noble cause, gilded by Victorian romanticism, but, as wars always do, it would turn out to be bloody, mean, and hard. The war would peel away the masks and pretenses people wore every day, wreck some families and bring some closer together, and change life's direction for many more. The war would slash through Ohio and its sister states of Indiana and Illinois like a ripsaw, cutting out whole strips of population from towns. It would end a horrifying number of lives—more than 35,000 men from Ohio alone, the equivalent in Ohio's population today of more than 175,000.

The war would permanently injure hundreds of thousands more, sending home legions of men who had lost arms, hands, legs, parts of their faces, their ability to work, their control of bodily functions, their *sanity*. Some of the men couldn't re-adjust to civilian life and would turn into tramps, wandering the American landscape like wraiths, mumbling to themselves. And some of those who had gone off to fight would simply disappear, as if sucked into a whirlpool, never to be heard from again.

But in April 1861 no one knew that. Across the nation, and throughout Ohio, the attack on Fort Sumter set men and women excitedly preparing for war.

In Galena, Illinois, Ulysses S. Grant's reaction to the attack on Fort Sumter was unambiguous. "I have but one sentiment now," he wrote his father. "That is, we have a Government, and laws and a flag, and they must all be sustained."[68] He told a brother, "I think I ought to go into the service."[69] Almost immediately, he was asked to preside at a meeting to raise volunteers from Galena. (The request surprised him, for he still considered himself a newcomer.)

A company of soldiers was quickly raised in Galena and Grant drilled the recruits. He even showed the ladies of Galena how to make their uniforms. Grant was offered the company's captaincy, but declined in order to search for another position. His military education and experience merited a greater responsibility. Although that search would take longer than he expected, Grant would never return to his job in the family's leather store.[70]

In St. Louis, Missouri, the news of war reached yet another West Pointer from Ohio who had abandoned a military career years before. Like Grant, William Tecumseh Sherman was unreservedly a Union man, but for the time being he stubbornly stayed put, president of a local street car line. He had been sulking since March, when President Lincoln had airily dismissed Sherman's warning about the rebellious mood of Louisianans—and, by implication, Sherman himself.

Moreover, Ohio—then creating officerships—"has always ignored me," Sherman grumbled to his brother, Sen. John Sherman.[71] Claiming he needed to honor his contract with the street car line and make money to pay debts, Sherman insisted he would not volunteer, but left himself a small opening: "If I am offered a place that suits me I may accept."[72]

Hundreds of miles away, in the Pacific Northwest, a hot-tempered young army lieutenant named Philip Henry Sheridan was squirming in frustration over events in the East. At their remote post in Indian country, Sheridan and his detachment were at the end of the information pipeline, so news of growing tension between North and South dribbled into camp only once a week. Sheridan, who came from Ohio, was a man born to fight and if a big one

Stationed in the remote Pacific Northwest, a pugnacious young Lt. Philip H. Sheridan itched to join the war.

was coming, he wanted to be in it, and soon. For now, however, all he could do was wait.

In Ohio, however, thousands of men and boys were brooking no delay. Planting season had begun, but thousands of farmers, their sons, and their hired men deserted the fields to enlist, leaving their womenfolk, youngsters, and the elderly to tend the farms. Offices, schoolrooms, and workshops emptied. Volunteers came from every sector of society.

In the city of Cleveland on a Monday evening, April 15, the day of the president's first call for volunteers, an Irish immigrant and apprentice cabinet maker named Thomas Francis Galwey enlisted as a private in the Hibernian Guards, a militia company of Irishmen.

A vibrant, energetic youth, Galwey took care not to disclose his true age. He was only fifteen.

In the Fairfield County shire town of Lancaster, a popular young shoemaker named Joab Stafford began a hurried effort Tuesday morning to enroll enough volunteers to fill out his undermanned militia company. Captain Stafford, who was married and the father of a three year old, needed one hundred men for his company to be accepted.

In the somnolent farming community of Cardington, meanwhile, a banker named John Beatty, age thirty-two, was recruiting an entire company of men from scratch, enlisting himself as a private. Almost immediately the recruits voted Beatty their captain and by Friday he could report his brand-new company ready for duty.

Within a fortnight, twenty-three-year-old Oscar Ladley, an unmarried dry goods clerk in Yellow Springs, bid farewell to his mother and two sisters, and headed to Columbus. He enrolled as a private in the 16th Ohio Volunteer Infantry. So it went throughout the state in the days after Fort Sumter.

It took a few weeks longer for some. In Poland, Ohio, a slim, dark-haired,

A teacher named William McKinley weighed his options, then went to war as a private.

bookish eighteen-year-old school teacher named William McKinley decided, by early summer, in his deliberative way to go off to war. First, he told his mother. Then he and a friend made their way to the training camp at Columbus where a famous explorer named John C. Frémont was in charge. "I remember he pounded my chest and looked square into my eyes, and finally pronounced me fit for a soldier," McKinley recalled.[73] The young schoolteacher was assigned to be an infantryman in the 23rd Ohio. William S. Rosecrans was the regiment's colonel and its major was named Rutherford B. Hayes.

Simmering on the sidelines in Washington, forty-six-year-old Edwin McMasters Stanton, the nation's former attorney general now in private life, was alternately seized by panic and frustration. On learning that secessionists in Charleston had opened fire on Fort Sumter, Stanton groaned, "We have war upon us! The impression is held by many: that, in less than thirty days [Confederate President Jefferson] Davis will be in possession of Washington."[74] To a friend in New York, he wrote of the risk to "this government [of] utter and complete extinction."[75]

Congressman Clement L. Vallandigham, Dayton lawyer, newspaper publisher, and very outspoken Democrat, heard the news about Fort Sumter with profound regret. Vallandigham and many Northern Democrats—among them, Sen. Stephen A. Douglas, the Little Giant from Illinois, Lincoln's opponent in the late race for the presidency—opposed abolitionism but desperately wished to avoid secession. Now they would have to decide whether to close ranks with the Republicans in defense of the Union … or do what?

Over succeeding years, tens of thousands of Ohioans would volunteer to serve in the war. Only a few would have to be drafted. By 1865, upwards of three-hundred thousand enlistments would have been counted in Ohio.

There would be about 190,000 in Indiana and 250,000 in Illinois.

Farmers, clerks, lawyers, mechanics, and men with names like Altman, Garfield, Hartzell, Opdycke, Spiegel, and Warner, would enlist. Glowing with the innocence of a romantic and optimistic age, they could not imagine the places they would go, or what they would be called on to do and to endure, or what they would bring home—and what they would leave behind.

The war would hasten the reshaping of Ohio's landscape from a pastoral land of small farmers wrapped in a bucolic haze to a place of factories and office buildings and cities, with farms as the interstices. Even the psychic energy of this place would be different, as the rhythms of life, governed so long by the seasons, slowly came under the influence of big industry, big government, and big media.

War changes everything.

To Learn More:

No state in the Union can show you more about the Underground Railroad than Ohio, slavery's great escape hatch in the West. One of the nation's newest, largest, and liveliest history museums, The National Underground Railroad Freedom Center, opened in 2004 in downtown Cincinnati (**http://www.freedomcenter. org/** or **513-333-7500**). An authentic slave pen is one of the exhibits. Cincinnati also offers the Harriet Beecher Stowe House (2950 Gilbert Ave.; **513-751-0651** or **http://ohiohistory.org/places/stowe/**), where the author of *Uncle Tom's Cabin* lived while she was learning about slavery close at hand. In little Ripley, about forty-five miles from Cincinnati, the Rankin House—now a museum—still keeps watch over the Ohio River where many escaping slaves (including Uncle Tom's Eliza) crossed (**http://www.ohiohistory.org/undergroundrr/** or **937-392-1627**). In Ripley you can also visit the home of John P. Parker, the former slave who helped many others escape. (**http://www.johnparkerhouse.org/index.shtml**).

Farther afield, the National Park Service is restoring Harpers Ferry, West Virginia (**http://www.nps.gov/archive/hafe/**or **304-535-6029**).

Thrilling true stories can be found in *His Promised Land: The Autobiography of John P. Parker, Former Slave and Conductor on the Underground Railroad.* John Brown's life is related in *To Purge This Land with Blood*, by Stephen B. Oates and his significance pointed out in *John Brown, Abolitionist: The Man Who Killed Slavery, Sparked the Civil War, and Seeded Civil Rights*, by David S. Reynolds.

Ohio in the early 1800s was a land of opportunity, where brave, ambitious people turned a raw frontier into a land of bounty.

3

WAR CHANGES
EVERYTHING

Mid-April to Early Summer 1861

Beautiful Ohio, thy wonders are in view,

Land where my dreams all come true!

(from the chorus of "Beautiful Ohio," the official state song)

At first, only the bravest white men and women, armed with "a Bible, a rifle and whisky jug," (as one historian put it) had dared settle in Ohio in the 1780s.[1] It still was Indian country, a land ruled by the Ottawa, Wyandot, Miami, Shawnee, Delaware, and Mingos.

Then, in 1794, Anthony Wayne, a general so fearless he was known as "Mad" Anthony, defeated the Indians once and for all at the Battle of Fallen Timbers, near Maumee. Word spread of Ohio's rich virgin soil: throw seed on the ground and stand back! Settlers streamed in, clambering over the rocks and ruts of muddy trails that tunneled through dark woods. Ohio, Conrad Richter wrote in his historical novel, *The Trees*, was "a sea of solid treetops. ... As far as the eye could reach, this lonely forest sea rolled on and on till its faint blue billows broke against an incredibly distant horizon."[2]

Some of Ohio's settlers were farmers from New England, New York, or Pennsylvania who had given up trying to wrest livings from hill farms good mostly for raising rocks and children. Some were small farmers from the Upper South who had worn out their soil or their patience with plantation society. Some were clerks and teachers and mechanics and lawyers and craftsmen from crowded Eastern cities or Europe who were looking for a way to get ahead.

Some were woodsmen from thinning forests, searching for new hunting grounds.

The newcomers left behind discouraged lives in the East, the South, Germany, and Ireland, and came to Ohio seeking one thing: a fresh start in a new place with *opportunity for everyone*. One of the framers of the Northwest Ordinance had predicted that the land between the Ohio River and Lake Erie would become "the garden of the world, the seat of wealth, and the *centre* of a great Empire."[3] By 1800, the number of settlers in Ohio had reached 45,365. Three years later, it passed sixty thousand and with a stroke of Pres. Thomas Jefferson's pen on February 19, 1803, Ohio achieved statehood. It was the first Northern state west of the Appalachian Mountains and the seventeenth state of all.[4]

The settlers kept coming from all parts, making Ohio an America in microcosm. "Old America seems to be breaking up and moving westward," the English traveler Morris Birkbeck marvelled in 1817. "We are seldom out of sight, as we travel this grand track toward the Ohio [River], of family groups behind and before us."[5]

Ohio attracted hard-working strivers. By 1860, these worker bees had transformed a howling wilderness into a pastoral landscape of small farms, a land of milk and honey and many other good things. So many dairy farms dotted the northeastern part of the state that it was nicknamed "Cheesedom."[6] Cattle and hogs fattened in the Miami and Scioto valleys and sheep by the million floated across the landscape like low-lying clouds. Huge fields of grain covered much of the state. Between Columbus and Portsmouth lay "one almost continuous … cornfield" stretching for ninety miles.[7] Almost every farmer had hives of honeybees. And here and there factories were taking root.

It was not all work among the settlers of Ohio. Writing his memories of life before the war, James Dalzell, who had served in the 116th Ohio, remembered, "There were frolics of all sorts, quilting parties, huskings, dances, wood choppings, raisings, merrymakings of all sorts in which the whole country-side joined; plenty of whisky in every house [but] nothing to bring the blush of shame to any cheek."[8]

As Ohio filled with settlers, some with itchy feet joined the stream of migrants coming from the east and headed still further west, filling in spaces in Indiana and Illinois. Indiana joined Ohio in statehood in 1816; Illinois in 1818. Sharing the Ohio River as their southern boundary, Ohio, Indiana, and Illinois formed a tier of states stretching nearly six hundred miles from the western slopes of the Appalachians to the Mississippi River.

With their farms and factories, Ohio and the Midwestern states would become a horn of plenty for the Union war machine. The Midwest would produce fighting men as well; Ohio alone would generate 313,000 enlistments in the Union armed forces, the third largest of any state. Almost all were volunteers from civilian life, not professional fighting men but "citizen soldiers." More than fifty generals, among them the two most important Union commanders, would have Ohio connections, as would nearly sixty more who would be "brevetted" as generals (honored with the title, but not the command authority, for outstanding service).

Hundreds of the Union army's colonels, the officers who personally led regiments or brigades into battle, would be Ohioans. They, too, were volunteers and they had to learn warfare in a hurry, studying in their tents at night, training their men during the day. Four members of Lincoln's Cabinet came from the Midwest, two of the most useful ones being Ohioans. Some of the most influential members of Congress came from Ohio. Settled recently compared to the eastern states, Ohio would make an extraordinary contribution to winning the war. Men and women with Ohio roots, joined by those from its two young neighbors, Indiana and Illinois, would doom the Rebellion.

By the eve of war, Ohio's population had grown nearly 5,100 percent since 1800, its 2,339,511 people in 1860 making it the third largest of the thirty-four states. (Illinois, with 1,711,951, ranked fourth, and Indiana, with 1,350,428, ranked fifth.) Drawing immigrants from everywhere, Ohio was a microcosm of the nation. "Shaped like a wind-rippled flag roll[ing] westward," in historian Walter Havighurst's memorable words, Ohio was a bountiful land of small farmers and nascent industry.

It was one of the more recently settled places, but Ohio already was one of the biggest—peaceful and yet alive with youthful energy, rich in resources, and bustling with business, a place where dreams could come true.

Commotion in Columbus

Henry Beebee Carrington—General Carrington, if you please, although the man had never seen a live battlefield—was the master of his universe, a scholarly, thoughtful, but jittery little man of law books and courts and, as Ohio's adjutant general, the methodical manager of the state's militia system until mid-April 1861, whereupon things went haywire.

His law partner, William Dennison, was a suave patrician, a banker and railroad executive whose slide into the governorship of Ohio in January 1860

Rattled by the war's demands, Ohio Adjutant General Carrington created a state of confusion.

had been as smooth as goose grease. No one expected Dennison the governor to produce much except a warm seat for the next occupant, but then came the unpleasantness at Fort Sumter.

And, until spring 1861, the Ohio legislature had been the usual Midwestern assortment of lawyers and men of affairs, some urbane and others country plain, a variegated lot that settled down now and then in Ohio's little capital city of Columbus to deal with affairs of state. Rivals by day, they would congregate in hotel lobbies at night to lollygag, spit tobacco juice, and drink whiskey. They were used to the droning debate by which such thrilling matters as the supervision of railroads and support of the common schools were decided ever … so … slowly … as the days turned into months and the months turned into yawns.

War changes everything. With the attack on Fort Sumter, Adjutant General Carrington became a roaring engine of activity, Governor Dennison morphed into a take-charge leader, and the General Assembly started making decisions, sometimes in a matter of hours. *Hours.* Columbus shook itself awake, electrified by solemn purpose as excited citizens swarmed its streets. One state senator seized the arm of another and exclaimed, "Mr. Cox, the people have gone stark mad!"[9]

Carrington had never faced a challenge like this but he did not go mad, just somewhat unglued. A Connecticut native and Yale graduate, he had been appointed adjutant general after his law partner, William Dennison, was elected governor. Carrington was an intelligent man with a fondness for things military, but his knowledge came from books. Carrington liked to be called "general," although his title simply meant he was the governor's assistant in charge of the militia "in general." He oversaw Ohio's militia system and reported to the governor, who was commander in chief.[10]

Closely watching Carrington, Dennison, and all the goings-on in Ohio's capital city during the first days of war was twenty-three-year-old Whitelaw Reid, a bright young native of Xenia and graduate of Miami University with a tart tongue and a ready pen. By 1861, "White" Reid was based in Columbus, scrambling in his three-headed role as correspondent for the *Cincinnati Daily Gazette*, the *Cincinnati Times*, and the *Cleveland Herald*, all Republican papers.[11]

According to Reid, Carrington was a small, nervous, easily excitable man of "good literary acquirements."[12] There is a photograph of Carrington in his adjutant general's uniform, complete with epaulets of dangling braid perched on each bony shoulder like enormous birds' nests. That and other pictures reveal a small man with a high forehead and a thin face disappearing into a thicket of chin whiskers. Carrington's deep-set eyes gave him a haunted look.

Until 1861, Ohio's militias had appealed mostly to townies who had time and money, and who enjoyed marching in fine uniforms before admiring eyes. These "military social clubs," as one historian called them, came in handy for suppressing the occasional riot and for turning out on ceremonial moments, but they were hardly combat-ready.[13]

Militia members elected their officers (which meant popularity or influence could trump ability) and gave their companies stern, if sometimes exotic, names (such as "Fencibles," meaning "home guards," and "Videttes," meaning "mounted sentinels"). Training consisted of little more than parade-ground maneuvers. Militias could choose their own uniforms, which produced comic-opera combinations of stiff, plumed hats called shakos, brass buttons, elaborate belting, and shirts and trousers in a spectrum of colors, including both blue and gray.

Until the Civil War, America's on-call militia system was a gossamer shield, existing more on paper than in reality. It let the United States thriftily keep an amazingly small standing army. On war's eve, this nation of thirty-four states and thirty-two million people straddled a continent and defended it with a regular army of only 15,322 enlisted men and 1,080 officers scattered among dozens of dusty frontier posts.[14] In the war to come, most of the armed forces would consist not of professional soldiers or sailors but of phalanxes of volunteers with no real military experience.

For these reasons, as smoke hung over a battered Fort Sumter, Adjutant General Carrington found himself facing two problems. On the one hand, the federal government could be expected, very soon, to demand that Ohio supply it with militiamen, the quota not yet known. The difficulty here was that Ohio's militia consisted of only a handful of under-strength companies scattered among the state's larger cities and towns. Their aggregate strength added up to scarcely a thousand men, most of whom had only a nodding acquaintance with military matters.

Thanks to the public uproar, however, Adjutant General Carrington was being bombarded with what seemed the solution to his first problem: excited offers from every corner of the state, dispatched by telegraph and in person, to straight away send existing militia units or recruit new ones. Carrington's office on Saturday, April 13, the *New York Times* reported, "was thronged by persons eagerly inquiring for the news, and offering their services."[15]

Another paper reported offers were flowing into Carrington's office "with electric speed." By the end of the week "a thousand" offers to serve had been received.[16] Knowing what to do with this bounty of fired-up gladiators was the adjutant general's second big problem. Understaffed and inexperienced, the Ohio adjutant general's office turned into a madhouse. Carrington's head was spinning.

On Monday, April 15, President Lincoln issued a call for seventy-five thousand state militiamen for ninety days of federal service. Ohio's quota was thirteen regiments of one thousand men each, the regiments to be organized in ten companies of one hundred men each. Simultaneously, Governor Dennison received a telegraphed plea to *immediately* send two of those regiments for the defense of Washington. Surrounded on all sides by slave states, the nation's capital feared capture by secessionists, a fear shared throughout Ohio. "The Federal City in Danger" was a typical headline in the state's worried newspapers.[17]

Governor Dennison and Adjutant General Carrington telegraphed fifteen of the state's most promising militia companies and gave them the order they'd been hoping for: come to Columbus at once, prepared to serve your country. That evening, they personally walked to the Columbus homes of the commanders of five more companies to deliver their call-up orders, governor and adjutant general not losing a minute.

"It must have been quite a sight," wrote Dennison's biographer, Thomas C. Mulligan, musing about "the jaunty little adjutant general in his natty uniform with his sword at his side ... marching resolutely through the gaslight, trailed by the tall gentleman governor with the grave countenance and silk hat."[18]

Ohio throbbed with enthusiasm for war. On just one day in Cincinnati, naturalized Frenchmen were reported forming their own home guard unit while the city's printers were rallying to organize a company to go to war.

Also organizing were members of the Young Men's Gymnastic Association, who would be "under the instruction of F. W. Lester, the fencing teacher."[19]

Handbills, newspaper announcements, and parades drummed up volunteers in towns and cities across the state. Community leaders collected contributions to support the families the soldiers were leaving behind. As young men flocked to the militia recruiters, older, wealthier, and pudgier citizens formed "home guard" units. In some cases, employers promised to hold the jobs of departed soldiers until they returned. Ohio by itself, Reid thought, could have supplied at least a third "or more" of the seventy-five thousand men Washington had requested from the nation.[20] An excited Carrington claimed the nation's entire quota could have been met by Ohio.[21]

But Carrington let this tsunami of volunteers overwhelm him. "As hour by hour the telegraph brought [Carrington] the offers of fresh companies, he promptly made answer to each, accepting them all," Reid wrote. A telegram requesting permission to organize a company would arrive and Carrington would fire back his assent within minutes. An hour after that he would receive a second wire, reporting the company complete.[22]

Working in a frenzy, the adjutant general accepted many more volunteers than the number requested by Washington. Carrington, Reid observed, "was … so excitable [as] to bewilder himself and those about him in the fog of his own raising."[23] The thirteen regiments Washington requested from Ohio soon filled, but volunteers kept coming to Columbus and to camps hastily created around the state. This was a people's movement, the volunteers coming from every station and walk of life and representing a cross-section of democracy. In the war to come, a cadre of West Pointers would provide much (though not all) of the generalship. A small number of regulars would serve in the ranks as well, but the rest were needed to fight Indians. Most of the officers on the firing line and the enlisted men under their command were inexperienced volunteers who only recently had stepped away from their plows or desks or classrooms.

Ohio's little country capital of Columbus, with its fewer than twenty thousand residents, was overrun with would-be soldiers and had nowhere to put them. Most volunteers were in civilian dress and some even wore top hats. Some of the volunteers arrived in the fanciful costumes of their volunteer units, giving the streets a carnival air. Perched on the sidelines like vultures were legions of opportunity seekers hoping to make a profit from the war one way or another.[24]

At last, a halt was called to new enrollments. To accommodate part of the flood and protect Ohio as well, Governor Dennison persuaded the legislature to approve, on the state's own authority and expense, ten additional regiments, enrolling ten thousand men. But even then Ohio had more volunteers than it could use.

To dispose of the surfeit of volunteers, thirty companies comprising three thousand men already accepted by Carrington and in camps around the state had to be disbanded. Permission to still others on their way to camp was hurriedly revoked. The disappointed volunteers went home, furiously cursing Governor Dennison and his staff for having sent them on a fool's errand.

Next, Carrington was stuck with the delicate problem of resolving issues of seniority. Prestige attached to those units that had volunteered first and therefore qualified for Company A in a low-numbered regiment. The hard-pressed Carrington didn't know in what order he had accepted militia companies or even when they had arrived in camp. Arguments erupted over whose unit had volunteered first.

Carrington was nothing if not dedicated, however, and somehow he sorted things out. To meet Washington's plea for defenders right away, Carrington whipped together the 1st and 2nd Ohio Volunteer Infantry regiments from the twenty existing militia companies he and Dennison had summoned. These militias, which typically enrolled only forty or fifty active members before the war, had spent frenzied hours recruiting in their hometowns to meet the minimum of one hundred men.[25]

Most of the newly enlarged companies called arrived in Columbus Wednesday, April 17, were organized into two regiments of one-thousand men each the next morning, and were on trains heading east before dawn on Friday, only a week after Fort Sumter was fired upon. Under the circumstances, it was a singular achievement.

While Carrington was racing about, other officers of the militia system were trying to feed and shelter the avalanche of volunteers arriving on the Statehouse's doorstep. They hurriedly booked every hotel room in town and commandeered public spaces in the Statehouse and other buildings. The so-called "million-dollar war bill" to finance the militia was rushed through the state legislature.

Then Carrington got a surprise. Governor Dennison deftly arranged for Carrington's appointment as colonel of a new regiment of the regular army, although the excitable adjutant general hadn't asked for it. In Carrington's place, Dennison appointed a new adjutant general, a former army officer who, presumably, was not so easily flustered.

Ohio's newly completed Statehouse in Columbus housed recruits in its halls and chambers during the war's first weeks.

With his typical boldness, U.S. Congressman Clement L. Vallandigham, Democrat from Dayton, rushed to Columbus to try to persuade Democratic legislators not to support the war. His effort availed him nothing and the Senate drove him off by passing, thanks to Sen. James A. Garfield, a bill defining treason that was aimed squarely at Vallandigham.

It was Ohio's good fortune to have William Dennison as its first "war governor." He had the executive skill and financial acumen needed to respond to the war's demands. Unlike the high-strung Carrington, Dennison kept his head in the crisis, quickly making Ohio a bulwark of the Union war effort.[26] Because of an ill-prepared federal government, the burden of raising and equipping the troops fell largely on the states and their governors at first. Despite some mistakes, Dennison proved more than up to the task, dispatching aides this way and that to buy equipment from other states.

Nevertheless, Dennison suffered a political handicap, and it was a serious one. Although he had been born in Cincinnati, his smarts and suave gave him a sophisticated "Eastern" air. To Ohio's shirt-sleeved and calloused voters, the handsome Dennison seemed as sleek as an otter and too pretty by half. He was "frittered in polish," as they put it. It was an era in which sectional tension existed between East and West as well as North and South. The former was not as virulent as the latter, but Dennison would find that seeming Eastern exacted a political price.

Under the militia call-up, Governor Dennison was entitled to name three brigadier generals and one major general to command Ohio's volunteers. Two of his selections for brigadier general were useful mostly for their political value and would soon fade away, but the man Dennison named to the third brigadier generalship would develop into an able military man. He was Jacob Dolson Cox, the state senator who had been startled by Abby Kelley Foster's triumphant "Glory be to God!" cry.

A skinny, fine-featured six-footer of many talents, Cox was one of those high-energy Victorians who rocketed from one role to another, unimpeded by a later age's rules for professional certification. A many-sided man, he was a lawyer well-read in military literature, fluent in French, a good horseman, and an excellent fencer. He also was married to the daughter of Charles Grandison Finney, a famed revivalist and abolitionist.

Elected to the Ohio Senate in 1859, Cox, together with another Oberlin graduate named Monroe, and a future president named James A. Garfield, formed an alliance that worked closely with Governor Dennison on political matters. Cox and Garfield shared lodging while they were in Columbus. Thoughtful men, they were more worried than thrilled by the war. Coming back to their boarding house after Senate work, the two would often find themselves groaning to each other, "Civil war in *our* land!"[27]

One of their worries was whether Northern Democrats, who had some sympathy for the South, would support the war effort. One night, Cox found himself leaning on a Statehouse railing, listening to the voice of an unseen Stephen A. Douglas. The famed Illinoisan was speaking from the shadows of a second-floor hotel room, his orotund voice rolling through the darkness to a hushed crowd gathered in Capitol Square. Lincoln had defeated Democrat Douglas for the presidency the year before, but now Douglas was pledging his loyalty and hearty support to the Union, Lincoln, and the war effort. Douglas declared this was a time for loyal Americans to stand together. Cox went home "breathing freer."[28]

Dennison needed more military know-how than his three brand-new brigadier generals could offer. Soon a young railroad executive in Cincinnati was being urged on him for the state's major generalship. A railroad executive himself at one time, Dennison scarcely knew the man, but the Cincinnatian's boosters were singing his praises.

The Cincinnatian was remarkably able, his supporters said. He was a West Point graduate from Philadelphia who had written an impressive analysis of the European armies while an officer in the regular army. He had retired a captain, moved to Cincinnati, and now, at thirty-four, was an official of the Ohio and Mississippi Railroad. His name was George B. McClellan.

McClellan would be a prize catch because every state, as well as the regular army, was scrambling for officers. Dennison invited him to Columbus and liked what he saw, for McClellan was a man who could make a very good first impression: he was polished, self-assured, and knowledgeable. Sitting in on Dennison's interview with McClellan, Cox found the Cincinnatian "quiet and modest" at first, "but when drawn out he showed no lack of confidence in himself"—a cockiness that would become a McClellan's hallmark.[29] Dennison offered his visitor Ohio's major generalship on the spot and McClellan accepted.

Dennison often worked into the small hours of the night. A stream of official visitors flowed through his Statehouse office. He dispatched emissaries east and west to purchase equipment for the Ohio troops, because it would be months before the national government could take responsibility for outfitting the soldiers. The Statehouse echoed to the sounds of militia men billeted in its chambers—singing, drilling, and skylarking. On the terraces outside, ranks of state legislators practiced military drills supervised by the of handful members with military experience.

Electrified by the war, Ohio's capital city was "in an uproar; business suspended," wrote one correspondent, adding, "The tramp of troops and the rattle of drums were heard all day;" while at night excited young soldiers were "yelling like fiends."[30] Ohio's newly minted Brigadier General Cox and Major General McClellan huddled together to figure out what it would take to properly equip Ohio's soldiers. At the State Arsenal they found only a few boxes of rusted and damaged muskets, some worn-out artillery pieces, and a pile of mildewed harnesses. McClellan remarked wryly, "A fine stock of munitions on which to begin a great war!"[31]

McClellan returned to Cincinnati, in southern Ohio, to create a large camp for training the militia units that had gathered in smaller camps around the state. Such a camp near the state's largest city would concentrate troops ready to defend it against whatever might hurtle over Ohio's all-too-close border with slave state Kentucky. McClellan diplomatically named his hastily erected collection of wooden huts and tents "Camp Dennison." It turned out to be no favor to the governor.

Construction of Camp Dennison began at the end of April and continued throughout May as regiments poured in from the outlying camps. Built on farm fields, the camp site became a sea of mud under spring downpours.

Meals prepared by inexperienced cooks turned the stomachs of young men accustomed to Ma's home cooking. Country boys became ill with childhood diseases carried into camp by city dwellers.

To make things worse, discontented ninety-day men tried to discourage others from enlisting for a longer term under President Lincoln's second call for troops. The newspapers seized on the camp's miseries and soon Governor Dennison was being blamed for Camp Dennison's problems, although he had not created them. The governor had other things on his mind. Ohio shared more than half its border with the slave states of Kentucky and Virginia (West Virginia did not yet exist). Only the Ohio River separated its namesake from secessionist territory. Governor Dennison sent an emissary to Kentucky's Governor Magoffin to discover his intentions. Magoffin made friendly noises indicating Kentucky was going to remain neutral.

Reassured, Dennison turned his eyes toward Virginia. There, prospects were more troubling.

The First Regiments Depart

At first it seemed like the biggest picnic the young Ohioans had ever been on, a grand adventure never dreamed of by farm boys, clerks, and craftsmen. With bands playing, flags waving, and orators singing their praises the men of the 1st and 2nd Ohio Volunteer Infantry rushed east to defend their nation's capital. One day they were planting corn, slopping hogs, making shoes, or clerking in stores—small lives with small jobs, mostly in small towns or nearby—and the next day they were being cheered as heroes.

Composed of twenty old militia companies enrolling two thousand men from around the state, the 1st and 2nd Ohio Volunteer Infantry regiments were the ones Carrington had hurriedly organized and shipped out in response to Washington's plea for defenders. They had departed Columbus before dawn, exactly one week after the secessionists had opened fire on Fort Sumter.

General Carrington created the 1st Ohio with three companies from the Dayton area (the "Lafayette Guards," the "Dayton Light Guards, and the "Montgomery Guards"), two from the Cleveland area (the "Grays" and the "Hibernian Guards"), and one each from Lancaster, Portsmouth, Zanesville, Mansfield, and Cincinnati. He organized the 2nd Ohio with three companies from the Cincinnati area ("Rover Guards," "Zouave Guards," and "Lafayette Guards"), two from the Columbus area ("Videttes" and "Fencibles"), and one each from Springfield, Steubenville, Urbana, Miami County, and Pickaway County.

Wiping tears from their eyes, Ohio families waved goodbye to their young soldiers as they rushed off to war. Some would never return.

The Lancaster Guards, led by thirty-year-old Capt. Joab Stafford, won Carrington's nod for the prestigious designation as Company A of the 1st Ohio. On receiving the call-up telegram on Tuesday, Captain Stafford's Guards had begun parading through the streets of Lancaster at dawn Wednesday, "stars and stripes floating proudly above them," to drum up additional members to fill out their ranks. The goal was quickly achieved.

By late afternoon on Wednesday, a crowd of three thousand watched proudly as 109 men, led by the Lancaster Brass Band, marched to the railroad depot and boarded a train for Columbus. One of their number described the aspiring soldiers as a diverse lot, drawn from the area's "shoemaker shops, saddler shops, tailor shops, brick yards, stores, cigar shops, billiard rooms, law offices, farms, carpenter shops, railroads, butcher shops, and printing offices."[32] Most were between the ages of eighteen and twenty-five, although one private was forty-one.

The train carrying the Lancaster contingent paused in Zanesville, where the volunteers were met by three bands, given "a most bounteous repast," and subjected to several speeches before being sent on their way to Columbus, arriving later that night.[33] Thursday was spent in getting organized under

Adjutant General Carrington's direction. Leaving Columbus between 3 and 4 a.m. Friday morning, three troop trains traveling by different routes delivered the eager recruits of the 1st and 2nd Ohio to Pittsburgh, where they spent a night before continuing to the Pennsylvania capital of Harrisburg.

Along the way, the Ohioans received the cheers and blessings of citizens at every stop, repeatedly hearing, "God bless you all and may you return safely home!"[34] The progress of Captain Stafford's Company A of the 1st Ohio was reported back to Lancaster by Harrison Comer, a waggish twenty-five-year-old private who called himself Harry and liked to write breezy letters to his hometown newspapers.

While the Ohioans were still in Pittsburgh, a jeering mob of street toughs and secessionists, some carrying Confederate flags, attacked the 6th Massachusetts volunteer regiment as it transited from one Baltimore railroad station to another on its way to Washington. At least four soldiers and nine civilians were killed before the shaken New Englanders escaped the rioters and reached the nation's capital.[35] Then Maryland secessionists cut telegraph lines and burned railroad bridges.

Cut off from Washington by the troubles in Maryland, the Ohioans bedded down for two nights in the Pennsylvania Statehouse and other public buildings in Harrisburg. By now, some of the recruits—including 19 of the 109 with which Company A of the 1st Ohio started—had lost their taste for the whole enterprise, dropped out, and returned home. Harrison Comer hastened to reassure the homefolks that Company A was steadfast and true.

The men remaining, he reported cheerfully, "are all in excellent spirits, well satisfied with themselves and their officers. ... Rest assured, that the boys will acquit themselves to ... the glory of the State of Ohio."[36] Spirits were lifted when the daughter of Pennsylvania's governor prettily tore her handkerchief into bits and, like a lady with her knights, gave the fragments to the soldiers.[37]

From Harrisburg the two Ohio regiments went to Lancaster, Pennsylvania, where they spent two nights in hotels and public buildings, then several more nights on straw in the horse stalls at the fairgrounds. They received "substantial" meals, augmented by "whisky smuggled into camp after our officers go to bed," plus "peanuts and apples stolen from peanut vendors."

For amusement, according to an ebullient Pvt. Harry Comer, "we have the best singers ... the most scientific card players ... and more fun than any other company. ... Our boys are all well but one, in good spirits, fat, hale and hearty."[38]

The morale of Company A, Comer reported, benefited from Capt. Joab

Stafford's brand of informal, Western-style leadership. "Captain Joe, as he is familiarly called by the boys, puts on no superfluous airs, and physically and socially surpasses any of the band box soldiery."[39]

It helped a lot when uniforms and guns arrived for distribution to the men. On April 29, the two Ohio regiments were mustered into Federal service and began to feel like real soldiers.[40] Like most new soldiers North and South, they were eager for combat. Harry Comer wrote home to the Lancaster newspaper, "The boys generally, are in for one fight at least; some of them 'spilin' for a muss."[41]

Still cut off from Washington, however, the two Ohio regiments were sent to Philadelphia and quartered in the stables and buildings of Suffolk Park. Here they passed the time with drill and parade, as well as fishing and bathing at a nearby bay.[42] By now, they were running low on rations.

Suffering hunger pangs, men knocked the boards off the rear of their quarters to go in search of food during the night. In response, a sympathetic Philadelphia citizenry sent them "load after load of provisions." Even then, some soldiers remained on the loose and about fifty had to be rounded up and marched back to the camp's guard house, with a band playing the "Rogue's March."[43]

Camp Harrison, established in 1861 six miles north of Cincinnati, was a typical collecting point for Ohio's newly enlisted soldiers.

Finally, however, the orders came to move on to Washington, and so the Ohioans, nervously remembering the rioters' attack on the 6th Massachusetts, prepared in late May to go through Baltimore.

A SECOND GREAT ARMY

Across Ohio during the spring and summer of 1861, eager young men were climbing aboard boxy wooden railroad cars and going off to camp. The departures were noisy affairs, with band music, speeches, cheers for the soldiers, and cheers for the speakers. Then the trains would disappear down the track, men leaning out of windows to wave hats at the crowd of fluttering handkerchiefs fading into the distance.

Saying proud, brave things to each other, parents, sweethearts, wives, and children—many with wet eyes—would drift away, then fall silent as icicles of fear began to prick their hearts. Most of their young men—many of them boys, really—had never been outside Ohio.

Those left behind did not want to be left out of the war effort. While state officials were organizing the troops, women with solemn faces were gathering in kitchens, parlors, and meeting rooms to do their part. They would create "a second great army" that, as one observer put it, would be "working scarcely less earnestly and efficiently for the same great end" as the men.[44]

The Soldiers' Aid Society of Cleveland, born on April 20, 1861, is said to be the first such group in the nation, formed even before the United States Sanitary Commission, the Red Cross of its day.[45] Other groups followed quickly throughout Ohio. Crying "Mothers! Wives! Sisters! Let us do our part in country's cause," three Columbus women organized a meeting to receive "contributions of money, flannel, woolen socks &c" to bring relief to soldiers.[46] Governor Dennison's wife was chosen president of the group, the first Soldiers' Aid society in the capital city.[47] On May 10, volunteers set up a military hospital on South High Street in Columbus and by July 15 it had served three hundred military recruits who had fallen ill.[48]

In Cincinnati, "a company of patriotic ladies" from the Sixth Ward offered to pay for "a number of forty-two-pounder rifle cannon" for fortifying the city.[49] In towns large and small, volunteer groups sprang up by the dozens. Some were no more than neighbors gathering with little ceremony in someone's kitchen, but others elected officers, collected dues, and gave their groups formal names.

Existing ladies' aid and other societies also turned their energies to the war effort. The women knit socks and mittens, made bandages and medical

Ohio women rushed to care for sick and wounded soldiers in the era's primitive military hospitals.

supplies, stitched quilts, collected food, and raised money for soldiers' aid.

Scarcely a week after the Lancaster Guards departed, the ladies of Lancaster organized a fund-raising concert for the benefit of soldiers and families. "The music," reported the *Lancaster Gazette* "was grand. ... When the 'Star Spangled Banner' was concluded the whole audience arose to their feet, and cheer after cheer went up in response to the glorious sentiments of the good old anthem."[50] A few weeks later, the Lancaster women collected "2,117 pounds of good things, such as cakes, fruits, nuts, butter, pickles, preserves, tobacco, segars, &c" for shipment to their soldiers near Washington.[51]

Ohio's women proved how quickly they could respond to sudden emergencies. Little more than a week after Fort Sumter had fallen, members of the newly formed Soldiers' Aid Society of Northern Ohio in Cleveland were making bandages and lint (a soft, fleecy material used in medical care) when they received an urgent appeal. One thousand new recruits were marching into a nearby camp and the men would have to spend the chilly April night on the ground with nothing to cover them. Blankets were needed immediately.

The women set out door to door on what they called a "blanket raid." By nightfall, they had collected 729 donated blankets for the men. The women continued collecting the next day and "before night every volunteer in Camp Taylor had been provided for."[52] Then, because uniforms were not yet ready for the soldiers, the women collected additional clothing for the young recruits, many of whom were farm boys who had only what they were wearing when they answered the call.

In Cincinnati, volunteers took over an unfurnished building in May and turned it into a hospital for sick soldiers. The hospital subsisted on donations until the federal government adopted it in August. At nearby Camp Dennison, women volunteers spent entire days in the sick bays, "bathing the fevered brows ... and bending as angels of mercy over the forms of the dying soldiers, whispering words of Christian comfort and consolation.'"[53]

By June 1861, New Yorkers had established a national body, the United States Sanitary Commission, a civilian organization in which women would fill many roles. After some initial reluctance (Lincoln and others thought the group would be a "fifth wheel" and a hindrance), the federal government gave the Sanitary Commission authority to inspect sanitary conditions in military camps, gather medical supplies, distribute food, and provide a variety of support services that the government was not doing well, if at all.

With a central office in Washington, the Sanitary Commission established major branches in ten of the largest Northern cities, which in turn linked up with seven thousand local aid societies. Of the ten branch offices of the "Sanitary," as it was called, Ohio had three, the most of any state. The Soldiers' Aid Society of Northern Ohio became the Cleveland branch; Columbus and Cincinnati became the other two. Private donations and fund-raising fairs financed the Sanitary Commission's work. The United States Christian Commission did similar work, with the addition of spiritual uplift.

Ohio's men at the front needed the love and moral support of their families. Wherever they went, they expected a stream of letters to follow them, and when it didn't—often because of wartime delays in delivery—the men sent home urgent appeals for more mail. When they weren't writing the long accounts of daily life their men craved, the women managed farms and businesses, scratched out bits of income to replace some of their men's lost earning power, and shipped their own packages of food, clothing, and little luxuries to the soldiers.

At first, the women stayed close to home, but as casualties mounted, some went to the front. They went to military hospitals near combat zones, some unofficially to care for their own men, others to become paid nurses for strangers. Sometimes the women brought their sick or wounded husbands and sons home with them.

Most of all, the women back home did the hardest thing—wait, watching the road and the mailbox, desperately hoping for word from their soldiers while dreading what the mail or newspaper might bring. For four bloody years, men from Ohio and the Midwest fought their way across the South. The women and children worked and worried and waited.

IN WASHINGTON AT LAST

In late May, the 1st and 2nd Ohio marched through Baltimore on their way to Washington at last. Remembering the deadly rioting that the 6th Massachusetts had encountered on April 19, the soldiers carried loaded muskets. There was muttering about burning the city if they were attacked, but the Ohioans drew little more than a few jeers and calls for Jeff Davis.[54] Arriving safely in the nation's capital, they began craning their necks at the sights.

The Ohioans were bivouacked north of the Capitol building. They set up camp near a Rhode Island regiment and soon Ohioans and Rhode Islanders were visiting each other. "This Rhode Island regiment was the best provided for of any I ever saw," Milton McCoy, captain of Co. I, 2nd Ohio, remembered. Thanks to their wealthy young governor, William Sprague, the Rhode Islanders had everything they needed—guns, clothing, cooking utensils—and even brick ovens with "regular cooks" to bake them soft, fresh bread.

The Ohioans were not so fortunate. They were wearing shoddy uniforms that had been hurriedly made and were trying to get used to a key part of their diet: the military staple known as hardtack. Hardtack was unleavened flour baked in crackers five or six inches in diameter and a quarter- or half-inch thick. It was so hard that soldiers soaked it in water overnight before using it. McCoy claimed he knew a Cincinnati boy "who constructed a wagon ... using four crackers for the wheels, which bore his weight when put together."

The Ohioans did have a convenient source of water. A Zouave company from Cincinnati dug a ditch and found the pipe supplying the Capitol building. (Zouave companies—and there were many in both armies—wore gaudy uniforms modeled on the Algerian light infantry troops that were widely admired at the time.) The Cincinnati Zouaves punched a hole in the Capitol's pipeline with a pickaxe and soon had "a fine flow of water for all purposes."[55]

Cincinnati's well-traveled Murat Halstead, sent to Washington by the *Cincinnati Daily Commercial*, wrote a scathing article about the Ohioans' shabby condition. They had not been paid and looked like paupers, with uniform seams that "could be pulled open with the fingers." Thanks to attention by the press, the Ohioans received new uniforms and a month's pay within a few days.[56]

Once in Washington, volunteers from throughout the North drilled in the capital's parks and public grounds.

When they weren't drilling, the Ohioans went sightseeing, visiting the White House, the Smithsonian, Patent Office, Treasury, and monuments. The Patent Office—soon to become an improvised military hospital—was "a sight worth seeing," commented an awestruck Ohio private. "There can be found all the curiosities in the way of patents ever invented."[57] The troops spent much of one day parading in a "grand review," marching through the White House grounds and past President Lincoln and other dignitaries standing on the White House steps.

The Ohioans must have been pleased to learn that they would be under the command of fellow Ohioans. Overseeing the Army of Northern Virginia, the Union's major force in the East, would be Brig. Gen. Irvin McDowell, a regular army man originally from Ohio. Within his force, the 1st and 2nd Ohio regiments would be brigaded with a New York regiment and a battery of regular army artillery that would be under the command of Brig. Gen. Robert C. Schenck, a fellow volunteer from Dayton.

Schenck was a well-known Dayton lawyer, "square, compact, and broad-chested [with] rugged features," and a man of many abilities.[58] He had graduated from Miami University, then stayed three years, working part-time as a tutor in Latin and French, to earn a master's degree—a rarity in those days. Schenck's powers of oratory as a young man helped him win a seat in the Ohio House and then several terms in the United States House of Representatives. After that, he served as minister to Brazil from 1851–1853.

Returning to private life, Schenck retained some political influence. Hearing Lincoln speak in Dayton in 1859, Schenck promptly told fellow Republicans that the Illinoisan would be a good man for the presidency. Lincoln was said to remember that as the first time anyone had suggested the idea publicly.

When Schenck, with no military experience, offered Lincoln his services at the war's outbreak, he was appointed a brigadier general.[59] That made him one of the war's first "political generals," a species whose ability to lead was questioned by the press and many officers of the regular army. Schenck would be put to the test soon enough.

A MAKING OF GENERALS

By 1861, Winfield Scott was a crumbling castle of man, most of his firepower gone, his defenses nearly in ruins. Once a strapping giant—six feet, four or five inches tall, weighing 230 pounds—Scott became old, fat, and infirm over a long army career. Now in his seventy-fifth year, he weighed more than three hundred pounds, suffered from painful edema and a puzzling dizziness, was so lame he could walk only a few steps, and sometimes would fall asleep in mid-conversation. He could no longer get on a horse.

Scott was, in the words of one historian, "a magnificent monument to the past and nearly as useless."[60] None of this would have meant much to the fate of the nation, except for one thing—in 1861 Winfield Scott was general in chief of the army of the United States at its moment of greatest peril.

Over a long military career, Scott had worked his way up from shavetail artillery lieutenant to commanding general. He was tough, smart, and bold, but he also had a hot temper, an ego to match his size, and a propensity for feuds. For his love of a fine uniform and his insistence on proper military appearances, Scott's soldiers called him—not without affection—"Old Fuss and Feathers." After brilliantly leading the United States Army to a quick victory in the Mexican War, Scott settled down to peacetime soldiering, interrupted only once for one brief, disastrous foray into politics as a candidate for president.

Scott was a physical wreck by 1861, but there was nothing wrong with his mind and he could see things more clearly than many. Contrary to popular opinion, both North and South, he did not think the war would be over quickly. He also had an idea for squeezing the Confederacy to death, with minimal casualties, by blockading it by sea and the Mississippi River.

Ohioan Robert C. Schenck, an early supporter of Lincoln for the presidency, was one of the war's first "political generals"—appointed without a military background.

The press dubbed this the "Anaconda Plan" and laughed it to death in 1861, but Scott would live just long enough to see it implemented after all.

Scott badly needed generals who were mobile, unlike himself, but some of the army's senior officers had defected to the South, while others were too old to be much use. Scott tried but failed to recruit a fellow Virginian, a brevet colonel named Robert E. Lee who broke his oath of loyalty to the United States to join the rebellion. Scott decided he would have to put some lower-ranking officers on the fast track. One of the first was a promising staff officer, a Ohioan named Irvin McDowell.

In May, therefore, Maj. Irvin McDowell was catapulted into a brigadier generalship and assigned command of the military Department of Northeastern Virginia, the army's most important assignment. On paper at least, McDowell looked as good to the Lincoln administration as any officer at hand, although that wasn't saying much. Most of the army's highest ranking officers had no experience in commanding large numbers of men in the field, and neither did McDowell.

At forty-three, McDowell was a stout six-foot-tall man who was plain-spoken, but somewhat affected in his dress. He was said to dress in the "French style" and was noticeable for an iron-gray tuft in a full head of thick dark hair. McDowell had been born in Franklinton, on the edge of Columbus, in 1818. He was the son of a former Kentuckian who carried himself as a haughty aristocrat, though he had never been a wealthy one. The son inherited some of the attitude.

McDowell had studied at a military school in France and gone to West Point. His polish earned him a long military career mostly of staff duty, holding the kind of jobs usually awarded promising young officers. He had performed well during the Mexican War and later taught military tactics at West Point. McDowell was an able and conscientious man, but years of staff duty had turned him into a rule-book, spit-and-polish kind of soldier with martinet tendencies.

McDowell also was aloof and famously "pure," for he neither drank nor played cards, nor even took tea or coffee, and was ridiculed by some "as the most faultlessly pure and temperate man in all things in the army."[61] Perhaps to compensate for his self-denials, McDowell was a glutton, famed for having consumed a watermelon at one sitting.

There was something more troubling about McDowell. In a war where most of the fighting would be done by volunteers thrown against a tenacious foe, McDowell had two serious flaws: he had a career officer's disdain for the volunteer soldiers and showed it, and he held the Southern soldier in contempt.

While Scott, puffing and wheezing, was trying to assemble the Union's forces and while McDowell was laboring, without much confidence, to turn his volunteer rabble into an army worthy of the name, there were certain other men whom almost no one had heard of but who soon would become very well known.

In Illinois, ex-soldier Sam Grant was struggling, clumsily, to win re-appointment to the army. He helped organize a company of volunteers from Galena and went off to camp to help train them, but turned down an offer to be their captain in hopes of winning a commission with more responsibility. None came.

Thirty-nine-year-old Grant lacked political guile and friends in high places.

He wrote to military authorities in Washington without effect. He went to Cincinnati and twice waited in vain in McClellan's outer office. McClellan did not even deign to see him, perhaps because in the small, gossipy pre-war army Grant had developed a reputation as a drinker.

"Blue as a whetstone," Grant finally thought of applying to the influential congressman from his district in Illinois, Elihu B. Washburne. Seeing the political value of having a military officer in his debt, Washburne pulled some strings and in June Grant was appointed to a colonelcy. Within a few weeks he was leading the 21st Illinois, a volunteer regiment, on its way to war in Missouri. Grant's wife, Julia, naively thought this would be no more than "a pleasant summer outing."[62]

In St. Louis, meanwhile, forty-one-year-old William Tecumseh Sherman remained in his transit line office, refusing to volunteer because he felt Lincoln —and Ohio—had slighted him. Like Grant, he felt his military experience qualified him for something more than the offers that came his way. For a few days, he sat tight.

Finally realizing his refusal to serve was raising questions about his loyalty, Sherman unbent on May 8. He offered his services to the Union so long as it did not involve volunteers. He was promised a colonelcy in the regular army in Washington, but wound up instead inspecting and organizing the volunteers pouring into the nation's capital.

Next, instead of a regiment of regulars, Sherman was assigned command of a brigade of volunteers, consisting of one Wisconsin and three New York City regiments, all green as grass. In the campaign to come, Sherman and Robert Schenck would lead two of the four brigades composing an army division commanded by a crusty old New Englander named Daniel W. Tyler. Tyler's division and four others would compose the army led by Irvin McDowell.

While Grant, Sherman, and others were beginning their Civil War service, thirty-year-old regular army Lt. Philip H. Sheridan was itching to leave his frontier post in the Pacific Northwest and get into the fray. When his regiment, the Fourth Infantry, was ordered east, Sheridan was left behind with a small detachment and told to hold the fort until relieved. His connection with the outside world was the mail received once a week from Portland. Early in the morning of every mail day Sheridan would climb to a high point to peer down the road for the first sign of the messenger. Good news for Sheridan would not come until September 1.

Back in Ohio, George B. McClellan was at work in May and June turning

Irvin McDowell, a career soldier from Franklinton, was rushed into high command with scant experience in combat leadership.

thousands of Ohio farm boys and clerks into soldiers. McClellan brought impressive credentials to the job, but what impressed Ohioans most was McClellan the man. He made up for his unremarkable height (five feet, eight inches) with youthful good looks and an air of self-assurance that instilled confidence in all who met him. Even today, George B. McClellan's photographs suggest a man who had no doubts whatsoever about George B. McClellan.

George B. McClellan (with his wife, Nelly) harbored no doubts about his ability to lead soldiers. Others would.

McClellan had served creditably in the Mexican War and the peacetime army afterwards, but had been discouraged by the glacial pace of promotions in the peacetime army. He resigned as a captain and began a civilian career as a railroad executive, moving to Cincinnati in 1860. It wasn't long until the military would call him back.

On April 23, thanks to Governor Dennison, McClellan had been given the major generalship of Ohio volunteers. Then, on May 3, Washington assigned McClellan command of the Department of the Ohio, which included the states of Ohio, Indiana, and Illinois (and would soon be expanded to include western Virginia).[63] But McClellan's meteoric rise was not over.

On May 14, Governor Dennison, McClellan, and several other men were in Cincinnati discussing Ohio's defense when the governor was handed a startling dispatch from Secretary of the Treasury Salmon P. Chase in Washington: "We have today had McClellan appointed a Major-General in the *regular* army." (Ranks in the regular army were considered higher than similar ranks in the volunteers.) This meant that thirty-four-year-old McClellan, a mere army captain scarcely four years earlier, now ranked second only to the general in chief, Winfield Scott.

Even the self-confident McClellan was stunned, for a look of utter amazement came over his face.[64] The next day Governor Dennison had to produce the telegram to convince Mrs. McClellan of the appointment. McClellan's charm, poise, and self-assurance had caught the eye of Winfield Scott, general in chief of the army. Probably McClellan's fellow Ohioan, Secretary Chase, had given him a boost as well.[65]

McClellan's astonishing rise had begun with his selection by Governor Dennison. It would not be long before the governor would be wondering about the wisdom of his choice.

GAZETTE

On June 8, 1861, Tennessee voters approved secession, completing the emergence of a new nation called the Confederate States of America. The CSA unequivocally claimed eleven states and, on slim grounds, two more, the sharply divided border states of Kentucky and Missouri. In the end, however, neither left the Union. The CSA adopted a flag with thirteen stars anyway. It established its capital at Richmond, Virginia (as if to taunt Washington, only 106 miles away).

In the North, Abraham Lincoln quickly followed his original call for seventy-five-thousand militiamen for ninety days with a call May 3 for three-hundred-thousand volunteers, most for three years. Although both Union and Confederate leaders seemed to expect a hard fight, opinion on streets in both the North and South was that it would be a short war, requiring only one quick victory to show the other side how resistance was futile. This popular expectation would die a painful death.

Lincoln's determination to wage war did not impress Edwin M. Stanton, sitting on the sidelines in Washington and worrying. The nation's former attorney general vented his wrath at the Lincoln Administration—as well as his anxiety for the nation—after being rudely turned away while trying to offer his services to the Treasury Department. "No one can imagine the deplorable condition of this city and the hazard of Government," he fulminated, "who did not witness the panic of the Administration, and the painful imbecility of Lincoln."[66]

Opinion among Northern Democrats was split between those who favored war to reunite the nation and those who demanded an immediate negotiated peace. Democratic Sen. Stephen A. Douglas chose to support the war; Ohio Democratic Congressman Clement L. Vallandigham chose not to. The Ohioan had feared secession, but he

Only recently civilians, Ohio's soldiers rushed to have their "likenesses" taken before going to war.

quickly and loudly made clear that he also opposed the war, for which he blamed Lincoln.

Vallandigham considered himself a patriot who believed that only a negotiated peace offered a chance for national reunion. Nonetheless, newspapers across Ohio branded him a traitor. Undaunted, Vallandigham —like Brown and Ruffin—never doubted he was right.

In another part of Virginia, Edmund Ruffin was basking in the celebrity firing the honorary "first shot" at Fort Sumter had brought him. He had joined a lightly armed and slow-footed home guard unit that spent its time looking for runaway slaves. Worried about black insurrection, Ruffin slept with a loaded pistol beside his pillow. Bored with this, in early July the sixty-seven-year-old firebrand donned his homespun uniform, hitched on a knapsack holding two blankets and some crackers, tied some cheese to his belt, and began hiking from Richmond to join his old friends in South Carolina's Palmetto Guards.

The South Carolineans and a lot of other Confederates were camped around a rail junction called Manassas, less than thirty miles from Washington. Nearby ran an obscure creek known only to those who lived nearby. Its name was Bull Run, and soon it would be famous.[67]

To Learn More:

Step into antebellum Ohio by visiting Hale Farm and Village, a recreated Ohio village with authentic buildings and costumed interpreters maintained in Bath, Ohio, at 2686 Oak Hill Road, Cleveland by the Western Reserve Historical Society (http://www.wrhs.org/halefarm/ or 330-666-3711). The Ohio Historical Center, operated at 1982 Velma Ave., in Columbus by the Ohio Historical Society, includes such Civil War artifacts as "weapons, uniforms, medical and camp equipment, and battle flags" among its many permanent exhibits. (http://www.ohiohistory. org/ or 800-686-6124.

Walter Havighurst's *Ohio: A History* is a readable introduction to the subject, while Andrew R.L. Cayton's more recent *Ohio: The History of a People* and George W. Knepper's older *Ohio and Its People*, are longer works. T. Harry Williams' classic *Lincoln and His Generals* describes Lincoln's development as a military strategist whose field commanders ranged from the confused to the brilliant.

4

An Improvised War

Summer and Fall 1861

As the spring of 1861 wheeled toward summer, heat shimmered off the classical facades of buildings in the nation's capital and clouds of dust seasoned with animal manure swirled in the streets. Washington was raw, unfinished, odorous, and flyspecked, hot and dry from spring to fall except when it was hot and wet. It was not a city carved in alabaster.

The men of the 1st and 2nd Ohio came tramping into the Federal city in late May and were dismayed by the weediness of it all. "I was sadly disappointed," wrote Pvt. Harry Comer of the 1st Ohio's company from Lancaster. "Expecting to see … a place to dazzle the eye … I found it in every way inferior to Dayton and far from rivaling Columbus."[1]

The Capitol, yet to receive its dome, looked headless, and the Washington Monument remained unfinished, with work halted at 156 feet. Monumental public buildings stood here and there, their intervals cluttered with town houses, boarding houses, and whorehouses side by side with saloons, stores, and workshops. Then as now, Washington was a mix of slums and elegance, the privileged and the power-hungry living near the disadvantaged and the just plain hungry.

Most streets were unpaved, roamed at will by pigs, cattle, and geese. The Washington Canal, a sink of sewage and swill, was a suppurating gouge across the city. On her arrival in Washington, Nettie Chase, thirteen-year-old daughter of Treasury Secretary Salmon P. Chase, found the wide avenues "literally flow with yellow mud; the contemplative cows and pigs meander through the streets." She pronounced herself disappointed by "the combination of grandiousness and squalor of Washington."[2] Writer George William Bagby called it a "paradise of paradoxes … a great, little, splendid, mean, extravagant, poverty-stricken barrack."[3]

The place had turned into a huge military base. "The town is full of soldiers," reported Cincinnati journalist Murat Halstead, who had come to spend a month watching history unfold. "It is a distinction to be in civilian dress."[4] Soldiers camped in and around public buildings and regiments paraded endlessly up and down Pennsylvania Avenue. "Officers in tinsel and gold lace were so thick [along] Pennsylvania Avenue that it was a severe trial for a private to walk there," wrote a Massachusetts soldier whose right arm grew weary from constant saluting.[5]

Feeling unprotected only a few weeks before, the "Federal city" held about forty regiments of volunteers by early June, Halstead estimated, "and still they come." Peering from his window, the Ohio newsman gave readers a sense of what Washington was like: "A mighty noise … three batteries of flying artillery were going by … the street white with a fog of dust, and reverberating with the thunder of wheels and hoofs. The horses … and the batteries go together like huge machines, swift and terrible."[6]

And yet there was a sense of unreality. Despite years of Southern threats to secede, Northerners had tended to dismiss the angry talk as bluster. Now secession had occurred and the war was real, but it seemed incredible to many that fellow citizens might soon attack each other on a battlefield.

The government had not been on a war footing when Fort Sumter was attacked. Its army was tiny, the state militias unprepared, and the contents of arsenals were mostly moth-eaten or rusty. Competing with each other for scarce resources, the states had to furnish most of the soldiers and supplies at first. In its early months, the war effort on both sides was such a helter-skelter endeavor by amateurs that it has been called "an improvised war."

By early summer in 1861 Washington was wrapped in anticipation. *Something* was going to happen, although the crowds clamoring for action had no idea of how swift and terrible it would be. People only knew they stood on the edge of a great, thrilling unknown. Then came a sign.

Late in June and into early July, an extraordinarily large comet appeared in the sky, skirting the northern horizon and trailing a broad, fiery tail millions of miles long. The comet was so bright it could be seen in full daylight. One Northern observer joked that this was "our new ally," but others worried and wondered about what it might signify. An editorialist wrote, "What means this visit—peace or war?"[7]

Rescuing Western Virginia

Almost everyone in Northwest Ohio had heard of James Blair Steedman, and more than a few had shared a laugh and a glass or two or three with him. So when "The General" (a title of courtesy, with the thinnest of foundations) climbed on his horse in April 1861 and galloped from town to town in Ohio's upper left corner, he was able to assemble an entire regiment—upwards of one thousand men, ten companies that had already been forming in Toledo and its hinterland.

Steedman, a Toledo Democrat, was an iconic nineteenth-century Western American—a man's man, big-chested and big-headed, an entrepreneur roaring ahead on pure nerve, quick to laugh or curse, and none too careful with his appearance or, some said, his scruples.

Born in Pennsylvania and orphaned at thirteen, Steedman had gone to work to support a sister and two younger brothers, then joined Sam

Untutored in war, rough in manner, but always a man's man, Toledo's James B. Steedman quickly proved to be an able soldier.

Houston's campaign to free Texas. From there he went to northwest Ohio, where he—scarcely twenty-one—won a contract to build a canal. But the energetic Steedman did more.

He started a newspaper in Defiance, was a railroad contractor, briefly joined the California gold rush, served two terms in the Ohio House, and was public printer to the U.S. House of Representatives until he got lippy with President Buchanan. Finally he settled in Toledo, where he used the *Toledo Daily Herald and Times* to enlighten the public with his opinions on all matters.

Steedman held the title of major general in the Ohio militia, a mostly ceremonial position ranking not too far above Kentucky colonel. As expected, he was chosen colonel of the new regiment, the 14th Ohio Volunteer Militia, one of the "extra" regiments Adjutant General Carrington had accepted at state expense. The 14th spent about a month drilling at Camp Taylor, near Cleveland, then headed southeast. Little more than a month after leaving their fields and shops, the farm boys, clerks, and mechanics of northwest Ohio were going to war. They were going to Virginia.

At the time, Virginia stretched more than 250 miles westward from the Atlantic Ocean, crossing the Allegheny Mountains to end at the Ohio River. There was no state of West Virginia. Virginia east of the Alleghenies—about two-thirds of the whole—was plantation and slave country and favored secession.

From the Alleghenies westward, however, Virginia was a wild and wooded terrain that someone had called "a succession of ridges and a medley of hills." It was home mostly to humble people scratching livings from rough country.[8] Most western Virginians favored the Union and liked their Ohio neighbors better than the eastern Virginians. Only a few owned slaves. They were very different from the Virginians to the east.

Nestled against Ohio and a corner of Pennsylvania, western Virginia looked like a wedge waiting to split the Union in two. Other things enhanced its strategic importance. The Baltimore & Ohio Railroad, connecting the Midwest to Washington, ran through it and so did a telegraph line and some turnpikes. Western Virginia was important to both North and South.

Because it was bounded on the east and south by Virginia and Kentucky, loyal Ohio was face-to-face for more than four-hundred miles with two potentially hostile slave states, separated from them by only a few watery feet of Ohio River. "No State in the Union is more exposed than Ohio," warned the *Cincinnati Weekly Gazette*.[9]

With Virginia's leaders planning a referendum on secession for May 23, western Virginians loyal to the Union began appealing frantically to Washington and Ohio for help. Not wanting to inflame eastern Virginians, who had yet to officially decide whether to join the Confederacy, Washington chose not to intervene. But Ohio's Governor Dennison, who had already declared, "I will defend Ohio beyond rather than on her border," implored

General McClellan to rush militiamen to western Virginia to protect its Unionists.[10]

Busy training soldiers at Camp Dennison and never one to hurry, McClellan replied, "I advise *delay* for the present. ... Don't let these frontier men hurry you on."[11] That troubled Dennison. "From the reception of that letter," he later wrote, "I dated the beginnings of my doubt as to McClellan's being, after all, a man of action."[12]

But in mid-May, Confederate forces moved into western Virginia to break up Unionist resistance and burn railroad bridges, and, on May 23, a majority of Virginia voters—except for the Westerners—ratified secession. With Washington urging action, McClellan finally ordered several of Ohio's "extra" militia regiments—including Steedman's 14th—plus some Indiana units, to cross the border into mountainous western Virginia. McClellan himself remained at Cincinnati.

Confederate Col. George A. Porterfield had arrived in the Unionist stronghold of Grafton in western Virginia on May 14, but on news that McClellan was sending Union forces, he moved to Philippi, a friendlier place a few miles south. Like Harpers Ferry, Philippi was nestled near a river in a bowl formed by mountains. It was not a good place for an army to be caught. Nonetheless, with about 600 raw infantrymen, 175 cavalrymen, and a scanty supply of ammunition, Porterfield settled down on the evening of June 2, planning to continue his strategic retreat the next morning. He assumed a pelting rain would delay Union force and protect him for the night.

He was wrong. Two Union columns were approaching through the rain and the dark. One, led by western Virginian Col. Benjamin Kelley, included the 1st (loyalist) Virginia, the 9th Indiana, and six companies of the 16th Ohio, a ninety-day unit from northeastern Ohio. (The ranks of the 9th Indiana included Pvt. Ambrose Bierce, who would become famous after the war for his sardonic wit. Born in Ohio, he had lived in Indiana from the age of six.)

The other column, led by Indiana Col. Ebenezer Dumont, included companies from the 6th and 7th Indiana, Steedman's 14th Ohio, the 15th Ohio, and the 1st Ohio Light Artillery.

The brand-new soldiers of the 14th Ohio would write home that they had had an exhausting but exhilarating night. Soaked to the skin, they had wearily slogged up hill and down through the deep mud and darkness. Officers on horseback galloped along the column urging the soldiers forward.

Many men threw away their blankets, knapsacks, and other equipment, and some fell by the roadside, unable to go any farther. But when the

In the valley town of Philippi in what is now West Virginia, Ohio soldiers shared in one of the first Union victories, a small battle that would lead to greater things.

advancing Union soldiers confronted enemy pickets, the Confederates fled without even warning their own camp, and by dawn the Ohio artillerymen were perched on a bluff overlooking Philippi.

As soon as the Ohioans began firing their artillery, the astonished Confederates below fled in disorder, some only partly dressed, Then, "with loud huzzahs," the newly revived 14th Ohioans rushed down the hill.[13] (All battles are followed by hyperbole. An officer of the 14th Ohio wrote home, "To the 14th Ohio Regiment and Cleveland artillery alone belongs the whole honor of the rout of the rebels."[14] Accounts vary.) That the terrified Southerners fled so quickly tickled Northern journalists and they dubbed the little engagement "the Philippi races."

Ambrose Bierce remarked after the war, "By the way, that battery of ours did nothing worse than take off a young Confederate's leg."[15] Nonetheless, to this day the little West Virginia town of Philippi proudly calls itself the site of the "first battle of the Civil War," although the small action hardly qualified as a battle.

But it was significant. Feeling safer, Unionist delegates from thirty-two western Virginia counties promptly met in Wheeling, declared all actions of the Richmond government null and void, and all state offices vacant.

They established their own so-called "restored government of Virginia," which, in reality, held sway only in western Virginia.

Alarmed by all this, Maj. Gen. Robert E. Lee in Richmond, commander of Virginia's troops, dispatched his aide, Gen. Robert S. Garnett, and some more soldiers to turn things around. Garnett quickly barricaded two key passes in the mountains, one at Rich Mountain on the important Staunton-Parkersburg Road, the other on a connecting road sixteen miles north at Laurel Hill.

By now, General McClellan had decided western Virginia merited his personal attention, so he left Cincinnati, promising his pregnant wife, Nelly, he would write every day. Glowing from cheers received at every rail station, the young general entered western Virginia about June 21, having collected some regiments along the Baltimore & Ohio Railroad and gotten others started. All in all, he now had sixteen regiments from Ohio, nine from Indiana, and two from western Virginia, plus some cavalry and artillery.

Most of these men, and those who would soon join them, were—to put it charitably—half-baked soldiers. As late as early July, men of the 8th Ohio were still wearing their own shirts and training at Camp Dennison with "wooden guns, wooden swords, and cornstalks with which to drill and mount guard," according to young Thomas F. Galwey of Company B.[16]

"Soldiers!" McClellan proclaimed, to the accompaniment of invisible trumpets, on his arrival in western Virginia, "I have heard there is danger here. I have come to place myself at your head and share it with you. I fear now but one thing—that you will not find foemen worthy of your steel."[17]

Among those assigned to help McClellan oppose the "foemen" was a new brigadier general named William S. Rosecrans. Born in Ohio's Delaware County in 1819, Rosecrans had graduated fifth in his class at West Point, spent eleven years as army engineer, then resigned to pursue a civilian career in the coal and oil business. McClellan had recruited him when the war broke out.

Tall and lean, Rosecrans' face had been permanently scarred, by an oil lamp explosion, into "a permanent smirk."[18] He was a talented but intense, excitable, and sharp-tempered man who incessantly chewed on a cigar. A devout convert to Catholicism, his favorite topic was religion, which he somehow squared with his fiery stock of profanity. Privately, the often acerbic McClellan called Rosecrans "a silly fussy goose."[19]

McClellan's first objective was Rich Mountain, near Beverly deep in western Virginia. There, General Garnett had positioned 1,300 Confederates led by twenty-nine-year-old Lt. Col. John Pegram. Pegram was supposed to block a vital turnpike where it narrowed at the mountain's western foot. It was there that McClellan planned to attack.

McClellan placed the largest part of his force in front of Pegram's camp and sent the rest sixteen miles north to Laurel Hill, where Garnett and his main force were resting. McClellan ordered this force to keep Garnett "amused" by skirmishes and artillery barrages while the main Union force dealt with the roadblock at Rich Mountain.

Back at Rich Mountain, McClellan tried sending the 9th Ohio, a highly regarded regiment of German-Americans from Cincinnati, to probe the defenses of the Confederate base camp.[20] The Germans found them formidable and fell back. As McClellan mulled what to do next, Rosecrans, aided by a loyal local man, discovered an obscure path through the woods. It bypassed the Confederate base camp and led to an enemy detachment stationed at the summit, a mile or two up the road from Pegram.

The two Union commanders chewed this information over and agreed that Rosecrans would use the path to make a surprise attack on the summit. When McClellan heard sounds of battle coming from the summit, he would launch a frontal attack on the base camp. Attacked from both front and rear, Pegram's forces would be trapped between Rosecrans and McClellan.

Drawing on his stock of profanity, Rosecrans sent his brigade plowing through thick shrubbery and up the mountainside in pouring rain shortly after dawn July 11. He had nearly two thousand men, including the 19th Ohio, Burdsal's Ohio Cavalry, and three Indiana regiments. At the summit, the smaller Rebel force put up a surprisingly stubborn fight of two hours, further enlivened when a Confederate dropped his pants and mooned the attackers. He was killed by a Union sharpshooter with a "centre shot."[21] Finally, a bayonet charge ordered by Rosecrans carried the day.

By now, McClellan should have attacked the Confederate base camp, but he displayed what became a hallmark of his behavior in battle. Lt. Col. John Beatty of the 3rd Ohio watched as McClellan "sat on his horse … indecision stamped on every line of his countenance. … Hours passed … ."[22] Beloved by his troops, and seemingly brimming with confidence, McClellan would repeatedly lose his nerve by imagining his enemy stronger than it was.

McClellan assumed, with no evidence, that Rosecrans had been defeated at the summit. In reality, Rosecrans had driven the Confederates off the summit and, as McClellan was speculating about events and doing little else, a dispirited Pegram was abandoning his base camp and escaping right under his nose. McClellan only learned the truth from a messenger sent by Rosecrans.

Pegram's loss of Rich Mountain meant that General Garnett's main position at Laurel Hill was untenable. Garnett's Confederates fled through the woods, struggling through heavy rain that turned narrow lanes into oozing sinkholes. A Union force, including the 14th Ohio, was sent in pursuit of the flying Confederates, following a trail of wrecked wagons and discarded equipment trampled into the mud.

Among the pursuers were the 8th Ohio and its under-age Sgt. Thomas F. Galwey of Company B. The Ohioans captured a number of stragglers "dressed in gorgeous state militia uniforms—gray and gold tinsel—all of them half dead from hunger and fright," Galwey recalled.[23] At Carrick's Ford, General Garnett himself was shot in the back and killed as he tried to bolster resistance by a rear guard.

The panicked Confederates kept running, leaving behind the body of their commander, the first general of either side to be killed in the war. Exhausted but triumphant, the Union forces finally gave up their pursuit. Elsewhere, after wandering aimlessly through the woods, Pegram surrendered nearly six hundred men near Beverly.

It was a clean sweep for the Federals and McClellan fired off an exaggerated telegram of triumph to Washington. A rosy penumbra surrounded the young general with the Northern press making him "the hero of the moment," as Jacob D. Cox would dryly put it after the war. (Trying to reconcile McClellan's extravagant "proclamations" with the official record at Rich Mountain is "a curious task," as Cox delicately expressed it.[24])

Soldiers in McClellan's command tried to calm their nerves after their first experience of battle.

"[O]f all the horid sights I ever looked upon this was the most horid," wrote an Ohio soldier on viewing the mangled bodies of the dead at Rich Mountain. A correspondent from the *Cincinnati Daily Commercial* exclaimed, "Oh horrible! most horrible!" on viewing the "ghastly spectacle" of the victims' contorted faces and lacerated flesh.[25]

With their ninety-day enlistments up, Colonel Steedman and his 14th Ohio returned to Toledo, where they were reorganized into a three-year unit and sent to Kentucky. Although there was more to do in western Virginia, McClellan suddenly was summoned to Washington, arriving there on July 26. The Union's "hero of the moment" was needed on the war's main stage. Brigadier General Rosecrans, the real hero of the moment, was left behind, in charge of keeping remote, hilly western Virginia safe from the Confederacy.

Among the Ohio troops to join Rosecrans was the 23rd Ohio. Organized at Camp Chase, near Columbus, the regiment had given its new colonel, Eliakim P. Scammon (Rosecrans' replacement), a memorable welcome when he arrived in June. Scammon, a West Pointer who had been born in Maine but immigrated to Ohio, was a small, fussy soldier with martinet tendencies.

Before Scammon's arrival, the 23rd had been training for weeks in increasingly ragged and dirty civilian clothes. Then the men of the 23rd received their first government issue—undershirts and drawers, but nothing else. Being Westerners uncowed by authority, they dressed only in undershirts and drawers for Scammon's first review of them. Scammon, it is recorded, "simply wilted" and dismissed the parade.[26]

Among Scammon's officers were two future presidents: Maj. Rutherford B. Hayes and Pvt. William McKinley. Within days of the attack on Fort Sumter, Hayes had joined Cincinnati's Burnet Rifles, a home defense company that included many of his literary friends. Hayes' men called him "Rud" and elected him captain. Hayes drilled the men diligently, but soon decided that staying home and drilling part-time wasn't enough. In a population seized by war fever, home defense companies enjoyed little respect.

Hayes told his diary on May 15, "I would prefer to go into it [the war] if I knew I was going to die, or be killed in the course of it, than to live through and after it without taking any part in it."[27] On June 7 came a telegram offering him the position of major, and soon he was delighting in the routine of Camp Chase. McKinley joined the regiment in June. Soon enough, young Private McKinley would catch Hayes' eye, and one future president would begin mentoring another.

On July 25, the 23rd Ohio departed for western Virginia. Peering back at his wife, Lucy, and her mother on the platform as his train left the station, Hayes saw, "Their eyes swam. I kept my emotions under control enough not to melt into tears."[28]

A Meeting in Vienna

During May, President Lincoln could look out a White House window and see a secessionist flag flying in Alexandria just across the Potomac River. Even though Virginia had not officially seceded, Lincoln knew its soldiers were standing guard at the other end of the bridge to Washington.

But on May 23, a majority of Virginia voters, except those in the western mountains, endorsed secession, so Lincoln sent Federal soldiers across the Potomac. Years later, a veteran of the 2nd Ohio remembered marching across Washington's Long Bridge, under a full moon, with the bridge "springing" up and down under thousands of feet moving in quickstep. Entering enemy territory was serious business.

"No more the jocund mirth and hilarious song of preceding marches," recalled the Ohioan, to whom the monotonous songs of the bullfrogs of the Potomac flats had sounded like "requiems."[29]

Rebel forces on the Virginia side hurriedly withdrew and the Federals occupied Arlington Heights and Alexandria with little resistance. They gained a foothold that included Robert E. Lee's family estate (now Arlington National Cemetery). The 1st and 2nd Ohio pitched its tents at a pleasant spot called Camp Upton, near a railroad and about three miles from Alexandria.

Friends, relatives, and politicians were frequent visitors to Camp Upton. Ohio Congressman Clement L. Vallandigham decided to drop in on the Ohioans despite his unpopularity as an opponent of the war. As he approached Captain Stafford's Company A of the 1st Ohio, a concealed band struck up "The Rogue's March." Vallandigham flushed with anger and saucily flipped the tails of his coat. Soldiers pelted him with raw potatoes and an officer rushed him back to his carriage, where he found a straw effigy labeled "Vallandigham the Traitor."[30]

When the commander of the Army of Northeastern Virginia, General McDowell, visited Camp Upton, Capt. George M. Finch of the 2nd Ohio extended his hand in greeting, a Western gesture of friendly equality. McDowell stared at it before reluctantly returning the gesture, but by then Finch had withdrawn his own hand.

Next, McDowell said he was concerned about soldiers pillaging the gardens of Virginians. Captain Finch denied his men would do such a thing. McDowell turned in the direction of soldiers who were enthusiastically stripping a field of its cabbages and asked, "What men are those?" They were from the 2nd Ohio, an embarrassed Finch admitted.[31]

Midwestern enlisted men were not in awe of officers. Determined to maintain good relations with local citizens, General Schenck confronted men of the 1st Ohio whose fingers were stained with strawberry juice. "Why did you steal this man's strawberries?" thundered Schenck. "Because he was a Reb, and we wanted 'em," was the answer.

Schenck kept trying. "Where is your home and what is your name?" he demanded of each. "Near Franklin [General Schenck's Ohio birthplace] and my name is Schenck," every one saucily replied. Finally, the general surrendered, muttering, "We might as well drop this case; it bears [damned] hard on the Schenck family."[32]

Robert C. Schenck, newly minted as a general, led his Ohioans into a trap near Vienna, Virginia, and had to beat a hasty retreat.

Northeastern Virginia was a rolling land of trees, scrubby brush, and rickety farms, a "country ... gone to seed" after plantation owners wore out the soil and departed.[33] Scouting parties from both sides roamed the emaciated area and occasionally clashed. Most of the Ohioans passed their time in Camp Upton drilling, entertaining visitors, foraging for food, or gambling on the sly. Then, on June 17, General McDowell told General Schenck to take one of his regiments aboard a commandeered train, advance a few miles in the direction of Vienna, Virginia, and, "moving ... with caution," see what would happen.

General Schenck chose the 1st Ohio—only 668 of its men and 29 of its officers were available for duty that day—and moved down the tracks with caution, though, it turned out, not quite enough. Along the way, he dropped off six companies to guard key points and to patrol roads.

The remaining four companies, numbering 271 men, stayed on the train, a collection of passenger and "platform" (flat) cars pushed by a tall-stacked, high-wheeled locomotive. Schenck did not think of sending scouting parties *ahead* of the train. After all, the railroad line had been safely scouted the day before.

At six in the evening the train was nearing Vienna, the Ohioans perched on the flat cars and seated in the passenger cars. The train's whistle was heard by some roaming Confederates led by Col. Maxcy Gregg. Gregg's force included infantry, a troop of cavalry, and two pieces of artillery—altogether, nearly seven hundred men, a formidable force. Rushing his men to where the track curved through a cut, Gregg hid his cannon on a wooded hill, positioned his men in the woods, and waited.

One moment the Ohioans were enjoying a ride in the late-afternoon June weather, the next they were being shelled by artillery they couldn't even see. Accounts differ as to how much, if any, resistance the startled Ohioans put up, but Colonel Gregg claimed that his artillery "would have been very destructive if the [Union] troops had not made a most rapid movement from the cars to the woods."[34]

Nine of the Ohioans were killed or mortally wounded, but none of the Confederates was killed. The Ohioans retreated through the woods to their base at Camp Upton, while the civilian engineer and part of his train, not bothering to wait for anyone, raced in reverse to home and safety. Colonel Gregg and his soldiers burned the railroad cars left behind.

All the killed and wounded belonged to Company G, which had been formed from the Portsmouth Guards, and Company H, the Zanesville Guards. (Captain Stafford's company from Lancaster suffered no losses.) The bodies were recovered and buried near Camp Upton. For the Ohio regiments, it was a painful introduction to war, but there was worse to come.

THE FIRST OF THE MIGHT-HAVE-BEENS

After the Civil War, Irvin McDowell would look back on the worst year of his life and sadly write, "I am one of the *'might-have-beens'* rather than one of those who *have been and are.*"[35] His dejection was prompted by a post-war speech during which William Tecumseh Sherman enumerated the contributions of various Ohioans to the Civil War and never mentioned McDowell. McDowell must have felt himself slipping into an abyss of obscurity.

This son of Ohio had had the misfortune to get what every career army officer wishes for, a generalship, but to get it too soon, and under the worst possible circumstances. He is remembered today as the Civil War general who lost the first big battle of the war and then, incredibly, proved a loser all over again in the same place little more than a year later. All things considered, obscurity might have been better than ignominy of that order.

In May 1861, the army catapulted McDowell from major to brigadier general and gave him command of its largest force, the Army of Northeastern Virginia. (Another Ohioan, Secretary of the Treasury Salmon P. Chase, may have influenced the choice.[36]) With little time to prepare, McDowell was told to venture into nearby Virginia and, under the gaze of Washington's grandees, win the war in one fell swoop. An army of thirty five thousand men, the largest in American history but woefully inexperienced, was to be led into battle by a forty-three-year-old long-time staff officer who had never commanded more than eight men.[37]

Northern newspapers were screaming, "Forward to Richmond!" the Confederate capital. Both sides wanted one big, climactic battle and they wanted it *now.* Under pressure from Lincoln, McDowell reluctantly proposed moving first on Manassas, Virginia, nearly thirty miles southwest of Washington. An important rail junction and a key to attacking Richmond, Manassas was under the command of Gen. P. G. T. Beauregard, the Confederates' fiery hero at Fort Sumter. Union strategy would be to overwhelm Beauregard with McDowell's larger army.

Meanwhile, in the Shenandoah Valley to the northwest, Gen. Robert Patterson, nearly seventy years old, was to use his eighteen-thousand-man force of Pennsylvanians to bottle up Confederate Gen. Joseph E. "Joe" Johnston's eleven thousand men and keep them from reinforcing Beauregard.

Most of McDowell's men had never seen combat and neither had eight of their thirteen top commanders.[38] With good reason, McDowell wanted more time to prepare, but Lincoln replied, "You are green, it is true; but they are green, also; you are all green alike."[39]

Almost all of McDowell's troops were untested volunteers, many of them short-termers near the end of their ninety-day enlistments. As Northerners waited impatiently for the decisive battle, McDowell hurriedly organized his army into five divisions, assigning the first to Brig. Gen. Daniel Tyler, a dry-as-dust Connecticut Yankee but a veteran soldier. Tyler's division was composed of four brigades, two of them led by Ohioans Schenck and Sherman.

With almost no time to drill his novice soldiers, Colonel Sherman's brigade was composed of three New York volunteer regiments and one from Wisconsin, plus some artillery from the regular army. Brig. Gen. Robert C. Schenck—a "political general" and the only one of Tyler's four brigade leaders with no military experience whatsoever—would lead a second brigade, composed of the 1st and 2nd Ohio Volunteer Infantry (the only Ohio troops in McDowell's army), the 2nd New York volunteers, and an artillery company of army regulars.

On the afternoon of Tuesday, July 16, McDowell's forces marched from Washington and Alexandria, heading for Manassas on the Warrenton Turnpike and nearby roads. The Army of Northeastern Virginia consisted mostly of eastern soldiers, half of them New Yorkers. Only a fifth of the infantry regiments came from west of the Appalachians.[40] The Union advance had a colorful, parade-day feel to it with soldiers wearing a medley of militia uniforms, many of them blue but some gray. There were colorful Zouave units in gaiters, baggy trousers, and turbans or fezzes. The Confederates awaiting them wore the same variety of costumes.

As marching men often did in those days, the soldiers sang at first, but heat and heavy dust put a stop to that. After a night's rest, the march resumed Wednesday morning, but to experienced eyes, McDowell's force was more a mob than an army. Capt. John C. Tidball, a veteran artillery officer who had spent his youth in Ohio, decided that McDowell's men were "not soldiers but civilians in uniform."[41] For some, hooligans would have a better word.

When Colonel Sherman's aides tried to stop men who were pilfering farms, they defiantly shouted, "Tell Colonel Sherman we will get all the water, pigs and chickens we want." As an officer of the 79th New York Highlanders chased a pig, his kilt flew up revealingly, drawing hoots of "Take off that petticoat! Put on your pants!"[42]

These "civilians in uniform" streamed eagerly down the roads to their first battle, boys and men who had never fired a shot in anger, gaggling along pretty much as they pleased, skylarking and having a high old time, except for the heat and the Virginia dust swirling around them. They laughed and hooted, charged with the kind of excitement that precedes a big sports match. And the dust settled on them like a shroud.

Beauregard's Confederates were arrayed on the far side of Bull Run Creek. McDowell planned to have two of his five divisions loop around several miles to the north, cross Bull Run Creek at Sudley Ford, and surprise the Confederates on their left flank.

Meanwhile, Tyler's division would remain behind, pretending to threaten a stone bridge where the Warrenton Turnpike crossed Bull Run. Instead of crossing over, however, they would simulate attacks in an effort to keep the Confederates occupied at their center and distracted from the attack coming on their left. McDowell's last two divisions would remain out of the battle but in reserve.

McDowell's plan was a worthy if complex scheme for new soldiers, but instead of quickly putting it in motion, the Union general spent Friday and Saturday accumulating supplies. While the Union army rested, Confederate reinforcements led by General Johnston were arriving by train at Manassas

Junction. They had given General Patterson the slip and left him unawares in the Shenandoah Valley. McDowell's clever plan was in trouble before the battle began.

Union forces began moving through the dark at 2:30 Sunday morning, July 21. Tyler's division moved first, Schenck's brigade feeling its way through the gloom and down the Warrenton Pike while Sherman's brigade followed. "Proceeding slowly and carefully," as McDowell had ordered, Schenck deployed five companies of skirmishers from the 1st and 2nd Ohio on either side of the turnpike. Captain Finch of the 2nd Ohio remembered "darkness so intense that, literally, you could not see your hand before your face." Finch's Ohioans kept stumbling into fences and trees and many had "bloody noses and bruised limbs from such collisions."[43]

Finally arriving within sight of Bull Run creek, Schenck arranged his Ohioans and New Yorkers in a line of battle on the left side of the road, while Sherman's brigade of Wisconsin and New York volunteers did the same on the right. Captain Finch happened to notice a mounted officer he didn't know. The rider was "a dignified and stern-looking man, with fiery red hair and whiskers," who rode about fearlessly as the Confederate skirmishers on the opposite side of the creek took pot shots at him. Finch thought the man must be crazy to take such chances. It was Col. William Tecumseh Sherman.

Meanwhile, the two divisions McDowell had detailed to sneak around and strike the Confederate left were moving ever so slowly. Traveling the narrow lane to Sudley Ford turned out to be a "toilsome march," with the men growing tired, hungry, and thirsty, pausing to pick berries or get drinks. It took them until about 9 a.m.—long past the planned time—to cross Sudley Ford and start their advance on the Confederates.

Schenck's Ohioans and New Yorkers were carrying out their part of the plan by pretending to threaten the stone bridge across Bull Run. "First we would advance and threaten to *force* a crossing, and then retire, take a little rest, and repeat the manoeuvre," one of the Ohioans recalled.[44] On the other side of Bull Run, Confederate Col. Nathan G. Evans (known in the pre-war army as "Shanks," for his skinny legs) was not fooled for long. Warned by a lookout of the Union's flanking contingent approaching on the left, he turned his force to meet McDowell's main attack.

For much of the morning, a furious battle followed on a hill near the Warrenton Turnpike, with the Union forces pushing the Confederates back by fits and starts. It was the first battle for most of the soldiers, and, having had no combat experience, they found it startling to actually "see men shooting

Fighting between green troops from the North and South waxed and waned on Henry Hill during the Battle of Bull Run, until Union forces retreated.

at us less than two hundred yards away."[45] Nonetheless, the green soldiers on both sides fought bravely. Outnumbered, hot, and tired, the Confederates by late morning had retreated across the turnpike to a plateau called Henry Hill.

About mid-day there was a lull in fighting as both Federals and Confederates regrouped. McDowell and his staff rode through their troops shouting "The day is ours! They are running!" At this point, McDowell's forces outnumbered the Confederates in the immediate area, but once again he delayed, allowing his troops to rest before pressing the attack.

While McDowell rested, Confederate Generals Johnston and Beauregard were bringing up reinforcements in large numbers, including those of a newly minted general named Thomas J. Jackson. Realizing this, Tyler ordered Sherman's brigade, and then another, to end the charade at the stone bridge and splash across Bull Run.

The newly enlarged forces on both sides turned Henry Hill into a chaotic battleground for most of the afternoon. It was here that Confederate Gen. Barnard E. Bee, Jr., shouted, "There is Jackson, standing like a stone wall!"[46] Others were not so steadfast. Some Union and Confederate units fell apart under the shock of battle and their men wandered off, confused by the smoke

Near Bull Run Creek in Virginia, the first major battle of the Civil War occurred in July 1861. Thirteen months later, a second battle in the area would dwarf it.

and the mix of gray and blue uniforms employed on both sides.[47] The 69th and 79th New York of Sherman's brigade even fired into the backs of the gray-clad 2nd Wisconsin, another of Sherman's units.[48]

A merciless sun beat down on the tired and thirsty soldiers, their faces blackened by gunpowder from tearing open paper cartridges with their teeth. Colonel Sherman noticed riderless horses dashing about wildly, their nostrils streaming blood. Other wounded animals, still hitched to artillery pieces, lay on the ground, gnawing at themselves.[49] The din from the rifles and cannons was deafening. Officers yelled orders amidst shouts of "Give it to 'em, boys! Kill them!"[50] Now and then one side or the other would send up a battle cry, the Virginians' sounding something like "who-WHOOOOO-ey!" and the Union's like "hoo-RAAAAY" or "heigh-ray!"[51]

Fearing death, a Confederate cried out, "Oh Lord! Have mercy on me!" quickly followed by someone nearby crying, "Me too, Lord! Me too, Lord!"[52] A Union soldier was bayoneted fourteen times as he lay helpless on the ground. A sergeant's arm was torn off by a cannonball and flung in the face of another soldier who thought the blood was his own. A bullet ripped through the neck of one of Sherman's men who cried out as he fell, "Oh, my poor mother!"[53] Another of Sherman's men shot "a tall rebel" in the breast and years later remembered how his "great blue eyes stared so wildly that I think of them often still, and presume I always will."[54]

Between 3:30 and 4 p.m., so many of Joe Johnston's Confederate reinforcements from the Shenandoah Valley had arrived at Henry Hill that Union forces were increasingly hard pressed. "Here … began the scene of confusion and disorder that characterized the rest of the day," Sherman wrote in his report.[55] "I do think it was impossible to stand long in that fire," he told his wife.[56] A Maine regiment retreated, triggering a cascade of Union forces falling back in confusion in the direction they had come.

Back at the stone bridge, the remaining men of Tyler's brigade had just cut through an enemy barricade of felled trees and were expecting to cross and join the battle when they realized McDowell's main force was fleeing. Tyler's division retreated in the order it came, with Schenck's brigade bringing up the rear, the 1st and 2nd Ohio "preserving their lines in good degree, rallying together and arriving in Centreville [on the way to Washington] with closed ranks, and sharing comparatively little in the panic …," according to Schenck.[57] At one point early in the retreat, Schenck's 2nd Ohio had to form a hollow square to beat off a cavalry attack.

Other units were not so orderly. The retreat became a panic. Army units lost their cohesion. Hysteria seized the crowd of civilian spectators from Washington who had followed the army, hoping to witness a great victory. Soldiers, teamsters, ambulance drivers, members of Congress, and private citizens jostled and elbowed their way, panting and perspiring, as they headed for the safety of Washington. Captain Tidball, assigned to one of the reserve brigades in the rear, watched civilian spectators rush from their vantage points to seize "the first carriage available [and drive] off as fast as lash and oaths could make their horses go. Carriages collided, tearing away wheels; then horses were cut loose and ridden without saddles."[58]

Now Beauregard rode about on Henry Hill, shouting, "The day is ours!"[59] Broken artillery pieces, guns, and the dead bodies of men and horses from both sides littered the battlefield. Some men, in their death throes, had torn up all the grass and weeds within reach. Mortally wounded Union soldiers, left behind in their army's frantic retreat, lay propped against trees, their lives draining out of them.

About this time, that Confederate gadfly, the fire-eater Edmund Ruffin, came on the scene, having ridden artillery caissons part of the way to the battlefield. The old man was given the honor of firing a cannon that was aimed at a small bridge on the Warrenton Turnpike. The shell burst perfectly over the bridge, overturning a wagon and momentarily disrupting the stream of fleeing Union soldiers, teamsters, and civilians. Ruffin would spend months in ghoulish research after the battle trying to ascertain how many Yankees his shot had killed and wounded.[60]

Back in Columbus, an immense, excited crowd had gathered outside the office of the *Ohio State Journal* to hear news of the battle as it progressed. They expected "sun shine and joy [but] instead came dispatches announcing disaster, and a most despondent gloom spread over their faces," a contemporary recalled. By evening, however, "a feeling of determination and revengeful resistance was aroused. 'I feel like going myself!' was the exclamation of everyone who spoke."[61]

During the retreat, Schenck's New York regiment had melted away, but his two Ohio regiments largely held together. They rested at Centreville for two hours, then resumed marching. As Schenck was leading their retreat, he was hailed by Sherman who was riding alone. Asked where his troops were, Sherman replied, "Heaven only knows—they're gone with the crowd." Sherman rode with Schenck the rest of the night."[62]

The men of the 1st and 2nd Ohio were back in Washington the next day. Their ninety-day enlistments up, they returned to Ohio, their jolliness forgotten. The Ohioans had suffered only light casualties at Bull Run—two killed, six wounded, and fifteen missing—but they were despondent.[63]

As Capt. Milton McCoy of the 2nd Ohio put it, the Ohioans came home "[c]overed with dust and dirt, but not the glorious victory we all had anticipated."[64] Captain Stafford's Lancastrians had lost one man, captured. Harry Comer's chirpy insouciance had gone silent. The Ohioans were no longer "spilin' for a muss."

Bull Run turned former Attorney General Edwin M. Stanton into a clanging alarm. To one correspondent he wrote, "The imbecility of this Administration culminated in that catastrophe—an irretrievable misfortune and national disgrace never to be forgotten. ... the capture of Washington seems now to be inevitable." [65] And yet even Stanton had hope, telling another correspondent that "with all the calamity that is upon us I still do not ... despair of the Republic ... if our people can bear with this Cabinet they will prove able to supprt [sic] a great many disasters."

After the battle, Lincoln told McDowell, "I have not lost a particle of confidence in you," but he had already summoned McClellan from western

Virginia, the heir apparent to McDowell's command.[66] In his memoirs, Sherman would write that Bull Run "was one of the best-planned battles of the war, but one of the worst fought," meaning the way it was directed during the fight. He had that right. Bull Run was a melee between two mobs of amateur fighters whose leaders, on both sides, made serious mistakes— and yet many of the novice soldiers, from both the North and the South, fought with great courage.

As Sherman and others saw it, the battle could have gone either way. If only "Granny" Patterson had held Joe Johnston's Confederates in the Shenandoah Valley … if only McDowell had moved faster … if only the Union forces (including reserves that were never used) had been fed into the fight massively instead of piecemeal … Bull Run might have been a Union victory instead of a lost opportunity. It was only the first of the war's might-have-beens.

THE MAN WHO COULD TALK TO HORSES

She called him "Ulys." He opened his letters to her with "Dearest Julia" and closed them with "Kisses for the children. Kisses for yourself. Your Ulys."[67] Whenever he could, he took Julia with him on his travels, and they were not often separated. He was a family man who liked to get down on the floor with his children to play horsey or wrestle. He abhorred the sight of blood (and wouldn't eat rare meat), avoided hunting, was reserved in manner and had sensitive feelings, and didn't much like army life. And yet he was a soldier, and his business was the hard business of death and conquest.

Ulysses S. Grant, who skillfully led the Union army to victory in the Civil War, has often been dismissed as a butcher, a drunkard, and a failed president, outclassed in every way by the mythic aura of that courtly Virginia aristocrat, the elegant Robert E. Lee. And yet Grant, the plain citizen, arguably was the better general.

Grant was something else as well. In his quiet resolve and unfailing decency, he was the embodiment of an American archetype—the plain-spoken, unassuming countryman who comes out of obscurity to do great things. He and Lincoln were two of a kind—unpretentious Midwesterners who emerged to save their country at its time of greatest need, a stroke of fortune some of us have yet to fully comprehend.

Grant was born in 1822 in Point Pleasant, a tiny southern Ohio town in Clermont County, not far from the Ohio River, east of Cincinnati. His father, Jesse, was an ambitious, grasping, self-involved leather merchant, gregarious

Ulysses S. Grant was born in Point Pleasant in 1822, where his father operated a tannery. The home is preserved today as a historic site.

but not easy to like. His mother, Hannah, was a strangely detached, phlegmatic woman of little apparent warmth, not easy to know. The Grants named their first child Hiram Ulysses Grant and within eighteen months moved to nearby Georgetown.

There, Jesse built a tannery across the street from his family's small brick house, from which the child could hear screams of the animals being slaughtered. Hiram Ulysses Grant grew up hating the tannery but loving horses. As a toddler, he played among their legs and flicked their tails. Unconcerned, his mother would only say to worried neighbors, "Horses seem to understand Ulysses."[68]

As Grant grew older, he developed a reputation for taming horses, connecting with them in ways other people couldn't. He calmly read them as individuals, not anonymous, dumb beasts of burden or fleet-footed beauties, and he sensed their needs as fellow creatures. The Grant boy became known for his ability to calm nervous animals. It seemed as if the youngster could talk with the horses.

Clearly, young Grant would never follow his father into the tannery business, so Jesse fished around, called on a political contact, and came up with an appointment to West Point for his son. The Point offered a professional education, tuition free. It had not been the younger Grant's idea, but he went, with no great enthusiasm, because his father told him to. Because of a mix-up, he was not enrolled as "Hiram Ulysses Grant," but as "Ulysses S. Grant," the first two initials bringing him the cadet nickname of "Sam" (for "Uncle Sam").

Sam Grant did not like West Point ("military life had no charms for me") and passed through it almost unnoticed. He was not unfriendly but he was taciturn, making no deep impression on the other cadets. One who did remember him said Grant was "a small fellow ... [with] a total absence of elegance, and naturally showed off badly in contrast with the young Southern men, who prided themselves on being finished in the ways of the world."[69] Grant graduated an undistinguished twenty-first out of thirty-nine students in the class of 1843. Horsemanship, unsurprisingly, and, art, surprisingly, were his best subjects.

On graduation, Lieutenant Grant was assigned to the army's Jefferson Barracks in St. Louis, Missouri, and while there he met Julia Dent, the sister of a West Point roommate. Daughter of a retired army colonel who owned a few slaves, Julia was plain-looking and afflicted with strabismus or "squint," the tendency for one eye to wander. The good-looking young Grant never seemed to notice that, however, instead falling in love with the inner Julia who had a bubbly, energetic personality and the determination to take her proper place in the world.

Ulysses and Julia behaved with all the charming foolishness of young couples in courtship. When her canary died, he made "a nice little coffin" for it, painted it yellow, and had eight officers attend the pet's "funeral."[70] For her part, Julia dreamed of Grant and in his honor "named one of my new bedstead posts for him."[71]

Ulysses and Julia became secretly engaged in 1844, exchanging his ring and a lock of her hair. Julia recalled, "He declared his love and told me that without me life would be insupportable." From the beginning, the self-assured Julia would give her partner an emotional anchor, a source of strength, a snug harbor.

During their engagement, Ulysses wrote her from New Orleans, "You can have but little idea of the influance you have over me Julia, even while so far away. If I feel tempted to do any thing that I think is not right I am shure to think, 'Well now if Julia saw me would I do so' and thus ... absent or

Young Lt. Ulysses S. Grant fell in love with Julia Dent, who was plain-looking but endowed with a lively personality.

present I am more or less governed by what I think is your will."[72]

The young soldier and the slave-holder's daughter married in 1848 after four years of courtship, much of it by mail while young Lieutenant Grant was in the service of his country. They were married within weeks of his return from the Mexican War. After four years together, during which the Grants' first child was born, Lieutenant Grant was ordered to the Pacific Coast. Julia was pregnant again, so he reluctantly left her behind.

Grant traveled by ship and among its passengers was an observant young woman, Mrs. Delia B. Sheffield. Of Grant, she remembered a man who was "an incessant smoker and very taciturn, thoughtful and serious, though affable in manner, and during every day and an early part of every night of the voyage, I would see him pacing the deck and smoking, silent and solitary."[73]

Young Captain Grant spent nearly two years with the 4th Infantry at isolated posts in Oregon territory and California, desperately missing his family and trying unsuccessfully to supplement his pay with farming ventures. In his loneliness, he drank heavily, the start of an unfounded reputation in the gossipy army as a chronic drunkard. He was not an alcoholic, but someone who used alcohol to escape from depression.* "You do not know how forsaken I feel," he wrote Julia.[74]

On April 11, 1854, Grant suddenly resigned from the army, very possibly to avoid punishment for seeming to be intoxicated while on duty.* Then, with

* Historians disagree on whether intoxication caused Grant's sudden resignation from the army. Jean Edward Smith, in his generally admiring and well-received biography, *Grant* (New York: Simon & Schuster, 2001), says on page eighty-seven, "The story rings true." Brooks D. Simpson, in *Ulysses S. Grant: Triumph Over Adversity, 1822–1865* (Boston: Houghton Mifflin Company, 2000), says on page sixty-one that what happened "remains unclear," and suggests that army gossip may have embellished the story.

no head for business, Grant spent nearly seven fruitless years in civilian life near St. Louis. He farmed, even building a crude farmhouse he tellingly called Hardscrabble, then had to give up when farming didn't pay. Two days before Christmas in 1857, he pawned his watch. By 1858, the Grants had four children and poor prospects.

Wearing his old army coat, Grant sold firewood on the street in St. Louis, attempted the real estate business but failed, and applied for but did not get a job as county engineer. Perhaps the hardest moment of all came in 1860 when the desperate thirty-seven-year-old West Point graduate, a failure in every line of work he had tried, was forced to ask his father for a job. In May 1860 he began work as a salesman in a leather goods store owned by his father and operated by his younger brothers in Galena, Illinois.

He was still there when war broke out. "Galena was throbbing with patriotism," Julia wrote in her memoirs. "The men were holding meetings and calling for volunteers. The boys were playing at war, wearing military caps, beating small drums, guarding the crossings, and demanding countersigns."[75]

On April 18, Grant presided over one of Galena's public meetings on the war. Then he began a quest for an officer's position appropriate to his education and experience. It was unavailing. He had no close friends in positions of power, his letter of application went unanswered by Washington, and General McClellan—perhaps remembering Grant's reputation as a drinker—would not even receive him in his Cincinnati office.

After initially resisting any use of influence, Grant finally saw his local congressman, and soon had the colonelcy of an Illinois militia regiment, a rowdy group that had driven its previous colonel into resigning. Grant—who could read soldiers the way he could read horses—treated the men with both firmness and consideration and soon tamed them.

Arriving in camp in civilian clothes—"an old coat, worn out at the elbows, and a badly dinged plug hat," he was mocked, but not for long, "and in a few days he reduced matters in camp to perfect order."[76] On June 28, most of the militia regiment volunteered to follow him into three years of U.S. service as the 21st Illinois.

On July 3, Colonel Grant and his regiment left for the unruly border state of Missouri. Battles seemed imminent, but none materialized. Approaching where an enemy force under Col. Thomas Harris was thought to be, Grant's "heart kept getting higher and higher until it felt to me as though it was in my throat .... I would have given anything then to have been back in Illinois." Then Grant found the enemy had departed.

My heart resumed its place. It occurred to me at once that Harris had been as much afraid of me as I had been of him. ... From that event to the close of the war, I never experienced trepidation upon confronting an enemy, though I always felt more or less anxiety. I never forgot that he had much reason to fear my forces as I had his. The lesson was valuable.[77]

Desperate for experienced commanders, in late July President Lincoln promoted a number of officers, including Grant, to brigadier general. Only a few weeks before a ragged civilian who was being ignored, General Grant now commanded all troops in southeast Missouri. On September 2, he established his headquarters in Cairo at the southernmost tip of Illinois. South of this point, where the Ohio River flowed into the Mississippi, Kentucky formed the east shore, Missouri the west. From here the preeminent general of the Civil War would begin to emerge.

Kentucky, torn between a governor who favored secession and a legislature that didn't, had declared itself neutral territory. In September, however, Confederate Gen. Leonidas Polk unwisely violated Kentucky's neutrality by seizing Columbus on the Mississippi River.

Polk's thoughtless move opened the door to a counter-invasion by Union forces. Acting quickly and without orders, on September 6 Grant occupied Paducah, at the mouth of the Tennessee River, and then Southland at the mouth of the Cumberland River. No blood was shed and Grant, by his swift action, had saved two important gateways to the South and blocked Polk.

The new brigadier general spent most of fall 1861 training his troops at Cairo and looking southward. On November 7, Grant led his troops to Belmont, Missouri, across the Mississippi from Columbus. The Federals overran the Confederate camp there, although they barely escaped when a larger Confederate force returned while the men were looting the camp.

From where Grant sat at Cairo, the Mississippi ran southward like a broad highway through the western Confederacy, all the way to the Gulf of Mexico. Near Cairo, the inviting mouths of the Tennessee and Cumberland rivers offered avenues into the very heart of the Confederacy. Clearly, Cairo was a place to consider the possibilities. When the general wasn't training soldiers or enjoying his family, who had joined him there, he would sit silently in his office, watching his cigar smoke curl in the air. There was a lot for Ulysses S. Grant to think about that fall.

"Granny" Lee's Bad Start

McClellan had hardly left western Virginia to pick up the pieces after Bull Run when Robert E. Lee—a Virginian blueblood not yet famous as a warrior—arrived to take personal charge of the Confederacy's sagging fortunes among the hills and valleys. The Confederacy had won at Bull Run, but here it was in trouble.

Lee's first objective was to break the Union's grip on the vital Staunton-Parkersburg Turnpike. He was delayed by disease among the troops, endless rain that turned roads into quagmires, and a shortage of supplies. When the weather improved in early September, Confederate hopes rose, and under Lee's watchful eye in this, his first military campaign, Rebel forces began assembling a complex, five-pronged assault.

Lee's key objective was the summit of Cheat Mountain. There, Union soldiers—pausing periodically to admire the fine views—had constructed a huge fort to guard the turnpike. Driving them away would reopen the road for the Confederates.

As if to mimic Union strategy at Rich Mountain, Confederate Col. Albert Rust set out with 2,500 green troops to push through thick woods under a chilling rain, hoping to surprise the Union forces on Cheat Mountain with a flank attack. Fewer than three hundred Federals, including some Ohioans, were inside the fort at the time. It seemed ripe for the plucking.

Unaware he was greatly outnumbered, however, Union Col. Nathan Kimball, an Indianan, sent two companies of skirmishers against Rust's much larger force. Thoroughly soaked and cold, the startled Confederates turned around and fled, littering the woods with their blankets, spare clothing, and guns.

Other prongs of the attack on Union positions were either driven back or withdrawn by Lee when he realized how cold, hungry, and demoralized his soldiers were. He suffered a personal blow when his aide-de-camp, Lt. Col. John A. Washington, great-grandnephew to George Washington, was shot and killed by Federal scouts.

Writing off Cheat Mountain as a "forlorn hope expedition," Lee turned his attention sixty-five miles southwesterly to the strategically important river valley of the Kanawha. Originating deep in western Virginian, the Kanawha was a water highway westward to the Ohio River. In the Kanawha Valley, Lee would face the combined forces of Rosecrans and ex-Senator, now Brig. Gen. Jacob Cox.[78]

State Sen. Jacob D. Cox proved to be an able general despite a lack of military experience.

McClellan had arrived in western Virginia in June, leaving Cox in charge of Camp Dennison back in Ohio. When the Confederates appeared in force in the Kanawha Valley, however, McClellan told Cox to join the fight.

Cox brought with him several Ohio regiments joined by the soldiers of the 1st and 2nd Kentucky, most of whom actually were Ohioans. Though officered by loyal Kentuckians, the men of the so-called Kentucky regiments were unemployed Ohio longshoremen and steamboaters, "mostly of a rough and ready class [who] gave a great deal of trouble by insubordination; but they did not lack courage," according to Cox.[79] Cox's force eventually would give rise to the hard-fighting Kanawha Division.

Lee's key commanders in the Kanawha region were Gens. Henry Wise and John Floyd, both of whom were aristocrats and ex-governors of Virginia. With that much in common, they might be expected to work together. They did not, for they were bitter enemies and feuded continually. "If [Wise] had been half as troublesome to me as he was to Floyd, I should indeed have had a hot time of it," Cox wrote in his memoirs.[80]

From July through September, Union and Confederate forces clashed repeatedly for control of the valley. A memorable moment occurred September 10 at Carnifex Ferry when Col. William Haines Lytle of the 10th Ohio was struck in the leg by a bullet that also hit his horse. The maddened animal threw off its rider, leaped over the Confederates' barricade, and dropped dead among the enemy soldiers, who fled. Lytle was an accomplished poet, lawyer, and politician from Cincinnati who would survive this wound. The end of the "poet-soldier" would come later in the war and have a haunting quality.

The engagement was also Pvt. William McKinley's first taste of serious action. The men of the 23rd plowed through cornfields and brush to face the enemy across a river, take some fire, and discover the next day the Confederates had retreated. "This was our first real fight," McKinley, always the careful

Cincinnatian William S. Rosecrans drew on his military education and experience to play a prominent role in the war, but with only mixed success.

At Carnifex Ferry in western Virginia's Kanawha Valley, Rosecrans' troops forced a Confederate retreat in 1861, furthering the cause of West Virginia statehood.

record keeper, recorded in his diary. "We learned that we could fight and whip the rebels on their own ground."[81]

For the next few weeks, Confederates under Lee and Federals under Rosecrans and Cox sparred ineffectually. On October 24, 1861, western Virginians approved a referendum for statehood by a margin of 18,408 to 781, lopsided in part because many opponents boycotted the election. That was the last straw for Lee. On October 30, he gave up trying to hold the area by force and departed.

Statehood would not come officially until June 20, 1863, and vicious guerilla fighting and occasional clashes between regulars would plague the region for the rest of the war. Within the first year of the war, however, the Confederacy had lost control of a significant portion of Virginia. Ohio troops and their commanders, particularly Rosecrans and Cox, had played the largest role in achieving it. Cox later wrote, "The line of the Alleghenies [dividing western Virginia from Confederate Virginia] became the northern frontier of the Confederacy in Virginia, and was never again seriously broken."[82]

Since coming to the mountains, the previously dark-haired, clean-shaven Lee had grown a beard and it had come in gray. Confederate efforts under his direction in western Virginia had failed dismally, so he departed western

Virginia to catcalls from the Southern press charging him with lack of aggressiveness. They called him "Granny" Lee. But Robert E. Lee would be heard from again in this war, and so would the Ohioans.

GAZETTE

As 1861 wound down, William Dennison could look back with both satisfaction and wistfulness on his two-year term as Ohio's governor. In the opening months of this "improvised war," the burden of raising troops and supporting them fell on the shoulders of state governors. Dennison emerged as a leader in the Midwest's support of the Union, managing Ohio's contributions with energy and efficiency. He was farsighted as well; at his request, neighboring governors assembled for a meeting in Ohio that urged the federal government to act quickly and neutralize the Confederacy in Kentucky and Tennessee.[83]

Dennison's reward was to be denied a second term by his own party. Ohio's determinedly down-to-earth voters still thought Dennison "frittered in polish" and blamed him more than he deserved for some initial bungling. Dennison was told his services weren't needed in Washington either. But the "gentleman governor," as he was derisively called, was nothing if not dignified, and in January 1862 he gracefully returned to private life.[84]

In only nine months as a war governor, Dennison—working almost from scratch—had overseen the enlisting of upwards of one hundred thousand recruits, supported them until the federal government took over their care, and established military camps throughout the state, all while keeping Ohio on a sound financial footing.[85] The state's regiments—including Carrington's "extras" that Dennison had persuaded the legislature to pay for—had been useful in protecting Unionists in the areas bordering Ohio, thereby protecting Ohio as well.

As 1861 waned, so did the fighting as North and South settled down to prepare for what was to come. Blustery optimism was being replaced by grim resolve, laced with anxiety. The Confederates had established a front line that stretched over one thousand miles, from tidewater Virginia to the Oklahoma Indian territory.

The debacle at Bull Run had been a useful corrective to naiveté on the Union side, but it created undeserved hubris among the Confederates. After the war, the Confederacy's Gen. Joe Johnston would write of First Bull Run that "our army was more disorganized by victory than that of the United States by defeat."[86]

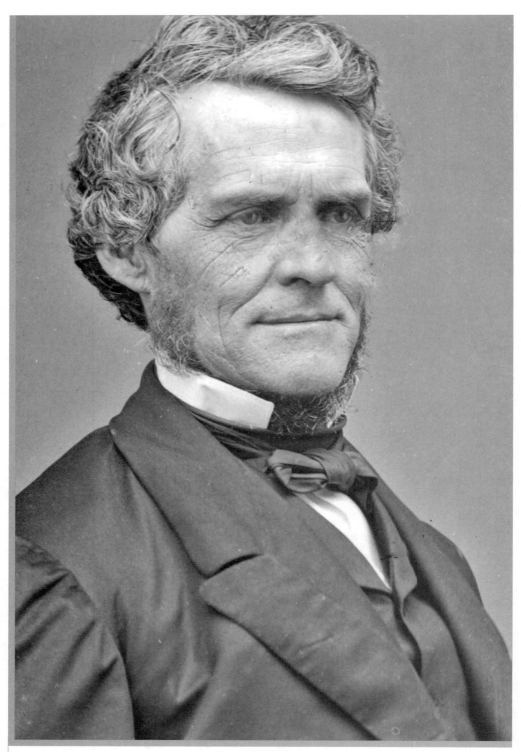

Ohio's rough-and-ready voters looked with disdain on their suave governor, William Dennison, but he proved an able war-time leader.

Underappreciated by publics on both sides was what had been happening in western Virginia. Thanks to that region's anti-secession majority and the military forces rushed them from Ohio and nearby states, the Confederacy had effectively lost an important chunk of territory—more than a third of Virginia—by the end of 1861.

Western Virginia was strategically important to both sides and the Confederates would keep trying until the end of the war to regain it, but with no lasting success. Outfought in the hills and valleys, the Confederacy had suffered its first major loss at the hands of Western troops. There would be many more.

To Learn More:

For a glimpse of the early life in Ohio of Ulysses S. Grant, visit his birthplace in Point Pleasant (http://www.ohiohistory.org/places/grantbir/ or 513-553-4911) and his schoolhouse in Georgetown (http://ohiohistory.org/places/grantsch/ or 937-378-4222).

In Ohio's next-door neighbor, the western portion of Virginia that is now West Virginia, many newly minted soldiers from the Buckeye state got their first taste of battle. Some battlegrounds, such as Rich Mountain and Cheat Summit, are little changed from 1861; Philippi offers a small museum as well. Travelling the state's up-and-down landscape suggests what marching was like for heavily laden soldiers. See the "West Virginia in the Civil War" Web site (http://www.wvcivilwar.com/ and the West Virginia Division of Tourism's site: http://www.wvtraditions.com/. T. Harry Williams' *Hayes of the Twenty-Third* ably describes the Civil War activities (largely in West Virginia) of Rutherford B. Hayes and his hard-marching regiment, the 23rd Ohio.

Further east in Virginia, the area where the first and second battles of Bull Run occurred and where the 1st and 2nd Ohio first saw combat is now the Manassas National Battlefield Park (http://www.nps.gov/mana/ or 703-361-1339). On Henry Hill, where so much desperate fighting took place, is a visitors' center offering an orientation film.

The First Battle of Bull Run is concisely outlined in JoAnna M. McDonald's *"We Shall Meet Again": The First Battle of Manassas (Bull Run), July 18-21, 1861*, and described in more depth in David Detzer's well-regarded *Donnybrook: The Battle of Bull Run, 1861*. "The Man Who Could Talk to Horses" comes to life in Jean Edward Smith's *Grant* and in Brooks D. Simpson's *Ulysses S. Grant: Triumph over Adversity, 1822-1865*.

Visitors to the Bull Run battlefield after the battle found soldiers' graves marked by boards from cracker boxes, with epitaphs written in pencil.

5

MINE EYES HAVE SEEN THE GLORY

Fall 1861 and Winter 1861–62

Cleveland moped through the fall and winter of 1861–62, depressed by squalls sweeping in from Lake Erie and a war that didn't seem to be going anywhere in particular, but one young Clevelander had other things on his mind. Early each morning and late each night, six days a week, he could be seen striding to and from his office, wrapped in his secret thoughts and hunched forward as if he were plowing through invisible obstacles.

Tall and whip-thin, the twenty-two-year-old had tightly drawn skin, smooth cheeks, and eyes as hard and bright as agates. When he looked up, it was like a snake popping out of its hole. Usually, he kept his emotions under wraps, but in an unguarded moment he burst out to an older businessman, "I am bound to be rich—bound to be rich—BOUND TO BE RICH!"[1] The young man's name was John D. Rockefeller. He would become the world's first billionaire.

The Ohio of young Rockefeller's time was nearly an Eden, a pastoral landscape of small farms, dirt roads, and little towns where life moved to the rhythm of the seasons. Islets of industry were appearing here and there, and Cincinnati, in the far southwest corner of the state, was a manufacturing and commercial giant, the biggest city in the Old Northwest, but the sensory truth was this: Ohio was the kind of agrarian Elysium imagined by Thomas Jefferson. It was a fertile, peaceable kingdom where most people spent their lives on small farms or in little villages, their feet planted firmly on the good earth, the fabric of their years woven by the weather, the rotation of the crops, and demands of animal husbandry.

Even young Rockefeller, destined to be a titan of oil, began his career in Ohio's wholesale produce industry, buying and selling the bounty of the land: "grain, fish, water, lime, plaster, coarse fine solar and dairy salt" as well as meat and other foodstuffs.[2]

In time, Eden-like Ohio would largely fade away, and the war's impact was only one reason. Go-getters like John D. Rockefeller were building a new country even as armies seemed bent on destroying the old. Although Rockefeller followed war news closely and opposed slavery, he was too busy to become a soldier. He hired a substitute for $300, a practice allowed at the time.

By the end of the war, Rockefeller would own Cleveland's biggest oil refinery and within a few years his Standard Oil Co. would make him the colossus of American business. While young men were learning how to kill each other and older men were studying their war maps in Washington and Richmond, men like Rockefeller were rising from humble backgrounds to build railroads, create factories, and pry riches from the earth. They were learning how to raise capital, get things made, and market them to the masses. They were practicing the art of the deal. They were building a new economy.

Son of a footloose flimflam man who was also a bigamist, John D. Rockefeller was rigidly moral himself. He was not just an ordinary Horatio Alger-like man of pluck and luck and good intentions, he was one of the biggest—one who made many others possible. He lubricated the wheels of industry and fueled the internal combustion engine. Plastics, the interstate highway, fertilizer, the daily commute, suburban sprawl, coast-to-coast travel in six and a half hours, farm tractors, and Big Ag are all part of a world he helped to make and we have today—life in the fast lane, 24/7.

Watching America industrialize itself, Henry Adams, a Yankee man of letters, would write within a few years about the "virgin and the dynamo," meaning a peaceful world of innocence displaced by a fevered modernity. In 1862, Ohio was the virgin, Rockefeller the dynamo.

MINE EYES HAVE SEEN THE GLORY

Julia Ward Howe was a plump little individualist, reputed to dye her hair red out of pure orneriness, so when the peppery Boston poet met the extraordinarily ornery John Brown in 1859, there must have been a frisson of excitement on both sides. Julia was married to a debonair adventurer and

Despite his execution in 1859, Ohioan John Brown was vividly recalled in the memories and songs of Union soldiers everywhere.

educator named Samuel Gridley Howe, one of Brown's "Secret Six" backers, and so the Ohioan came calling on the Howes.

Meeting Brown at her front door, Julia beheld "a Puritan of the Puritans, forceful, concentrated, and self-contained." She felt "great gratification at meeting one of whom I had heard so good an account."[3] Brown liked her too. Soon, however, Brown would be only a memory.

After war broke out in April 1861, a Massachusetts militia unit was ordered to repair old Fort Warren in Boston Harbor. In this simpler age, soldiers got their music by making it themselves, spontaneously joining in chorus while working or marching. Laboring on the fort, the young soldiers sang favorite songs, including an old Methodist hymn with a catchy tune titled, "Say, Brothers, Will You Meet Us?"

Bored, the soldiers concocted new verses to tease one of their fellows, a good-natured Scot named John Brown. The coincidence of names with the notorious John Brown caught the soldiers' fancy, producing such lines as *"John Brown's body lies a-mouldering in the grave, His soul's marching on,"* followed by lusty choruses of *"Glory Hally, Hallejuah!"*[4] A hit with everyone who was reminded of Ohio's notorious Brown, the song spread throughout the Union army.

Late in 1861, the Howes visited Washington. A carriage carrying Mrs.

Howe and several friends was delayed by troops crowding the road, so the Howe party passed the time by singing snatches of army songs, including "John Brown's Body." Someone suggested that Julia "write some good words for that stirring tune." The words came to her as she lay in bed early the next morning and within a few months she published "The Battle Hymn of the Republic."

Howe's "Battle Hymn" became the semi-official anthem of the Union army, as powerful in stirring Northern emotions as *Uncle Tom's Cabin* had been years before. Thousands of Ohio soldiers sang it as they marched off to battle.

"John Brown's Body" was sung in spirited 4/4 time, a mocking song that helped soldiers march along. Julia slowed her version down to a religious processional—and a grim warning to the South:

Mine eyes have seen the glory of the coming of the Lord
He is trampling out the vintage where the grapes of wrath are stored,
He has loosed the fateful lightening of His terrible swift sword …

I have seen Him in the watch-fires of a hundred circling camps
They have builded Him an altar in the evening dews and damps
I can read His righteous sentence by the dim and flaring lamps …

I have read a fiery gospel writ in burnish'd rows of steel,
"As ye deal with my contemners, So with you my grace shall deal;"
Let the Hero, born of woman, crush the serpent with his heel …

Glory! Glory! Hallelujah
His truth is marching on.[5]

Before his execution in December 1859, John Brown had issued a warning: the crimes of "this guilty land" would be purged away with blood. Now, as soldiers invaded the South and trampled out the grapes of wrath, his truth was marching on in song and deed.

THE HARD DRIVERS

Despite the uneasiness in his soul, or perhaps because of it, James Abram Garfield hungered to get ahead and had the brains, energy, and (as someone once said of another shooting star) all the disadvantages you need to succeed. In one lifetime, he achieved one of America's great success stories and one of its tragedies.

Born in 1831 in a log cabin in the malarial Cuyahoga Valley in northeastern Ohio, Garfield was only twelve when his father died, leaving

Born in a log cabin but highly gifted, James A. Garfield enjoyed early success in politics and war, but less as a young husband.

his family in poverty. Endowed with a prodigious intelligence, the boy lost himself in books, then left home at seventeen to work on canal boats. His intelligence attracted attention, however, and like a leaf on a rushing stream, he was carried along by others from one educational opportunity to another. Graduating with honors from Williams College in 1856, Garfield returned to Ohio and, only twenty-five years old, became the head of the Western Reserve Eclectic Institute (now Hiram College).

Garfield achieved success after success, but—perhaps because it came so early and easily—he never was completely free of a certain discontent, a feeling there was always "Something Else" to be won. That made him restless, in matters of the heart particularly, and it repeatedly caused problems. The first occurred late in 1852 when he broke off a romantic relationship with one Mary Hubbell of Hiram.

To Mary Hubbell, Garfield had offered "my fondest affections ... [t]o no other being but yourself, on earth."[6] With language like that, Mary thought they were engaged, but he did not. His jilting her caused Mary and her local sympathizers to be loudly outraged. For a time, the young women of Hiram boycotted Garfield.

The public fallout from the Hubbell breakup had rattled young Garfield, but by late 1853 he was involved with a fellow Eclectic student, the dark, serious, and lovely Lucretia Rudolph, nicknamed "Crete." Then followed five uneasy years of procrastination, during which he maintained a warm, probably romantic correspondence with one Roberta Selleck in New York State while never quite resolving his relationship with Crete.

In 1858, Garfield finally married Crete, not so much because he wanted to, apparently, but because it seemed to be expected of him. (The summer before they married, Crete wrote James, "[M]y heart almost breaks with the cruel thought that our marriage is based upon the cold stern word *duty*."[7]) During this time he was also maintaining a warm friendship with a woman named Almeda Booth, a professional colleague at Hiram. It did not appear to be a romantic relationship, but its closeness disturbed Crete nonetheless.

It wasn't long until Garfield the married man was away from home, on school and other business, more than he was home. Crete and "my dear Jamie," as she called her husband, maintained a steady correspondence during his absences, but the tone of their letters suggests that she loved him more than he did her. (She signed her letters to him, "Your loving wife," he with a more oblique "Ever, James.")[8] Garfield did return home now and then, because in the summer of 1860 Crete gave birth to daughter Eliza. The Garfields nicknamed her "Little Trot," after a character in the Dickens best-seller *David Copperfield*.

Garfield had been persuaded in 1859 to run for the Ohio Senate on the Republican ticket. Passionately opposed to slavery, he made thirty campaign speeches on the subject in a district that needed little persuading. Easily winning the election, he went to Ohio's capital, where his speaking skills and friendly manner (a husky six-footer, he was fond of giving friends bear hugs) won him popularity. The evil of slavery was never far from his mind. John Brown had lived in Garfield's district, and when the raider of Harpers Ferry was sentenced to hang, Garfield wrote in his diary, "Brave man, Old Hero, Farewell!"[9]

Letters between the Garfields reveal a marriage under stress. On March 14, 1860, James dutifully wrote Crete, "Much of the time since I left home I have felt sad and unhappy ... [but] I shall try to make life for you and myself as pleasant as possible."[10] His last visit home had not gone well. She replied that "it seems a little hard to have you tell me ... that you had for several months felt that it was probably a great mistake that we had ever tried a married life. But, Jamie, I will not treasure it up against you."[11]

When war broke out, Senator Garfield—then in Columbus, as usual—wrote Crete, who had remained in Hiram, as usual, that "it makes me long to be in the strife and fight it out."[12] He helped raise volunteers for the 7th Ohio Volunteer Infantry and was expecting the men to elect him their colonel (which was customary in militia units at the time) when Governor Dennison sent him on a secret mission to Illinois.

Garfield's mission was highly successful. Not only did he procure five thousand badly needed muskets for Ohio's new soldiers, but he also persuaded the governors of Illinois and Indiana to place their recruits under the command of General McClellan of Ohio. When Garfield returned home, however, he found that someone else had won command of the 7th Ohio.

Then, Garfield failed to win a similar position with the 19th Ohio and, when he continued seeking a command, onlookers faulted him for unseemly ambition. Finally, after weeks of frustration, he was offered the lieutenant colonelcy—the second in command—of a regiment then forming, the 41st Ohio.

Enter William Babcock Hazen. A boyhood friend of Garfield's in Hiram, Hazen had graduated from West Point with the class of 1855 (ranking only twenty-eight of thirty-four, although he had been a serious student). Sent west, he became a fierce fighter of Indians. While he recovered from a serious bullet wound, Hazen was assigned to teach infantry tactics at West Point. At war's

William Babcock Hazen was a hard-driving commander as "insensible to fatigue as a threshing machine." His well-drilled soldiers appreciated him after experiencing combat.

outbreak, he desperately sought a command, but it wasn't until September of 1861 that he received it—the unfilled colonelcy of the still-forming 41st Ohio, perhaps at the instigation of the regiment's lieutenant colonel, his old friend Garfield.

With the army's need for leaders escalating, Garfield almost immediately was given the top command of the 42nd Ohio, at the moment existing in name only. He quickly recruited sixty of his Eclectic students, draining the Hiram institution of most of its males, and used them to form the nucleus of Company A. By November the regiment had reached full strength and was undergoing rigorous training by its schoolmaster commander.

Garfield taught himself the military basics by whittling a set of wooden blocks, which he maneuvered on his desk to simulate marching. Then he used the blocks to teach his officers, who spent six to eight exhausting hours a day ordering their awkward recruits back and forth across the alternately dusty and muddy fields of Camp Chase. Garfield's new soldiers were convinced of his military prowess and became fond of him as well. Nevertheless, the gregarious Garfield disliked the loneliness of command. For a while, patting his horses and whispering in their ears had to serve instead.[13]

As Garfield was putting the 42nd Ohio through hard drills at Camp Chase, Hazen was pressing the 41st Ohio even harder at Camp Wood near Cleveland. Photographs of Hazen reveal a man with a pointed mustache and drill-sergeant eyes so piercing that photographers usually told him to avoid looking at the camera.

The thirty-year-old Hazen had barely arrived in camp before he began firing off orders. "The first principle of the soldier," Hazen told his men, is "obedience to commands." He was a man with many commands, on everything from cleanliness and neatness (bare feet, unbuttoned shirts, and long hair would not be tolerated), to drill, endless drill.

"[A]s insensible to fatigue as a threshing machine," according to two veterans of the 41st, Hazen drove his men from reveille to lights-out. Bugle calls hurried the volunteers from one duty to another. The veterans recalled that "the men began to wonder if two days' work was not crowded into the twelve-hour program."[14] Hazen purchased books of "military reading," which the men had to study in preparation for recitations.[15] He believed that his "rigid enforcement made the regiment one of the best ever in any service."[16] After they had experienced combat, Hazen's well-prepared soldiers had to admit the battle-scarred Indian fighter knew what he was doing.

Sweating with the rest while absorbing Hazen's tough methods was a thirty-one-year-old merchant named Emerson Opdycke. Opdycke had enlisted early as a private in the 41st, but proved so promising a soldier that within weeks his fellows elected him first lieutenant of their company. He had grown up sharing the hard life of a pioneer family in the wilderness of northeastern Ohio's Trumbull County. Except for time out to join the California gold rush, he had spent most of his early career in the saddle and harness business in Warren.

Impressed by Hazen's command style, former businessman Opdycke became a tough, successful commander on the battlefield.

At war's outbreak, Opdycke—married and father of a young son—helped recruit a company of volunteers from Trumbull and Cuyahoga counties. On August 26 at Camp Wood the men were mustered in as Company A of Hazen's 41st Ohio. Almost six feet tall, endowed with a receding hairline and a parade-ground voice, Opdycke was the kind of officer Hazen liked, a hard-driving, no-nonsense, and highly ambitious soldier who seemed born to command.

As the winter of 1861–1862 neared, Hazen's 41st Ohio and Garfield's 42nd Ohio were deemed ready to go to war. Both were ordered to join Brig. Gen. Don Carlos Buell's Army of the Ohio, then in Kentucky, the 41st to Louisville and the 42nd to Kentucky's border with western Virginia. In time, Hazen, the military professional, and Garfield, the self-taught commander, would be tested in battle.

In the Hills and Valleys

With the approach of winter in late 1861, war-torn western Virginia quieted as snow swirled around its mountain tops and settled into the valleys. Lee had given up and departed, the region's voters were demanding statehood within the Union, and if the Confederacy had not written off western Virginia, it certainly was losing interest. "This country is not worth fighting for," wrote one unhappy Confederate warrior stuck in the mountains.[17] Another called western Virginia "the most God forsaken Country I ever laid eyes on that is certain."[18]

With remnants of Lee's Confederates still in the region, Federal troops from half a dozen states—the largest number from Ohio—were ordered to protect western Virginia while it sought to become a state of its own. Gen. William Rosecrans, who became the region's highest Union officer after McClellan, went to Washington and set up headquarters in Wheeling near the Ohio line. A dispirited Cox, yearning to join the action somewhere—anywhere—else, was bluntly ordered by Rosecrans to stay put in the Kanawha Valley.

In late October, the 8th Ohio saw some action when it ventured into the extreme eastern portion of western Virginia and chased the Confederates out of Romney, but within two months the Federals pulled back, threatened by a certain Confederate named Jackson.

The 23rd Ohio spent the winter in tents and huts scattered among strategic points in the Kanawha Valley. Rutherford Hayes, recently promoted to lieutenant colonel of the 23rd, was relishing the military experience. He hadn't shaved since summer, often slept in his clothes, and sometimes even in his boots.[19] It seemed to thrill him.

Others were thrilled just to get away from the place. Young Thomas F. Galwey of the 8th Ohio spent "two delightful months" recruiting in Columbus, escaping much of western Virginia's winter.[20] Lt. Col. John Beatty and the Third Ohio also escaped from wintry western Virginia when they were transferred to Buell's army in Kentucky in November. The Midwesterners remaining in the Department of Western Virginia shivered and yawned their way through the winter.

In this frozen up-and-down region, the wisest thing for soldiers to do was to settle into winter quarters and venture out no more than they had to. The winter of 1861–1862 was exceptionally harsh. With snow drifting over the huts they had built for themselves, soldiers on both sides spent a lot of time trying to stay warm as they listened to each other cough. "I don't know of anything interesting to write," a bored Sgt. Oscar D. Ladley of the 75th Ohio wrote his mother and sisters in Yellow Springs.[21]

The soldiers held stag dances, gambled, played chess and checkers, and engaged in what one called "the supreme passion"—carving pipes, rings, and other small objects from the roots of laurel or rhododendron bushes to send home.[22] In spells of good weather, they went foraging, hunting, fishing, or exploring. ("Yesterday myself with two other boys of our company went up on a high hill and had a splendid view for 25 or 30 miles," according to Sergeant Ladley, grateful to finally have something to write about.[23]) But as the winter wore on and morale fell, the men grew morose, desperate for a change.

A nasty little engagement on December 11 and 12 reminded them there still was a war going on. Ohio, Indiana, and loyal western Virginia soldiers trudged through the snow from the Union camp on Cheat Mountain for a surprise attack on the Confederate camp on 4,500-foot Allegheny Mountain, 20 miles away. Poor coordination doomed the attack. Twenty Federals were killed and 107 wounded.

The discouraged attackers plodded back to their own camp and stayed there. After that, the winter settled down to a series of skirmishes every few days, with only an occasional casualty or two. Things would not change until spring.

GOING TO SOLDIER

On November 1, 1861, the once-mighty fortress that was Winfield Scott, commander of all the nation's armies, tottered off to retirement. Waiting to take his place was thirty-four-year-old George B. McClellan. Summoned from the mountains of western Virginia in July, McClellan had spent his time since then revitalizing the wrecked, demoralized army left him by Irvin McDowell. All the while he had been snubbing his one-time supporter Scott ("a perfect imbecile"), privately sneering at Lincoln ("a well-meaning baboon"), and telling intimates the war should not be wasted saving "the nigger."[24]

On the same day Scott retired as head of all the armies, Lincoln summoned McClellan to the White House and asked him if he could take over the army's top command. He would have to oversee the Union's forces in theaters across the nation while he personally led McDowell's old command, now called the Army of the Potomac. It was a tall order, but McClellan—who scarcely five years before had been a mere captain—did not hesitate. "I can do it all," he told Lincoln.[25]

He could do it all. McClellan had cockiness in buckets, but in this he was different more in degree than kind with the thousands of young men hurrying to enlist in the Union armies. With the innocence and enthusiasm of youth, they wanted to join the great cause of holding the nation together by defeating the traitors of the South. Yes, the North had suffered defeats here and there, but no, youth would not be denied the opportunity to set things right. They could do it all.

Men young and old and in various conditions poured into the camps. A visitor to the camp in Columbus reported, "They are of all ages, from the man whose head is already gray to the boy on whose cheeks has not obscured the bloom. All the faces are resolute and there is fight in them."[26] Officers tried to expel a one-eyed man who had joined one regiment, but he wept so hard and was supported so strongly by his fellows that he was allowed to stay. Physical exams were cursory. If a man breathed, walked, and had enough teeth to tear open the paper that held the powder for each bullet, he would probably be enrolled.

The Lincoln administration doubted the war could be won quickly or cheaply. Beginning in May with a call for five hundred thousand volunteers, most for three years of service, Lincoln was turning the Union's improvised war machine into something more formidable. Ohio's quota this time was 67,365; Indiana's 38,832, and Illinois was asked to send 47,785.[27]

The Midwestern volunteers received rudimentary training at camps that sprang up in farm fields and fairgrounds around their states. Men were housed in tents or animal stalls. Bigger, more elaborate facilities, featuring new wooden barracks hastily built in muddy fields, were created at Camp Chase near

New enlistees, still in their civilian clothes and innocent of all things military, were formed into "awkward squads" for their initial training.

Relaxing with camp gossip—also known as "the bull session"—is a time-honored way of passing time in the military.

Columbus, and Camp Dennison near Cincinnati. These camps organized some raw regiments of their own while serving as way-stations for those from the state's smaller outlying camps. Camp Chase also held Confederate prisoners in one corner and it became a place for returning Ohio regiments to be mustered out and paid off.

Depending on the weather, Camps Chase and Dennison were either bogged down in mud or obscured by clouds of dust, but to farm boys and small-town clerks whose heads were filled with the romance of war, they were exciting places. Andrew Altman, a farm lad from northwest Ohio, arrived at Camp Chase in late January 1862 with the 68th Ohio, formed a few weeks earlier at Camp Latta near Napoleon.

Delighted to trade the drudgery of farm life for military adventure, Private Altman wrote his family, "I like it first rate," although the mud at Camp Chase was "shoe top deep."[28] A few days later he added, "If … you was here and drild with us a while and here the band and the drums sound, you would … feel like shootin a rebel."[29] Soon after, he wrote, "I love camp life very well. We have all to eat we want, plenty to ware, and good times and great prospects of the war a ending." [30]

Altman explained that Camp Chase housed three to four thousand Union volunteers at the moment, while a high board fence penned in three hundred Confederate prisoners (a number that would rise as high as 9,416 near the end of the war).[31] The young soldier was briefly put to work guarding the Confederates, a thin and ragged lot dressed mostly in civilian clothes. "They are uneasy as a parsel of turkeys that has been caut in a trap," he wrote.[32]

Another member of the 68th Ohio, Sgt. Jacob Bruner from Antwerp, Ohio, termed the amenities of Camp Chase as much ahead of Camp Latta as a "mansion is ahead of a hovel." Like some others, Bruner had volunteered partly for the army's dependable, if small, income. A struggling lawyer whose financial problems had admittedly made him "snappish" with his family, Bruner earned extra income in camp by writing songs for the regiment, among them a stirring ditty called "Root Hog or Die." The enterprising Bruner printed one thousand copies of his song and sold $12.84 worth in one day.[33]

Another satisfied guest of Camp Chase was Marcus M. Spiegel, a commission merchant from Millersburg. Spiegel had recruited a number of Holmes County's War Democrats for service and been chosen captain of Company C of the 67th Ohio Volunteer Infantry. Spiegel, who had emigrated from Germany in 1849, was thrilled to be (as he described himself) "a bold Soldier Boy" who delighted in the "Barracks large & Comodius." Each barrack accommodated eighteen men in stacked bunks, three men to a bunk.[34]

Avoiding the laconic style of his fellow Midwesterners, Spiegel began his letters home with a flourish: "My dear & much beloved Wife and Children!" Like Altman, Spiegel was caught up in the martial spirit of the place: "While I write you I can hear 2 Bands playing and the drummers beating. This is a most magnificent day and the Guard mounting & dress parade to day was splendit."[35]

Four miles west of Columbus, Camp Chase occupied 160 acres and was described as "a liberally sized town with a great uniformity of houses [barracks], about 160 in number."[36]

Eighty-five miles southwest, sixteen miles from Cincinnati, was Camp Dennison, Ohio's other large training facility. It, too, consisted of long rows of wooden barracks facing a parade ground. It attracted crowds of spectators delivered by excursion trains from Cincinnati. "We have a very pleasant place

In snow, rain, or a blazing sun, drummers summoned soldiers to their duties throughout the Civil War.

here. hils al around us. the ralrod runs through the center of camp,"
a soldier wrote his wife in mid-November, 1861.[37] His barrack had a kitchen
and bunks for ninety-eight men.

Soldiers typically spent five hours to seven hours a day in training. A
veteran of Camp Dennison recalled that the "every day duty of the Regiment
was squad, company and [sometimes] battalion drill, with dress parade in the
evening, besides regular guard and fatigue duty [cooking, cleaning, and other
chores]." Soldiers in the camps typically were awakened by bugle calls at 5
or 6 a.m. and sent to bed by another bugle call around 8 or 9 p.m.[38]

The training left a lot to be desired. Much of it was old-fashioned close-
order drill at the regimental level, with rows of men moving elbow to elbow
like automatons across an open field and firing their weapons in volleys.
The idea was to maximize the firepower of the soldiers' inaccurate short-range
muskets. (As weapons improved in accuracy and range in the course of the
war, soldiers learned to throw up defensive works and take shelter whenever
they could.)

Most of the officers were as lacking in military knowledge as their men and
had to study manuals each night to learn what they would teach the next day.
Physical conditioning for its own sake was ignored and weapons training was
so scanty that some units reached the front having scarcely learned how to load
and fire their guns.

Not every one was captivated with army life. Sgt. John E. Richardson, a
member of the 48th Ohio, a unit enlisted from the state at large, regularly wrote
loving letters from Camp Dennison to his wife, Rosetta, expressing acceptance
of army life, but not enthusiasm. He told her, "We have plenty to eat sutch as it
is," including bread, meat, potatoes, rice, hominy, coffee, and sugar.

Addressing Rosetta alternately as "Deare Companion" or "Mi Deare
Wife," Richardson signed himself "your lovin husband," and told her to "kiss
the baby six ten times for mi." In her replies, the more literate Rosetta ("your
affectionate wife") promised to kiss the baby "sixteen times and a half for
you" and asked him to "write as often as you can if not oftener."
She playfully urged her husband to "be a good boy & do your bidding."[39]

The 48th had been at Camp Chase since early November 1861, drilling
and waiting for volunteers to complete its ranks. By mid-February the "close
confinement to camp, and the strict discipline made the Regiment very
restless," wrote Sgt. John A. Bering.[40] The young soldiers enviously watched
other units depart. Finally, however, the regiment was complete, and on
February 17 the 48th shipped out.

By March 19 the 48th Ohio had arrived at a place on the Tennessee River called Pittsburg Landing near a small, crude church known as the Shiloh meeting house. Remembering the regiment's impatience to see action, a veteran later wrote, "The general opinion of the rank and file seemed to be, 'The war will be over before we can get into it.' Alas! How little any of us dreamed of what was to come."[41]

THE BLOODHOUND FROM OHIO

In late December 1861, a group of three United States senators and four members of the House of Representatives met for the first time in the basement of the U.S. Capitol. What was said there was supposed to remain secret, which, in the ways of Washington, meant that it would not.

The Union army even drilled its soldiers in the shadow of the unfinished dome of the U.S. Capitol.

Throughout the war, a steady procession of Union generals, privates, and government officials would be summoned to the basement room where they would be grilled in an atmosphere that some likened to Britain's oppressive Star Chamber. The committee's subjects would return to public life, sometimes badly shaken. This inquisitorial body was the Joint Committee on the Conduct of the War ("the CCW") and its chairman was a senator from Ashtabula County in northeastern Ohio, Benjamin F. Wade, and one of the nation's loudest voices for an aggressive war and an end to slavery.

The New England-born Wade carried the nickname "Bluff Ben" for good reason. Possessed of bottomless stores of profanity and insults, he was infuriatingly self-righteous, and, having once taken a position on an issue, was no more moveable than a very large mountain. His photograph shows a man with a firmly down-turned mouth and hard eyes staring from under bushy eyebrows.

Even some fellow abolitionists thought Wade too aggressive, "bitten with Presidential fever," and "a bloodhound" for his persistence.[42] Wade once told

"Bluff Ben" Wade, senator from Ohio, was a Radical Republican, determined to force Lincoln to free the slaves before he was ready.

Lincoln to his face that the president was responsible for every military mistake that had been made in the war and that Lincoln was not one mile from Hell at the moment. (Lincoln replied that, in his opinion, Hell was indeed only a mile from the White House—by which he meant the distance to Wade's Capitol Hill.)[43]

The committee was the brainchild of Radical Republicans, those agitators who plagued Lincoln with demands for an immediate end to slavery and a stepped-up fight against the South, to be followed with punitive measures after the war. The Radicals cared little for the political realities with which Lincoln had to deal and they scorned the quality of his mercy. Wade dismissed Lincoln's leadership as "your rose-water war."[44]

Making progress incrementally by following facts, not wishes, Lincoln caught abuse from all sides. Anti-war Democrats—among whom the so-called "Copperheads" were most bitter—harassed Lincoln for prosecuting the war while the Radical Republicans assailed him for not prosecuting it harshly enough.

Disappointment lingering after the debacle at Bull Run in July 1861 was one reason for the CCW. Another was a Federal disaster at Ball's Bluff, Virginia, on October 21. There, Col. Edward D. Baker, a former senator from Oregon, a close friend of Lincoln, and a brave but inept soldier, had allowed himself to be ambushed, suffer over nine hundred casualties, and lose his own life.

Somehow, the CCW and Secretary of War Stanton convinced themselves that Baker's superior, Gen. Charles P. Stone, was treacherously to blame for this. In a flagrant example of the kind of abuse of civil rights that can arise from wartime hysteria, the innocent Stone was imprisoned for 189 days without charges or trial, then released without explanation.

Wade was no paper tiger. After the fall of Fort Sumter, he had tried to join the Union army, but he was sixty years old and disqualified. In July, like other members of Congress, he had journeyed down the Warrenton Pike to watch the battle of Bull Run. Unlike many other spectators and soldiers, however, he refused to flee, instead brandishing a squirrel rifle while bellowing "Boys, let's stop this damned runaway" and trying, with little success, to turn around the panicked soldiers.[45]

Throughout the war, Wade's committee damaged reputations, meddled in military affairs although it had no military expertise to offer, and stirred up trouble where no trouble was needed. On the other hand, it pressed for the abolition of slavery when it was unpopular to do so and served as a necessary watchdog on the military. Wade and his committee were always a force the Lincoln administration had to reckon with. To some today, the CCW has the bad odor of McCarthyism, but not everyone would agree.

In their biography of Lincoln, the president's former secretaries and strong supporters, John G. Nicolay and John Hay, expressed their own view of the CCW: "It was often hasty and unjust in its judgment. But [it was] always earnest, patriotic, and honest … and on the whole it must be said to have merited more praise than blame."[46] Perhaps.

THE QUIET MAN

Ulysses Grant tended to be uneasy when his family wasn't nearby. Since making his headquarters at Cairo, Illinois, in early September 1861, he had been writing to Julia in Galena, 350 miles to the north, asking her to join him and bring their four children. Julia had procrastinated, afraid of getting closer to the war zone, but finally, "with much timidity," agreed.

As Julia was packing in Galena on Thursday, November 7, she felt weary, lay down for a while, and then (she recalled in her autobiography) she "distinctly saw Ulys a few rods from me … as if he were on horseback. He looked at me so earnestly and, I thought, reproachfully, that I started up and said 'Ulys!'"

The next day Ulysses met Julia at the Cairo train station and she told him of her vision. "That is singular," he replied. "Just at that time I was on horseback and in great peril and I thought of you and the children and what would become of you if I were lost. I was thinking of you, my dear Julia, and very earnestly, too."[47]

In fact, Grant had come close to being killed the previous day. Without orders, he had taken his soldiers and steamed a few miles down the Mississippi River to attack a Confederate camp at Belmont, Missouri. He easily drove off Belmont's defenders and destroyed the camp, but was caught off-guard when enemy reinforcements arrived from across the river.

It was a close thing. Grant had to stage a risky break-out and hightail it with his men back to Cairo. The last man to board the steamboat, Grant learned later that the Confederates had spotted him when he was alone and easily could have shot him.[48]

Grant was still learning the art of war and making mistakes, but he was demonstrating qualities of leadership the Union badly needed: initiative, courage, and the ability to lead men. Humbled by his years of civilian struggle, Grant understood his volunteer citizen-soldiers in a way

A new brigadier general, Ulysses Grant posed for his "likeness" in a finer uniform than he would wear on the field.

many other officers did not. He preferred to lead them with firm but low-key common sense instead of harsh discipline. ("We called him 'the quiet man,'" a soldier remembered.)[49]

Grant's men had learned how quick and bold "the quiet man" could be. Two months before the engagement at Belmont, Grant had occupied nearby Paducah, Kentucky, within forty-eight hours of learning that it was threatened by forces led by the Confederacy's "bishop-general," Leonidas Polk. Polk's invasion of neutral Kentucky was a mistake, because it turned the supposedly neutral state into a war zone open to Northern invasion. Because of Grant's quick action, Polk's advance had stalled at Columbus, Kentucky.

Grant had shown speed and aggressiveness at Paducah and Belmont, but he had bigger things in mind. Months earlier, Ohio's William Dennison and his fellow Midwestern governors had urged Washington to invade the Confederacy from the west. Now Grant was in a position to do exactly that, but at Cairo. Not only was he on the shore of the mighty Mississippi River, but also, he had convenient access to two other rivers just waiting to be followed into the heart of Dixie, the Tennessee and the Cumberland.

The 652-mile Tennessee River rose in eastern Tennessee, flowed through northern Alabama and western Tennessee, and emptied into the Ohio River at Paducah, an easy fifty miles by steamboat from Cairo. Only a few miles further up the Ohio was the mouth of the Cumberland River, which flowed 687 miles through Tennessee and Kentucky. In an era of notoriously poor and undependable roads on land, these two rivers were like superhighways into the Confederacy.

In August 1861, Grant met with the flamboyant John C. Frémont, a famed explorer and former presidential candidate who now was Union commander in the West. They discussed invading the South via the Mississippi. Grant impressed Frémont as "a man of unassuming character, not given to self-elation, of dogged persistence, and of iron will."[50] He was exactly right, but Washington had come to view Frémont as a loose cannon and a sloppy administrator to boot, so by early November he was replaced by Maj. Gen. Henry W. Halleck. Halleck was ordered to clean up the mess "the Pathfinder" had left behind and that, for the time being, was the end of Grant's Mississippi River invasion plan.

Halleck, popeyed and balding, was an irascible administrator known throughout the army as "Old Brains" for his impressive knowledge of all things military. Like many other West Pointers before the war, Halleck had resigned from the calcified army to find his fortune in civilian life and had actually made one as a lawyer in California. On his return to service at the outbreak of hostilities, he was commissioned a major general. But he was a desk soldier and an excessively cautious one at that, while Grant was a man of action. That would cause problems.

"UNCONDITIONAL SURRENDER" GRANT

By January 1862, Grant had grown tired of waiting for Halleck to order him into battle, so he temporarily turned over command in Cairo to Brig. Gen. John A. McClernand of Illinois (a political conniver who bore close watching) and traveled to Halleck's St. Louis headquarters. There he presented a new plan for invading the South, this time by way of the Tennessee River. Perhaps remembering Grant's reputation as a drinker, Halleck listened impatiently, said no, and sent Grant back to Cairo, "very much crestfallen."[51]

However, Navy Capt. Andrew Hull Foote, a tough old salt from Connecticut who was on better terms with Halleck, liked Grant's idea. Foote sent Halleck a proposal for a joint naval-army expedition up the Tennessee River. Coincidentally, Lincoln was growing increasingly impatient with the lack of action in both the Eastern and Western theaters and had issued "General War Order No. 1," ordering the Union's inert forces forward on all fronts—McClellan in the East, Halleck and Buell in the West.

Now wide awake, Halleck wired Grant on January 30 "to take and hold Fort Henry," a Confederate fortress in northwestern Tennessee. Fort Henry had been built to blockade the Tennessee River, so capturing it would be like throwing open a back door to the Confederacy. Grant leaped into action. By February 2, Foote, with seven Union gunboats, and Grant, leading fifteen thousand soldiers, most of them Illinoisans, were traveling on steamboats, southward through Kentucky, heading for the fort via the river.

This earthen fort was a weak link in the South's defenses. Poorly situated on low land, Fort Henry was equipped with old guns and partly flooded, with the river threatening to flood the rest. On February 4 and 5 Grant landed his troops near the fort and Foote's ironclad gunboats began a bombardment. The strange-looking, heavily armored gunboats were nicknamed "Pook's Turtles," after their designer. Loaf-shaped and bristling with cannon, they looked like enormous Hostess Twinkies with quills.

Foote's gunboats quickly knocked out most of Fort Henry's heavy guns while absorbing relatively little damage themselves. A large part of the Confederate commander's garrison retreated to Fort Donelson, about eleven miles away.

After less than two hours of bombardment, Fort Henry surrendered and Grant marched in. His soldiers hadn't fired a shot. To Julia, Grant wrote, "Fort Henry is taken and I am not hurt. This is news enough for to-night …. Kiss the children for me. Ulys."[52]

Having shown the army how it got things done, the navy chugged back to the Ohio River, executed a U-turn, and sailed up the Cumberland River to attack Fort Donelson, a very different proposition. Guardian of the Cumberland, which paralleled the Tennessee River in this part of Tennessee, it had, compared to Fort Henry, far more troops, better guns, rings of trenches outside its walls, and a commanding position atop a ridge.

Although the ever-cautious Halleck wanted Grant to stay put and "hold onto Fort Henry at all hazards," Grant wanted to attack Donelson.[53] After

Grant's capture of Fort Donelson in Tennessee early in 1862 gave the North a longed-for victory and made him famous as "Unconditional Surrender" Grant.

waiting a week and receiving neither approval nor disapproval from Halleck, Grant moved his forces cross-country to besiege the fort.

Again, Foote's gunboats led the attack, but this time did little damage and were forced to withdraw after being badly battered by return fire. Now it was up to Grant's green troops, newly enlarged by several thousand reinforcements. In mapping the terrain around the Donelson battlefield, Grant was fortunate to have the assistance of a talented young military engineer from Clyde, Ohio, named James Birdseye McPherson. A winning personality, McPherson would become a great favorite of both his commanders and those he commanded.

During a warm march from Fort Henry, many of Grant's men had discarded their coats and blankets, but then temperatures dropped and snow and freezing rain fell, causing much suffering. Nonetheless, two of Grant's division commanders launched attacks on the fort's supposed weak spots, only to be driven back with heavy losses. "The taking of Fort Donelson bids fair to be a long job," Grant wrote Julia.[54]

It wasn't. The fort happened to be under the command of a Confederate politician-turned-general named John B. Floyd, an inept veteran of western Virginia operations who, in Grant's view, was "no soldier."[55] Floyd's second in command, Gideon Pillow, did have experience as a soldier but was incompetent anyway, in Grant's opinion. The only competent and experienced soldier at Fort Donelson was Simon B. Buckner, an old army acquaintance of Grant. (Buckner had once lent money to the perpetually straitened Grant.) But Buckner was only third in command in the fort.

Although the Confederates were in a strong position, their supplies were running low, they believed Grant's forces were larger than they really were, and they feared the Union navy would come back. Worst of all, Floyd wanted only to escape. He had been secretary of war under President Buchanan and worried that, if captured, he would be charged with treason.

Floyd ordered Pillow to attempt a breakout that would open up an escape route. Pillow furiously attacked Grant's right and temporarily broke through the Union line. Then, Floyd foolishly ordered his forces back to the fort to retrieve their baggage.

Notified of Pillow's successful attack, Grant hurried back to the battlefield from a strategy session he had been having with Foote. Surveying the disarray on the Union right, he displayed the steadfastness under pressure for which he would become noted. Calmly, he turned to Gen. Charles F. Smith, and told him, "General Smith, all has failed to our right. You must take Fort Donelson."

Replying, "I will do it, General," the old soldier rode forward, ramrod straight in his saddle. Holding his sword aloft, Smith ignored bullets whistling by him as he charged. His soldiers could see Smith's long white moustache over his shoulder and followed him with bayonets fixed. Swarming over the Confederates' outer defense line, they took it without firing a shot.

Grant's force was composed largely of Illinois troops, with a scattering of other Midwesterners, including three Ohio regiments who witnessed the action but were not greatly involved. Among the Ohioans was Pvt. Andrew Altman of the 68th Infantry. Altman watched as Union troops "charged bayonets on them and you ought to a seen them run over the Bres works. They went like Deer." The young soldier wrote his family that "the guns cracked gust as fast as though you would put pop corn in the ovin."[56]

By nightfall, dead and wounded littered the ground to both the right and the left of the fort. Grant told his chief of staff, "Let's get away from this awful place. I suppose this work is part of the devil that is left in us all."[57] During the night Floyd, Pillow, and some Confederate troops slipped away by boat, leaving Buckner holding the bag. The next morning, Buckner asked for terms of "an armistice" to arrange terms of capitulation. Grant replied, "No terms except complete and unconditional surrender can be accepted. I propose to move immediately upon your works."[58]

The rules of this war were beginning to change. Romantic ideas of gallantry and gentlemanly conduct were giving way to something new—the idea that war had to be all-out and was not a game for the genteel. Compelled to accept Grant's terms, Buckner groused that they were "ungenerous and unchivalrous."[59] Later, however, one of the Confederate officers described Grant as "a modest, amiable, kind-hearted but resolute man."[60] According to Grant, about fifteen thousand Confederates surrendered, the largest capitulation of troops to date.

Throughout the North, guns boomed and bells tolled in celebration. Grant was an overnight sensation. His stern terms to Buckner delighted victory-starved Northerners and they took to calling him "Unconditional Surrender" Grant.

Halleck, Grant's immediate superior, sent no congratulations, but Washington promoted Grant to major general. In less than a year, the leather-goods clerk and ex-captain with a blot on his past had risen to the highest grade the army ordinarily conferred.

Cump Loses His Grip, Then Regains It

On February 8, 1820, a red-headed baby boy was born in Lancaster, Ohio, third son to Judge Charles and Mary Sherman. They named him Tecumseh Sherman. When someone chided the judge for naming his son after a "savage," the father replied simply, "Tecumseh was a great warrior" and discussed it no more.[61]

Charming and well-read, Charles Sherman had a talent for everything except managing money. When he died suddenly in 1829 at age forty-one, he left a widow, eleven children including nine too young to leave home, and a mountain of debt. Overwhelmed, Mrs. Sherman kept the three youngest children but farmed out the rest to friends and relatives.

Nine-year-old "Cumpy," as little Tecumseh was called, went to a prosperous lawyer named Thomas Ewing, whose large, fine house was only a few doors up the hill from the humble Sherman home. The Ewings had six children of their own, including Eleanor, known to everyone as Ellen. The Ewings called the boy Cump and treated him kindly, but added "William" to his name so he could be baptized into their Roman Catholic faith.

Charles Sherman had envisioned a military career for Tecumseh, so the influential Ewing obtained the boy an appointment to West Point. Shy, sensitive, and studious in Lancaster, young Sherman blossomed into a popular cut-up and a more-than-able student at the academy. Cadet Sherman and Ellen, who was only fourteen at the time, began a correspondence.

William Tecumseh Sherman was born in Lancaster in an unpretentious dwelling that, enlarged, stands today, serving as a museum.

In 1840, William Tecumseh Sherman graduated sixth of forty-two in his class, despite having had piled up hundreds of demerits for youthful transgressions. Sherman was in his final year at West Point when Ulysses S. Grant entered, but it is doubtful the exuberant Sherman spent any time with the quiet Grant. That would come later.

Like many graduates of the Point, Sherman spent a few years in the arteriosclerotic army of the 1800s, then resigned in 1849 to search for better things. In 1850 he married his foster sister Ellen Ewing. It was a curious kind of marriage, appearing to lack the romance of the Grants and strained by disagreements over religion, his career, and her desire to live in Lancaster forever. But there was a mutual dependence as well. Always addressing Sherman as Cump, she liked to describe him as her "protector."[62] Later, she would come forward as Cump's protector.

Sherman finally resigned from the army, as Ellen had been hoping, to take a job managing a bank in gold-rush California. It was a position that soared briefly, then fell to earth by 1857. Next came a few years of this and that, with Sherman determined above all to avoid returning to Lancaster where "I can only be Cump Sherman." His objection may have grown out of resentment or envy of his highly successful foster father. In any case, he said, "For that part of Ohio I had no fancy."[63]

Sherman's face—always a study in wrinkles and whiskers—became even more worn under the pressure of war.

In 1859 he accepted appointment as the first superintendent of a new Louisiana military college, known today as Louisiana State University. Although he had no quarrel with slavery, Sherman was a rock-solid Unionist, so when Louisiana joined the secessionist states in January 1861, he resigned and returned north, there to become head of a St. Louis street railway company.

Unlike Grant, Sherman had loved West Point and felt at home in the army, but he resisted returning to duty when the war broke out. Miffed that Lincoln hadn't seemed to take him seriously at a brief meeting in Washington, he also didn't want to risk his reputation leading green volunteers.

Ellen, however, was convinced that "he will never be happy out of the Army" and, indeed, on May 8, 1861, Sherman succumbed, writing to Secretary of War Cameron to offer his services.[64] He was promised the colonelcy of a new regiment in the regular army, but wound up spending most of June as Winfield Scott's inspector of units and installations around Washington. Then he was suddenly put in command of one of the brigades of volunteers in the army General McDowell was assembling to invade Virginia.

Colonel Sherman showed courage and initiative in commanding a brigade at Bull Run, but his green, short-term soldiers were hard to lead. ("The volunteers test my patience," he wrote his brother John.) He left the battlefield discouraged at his performance and feeling "mortification of the rout." He wrote Ellen, "Well as I am sufficiently disgraced now, I suppose I soon can sneak into some quiet corner."[65]

But "a quiet corner" was not to be. Sherman had been mentioned favorably in reports from the battlefield. With the army desperate for experienced commanders, Sherman, like Grant and a number of others, was promoted to brigadier general in August. Then, Gen. Robert Anderson—the hero of Fort Sumter—asked Sherman to be his second in command of the Department of the Cumberland in Kentucky, assigned to keeping that border state secure for the Union.

Troubled by memories of Bull Run and harboring doubts about himself, Sherman was happy to take a supporting role. "Not 'til I see daylight ahead do I want to lead," he wrote Ellen.[66] But within a few weeks Anderson, badly shaken by his ordeal at Fort Sumter, asked to be relieved. His command—much of Kentucky—was turned over to Sherman.

The dismayed Sherman was faced with a shortage of supplies right down to maps, a lack of experienced officers who could train the raw troops pouring into Kentucky, a civilian population of mixed loyalties, and a shadowy enemy that was poking its nose into Kentucky at several points.

It was a daunting prospect, and Sherman was in no shape emotionally to deal with it. His attention-getting appearance and manner worked against him as well. A tall man, Sherman had an unruly thatch of reddish-brown hair, sharp bright eyes, a sharp red nose over a stubbly beard, and a prematurely wrinkled face resembling nothing so much as an unmade bed. His coat was usually unbuttoned, his uniform—though well tailored—usually soiled and wrinkled.

Even more noticeable was Sherman's manner. Always restless, he "jerked himself along" as he walked and wasn't quiet even when he sat, his eyes darting to and fro, his hands and feet moving. He fired off words in bursts like a Gatling gun. To onlookers, Sherman seemed a human volcano, always threatening to erupt, and perhaps in dangerous ways. And this was how journalists, fascinated by this strange man, began to see him—and to describe him.

Secretary of War Cameron called on Sherman, asking how many troops he needed to clear Kentucky and invade Tennessee. Two hundred thousand, Sherman replied as Cameron gasped. The estimate was not unrealistic but at this early stage in the war it sounded alarmist to the newspaper reporters who sat in on the meeting. Sherman, with his herky-jerky manner, seemed overwrought to them.

It didn't help that Sherman disliked press attention and routinely brushed off reporters. "He is cold, distant, and of a brusqueness of manner … that is absolutely repulsive," wrote a correspondent of the *Cincinnati Daily Commercial*.[67] "If I had my choice," Sherman reportedly once said, "I would kill every reporter in the world, but I am sure we would be getting reports from Hell before breakfast."[68] The frustrated reporters noticed Sherman haunting the Louisville telegraph office, pacing the floor as he awaited dispatches, chewing his cigar, muttering to himself, and talking about unseen enemy armies. The idea grew that Sherman was mentally unbalanced. In fact, he was breaking emotionally.

On November 1 he wrote Ellen wishing that "we might hide ourselves in some quiet corner of the world. ... [N]ow I find myself riding a whirlwind unable to guide the Storm."[69] Within the week an aide to Sherman sent an urgent-sounding message to Ellen's father: "Send Mrs. Sherman … to Louisville. [I]t is necessary to turn Genl Shermans Mind from responsibility now resting upon him."[70]

Ellen apparently rushed to Sherman's headquarters where, she wrote, "Knowing insanity to be in the family & having seen Cump in the seize of it in California, I can assure you I was tortured by fears which have been *only in part* relieved."[71]

The stress of too much to do and too little with which to do it was overwhelming Sherman, and after only a month in command he asked to be relieved. Replacing him was Brig. Gen. Don Carlos Buell, sent down from the Army of the Potomac by McClellan to take charge of an enlarged Department of Ohio, incorporating the "near Midwest" plus Tennessee and eastern Kentucky.

Yet another prominent Union commander from Ohio, Buell had been born near Marietta and graduated from West Point in 1841, ranking thirty-second of fifty-two graduates. One of the few peacetime officers to make the army his career, Buell had been a lieutenant colonel commanding a desk in Washington when the Civil War broke out.

An uninspiring introvert and a stickler for the rules, Buell was primarily an organizer and administrator, excellent to the point of tedium. He also had the misfortune to be a friend of McClellan's and a clone in both McClellan's strategic thinking and his kind feelings for the South. It was an association that would do him no good.

Sherman was sent to less stressful duty at the St. Louis headquarters of Henry W. Halleck, commander of the new Department of the Missouri, incorporating almost everything west of Buell's department. Wonder of wonders, the irascible Halleck not only knew Sherman from long ago, but also even liked and respected him. So when Sherman began showing signs of hysteria all over again, Halleck sympathetically sent him home to Ellen for twenty days' leave. While in Lancaster, Sherman picked up a copy of the *Cincinnati Commercial* only to discover an article by Whitelaw Reid with the headline, "Gen. William T. Sherman Insane." (It would be picked up and published throughout the country.) Sherman was furious.

With this, Ellen showed her mettle. She, her father, and other family members demanded retractions from newspapers across the country that had printed the story. Sherman's foster brother Philemon met with Reid, who then published Philemon's rebuttal. According to historian John F. Marszalek, Ellen not only wrote President Lincoln, but also went to see him personally on Cump's behalf.[72]

Sherman may have had a nervous breakdown, but he was not "insane." Lee Kennett, a modern biographer, has found Sherman's correspondence during this time to be lucid and rational, his fears not unfounded, and his responses to those fears appropriate.[73] However, Sherman was unusually excitable and

A fanciful lithograph published early in the war shows ranks of patriotic "Uncle Sams" marching confidently to battle the Southern rebellion.

emotive. He experienced mood swings, perhaps aggravated by overwork and lack of sleep. An underlying factor might have been debilitating childhood memories of losing both parents, resentment and jealousy of his foster father, failures in his civilian career and, most recently, his disappointment with himself at Bull Run.

Rested and recovered from the strains of high command, by January 1862 Sherman felt ready for duty. His friend Halleck assigned him to a safe backwater, the training camp at Benton Barracks outside St. Louis. In this low-pressure atmosphere, Sherman's spirits gradually rose.

Then, keeping a promise to his old friend that "you will not be forgotten," Halleck sent Sherman to Paducah to organize an army division of twelve new infantry regiments (nine from Ohio), plus some cavalry and artillery. On March 6, Halleck ordered Sherman to lead his division southward on the Tennessee River and join forces under Grant for an attack on the rail junction of Corinth, Mississippi.

Meanwhile, Grant had been restored to command after a short suspension by Halleck caused by communication problems and misunderstandings. Quite possibly, however, Halleck's jealousy of Grant's successes aggravated the relationship.

In mid-March, Sherman arrived at Pittsburg Landing where, ominously, flocks of vultures were circling overhead.[74] He was commander of what would become the Fifth Division of the Army of the Tennessee, under Grant's overall command. That Grant was Sherman's junior by a couple of years was not a problem for the older man, still uneasy about assuming too much responsibility.

On Thursday, April 3, Sherman wrote "Dearest Ellen" from Pittsburg Landing, disavowing any ambition "to guide events" but sounding cheerful. Sherman and his men were encamped near a crude log house of worship. "The weather is now springlike, apples & peaches in blossom and trees beginning to leave," he wrote Ellen. "Bluebirds singing and spring weather upon the hillsides."[75] The church's name was Shiloh.

TO LEARN MORE:

Historic Lancaster, Ohio, offers house tours, including William Tecumseh Sherman's humble birthplace (http://www.shermanhouse.org/ or 740-687-5891). The house has been restored to its early appearance and family and Civil War memorabilia is also displayed. Only a short walk up the street is the elegant home of the Ewings, who became his foster parents when "Cumpy" was nine. Walk a short distance in the opposite direction to see Sherman's statue firmly grounded before the Chamber of Commerce. Travelling further afield, you can visit the site of Grant's first great triumph at the Fort Donelson National Battlefield near Dover, Tennessee (http://www.nps.gov/fodo/ or 931-232-5706). (Nearby Fort Henry is now under water.)

The life of the complex, puzzling—but never dull—William Tecumseh Sherman is recounted in Stanley P. Hirshson's *The White Tecumseh: A Biography of General William. T. Sherman*. Sherman speaks for himself (sounding very Shermanish) in his memoirs, ably introduced by Michael Fellman. Benjamin Franklin Cooling points to the importance of Grant's first major campaign in *Forts Henry and Donelson: The Key to the Confederate Heartland*.

In *All for the Regiment: The Army of the Ohio, 1861-1862*, Gerald J. Prokopowicz shows how a large fighting force in the Western Theater was recruited, trained, and introduced to combat.

Whenever the war permitted, streams of mail flowed between soldiers and their families and friends. Young men seized quiet moments in camp to write their letters.

6

THE BLOODY WORK OF WAR

Spring 1862

At mail call, soldiers would drop whatever they were doing and rush forward, hoping to get letters from home filled with the minutiae of everyday life: *the corn's been planted, baby's feeling better, Will Johnson has joined up, and about time, too.* Letters from home were read, re-read, and passed around the campfire.

Back home, people would haunt post offices, waiting anxiously for envelopes from husbands, sons, and sweethearts, each an affidavit that a cherished someone was alive. People at home dreaded the envelopes from officers because they almost always brought bad news. The good letters would be read and re-read, circulated among family and friends, and sometimes published in the local newspaper. Letters from soldiers were preserved as family treasures—and sometimes as the last record of a life departed.

Early in the war, Ulysses S. Grant noticed that his "officers and men were in constant communication with kindred and friends at home." Grant, a regular correspondent with Julia, arranged with postal authorities to give soldiers' mail priority.[1] Mail's importance to morale was well recognized. Montgomery Blair, Lincoln's postmaster general for much of the war, introduced special services such as money orders and "soldier's mail," which shifted payment of postage from the impecunious soldier to the recipient. In 1864, Radical Republicans bent on political purity forced Democrat Blair out, even though he was highly effective, and replaced him with former Ohio Gov. William Dennison.

Throughout the war, young men in uniform who had hardly put a word on paper since leaving school found themselves struggling with pencil or pen and ink to scratch out messages by candlelight while using haversacks as desks. Searching for words, they fell back on formulas faintly remembered from their school days. Countless letters home began with, "It is with pleasure that I take pen in hand to tell you that I am well at present."

As well as campground gossip and speculation, soldiers' letters home, like those of the 68th Ohio's Pvt. Andrew Altman, included promises to fight fiercely ("I will do my best Durty tricks to Shoot a Reble"), words of wisdom to younger siblings ("you must not cut up [in school] al thou I would rather you would cut up than to be Sick"), promises to bring home war booty ("I have two Secesh Coats, one for me and one for you"), and wildly optimistic predictions of war's end ("we will be home by the forth of July," written three years before it happened).

As the 68th Ohio left camp for the front early in 1862, Private Altman promised his family on the farm in Napoleon, "I will wright once a week to you when I can Send them." Soldiers counted letters sent and received, the better to coax the folks back home to write. Over time, Altman's pleas would grow in urgency. On February 18, he grumbled, "I have not got a letter from you yet, I don't See why. I Rote you three. I will Rite every chance I have." Three weeks later he was sounding desperate: "Write to me if you Pleas write a way."[2]

Another young private, Isaac Jackson of the 83rd Ohio, wrote a sister after only a few weeks away from home, "[Y]ou do not know how much good it does a soldier to receive a letter. ... You cannot send too many, and you must be sure to tell all the news for we love to hear the news from home."[3] Even top brass pleaded for letters/ From the field, Brig. Gen. Garfield wrote a friend, "I beg of you not to stop writing me, even if I am not able to get my letters through to you."[4]

A lack of mail usually was due to the problems war caused the delivery system, but whenever the channels were working, floodtides of news and gossip flowed between home and the armies. What counted most to families and friends was any message evidencing that their soldier was safe. For a tired, scared, and lonely soldier far from home, knowing he was still cared for was the most important message he could receive.

Among the men of the 110th Ohio was a forty-one-year-old corporal named John R. Rhoades. A farmer in the Miami County village of Fletcher, Rhoades left behind a wife named Sarah, a small boy called Willie, and an infant daughter nicknamed Rella. In October 1862, the 110th was sent to keep the peace in western Virginia. Like other soldiers, Rhoades was quick to grumble when the mail brought nothing from home.

Sarah was not strong on spelling but she could write voluminous letters in a neat hand that told John what he needed to hear: "You say you feel bad you get no letters from home when others around you are getting [them]. You cant fell no worse than I do when … they tell you, you got non of mine."

Most of all, John needed caring words and Sarah knew it. In November 1862, she wrote, "I have not forgotten you by no means for I am thinking of you nearly all the time when I go to bed at night I wonder where you are & what you are doing & in the morning the same way for I know you are in the enemys land …. Night & morning on my knees I ask God to protect you & others from want from perals and danger & give helth & strength & prosperity & bring you all safe home."[5]

Too close to the action to see war's big picture, soldiers craved newspapers, sometimes even trading them with Confederates during brief truces.

Relatively few letters received by soldiers survived the hardships of war, but that one did, carried by John for more than two and a half years until it was creased, stained, and worn by constant re-reading of its message: *"I have not forgotten you by no means."*

Rhoades came home to Sarah, Willie, and Rella in June 1865.

THE DEVIL'S OWN DAY

The sun was just beginning to show through the trees near Shiloh Church when a half-dressed 1st Lt. Frances Marion Posegate of the 48th Ohio sat down in front of his tent for a cup of strong, black coffee. Posegate's unit and most other regiments of Sherman's division of Grant's army were camped along a ridge about two and a half miles inland from Pittsburg Landing on the Tennessee River.

It was Sunday morning, April 6, 1862, and Posegate, a printer in civilian life, was enjoying "the soft, shimmering opening of a typical Southern spring day" while listening to the birds and admiring nearby wildflowers that were nodding in a gossamer breeze.

Before Posegate could raise the cup to his lips, the long roll of a drummer's alarm burst out in a neighboring brigade and came thundering down the line of encampments, accompanied by the sound of distant gunshots—some scattered, some in short volleys. Posegate yanked on his uniform shirt, buckled on a sword, and told the cook to keep his breakfast warm. He was acting adjutant of the 48th, so he hurriedly began forming up the regiment.

Posegate was still trying to make a count of men ready for battle when the regiment's brave but impetuous colonel, a Cincinnati lawyer named Peter J. Sullivan, rushed up and ordered the soldiers down a slope in the direction of the firing. The Ohioans obeyed, but when they discovered how close the tide of oncoming Confederates was, they ran back.

The Union soldiers had scarcely reached the crest of their ridge when the Confederates fired a volley, which sounded to Posegate "as if a whirlwind of bees had passed over us." The Ohioans formed their line of battle along the ridge.

Posegate was passing along the 48th's line, waving his sword and urging the nervous men to stand fast, when he was distracted by a bullet grazing his knuckle. When he looked up, the line of battle was gone. After firing an initial volley standing up, his men sensibly had taken shelter behind trees and fallen trunks, and were aiming carefully and firing at will.[6]

For one Ohio regiment, that was the beginning of the great Battle of Shiloh

On the morning of April 6, 1862, unprepared Union soldiers found themselves fighting Confederate attackers rushing into their campgrounds around Shiloh Church.

(which contemporaries called the Battle of Pittsburg Landing), a two-day struggle in southwestern Tennessee that would shock North and South alike for its ferocity. More than one hundred thousand Union and Confederate soldiers would fight there and twenty-four thousand would be killed, wounded, or captured.

Shiloh would prove the costliest two-day battle of the war, one that took more lives than all previous American wars put together.[7] After Shiloh, Grant wrote in his memoirs, "I gave up all idea of saving the Union except by complete conquest."[8] But that was not the only lesson to be learned.

Generals are not stupid or they wouldn't be generals, but, like the rest of us, they are capable of stupidity. The difference is their foolish mistakes can kill thousands of people, sometimes including themselves. Shiloh offers a textbook case. The gravestones in the Shiloh National Military Cemetery provide the illustrations.

Acts of stupidity have their causes, of course, and at Shiloh they had everything to do with the states of mind of four men: Maj. Gen. Ulysses S. Grant and Brig. Gen. William Tecumseh Sherman on the Union side, and Gen. Albert Sidney Johnston and Gen. P.G.T. Beauregard on the Confederate side. Grant was a hard-to-rattle, heads-down slugger who thought more about what he was going to do than what the enemy might do—sometimes to his regret.

Sherman was more cerebral than Grant, but plagued by oscillating emotions. Until recently, Sherman had worried too much about what the enemy might do. Now he reversed himself and, as if to compensate for the past, didn't worry enough.

On the Confederate side, the tall, calm, and distinguished-looking Johnston had enjoyed a sterling reputation until the losses at Forts Henry and Donelson and elsewhere. Now, because of recent strategic decisions, he was suffering shrill attacks from the Southern public, charging him with cowardice, incompetence, and disloyalty. The cries tormented him.

Johnston's second in command at Shiloh was P.G.T. Beauregard, the hero of Fort Sumter and Bull Run. Called "the little Creole," the fiery Beauregard sometimes was ruled by common sense and other times by pigheadedness. Carrying their psychological baggage with them, these four would set the stage at Shiloh and direct what happened on it.

The miseries of Johnston, commander of all Confederate forces west of the Appalachians, had begun in January. Until then, the Confederates in the Western Theater had an impressively long frontier that stretched westward from southeastern Kentucky, through southern Missouri and as far as the Oklahoma Indian Territory. But this front line was tissue-paper thin because Johnston didn't have enough men to defend its seven hundred miles.

In January, the tissue began to tear in Kentucky. By now, Ohio's James Garfield, who had left training camp barely a month before and was largely a self-taught soldier, already commanded a brigade of several regiments in Don Carlos Buell's Army of the Ohio. In mid-January, Garfield's brigade had a brush in eastern Kentucky with a poorly equipped Confederate force that quickly decided to withdraw.[9] It was a minor affair, but enough, apparently, to justify promotion to brigadier general for the politically connected Garfield.

Then, another Union force from Buell's army slogged through mud for eighteen days to confront the Confederates in southern Kentucky in the battle of Mill Springs on January 19. The Federals defeated an equal number of poorly equipped enemy soldiers, killed their general, and sent the Rebels flying in unseemly haste. Ohioans played an important role in the encounter.

The 9th Ohio, Cincinnati's first all-German regiment, had turned the enemy left with a daring bayonet charge. Col. James B. Steedman's 14th Ohio led a charge into the Confederates' defenses and pursued "the flying enemy," firing into the rear of their retreating column.[10] With the Union victory at Mill Springs, the right flank of the Confederates' western line had collapsed.

That loss, followed by Grant's capture of Forts Henry and Donelson in Tennessee, persuaded the hard-pressed Confederates they had to concentrate their scattered forces in the West. Drawing troops from all directions, Johnston assembled an army at the vital rail junction of Corinth in northeastern Mississippi. From there, Johnston, with Beauregard second in command, planned to launch a massive drive to regain territory.

To assemble his army, however, Johnston had had to temporarily concede Kentucky to the Union and give up a large chunk of western Tennessee, including—heart-wrenchingly—the Confederate state's capital at Nashville. This three-month cascade of defeats and retreats infuriated the Southern public and demoralized its soldiers.

Although the western Confederacy was sagging badly under Federal pressure, by the end of March Johnston had forty thousand soldiers massed at Corinth and a plan to hit back. Corinth was little more than twenty miles south of Pittsburg Landing, Tennessee, where the main body of Grant's Army of the Tennessee was awaiting Buell and his Army of the Ohio.

Buell was coming down from Nashville to join Grant in crushing Johnston's Confederates, who were expected to obligingly await their fate at Corinth. Until Buell arrived, Grant intended to pass the time training his green-as-grass troops, many of whom had been farm boys and clerks only weeks before.

Tucked against a bluff on the west bank of the Tennessee River, Pittsburg Landing was a stopping place for commercial boats. Rolling back from the landing was forest and brush land interrupted by an occasional farm and crisscrossed by creeks, ravines, and country roads. Peach blossoms and dogwood pleasantly scented the air, but this was not rich farm country. Unimpressed Ohio farm boys turned up their noses at it.

Here, five of Grant's six divisions of the forty-nine-thousand-man Army of the Tennessee, including Sherman's Fifth Division, were encamped before the big push to Corinth. Except for a few regular army cavalrymen, Grant's army consisted entirely of Midwesterners, nearly two-thirds of them from Illinois, Ohio, and Indiana. Arranged more for convenience than defense, the Union camps were scattered over several square miles between the river and Shiloh Church.

A sixth division, under Gen. Lew Wallace (future author of *Ben Hur*) was stationed five miles north at Crump's Landing. Four miles still further north, Grant had docked his headquarters boat at Savannah, there to await Buell. Grant spentmost of his days at Pittsburg Landing, returning to Savannah at night.

It didn't bother Grant or Sherman that their camp at Pittsburg Landing and

For most of the first day of the Battle of Shiloh, Union defenders fought bravely along the Sunken Road and the "Hornets' Nest," but eventually were overwhelmed.

the Confederates' at Corinth were on the same side of the river and connected by roads, separated by only one day's march in good weather. No defenses were built around Union camps, pickets were sent out only short distances, and scouting was sporadic. All this despite signs that something was going on at Corinth; trains had been delivering enemy troops there and the nearby countryside seemed eerily deserted.

On Monday, March 31, Johnston's Confederates began skirmishing in the direction of the Union camp. Almost daily the nipping and probing was ratcheted upward. Grant heard estimates of Confederate troop strength ranging from forty thousand (which was about right) to as high as eighty thousand.[11] Even though that suggested Confederates might outnumber him by two-to-one, Grant wasn't concerned. He kept on calmly planning the attack on Corinth. In his mind, being attacked was out of the question.

But Johnston was determined to surprise Grant before Buell's reinforcements arrived, so on April 3 he started the main body of his troops northward. Whipped by winds, pelted with rain and hail, and forced to slog through mud, the inexperienced Confederates took two days longer than expected to approach the Union camps. The undisciplined young soldiers sloshed noisily along, hooting at the occasional deer, blasting stumps and squirrels with revolvers, and test-firing their damp rifles.

Beauregard was not one to shrink from battle, but he began to worry that Union forces had detected the Confederates' heavy-footed advance. He urged Johnston to abandon the attack. But Johnston, smarting from criticism by an angry Southern public, seemed determined to prove the complainers wrong. He would fight the Yankees if they were a million, he said, promising his officers they soon would water their horses in the Tennessee River. With thousands of lives at stake, Johnston was determined to redeem his reputation.

Even as the Confederates lurched noisily toward the Union camp with Beauregard fretting and fussing, Sherman was swatting away all warning signs. Of all Grant's division commanders, Sherman should have been the most concerned. His 7,900 men, a majority of them Ohioans, were untested in battle and their camps were on the leading edge of the Union position. They straddled the Corinth Road, facing the direction an attacker probably would come. And tell-tale brushes between Federals and Confederates had been occurring almost daily.

On Friday, April 4, Confederate scouts peppered an Iowa company on picket, wounding one soldier. On the same day Col. Ralph Buckland, a Fremont attorney and politician, took his brigade of three Ohio regiments on a training exercise. Venturing down the Corinth Road three or four miles, he found the woods full of Confederates and got into a fight.

By day's end, three of Buckland's officers and nine enlisted men had been captured by the enemy, eight wounded, and one killed. Sent to help Buckland, Maj. Elbridge G. Ricker of the 5th Ohio Cavalry came back with nine Confederate prisoners and the worrisome estimate that two thousand Confederate infantrymen, some cavalry and artillery, were nearby.

But Sherman was irate that Buckland had caused a fight prematurely. When Buckland and Ricker warned him a Confederate advance could be in the offing, Sherman retorted "it could not be possible … it was a mere reconnaissance in force."[12] He sneered, "Oh, tut; tut. You militia officers get scared too easily."[13]

Nothing seemed to alarm Sherman, who only months before had been imagining threats from every direction. When three members of the 77th Ohio took a short stroll beyond their picket line, they spotted a swarm of

Confederates in the distance. One of the Ohioans went to warn Sherman, but he exploded with an order (later rescinded) to arrest the messenger for spreading a false alarm.

Despite Sherman's denials, by Saturday, April 5, the Union camp was buzzing with speculation about an impending attack. Confederate prisoners had boasted to their captors of an impending attack. One prisoner, dying, warned in his last words that "many more [will be] killed."[14]

Some lower-level Union officers were growing nervous, but none caught as much obloquy as Col. Jesse J. Appler, commander of the 53rd Ohio, an infantry outfit from southern Ohio. Appler, near fifty years of age, was said to be a "business gentleman and honorable citizen of the city [of] Portsmouth, Ohio."[15]

Appler had been a captain in a ninety-day regiment, then re-joined as colonel of the 53rd, a three-year outfit.[16] He must have looked like a leader, because the 53rd was able to attract a large number of recruits.[17] Several Methodist ministers were among the unit's officers, so card playing and drinking were prohibited, and prayer meetings were common in the regiment.

One of the ministers proudly observed that "the spirituality and Christianity of this regiment ... certainly could not be surpassed."[18] The regiment's purity did nothing to protect it from sickness from polluted water at Pittsburg Landing, however, and at one point two-thirds of its members were unfit for service.[19]

By Saturday, Appler must have been frazzled by his regiment's health problems. Perhaps he had been sick himself. It "was a day of rumors" about enemy activity, and, one veteran recalled, "Colonel Appler was very uneasy." When scouts reported being fired on by a picket line of Confederates, Appler ordered his regiment into a line of battle and sent the quartermaster to notify Sherman.

Returning, the quartermaster repeated Sherman's message loudly: "Take your [damned] regiment to Ohio. There is no enemy nearer than Corinth." That made Appler's men laugh and, without even waiting for orders, they broke ranks.[20]

While Sherman was brushing off warning signs, he was sending reassuring reports to Grant. On Saturday afternoon he told Grant the bare facts of Ricker's worried report, minus Ricker's interpretation. Sherman believed the enemy was only being "saucy," concluding, "I do not apprehend anything like an attack on our position."[21]

That evening, however, Johnston's Confederate army of forty-four thousand was resting within two miles of the Union camp, its members pondering their commander's message: "I have put you in motion to offer battle to the invaders of your country. Remember … your mothers, your wives, your sisters, and your children."[22]

Even as Johnston and his men were preparing to pounce, Grant was writing to Halleck in St. Louis, "I have scarsley the faintest idea of an attack, (general one) being made upon us, but will be prepared should such a thing take place."[23] Earlier in the day, Grant had sent word to an advance brigade of Buell's not to hurry to join him. "There will be no fight at Pittsburg Landing," he told them. "We will have to go to Corinth, where the rebels are fortified."[24]

On Saturday evening, April 5, the Confederates lying near Grant's main force were trying to catch some sleep. At 3 o'clock the next morning, Johnston ordered their advance. Appler hadn't been able to sleep that night. At about 4 o'clock in the morning, he awoke his adjutant, 1st Lt. Ephraim C. Dawes, and they walked to a point where they could hear distant gunfire. Some pickets told Appler they were sure a large enemy force was nearby.

A worried Colonel Peabody of a nearby division dispatched three companies to see what might be out there. Stumbling through the darkness, Peabody's probing force got into an hour-long fight at about 5:15 a.m. One of the men, shot in the arm, came running into Appler's camp, shouting "Get into line; the rebels are coming!"

No longer hesitant, Colonel Appler ordered the long drum roll of alarm, formed the regiment in line of battle, and, swallowing his pride, sent his quartermaster to Sherman once more. Again, the quartermaster returned with a curt dismissal, delivered more softly this time: "General Sherman says you must be badly scared over there."

But the warning signs grew more ominous. A half-dressed officer came running to Appler, crying, "Colonel, the rebels are crossing the field!" Another officer returned from the picket line to exclaim, "The rebels out there are thicker than fleas on a dog's back." Appler ordered the regiment to face one way, then realized that was wrong when "bright gun barrels" were spotted through the foliage in another direction. He ordered an about face, exclaiming, "This is no place for us."[25]

At about 7 a.m. Sherman and his staff appeared on horseback at Appler's position. At about the same time, Confederate skirmishers emerged from brush within sight and raised their weapons. When an officer of the 53rd cried out, "General, look to your right," Sherman dropped his spyglass, raised his hand, and exclaimed, "My God, we are attacked!"

Shots rang out, Sherman's orderly fell dead, and Sherman himself was hit in the hand by buckshot. The general wrapped his hand in handkerchief, wheeled about and galloped away, shouting as he passed the 53rd's colonel, "Appler, hold your position; I will support you."[26]

Now the rest of Sherman's division and the one next to it, a mix of troops from seven Midwestern states commanded by Illinoisan Benjamin M. Prentiss, began springing into position. From his place on the ridge, the 53rd Ohio's Dawes had a view that "was one never to be forgotten."[27] To his right, Sherman's regiments were forming a line of battle, but it had large gaps left by soldiers convalescing from illness.

Behind the ragged Union line of battle, servants, teamsters, and other noncombatants, joined by some fleeing soldiers, were running to the rear. Directly in front of Dawes were the oncoming lines of Hardee's corps of Confederates, marching on a three-mile front, solid rows of men extending left and right until lost to sight in the woods.[28]

An Ohio veteran recalled the same view years later, "We could see them everywhere, their guns, bayonets, swords and artillery were glistening in the morning sun. After all eyes had looked earnestly to the front for a few moments, they then turned and looked each other square in the face, as soldiers invariably do before going on a charge."[29]

The 53rd fired two volleys, slowing the oncoming Confederates, but then the panicky Appler cried out, "Retreat, and save yourselves."[30] Two companies didn't hear his order and continued to fight, while the rest fled past an Illinois regiment in their rear, only to gather behind it. Appler again told his men to "Retreat, and save yourselves." Then he disappeared.

Dawes found Appler lying behind a tree, his face "like ashes," his voice trembling. "[O]ur colonel was a coward," Dawes decided, and swore at Appler, who "jumped to his feet and literally ran away."[31] Dawes rushed to help another Ohio regiment that was giving way under the Confederate assault.[32]

Grant's army seemed doomed. None of the men in the front line formed by Sherman and Prentiss's divisions had seen combat before and many had had only a little training. The 53rd had never even drilled with another unit.[33] The Confederates not only had the advantage of surprise at Pittsburg Landing, but also, at this point, with Lew Wallace's Union divison a few miles downriver, a slightly larger number of men.

The Confederates' advantage grew larger as panic spread among Grant's soldiers, thousands fleeing to hide under the bluff at the boat landing. Grant later estimated the runaways at five thousand, while Don Carlos Buell put the figure at closer to fifteen thousand. However, some of the runaways returned to the battle later.

The majority of Grant's inexperienced and unprepared soldiers did what their preservation instincts told them *not* to do—stay and fight. They were bolstered by commanders who threw themselves into the battle wholeheartedly, galloping from position to position, shouting orders to the officers and words of encouragement to the men. All doubt and inaction behind him, Sherman furiously crisscrossed the field to direct his division. Grant, who had injured his leg the day before when his horse fell, dashed back and forth on horseback, his crutch held up like a lance.

From 7 to 10 a.m., Sherman's division gave ground only grudgingly, flinging back the Confederates with heavy casualties. Confederate General Hardee later wrote that Sherman's green troops kept up such "a terrific fire" that one of his regiments lost more than three hundred killed or wounded out of a total force of four hundred twenty-five.[34] Finally forced to backpedal a short distance to a new position, Sherman's men fought on another hour and a half before moving still further back.

Exposing himself fearlessly, Sherman was wounded slightly twice during the day and had three horses shot out from under him.[35] As the day wore on, however, the Confederates kept attacking "with such a disregard of losses on their own side that our line of tents soon fell into their hands," Grant remembered.[36] The blossoms Sherman had admired a few days earlier fell to the ground as Confederate bullets ripped through the trees like hail.

Col. Jesse Hildebrand's brigade, composed of the 53rd, 57th, and 77th Ohio, "had substantially disappeared from the field" by 10:30 a.m., according to Sherman. (Although, Sherman learned later, the 53rd had rallied and joined with the 48th Ohio in fighting the Confederates.) Sherman's three other brigades mostly retained their cohesion, although some individuals fled the field. Because color bearers were chosen for their bravery, Lieutenant Posegate was shocked to see his regiment's color bearer run away. Later in the day, the 48th would flee to the river's edge, but return to Grant's defensive line.

Enemy fire was so heavy, Posegate remembered, that a heavy thicket of hazel brush in front of his position looked as if it had "been cut down with a dull sickle," not a stalk left standing. Every tree behind which one of his men had stood "was peppered with bullets, one on top of the other, from about the height of a man to several feet above. ... Our salvation was that the Johnnies fired too high," he concluded.[37] But Posegate would not escape unharmed.

One bullet ripped the rain cover from his hat and another hit him under

Ulysses S. Grant went to West Point reluctantly and didn't care much for army life—but he rose from obscurity to become the greatest general of the Civil War.

the left shoulder blade, exiting under his arm. Posegate kept fighting for an hour then collapsed. A field surgeon stuffed the wound with dry lint and sent him to the river in an ambulance. When Posegate reached the river, he could see a hospital tent atop one of the bluffs. Bloody arms and legs were piling up outside like cordwood, and from inside the tent came "heart-rending screams and despairing groans."[38]

To Sherman's far left, Prentiss's division fell back to a sunken road, where, for most of the day, the inexperienced soldiers fought so determinedly that the Southerners dubbed the place the "Hornet's Nest." Ordered by Grant to hold his position, Prentiss did exactly that, repelling twelve charges.

Only in the late afternoon, when a massive artillery barrage began to sweep the sunken road, did Prentiss surrender the 2,200 men of his division who remained. By his steadfastness he and his mix of Midwesterners had bought Grant's army the invaluable gift of time.

Johnston and Beauregard had planned to force the Union line back far enough to trap it against the fast-rushing Owl Creek, separating the Federals from their escape hatch at Pittsburg Landing. Johnston had told President Davis that he planned a three-pronged attack, simultaneously launching three corps while holding a fourth in reserve. But, inexplicably, Johnston didn't follow his own plan. Instead, he arranged his army into four successive *rows*, spreading them evenly across the Union's entire front and rolling them forward one after another, like waves falling on a beach.

Attacking by long, thin rows instead of three hard-hitting columns advancing in parallel was Johnston's first mistake of the day. As the broad Confederate front rolled ahead, uneven terrain and opposing fire upset the alignment of its rows. Troops from different commands became jumbled together in confusion and officers lost touch with their men. Adding to the disarray were hungry, poorly supplied Confederates who slowed to loot the Union camps.

Prentiss's Federals held their position so stubbornly that Johnston became preoccupied with them. Neglecting the rest of the field to direct the fight with Prentiss was Johnston's second mistake. His inattention to the larger picture allowed the Confederate attack to become even more disorganized. Instead of the massive, simultaneous concentration of force Johnston intended, the battle turned into smaller struggles erupting sporadically at various points along the battle line. "There was no hour during the day when there was not heavy firing and generally hard fighting at some point along the line, but seldom at all points at the same time," Grant recalled.[39]

Johnston's third mistake was fatal to himself. Riding bravely (but "uselessly," in Beauregard's opinion) close to the fighting, Johnston was wounded. At about 2 p.m. a bullet cut an artery in Johnston's leg without his realizing it. An old wound had numbed the leg and his boot concealed the bleeding. Only when he began to sway in his saddle as blood dripped from his heel, did Johnston consent to be lowered to the ground in a sheltered ravine.

Johnston's blood ran in a stream six-to-eight feet from his body, collecting in a pool. Within half an hour, he was dead and the surrounding officers' staff burst into tears. One of them collected himself enough to send a message to Beauregard: "It now devolves on you to complete the victory."[40] To hide the loss from the troops, Johnston's body was taken from the field hidden in a blanket.

By late afternoon, the Confederates, under Beauregard's command, had pushed Grant's army far back, but not quite as far as the Confederates planned. Union forces still held Pittsburg Landing and formed a defense line that was bristling with artillery and partly protected by a deep ravine. Now it was Beauregard's turn to make ill-founded assumptions.

The new commander decided his tired and hungry Confederates had done enough for one day. He assumed, from misinformation, that Buell's reinforcements were not coming after all. Beauregard also failed to personally check on his front line and determine whether another hour of fighting was possible before dark.

Confident he could finish off Grant's army in the morning, Beauregard called off the fighting at 6 p.m. and sent a telegram to Richmond announcing the Confederates had "gained a complete victory."[41] Then he went to sleep in Sherman's abandoned tent.

Backed into a corner, Union forces held only a fraction of their original campground. "Well, Grant, we've had the devil's own day, haven't we?" Sherman said. Smoking his customary cigar, Grant quietly replied, "Yes, lick 'em tomorrow, though."[42] The quiet confidence was typical of the man who seemed unflappable in the most daunting of circumstances. By the end of the war, it was a quality that had more than redeemed his errors.

His swollen ankle throbbing from the fall of his horse, the rain falling in torrents, Grant spent the night, sleepless, under a tree a few hundred yards from the river. He tried taking shelter in a building where wounded men were undergoing amputations. "The sight was more unendurable than encountering the enemy's fire," Grant recalled, "and I returned to my tree in the rain."[43]

"Lick 'em tomorrow, though," a calm Grant told Sherman after the disastrous first day of fighting at Shiloh. On the second day, they did.

REVERSALS OF FORTUNE

On the day before Johnston's attack at Shiloh, Buell's Army of the Ohio had arrived downriver at Savannah. Buell brought about seventeen thousand men, most of them Midwesterners, more than half from Ohio, Indiana, and Illinois. Among Buell's commanders was Col. William B. Hazen, bumped up from taskmaster of one regiment to taskmaster of a brigade of three. Hazen's brigade included his old 41st Infantry, in which Emerson Opdycke was now a captain and acting major.

Commanding another brigade in Buell's army was James A. Garfield, raised from regimental command as well and promoted to brigadier general, thanks in part to his performance in a skirmish in January, and in no small part to a campaign on his behalf by well-connected friends in Columbus and Washington.[44]

Buell's men had spent the night in peaceful slumber at Savannah and awoke expecting a lazy Sunday in the bright, warm sunshine. But then, wrote Sgt. Ambrose Bierce of the 9th Indiana, they heard "a dull, distant sound like the heavy breathing of some great animal below the horizon." Listening, Buell's men rose to their feet. "[T]he sound of the great guns now came in regular throbbings—the strong, full pulse of the fever of battle," Bierce wrote.[45]

Then bugle calls sounded across the camp and the men ran to their arms

Hospital boats sent from Cincinnati and other Northern cities rushed to Pittsburg Landing to collect thousands of wounded after the Battle of Shiloh.

and prepared to march. By dusk, an advance brigade of Buell's force had arrived on the shore opposite Pittsburg Landing.

Buell's advance force was commanded by Col. Jacob Ammen, an Ohioan and West Pointer turned college professor. His men affectionately called him "Uncle Jake." Soon, Ammen's three regiments were being ferried across the river and fed into the left of Grant's line. To Bierce, the new arrivals formed "black, sinuous lines, creeping like a giant serpent beneath the trees," stumbling through a pitch-black night as rain fell, tripping over dead bodies and an occasional wounded one.

The only light Bierce could see came from candles in surgical tents, where, as pairs of litter bearers came and went, "low moans [issued] from within and … long rows of dead [lay] with covered faces outside."[46]

Lew Wallace's 7,600-man division, composed mostly of Iowa and Illinois men, arrived after a march from Crump's Landing delayed by miscommunication. One of Wallace's few Ohio regiments, the 68th (to which Andrew Altman belonged), was so reduced by illness it had to be left behind as camp guard. "[T]he officers had us out on [dress] parade this after noon and there was oneley about one hundred or two hundred any how. The rest is sick," Altman wrote his brother.[47]

Throughout the night, crowded steamers shuttled Buell's men from Savannah to Pittsburg Landing. The new arrivals marched past thousands of runaway soldiers—"dead to shame," according to Bierce—huddled under the bluff. Some skulkers taunted Buell's men with warnings of doom. Others tried to force their way onto the boats and had to be driven back with bayonets. From above the bluff rose the groans and screams of men undergoing amputations in the surgical tents.

At regular intervals throughout the night, with blinding flashes and shuddering reports, two Union gunboats fired shells in the direction of the out-of-sight Confederates. The intent was more to ruin their rest and rattle their nerves than do damage. From his mattress aboard a relief boat, the wounded Posegate watched one of the gunboats position herself for action. The gunboat reminded him of "a huge, black vulture sailing near the earth and yet, with cocked eye, looking upward for its prey."[48]

The 72nd Ohio had established a hospital near the landing, sheltered by the bluff. Here, among hundreds of wounded, worked Dr. John B. Rice, a physician from Fremont, and Hospital Steward William Caldwell (later assistant surgeon and, after the war, a prominent Fremont physician). Dr. Rice probed the wounds and performed the amputations while Caldwell applied the bandages.

Later that night, after their work was done, Caldwell wrote his father, "We lay on the bank of the Tennessee on the night of that first day of death with the enemy's camp fires and the gun-boats throwing their fiery storm over our heads to keep them at bay," Unable to get Shiloh out of his mind a year later, Caldwell told his sister, "I would gladly blot from my memory the horrors of those two days."[49]

The next morning, Bierce's regiment moved across the battlefield, passing trees with riddled bark and branches turned into hand-like bunches of splinters. Knapsacks, blankets, hats, and broken rifles had been beaten into the mud and "[d]ead horses were everywhere," Bierce wrote. So were corpses and wounded men waiting for care.

Bierce came upon a Union sergeant, who must have been "a fine giant in his time." The man lay on his back, taking his breath in spasmodic snorts and blowing it out in froth. His skull had been cracked open by a bullet and his brains were leaking out "in flakes and strings." One of Bierce's men offered to put him out of his misery with a bayonet thrust. Bierce said no, for "it was unusual, and too many were looking."[50]

Compared to Sunday's battle, the shoe was on the other foot in Monday's. The Union army had twenty-five thousand fresh reinforcements; Beauregard had none. A Union attack was ordered at daylight and now it was the Confederates' turn to be scattered and surprised. The Confederates fought stubbornly, but Union forces gradually recovered the ground lost the day before, though at a price. Hazen's brigade was hit especially hard, with his 41st Ohio suffering 140 killed and wounded out of 371 soldiers present for duty.[51]

Acting Major Emerson Opdycke distinguished himself by seizing the regiment's colors after the color-bearer had fallen, and shouting, "Forty-First Ohio, follow your colors!"[52] He was wounded twice. "To go over our … ground now, it seems miraculous how one of us escaped," Opdycke wrote his wife. "On Monday morning, I was within a few inches of thousands of whistling bullets, cannon balls, and bursting shells." He mentioned that his son's picture "was in my coat pocket during the battle, a little charm for me."[53]

Garfield rushed to battle at the head of his brigade, dodging shells and bullets, but arrived too late for serious action. Chastened, perhaps, by combat, his letters to Crete were more affectionate. Now she was "My Dear Crete" and he signed himself, "Ever and forever, Your James." Still, he reserved his most fervent declarations for their daughter: "Kiss our precious little Trot for me a hundred times," he wrote.[54]

At 2:30 Monday afternoon, Thomas Jordan, adjutant general in Beauregard's army, spoke to him: "General, do you not think our troops are very much in the condition of a lump of sugar thoroughly soaked with water …. ready to dissolve? Would it not be judicious to get away with what we have?"[55] Beauregard replied that he was about to order a retreat.

The Confederates had suffered a staggering twenty-four percent casualty rate, the majority killed or wounded. Grant's army, including Sherman's division, had suffered a twenty-two percent casualty rate, but the largest number were prisoners and there were far fewer killed or wounded than the Confederates. Buell's army, not all of which were fully engaged, lost about twelve percent.

At first, news of the battle was saluted in the North as "a glorious victory."[56] After all, the Union forces retained possession of the battlefield. But soon another story emerged, much of it inspired by Whitelaw Reid of the *Cincinnati Gazette* who had arrived on the battlefield the second day. Reid wrote that Grant was caught by surprise and saved by Buell, and that story spread quickly, reinforced by letters from soldiers who had been there.

Buell claimed credit for saving Grant (Grant disagreed), and Illinois Gen. John A. McClernand, ever the conniver, did his best to stir the pot on his own behalf. Old suspicions of drunkenness by Grant surfaced again. (There was even a rumor, Julia Grant said, that Grant had been in some dance house instead of on the field. "The idea!," she sputtered. "dear Ulys! So earnest and serious; he never went to a party of any kind, except to take me."[57]) As public criticism of Grant spread, Sherman—whose battlefield performance his friend Halleck went out of his way to praise—came to Grant's defense via what he told the newspapers.

Sherman's battlefield performance so fully restored his self-confidence that one biographer has called it "a major turning point in his life."[58] On April 11, he wrote "Dearest Ellen," laconically reporting, "Well we have had a big battle where they Shot real bullets and I am safe, except for a buckshot wound in the hand and a bruised shoulder from a spent ball."

Three horses had been killed under Sherman and it seemed to him that half his men had run away, but he was more than satisfied with his own performance. The experience raised his expectations for himself: "I have worked hard to Keep down but somehow I am forced into prominence and might as well submit," he decided.[59]

Sherman crowed to Ellen about the praise he had won from Grant and the soldiers, but even he was shaken by the carnage. It "would have cured anybody of war," he told her. "Mangled bodies, dead, dying, in every conceivable shape, without heads, legs; and [the] horses!"[60]

Ellen, who didn't receive his letter until late on Saturday, April 19, quickly wrote back how happy she was that "Dearest Cump" had survived the battle. Just as quickly, she shifted into managerial mode: "Do not expose yourself unnecessarily & do recommend your soul with contrition to God every day. Do not go into battle a heathen," she told her husband. It did no good. Dearest Cump remained a heathen.[61]

In Washington, pressure grew on Lincoln to remove Grant. The president endorsed Halleck's decision to move Grant to a sideline position that amounted, one historian has written, to "a de-facto suspension."[62] But Lincoln refused demands to fire Grant. He had never met Grant, but the commander in chief understood something others didn't. Too many of his generals avoided battle or were easily discouraged. Grant was different; nothing stopped him.

Late one evening Lincoln listened for two hours as a close friend and advisor urged him to dismiss Grant. Unshakeable, the president made a

Gen. Ormsby M. Mitchel, the "astronomer-soldier" from Ohio, was a resourceful commander who came to an untimely end.

decision that would make all the difference in the war yet to come: "I can't spare this man; he fights."[63]

At Shiloh, those who had not been spared were laid out in long rows and then hurriedly buried to avoid decay in the heat. Thousands of the survivors were permanently maimed in mind or body. Some were angry. A furious Emerson Opdycke wrote his wife, "Such inexcusable inefficiency ought to cost General Grant his office if not his life. No good officer need ever be surprised to the extent that he was if he but regard the plainest rules of war."[64]

Whitelaw Reid wrote after the war that Grant's "neglect of pickets and out-posts approached criminality."[65]

In civilian life, severe harm to life and limb that could have been avoided would be called criminal negligence. In war, it's just stupidity.

THE GREAT LOCOMOTIVE CHASE

Ormsby MacKnight Mitchel was a shooting star who came out of nowhere, streaked across the sky, and disappeared. A gifted child, he was reading Virgil at age nine. His widowed mother left him alone with his books as long as she could, but at twelve he had to go to work in a store in Lebanon, Ohio, for twenty-five cents a week.

A relative secured young Mitchel a place at West Point, although the boy was only fifteen. He graduated in the upper third of a class that included Robert E. Lee and Joseph E. Johnston. After four years' army service, Mitchel resigned and became a well-known professor of mathematics, natural philosophy, and astronomy at Cincinnati College (today's University of Cincinnati).

Professor Mitchel was a spellbinding speaker, the kind who could attract and hold audiences for subjects they didn't think they were interested in. He raised money to build an astronomical observatory in Cincinnati that was considered the finest in the nation. A Carl Sagan of his time, Mitchel published several popular books on the stars and planets, did engineering work for railroads, and built an international reputation as a man of science and technology.

A militia man for several years, Mitchel jumped into the war in August 1861 as a brigadier general of volunteers. While Grant was moving on Forts Henry and Donelson in Tennessee, Mitchel was leading a division of Don Carlos Buell's army that occupied Bowling Green, Kentucky, and Nashville, Tennessee, without opposition.

After that, Mitchel headed for Huntsville, Alabama, where he surprised and drove out a small force of Confederates. Before Mitchel's enterprising brigade had finished, Union forces had grabbed most of the vital east-west Confederate rail line from Mississippi to Tennessee.

It was then that one of the war's strangest episodes took place. Hoping to weaken Chattanooga's defenses, Mitchel—perhaps at Buell's behest—ordered a small band of volunteers to slip into Georgia and steal a train. By heading north and destroying railroad bridges behind them, they could prevent quick Confederate reinforcement of Chattanooga, reducing its ability to resist attack by Buell. It was the kind of exciting, deceptively simple idea that attracted daring young men.

Twenty-two men from three Ohio regiments—the 2nd, 21st, and 33rd Infantry—volunteered and were put under the leadership of James J. Andrews, a Union spy. The soldiers changed into civilian clothes, and, claiming to be Kentuckians going to join the Confederate army, worked their way through enemy territory to Marietta, Georgia.

A few men failed to make it to Marietta, but on April 12 Andrews and the rest bought tickets and boarded a northbound train. At Big Shanty, eight miles north, the train's crew and passengers left the train for breakfast. As an unwitting Confederate sentinel stood by, Andrews's men uncoupled the last few cars and climbed aboard the remaining train, a locomotive named the *General*

Out of fuel, Union soldiers who had stolen the Confederate train scattered into the woods, but were soon captured.

pulling a tender carrying fuel, water, and three boxcars. The train with its new crew took off with a screech.

To succeed, the raiders would have to dovetail their progress northward with trains bound south on the same track. That assumed everything was running on time that day. It was not.

At first, things went well, with the stolen train breezing through enemy territory, pausing now and then so the raiders could cut telegraph wires, tear up track, and take on wood and water. But south-bound trains repeatedly forced the raiders to wait on sidings. Meanwhile, two determined Southern trainmen began chasing the *General* with a hand-car, switching to a locomotive at Etowah. Changing to yet another, faster engine, the *Texas*, the pursuers picked up armed men and raced north after the Yankees, pausing to put out fires set by the raiders and to put back rails they had pulled up.

To foil the pursuit, Andrews's raiders threw debris on the track and left behind boxcars they had set on fire. Doggedly pushing the obstacles out of the way, the Confederates continued the chase. Finally, the *General* ran out of fuel near Ringgold, Georgia, near the Tennessee border. The raiders scattered into the woods, but all were caught and imprisoned.

Eight raiders, including Andrews, were executed and buried in Chattanooga. Eight others escaped from an Atlanta jail in October 1862, and six were exchanged in March 1863. The great adventure had failed, but the raiders were heroes to the North. The first Medals of Honor ever authorized by Congress were awarded to nineteen members of the raiding party.

The first medal of all was pinned on the chest of Jacob Parrott, at eighteen the youngest raider. He had been badly beaten by his captors trying, unsuccessfully, to make him talk. Parrott, a cabinet maker, had been born near Columbus and was a member of the 33rd Ohio, a unit formed in Portsmouth. After the war he lived in Kenton.

The Andrews raid lives on in America's memory. In 1927 Hollywood released a comedy-drama starring Buster Keaton and the *General,* and years later Walt Disney produced *The Great Locomotive Chase.* Gen. Ormsby Mitchel did not fare as well. Praised for a successful occupation of Huntsville, Alabama, promoted to major general, and pronounced one of the Union's ablest commanders, he ran headlong into the hostility of Henry W. Halleck, recently called east to be the Union's general in chief.

Halleck, the quintessential desk soldier and linear thinker, "had a profound contempt for success won in such irregular methods as Mitchel had employed and a profound distrust for the men who employed them," Whitelaw Reid wrote after the war. "He considered Mitchel reckless and Quixotic—lucky, perhaps, thus far … but utterly unsafe."

There may have been other factors involved. In any case, instead of giving Mitchel the new command he requested, Halleck kept him twiddling his thumbs for six weeks, then sent him to the relatively unimportant command of the Department of South Carolina.[66]

Undeterred, Mitchel, known to the public as the "astronomer-soldier," set to work with a will, visiting camps the Union forces had chipped out of the Carolina coast, launching expeditions against the Confederates, even developing a comfortable village for runaway slaves.

On the 26th of October 1862, however, Mitchel contracted yellow fever and on the 30th he died. Ohio's celebrated astronomer-soldier never returned home. The Union commander was buried in Beaufort, South Carolina, not far from the homes of those pillars of the secessionist Old South, the Barnwells and the Rhetts.

ON TO CORINTH

Union soldiers were still cleaning up the mess after the battle at Pittsburg Landing when "Old Brains" Henry Halleck, commander of the army's sprawling Department of the Mississippi, left his desk in St. Louis and took personal command of Grant's army. To serve out his de facto suspension, Grant

In an excess of caution, General Halleck took a month to advance twenty-two miles against Corinth, Mississippi. Corinth's Confederate defenders escaped unharmed.

was made "second in command," a meaningless position with no authority.

There, Halleck assembled a huge force to resume the advance to Corinth. To Grant's former command, the Army of the Tennessee, Halleck added Buell's Army of the Ohio, and John Pope's Army of the Mississippi, fresh from an impressive victory at New Madrid and Island Number Tenth on the Mississippi River.

Halleck now had 120,000 men, a force so big nothing the Confederates had in the West could have stopped it. In moving against Corinth, where Beauregard's battered, sick, and demoralized Confederates were huddled, the Union had the men and the momentum to smash Beauregard and doom the western Confederacy. *This* was the moment.

And then it was gone.

Instead of crushing Beauregard with one quick blow, Halleck concentrated on making sure his Union army would never, ever be surprised again. Over-compensating for what happened at Shiloh, he moved his huge force so gingerly, throwing up new earthworks every day, that it took a month to advance twenty-two miles to Corinth. Just as Halleck was arriving on Beauregard's doorstep at the end of May, the Confederates slipped away, abandoning Corinth but escaping to fight another day.

Halleck had frittered away his opportunity to destroy an entire army and deal a staggering blow to the Confederacy. In the process, he almost frittered away the man who would prove to be the Union's most effective general. "I was little more than an observer," Grant recalled in his memoirs. "My position was so embarrassing in fact that I made several applications … to be relieved."[67] As second in command with no real authority, Grant believed "my position differs but little from one in arrest."[68] Intending to go home, he told Sherman, "I have stood it as long as I can, and can endure it no longer."[69]

Sherman, however, was developing a warm bond with Grant. He had already publicly come to Grant's defense over his lack of preparedness at Shiloh (for which, of course, Sherman bore some responsibility). Now Sherman "begged him to stay," saying "some happy accident might restore him," just as Shiloh had Sherman. Shiloh had shown Cump he could lead men in the heat of battle under difficult circumstances. His doubts about himself swept away, the buoyant Sherman described himself as "in high feather." He told Grant his fortunes might well change.

The pep-talk worked. In a few days Grant told Sherman he would not go home.[70] The two men were developing a friendship that would sustain both throughout the war. Sherman was grateful that Grant had not shifted blame to him for the surprise at Shiloh; in return, Sherman argued Grant's case via the public prints.[71] Later, Sherman is said to have dismissed rumors that long troubled both men by saying, in exaggerated fashion, "Grant stood by me when I was crazy, and I stood by him when he was drunk, and now we stand by each other always."[72]

THEATERS OF WAR

War changes everything, including war. By the winter of 1861–62, Americans North and South were learning the quick and easy conflict they had expected was nowhere to be found. It was beginning to look like a long, hard slog. Among military commanders, the idea was being advanced—notably, by Grant—that war was not a gentlemen's game. The idea wasn't just to win, it was to eliminate the opposing force's ability to fight. And, for those who could see it, a pattern was emerging in the war's geography. The conflict was sorting itself into theaters of operation.

There were at least four such theaters, two of which played lesser, though not insignificant, roles. Playing the lesser roles were the Lower Seaboard and Gulf Approach Theater, encompassing the Gulf and Atlantic coasts and the high seas, and the Trans-Mississippi Theater, which stretched from Louisiana west of the Mississippi to the Indian territories. Lying between these grim sideshows, however, were the war's main stages—the Eastern Theater and the Western Theater. To this day, one of these theaters has received the lion's share of attention from historians and the public when what mattered most took place in the other.

In the region of the United States between the Mississippi River and the Atlantic coast, the great divider is the Appalachian Mountains. On the east side of this chain were fought the battles of the Civil War's *Eastern Theater*. The fighting was concentrated in what is Virginia today, although occasionally it spread to parts of Maryland and Pennsylvania.

West of the Appalachians to the Mississippi lies the "near Midwest," although nineteenth-century Easterners considered everything beyond the mountains to be the "Great West." This area formed part of the *Western Theater,* but only part. To it must be added several states we usually think of as Southern or Southeastern: Kentucky, Tennessee, Mississippi, Alabama, Georgia, and the Carolinas.

Historians consider these southern states part of the Western Theater because it was the area of operations for Federal troops who came largely from the states *west* of the Appalachians (and, in largest numbers, from the Midwestern sister states of Ohio, Indiana, and Illinois). For that reason, West Virginia should also be considered part of the Western Theater.

Because of its large populations, press corps, and location of Washington, the Eastern Theater got the most attention during the war, as it does to this day. To many Americans, Gettysburg was the turning point of the war. It was not. Virginia boasts it hosted more battles than any other state, as if to say it had the most important role in the war. It did not. Virginia was a slaughterhouse for troops from both the North and the South, producing widows and orphans and little else for much of the war.

The fate of the Confederacy was sealed in the Western Theater. That task was largely accomplished by the end of 1864, primarily by Western troops led by Western officers, most of all by generals with Ohio roots. The war's final chapter—almost an anti-climax, though a very bloody one—was written in 1865 by three Western generals who came east to finish the job.

Easterners do not like to hear this, but it is true.

GAZETTE

In Ohio, 1862 began with a change signifying there would be no change in the state's support for the war. Republican Gov. William Dennison's unpopularity meant he could not be re-elected, so Republicans had gritted their teeth, stopped talking about slavery for the time being, and joined War Democrats the previous fall to form a coalition of convenience called the Union Party. For governor, the Union Party nominated an experienced Democratic politician and businessman, David Tod from Mahoning County.

In the fall 1861 elections, Tod had coasted to victory on a platform that supported the war while carefully saying nothing about the trickier subject of slavery. Union Party candidates took control of the Ohio legislature as well. Clearly, Ohioans—including many Democrats—wanted the war to go on and

At full strength, a thousand-man Civil War regiment, like the 51st Ohio on dress parade in Nashville early in 1862, made an impressive sight.

the Union restored. Governor Tod got down to business, focusing on the war effort. He created agencies to aid veterans, fired off telegrams to Washington demanding better care of Ohio soldiers, and recruited still more Ohioans for the service.

As busy as Lincoln and the Republican Congress were with the war, they also were working to keep the nation growing. On May 20, 1862, Lincoln signed the Homestead Act to encourage settlement of the West. Beginning the following January 1, individuals could claim 160-acre farms in the West for a nominal sum. They only had to settle on their land and improve it. The Homestead Act triggered a land rush that would fill the middle of the country with settlers.

There were other signs of a forward-looking nation. On July 1, 1862, Lincoln signed the Pacific Railroad Act, authorizing a rail link between Chicago and California. Now Ohioans could foresee a time when they could step on a train in Cleveland or Cincinnati and cross the continent in days instead of weeks. One day later, Lincoln signed the Morrill Act, granting loyal states public lands they could sell to build public universities, the objective being to offer higher education to all at an affordable price.

Lincoln also was making changes in the war's managers. Early in January 1862 he appointed Secretary of War Simon Cameron minister to Russia,

Russia being about as far as Lincoln could send him. Willing to forget past insults, Lincoln chose Edwin M. Stanton to take Cameron's place. Wearied by McClellan's procrastination and complaining, on March 11 Lincoln—with Stanton's encouragement—relieved the "Young Napoleon" of his duties as general in chief. Lincoln said it was so McClellan could concentrate on leading the Army of the Potomac. But McClellan should have taken it as a warning; Lincoln's patience had its limits.

As Sherman predicted, Grant was returned to command in early June. Having occupied Corinth and failed to pursue Beauregard's tattered army, Halleck made another mistake. Instead of keeping his huge force intact and using it to overwhelm the Confederates in the Western Theater, he broke it up, dispersing it to hold territory. Grant was put back in charge of his Army of the Tennessee and sent to Memphis, ordered to spread out his forces along the Mississippi-Tennessee border. That denied him the ability to mount attacks.

Meanwhile, Lincoln and Stanton realized, after several weeks of trying to get along without a general in chief, that they needed an experienced military man. They summoned Halleck east and Halleck, in turn, summoned Grant to replace him in the West. That put Grant in command of both his own Army of the Tennessee and Pope's old Army of the Mississippi, now under Rosecrans.

Buell would continue to command the Army of the Ohio, reporting to Halleck, not Grant. With Western Theater forces weakened by being spread all over the map by order of Halleck, Bragg and other Confederate commanders began planning to invade Kentucky, recapture Corinth, and just possibly cross the Ohio River. Unable to take the initiative himself, Grant remembered the summer of 1862 as "the most anxious period of the war."[73]

Eventually, Grant would be freed to make the bold strategic moves Halleck couldn't seem to make. Even Whitelaw Reid, who had been shocked by Grant's lack of vigilance at Shiloh, was impressed by his coolness under pressure. At Shiloh, "Grant rose to the height of a hero," Reid decided. "The man who amid the disasters of that day could calmly reason out the certainty of success to-morrow, gave proof, in spite of blunders ... of his capacity to lead the hosts of Freedom in greater struggles yet to come."

From that battle Reid wrote, "I date, in my own case at least, the beginnings of any belief in Grant's greatness."[74]

To Learn More:

Shiloh—Sherman called its opening engagement "The Devil's Own Day"—
stunned North and South alike by its size and ferocity. This bloodsoaked
battleground where so many Ohioans fought and died is preserved in the Shiloh
National Military Park (**http://www.nps.gov/shil/** or **731-689-5696**). Nearby
Corinth, Mississippi, is part of the park.

An unusual monument to Andrew's Raiders, including a handsome replica
(reduced in size) of the locomotive called *The General* is in the Chattanooga
National Cemetery, 1200 Bailey Ave., Chattanooga, Tennessee (**http://www.cem.
va.gov/cems/nchp/chattanooga.asp** or **423-855-6590**). *The General* itself in all
its shiny glory can be seen at the Southern Museum of Civil War and Locomotive
History in Kennesaw, Georgia (**www.southernmuseum.org** or **770-427-2117**).

Wiley Sword's *Shiloh: Bloody April* is a classic, but a more recent treatment,
Larry J. Daniel's *Shiloh: The Battle That Changed the Civil War* is also well
regarded. The ill-fated attempt by Andrews' Raiders to steal a Confederate train
is chronicled in *Stealing the General: The Great Locomotive Chase and the First
Medal of Honor* by Russell S. Bonds.

"The empty chair" was one of the ways sentimental Victorians symbolized a death visited them by war.

7

I Am in Command Again!

Spring and Summer 1862

Death was life's companion in the nineteenth century in ways hard to imagine in the twenty-first. There were, of course, the usual outcomes from water accidents, cirrhotic livers, and the morbidly depressed, not to mention the elderly who ran out life's string more or less as expected. But with a familiarity we cannot know, death in the Victorian era sat down at every dinner table, lay in every bed, studied the clerk at his desk and the farmer in his field, and did what death does always: watch and wait.

But it waited less patiently back then. Barefooted children stepped on rusty nails, E.coli stalked the food supply, thunderclaps exploded in men's chests, and lumps grew undisturbed in women's breasts. Death was everywhere and the medical profession offered only a few defenses. Historians have called Civil War-era medicine "more medieval than modern."[1] Health care was primitive in an age priding itself on innovations and improvements such as the telegraph, a vast rail network, and the propeller-driven steamship. Ignorant of germ theory and armed with a handful of crude remedies, doctors relied when they could on medical practice by committee. The very sick could expect several physicians to gather around the bedstead, murmur thoughtful hmmms, and pool their ignorance.

Medical care was even worse in warfare. The United States Army lacked skilled doctors, supplies, and organizations to treat huge numbers of patients. Far from supply depots, Western armies were even less well provided for than Eastern ones. Soldiers fell ill and died from so-called childhood diseases when farm boys mingled with city youth carrying diseases to which the farmers had

Stonewall Jackson's brilliant Shenandoah Valley Campaign of 1862 forced Union Gen. Frémont's poorly led soldiers into retreat.

no immunities. Soldiers drank foul water, ate wretched diets, and lived amidst filth. Probably twice as many men of the Union and Confederate armies died from disease as died from wounds.[2]

We're not sure of the exact number of men who served in the Civil War—problems with the records prevent it. Depending on the source consulted, we can say there may have been as many as 2,800,000 enlistments—some of them repeats—or as few as 2,100,000 for the Union cause; there were somewhere around one million for the Confederacy. According to one authoritative source, Louisiana State University's "U. S. Civil War Center," about 185,000 men on both sides are thought to have died from wounds, while twice as many succumbed from other causes. Another 412,000 men survived wounds, many disfigured or disabled for life.

The dead and wounded for both sides may have totaled nearly six-hundred thousand, more than ALL other American wars combined, leaving out only World War II.[3] Moreover, 14.5 percent of all Civil War soldiers died from all causes, making it far more lethal than World War II, in which 2.5 percent died.[3]

At least one of every four Civil War soldiers was killed or wounded. In some communities, entire generations of young men were wiped out or maimed. According to figures quoted by Nan Card, curator of manuscripts at the Rutherford B. Hayes Presidential Center, "Eight percent of all white males enumerated in the 1860 United States Federal Census between the ages of thirteen and forty-three died in the conflict."[4]

Card examined the "experience of death in the Civil War" in Fremont and the surrounding Sandusky County. Before the war, Sandusky Countians had the "Good Death" as a romantic ideal, a belief that courage on behalf of a noble cause could redeem death and bring solace to the survivors.

Tradition dictated elaborate rituals during mourning, influenced by the Romantic tradition of *Weltschmerz*, a mood of sentimental sadness. Popular art, music, and drama fostered an ideal in which soldiers were expected to show the fight bravely, show the gallantry of King Arthur's knights, and die nobly on antiseptically clean battlefields. Lithographs showed well-organized ranks of neatly uniformed soldiers marching under fluttering flags, led by sword-wielding officers on prancing horses. Legions of young men marched away from home promising to die, if they had to, with their "faces to the enemy" while defending their community's honor. "Honor" was very important to them all.

That changed when harsh realities intruded on the fantasies of soldiers and civilians. The banality and brutality of war, its stink and misery, stunned new soldiers.[5] What happened on the fighting fields was ugly, and hardship and boredom filled the intervals between battles. After a fight, companions with whom young men had laughed and shared meals were found lying in the mud, entrails spilling from their abdomens. The wounded cried for their mothers and tore up the grass in their agony.

The quality of medical care was highly uneven and often scarce. In June 1864, a volunteer nurse described what she saw during the siege of Petersburg, Virginia: On the field "dead and dying lay … and they were carried under tents and rolled together like the logs on a corduroy road …. Worms soon bred in the fresh wounds [of the injured]; the sun burned their faces till

Homes and barns were commandeered as field hospitals for the typical battle's hordes of wounded.

the skin pealed away, and in the agony of thirst and fever it seemed like a merciful relief when their spirits rid themselves of the mortal and mutilated bodies."[6]

Almost as shocking were those soldiers who had vowed never to show the white feather but turned and ran in the face of the enemy. Others disappeared unnoticed. They had deserted, been captured, or killed, their bodies left behind to be buried by strangers. What soldiers experienced on the battlefield didn't match the lithographs.

For Sandusky Countians, both soldiers and civilians, Shiloh was a brutal awakening. To the end of their days, veterans would remember the sight of arms and legs piling up outside hospital tents from which screams and moans were issuing.

Established traditions of mourning and burial were shattered by the need for quick burial in hot weather. When they could, soldiers would mark a grave with a name scratched on a scrap of wood from a cracker or ammunition box. Sometimes, however, the dead had to be buried in impersonal trenches.

As the war went on, the fortunes of battle meant that some corpses had to be left behind—unburied, unidentified and unmourned. Coming across an unrecognized corpse, all that soldiers could say sometimes was, "There's somebody's darlin'."

Confronted by war's miseries, Card believes, Sandusky Countians "turned away from the antebellum Romantic vision of death and moved toward cultural, secular mourning practices."[7] Some of the mourners sought comfort in religion, while others began to question the war's leaders and their purposes. Maintaining morale on the home front in the face of battlefield defeats and mounting casualties was one of Lincoln's biggest headaches.

Compounding the misery for civilians was incessant rumor-mongering and searching for scapegoats. Families and friends of the 72nd Ohio Volunteer Infantry not only grieved for its losses at Shiloh, but also for its honor. In many minds, shame was as bad as death. Early, incomplete reports suggested the 72nd Ohio had run away on the first day at Shiloh. Symbolizing the regiment's supposed shame was the loss of its "colors," the battle flag stitched by women of the county.

In reality, the startled 72nd had taken much of the brunt of the Confederate attack, fighting bravely and well for two hours in the heart of the battle before being ordered to retreat, after which it lost some of its organization. Col. Ralph P. Buckland, commander of the brigade to which the 72nd belonged, had to write a "detailed explanation of events," published in a county newspaper to quiet some of the criticism.[8]

The rumors in Shiloh's aftermath spread like bloodstains, imputing cowardice, failures of leadership, and other ugliness to men who deserved better. These hometown rumors filtered back to the soldiers, causing army surgeon Dr. John B. Rice to write his wife in Fremont, "[Y]ou cannot believe how deep a gloom it casts … to find that after all our labors, dangers, & sacrifice, we were denounced as cowards."[9] Sadly, Rice himself was one of the victims of baseless rumor and in one of the cruelest ways possible.

Rice's success in stemming illness among his troops made him one of the ablest physicians in the army. His skill and courage would bring him repeated promotions, ultimately to chief medical officer of the District of Memphis, overseeing 150 surgeons caring for 15,000 patients. At Shiloh, however, Rice was only the surgeon of the 72nd Ohio. He and his medical colleagues braved Confederate shot and shell, narrowly escaping capture in a successful struggle to bring 230 sick and wounded men to safety.

Despite Rice's service, fictions erupted at home that he had employed donated medical supplies for personal profit and demanded payment to treat the wounded.[10] Exhausted and frustrated by a shortage of supplies, Dr. Rice replied he could bear the rumors so long as his family supported him. Shortly before leaving for war, the thirty-year-old Rice had married nineteen-year-old Sarah Wilson, daughter of a prominent Fremont physician. In his absence, his young wife had enjoyed parties, weddings, and other social events as if there was no war.

The poisonous rumors flying around Sandusky County after Shiloh apparently caused even the doctor's young wife to question his integrity for a time. "Fraught" by her lack of faith in him, he sadly replied, "It is fortunate that my heart is familiar with that sorrow, which comes from a sense of neglect, coldness, and unmerited chastisement. Though the worst may come, I trust while I live that I shall remain faithfully, your loving husband."[11]

Then Dr. Rice went back to his patients.

THE ENIGMA FROM OHIO

Next to Lincoln, the most important man in Washington during most of the war was an enigma from Ohio named Edwin McMasters Stanton. Historians have had a hard time pinning down the man and even eye-witnesses couldn't agree on him; they variously described him as hard-hearted or kind, honest or conniving, humorless or witty.

The rages of Secretary of War Edwin M. Stanton were legendary. Glasses pushed to his forehead, Stanton's face became a thundercloud as he glared at malefactors.

Historians do agree on this, however: Stanton was a tough, crafty engine of energy, a man many found hard to like and most found hard to resist, and he was exactly what the Republic needed. Stanton was Lincoln's secretary of war and the man whom Lincoln spent more time with than any other man in his administration. Congressman Henry L. Dawes of Massachusetts, who knew both, observed, "If Lincoln was essential to the success of the Union, it is no less true that Stanton was essential to the success of Lincoln."[12]

Born in 1814 in Steubenville on Ohio's eastern border with western Virginia, Stanton was the oldest child of a village doctor who was an opponent of slavery and who died when the boy was thirteen. Even as a child, Stanton could be brusque and imperious, perhaps to cover for the limits imposed on him by myopia and asthma. But he also was smart and energetic, a promising if especially assertive youth.

Before he was twenty-two, the precocious Stanton had been admitted to the bar, joined a practice in Cadiz, and begun building a reputation for himself. He was a stocky young man of average height and abundant wavy hair, who peered through thick glasses. He married Mary Lamson, whom he had met in Columbus, and not long after that he joined the law practice of Judge Benjamin Tappan, one of the state's most prominent jurists.

Edwin and Mary were very much in love. In 1840 they had a baby they named Lucy Lamson Stanton. His middle twenties, Stanton later recalled, were the happiest years of his life. A journalist described him at that time as "young, ardent, and of a most joyful nature," with a keen sense of humor.[13]

But in 1841, little Lucy died. The Stantons had a healthy son after that, but early in 1844, mother Mary became ill with "bilious fever." For

The son of a doctor, Edwin M. Stanton was born in this house in Steubenville in 1814.

Appointed early in 1862, Secretary of War Stanton quickly expanded the functions of the War Department and enlarged its headquarters building.

two weeks, Edwin scarcely left Mary's bedside, but she, too, died. Shattered by grief, he still had not fully recovered from her death when a younger brother, Dr. Darwin Stanton, cut his own throat, his blood "spouting up to the ceiling."[14] Stanton's cascade of losses briefly drove him to the brink of insanity.

Stanton moved to Pittsburgh and dealt with his sorrow by diving into legal work. His hard-driving talent won him clients throughout the Ohio Valley, Pennsylvania, and the East Coast, but embittered by personal loss, his personality turned offensive. At his best, he was aloof, at his worst, "haughty, severe, domineering, and rude."[15] Always playing hardball in his legal work, he struck others as "unpleasantly intense."[16] Those he had insulted sometimes threatened him with violence. His practice grew nonetheless, for he was a prodigious worker and an excellent legal mind—but his was a lonely existence.

In 1855 Stanton was hired as one of the defense attorneys in a patent infringement suit over the mechanical reaper. He was disgusted to find that a member of his legal team was a gawky rube from Illinois named Abraham Lincoln. In the course of the legal battle in a Cincinnati court, Stanton snubbed Lincoln repeatedly, sneering at him as "a long, lank creature" and a "giraffe."[17]

However, Stanton retained enough of the social graces needed to meet, woo, and, in 1856, wed Ellen Hutchinson, daughter of a socially prominent Pittsburgh family and sixteen years his junior. The Stantons moved to

Washington where he had been finding an increasing number of clients.

Apparently Stanton had found a soul-mate in Ellen, for a few years later Lincoln Secretary John Hay described her as "a pretty wife as white and cold and motionless as marble, whose rare smiles seemed to pain her."[18] (A photograph taken around 1865 shows a woman whose tightly combed hair, direct gaze, and firm mouth suggests someone very much in control of herself.[19])

Stanton's legal abilities caught the eye of the Buchanan government. In 1858 he was hired to go to California and clean up an "Augean stable" of conflicting land claims. Stanton spent a year working it out, returned to a grateful government, and then won public attention by successfully defending Congressman Dan Sickles of New York, an incorrigible rascal charged with the murder of his wife's lover. Stanton won an acquittal for Sickles by reason of temporary insanity, the first successful use of the defense.

Although he was a Democrat, Stanton was resolutely opposed to slavery. He kept quiet during the public debate over it, but privately remarked he would have gladly defended John Brown in his trial for the raid on Harpers Ferry.

In December 1859, Stanton was brought into Buchanan's administration as attorney general. To Stanton's dismay, Buchanan was alternately stubborn and vacillating in the face of the South's secessionist threats. His Cabinet was fractured as well, a mix of Unionist, secessionist, and undecided positions. Stanton was a Democrat, but he was as strongly pro-Union and as anti-slavery as any Republican, and he was outraged by the confusion he found in the Buchanan administration.

Democrat Stanton had to decide between his pro-Union beliefs and his obligations to President Buchanan. Choosing a daring course, he began secret communications with Congress and its pro-Union element. Almost daily, Democrat Stanton sent insider information on administration doings to such Republican stalwarts as New York Sen. William H. Seward. Seward, in turn, kept President-elect Lincoln informed.

Working secretly, Stanton also headed off a treacherous effort by Secretary of War John B. Floyd to divert 124 Federal cannons to the South. All the while Stanton was doing his best to stiffen Buchanan's spine in the face of the growing threat from the South.

Stanton lost his post when Lincoln and the Republicans took over, of course, but the former attorney general was relieved that a Unionist, anti-slavery Republican had become the nation's chief executive. Soon, however, he was angrier at Lincoln than he had been at Buchanan. Lincoln, trying to hang onto border states wavering between the Union and the Confederacy, was taking a conciliatory approach toward slavery. A hard-liner by nature, Stanton considered that weak and hypocritical. Fuming, he recalled the president's Midwestern gawkiness and mocked "the imbecility of this administration."[20]

For political reasons, Lincoln had chosen a wily Pennsylvania politician named Simon Cameron to be his secretary of war. Cameron, concerned most of all with what profited Simon Cameron, turned out to be completely inept and thoroughly corrupt. After suffering this for months, in January 1862 Lincoln made Cameron minister to Russia. Overlooking past insults and rudeness, Lincoln replaced Cameron with Stanton.

Warned that the hard-headed Stanton might "run away with the whole concern," Lincoln recalled a Midwestern preacher so energetic that some parishioners wanted to put bricks in his pockets to hold him down. "I may have to do that with Stanton," Lincoln said, "but if I do, bricks in his pocket will be better than bricks in his hat. I'll risk him for a while without either."[21]

Cameron had made "a rats' nest" of the limp bureaucracy known as the War Department, a disgusted Stanton discovered on taking office. "We have had no war," he moaned. "We have not even been playing war."[22] The War Department's job was to recruit troops and keep them supplied. In his usual hard-hitting way, Stanton quickly reorganized the bureaucracy and reformed the way it did business.

Stanton dove into his work with such determination that he did not see his wife for days at a time. Democratic newspapers loyal to the Union rejoiced at his appointment. Claiming Stanton "has more of the Bonaparte in him than any other man in America," the *Cleveland Plain Dealer* boasted that the "talking and stealing may be done by Republican stump speakers and army contractors, but the fighting will be done by Democrats and the conservative masses."[23] An early observer called Stanton "the most popular man in Washington" but wondered, "will it last?"[24]

It would not, for Stanton attacked problems with a ferocious disregard for his own popularity. His abrasive personality brought a chorus of press criticism. Stanton knew how to work effectively behind the scenes, however, and, as one historian has observed, he had "a certain congenital duplicity."[25]

Stanton and General McClellan had so close a relationship at first that "Little Mac" (a fellow Democrat who had urged Stanton to take the secretary's job), assumed Stanton was his protector. McClellan didn't know Stanton was conferring with Radical Republicans troubled over the "Young

Napoleon." Worse, Stanton and the Radicals became secret allies in pressing for McClellan's removal from command.

Stanton sat in on many of the Joint Committee on the Conduct of the War's secret, unrecorded meetings. Carefully cultivated by Stanton, a balky Congress became more cooperative with the White House. Democrat Stanton even successfully pushed for the re-election of Ohio's Benjamin Wade when the Republican senator's future was in doubt.

The new secretary of war quickly enlarged his department's staff and the building to house them, took charge of the country's telegraph system, reformed government purchasing of war materials, and assumed responsibility for the nation's internal security. Corruption and favoritism in purchasing and hiring was stamped out, for if Stanton suffered from a "congenital duplicity" when it served a larger purpose, he also was a congenitally honest manager.

The productivity of the bureaucracy accelerated under the Ohioan's boundless energy and rapid-fire decision-making. Despite Lincoln's playful remark that he, Lincoln, "had no influence with this administration," the president proved perfectly capable of managing his willful secretary of war. Working closely with Lincoln, Stanton's contempt dissolved as he discovered the core of the man hidden by his rough exterior. He came to deeply respect the president's wisdom, yielding to no one but him. The two men became close friends.[26]

Stanton preferred to work standing at a high, inclined table in his plain corner office, seldom leaving before 9 or 10 p.m. at night. He ate many of his meals here. Visitors were daunted by his grim visage, icy voice, and unblinking stare through thick glasses. When provoked, Stanton would thrust his glasses up his forehead while his face became a thundercloud, and his voice trembled with passion. With his brushy appearance—sidecars of hair riding over his ears and a tangly beard tumbling down his chest—Stanton resembled an angry bear peering shortsightedly from a briar patch.

Stanton had a sense of humor that could be mordant. When a man wearing a false uniform and posing as a field officer was brought before him, Stanton called for a saber and handled it thoughtfully as the malefactor trembled. Then Stanton cut the shoulder straps and buttons from the quivering impostor's coat and sent him off, unharmed, to a military prison.[27]

Seldom noticed was how the busy secretary would personally hear appeals from wounded soldiers, widows and mothers, and handle their problems gently. He regularly opened his office to visitors, who would stand around the room while each petitioner stepped up to his table, stated his business, and got an immediate answer.[28] Stanton reserved his wrath for the dishonest, the lazy, and the incompetent.

One evening in March 1862, Lincoln decided to relieve McClellan of his duties as general in chief, so he could concentrate on leading the Army of the Potomac's Peninsula campaign. It probably was no coincidence that earlier that day Stanton had complained bitterly to Lincoln about the slow-moving McClellan. Stanton also had been taking notice of an obscure Union general in the West. When news of Grant's capture of Fort Donelson reached the War Department, Stanton led his staff in three cheers for Grant that were so loud they "shook the old walls."[29]

For some time Grant would remain a secondary, though rising, figure in the eyes of the Lincoln administration. After removing McClellan from the office, Stanton and Lincoln tried functioning as co-generals in chief, but soon realized they needed a man with military know-how in the job. Irascible, buggy-eyed Henry Halleck, who had been claiming credit for the successes of others in the West, was called east in July 1862.

The fussy, cautious Halleck, as devoid of charisma as McClellan was endowed with it, soon was competing with Stanton for the title as the most unpopular man in Washington. As a military man, he had the president's ear at first, shutting Stanton out of the innermost councils of war for a while. Faced with all the war's complexity, however, Halleck's energies flagged and by the end of August Stanton was back at Lincoln's side. Despite his general in chief title, Halleck functioned more as a bureaucrat, though a useful one, than a leader.

Even as he ran the Union logistical machine, pumping men and supplies at full throttle to the armies in the field, Stanton consulted with Lincoln about the direction of the war, with Lincoln having the last word. Sometimes referred to as Lincoln's "Mars"(the god of war), Stanton puzzled his contemporaries. George Templeton Strong, a wealthy New Yorker who helped found the United States Sanitary Commission and was a keen observer of events, thought Stanton "honest, patriotic, able, indefatigable, warm-hearted, unselfish, incorruptible."

But Strong had trouble summing up Stanton, because he also considered the secretary of war "arbitrary, capricious, tyrannical, vindictive, hateful and cruel."[30] Confronted with this description, Stanton would not have cared. What counted with Lincoln's secretary of war were results. Washington's provost marshal, William E. Doster, well acquainted with Stanton, said the secretary knew that, "no matter what he did, all would be right, if

Each Union artilleryman, like these Eastern Theater soldiers, had his assigned position and duties during battle.

he secured the verdict—suppression of the rebellion was the goal. Nothing else mattered."[31]

STONEWALL COMES TO THE SHENANDOAH VALLEY

Professor Thomas Jonathan Jackson was a peculiar man, just about everyone at the Virginia Military Institute agreed on that. The signs were there to see. Obsessed with his health, he would suddenly and violently pump an arm in the air—to create better circulation of the blood, he said. He wore clothes wrong for the season, walked with a strange stride, and sometimes forgot to eat. And he was consumed by the hard-hearted religiosity of an Old Testament God whose mercies, in Jackson's mind, would come to include the slaughter of Yankees in combat.

A six-foot-tall man with a long black beard, blade-like nose, intense pale-blue eyes, and a high-pitched voice, Jackson in the classroom was a humorless, uninspiring disciplinarian. Students called him "Tom Fool" and "the worst teacher God ever made."[32]

But he would emerge as one of the war's finest generals. Scarcely two weeks after the attack on Fort Sumter Jackson left the classroom and joined the Confederate army as a lieutenant colonel. He was promoted to brigadier general just in time for First Bull Run, where his steadiness earned him the sobriquet "Stonewall" (which, as an aggressive commander, he never was quite sure he liked). Having shown great promise, by November 1861 he was a major general in charge of Virginia's Shenandoah Valley.

A lush and beautiful breadbasket for the Confederacy, the Valley also was strategically important to the Union. Screened by mountains, it formed a natural passageway for a marauding army to threaten Washington and points north. With a small and steadily dwindling force, Jackson spent the winter of 1861–1862 trying to beat off, without much success, Federals who were nibbling away at the Valley's northern end.

Things changed in the spring when Robert E. Lee gave Jackson an assignment. Given additional troops—some brought down from their isolation on Allegheny Mountain—Jackson was ordered to keep Federal troops so busy in the Valley they couldn't leave and reinforce McClellan who was leading the Army of the Potomac up the Virginia Peninsula towards Richmond. But the Valley also was important in its own right and no one knew it better than Jackson who had been born in western Virginia. "If this valley is lost, Virginia is lost," he said.[33]

What followed was a virtuoso demonstration of how a small army could run circles around a larger one. The individual battles fought in the Shenandoah Valley between March and early June 1862 were not big ones, but together they turned Jackson into a living legend, feared in North and worshipped in the South, where Robert E. Lee had yet to take center stage.

To fight Jackson, the Union pulled in troops from several directions, including Ohioans from far western Virginia. Unfortunately, Union forces in the Valley would be led by inept generals. One was Gen. Nathaniel P. Banks, a Massachusetts politician of many parts, none of which had anything to do with leading soldiers. Banks would botch every engagement given him, saved from dismissal only by his political prominence.

Another Union commander in the Valley was John C. Frémont, the flamboyant, famous explorer whose fighting qualities made him, a modern writer has observed, "one of the North's greatest embarrassments."[34] Just plain unlucky was a third Union commander, Brig. Gen. James Shields, an Irish immigrant and politician from Minnesota who was given field command of Union forces in several battles.

Jackson's Shenandoah Valley campaign of 1862 appeared to start badly, for he suffered a tactical defeat at Kernstown on March 23. Outnumbered by a larger hard-fighting Union force drawn from both Eastern and Midwestern states, Jackson had to retreat in a hurry, losing a number of men. But he had put a scare into the nation's capital, causing Washington to weaken McClellan by taking some of his troops from the Virginia Peninsula to defend itself. Jackson's "loss" at Kernstown actually benefited the Confederates more than the Federals.

During April, all Jackson did was worry the Federals. "Alarms are sounded almost every night," wrote Thomas F. Galwey, whose 8th Ohio was one of the Midwestern regiments sent to the Valley. "Jackson is moving somewhere all the time, as lively as a flea,"[35] and as hard to catch—to mislead the Union forces on one occasion, the wily Jackson marched part of his newly reinforced command out of the Valley, then reversed course and rushed back by train.

On May 8, Jackson and Robert C. Schenck clashed near McDowell. The Federals, most of whom in this engagement were from Ohio, fought bravely and inflicted more casualties on Jackson than they took, but they were outnumbered and had to retreat.

As he was in the classroom, Jackson was a stern taskmaster, forcing his soldiers to march so fast and so far, to unexpectedly pop up here and there, that they were nicknamed "Jackson's foot cavalry."

Sgt. Oscar D. Ladley of the 75th Ohio wrote his mother and sisters about how "the movements in the valey are strange. First we drive the Rebels up and they drive us back, then we drive them up again and then fall back. I dont understand what it means."[36] Jackson, of course, understood full well that it meant he was keeping the Federals busy in the Valley and unable to support McClellan.

Thanks to his adroit maneuvering, Jackson scored more Confederate victories. Bobbing and weaving to catch the Federal forces in smaller parts, Jackson's sixteen thousand men pounced on a force of only one thousand Union soldiers at Front Royal on May 23 and killed, wounded, or captured almost all of them. On May 25, Jackson attacked Banks at Winchester, outnumbering the Federals—all from Eastern states—by two-to-one and capturing two thousand of the eight thousand Union men.

Jackson wound up his Shenandoah Valley campaign with victories at Cross Keys on June 8 and Port Republic on June 9. Federal forces in both cases were a mix of Eastern and Midwestern units, including several Ohio infantry regiments, among them the 8th Ohio cavalry. By moving in two columns,

Frémont and Shields thought they could trap Jackson, but they wound up beaten instead. "Thus ends our unfortunate attempt to catch Jackson," Sergeant Galwey dryly noted.[37]

Things quieted in the Valley while Jackson allowed his men to catch their breaths. Sergeant Ladley used the interlude to visit an elderly aunt and some cousins who "welcomed me cordially, notwithstanding they are Secesh." Although two of Ladley's cousins had been serving in the Confederate army, his aunt had been caring for a sick soldier from the 75th Ohio. Ladley and his relatives had a pleasant chat and then went back to their respective sides of the war.[38]

On June 17, Jackson was ordered to join Lee in holding back McClellan on the Peninsula. It took until June 24 for the Federals to realize Jackson had left the Shenandoah Valley. During the next two years, combat in the region receded to the war's margins, but neither the Confederacy nor the Union had finished here. In 1864, destruction and death would sweep this beautiful place again.

A Campaign Comes to Nothing

In July 1861, a shaken Washington had still been trying to sort out what had happened at Bull Run when a supremely confident George B. McClellan arrived to take command of McDowell's battered, demoralized army. McClellan wrote his wife Ellen, who had remained in Cincinnati, that "I find myself in a new & strange position here—Presdt, Cabinet, Genl Scott & all deferring to me .... I seem to have become *the* power of the land."[39]

Endowed with charisma and organizational skills, McClellan went to work reinforcing Washington's fortifications and turning his forces into a model army. Soon he was staging grand reviews of the shiny new Army of the Potomac, created by combining McDowell's old Army of Northeastern Virginia with troops originally assigned to the defense of Washington. The Young Napoleon could put on quite a show.

Dignitaries were impressed by tens of thousands of men in blue marching smartly, bayonets gleaming, as McClellan galloped back and forth directing the spectacle. By making his men feel good about themselves, McClellan redeemed them from the shame of Bull Run. Loving him for it, they called him "Little Mac."

And yet the army did not advance. It grew bigger and better, but weeks and months went by and nothing happened. By winter, McClellan's repeated announcement of "All quiet on the Potomac" had been turned into a term of derision against him. Insisting he would not move until the time was right, McClellan claimed again and again—erroneously—that he was outnumbered by the Confederates in nearby Virginia. The country fidgeted, Congress fretted, and Benjamin Wade's Committee on the Conduct of the War watched McClellan through narrowing eyes. Lincoln said that if McClellan was not going to use the army, he would like to borrow it.

By January 1862 Lincoln had run out of patience. On the 27th he issued General Order No. 1, intended to get his resting armies moving. Lincoln thought McClellan should advance on Richmond by crushing Joe Johnston's Confederates dug in at Manassas—the Bull Run approach all over again.

McClellan had a different idea. He would move his army by ship to Fort Monroe at the tip of the Virginia Peninsula, southeast of Washington. From there, he argued, he could quickly march up the Peninsula and attack Richmond, from the opposite direction, before it could be reinforced.

McClellan was acquiring a reputation for doing nothing quickly, but Lincoln—still deferring to military expertise—reluctantly agreed on condition that enough troops remain behind to protect the nation's capital. In late March, 133,000 soldiers, 44 artillery batteries, and 15,000 horses were loaded onto a fleet of steamships, sailing vessels, and barges in the ponderous beginning of McClellan's Peninsula Campaign.

What ensued was a full-dress demonstration of McClellan's delicate approach to warfare, beginning with a revelation at nearby Manassas. Catching wind of McClellan's plans, Joe Johnston abandoned his Manassas fortifications and promptly re-positioned himself to protect Richmond from a Peninsula approach. McClellan's detractors hooted when Johnston's abandoned works at Manassas yielded "Quaker guns" (tree trunks carved and painted to resemble cannons) and other signs the Confederates had had nowhere near the strength there that McClellan claimed.

By early April 1862, the Army of the Potomac—composed almost entirely of Eastern troops and no Ohio units—started trundling up the Peninsula to within seventy-five miles of Richmond. Almost immediately McClellan ran into a roadblock. Confederate Gen. John B. Magruder, another colorful character among the many in this war, had stretched a thin line of defenses across the Peninsula at Yorktown. A dandy with a penchant for playacting, Magruder then shuffled his troops back and forth to create the impression he had more men than he really did. In a situation where Grant would have attacked, McClellan froze in place, then spent more than a month arranging his artillery for a siege.

Trains carried away casualties from the fighting at Fair Oaks and Seven Pines, one of the battles in McClellan's ill-fated Peninsular Campaign of 1862.

Believing himself outnumbered, as usual, McClellan also resumed another of his hallmark behaviors: demands for reinforcements while he sat motionless. Lincoln, who had discovered that McClellan had left significantly fewer troops to defend Washington than he had promised, was not impressed. On April 9, as the president digested the news from Shiloh, he wrote McClellan, *"You must act."*[40]

Just as McClellan was about to assault the Confederate lines, Magruder scuttled away from Yorktown. McClellan had wasted a month preparing a siege that would never happen. He resumed plodding north towards Richmond, the Confederates backpedaling, until, by late May, he was within a few miles of the Confederate capital.

Suddenly, on May 31, the Confederates' Joe Johnston attacked and the Battle of Seven Pines erupted for two days. The encounter was marked by a series of costly errors by the Confederates, but wound up changing nothing for either side, except for one thing: it took Joe Johnston out of the fight, for he was wounded on the first day.

Johnston's wounding marked a turning point in the Confederacy's war effort. It brought Robert E. Lee, who had been serving, in relative obscurity, as an adjutant and military advisor to Jefferson Davis, back to command in the field. And the rest, as they say, is history.

As usual, McClellan outnumbered the Confederates, and, as usual, he continued to overestimate their strength. After procrastinating until June 25, his efforts to start moving again produced the Seven Days' Battles, in which, day by day, Lee skillfully drove the Federals away from Richmond.

On July 1, McClellan's campaign was effectively ended at Malvern Hill, the last of the battles of the Seven Days. Malvern Hill left both armies badly hurt—Lee's more so—but now the Army of the Potomac pulled back and hunkered down, the fight gone out of it. A gloom settled on Washington as it wondered where all that parade-ground brilliance had gone.

THE LONG, HOT SUMMER

In June 1862, General John Pope, an Illinoisan who commanded the Union's Army of the Mississippi, was enjoying a furlough with his family in St. Louis, when a telegram came from Secretary of War Stanton. "I would be glad to see you in Washington," it said, a communiqué from Olympus signifying something more than an invitation to tea.

Pope rushed to the nation's capital, where he found Stanton looking like "a man who had lost much sleep and was tired both in body and mind ... his manner was abrupt and his speech short and rather dictatorial."[41] The two men sat alone while the secretary of war outlined the situation.

McClellan's huge Army of the Potomac on the Virginia Peninsula was menacing Richmond while seeming to never quite get there, while three smaller Union armies—under Frémont, Banks, and McDowell—were floating around elsewhere in Virginia and not getting much done. Thanks to Stonewall Jackson's brilliant campaign in the Shenandoah Valley, the three independent armies and their hard-luck commanders had known little but defeat.

Pope, on the other hand, was the Union's newest hero. While McClellan was dithering on the Virginia Peninsula, Pope captured New Madrid, Missouri, and nearby Island Number Ten, a vital choke point on the Mississippi River. Pope had shown ingenuity and persistence in his river adventure, finishing just in time to join Halleck's elephantine advance from Shiloh to Corinth. Stanton had a request. Would Pope come east and combine the three smaller armies there, then get something going, eventually, perhaps, with McClellan?

Pope, unacquainted with the Eastern armies and their commanders, didn't like the sound of it, especially the part about McClellan, whom he didn't care for (and who reciprocated the feeling). However, duty called and Pope, a big man with an immense black beard and a thunderous voice, knew of no one who could do the job better.

With that decision, Pope began attracting bad luck the way a magnet attracts iron filings. The war, which began as a haphazard brawl between amateur soldiers with amateur leaders, was turning into a whirlwind that could elude the grasp of most men. In only a few weeks it would elude John Pope's.

As Pope left for the East, one of his Western commanders ominously remarked, "Good-bye Pope, your grave is made."[42] Pope promptly got off on the wrong foot by addressing his victory-starved Eastern soldiers condescendingly: "I have come to you from the West, where we have always seen the backs of our enemies; from an army ... whose policy has been attack and not defense." He ordered them to dismiss from their minds all thoughts "much in vogue amongst you" of defense or retreat and think instead of advancing on the enemy.[43]

That a Western roughneck could think he had anything to teach well-trained Easterners was beyond the comprehension of Pope's audience; that he stressed the Easterners' failings more than their talents was insulting. Pope even infuriated Robert E. Lee by warning Confederate civilians they would feel his iron fist for their disloyalty. To cap it off, Pope told a reporter that his headquarters would be "in the saddle," reviving an ancient military wisecrack that his headquarters were where his hindquarters ought to be.[44]

By early August, Pope had the three corps of his newly created Army of Virginia midway between Washington and Richmond, planning to sit tight until McClellan returned from the Peninsula. McClellan had been stymied by Lee, so Halleck ordered him to leave the Peninsula and head for Washington to join Pope. Halleck's order met with loud protests from the Young Napoleon, but, dragging his feet, he finally began turning his leviathan of an army northward.

Seeing McClellan's threat to Richmond removed, Lee decided to rush northward as well. With Stonewall Jackson in the vanguard, Lee intended to "suppress" (as he put it) the obnoxious Pope before he could join forces with McClellan.

Almost immediately, Lee benefited from a Union general's foolishness. One of the three corps in Pope's new Army of Virginia was commanded by Nathaniel P. Banks, the political general from Massachusetts with more courage than sense. Itching to make up for his drubbing by Jackson in the Shenandoah Valley, the impetuous Banks—against orders—launched a surprise assault on Jackson on August 9.

The attack near Cedar Mountain (about seventy-five miles northwest of Richmond) worked well enough at first, but Banks had no reserves and Jackson did. That made all the difference.

Banks' II Corps consisted mostly of Eastern troops, but one of his infantry brigades was made up of four regiments of Ohioans, including the 66th Ohio Volunteers. Recruited from Champaign, Delaware, Union, and Logan counties in the state's midsection, the 66th had joined the war only seven months earlier, but had acquitted itself well in the Shenandoah Valley.

Now, under a scorching late-afternoon sun, these hapless Buckeyes were ordered to advance on Jackson through a cornfield. Taking heavy musket fire from left, right, and center while artillery shells plunged from above, the parched Ohioans crashed through dense cornstalks, the rough leaves slapping their sweaty faces. Coming out on the field's far side, they soon realized they were outnumbered. Retreating through the corn, they dragged as many wounded as they could.

Emerging where they had started, the tired, thirsty, and hungry Ohioans encountered more gunfire. They scattered into the woods where some hid for the night. Survivors assembling the next day learned almost half their number had been killed, wounded, or captured. Some men had died of sun stroke.[45]

The 66th Ohio had taken so many casualties that not one company had enough men left to mount a color guard. Company B had been reduced to one man. Quick reinforcement by Pope saved the rest of Banks' II Corps from being vaporized, but the corps was so badly chewed up and demoralized that it had to be sent to the rear for recuperation. Pope was disgusted, with good reason: he had scarcely taken command and already one of his three corps was effectively out of service.

The Battle of Cedar Mountain yielded sad truths. One was that the war had morphed into something so huge that this fight was no more than one of the smaller bloodlettings. Cedar Mountain's 2,700 casualties on both sides weighed rather lightly in the balance. In the larger scheme of things, Cedar Mountain didn't mean much, except for another truth: something worse was about to happen.

REPRISE

With an astonishing talent for putting his foot in his mouth, John Pope began his Eastern service badly and went downhill from there. Profane, loud-mouthed, and impatient, Pope quickly alienated his soldiers and even his highest officers. A brigade commander called him "[o]ur miserable humbug

In just one of the embarrassments suffered by Gen. John Pope of Illinois, Confederates pillaged the Union supply depot at Manassas.

bag of gas" and another general remarked, "I don't care for John Pope one pinch of owl dung!"[46]

To make things worse, Pope's soldiers may have wondered if he was a "Jonah"—slang for the maladroit or luckless soldier who was forever spilling his soup or charging in the wrong direction.

The costly foul-up by Nathaniel P. Banks at Cedar Mountain, the first of Pope's misfortunes, took Bankss' corps out of action, leaving Pope with only two corps, one led by Franz Sigel, the other by Irvin McDowell. The next misfortune occurred when Confederate cavalry under Maj. Gen. Jeb Stuart made a lightning strike on Pope's headquarters. Narrowly missing Pope himself, Stuart captured his baggage train, a wad of cash, the general's dress coat, and, worst of all, valuable papers detailing Pope's plans.[47]

Pope's army was amused, not sympathetic, at their commander's losses. No one was amused when Stonewall Jackson's "foot cavalry," nimble as always, slipped around Pope and fell like locusts on his massive supply base at Manassas Junction. The Confederates had a fine time looting the Union's prodigious supply of stores and burning what they couldn't eat, drink, or carry away. Meanwhile, Pope scratched his head, wondering where Jackson had gone.

Pope's bad luck was contagious. Two Ohio and four New Jersey regiments on their way to join him stumbled into Jackson's plundering Confederates at Manassas. The startled Jerseymen fled, leaving only the badly outnumbered 11th and 12th Ohio to fight it out before they, too, retreated to the defenses of Washington.[48] The frazzled Ohioans had barely reached safety when they could hear the rumble of artillery in the distance. It was August 28, 1862, and the Second Battle of Bull Run was about to begin.

Having had a fine time at Manassas, Jackson's force withdrew to the Warrenton Pike (down which Irvin McDowell's ill-fated army had marched to its doom a year before). Befuddled when he found Jackson gone from Manassas Junction and unable to find him, Pope fired off confusing orders to his troops.

Hidden behind a nearby railroad embankment, Jackson's forces spotted one of McDowell's columns crossing in front of them and pounced. Hard fighting continued until after dark, the encounter ending in a stalemate costly to both sides. Somehow, that gave Pope the idea he had Jackson trapped and retreating. In reality, he neither understood Jackson's position nor even the location of all his own troops.[49]

Pope spent the next day, August 29, launching piecemeal, uncoordinated assaults on Jackson's position, succeeding mostly in chewing up his own forces. Meanwhile, reinforcements under Confederate Gen. James Longstreet had arrived and, under Lee's direction, were at Jackson's side ready to fight. Three times an anxious Lincoln wired Pope, "What news?"

Although he knew Longstreet had arrived, Pope still thought the Confederates were retreating. After vacillating all morning on Saturday, August 30, the Union commander launched a massive ten-thousand-man attack at 3 p.m. The Union troops attacked the railroad embankment three times and were repulsed three times, the fighting so desperate that, between attacks, Confederates scrambled from their defenses to strip ammunition from dead and wounded Federals. Some of the Confederates were reduced to lobbing rocks blindly over the embankment. Their intended victims picked up the rocks and threw them back.[50]

Pope's attack was too little, too late. It failed and then Lee replied by launching the largest single attack of the war, sending twenty-eight thousand to thirty thousand men against the Union left. Resisting the huge force was like trying to stop a steamroller. Pope's army began to crumble.

Pope's "bad luck" was no coincidence. That a general could succeed in one kind of operation—as Pope had with his methodical siege and capture of Island Number Ten and New Madrid—didn't mean he could in another, such as a fast-moving battle covering a lot of ground. Nor did a general's ability to lead a single corps of several thousand men mean he could direct an army of *several* corps with tens of thousands of men. Pope would prove both maxims. By the summer of 1862, he had reached his level of incapacity.

It didn't help that Pope's second in command at Second Bull Run was none other than Irvin McDowell, back in the neighborhood where he had been humiliated the year before. McDowell performed no better than he had before, spending much of his time ineffectually moving his troops back and forth.

Meanwhile, McClellan's army was returning from his failed Peninsula Campaign. The sullen McClellan moved so slowly that he proved of limited help to Pope. The Young Napoleon suggested to a dismayed Lincoln that

Huge numbers of men filled Union camps in the Eastern Theater, but had only limited success against Confederate forces for the first three years of the war.

Out-generaled by Confederates Lee and Jackson, Union General Pope was forced into ignominious retreat from the Second Battle of Bull Run.

an alternative to reinforcing Pope was simply "to leave Pope to get out of his scrape." To his wife, Ellen, McClellan confided he now had "a terrible task" on his hands, with "perfect imbecility to correct."[51] Little Mac was always having to cope with the "imbecility" of others.

Under Lee's huge attack, Pope's Union soldiers were pushed back steadily. The Confederates were slowed only when Pope cobbled together a defensive line that held together just long enough to let the rest of his army get off the field. At the dangerous center of this desperate, last-ditch defense was an all-Ohio brigade.

Col. Nathaniel C. McLean commanded the brigade. A Cincinnatian who lived and breathed the law, McLean not only was the son of a judge, but also was married to a judge's daughter. He had organized the 75th Ohio in January and become its first colonel. Now he commanded a force of several Ohio regiments that were battle hardened, but sadly diminished in number by sickness and combat.

As best he could, McLean hurriedly deployed his men in a line along the crest of Chinn Ridge, the 73rd and 25th Ohio on the left, Battery K of the 1st Ohio Light Artillery in the center, and the 75th and the 55th Ohio to the right. Then he began taking punishment in a desperate effort to hold back the Confederates.

General Schenck, the division commander, arrived to encourage McLean's defense, but as Schenck waved his sword, a bullet hit near his right wrist, breaking the arm. Schenck was helped to the rear. McLean's position on the ridge was a good one, but the 1,200 men of his worn-down brigade were

After Second Bull Run, the woods and fields near Manassas, Virginia, were littered with Union dead.

outnumbered. Still, for much of the afternoon they were able to fight off the attackers. Finally, the Confederates swarmed around the right flank of the 55th Ohio, a Confederate colonel yelling, "Up to the fence and give them hell!"

As the attackers poured volley after volley into the flank of the 55th, the regiment collapsed. By now, more than a third of McLean's men were casualties, and, "swearing and gesticulating," he had to lead the survivors rearward. The Ohioans' stubborn resistance, however, had bought enough time for Pope's army to escape.

In a book devoted to the second battle of Bull Run, historian John J. Hennessy wrote that no Union brigade played "a more critical role in the battle than McLean's, and no regiment more than the 55th [Ohio]"[52]

That night, Pope led his whipped army back to Washington, crossing the old Stone Bridge over Bull Run Creek, the last men across blowing up the bridge behind them. The Second Battle of Bull Run made the first look like skirmish, for the Union suffered five times as many casualties as it had in its loss the year before. Thanks to Pope's flailing defense, his own army's lack of confidence in him, and the enemy's better generalship, 22,100 of the men in blue were lost to death, wounds, or capture, while 8,350 of the Confederates were lost. Thousands of wounded overwhelmed Washington's makeshift hospitals.

Most of Pope's army eluded pursuit by escaping behind Washington's fortifications. Denied the opportunity to finish off Pope, Lee bypassed Washington and headed north. Lincoln sent Pope off to fight the Indians on the frontier. Pope left behind a maelstrom of recriminations and finger-pointing. Commanders blamed each other and Pope most of all.

Cries also arose that McDowell was a traitor, some over-wrought civilians claiming that an oddly shaped hat he wore in battle was a secret signal to the Confederates. McDowell was cleared by a military court of inquiry, but he was sidelined for the rest of the war.

Then Lincoln did something stunning. Wade's Congressional Committee on the Conduct of the War, Stanton, and even Mrs. Lincoln wanted McClellan's head for his failure on the Peninsula and his slowness in coming to Pope's aid. However, Lincoln never lacked the courage to make unpopular decisions. For all McClellan's failings, Lincoln realized his charisma and organizational skills were needed to revitalize Pope's demoralized soldiers and fold them into the Army of the Potomac. He called McClellan to the White House.

Since his recall from the Peninsula, McClellan had been wrapped in gloom, fearing removal from command. But a few days later McClellan came riding jauntily into Brig. Gen. Jacob D. Cox's camp outside Washington. He wore the yellow sash denoting high office and his face was animated as he greeted Cox.

"Well, General," he said. "I am in command again!"[53]

A Cyclone Called Mother

In 1861, a fast-moving object named Mary Ann Bickerdyke descended on the Union army, shaking things up in a way that would make her a legend. As befits a legend, many stories are told about "Mother Bickerdyke," and some of them are even true. We're not always sure which ones, but the most important thing about Mary Ann Bickerdyke is this: she was the angel of mercy to which many soldiers prayed.

Mary Ann Ball was born on a farm in Knox County, Ohio, in 1817, and in 1847 she married Robert Bickerdyke in Cincinnati. By 1861 she was a widow with two children living in Galesburg, Illinois, scratching away at small jobs to make a living. She must have wanted something more than being a servant, nurse, or laundress, however. She eagerly accepted her church's mission to take food and other supplies to the sick soldiers in the Union military base at Cairo, Illinois.[54]

The filth, lack of care, and shortage of supplies Bickerdyke found in the Cairo soldiers' hospital shocked her. Instead of resuming her life in Galesburg, she set to work cleaning the hospital, personally washing the "dirt-encrusted bodies of every patient" and replacing the hospital's pestiferous male nurses with healthy ones.[55]

Doing things her own way, she ignored the hospital's medical officials, who tried to stop her, then complained to the commanding general. Not an easy woman to resist, she talked the commander into her way of seeing things and went back to doing things the way she wanted. That set the pattern for the rest of her war.

After Grant's capture of Fort Donelson, Bickerdyke made five round trips to the place, traveling as a nurse on a hospital steamer sent to pick up the wounded. She insisted on personally touring the battlefield at midnight to make sure no soldier had been left behind. She worked in the field hospitals at Shiloh, then—at Grant's suggestion—moved on to the military hospitals in Memphis. Next, she took charge of an isolation ward for smallpox victims. Once again, she found filth and neglect. To clean the building, Mrs. Bickerdyke recruited a force of African-American men who had survived smallpox and therefore were immunized.

Bickerdyke's grateful patients called her "Mother." When she could, she fed them fresh produce and treated them with herbs. From time to time, she returned to Illinois to gather donations of food, clothing, and medical supplies. More concerned with results than protocol, she became notorious for seizing the supplies she needed without going through channels or bothering with requisitions.

In 1863 Mother Bickerdyke nursed the sick and wounded during Grant's siege of Vicksburg and joined Sherman's march to Chattanooga, where she was said to be the only woman on the front lines during the battles of Lookout Mountain and Missionary Ridge. Later, she accompanied Sherman's army on its drive to Atlanta, then did a stint of lectures for the United States Sanitary Commission, followed by nursing of Union prisoners returning from Andersonville.

Many stories, of uncertain provenance, are told of Mother Bickerdycke. To stop pesky soldiers from filching pies she'd baked for her patients, she was said to have put out pies laced with laxative. The thefts stopped. Spotting a healthy young officer wearing a shirt stolen from Sanitary Commission supplies, she supposedly threw him on the floor, sat on him, and yanked off the shirt. She was said to be capable of baking hundreds of pies or loaves of bread in a single day.

Whether true or not, stories told about her typify her spirit. She was such a take-charge person that a medical officer remarked, "We all had an impression that she held a commission from the Secretary of War, or at least from the Governor of Illinois."[56] She had no earthly commission, of course, but when a cheeky young doctor demanded to know where she got her authority, she shot back, "I have received my authority from the Lord God Almighty. Have you anything that ranks higher than that?"[57]

Major General Sherman—it was said that she addressed him as "Bill"— captured her spirit best. Asked why he let her ride roughshod over army regulations, he replied simply, "She ranks me."[58]

GAZETTE

Across the Mississippi, in March 1862, a Federal force had whipped its Confederate attackers at Pea Ridge, Arkansas. In the Atlantic and Gulf Coast Theater, meanwhile, joint army-navy operations by Union forces chewed off slivers of coastline. The greatest success in that theater was the capture of New Orleans and the mouth of the Mississippi, thanks to a daring attack by old Adm. David G. Farragut, a veteran of the War of 1812.

Beginning with the Union victory at Mill Springs, Kentucky, the Western

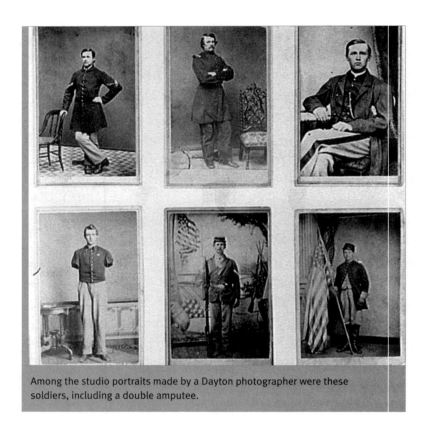
Among the studio portraits made by a Dayton photographer were these soldiers, including a double amputee.

armies had achieved success at Forts Henry and Donelson, Shiloh (with much bloodshed), and Corinth (with much caution). Elsewhere in the Western Theater, meanwhile, John Pope and his Midwestern troops had masterfully engineered the capture of New Madrid, Missouri, and Island Number Ten in March and April, opening much of the upper Mississippi to navigation. A strategic disaster for the Confederacy, Pope's achievement was a huge success for the Union at very little cost.

By early June 1862, the wartime map of the United States had changed dramatically. In western Virginia a new state was forming. West of the Appalachians, the Confederates had been pushed out of Kentucky, much of Tennessee, the northern edge of Alabama, and much of the Mississippi River Valley. Although they would see more fighting, the border states of Kentucky and Missouri were unlikely to leave the Union. Beyond the Mississippi, the far western Confederacy was close to being cut off and isolated.

It was a different picture east of the Appalachians. After the debacle at Bull Run and McClellan's failure on the Virginia Peninsula, Richmond seemed no closer to capture than it ever was. Confederates had good reason to cheer. Events in the Western Theater loomed so large, however, that a worried

Edmund Ruffin had told his diary on April 30, 1862, "I cannot now help admitting … the *possibility* of the subjugation of the southern states & the ruin of their cause."[59]

In fact, the Confederacy was caving in from the west, but nervous Northeasterners, licking their wounds, were preoccupied with capturing Richmond. Despite a year of effort, the Confederate capital was still there, rebellious, insulting, and *damned impertinent!*—right under the noses of loyal Americans. Instead of gazing longingly at Richmond, Easterners should have turned their eyes westward. Slowly but surely, help was on the way.

TO LEARN MORE:

You can meet the bearish Edwin M. Stanton, almost face to face, in Steubenville, the city of his birth. Shined up and rededicated, Lincoln's fearsome secretary of war stands rooted in front of the Jefferson County Courthouse (corner of Market and 3rd streets). After escaping Stanton's wrath, you can see one of his desks in the Jefferson County Historical Association's museum if you've made arrangements in advance (**740-283-1133**). Stanton's career is exhaustively treated in *Stanton: The Life and Times of Lincoln's Secretary of War*, by Benjamin P. Thomas and Harold M. Hyman.

For breathtaking views of the valley where so much blood was shed by Stonewall Jackson and Phil Sheridan, drive the 105-mile Skyline Drive (the speed limit is 35 miles per hour), between Front Royal and Waynesboro, Virginia, in the Shenandoah Valley National Park (**www.nps.gov/shen/** or **540-999-3500**). Descend into the Valley to visit several of its battlefields (visit **www.shendandoahatwar.org** for directions).

The battleground of Second Bull Run (or Second Manassas), where the 55th Ohio fought so bravely, can be visited at the Manassas National Battlefield Park, not far from Washington, D.C. (**www.nps.gov/mana/** or **703-361-1339**).

The story of Second Bun Run is recounted in detail in John J. Hennessy's *Return to Bull Run: the Campaign and Battle of Second Manassas*. Nina (Brown) Baker wrote *Cyclone in Calico: The Story of Mary Ann Bickerdyke*. The long, hard war of the 66th Ohio is related in detail by David T. Thackery in *A Light and Uncertain Hold: A History of the Sixty-Sixth Ohio Volunteer Infantry*.

Men did the fighting, but women provided badly needed support. The determined spirit of Union women is symbolized in this patriotic image.

8

THIS WAR IS AN AWFUL THING

Autumn 1862

The nineteenth-century American woman was a wondrous creature, prized in her femininity and defended for her fragility, so worshipped in motherhood that she seemed the jeweled bearing on which American civilization turned.

And yet ... she was so marginalized. She could not vote or hold office, expect equal justice under the law, attend most colleges, or aspire to all but a few low-paid occupations. Cherished, constrained, and corseted, women had soft power at home, but no right to a voice in public policy. Women seemed as goddesses—almost ethereal beings—while at ground level man was head of the household. It was very curious.

War changes everything, sometimes for the better. The Civil War was a chance, unrequested, for women to show they were worthy of more than they were being given. By necessity, they took over farm, factory, and office jobs left by men who had gone to war. They used their ingenuity to scrape together pennies to keep their families afloat. Alone, they put food on the table, herded cows, darned socks, comforted crying children, and shepherded teenagers through adolescence. They did all that as well as their traditional chores, and then they did more.[1]

Seizing moments between canning the harvest, balancing account books, and baking bread, women volunteered at the local soldiers' aid societies where they did still more canning, sewing, and knitting. Then, when the day should have been done, they sat by flickering lamp light to write the long letters for which their homesick soldiers pleaded.

Women of the Civil War era had it all, though not quite the way feminists today would want it. On the spectrum of human rights it didn't look as if women moved very much during the Civil War. And yet the moral weight was slowly shifting, the contrast illustrated by the spectrum's extremes. At one end was the Princess, usually a woman of means with no aspirations to authority, content with her sheltered role. At the other, the Activist, be she loud or soft-spoken, beating her fist, literally or figuratively, on the doors to power.

Sarah Wilson Rice was a Princess, the pampered daughter of a prosperous Fremont doctor, married in 1861, age nineteen, to thirty-year-old Dr. John Rice. He left so soon to join the war that they never had the wedding trip she expected. She remained in Fremont with her parents while Dr. Rice cared for sick and wounded soldiers—first in western Virginia, then with the 72nd Ohio at Shiloh and other points in the Western Theater. Meanwhile, she enjoyed a life of sleigh rides, "sociables" that included dancing with other men, weddings, and visits with friends.

Young Mrs. Rice—who called herself "Lizzie"—was a prodigious writer of letters to "My own darling husband" and they were always cheery, except for a bad patch, passed soon enough, when local gossip smeared her husband. Typically one thousand words or more long, Lizzie's letters rambled on with rare pauses for paragraphs, girlishly skipping from one topic to the next, weaving together local news and gossip, flirting, and teasing. "Have always wondered how it was, that anyone with as much sense as you have, ever took a fancy to such a giddy chatter-box as I am," she confessed.[2]

Lizzie's letters mention almost no volunteer work for the war effort and so little around the house that her first effort at baking a cake was occasion for a proud announcement ("You know that was my first attempt at anything of the kind").[3] Lizzie was a Princess.

Very different from Lizzie Rice was Dr. Mary Edwards Walker. While Mrs. Rice spent the war years visiting, dancing, and flirting, enjoying the sheltered life of a woman of privilege, Walker was forcing her way into the bloody and dangerous world of men at war. An upstate New Yorker, Walker was a rare nineteenth-century female—a medical college graduate who had established and maintained a medical practice.

When the war broke out, Dr. Walker hurried to Washington to treat the wounded from the battle of Bull Run. Sexism allowed her only to be a volunteer nurse, working in a temporary hospital set up in Washington. By December 1862—probably operating on pure nerve and some deception—

she was treating the wounded at Fredricksburg as a doctor, dressed in uniform with surgeon's sash.[4]

It was likely she had no commission, although she may have been given permission to practice by a regional commander. That ended when an army medical board pronounced her "utterly unqualified for the position of medical officer." Nonetheless, the indefatigable Dr. Walker kept showing up at battles and in military camps, acting as if she belonged there.

In 1864, the 52nd Ohio was camped in northern Georgia when, as Sgt. Nixon B. Stewart recalled, "we were shocked" to be introduced to the regiment's new assistant surgeon. It was Dr. Walker. Slender and "rather frail looking," she wore a dark blue uniform with a strip of gold lace down the side of her trousers.[5] She had been commissioned by General George H. Thomas, commander of the Army of the Cumberland and held the rank of 1st lieutenant.

Unable, perhaps, to accept the idea of a woman doctor, especially one with an assertive personality, the men of the 52nd Ohio decided they didn't like her. She turned her attention to sick Confederate civilians, passing through the picket lines every day to treat them. She was taken prisoner, accused of spying, and held by the Confederates for four months before being exchanged. After the war, she was awarded the Medal of Honor for her service. She further distinguished herself by wearing only men's clothes and becoming an advocate for women's rights.[6]

Other women left home and went off to war as well. About twenty thousand worked fulltime as nurses, cooks, and laundresses in military hospitals.[7] Several hundred are thought to have disguised themselves as soldiers and joined the men. A few served as spies.

George Sala, an English writer touring the United States during the war, wondered "whether either ancient or modern history can furnish an example of a conflict which was so much a 'woman's war' as this."[8] It would be many years before women would win the right to vote and, as of 2007, still have not been able to pass the Equal Rights Amendment to the Constitution. But Sala had sensed something; the ground was shifting under the feet of men and women, slowly but inexorably.

Most women still went quietly about their lives, accepting the state of affairs and trying to fill out the limited roles men allotted them. And yet there had been a raising of consciousness, a dawning exemplified by Lucretia Garfield, a thoughtful woman who insisted she was not a feminist. In a reflective moment she wrote, "It is horrible to be a man but *the grinding misery of being a woman between the upper and nether millstones of household cares and training children* is almost as bad. To be half civilized with some aspirations for enlightenment, and obliged to spend the largest part of the time the victim of young barbarians keeps one in a perpetual ferment!"[9]

For someone who claimed not to be a women's-rights activist, it sounded like a cry of pain.

"GIVE THE SONS OF BITCHES HELL!"

While McClellan shaped up his newly enlarged Army of the Potomac—well-provisioned, thanks to Stanton's War Department—Lee moved north, his soldiers ragged, hungry, and often barefooted. Maryland held the promise of food, clothing, and shoes, and possibly volunteers. Refreshed, Lee might crush McClellan's army and turn to threatening Harrisburg, Philadelphia, or even Washington. That could bring recognition of the Confederacy by Britain and France, who were waiting to see who would win the next battle.

Crossing into Maryland on September 4, Lee divided his forces, sending Stonewall Jackson to capture Harpers Ferry. Marylanders received Lee with a lack of enthusiasm, however, and then McClellan had a stroke of luck. A careless Confederate lost a copy of one of Lee's orders, and McClellan's men found it.

Learning what the opposing forces were up to, McClellan exulted, "If I cannot whip Bobbie Lee, I will be willing to go home."[10] As usual, however, McClellan let precious hours drift away, allowing "Bobbie Lee" to seize high ground along Antietam Creek, near Sharpsburg, and block three important passes at South Mountain, a 1,300-foot ridge nearby.

Before he could attack Lee, McClellan needed those passes to protect his flank. The result on a bright Sunday, September 14, were three simultaneous battles at high elevations. The attack at Fox's Gap was led by Brig. Gen. Jacob Cox and his "Kanawha Division." For nearly a year, the former Ohio legislator had commanded a brigade in western Virginia that grew into a division of two brigades. Named after the river valley where it operated, the division was dominated by Ohioans, tanned and muscular from months of living like mountain goats.

Cox ordered Col. Rutherford B. Hayes and his 23rd Ohio to lead the attack, hitting the Confederates at their strongest point. Yelling "Give them hell! Give the sons of bitches hell!" Hayes spurred his horse forward. Heavy fire forced his Ohioans to pause three times, but they reformed and charged again. Hayes was about to order a fourth charge when a bullet hit his left arm just above the elbow, breaking the bone and leaving a gaping hole.

Feeling faint, Hayes sank to the ground. A wounded Confederate lay nearby and the two enemies had a friendly conversation as the battle raged around them. Hayes asked the Confederate to send a message to Lucy Hayes if he died on the battlefield.[11] During a pause in the battle, however, Hayes was rescued by his men.

By noon, the Ohioans were exhausted and the Confederates were in disorder. A two-hour lull ensued while both sides caught their breaths and brought up reinforcements. Artillery kept up the fight, however, and the Confederates' canister shot

Rutherford Hayes was a Cincinnati lawyer who savored military life and rose to general.

cutting furrows in the sod "with a noise like the cutting of a melon rind," Cox remembered.[12] A Confederate counter-attack in the afternoon was repulsed with heavy losses. The fighting ended at dark when the Confederates, sensing they were outnumbered, slipped away in the night, abandoning Fox's Gap to the Federals.

Union forces captured South Mountain's two other passes as well. That success was offset by Jackson's easy capture of Harpers Ferry and 12,500 of its defenders, the largest surrender of Federal troops in the war. (Union soldiers' anger at the lack of fight shown by their commander, Dixon Miles, may have caused his being mortally wounded by "friendly fire."[13]) An Ohio battery and three infantry regiments were among those captured at Harpers Ferry. All four units were exchanged or paroled within a few months and many members rejoined the service.

Colonel Hayes had his wound dressed at a field hospital and an ambulance took him to recuperate with a Union loyalist in a nearby town. Anxious for news from the battle erupting at Antietam Creek, Hayes paid two boys a dollar each to stand by his bedroom window and gather news from passersby. After

A bridge over Antietam Creek was the scene of fierce fighting involving Ohio troops.

a few days, a worried Lucy Hayes arrived and, when she was not caring for her husband, she visited other wounded soldiers. Then Hayes was granted permission to return home on medical leave.

THE BLOODIEST DAY

Early on the morning of Wednesday, September 17, 1862, a thin line of men, armed and nervous, moved across misty Maryland farmland, peering into the patchy fog. They were all that was left of the 66th Ohio, a regiment that had departed Ohio nine months earlier with one thousand men, been decimated at Cedar Mountain, and now could count only 120 soldiers.

Moving on a broad front with the 66th were two other worn-down regiments: the 7th Ohio to the right, and the 5th Ohio to the left. Strung out still further to the left and completing the brigade was a unit bigger than all the Ohioans put together, the 800 men of the 28th Pennsylvania going into battle for the first time. The Pennsylvanians could only imagine what a battle was like, but the veteran Ohioans already knew.

Earlier that morning, while drinking their coffee and waiting for orders, members of the brigade could hear heavy firing a mile away. Maj. Gen. Joseph Hooker's I Corps was attacking Stonewall Jackson's Confederates. The Ohioans watched wounded Federals filter back through their lines, bringing word that Hooker's attack had failed. Before the men of the Union brigade had time to finish their coffee, they were ordered to head in the direction Hooker's men were coming from.

Maintaining a broad front, the brigade's Pennsylvanians disappeared into some woods as the Ohioans crossed open land. Col. Eugene Powell, a young native of Delaware, Ohio, and commander of the 66th, was riding side by side with Maj. Orrin Crane who was leading the 7th Ohio. The two men chatted quietly as they rode along searching the fog for Confederates.

Suddenly, Powell and Crane saw something startling in the mist: a brigade of soldiers poised behind a rail fence at the edge of a cornfield. Less than one hundred feet away, the men faced away from the Ohioans and seemed unaware they were approaching. For a moment, the two Union officers argued quietly. Crane thought they had come across Union soldiers; Powell was sure they were enemy and wanted to start shooting. Powell won the argument and ordered the 66th to fire.

Powell was right. The strangers were several regiments of Georgians caught by surprise and stunned by the volley from the Ohioans who fired at almost point-blank range. Adding to the carnage was the 28th Pennsylvania, which rushed up and delivered a terrific volley of its own. Colonel Powell later wrote the scene was "awful beyond description" with "dead men ... literally piled upon and across each other."[14] (By the end of this day, the 6th Georgia—which had been the closest regiment to the approaching Ohioans—would suffer ninety percent casualties.[15])

The Union soldiers accelerated their advance, knocking down fences and firing as they pursued the fleeing Georgians. "The retreat of this line of the enemy soon became a rout," Powell wrote in his after-action report. "My regiment took a number of prisoners, who were sent to the rear."[16]

After wrecking the Georgian brigade, the Ohioans and Pennsylvanians arrived across the road from a white building known as the Dunker Church. The ground nearby was carpeted with bodies both blue and gray from the earlier battle between Hooker and Stonewall Jackson. Reinforced by a second brigade and some artillery, the Ohioans and Pennsylvanians held their ground until early afternoon.

By then, however, the soldiers near the Dunker Church realized they would get no more support and were in danger of being surrounded, so they returned to Federal lines. The Ohioans and Pennsylvanians remained in reserve the rest of the day. Colonel Powell went off to the nearest field hospital. He had been hit by a bullet "along the cheek and neck," coming so close to his jugular vein that a surgeon told him "there was the thickness of thin paper between me and eternity."[17]

The experiences of Powell and his 66th Ohio occurred, geographically, at one end of the struggle between Lee and McClellan known as the Battle of Antietam. Because McClellan had not moved quickly after finding Lee's lost order, Lee was able to position his 41,000 men on high ground near the little town of Sharpsburg about 60 miles northwest of Washington. Lee's Confederates formed a four-mile line running north and south on a ridge overlooking Antietam Creek. Union forces would have to cross the creek and attack uphill.

To carry the Union's fight, McClellan's Army of the Potomac had seventy-one thousand men organized in six big army corps. McClellan's army was composed mostly of Eastern soldiers—New Yorkers and Pennsylvanians most of all—so only a handful of Midwestern units fought at Antietam. The 5th, 7th, and 66th Ohio Volunteer Infantry regiments had been positioned near the northern end of Lee's line. About a mile south, the 8th Ohio faced the center of the line. Another mile or so south, Jacob Cox's Kanawha Division was among the troops confronting the southern end of Lee's line.

The battle of Antietam had opened at 6 a.m. on Wednesday, September 17, with Hooker's attack against Stonewall Jackson at the northern end of Lee's line. His I Corps had made the first effort, the XII Corps, including the three small Ohio regiments, the second. The two attacks produced little except thirteen thousand men wounded or killed on both sides.

About mid-morning, the action shifted south to the center of Lee's line where two Union divisions—one including the 8th Ohio—were ordered to attack. Key to the defenders' position was an eroded lane known then as the Sunken Road and ever since as Bloody Lane. Awakened early "for this day's merry-making," as Sergeant Galwey of the 8th Ohio wryly called it, the men barely had time for breakfast before being ordered forward.

They arrived overlooking a cornfield, with the Dunker Church four hundred yards to their right. Along with the rest of the brigade, which was commanded by Brig. Gen. Nathan Kimball, Galwey and the 8th Ohioans vaulted fences and filed through an apple orchard until Confederate riflemen popped up from the Sunken Road and fired at them. Men around Galwey began to drop. With no reinforcements to help them, Galwey told his diary, the Ohioans "go forward on the run, heads downward as if under a pelting rain."[18] Heavy fire forced them to pause about fifty yards from the Sunken Road.

"Our men are falling by the hundreds," Galwey wrote. "Jack Sheppard, my old mess-mate, jovial companion, and a favorite with everyone, drops ... shot in a dozen places. He never even groaned! This morning he boastingly said that the bullet was not yet [made] that was to kill him!" Wounded soldiers were everywhere. Galwey saw the regiment's orderly sergeant sticking to his position, although his face is "streaming blood."[19]

Kneeling in the grass, Galwey noticed "almost every blade ... is moving" and remarked, innocently, that it must be caused by "merry crickets." A companion laughed, because the hailstorm of enemy bullets was making the grass sway. Stunned by the thunder of exploding shells, Galwey paused and looked around. He saw Lieutenant Delaney shot through the bowels. A shell took off the top of Lieutenant Lantry's head. Jim Gallagher's head was grazed and he rolled into a ditch, curled in a ball. Riding past Galwey, General Kimball muttered, "God save my poor boys."[20]

The 8th Ohio was ordered to charge again, but intense Confederate fire drove it back. Attempting its fourth or fifth attack, the Union brigade fixed bayonets and charged the Sunken Road again. "We raise a savage yell and advance on the run," Galwey wrote, and this time they reached the road, only to find it abandoned by the Confederates. The defenders had left behind "six hundred dead bodies lying within four hundred yards of bloody sand."[21]

Crossing the Sunken Road, the Federals reached the crest of the ridge formerly occupied by Lee's army. Then they saw fresh Confederate troops approaching. With only three rounds of ammunition left per man, the Union soldiers turned around and fled through heavy enemy fire, reassembling behind a barn that was being used as a hospital.

Galwey's company had gone into action that morning with thirty-two men. Only four, including Galwey, remained unharmed. The division commander, William H. French walked up to the brigade with his eyes wet with tears. He told the men that Maj. Gen. Edwin V. Sumner, the corps commander, was calling Kimball's brigade "the Gibralter Brigade"—a tribute to its steadfastness and one of the highest compliments that could be paid at the time.[22] The brigade rested as the action shifted elsewhere.

Waiting near the southern end of the battleground was Ambrose Burnside's corps, which now included Jacob Cox's Kanawha Division. Shortly after noon, Burnside tried twice to force his way across a stone bridge over Antietam Creek using the Kanawha Brigade to lead one of the thrusts. In mid-afternoon, however, the Federals discovered they could ford the creek instead and by 3 p.m. they had crossed, pushing Lee's right wing back and heading for the Potomac.

Confederate dead lie along a fence line attacked by Union forces in the Battle of Antietam.

If he reached the Potomac, Burnside could cut off Lee's retreat. The Confederates were in grave danger. But then, wearing blue uniforms taken from Harpers Ferry, enemy reinforcements commanded by A. P. Hill arrived just in time to push Burnside's men back across Antietam Creek and save Lee's army. With that, the day's fighting was over.

(Conspicuous for his gallantry during the battle was William McKinley of the 23rd Ohio. By this time, McKinley's diligence and attention to detail had won him the post of commissary sergeant. At Antietam, McKinley daringly drove his wagon through enemy fire to bring coffee and food to the fighting men. Colonel Hayes was so impressed that he recommended the young soldier for promotion to second lieutenant.[23])

On this day Union forces had suffered 12,400 casualties and the Confederates 10,500. Shiloh would stand forever as the costliest two-day battle of the Civil War, but Antietam would be recorded as the bloodiest single-day battle. The war had started with both sides believing it would be over quickly and cheaply. Wars are seldom quick and never cheap, and this one was destroying staggering numbers of lives. Sadly, men were getting used to it.

Soldiers who had been shocked by their first sight of dead and mangled bodies after a battle no longer were. Pvt. Joseph Diltz of the 66th Ohio, a farm laborer from Champaign County, wrote his father-in-law,

> *We don't mind the sight of dead men no more than if they wair dead hogs. Why thair at Antietam the rebels was laying over the field bloated up as big as a horse and as black as a negro and the boys run over them and serch their pockets as unconcerned ...I ran across a big grayback as black as the ase of spade. It startled me a little at first but I stopd to see what he had but he had bin tended too and so I past on my way rejoicing.[24]*

But the battle had frightened Diltz. "Mary," he wrote his wife, "I went in to the fight in good hart but I never want to get in another. It was offal Mary. You cant form eny idy how it was."[25]

Both sides spent the next day pulling themselves together, but Lee's army had taken a staggering number of casualties and he knew he was outnumbered. That night he slipped away, heading south. For the umpteenth time, McClellan was convinced that *he* was outnumbered, and—to Lincoln's great frustration—did not pursue the weakened Lee.

Antietam was yet another of the war's many hollow victories, in which one side or the other retained the field but failed to exploit its opportunity and let the enemy army escape to fight another day.

Like all such victories, it was wrapped in if-onlies. If only McClellan had seized the high ground before Lee did. If only McClellan had sent in reinforcements to exploit one of his breakthroughs—either the one that crossed Bloody Lane or the one that drove past Sharpsburg before encountering D.H. Hill. If only McClellan had committed to battle his many unused reserves. But once again McClellan proved incapable of risking his beautiful army in all-out warfare. Once again he showed the lack of resolve needed to both win a battle and exploit the victory.

Even hollow victories confer advantages and this had several. Lee's invasion of the North had been halted. The possibility that Britain and France would

Confederates wounded and captured at Antietam were cared for in an improvised Union field hospital.

move closer to diplomatic recognition of the Confederacy had evaporated, at least for the moment. And Lincoln could claim Antietam as the victory he needed to make a proclamation that would shape the course of history.

THE RELUCTANT COMMANDER

By fall 1862, McClellan's fate was sealed. Lincoln waited until the elections were over then sent the popular "Young Napoleon" an order, arriving November 5, that relieved him of all command. McClellan appeared to take it well, but privately mourned, "[A]las for my poor country—I know in my innermost heart she never had a truer servant. ... if we have failed it was not our fault."[26] Nothing ever was, of course, for McClellan was one of those leaders who could never admit a mistake.

Encouraged by Stanton and others, Lincoln saw things differently. Not only had McClellan failed to take Richmond or destroy Lee when he had the chance at Antietam, he was becoming politically dangerous. He was developing a cult of personality with his men and enjoying the favor of conservative Democrats who opposed Lincoln. McClellan was even treacherously encouraging newspaper attacks on Stanton. The removal of Little Mac may have come just in time. "In a few more weeks," Halleck speculated, "he would have broken down the government."[27]

McClellan was replaced by Maj. Gen. Ambrose Burnside, a Rhode Island businessman whose commanding height, bald dome, and luxuriant mutton-chop whiskers made him handsome in nineteenth-century eyes. A warm, friendly gentleman who everyone found easy to like, Burnside accepted command of the huge Army of the Potomac reluctantly. He just didn't think himself worthy of it. He would be proven right the very next month in battle at Fredricksburg, a large town on the Rappahannock half-way between Washington and Richmond.

With an army of 115,000, Burnside intended to cross the river with pontoon boats, take Fredricksburg, and then move directly south to attack the Confederate capital. The pontoons arrived late, forcing Burnside's men to watch as Lee moved, unopposed, onto high ground on the other side of the river. Burnside finally got his pontoons, but he was a stay-the-course kind of commander and wouldn't modify his battle plan to reflect the new realities. (A West Point military historian wrote, "One of Ambrose Burnside's foibles was that once committed to an idea or plan, he had difficulty changing it.")[28]

Burnside began the attack on Fredricksburg on December 11 with artillery fire against the innocent town itself. Ohioans in just one battery fired one

Rhode Islander Ambrose Burnside doubted his own abilities and proved he was right to do so by botching an attack on Lee at Fredricksburg.

thousand shells across the river, doing more harm to historic buildings than the Confederates. In the face of fire from a well-dug-in enemy, Union forces crossed the river and occupied the battered city. On the 13th, Burnside ordered attacks on the Confederates securely entrenched on the high ground each side of the town and, behind the town, in a sunken road behind a stone wall on Marye's Heights.

Burnside's huge army was composed mostly of Eastern troops, with New Yorkers and Pennsylvanians forming a majority. Five Midwestern states were represented by much smaller numbers and the 4th and 8th Ohio were the only infantry units from the Buckeye state. The Ohioans were in what was left of the "Gibralter Brigade" led by Nathan Kimball in the attack on Bloody Lane at Antietam. (The 5th and 7th Ohio had been ordered into winter quarters.) Now Kimball's brigade would lead the attack on Marye's Heights and encounter a new "bloody lane."

After spending the night in the ruined town, Kimball sent the Ohioans and a Delaware unit through Fredricksburg's outskirts as skirmishers. He advanced the rest of his brigade under "a most murderous fire" from Confederate artillery. Shells that burst directly in the Union ranks destroyed "a company at a time."[29]

Thomas Galwey and the 8th Ohio were able to reach a small brick grocery

In the turmoil of war, only a few of the dead were given a coffin and a dignified burial.

store, drag their wounded into it, and take shelter as exploding shells shattered every window and bullets whistled through the building. The Ohioans were amazed to find a woman hiding in the cellar. When wounded men began to beg for water, the soldiers forced the woman outdoors "into the pelting shower of missiles" to point out the well.[30]

Meanwhile, the 4th Ohio was struggling up Marye Heights as man after man fell to heavy fire. Pvt. William Kepler of Company C noticed "a plucky little fellow of some sixteen summers" returning from the front, swinging the stub of an arm from which his hand hung by a thread as spurting blood traced circles on the ground. He was shouting "Hurrah for the Union!" The boy sank to earth and Kepler never saw him again. Some Union soldiers got within twenty-five paces of the stone wall sheltering the Confederates in the sunken road behind it … but no further.[31]

Galwey's company spent most of the day in the brick store, firing whenever the smoke cleared to reveal a target. Out of ammunition, they returned to the riverbank to light fires and boil their coffee as darkness fell. "Every building in the town is a hospital," Galwey wrote. "Their floors are spattered with blood. Surgeons are operating everywhere; ambulances are coming and going."[32] The Ohioans were able to rest the next day, "our army … too much shattered to attempt another assault."[33]

Under pressure from his subordinates, on December 15 Burnside gave up his entire offensive and retreated across the river, his army and his reputation badly damaged. The Union forces had suffered thirteen thousand killed, wounded, or captured, the Confederates one-third as many. The 4th Ohio had lost nearly half its members, the 8th Ohio about one third.

There was more misery. When Galwey and his companions returned to the huts they had occupied for a month before the attack, they found them empty, pillaged by camp followers "leaving nothing but mere shells."[34]

If they had only known, the Ohioans could have taken grim satisfaction from one outcome of the battle. Among lives ended at Fredericksburg was that of Confederate Gen. Maxcy Gregg, the South Carolinean who had ambushed Schenck's 1st Ohio at Vienna in 1861. Gregg, an erudite South Carolina lawyer with a taste for Greek drama and astronomy, was hit by a bullet near his spine and died two days later.

CAVALIERS AND SQUIRREL HUNTERS

In the stories the South likes to tell itself, the cavalier plays a leading role, impressing men with his devil-may-care dash and skill with horses while attracting women with a courtliness spiced by the possibility that a bodice could be ripped at any moment. Shards of this cherished bravado can be found today in such varied forms as Andy Griffith, those soldiers who savor the smell of napalm in the morning, and the endlessly circling knights of NASCAR.

Kentuckian John Hunt Morgan was a cavalier who scared the daylights out of Ohio. Raised in Lexington, Morgan was a tall, handsome gentleman whose drawling courtesy concealed the restlessness of an adventurer. Early in the war he formed "Morgan's Raiders," a cavalry squadron that grew in size and ferocity—and ambition.

In July 1862 Morgan led a thousand-mile whirlwind of hit-and-run attacks on Federal camps in Kentucky. That threw Cincinnati—just across the Ohio River from Kentucky—into such a tizzy that city police and firemen, dragging a lone cannon, went south intending to head off Morgan. Instead, he captured the cannon. Morgan returned to his Tennessee base without touching Ohio.[35]

Within weeks, however, a new threat arose. Confederate Gen. Edmund Kirby Smith led a large army into Kentucky, alarming Ohio all over again. When Smith easily defeated a Federal force at Richmond, Cincinnati panicked. This time, Maj. Gen. Lew Wallace took charge of the city's defenses.[36] Martial law was declared, businesses were closed, and citizens began drilling in the streets.

On both sides of the Ohio River a "Black Brigade" of a thousand African Americans threw up fortifications, the North's first organized use of blacks in the war effort. Cincinnati and Covington, across the river, quivered with anticipation.

The Union's veteran armies were tied down elsewhere, so Ohio's military camps rushed partly trained troops to Cincinnati. Governor Tod issued an urgent call for armed civilians as well.[37] What he got were the "Squirrel Hunters," nearly sixteen thousand clerks, woodchoppers, and farmers of various sizes, shapes, and ages, wearing "all manner of garb" and lugging ancient muskets, shotguns, horse-pistols, and weapons better suited for shooting rodents.[38] Throughout Ohio, would-be warriors in overalls and waistcoats boarded trains heading for Cincinnati.

Elements of Smith's Confederates approached Union earthworks that had been thrown up at Covington, but after a bit of skirmishing, they withdrew, needed elsewhere. Suddenly, the danger to Cincinnati was over.

As the good news spread through Union lines on September 11, "John Brown's Body" arose spontaneously from thousands of throats, a chorus without a director, rising to the heavens and reverberating "from hill and valley, now dying away, now coming back with increased volume and force."[39] It was a musical cry of triumph and a reminder that the spirit of "Old Brown" still lingered in the land.

The unblooded Squirrel Hunters disappeared into the city's taverns and it was days before Cincinnatians could sweep the last of them out of town.[40] But Ohio would hear from John Hunt Morgan again.

THE BATTLE AT CORINTH

For the Confederates inhabiting it in the spring of 1862, the Mississippi town of Corinth had been a hell-hole and a death trap. Few men in gray would have regretted leaving the place after Halleck's huge Union force crept up on them in June. The town's slow-draining lowland and oily, oozy, putrid well water caused soldiers to die by the score from typhoid and chronic dysentery. At one time, eighteen thousand of Beauregard's seventy-three thousand Confederates were on the sick list.[41] Put off by what he saw of the region, Ambrose Bierce called its inhabitants "swamp-dwellers" who were forced to share the countryside with alligators.

But the Confederates wanted Corinth back.

For all its miseries, the pestiferous place was a vital rail center, the intersection of one Confederate rail line running north and south and another that ran east and west. The second line connected the Confederacy east of the Mississippi to that west of it. Losing Corinth permanently would be a serious setback to the Rebellion.

Corinth was, of course, only part of a much bigger picture for the Confederacy. For a few weeks between August and October 1862, Confederates launched a series of attacks that badly shook Union forces both east and west. The first was Lee's Maryland campaign, halted in September only at great cost at the battle of Antietam. That merely returned things in the Eastern Theater to the status quo ante. But then, in October, came two hard punches—one in Mississippi and the other in Kentucky—intended to wipe out Union successes in the Western Theater.

When Confederate forces appeared to threaten Cincinnati, nearly sixteen thousand untrained civilians from throughout Ohio, nicknamed "Squirrel Hunters," rushed to defend the city.

About 10 in the morning of a hot Saturday, October 3, twenty-two thousand Confederates under Gens. Earl ("Buck") Van Dorn and Sterling ("Pap") Price began their attack on the Federals entrenched at Corinth. Defending the railroad town were about twenty-three thousand Midwestern soldiers under Maj. Gen. William S. Rosecrans. (Old Rosy had been brought down from western Virginia the previous June to command the Army of the Mississippi.) By afternoon, the screaming Confederates, typically heedless of their losses, had overrun Union entrenchments and pushed the defending forces backwards two miles to their innermost defense line.

Certain that victory was in his grasp, Van Dorn suspended operations for the day so his exhausted troops could recover from the heat. The next morning, Van Dorn's men attacked on a broad front, centering on a fortified artillery placement called Battery Robinett.

Protecting the Union gunners on their right was the 63rd Ohio Volunteer Infantry. The 43rd Ohio defended the battery's left. Oscar L. Jackson, captain of the 63rd's Company H, watched columns of Confederates emerge from the woods, marching toward him with a firm, deliberate step. Jackson's men nervously shifted from foot to foot, pulled at their blouses, and checked their equipment as they waited for the order to fire. "In my campaigning I had never seen anything so hard to stand as that slow, steady tramp," Jackson recalled.[42]

Twice the Confederates charged, throwing themselves "against us like water against a rock," before being repulsed. They came so close a Confederate general fell dead at Jackson's feet. His Company H was moved next to a pair of cannons after the previous company guarding them was nearly annihilated.

Then one hundred Texas Rangers attacked Company H, by now reduced to twenty-four men. "The Texans began yelling like savages and rushed at us without firing," Jackson remembered. His men fired one volley and then, with bayonets fixed, counter-charged the oncoming Confederates.

Fighting between the Texans and the Ohioans turned hand-to-hand, the two sides slashing at each other with bayonets while Captain Jackson fired his pistol in the attackers' faces. His company was reduced to eleven men, but a Missouri company came to its aid, forcing the Texans to retreat. Struck by a projectile that broke a cheek bone and tore through an optic nerve, Jackson

Month after Halleck's Union army captured Corinth, Mississippi, Confederates made a desperate, failed attempt to recapture the rail junction.

walked a short distance to the rear, collapsed, and awoke two days later in a field hospital.[43]

Desperate fighting eventually forced Van Dorn's Confederates back and into a general retreat. Rosecrans waited until the next day before pursuing Van Dorn. Finally getting going,

Many Confederates fell in fierce fighting around Battery Robinett at Corinth.

Rosecrans defeated the Confederates at nearby Hatchie Bridge, but failed to wipe them out. Though unsuccessful, the Confederate siege of Corinth had exacted a heavy toll from the Union defenders.

Nearly half of the 63rd Ohio's members had become casualties, as had a fourth of the 43rd Ohio, including its commander, Col. Joseph L. Kirby Smith. Smith, who died of his wounds several days after the battle, was a West Pointer and a nephew of Confederate Maj. Gen. Edmund Kirby Smith. While Joseph L. Kirby Smith was fighting off the Confederates in Mississippi, his uncle was making trouble for Union forces in Kentucky.

"WHAT A BATTLE IS"

On a hot, dry Tuesday, October 7, streams of wagons hurriedly loaded with household goods and driven by frantic citizens rattled out of the central Kentucky market town of Perryville. On one of the wagons rode "a handsome maiden [whose] features were contorted with fright [and] whose heartrending screams" would long haunt the Union cavalryman who observed her. On another road, a fleeing Methodist minister drove his wagon out of Perryville in such a rush that he left a daughter behind. A few citizens remained hidden in the town, but by Wednesday morning Perryville was almost deserted.[44]

The area surrounding the town was about to become a battlefield. For days, two thirsty armies had been looking for each other as they trudged through a landscape scorched brown by a relentless drought. Approaching Perryville from the west was the Army of the Ohio led by Maj. Gen. Don Carlos Buell. Approaching it from the east were the Confederate armies of Gen. Braxton Bragg and Maj. Gen. Edmund Kirby Smith.

In one of the war's many strange coincidences and intersections, Buell and Bragg were brothers-in-law. When their battle was over, they would share something else—the belief by their governments that they had failed.

In late June, Bragg had replaced the impetuous Gen. Pierre Gustave Toutant Beauregard as commander of the Army of Tennessee. The new commander was a sickly, quarrelsome disciplinarian whose beard looked as if it were made out of wire and whose coal-black eyes glared out from dark thick brows. Bragg had a talent for making enemies. Twice during the Mexican War his own troops had tried to assassinate him.

In August, Bragg and Kirby Smith launched a two-pronged invasion of Kentucky, where they thought Confederate loyalists would rush to join them in claiming the state for the Confederacy. Then, Earl Van Dorn and Sterling Price—if they were victorious in Mississippi—could march north, join Bragg and Smith, and invade Ohio. Lincoln realized what was at stake. To lose Kentucky, he said, "is very nearly the same as to lose the whole game."[45]

Like his friend McClellan, Don Carlos Buell did not like to move quickly and it took repeated prodding from Washington before he finally led his Army of the Ohio out of Nashville. Reinforced by a number of green regiments rushed from Ohio and other states, Buell went looking for Bragg and Price. The Confederates had scored a string of victories since invading Kentucky, but gathered almost no recruits.

On the evening of Monday, October 6, part of Bragg's army tramped wearily into Perryville and fell asleep in and around the town. Meanwhile, Buell's army was approaching, in three columns, and in the morning elements both armies began poking at each other. Frightened by gunfire in the distance and by the ragged, hungry, and thirsty Confederate soldiers roaming the town looking for food, most of Perryville's residents fled on Tuesday; the main battle would occur the next day.

The Chaplin Hills, a region of swales and hillocks, lies just west of Perryville. It was in this place of rolling woods and farmland that the two armies would collide, the panting soldiers pursuing each other up and down ridges and through cornfields and trees in a confused, swirling, vicious struggle.

It was the largest battle fought in Kentucky. Military historians have called it a "meeting engagement," meaning it just sort of happened without much planning.[46] Thirst provided the trigger. The land had been drought-stricken for months, leaving only stagnant pools of water for thousands of parched soldiers.

Searching for water on the night of October 7–8, Philip Sheridan's division of Buell's army ran into thirsty Confederates doing the same. At 3 a.m. Sheridan's men drove the Confederates away from a creek, the opening act in the battle of Perryville.

Heavier fighting erupted at 2 p.m. the next day when Confederates attacked an inexperienced Union brigade commanded by Brig. Gen. William Terrill. Terrill's green brigade anchored the north flank of I Corps commander

Union skirmishers move forward at Perryville, where the biggest battle in Kentucky was about to be fought.

Maj. Gen. Alexander McCook, one of Ohio's family of "Fighting McCooks." Terrill's brigade included the 105th Ohio, organized only a few weeks before, and Pvt. Josiah Ayre of Company E recorded in his diary what happened that afternoon:

> *By some reason or other we could not form into proper line and after going through several maneuvers in order to do so we became mixed and confused, not knowing what our officers said or anything about it. Finally we were ordered to load and fire.*

Ayre fired two or three times until the "steadily advancing" enemy was no more than 250 feet away.

> *By this time every man seemed to be looking out for himself as we were all broken up. For my part I could not tell if we had any regiment or not. After falling back … we came to a kind of grove so getting behind the first tree I saw I gave them a few more rounds. … [A]musket or rifle ball struck me in my left leg just below the calf breaking it and passing clear through. I of course fell and that finished my fighting.*

Ayre, only twenty-one years old, died a few days later from complications from the wound.[47]

Supporting Terrill's brigade was "Parsons' Battery," an improvised artillery unit organized just weeks before and manned by infantrymen from the 105th Ohio with scarcely a week's training on the guns. The novice gunners provided slow but deadly fire at first, but fled after losing their infantry defenders. That

An artillery piece stands on the Perryville battlefield where the inexperienced men of "Parsons' battery" tried to hold back oncoming Confederates emerging from the tree line in the distance.

left Lieutenant Parsons almost alone, struggling to save one of his guns by himself. Other soldiers had to drag the feisty Parsons to safety.

Terrill's brigade was driven back in intense fighting and Terrill himself was killed, struck in the chest and side by a shell fragment.[48] Terrill had been the cadet officer Sheridan had threatened at West Point. The grudge was ended when they had met again a few days before Perryville and shook hands. Two years later Terrill's younger brother, a Confederate general, also would be killed, and the Terrill family would erect a joint headstone reading, "God alone knows which was right."[49]

A little further south on the battlefield, John Beatty, the banker from Cardington who had become colonel of the 3rd Ohio, was holding fast but paying the price. "For a time … it seemed as if all hell had broken loose," Beatty remembered. "[T]he air was filled with hissing balls; shells were exploding continually and the noise of the guns was deafening; finally the barn on the right took fire, and the flames … threw the right of the regiment into disorder; the confusion, however, was but temporary."

Then, Beatty remembered, "The boys closed up on the left, steadied themselves on the colors, and stood bravely to the work. Nearly two hundred of my five hundred men now lay dead and wounded on the little strip of ground over which we fought."[50] After the battle had subsided in the evening, division commander Gen. Lovell H. Rousseau rode up in the dark and said, "in a voice tremulous with emotion, 'Boys of the Third, you stood in that withering fire like men of iron.'"[51]

But men of iron could weep. Nineteenth-century manliness allowed for tears in times of loss or great disappointment, as Beatty recalled in his war memoir:

> *Men are already digging trenches, and in a little while the dead are gathered for interment. We have looked upon such scenes before; but then the faces were strange to us. Now they are the familiar faces of intimate personal friends, to whom we are indebted for many kindly acts. We hear convulsive sobs, see eyes swollen and streaming with tears ... as our fallen comrades are deposited in their narrow grave.*[52]

By such hard lessons Beatty's novice soldiers were learning war's truth. Before the battle, Beatty recalled, the "boys marched well and were in high spirits; the long-looked-for battle appeared really near ... [E]very eye peered eagerly through the woods to catch a glimpse of the enemy."[53] Their first battle was the end of innocence. Now, said Beatty, "they really realize what a battle is. They see it is to men what an arctic wind is to autumn leaves ...."[54]

Still further south on the battlefield, the Confederates attacked General McCook's right flank and, in McCook's own words, "badly whipped" him. Elsewhere, however, Generals Sheridan and Steedman had more success. Sheridan's division fought aggressively during the day, repelling an attack and then counterattacking, chasing the Confederates through the streets of Perryville. Toledo's James Steedman, now commanding a brigade of five regiments, rushed to reinforce other units under pressure, dramatically barking at one point, "Don't fire until you can see the whites of their eyes."[55]

Perryville was a hard-fought but confused battle. For a long time, Bragg failed to understand how large an enemy he faced. For his part, Buell lost contact with the part of his army doing the actual fighting. With headquarters only two-and-a-half miles from the battle, he didn't hear its sounds because of an atmospheric phenomenon known as an "acoustic shadow." That, together with an amazing failure to maintain communication with his forces, kept Buell and two of his three corps commanders from realizing, until late in the day, that a battle was occurring. Of the twenty-four brigades Buell had rushed to the area, only nine were engaged in heavy fighting. They took heavy losses while fifteen other brigades languished nearby.[56]

Shelves groan with books detailing, minute by minute, the decisions made

Although the Confederates withdrew from the field, Union Gen. Don Carlos Buell, an Ohioan, was relieved of duty not long after the battle of Perryville.

in the heat of every Civil War battle. Often, however, the decisions made *after* the battle count the most. At Perryville, Bragg had achieved a tactical victory over the woefully out-of-touch Buell. Nonetheless, the Confederate commander had finally gotten a fix on his opponent and decided he would soon be outnumbered. He ordered a retreat to Tennessee over the protests of his officers. The withdrawal from Kentucky infuriated Confederate soldiers and civilians alike, for they believed Bragg had had the upper hand at Perryville.

The Lincoln administration was not much happier. Acoustic shadow or not, Buell should have been in closer touch with his forces. Moreover, Perryville looked like another hollow victory, for Buell failed to aggressively pursue the retreating Bragg. It didn't help that Buell was argumentative with Washington, a martinet unpopular with his own troops, unwilling to commit to total warfare against the South, and a close friend of the underwhelming McClellan, who was on a slippery slope himself after Antietam.

In the bright moonlight the night after the battle, a soldier remembered seeing the dead: "Their faces were very pale, and the light of the moon glittered in their eyes."[57] The lanterns of parties searching for the wounded flickered among the ridges, and groans and cries mixed with the occasional gunshot of a nervous picket.

As so often happened in the Civil War, the citizenry around Perryville was left to clean up most of the mess after the armies departed in search of new killing fields. The morning following Bragg's retreat, the dead and wounded were found scattered over hundreds of acres of fields and pastures. A Union soldier crossing the battlefield found that "[f]or four miles the fields are strewn with the dead of both parties, some ... torn to pieces and some in the dying agonies of death."

With little capacity of its own for medical care—because Buell had ordered most supplies left behind—the Union army relied on Sanitary Commission volunteers and the kindness of local citizens. "Every house was a hospital, all crowded with very little to eat," one doctor recalled, while another observed that "sick and wounded were scattered about the country in houses, barns, stables, sheds, or wherever they could obtain shelter... ." Short of food and supplies themselves, local civilians cared for the sick and wounded for five months after the battle, struggling to cope with the deaths almost daily of the men they could not save.[58]

Union soldiers quickly buried their dead and marked the graves with wooden headboards, but they felt no obligation to the departed Confederates, who they accused of looting Union corpses. Henry P. Bottom, a prominent citizen, found hundreds of dead Confederates on his land and buried them himself in two large pits. A week after the battle, many other still lay in the hot sun, the smell of decay hanging in the air along with the awful sound of feral hogs feeding on the bodies until they, too, sickened and died.[59]

By experiences such as these, soldiers and civilians who had gone to war with romantic notions were learning—as John Beatty put it—"what a battle is."

"THIS WAR IS AN AWFUL THING"

In November 1862, a Fremont farmer and school teacher named Ammi Williams went on a rescue mission to Harpers Ferry in western Virginia. Angered by the poor medical care his nineteen-year-old son, Joseph, was getting in the army, Williams daringly had decided to bring his boy home to Fremont "without leave or license."

"I had an awful job getting him home," Williams wrote his brother Henry in New York the day after returning to Fremont. The young soldier was suffering from "camp dysentery," rheumatism, and a severe cough. "His bowels run every hour night and day," his father wrote. "He could not wait a minute for he had no control of himself. I was gone 9 days, & did not have one nights sleep, & I am tired out. I thought he would die on the road in spite of everything I could do, but I made out to get him home alive. ... Everything will be done for him that parental care can devise."

But parental care was not enough. Two weeks later, Williams wrote Henry, "I am grieving for my son, poor Joseph is dead. ... I can hardly write my eyes are so blinded with tears. Indeed everything was done for him that love and affection & medicine could do, but it was no avail." Joseph had died on Saturday, November 29, and been buried the next day.

Second oldest of the seven Williams children, Joseph Ammi Williams had been among the first Ohioans to respond to the call to arms after Fort Sumter. On April 24 he slipped into the army under age, several months short of his eighteenth birthday, and was mustered into Company G of the 8th Ohio. The 8th Ohio never left the state during its term as a ninety-day regiment. On June 5 Joseph was among the men who re-enlisted for three years when the regiment was reorganized.

Sent to western Virginia to guard the Baltimore and Ohio Railroad, the 8th Ohio was ravaged by typhoid fever, probably contracted at an unhealthy campground the men called "Maggotty Hollow." Joseph was among the victims.

"Follow me!" this Union flag bearer seems to telling young men who had yet to join the army.

Young Williams spent six weeks in a military hospital at Grafton, then fled the hospital for fear he would die there (a not unrealistic expectation, given the primitive condition of many army hospitals). Joseph was a walking skeleton when he returned to duty, unrecognized at first by his fellow soldiers because "he was so emaciated & looked like a ghost."

In the spring of 1862, the 8th was among the Union forces attempting to counter Stonewall Jackson's Shenandoah Campaign. By September the regiment would be in the center of the Union line at the Battle of Antietam, but Joseph was spared the bloodletting because he was ill again. For three months Joseph's military doctor "would neither give him any medicine or give him a furlough," Williams complained to brother Henry.

Once Joseph had been spirited away from the military and taken home, Williams and his wife, Nancy, did all "that love and affection & medicine could do." It became clear there was no hope. Williams had to tell his son that "he could not live & that he must look to heaven for help … [Joseph] replied, let God's will be done, for it was all right & just … ."

Williams supported the war and earlier in the year had run, successfully, for school director in Fremont on the "Union ticket." But even he was growing heartsick at the toll the war was taking. He would express to Henry the thought shared by many sorrowful families throughout the ages: "This war is an awful thing. We can never know the half of the misery it cost."[60]

GAZETTE

As 1862 faded away, gloom settled on Northerners and Southerners alike. In the East, Stonewall Jackson's fancy footwork in the Shenandoah, McClellan's failed Peninsula Campaign, and Pope's blundering at Second Bull Run had cheered the South and depressed the North. Burnside's debacle at Fredricksburg in December was the last, brutal blow of the year. Not only Northerners were depressed, however.

Lee's invasion of the North had been repelled at Antietam and he returned home with his army lacerated, his soldiers still hungry and threadbare. Inflation and shortages of just about everything were plaguing civilians in the South. And if the Union's capture of Richmond was nowhere in sight, neither was the diplomatic recognition by Britain and France that the Confederacy yearned for. East of the Appalachians, whether North or South, Christmas cheer would be hard to find in December 1862.

In Virginia, Edmund Ruffin fulminated about the North's "malignant and villainous designs" in declaring emancipation of the slaves.[61] Still, he took satisfaction in the fact that slave prices remained high nonetheless. Despite failed efforts at Antietam and Perryville, moreover, "we have at least struck terror throughout the assailable northern territory."[62]

If only Northerners could have appreciated it, the picture was brighter in the Western Theater beyond the Appalachians. Mill Springs, Forts Henry and Donelson, Shiloh, and the capture of Corinth had all been Union victories, if not always complete triumphs. Much of the Mississippi River had fallen into Union hands. The Confederates had been repelled at Corinth and Perrysburg. Kentucky had been saved for the Union, meaning its neighbors north of the Ohio River could sleep at night.

In the Trans-Mississippi Theater, a Union victory at Prairie Grove, Arkansas, had been a staggering blow to the far western Confederacy. And, by the end of 1862, Grant had begun a never-say-die campaign against Vicksburg just as Rosecrans was menacing Bragg in central Tennessee.

There were other signs. Under its intense new secretary of war, Edwin Stanton, the Union's war machine had finally shifted into high gear. Lincoln was showing a willingness to dismiss generals who weren't performing and replace them with ones who might. The big picture was this: everywhere the Confederacy was on the defensive and if victories lately had seemed to elude the Union in the East, things were different in the West.

Even among discouraged Northerners, however, a hard core of grim resolve remained, waiting to be encouraged. There was an almost unbroken record of success beyond the Appalachians that could do just that, if only the doubters would pay attention. The Confederacy would continue to fight and succeed in the East, but as its Western domain dissolved, its lifeblood, like Albert Sidney Johnston's, was draining away.

TO LEARN MORE:

The September 1862 battleground near Antietam Creek in Maryland, where so many men of the 8th Ohio were killed or wounded, is carefully preserved by the National Park Service (**www.nps.gov/anti/** or **301-432-5124**). A trove of information also can be found at "Antietam on the Web," (**http://aotw.org/**). An important but little noticed battle in the Western Theater occurred at Perryville, Kentucky, in October (**http://www.battleof Perryville.com/**). Ohioans died here, and, two months later, still more Ohioans died in Burnside's failed attack on Fredricksburg, Virginia. That battleground and several others are preserved in the Fredricksburg and Spotsylvania County Battlefield Memorial (**http://www. nps.gov/frsp/** or **540-371-1907**).

Stephen W. Sears wrote the classic *Landscape Turned Red: The Battle of Antietam*. Burnside's disaster is grippingly described by George C. Rable in *Fredricksburg! Fredricksburg!*, while Kenneth W. Noe did the same for a major western clash in *Perryville: This Grand Havoc of Battle*. A vivid—and remarkably candid—eyewitness account by an Ohio commander at Perrysville and other Western Theater battles can be found in John Beatty's *Memoirs of a Volunteer 1861-1863*.

Soldiers from Sherman's XV Corps joined others under Grant's overall command in attacking Confederate lines at Vicksburg on May 19, 1863.

9

REMEMBER ME, MY DEAR WIFE

January to July 1863

It was the custom in Washington for presidents and cabinet members
to throw open their front doors on New Year's Day and receive visitors,
and so, from 11 to 2 o'clock on January 1, 1863, President Lincoln composed
himself to greet a stream of dignitaries and ordinary citizens and give them
a confident expression, a firm handshake, and a friendly comment. It could
not have been easy, for Lincoln was anguishing over Burnside's bloody
debacle at Fredricksburg, a little more than two weeks before, and grieving for
his son, Willie, who had died on February 20. "If there is a worse place than
hell, I am in it," he remarked.[1]

Finally, the doors of the White House swung shut and Lincoln turned to
the most important task of the day. His hand swollen by hours of shaking
hands, he sat down to sign the Emancipation Proclamation, which declared
that henceforth slaves in Confederate territory were free and blacks could be
enlisted in the Union's armed forces. Concerned that later generations would
say his hand shook, Lincoln steadied himself and slowly and deliberately signed
with a sure, strong hand.

The Proclamation was a bold, risky stroke at a low point in the Union's
fortunes, but it was a turning point in the war and the nation's history. Partly,
it was driven by military strategy, because slave labor freed white men for the
Confederate army. It also expanded the war into a moral crusade, as well as
one to save the Union. That would play well in Europe, where Confederate

pretensions to aristocracy enjoyed a certain cachet but slavery did not.

The Emancipation Proclamation was pragmatism in the service of compassion. Critics then and detractors today have pointed out that did not free slaves in the Border States, but given the delicate political climate of the times, Lincoln had to practice the art of the possible. The Union couldn't afford to alienate the slave-holding Border States and voters who were not abolitionists.

Ohio fingerprints can be found on the Proclamation. Secretary of the Treasury Chase, the Cabinet's resident Radical Republican, had long pushed for it, arguing especially for black troops. He also had advised Lincoln on some of the phraseology.[2] The Confiscation Act of July 17, 1862, a conceptual ancestor of the Proclamation, had been instigated by Secretary of War Stanton who joined Chase in pressing Lincoln for both emancipation and black troops.[3]

In Ohio, supporters of the war greeted 1863 cheerlessly, although the *Ohio State Journal* in Columbus tried to put its best face on things ("The New Year Day was bright and beautiful. ... We have trouble among our people, but they are not cast down ... . Let us ... march manfully on").[4] Nonetheless, the Proclamation came with a political cost.

Lincoln's proposal for the Proclamation, announced after Antietam the previous September, had combined with military reverses to energize Democratic opposition to the war. In recent elections in Ohio, the Union party—an alliance of Republicans and War Democrats—had lost fourteen out of nineteen Congressional seats to the Democrats as well as important state offices ranging from attorney general to supreme court justice.[5]

At times like these, President Lincoln sought relief in humor. If he had known about it, the president might have smiled at some tortured but worshipful verse that appeared in the *Cleveland Herald* three weeks after the Proclamation:

> *But American history will proudly tell*
> *How Abraham Lincoln felt the swell*
> *Of humanity's heart and when time was ripe*
> *Grasped his old steel pen with a manly gripe,*
> *And signed for a nation's honor.*[6]

GIVE THEM A WHOOP AND A YELL!

On a night so cold the air seemed to crackle, the notes of "Home Sweet Home" rose into the clear sky and hung there with the stars before falling on Union

Lines on the Union left, primarily Hazen's brigade, held firm while others were falling apart at Stones River on the morning of December 31, 1862.

and Confederate soldiers alike, a final blessing before they died.

The music came from army bands playing among the cedars and rock outcroppings near the Stones River in central Tennessee. It was Tuesday night, five days after Christmas 1862, and the two shivering armies were here to greet the new year by trying to destroy each other. But first, the Union and Confederate bands, out of sight but not earshot, had joined spontaneously in playing one song together.

Sound carried far in the cold night air. Just before the closing bugle call of the day, military bands on both sides had begun to play. Ignoring each other at first, the brass bands tootled and beat out their soldiers' favorites, the notes of "John Brown's Body" from the Union side mingling with "Bonnie Blue Flag" from the Confederates.

A Confederate soldier recorded what happened next:

At every pause on our side, far away could be heard the military bands of the other. Finally one of them struck up "Home Sweet Home." As if by common consent, all other airs ceased, and the bands of both armies as far as the ear could reach, joined in the refrain.[7]

A shared moment of communion—and then the music ended. The cold, tired, and homesick soldiers, united ever so briefly, tried to go to sleep, each side knowing that in the morning it would attack the other.

Leading the Confederates was quarrelsome, quirky Braxton Bragg, still

The recreation of a wrecked artillery piece is an exhibit at the Stones River National Battlefield.

in command after his unpopular decision to retreat from Kentucky after the battle of Perryville. Bragg had taken his disappointed army into winter quarters in Murfreesboro where a railroad line, an important turnpike, and the Stones River converged. There, Confederate officers enjoyed a round of balls highlighted by the storybook wedding of John Hunt Morgan, the thirty-six-year-old cavalier, to a seventeen-year-old beauty named Mattie Ready. Bragg expected no attack before spring.

On the Union side, however, there had been a change of command. Fed up with generals who would rather maneuver than fight, the Lincoln administration yanked both Don Carlos Buell and George B. McClellan from command within two weeks of each other. In Yellow Springs, Oscar D. Ladley's mother wrote him, then in Virginia, the view from the home front: "Buel has been relieved. … his men are down on him. … they say he might have baged the whole rebel army if he had a mind too, but he would not. … he is looked upon as a traitor by a great many."[8]

That was overstating the case against Buell, who stands properly indicted, not for disloyalty, but for slowfootedness, quarrelsomeness, and a preference for "soft warfare," the gentlemanly art of winning without harming your enemy *too* much—especially the South for which Buell and McClellan shared a certain amount of sympathy. Like Grant, the Lincoln administration was coming to understand that something else was needed to win this war. We know it as "total war." It would be the price the South paid for its rebellion.

To take Buell's place, the Union called in still another Ohioan, Maj. Gen. William Rosecrans, the recent victor at Iuka and Corinth in Mississippi. Rosecrans hadn't lived up to Grant's expectations in either affair, but from where Washington sat he looked like a winner.

Soldiers in the Army of the Ohio cheered when they heard Rosecrans was replacing Buell. Buell was a fussy, cold martinet; Rosecrans listened to his enlisted men—even pandered to them, in the opinion of journalist William F. G. Shanks, who had taken an instant and excessive disliking to Old Rosy:

> *Rosecrans was not an impressive man. It was too apparent that all he did was for "effect," in the theatrical sense. He possessed very little dignity. ... He never passed a regiment without having a pleasant word for the men. He chatted freely and even jocularly with them. ... All this pleased the men ... [b]ut all this admiration died out on the first apparent failure of the idol.*[9]

Shanks was too harsh. Jollying of the men may have stemmed from a genuine affection for them and been one way Rosecrans used up some of the electricity with which he was charged. Tightly wound and fueled by a deep reservoir of nervous energy, Rosecrans set a daily pace that exhausted the members of his staff. Then they were expected to sit up much of the night listening to his ruminations on theology. (Rosecrans had converted to Catholicism years before and remained engrossed by it.)

While Bragg and his army enjoyed themselves in Murfreesborough, in Nashville Rosecrans was methodically reorganizing and refitting the demoralized, tattered Army of the Ohio. All the while, he was swatting away demands from Washington that he go after Bragg before he was good and ready. Rosecrans's troops found him friendly and obliging, but to his superiors he could be stubborn to the point of pigheadedness. "To threats of removal or the like ... I am insensible," he loftily told the general in chief, Halleck.[10] Halleck clamped his mouth shut, but kept one eye on the calendar.

Finally, on December 26, Rosecrans's army of more than forty thousand— re-christened the XIV Corps and known to history as the Army of the Cumberland—stepped out from Nashville, heading southeast. By December 30 it had halted two miles north of Murfreesboro, where Bragg's Confederates waited, torn from their rest.

Rosecrans had divided his army into three parts, each led by a career soldier. His left wing was led by Maj. Gen. Thomas L. Crittenden, the center by Maj. Gen. George H. Thomas, and the right by Maj. Gen. Alexander M. McCook, one of Ohio's "Fighting McCooks," a clan that produced an astonishing number of soldiers. "Pap" Thomas was widely respected, but the other two commanders, inherited from Buell, were not. Col. John Beatty, formerly commander of the 3rd Ohio and now one of Thomas's brigade commanders, especially regarded the jovial, "fleshy" McCook as "a chucklehead" who just might be "deficient in the upper story."[11]

Fortunately for McCook, one of his three division commanders was a bandy-legged little career soldier, the Ohio-born Philip H. Sheridan. Sheridan was emerging as one of the Union's most aggressive generals. Only thirty-one, he was said to be the youngest division commander in the Union army. In his *Personal Recollections of Distinguished Generals,* the journalist Shanks praised Sheridan as "a quick, dashing, stubborn fighter."[12] As Shanks put it, "Sheridan goes into battle not from necessity merely. The first smell of gunpowder arouses him, and he rushes to the front of the field."[13] Shanks had put his finger on Sheridan's love of a fight.

About ten thousand men, a fourth of Rosecrans' army, were Ohioans, distributed among thirty-four infantry regiments, nine artillery batteries, and three cavalry regiments. Several of his key officers were Ohioans as well.[14] Three of Thomas's brigade commanders—Beatty, Brig. Gen. James B. Steedman, and Col. Daniel McCook (a younger brother of Alexander) were from the Buckeye state. A brigade in Crittenden's left wing was commanded by that tough spit-and-polish career soldier, Col. William B. Hazen. Except for a handful of Eastern units, the rest of Rosecrans's army were Midwesterners, the largest numbers, after Ohio, coming from Illinois and Indiana.

With the two armies parked almost eyeball to eyeball, Rosecrans shouldn't have been surprised on the morning of Wednesday, December 31, but he was. Both armies had planned attacks, but Bragg moved first. Shortly after 6 a.m., as Union soldiers boiled their coffee and fried their bacon in the cold, foggy dawn, a solid wall of Confederates burst from the cedar thickets in front of McCook's lines on the Union right. Some Federals were able to fire a volley, but others fled, leaving their breakfasts for the hungry Confederates.

Near the outermost end of McCook's line were the 15th and 49th Ohio infantry regiments. With no time to even load its weapons, the 49th collapsed under the shock and scattered, nearly half its members killed, wounded, or captured. The 15th Ohio held its ground long enough to fire several volleys, allowing some other regiments to escape. Finally forced to retreat themselves, many men of the 15th became casualties as they tried to force their way through a tall picket fence blocking their escape route.

The Confederates pushed some Union regiments back two miles. James Cole of the 26th Ohio recalled, "Oh, such a sight I never want to see again. Just think … men running every way and no one knew where to go but to try to get out of danger."[15]

There were pockets of stubborn resistance along the Union's right wing. Those men of the 15th Ohio who managed to get through the picket fence rallied around the flag on the other side and made a new stand. Stationed a few hundred yards behind the initial line of battle, Joab Stafford—now a major—and his 1st Ohio braced themselves and held back three Confederate regiments for twenty minutes before retreating, the last in their area to do so.

Positioned nearer the center of the Union line, Sheridan had suspected that morning would bring an attack and he had roused his men at 4 a.m. Thus prepared, Sheridan's division held back the attackers for much of the morning, not retreating until they had exhausted their ammunition. Although McCook was seldom seen near the front lines, an excited Rosecrans seemed to be everywhere, rallying the troops, and barking orders. "This battle must be won!" Rosecrans shouted as he galloped back and forth with little regard for his own safety.

He scarcely noticed when a cannonball beheaded his chief of staff, splattering him with the man's blood.

By mid-day, the Union line, alternately fighting and retreating, had been jackknifed into an acute angle, one leg longer than the other. Here the Federals stood like a stone wall. The pivot point for the two legs was Colonel Hazen's brigade. Stationed by a wood known as the "Round Forest" (and dubbed "Hell's Half-acre" by the soldiers), Hazen formed the nucleus of a tenacious defense. Typical of the defenders was the 41st Ohio, which would lose more than a fourth of its 413 officers and men before the battle was over.[16]

Having driven the rest of the Union line as far as it would go, Bragg ordered four bludgeoning Confederate attacks on Hazen's position to no avail. As the afternoon wore on, the fighting became more sporadic and by nightfall the Confederate commander was ready to declare victory and call it a day. Expecting Rosecrans to retreat, Bragg wired Richmond that the Confederacy had scored a win.[17]

But the next day—New Year's Day—the Union army was still there. Rosecrans had decided to stay and fight. To strengthen his left, Rosecrans moved artillery and troops across the shallow Stones River to a strategic hill that Bragg had neglected to occupy. No more than light skirmishing occurred on New Year's Day, but on January 2 Bragg obstinately ordered an assault on the newly reinforced Union left, ignoring warnings from his own commanders that it would be disastrous. At first, the Confederates pushed back Union defenders, but their initial success quickly turned into chaos. The Confederates had been lured into a killing zone.

Waiting on their hill overlooking the advancing Confederates were Union artillerymen with fifty-eight cannons, protected by infantry. When the Union gunners simultaneously opened fire, the earth trembled and the din deafened the Confederates caught in a hailstorm of rifle and artillery fire. The gray-clad ranks dissolved, turned, and fled, chased by the Union soldiers.

Galloping about in the thick of the fight, sweating profusely and snapping out rapid-fire orders, Rosecrans told one of his commanders, "Go at them with a whoop and a yell!" Within forty minutes, the shocked Confederates were back where they started, completely disorganized, a third of their number dead or wounded.

With that, the battle of Stones River was over, its 23,000 casualties making it almost as costly as Shiloh. The Union suffered 13,249 of the killed, wounded, missing or captured. (If Stones River was a "victory," Grant told Lincoln later in the war, it was not one that the Union could afford very many of.) Stones River was one of the war's costliest battles for Ohioans, who accounted for a fourth of the casualties. The Battle of Stones River had been a tactical draw, but by retreating once again, Bragg turned it into yet another strategic victory for the Union. Stones River paved the way for the Union's advance through eastern Tennessee, and eventually to Atlanta and then to the sea. The capture of Fort Donelson had opened a back door to the Confederacy. With

Surrounded by the graves of Union soldiers, the Hazen Brigade Monument marks a gallant defense and is the nation's oldest intact Civil War monument.

Stones River, the Union was through the door and headed for the Southern heartland.

Two days after the battle, Colonel Beatty roamed the battlefield, finding the dead bodies of "National and Confederates, young, middle-aged, and old ... scattered over the woods and fields for miles." Someone told him that a mule "had a leg blown off on the first day's battle; next morning it was on the spot where first wounded; at night it was still there ... patiently suffering."[18] Beatty must have wondered how long it would take the beast to die.

MY PLANS ARE PERFECT

If truth is the first casualty in war, a close second is magical thinking, the substitution of wishful imagining for a thoughtful examination of the facts. In the spring of 1863, Union Maj. Gen. Joseph Hooker became enchanted with the blue-sky possibilities instead of the down-to-earth probabilities, only to run head-first into reality. It happened in an eerie place Virginians called the Wilderness.

The Wilderness was an ugly tangle of second-growth trees and brush crossed by the Orange Turnpike. Hooker's Army of the Potomac was spread over several miles, with his XI Corps, which counted a number of regiments of Ohioans among its men, anchoring his far right. As the sun sank over their right shoulders on Saturday, May 2, most of the Ohioans positioned along the road had stacked their arms and were whiling away time in the usual ways. Some were cooking supper while others played draw poker. Nearby, a regimental band was playing.

Suddenly, deer and small game came bursting out of the woods. An artillery shell flew down the road and burst over the heads of the startled soldiers. Then came bullets that "whistled like a shower of hail." The Ohioans dropped their cards, grabbed their weapons, and struggled to form a line of battle in the face of hundreds of fellow soldiers from neighboring regiments fleeing through their lines. Whether from panic or intent, some of the fugitives fired their weapons at the men who tried to stop them.[19]

The startled Midwesterners belonged to four regiments from Ohio, which, with one from Connecticut, formed a so-called "Ohio Brigade" of more than one thousand men commanded by Brig. Gen. Nathaniel C. McLean. McLean had won the respect of his men during the Shenandoah Valley Campaign of 1862, Second Bull Run, Antietam, and Fredericksburg. One of his best junior officers, 1st Lt. Oscar D. Ladley, later called him a "noble, brave, and patriotic soldier, one who was beloved by all."[20]

McLean had seen a lot of hard fighting in this war and was about to see more. McLean's Ohio Brigade, as well as a brigade of inexperienced New York and Pennsylvania short-termers, belonged to the XI Corps commanded by Oliver O. Howard, a career soldier from Maine. Howard's XI Corps dangled at the western, outermost end of a line of troops positioned along the Orange Turnpike in the Wilderness. It was a barren, forbidding landscape suitable for a nightmare.

In charge of everything on the Union side here was Maj. Gen. Hooker. After his disastrous campaign against Fredricksburg, Ambrose Burnside had been quickly replaced by Hooker, a West Pointer who had been born in Massachusetts and most recently was a Californian. Hooker's nickname was "Fighting Joe," which set the tone Washington wanted.

The forty-nine-year-old Hooker, handsome in a dissolute sort of way, was an opinionated, loud-mouthed, and hard-drinking political conniver much disliked by his fellow officers. Lincoln had been warned about Hooker's bad habits and told him so, but said he was giving him a chance anyway. Remembering that Hooker had once said that "[n]othing would go right until we had a dictator," Lincoln told him, "What I ask of you is military success, and I will risk the dictatorship."[21]

To Hooker's credit, he smartly revitalized the worn-out, demoralized Army of the Potomac he had inherited from Burnside. Then he maneuvered it across the Rappahannock River, arriving on Lee's left flank with a deftness that historians have called "brilliant."[22] No doubt Hooker would agree. Earlier, he had boasted, "I have the finest army the sun ever shone on. My plans are perfect, and when I start to carry them out, may God have mercy on General Lee, for I will have none."[23] Now he trumpeted, "our enemy must either ingloriously fly, or … give us battle on our own ground, where certain destruction awaits him."[24]

And that was where Hooker's grand campaign was doomed. To assume—even for a moment—that the talented Robert E. Lee and Stonewall Jackson would agree Hooker's plans were "perfect" was a fatal eruption of the imagination. To think that, merely faced with Hooker's army, they might "ingloriously fly" was to indulge in magical thinking.

But over-confidence was only Hooker's first mistake. His second was to think he didn't need his cavalry. He had sent almost all of it, ten thousand strong, on what would turn out to be a wild-goose chase to cut Lee's supply lines. That deprived Hooker of his eyes and ears, the cavalry scouts who could gather valuable intelligence. It deprived Lee of very little.

Stonewall Jackson's surprise attack on the Union XI Corps at Chancellorsville caused some poorly positioned troops to panic and run, while others fought bravely.

After sending off the cavalry, Hooker still had 110,000 men, twice as many as Lee. He even outnumbered Lee after sending forty thousand more men, under Maj. Gen. John Sedgwick, to attack Fredericksburg and—presumably— divert Lee's attention. Having done all that, Hooker moved his remaining seventy thousand men into a commanding position on open ground. There his advance units began skirmishing with the Confederates. Hooker had everything going for him. At this point, he could have brought his superior numbers of men and big guns to bear on Lee and crushed him.

He didn't. Disconcerted because the skirmishing meant Lee hadn't "ingloriously" fled after all, Hooker made another mistake. To the astonishment of his own commanders, he suddenly ordered his army to leave the advantageous open ground and pull back into defensive positions in the Wilderness.

Caught in thickets that limited visibility and maneuverability, Hooker's army immediately lost its advantage in men and artillery pieces. Maj. Gen. Darius N. Couch, the commander of the II Corps, listened to Hooker's lame explanation for the withdrawal and concluded, "I retired from his presence with the belief that my commander was a whipped man."[25]

Throughout the war, wounded men like these who survived an eastern battle in 1864, had to recuperate wherever they could, including outdoors under trees.

Having retreated into the Wilderness, Hooker now formed a battle line by stringing three of his corps along the Orange Turnpike, the XI Corps and its many Ohioans at the far right end. Hooker made his headquarters near the center of the line, in the home of a family named Chancellor at a crossroads called Chancellorsville, and positioned several other corps in reserve nearby.

Lee quickly figured out what Hooker was thinking and, defying conventional military wisdom, split his army into three parts. He sent a small force to keep Sedgwick occupied at Fredericksburg and positioned another in Hooker's front to hold him in place. Then he sent his largest force, under Stonewall Jackson, to circle around Hooker and fall on his poorly positioned right flank. At this, Hooker made yet another mistake. Assuming what he heard was what he wished for, he jumped to the conclusion that the reports he was receiving of Jackson's troops in motion meant Lee's army was in retreat. It was not.

The truth of the matter emerged on the evening of May 2. It was the misfortune of McLean's Ohio Brigade to be positioned on the right side of Howard's XI Corps. Just beyond McLean, the brigade of inexperienced New Yorkers and Pennsylvanians formed the very tip of Hooker's line. In soldiers' language, Howard's XI Corps was "in the air," meaning it was exposed to a flank attack.

Fourteen Ohio regiments and four artillery batteries were among Hooker's more than two hundred infantry regiments and many artillery batteries. Ohioans formed the largest single contingent of Midwesterners in Hooker's army, but there were also seventeen infantry regiments, plus some cavalry and sharpshooters from Illinois, Indiana, Michigan, and Wisconsin. The rest of Hooker's army were Easterners.

During the night of May 1–2, pickets from the XI Corps spied Jackson's troops moving nearby. Ohio officers confirmed what the pickets reported. Highly alarmed, the Ohioans tried to warn their division commander, Brig. Gen. Charles Devens, Jr., of Massachusetts.

In a repetition of Sherman's obtuseness before Shiloh, Devens told Col. John C. Lee, commander of the 55th Ohio, "You are frightened, sir," and brushed off the concerns of Col. Robert Reily of the 75th Ohio and Col. William P. Richardson of the 25th Ohio. When Hooker, in a moment of clear thinking, sent cautionary messages to General Howard advising him to strengthen his flank, Howard ignored the warnings.

All states of denial were shattered when the dreaded Stonewall Jackson attacked the exposed right side of the XI Corps, the Rebels forming a semi-circle that threatened to envelop Devens's entire division. First to receive the attack, the inexperienced New York and Pennsylvania soldiers turned and fled through McLean's Ohio brigade. The Ohio brigade kept up a steady fire until it realized it was surrounded on three sides. Then it, too, retreated, leaving more than half its men on the ground, dead or dying. A veteran of the 75th Ohio recalled that the Confederates came at the Ohioans "like an avalanche."[26]

Jackson steadily pushed the Union's XI Corps down the Orange Turnpike, collapsing the regiments like dominos, although Jackson's right wing ran into trouble for a while. There, James R. Lowe, a second lieutenant promoted from sergeant and wearing shoulder straps for the first time, commanded forty men of the 55th Ohio in a skirmish line. Toughened, perhaps, by its desperate stand at Second Bull Run, this handful of soldiers put up such a fight that two Confederate brigades, probably numbering over one thousand men, thought they were facing a larger force and delayed their advance. Lowe's tiny force bought McLean's brigade enough time to keep it from being completely enveloped.[27]

Further down the Union battle line, Sgt. J. H. Peabody of the 61st Ohio was carried along by the wave of fleeing soldiers until he emerged in an open field. There he saw a sight "I shall never forget as long as I live," a swirling mass of panicked, disorganized Union regiments. In the midst of frantic runaways was Maj. Gen. Howard swinging a revolver in his left hand and crying, "Halt! Halt! I'm ruined, I'm ruined; I'll shoot you if you don't stop; I'm ruined, I'm ruined."[28] (A Pennsylvania cavalryman saw Howard clutching an abandoned stand of colors and "pleading with his soldiers, literally weeping as he entreated the unheeding horde.")[29]

On the far western edge of the field, however, McLean's battle-hardened Ohio Brigade had taken a new stand and was making "a desperate effort" to hold back the attackers.[30] Nothing could resist the tide of frightened men, however, and soon both Howard and the Ohio Brigade were swept away.

Still further from the point of Jackson's attack and near the center of Hooker's army, men of the 4th Ohio could hear the thunder of artillery and the rattle of musketry moving in their direction. Suddenly, crowds of panicked Union men, tearing off their badges of rank as they ran, descended on them. The 4th was formed into a line in attempt to stop the runaways, but, as one veteran recalled, "some poor fellows, with eyes starting from their sockets and the expression of maniacs, rushed through our lines" in spite of threats and fixed bayonets.[31]

Jackson's Confederates collapsed the Union right for two miles until a new defensive line, cobbled together by Howard and Hooker, combined with darkness to halt attacks for the night. The Union men would have regained some confidence if they had learned that Lee lost his "right arm" that night. Stonewall Jackson, prowling in the dark, had been mistakenly fired upon by his own men and mortally wounded.

The next morning saw stronger resistance to the Confederates, for many Union soldiers had recovered their poise. But there was something they couldn't overcome, as a battalion made up of the 4th Ohio, 14th Indiana, and 7th West Virginia discovered. This force had advanced into the woods near the center of the Union position and was making steady progress in the face of bitter Confederate opposition when suddenly, without explanation, it was ordered to fall back. "[T]he boys were loth to do so, feeling sure if we only were supported we could have things our own way, as the rebels were evidently at the point of giving up in despair," William Kepler, a private in the 4th Ohio, recalled years later.[32] Why the battalion was not allowed to continue its advance had everything to do with the state of mind of Fighting Joe Hooker.

Two days earlier, Hooker had surrendered the initiative and withdrawn from a strong offensive position to the defensive one in the Wilderness. He followed that by failing to put his reserves into fighting during the next two days. Forty thousand Union soldiers, of Hooker's seventy thousand, never fired a shot at Chancellorsville. While Lee and Stuart threw everything they had at Hooker in his defensive crouch, Fighting Joe steadily retreated, abandoning his headquarters at Chancellorsville. Then, while Lee was temporarily diverted, he pulled back Kepler's battalion and the rest of his forces, leading the demoralized Army of the Potomac back across the Rappahannock under the cover of darkness.

By his almost uncanny ability to plumb his opponent's state of mind and by daring to divide his forces in the face of a larger foe, Lee had won his most brilliant victory. Hooker's performance at Chancellorsville also stands as the most inglorious performance by a Union general in a major battle. He had lost his nerve when Lee didn't "ingloriously fly" as expected. General Couch recalled, "Hooker became very despondent. I think that his being outgeneraled by Lee had a good deal to do with his depression."[33] A possible contributing factor was a concussion Hooker may have suffered when a shell exploded nearby.

On May 6, Oscar D. Ladley, the dry goods clerk from Yellow Springs serving in the 75th Ohio, wrote his family, "We have through the ignorance of our generals suffered a complete surprise and was compelled to fall back. ... I don't know who to blame, whether Hooker, Howard, Devens, or who, but whosoever fault it was they have brought disgrace to our corps."[34]

Indeed they had. Because of the panic of its New York and Pennsylvania regiments, caught off guard thanks to Generals Devens, Howard, and Hooker, the XI Corps caught much of the blame for the Chancellorsville disaster. The press derided it for a cowardly stampede in the face of Jackson's attack. Fellow soldiers sneered at it long after the battle and even after the war.

For the Ohioans, who had generally fought well and suffered heavy losses, the scorn must have been especially hard to bear. More than 1,100 of them had been killed, wounded, or were missing after the battle, about 10 percent of all Union casualties. Hit hard by Stonewall Jackson, McLean's Ohio Brigade had suffered half the Ohio casualties. Col. Robert Reily, commander of the 75th Ohio was killed and all three of the Ohio Brigade's other regimental commanders had been wounded. All had tried to warn Devens and been rebuffed.

If Ladley wasn't sure who to fault for the debacle at Chancellorsville, others knew where the blame lay. Lt. E. C. Culp of the 25th Ohio said it lay in the "unpardonable stupidity of two general officers, a division and [a] corps commander [Devens and Howard]."[35] Most of all, of course, it lay with Hooker. Two months later, Fighting Joe was replaced as commander of the

Army of the Potomac, the Union's latest braggart to fail.

More than forty years after the battle, Hartwell Osborn of the 55th Ohio recalled a memory that epitomized Chancellorsville for him:

> I heard a peculiar noise close at hand, somewhat resembling the sound of a smart slap on the face with an open hand … and turning toward it I saw, almost within the touch of my extended arm, an infantryman of splendid physique, still standing erect as a soldier at attention, with a hole squarely through the centre of his forehead as large as a silver half-dollar. He was dead, of course, and must have fallen almost immediately, but not before my gaze left him, and in my mental vision he stands there yet, and ever will … a monument to the wretched mismanagement that sent him to his death.[36]

THIS WILL ALL COME OUT RIGHT

Julia Dent Grant was not only her husband's strongest defender against criticism, but also his closest personal counselor, and now and then she extended her franchise to include military strategy. From February to April 1863, Grant had been occupied with schemes to get at the Confederate fortress at Vicksburg, on the Mississippi, by digging canals or forcing river boats through swamps and bayous. Impatient with all this, Julia told her husband, "Do stop digging at this old canal. Mass your troops in a solid phalanx at a point north of the fortress, rush upon it, and they will be obliged to surrender."

A smiling Grant told Julia not to worry. "I will not use the canal. I never expected to, but started it to give the army occupation and amuse the country until the waters [from winter's floods] should subside sufficiently to give me a foothold and then, Mrs. Grant, I will move upon Vicksburg and will take it, too. This will all come out right in good time."[37]

But the country was not "amused." Lincoln was being bombarded with warnings that Grant was "frittering away time and strength to no purpose."[38] Murat Halstead called Grant "a jackass in the original package. He is a poor drunken imbecile."[39] Grant's reputation also was suffering from an ill-conceived order barring Jewish traders from his department. It had brought down a firestorm of criticism.

"I think Grant has hardly a friend left, except myself," Lincoln said. "What I want, and what the people want, is generals who will fight battles and win victories. Grant has done this and I propose to stand by him"[40] The order against Jewish traders was quickly rescinded by a chastened Grant and in April he launched yet another offensive against Vicksburg, one that would, as he had promised, "come out right." It would be the Union's greatest triumph yet and this time the word "brilliant," recently conferred on Lee for Chancellorsville, would now belong to Grant.

Though somewhat fanciful, this lithograph captures something of the unrestrained fury of a Union attack on Confederate lines at Vicksburg.

Vicksburg was the Confederacy's last great stronghold on the Mississippi River and a link to the Confederacy west of the river. It stood on high bluffs on the east side of the river and Confederates called it the Gibraltar of the Mississippi.

The Union navy, which controlled the river north and south of Vicksburg, had tried shelling the city with no success. No one could imagine infantrymen scrambling up those bluffs, either.

For the Union to capture this place would be to command the nation's main water highway in its entirety and split the Confederacy in the process. Lincoln declared, "See what a lot of land these fellows hold, of which Vicksburg is the key! The war can never be brought to a close until that key is in our pocket."[41]

Grant stopped digging his canal in March. On April 11 Gen. John C. Pemberton, in command at Vicksburg, notified Gen. Joseph Johnston, the Confederacy's commander in the West, that "Grant's forces are being withdrawn to Memphis." On April 16 the *Vicksburg Whig* boasted that "there is no danger here." That evening, Confederate officers and Vicksburg's elite celebrated with a festive ball. Suddenly, loud explosions rocked the hall as Vicksburg's batteries opened up on eight Union gunboats and three transports moving down the river.

Grant hadn't given up at all. He simply had a new plan and was moving his supplies to a new staging area south of the city. As the gunboats and Confederate batteries exchanged fire to little effect, Grant and his family sat on his headquarters boat, anchored just out of range, and viewed the fireworks. Holding Julia's hand, Grant sat quietly smoking, with twelve-year-old son, Fred, seated next to him and ten-year-old Ulysses Jr. in the lap of a staff officer.[42]

A few nights later, a second Union water convoy slipped by Vicksburg. With that accomplished, Grant marched his army to a point on the Mississippi's opposite bank south of Vicksburg, and there the Union fleet ferried the army back across the river unopposed. Instead of immediately turning north to Vicksburg itself, however, Grant first attacked Confederate support forces at other points, among them Jackson, capital of Mississippi, and Champion's Hill, a knoll guarding roads to Vicksburg from the east. He succeeded at every turn.

In only seventeen days Grant marched 180 miles, won five battles, inflicted 7,200 casualties, captured many pieces of artillery, and cooped up Pemberton in Vicksburg, cutting off his supply lines while he, Grant, opened up his own.[43] Grant was looking better every day to Washington, thanks partly to Assistant Secretary of War Charles A. Dana, whom Stanton had planted as a spy in Grant's camp. Acting as Stanton's eyes and ears, Dana was thoroughly taken with Grant's modesty and determination. Dana became a useful interlocutor between Stanton and the general.

Grant's soldiers were taken with him, too, liking and respecting but not worshipping him the way Eastern armies had McClellan. The quiet, plain-spoken Grant with his slouch hat, ever-present cigar, ordinary soldier's blouse, and old pants stuffed in muddy boots had none of the bluster or loftiness of other generals.

The men viewed him as "a friendly partner" and instead of cheering him when he passed would greet him like a neighbor: 'Good morning, General' or 'Pleasant day, General.'[44] There was something very Western about that.

Having largely disposed of forces that could come to Vicksburg's assistance, by May 19 Grant moved onto Vicksburg's doorstep. His Army of the Tennessee, which would eventually number seventy-one thousand here, was divided into five corps, two of them commanded by Ohioans William Tecumseh Sherman and James B. McPherson. Ohio also had supplied Grant's army with thirteen batteries of artillery, twelve companies of cavalry, and thirty regiments of infantry.

Of the rest of Grant's forces, all but a few came from the Western Theater, the largest number from Illinois and Indiana.

Vicksburg was a tough nut to crack. Confederate engineers had surrounded the city with a nine-mile semi-circle of defensive lines that included nine forts connected by rifle pits and a ditch fifteen feet wide and ten feet deep. More than thirty thousand soldiers well supplied with ammunition and artillery secured these defenses.

Grant tried two frontal assaults on Confederate defenses, one on May 19th and another on the 22nd. Col. Marcus Spiegel and his 120th Ohio led a Union column and what they faced, he wrote his wife, was "perfectly terrific awful; I never saw shot, shell, crape [grapeshot] and Bullets fly thicker in my life."[45]

Here and there, attackers gained a parapet and the 48th Ohio briefly planted its colors on one of the forts. But the attackers were soon driven back. Trapped in a road cut, men of the 20th Ohio spent hours pressing their backs against the earth, bullets whistling by their knees, as they waited for dark to cover their retreat. Grant's two attacks had cost four thousand casualties and gained little ground. Union dead lay where they fell, out of reach in the no-man's-land between the lines. Some of the bodies, untouched for up to nine days, swelled and burst in the heat. A severely wounded young lieutenant lay in the hot sun for three days, untended, lacking water and food, until death mercifully took him.[46]

Undaunted, Grant decided to wear down and starve out Pemberton by laying siege to Vicksburg. Richard W. Burt, a grocer from Newark and first lieutenant in the 76th Ohio, wrote home, "We can't get in yet … and they can't get out, for we have them entirely surrounded. ... [W]e have plentiful supplies, and can stay on these heights as long as Gen. Grant thinks best. The Rebels may have three days, three weeks, or it may be three months rations but they can't last always."[47]

The siege went on for six weeks, the ten square miles within Vicksburg's defenses a living hell of privation and danger. The rolling terrain of Union territory surrounding Vicksburg became a moonscape, denuded of trees and grass, pitted with shell craters, crevassed by zigzag trenches, and littered with the trash of thousands of men blown about by hot winds. From a distance, the horizon shimmered in the heat, seeming to undulate with thousands of ants that were actually soldiers. Under the blazing sun, men used their rubber sleeping mats to make shelters propped up with sticks. Embankments were riddled with sleeping holes the men had dug, "very much like graves with one end out," as one occupant put it.[48]

The terrain trembled with activity. Twice, soldiers who had been miners tunneled under Confederate forts to detonate huge amounts of gunpowder. Numbers of Confederates were killed, but the defenses were not breached. Protected by rolling cylinders of wood or wicker called "saprollers," some Union men kept busy digging trenches to get nearer to Confederate defenses.

Called "sharpshooters" during the Civil War, snipers like these in the Eastern Theater plied their trade with deadly effect. They "are constantly popping away," a soldier at Vicksburg wrote.

Sometimes they got so close that the soldiers could toss improvised hand grenades over the parapets. On one occasion, the busy diggers glanced up to see Confederates grinning down at them. A truce was hastily arranged until everyone could realign themselves.[49]

A member of the 20th Ohio built a wooden mortar, which could be used with a small charge of powder, to lift a bombshell over a Confederate parapet.[50] Some missiles were more annoying than deadly. "The rebs threw their whiskey bottles out of [their] fort on our men and our men threw it back. They are that clost to one another," Andrew Altman wrote.[51]

Snipers made life miserable for men on both sides. "The sharpshooters are constantly popping away, it sounds like shingling a house. First one pops and then another," wrote Isaac Jackson, an apprentice tinsmith from Harrison and a member of the 83rd Ohio.[52] He claimed that the "Rebels dare not poke their heads up to shoot so they hold up their guns and pull their triggers. Sometimes they get their hands shot off." [53]

A 20th Ohioan known to have a good eye was given a "Henry rifle," a repeating rifle favored by sharpshooters, and detached from regular duty to do what damage he could. He kept busy, but one day the dejected soldier reported, "Colonel, I aint had no luck today. I haint killed a feller."[54]

Sharpshooting went both ways, of course. A lieutenant of the 76th Ohio peered through a small opening to see the effect of an artillery shell.

A Confederate bullet hit him in the mouth and passed out the back of his neck. He died within twenty minutes.

A typical day's shelling by Union artillery might start at 4 a.m. and continue for six hours. In one such episode, seventy shells were seen to burst in one Confederate fort alone. A Union mortar fleet on the river provided "a magnificent spectacle at night," a private in the 76th Ohio remembered. "The fuses of the bombs could be clearly seen as they made their graceful curve through the sky—sometimes three or four in the air at once like flying stars; the detonation as they exploded in and over the city shaking the very hills."[55]

The Confederates were able to smuggle messages in and out Vicksburg, but food and medicine could not reach the city. Sickness, wounds, and hunger incapacitated half the defenders. So much Union artillery fire smashed into the city that civilians took to living in dirt caves dug out of hillsides, sometimes dying anyway when Union shells collapsed their burrows. The city's newspaper had to be printed on the reverse side of wallpaper. Mules had to be slaughtered and rats caught for food.

Early on, Gen. Joe Johnston had advised Pemberton to abandon Vicksburg, but Pemberton refused. In turn, repeated pleas from Pemberton to Johnston, only a few miles away, to come to the aid of Vicksburg were ignored. Most of Johnston's soldiers were raw recruits poorly supplied and equipped, and in no condition to take on Grant. On June 15, Johnston told Richmond that Vicksburg could not be saved, but on July 1 he attempted an attack nonetheless, which Sherman easily rebuffed.

Union soldiers were well supplied, but it was no picnic on the siege lines. A soldier in the 20th Ohio noted that by June 7 the men had spent a month and a half in mud and dust with no chance to bathe and no change of underclothing. "Our bodily condition can be imagined," he said. "The 'greybacks' [lice] swarmed and were no disgrace to us as it was simply impossible to get rid of these."[56]

Finally, even the stubborn Pemberton realized Vicksburg could hold out no longer. His starving troops were on the verge of mutiny. After a

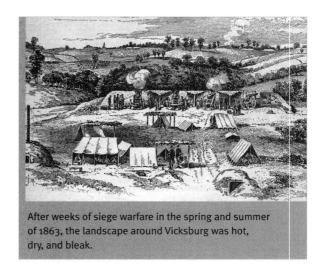

After weeks of siege warfare in the spring and summer of 1863, the landscape around Vicksburg was hot, dry, and bleak.

day of negotiations, Pemberton surrendered on July 4. Rather than burden the North with a huge number of prisoners, Grant paroled Pemberton's army, meaning its members could not return to combat until exchanged for Union parolees or captives. He expected, correctly, that many parolees would simply melt away as they were marched away from Vicksburg. Beginning at 10 a.m. on July 4, the Confederates marched out with their colors flying and bands playing, and stacked their arms as Union soldiers watched quietly. (In an illustration of the tribalism of Southerners at the time, Pemberton had never been completely trusted because he had been born in the North. After the fall of Vicksburg, he was unjustly suspected of treason.)

At 11 a.m., Union Gen. "Black Jack" Logan's division (among whose regiments were the 20th, 32nd, 68th, and 78th Ohio Infantry and the 3rd battery of the Ohio Light Artillery) was sent into the city to take possession. Shocked by the gaunt look of the citizens, the Union men began handing out their own rations. Isaac Jackson said the Confederate soldiers were "a hard looking set … nearly starved. I was talking with one who had been eating mule meat for four days & but one biscuit per day for over a week." He met some children who had been living in a cave and eating "mule meat, and peas & corn bread."[57]

Jackson was stunned by the damage Union shelling had done to the city. Civilians had not been targeted deliberately, but the notoriously inaccurate artillery made precision impossible. Vicksburg "was a desolate looking place," he wrote his brother and sister. "I did not notice a house but that was shot through." Shells had gouged six-foot holes in the ground; artillery had punched holes in houses and exploded inside, shattering walls, ceilings, and floors.[58]

Outside the city, Union and Confederate enlisted men mingled easily, talking and joking. Isaac Jackson later wrote, "I never spent a happier fourth than the one I spent in the noted city of Vicksburg."[59]

A few days later, a subsidiary Confederate base at Port Hudson, Louisiana, unable to stand by itself, surrendered. The Mississippi River, the vital river highway of the western United States, had been cleared of Confederates. After the first Northern vessel sailed unhindered down the river, Lincoln exulted, "The Father of the Waters again goes unvexed to the sea."[60]

Within a few days, the president wrote Grant this way: "My Dear General: I do not remember that you and I ever met personally. I write this now as a grateful acknowledgement for the almost inestimable service you have done the country."[61] As welcome as Lincoln's message was, the general probably would have enjoyed even more what Marcus Spiegel wrote his wife: "Grant is the greatest Chieftain of the Age; the boys worship him."[62]

Northerners who actively opposed the war and appeared to sympathize with the Confederacy were called "Copperheads" and caricatured with pens dipped in acid.

VALLANDIGHAM AND THE COPPERHEADS

There were those who observed that Ohio Congressman Clement Laird Vallandigham had a very large mouth, by which they meant the aperture through which he spoke, but there were many others who meant that Congressman Vallandigham had far too much to say, that he said it much too loudly, and that *whatever* he had to say was not only wrong but traitorous.

But no matter how they derided the Congressman from the Dayton area, what his critics feared—with justification—was that Vallandigham dared to say what many people believed but could not say themselves. And that, in his critics' opinion, made him very dangerous, a subverter of the Union's war effort. As the gloomy days of winter 1862–63 turned into uncertain days of spring, the thought arose in certain minds that something had to be done about this man.

Born in Lisbon, Ohio in 1820, Vallandigham became a lawyer, was twice elected to the Ohio legislature, and from 1847–1849 edited the *Dayton Empire,* a weekly Democratic newspaper. Of average height but strongly built, he had a dark complexion topped by a fine head of "dark, glossy hair."

In 1858, Val, as his friends called him, was elected to Congress as a Democrat and, according to a New York reporter, soon rose to prominence as one who was "quick, ruthless, sagacious and never inclined to hesitate where any prospect of advantage is held out." His chief fault, the reporter wrote, was "a great egotism of manner, and a long monotony of loud and vigorous language. He is too fond of mistaking himself for the whole Western Democracy."[63]

No one doubted Vallandigham's sincerity. He was a traditional conservative Democrat of that time, a believer in states rights and a strong defender of Western sectionalism against the supposed plots of New England's moneyed industrialists. He harassed the North's war effort by hectoring Lincoln and the Republicans while playing the obstructionist in Congress.

Because of its potential to split the Union, abolitionism especially infuriated Vallandigham. For that, he had strong support from immigrant Irish and Germans as well as white Southerners who had moved north and were nicknamed "Butternuts." These small farmers and humble mechanics were suffering from the wartime loss of Southern markets and they feared freed blacks would compete with them for jobs.

By giving voice to Negrophobia and those who regarded the war as a misguided effort that was likely to fail, Vallandigham emerged as the western leader of opposition to Lincoln, the Republicans, and the war. That made him the most prominent member of the Copperheads, the derogatory term applied to Northern opponents of the war. The term may have originated more innocently, but many took it to mean the qualities of a snake.

Vallandigham was a nettlesome critic of Lincoln and the war, but in fact he was loyal to the North and thought the South was wrong to secede. However, he favored a negotiated peace, rather than military victory. Doing so put him in the unfortunate company of those loyal citizens who, in time of war, are often labeled traitors for disagreeing with their government.

To remove Vallandigham from the stage in the fall 1862 elections, the Republicans fielded a war hero, Robert C. Schenck, the political general who had been seriously wounded at Second Bull Run in August. The ugly wound healed but Schenck never recovered full use of one hand. Until then, Schenck had rejected urgings that he put an end to the troublesome Vallandigham's career in Washington by running against him in the fall election. After his wounding, however, he succumbed to the urgings of Salmon Chase and President Lincoln, and soon the electoral battle was joined.

In the campaign of fall 1862, Vallandigham—never the most temperate of speakers—had pulled out all the stops in appealing to the racial prejudices of the voters. It was a fertile field to plow after Lincoln's announcement in

September of plans to issue the Emancipation Proclamation. Racial riots had exploded in Toledo and Cincinnati.

The Schenck-Vallandigham contest was fought with calumny, rumors, and lies flying in both directions. Earlier Democratic wins in a number of other states suggested a rising tide of opposition to emancipation and a decline in support for the war. War weariness gained Democrats fourteen of Ohio's nineteen Congressional seats in the October election—but it failed to save Vallandigham's. Schenck's personal popularity, plus some gerrymandering, helped him narrowly defeat the incumbent Democrat from Dayton. Suddenly, Vallandigham was a lame duck whose term would end in January 1863.

Vallandigham didn't leave Congress quietly. On Wednesday, January 14, 1863, he rose from his seat in the House of Representatives and moved directly in front of the Republican side as the chamber hushed to hear him. Speaking directly to the Republicans, he boldly called for an armistice, withdrawal of Northern troops from Southern states, and the reopening of trade, travel, and communication between the regions. In this way, Vallandigham argued, time would dry tears, dispel sorrows, and permit herbs and grass and trees to grow again "upon the hundred battlefields of this terrible war."[64]

Vallandigham's ideas were both vague and impractical. Republicans and many War Democrats showered him with criticism. Nonetheless, peace sentiment was rising in the Midwest, and Vallandigham began to think ahead to new opportunities. In early March 1863, the ex-congressman returned to Ohio and hit the ground running. He was going to seek the governorship. An extravagant homecoming reception in Dayton lifted his heart as speakers showered praise on his head.

But there were danger signs. On March 5, about one hundred soldiers from Camp Chase trashed the Columbus office of the *Crisis,* a newspaper opposed to the war. The office of the *Marietta Democrat* was wrecked as well. Meanwhile, Gen. Ambrose E. Burnside, idled since his replacement by Hooker as commander of the Army of the Potomac, had been sent west to take command of the military's Department of the Ohio and was determined to redeem himself. Soon Col. Henry B. Carrington, now commander of the military's District of Indiana, was filling Burnside's ears with overheated warnings about Vallandigham and hints of conspiracy.

Persuaded that disaffection and disloyalty were being stirred up in Ohio, Burnside issued his General Order No. 38 on April 13. Those civilians with the "habit of declaring sympathy for the enemy" would be arrested and tried in military court, Burnside announced, meaning he was establishing himself

Ohioan John Mercer Langston became one of the most prominent advocates of black participation in fighting the Civil War.

as public censor and intended to ride roughshod over civil liberties.[65] It was as if the Bill of Rights had been unilaterally suspended.

Outraged, Vallandigham and allies began baiting Burnside in a way that made even that affable man's ears burn. At a political rally in Mount Vernon on May 1, Vallandigham deliberately criticized Burnside and his order while Burnside's agent took notes. On the night of May 4, a special train of soldiers from Cincinnati came to Dayton. Within thirty minutes they broke down

Valladingham's back door, arrested him, and removed him to the train to be locked up in Cincinnati.

Outraged by the arrest, the *Dayton Empire* published inflammatory articles, and soon excited crowds were gathering on street corners. Eventually, they formed in front of the *Dayton Journal* office, a Republican paper and political opponent of Vallandigham. They set the place on fire and the fire spread to destroy half a block. Burnside's troops arrived, declared martial law, calmed things down, and suspended publication of the *Empire*.

Vallandigham was no more tractable in his Cincinnati cell than he had been outside. He surreptitiously wrote a ringing declaration of rights addressed "To the Democracy of Ohio" and smuggled it out to wide publication in friendly newspapers. When his court martial began on May 6, he denied the military had jurisdiction over a civilian, demanded a civil trial, and refused to enter a plea. The court plowed ahead nonetheless, finding Vallandigham guilty of violating Burnside's General Order No. 38 by "declaring disloyal sentiments and opinions, with the object and purpose of weakening the power of the Government in its effort to suppress the unlawful rebellion."[66] The court agreed on imprisonment rather than execution.[67]

By now, however, even Republicans were criticizing Burnside's highhanded actions and expressing concern about civil rights. Vallandigham was becoming an embarrassment the Lincoln government didn't need. As the authorities pondered what to do with him, Val sat in his cell and waited.

JOHN MERCER LANGSTON AND A "BAPTISM OF BLOOD"

From late April through early June 1863, a young man with a mind honed by the law and a voice that could reach the heavens roamed Ohio, Indiana, and Illinois looking for African Americans. He was neither slave-catcher, nor law enforcement officer, nor preacher, but he had a mission nonetheless. His name was John Mercer Langston and he intended to make sure that one of the promises of the Emancipation Proclamation was kept.

The best-known and most respected black man in Ohio, Langston's life had been remarkable from birth. He had been born a free person in Virginia in 1829, son of a prosperous white planter and an emancipated slave of mixed African and Indian blood. When both parents died in 1834, he received an inheritance large enough to make him financially independent.

For four years, a friend of Langston's father raised the child in Chillicothe, Ohio, as if he were white. It was a pleasant time, but then the boy experienced what he later would call "The Great Change." It had been decided that he was old enough to be treated for what he really was supposed to be: an untouchable person of color. He was sent to Cincinnati for the rest of his rearing and shared in the bigotry suffered by the black community there.

Thanks to his high intelligence and financial assets, at age fourteen Langston was enrolled in the preparatory department of what is now Oberlin College in Oberlin, Ohio. This institution had been an unusual place from the very start. Founded in 1833 to train teachers and ministers, it decided in 1835 to admit blacks as a matter of policy and in 1837 began admitting women—extraordinary decisions for a college at that time. Conservatives derided its liberalism.

Antislavery students and faculty who flocked to Oberlin turned the school and the little town surrounding it into a hotbed of abolitionist feeling. Young Langston excelled at debate and in 1848, not yet a college graduate, gave a well-received impromptu speech at the National Black Convention in Cleveland. In 1849 he graduated from the Oberlin Collegiate Department. Langston followed that by earning a master's degree in theology at Oberlin. Next, he read law in the office of an antislavery lawyer in nearby Elyria and in 1854 passed the Ohio bar examination to become the state's first black lawyer. Langston established a law practice in the Lorain County village of Brownhelm where he was elected town clerk, becoming perhaps the first black elected to any office in the United States. Then he moved back to Oberlin in 1856, where he established a successful law practice and vigorously supported Republican candidates for office at every level.

All the while, Langston was becoming known as a compelling speaker on black issues and a campaigner for antislavery candidates. He organized antislavery societies and participated in the Underground Railroad. He met with John Brown who tried to recruit him for his raid on Harpers Ferry—an opportunity Langston wisely declined. Nonetheless, Langston later called the raid "heroic" and "patriotic" and lauded Brown as "noble and Christ-like."[68]

Following the Emancipation Proclamation, the Lincoln government authorized several states to raise regiments of African Americans. Washington did not include Ohio among them, because Democratic opposition to the war and abolition had caused an electoral backlash in the Ohio elections of fall 1862. Massachusetts was authorized to recruit blacks, but, with a small black population, was having trouble finding them. Massachusetts decided it had to go looking in other states.

Langston was enlisted as the Bay State's chief agent in Ohio, Indiana, and Illinois. The Midwest looked like fertile territory for recruiting blacks.

In an 1861 abolitionist lithograph, a black man is lifted out of slavery. Flags bear the mottoes "All Men Are Created Equal" and "Stand By the Declaration."

Census data suggested Langston's own state of Ohio had seven thousand potential recruits, more than any other Northern state except New York and Pennsylvania.

But Langston faced an uphill struggle. Blatant racism and the memory of earlier rebuffs had made African Americans wary of white promises. It didn't help to hear whites gratified that now African-American soldiers could take bullets intended for white men. During spring 1863 Langston traveled throughout the Midwest, appealing to black pride. A trained advocate, he knew how to make a case.

Given the opportunity to demonstrate their worth, black soldiers quickly proved to be dedicated, able soldiers.

Ex-slaves were enrolling in the army, Langston said, and free "black northerners should not stand aloof from this contest." He argued that the government "cannot crush out this wicked rebellion without the help of the Negro," insisting that "they should be willing to pass through a baptism of blood, if need be, that the nation might at last come out purified."[69]

Langston's brother Charles became a recruiter. An Oberlin cobbler named O.S.B. Wall, son of a slave and a white slave owner, suspended work to serve as Ohio state agent, based in Columbus, and aided by several sub-agents. Langston had the greatest credibility, for he was a powerful speaker with a believable manner. Two days after he addressed a mass meeting in Cleveland, thirty men left to join the black 54th Massachusetts. Twenty Oberlin blacks set off to join the 54th, each armed with a gift of $4 and a Bible. Forty-five black Chicagoans volunteered after a Langston speech.

When the 54th Massachusetts was fully enrolled, Langston began recruiting for the 55th, enjoying marked success in central and southern Ohio. The 54th counted 214 recruits from Langston's territory, 158 of them Ohioans, while the 55th enrolled 375 Midwesterners, 222 of them Ohioans.

While Langston recruited in the Midwest, Secretary of War Stanton sent Adj. Gen. Lorenzo Thomas to the Mississippi Valley to assure the welfare of black refugees from slavery. Interpreting his mandate broadly, Thomas soon was organizing regiments of former slaves. White Union soldiers, who once would have scorned the idea, now saw it as good strategy.

When the 68th Ohio was camped in Louisiana, Andrew Altman wrote his father that four regiments of ex-slaves soon would be joining the Union army. "That keeps them from raising produce for the rebbles and then yet they fight a gainst them," Altman observed. "I say that is right, is it not? If they had a don that long a go this war would a have been don by this time."[70]

The idea was catching on throughout the North. By mid-June, Ohio Governor Tod, who initially had opposed recruiting a black regiment under Ohio's authority, changed his mind and asked Langston to do just that. Soon Langston was recruiting African Americans for their own regiment, the 127th Ohio.

THE DEATH OF JACOB BRUNER

On April 15, 1863, Jacob Bruner wrote his wife, Martha, in Antwerp, Ohio, with exciting news. He had just accepted a first lieutenancy in one of the new Negro regiments and "my wages will be one hundred and ten dollars and fifty cents a month or thirteen hundred and twenty six dollars per year!" Bruner exulted, "Thank God the way is now clear. If I am spared, [I can] raise you, myself and our children above want and penury."

A country lawyer, Bruner had a romantic, imaginative soul, not an attorney's. He had courted his wife with poetry he wrote himself and decorated with fancy lettering, streamers, and flowers. His law practice had brought in so little income that he joined the 68th Ohio in November 1861 to get a private's paltry $13 monthly wage. Within a few months he became the regiment's quartermaster sergeant with a wage of about $20 a month.

Only white officers were allowed to lead black regiments. Bruner's was the 9ᵗʰ Louisiana Volunteer Infantry (African Descent), filled with former slaves and based at Milliken's Bend in northeastern Louisiana. Bruner was first lieutenant in Company E under Capt. Lyman J. Hissong. Like many soldiers, Bruner's attitude toward blacks had changed. He had begun the war believing slavery was best for blacks in a white society, but by early 1863 was praising the Emancipation Proclamation and the arming of African Americans.

Buoyed by his lieutenancy and ever the romantic, Bruner enclosed two dried roses in one of his letters to Martha and, in another, some dark brown hair "from those locks you once so admired." One of his last letters closed with a passionate, "Here is a thousand kisses!" Clearly, Jacob adored his wife. By contrast, her letters to him were drab and largely concerned with the problems of civilian life.

Milliken's Bend, on the Mississippi River twenty-five miles north of Vicksburg, had once served as Grant's headquarters. By late spring 1863, however, it held only a garrison of 1,410 men, all but 160 of them ex-slaves from cotton plantations along the river. Organized into four regiments that were still filling, the blacks were well clothed, armed, and fed, but hadn't received much training. Some had only fired their guns twice.

Alerted on June 6 that a Confederate division from Texas was nearby, the Milliken's Bend garrison of mostly novice soldiers huddled behind a thorny hedgerow and an eight-foot-high levee and nervously awaited attack. The black recruits of Bruner's 9ᵗʰ Louisiana anchored the left of the Federal line while the 11ᵗʰ Louisiana anchored the right, with the 1ˢᵗ Mississippi, 13ᵗʰ Louisiana, and the white 23ʳᵈ Iowa completing the line between them.

In the early morning light on June 7, a Confederate brigade attacked Milliken's Bend "with yells that would make faint hearts quail."[71] Pushing through the hedgerow, the Confederates raced up the front slope of the levee, where they fired their guns for the first time. The inexperienced African Americans couldn't reload fast enough and the struggle turned into savage hand-to-hand combat with bayonets and clubbed rifles.

The inexperienced defenders fought bravely, but had to retreat, taking a stand behind the natural defense offered by the riverbank. Unable to dislodge the Union soldiers, taking fire from Union gunboats, and exhausted by ninety-five-degree heat, the Confederates gave up and left.

Milliken's Bend was one of the bloodiest small engagements of the war, important for its demonstration to doubters of how bravely blacks would fight. The 9ᵗʰ Louisiana suffered severely, with two-thirds of its 285 men killed or wounded. One of the fatalities was Jacob Bruner, shot through the head in the

Like many of their white counterparts, black soldiers had their "likenesses" taken in their new uniforms.

thick of the fight. Before retreating, the Confederates emptied his pockets and looted his tent.

Four days later, Company E's Captain Hissong wrote Martha Bruner with the sad news. In subsequent letters, he explained a bureaucratic cruelty: she probably couldn't expect to receive the officer's pay owed Bruner because the regiment hadn't completed recruiting and therefore had not been officially accepted into United States service. She might get pay owed Bruner as a sergeant and also what was left of his personal effects—old trousers, books, and pictures—if she wished them. He told her the soldiers had buried Bruner and, given the heat, it was best the body not be returned, at least not until cooler weather.

Still in her early twenties, Martha Bruner was left with three children and little else from her husband, except his letters, including one he had written only a few weeks before his death:

> *Remember me my dear wife as I know you do in your prayers. [P]ray for my success and happy return to your arms. ... Continue in an abiding faith that all will be well and that our last days may be our best.*[72]

To Learn more:

The rigorous training William B. Hazen put the 41st Ohio through paid off at Stones River, Tennessee, where the regiment played a decisive role. The History of the 41st Ohio Veteran Volunteer Infantry is recounted by two of its officers: Robert L. Kimberly and Ephraim S. Holloway. This important but under-reported battle is carefully treated by a modern historian in *No Better Place to Die: The Battle of Stones River*, by Peter Cozzens. The Stones River National Battlefield (**http://www.nps.gov/stri/** or **615-893-9501**) and its National Cemetery are beautifully kept memorials.

Correspondence between a soldier of the 75th Ohio at Chancellorsville and his family in Yellow Springs is laid out in *Hearth and Knapsack: The Ladley Letters*, 1857-1880. That strange battle is explained by Ernest B. Furgurson in *Chancellorsville, 1863: The Souls of the Brave*. The Chancellorsville battleground is part of the Fredricksburg and Spotsylvania County Battlefield Memorial (**http://www.nps.gov/frsp/** or **540-371-1907**).

The stories of Grant's brilliant Vicksburg campaign in Mississippi and Meade's defensive victory at Gettysburg, Pennsylvania—both of which culminated on July 4, 1863—are related in *The Most Glorious Fourth* by Duane Schultz.

Ohio's notorious Clement L. Vallandigham, who sorely tested the North's tolerance for domestic opposition to the war, receives a friendly examination from Frank L. Klement in *The Limits of Dissent*. The story of an energetic Ohioan who did so much for the war effort and African Americans is related by William Cheek and Aimee Lee Cheek in *John Mercer Langston and the Fight for Black Freedom, 1829-65*.

10

RIVERS OF DEATH

July to November 1863

In 1863, Holmes County floated in the air like a hot-air balloon rising heavenward, tethered to Mother Earth and Ohio by no more than a single rail spur and a few winding dirt roads. Localism ruled America in those days and for most Ohioans the horizon ended at the county line. But Holmes County had an other-worldliness all its own: many Amish and Mennonites lived there, as they do today, mostly ignoring the outside world as they tended to the soil and their souls. Pacifists, they did not support the war.

Nor did many other residents of Holmes County. They were Peace Democrats, many of them German and French immigrants still trying to climb the language barrier. Their opposition was not religious but political. In 1860, the county had voted overwhelmingly for Douglas, Lincoln's opponent, and on the day President Lincoln signed the Emancipation Proclamation, the *Holmes County Farmer* snapped, "Niggers may rejoice, but this is the darkest day for white men ever beheld in this country."[1]

So it was that in 1863 Holmes County, a thinly populated region of small farms and many gentle people, spun in its own orbit paying little attention to what lay beyond and not liking a lot of what it saw when it did. Then, on Friday, June 5, 1863, a federal official named Elias W. Robinson rode up to a group of men who were laying a stone foundation in an area called French Ridge.

By this time, war weariness was widespread among Northerners, regardless of political affiliation. Its harsh realities had cost war some of its early charms. Few men were volunteering, so Congress passed a conscription law in March 1863. Each state had a quota to be filled with the willing, if possible, and if not, the unwilling drawn by lot. But the draft was highly unpopular. To nineteenth-century Americans, forced military service seemed shameful and un-American.

Threatened with a draft, Ohio communities worked frantically to persuade men to volunteer instead, offering handsome "bounties" of hundreds of dollars on top of the federal bounty of one hundred dollars. Greed plagued the system with corrupt enlistment brokers and "bounty jumpers" who repeatedly enlisted, deserted, then re-enlisted.

Robinson was an enrollment officer charged with carrying out the conscription law. He provoked the men working on French Ridge by asking if there were any "Copperheads" in the area. Somebody hit him with a stone and the officer galloped away as the men laughed and hooted, one of them firing a pistol into the air. Within a few days, a provost marshal arrested several of the men, but a party of armed Holmes County men quickly forced him to give up his prisoners.

That was the birth of Ohio's "Holmes County Rebellion," sometimes grandiloquently called the "Holmes County War." Knowing the authorities would return in force, some armed Holmes Countians gathered at Lorenzo Blanchard's farm on French Ridge. To deal with them, a patchwork army of four hundred U.S. soldiers led by Col. William Wallace arrived from Columbus. At first, "bushwhackers" hiding in the woods fired on the little army, but the experienced soldiers were unperturbed, pushing on to Blanchard's farm until the rebels "were flying in all directions." There were few casualties.

The rebels realized they were no match for the soldiers. The next day, several leading men came to the army camp seeking peace and ready to make concessions. The stone-throwers were delivered to Colonel Wallace, he departed, and with that, draft resistance faded away in Holmes County. In punishing the rebels, the federal government was inclined to be charitable. Of the forty or more participants indicted, only two were tried and only one— Lorenzo Blanchard—was convicted, sentenced to six months in prison and a fine of $500. To Blanchard's everlasting embarrassment, his farm acquired the nickname "Fort Fizzle."

Shocked by the news from his home county, Marcus Spiegel, who was then near Vicksburg with the 120th Ohio, wrote his wife urging her to sell their home in Millersburg and move away. (She did not.)[2]

More serious resistance to the draft erupted elsewhere, the worst in New York City in mid-July. Mobs lynched eleven blacks, burned buildings, wrecked the home of the provost marshal, and terrorized neighborhoods. ("It was the awfullest thing I ever heard of," Mary Ladley in Yellow Springs wrote her soldier brother, Oscar.)[3] Soldiers who had just finished fighting at Gettysburg were rushed to New York. Their volleys of deadly gunfire ended all resistance. They were followed by several Ohio regiments sent to make sure the lid stayed on. The fight had gone out of the protestors, however, so the Ohioans passed the time parading, sightseeing, and having their "likenesses" taken in the city's photography studios.

The drafts produced barely 168,000 soldiers nationwide (and only 4,250 in Ohio, out of the 300,000 Ohioans who went to war), but the threat of the draft is thought to have boosted *voluntary* enlistments by more than a million men.[4] Bounties made a difference as well. Nonetheless, a modern historian has concluded that the corruption infesting the Civil War's bounty system should teach us "that universal conscription [is] the only fair and effective way to build a citizens' army."[5]

After using drafts successfully in the twentieth century, the United States has returned to an all-volunteer army. That sidesteps a politically unpopular draft by attracting part of the population with … bounties. Only we call them "enlistment bonuses."

GETTYSBURG

From the air, they must have looked like rivers on a winter morning, steam rising as they glided northward through the battle-worn landscape of Virginia. On the ground, they were seven corps of Union soldiers, thousands of infantrymen wearing hot woolen uniforms soaked with sweat and whitened with dust. The soldiers licked their dry lips with dry tongues, and, choking on the clouds of dust they kicked up, struggled to keep moving in the hellfire of a southern June. Army ambulances roamed the roadsides picking up soldiers who had collapsed. Dozens died from exhaustion and heat stroke.

This was the Union's Army of the Potomac, on the march again and looking for redemption. Shaken by defeat at Chancellorsville—which "Fighting Joe" Hooker had promised would be a triumph—the men had needed weeks in camps north of the Rappahannock to start feeling better about themselves. Troubled most of all were the men of Maj. Gen. Howard's XI Corps, taunted for folding under Stonewall Jackson's surprise attack. An officer remembered sobbing in frustration and humiliation during the retreat from Chancellorsville.[6] Hooker and the army brass didn't seem to mind that the XI Corps rank and file, many of them Ohioans, were being made scapegoats for failures of command.

Then, on June 3, 1863, Lee's Army of the Northern Virginia slipped out of its camps south of the Rappahannock and headed north through the Shenandoah Valley, hidden from prying eyes by the Blue Ridge Mountains. Once again, Lee had decided on a high-risk invasion of the North, intending to scoop up some of the countryside's bounty, catch the pixilated Hooker and destroy his army, and, by threatening major cities of the North, perhaps push a demoralized Union into suing for peace. It was a long shot, but long shots were what the Confederacy was reduced to.

Hooker had been ordered to shadow Lee and stay between him and Washington, but by June 28, Lincoln's patience with disputatious Fighting Joe, Chancellorsville's failed commander, ran out. Hooker was replaced by one of his corps commanders, Maj. Gen. George G. Meade, a goggly-eyed, irascible Pennsylvanian nicknamed "Old Snapping Turtle." To oppose him, Lee had about seventy thousand men, ragged and hungry but cocksure they and Bobby Lee were unbeatable. The Army of the Potomac had about ninety thousand mostly battle-tested veterans confident they knew how to fight even if their leaders didn't. Between four and five thousand were Ohioans. There were smaller numbers from Indiana, Illinois, and three other Midwestern states.

While tramping north, the dust-covered men of the 4th and 8th Ohio regiments, looking like ghosts, had a portent of things to come. Transiting the old Second Bull Run battlefield, they found a city of the dead. Arms of half-buried soldiers reached imploringly from the earth. A shoe protruded from the ground, the sole peeled back to reveal a bony foot pointing to the sky. Skeletons in remnants of uniforms lay about, silent screams seeming to rise from their gaping jaws.[7]

By late June, the Army of the Potomac was crossing the river for which it was named and coming gratefully into western Maryland's fruited land, a place where girls rushed to the roadside to offer cups of water. Coming across some aromatic cheeses shaped like baseballs, men of the 66th Ohio boyishly used them for an odoriferous food fight.[8] But exhausted soldiers, like Sgt. Luther B. Mesnard of the 55th Ohio, were still collapsing on the road. Mesnard, 26, a farmer from Norwalk, was unconscious for thirty minutes. He awoke in an ambulance and stayed there for two days.

Meanwhile, Lee's famished Confederates were slicing into south-central Pennsylvania, brushing aside the state's militia, plundering the countryside, and heading for the state capital of Harrisburg. Convinced of the superiority of all things Southern, the invaders were astonished at the lush countryside, well kept without slaves, wheat fields glittering like the gold of Midas, thick leaves of corn resembling swords pointing to the sky, and cherry trees dripping with fruit the color of blood. Thin, scraggly haired men in tattered uniforms, many barefooted and hatless, the Confederates sniffed the air like wolves, their grins revealing yellowed teeth as they looked hungrily at the bounty surrounding them.

On July 1, a party of Confederates heading for Gettysburg, Pennsylvania, in search of shoes ran into a Union scouting force determined to hold the strategic little crossroads town. So began the three-day battle of Gettysburg, the costliest of the war. Soon the Union I Corps arrived to join the fight, followed by Howard's XI Corps.

Two of Howard's three divisions—including, among others, the 25th, 61st, 75th, 82nd, and 107th Ohio regiments, plus Capt. Hubert Dilger's artillery battery—flowed northward through the streets of Gettysburg "at millrace speed" and out into the fields beyond.[9] Frightened townspeople lined the town's streets, cheering the Union soldiers as their deliverers from the Confederates, and giving them food and water. The third of Howard's divisions, which included the 55th and 73rd Ohio, remained in reserve on Cemetery Hill on the southern edge of town.[10]

The men of XI Corps yearned to win back their honor, taken from them at Chancellorsville, but in a terrible irony, their right flank once again was left "in the air," unsupported before a larger enemy force. An officer recalled Confederates and Federals coming so close that they could look in each other's eyes while "firing literally in one another's faces." Anna Mary Young, who lived nearby, remembered "that for every gun fired there was a shriek. ... All I could do was sit in a cellar corner and cry."[11]

Battery I of the 1st Ohio Light Artillery was under the command of Capt. Dilger, known as "Old Leather Breeches" and considered by some to be the best artilleryman in the Union army. As he had at Chancellorsville, Dilger was able to slow the Confederate advance, but was unable to stop it. A Confederate told how the XI Corps infantrymen fought bravely until the battle turned into "a fearful slaughter[;] the golden wheat fields, a few minutes before in beauty, now gone, and the ground covered with the dead and wounded in blue."[12] By late afternoon, the XI Corps, joined by the I Corps, was retreating—again.

Orderly at first, the retreating soldiers paused now and then to turn and fire at the pursuing Confederates. As thousands of Union men clogged Gettysburg streets, slowing their retreat, panicked soldiers struggled to escape.[13] Civilians huddled in basements, watching shadows fly by their cellar windows and listening to the screams of the chasers and the chased crashing through

Union soldiers fight their way through a wheat field in the Eastern Theater.

their houses.[14] A fleeing regiment ran into a blind alley, then turned to see Confederates blocking the entrance with the bodies of dead Union soldiers.[15]

Some men entered homes and hid under beds and in closets. Searching for them, Confederates descended into cellars, their eyes glittering in the gloom as the civilians cowered. An XI Corps general hid in a pigsty for three days.[16] The two XI Corps divisions engaged on the first day lost about half their men.[17] By the time the 82nd Ohio reached safety on Cemetery Hill, it had lost 150 of its 258 men.[18]

Those who escaped from town gathered on Cemetery Hill, joining the reserves Howard had left to hold the high ground. With its stonewalls and vistas of the countryside, Cemetery Hill—where many of the Ohioans would be positioned in fighting yet to come—anchored a superb defensive position. To the east, the land dipped and rose again to become Culp's Hill, about a mile away, and to the south, Cemetery Hill turned into Cemetery Ridge, declining for about two miles to end near rocky mounts called Round Top and Little Round Top.

As the main body of Meade's Army of the Potomac arrived later in the day, it was posted along the heights to form a defensive line shaped like an enormous inverted fish hook. Some arriving Union artillery went crashing through Evergreen Cemetery scattering headstones. Exhausted Ohioans lay down to sleep that night among the graves. "How we did sleep and rest!" Sergeant Mesnard recalled.[19] But to the west, campfires flickered along Seminary Ridge. They were Confederate, and they were only a mile away.

The next morning—Thursday, July 2—Harriet Bayly and her niece left the Bayly farmhouse with a basket of bread and butter, wine, and bandages. Picking their way among corpses turning black in the heat, they attended the Union wounded who had been left lying on yesterday's battlefield. Some had crawled into fence corners to escape the blazing sun; all were crying for water. Mrs. Bayly shamed some Confederates into bringing water to the thirsty casualties.

South of town, a girl named Tillie Pierce noticed "numerous rough boxes" had been stacked outside her garden fence. They were coffins, ready for use. Passing soldiers made grim jokes about army efficiency.[20]

Later that day, Lee attempted to cave in Union forces on both flanks. His fierce late-afternoon attacks on the Union left (where no Ohio infantrymen were positioned) came close to breaking through, but by early evening the battered Confederates were forced to withdraw, leaving behind a trail of bodies and a list of blood-stained names for the history books: the Peach Orchard, the Wheatfield, Roundtop and Little Roundtop, and the Devil's Den. "The blood stood in puddles in some places on the rocks," one soldier recalled.[21]

Further north, in the center of the Union line of battle, action was limited to high-intensity skirmishing and sharp-shooting. Men of the 8th Ohio formed small groups to fire simultaneously at each suspected sniper, a tactic they called "Turning a Jack." They claimed great success in silencing "poor Johnny."[22] Pvt. Charles Stacey from Norwalk, a 55th Ohioan, hid behind a stump and popped up twenty-three times in four hours to target enemy sharp-shooters, quickly ducking to escape return fire. Rebel sniping in his sector ceased.[23]

Now and then a sacred moment occurred when the men were reminded

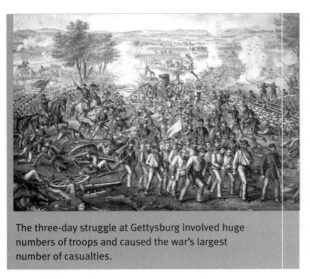

The three-day struggle at Gettysburg involved huge numbers of troops and caused the war's largest number of casualties.

of their common humanity. Lt. Thomas F. Galwey of the 8th Ohio remembered watching a Confederate sharpshooter emerge from his lair behind a tree to shouts from his fellows of, "Don't fire, Yanks!" As the men of the 8th Ohio watched, the Confederate approached a wounded Union soldier who lay exposed to the sun in a free-fire zone and gave him a drink from his canteen. Shooting had ceased and men on both sides stood up to witness the little act of compassion. As the Union men cheered the Rebel soldier, he returned to his tree and shouted, "Down Yanks, we're going to fire." And the men lay down again.[24]

For every grace note, however, the battle exacted a price, with horrifying wounds among the most common. Lt. Col. Eugene Powell of the 66th Ohio remembered how an overhead explosion caught Sgt. William M. Scott in the face, tearing away his nose and upper left jaw. "As he breathed his cheeks seemed to meet, as there was not anything to keep them apart," Colonel Powell said. Amazingly, Scott survived, was discharged for disability, and, terribly disfigured and unable to speak, went home to Logan County where he lived many years.[25]

George Enderlin, a bugler in the 73rd Ohio, crawled into a free-fire zone to rescue a wounded comrade, Pvt. George Nixon. Nixon died within two days, but left a son whose grandson Richard would be elected president of the United State 105 years later. Swirling around these little events, the fighting went on with no interruption. Leading skirmishers into the dangerous territory between the lines, the 55th Ohio's Sergeant Mesnard was wounded in his right arm. Loping along Cemetery Hill in search of a field hospital, the wounded Mesnard looked left and saw Federal and Confederate soldiers fighting hand to hand among the Union cannons stationed near the cemetery gatehouse.

This was the attack Lee had ordered on the Union's *right* flank. In what must have seemed an endlessly looping nightmare, two Union brigades from the XI Corps were attacked on Cemetery Hill by the same Rebel brigades that had lacerated them the day before north of town. The weary soldiers of the 25th, 75th, and 107th Ohio and their fellow regiments fought desperately, but they were too few and were overrun. The Confederates "put their big feet on the stone wall and went over like deer, over the heads of the whole … regiment," Sgt. George Clements of the 25th Ohio recalled.

Oscar D. Ladley, now a lieutenant in the 75th Ohio, wrote home, "A Rebel officer made at me with a revolver … I had no pistol nothing but my sword. [O]ne of our boys run him through the body so saved me. There was a good man killed in that way."[26] The fighting among the Union artillery pieces turned into a swirling mass of men using their muskets as clubs, throwing rocks, firing pistols, and, in the case of the artillerymen, swinging their rammers like baseball bats. When darkness fell, Confederates and Federals fired blindly, sometimes at their own men. Finally, Union reinforcements, including the 4th Ohio, helped the XI Corps men drive the attackers back down the hill "in a headlong dash in the dark."[27]

A mile east, a parallel Confederate attack fell upon Culp's Hill but stalled on the lower slope, unable to gain the crest that night. In the early Friday morning darkness, so many Union reinforcements arrived that they had

On Cemetery Hill, Union artillerymen found themselves fighting Confederates hand-to-hand in the second day of the Gettysburg battle.

to operate in shifts behind their breastworks—"a pretty good way to fight," an officer remarked."[28] The 66th Ohio decided to move outside the trenches. "My God! If you go out there the enemy will simply swallow you!" someone warned them.[29] Having seen worse, the Ohioans were fatalistic by now, so they went anyway, hiding among rocky outcroppings to pour flanking fire on attackers. They returned safely and watched as the surviving Confederates withdrew, marking the failure of Lee's attack on the Union right.

Elsewhere, Sergeant Mesnard of the 55th Ohio had had his wound dressed and, after spending the night in a haystack, went sightseeing along Union lines on Friday. An ominous silence had settled on the battlefield. Waiting for what might come next, the men shaded themselves from the burning sun by stretching cloths over muskets bayoneted into the ground. Then two signal guns broke the silence about 1 p.m. and 120 Confederate cannons opened fire on the Union center, followed by an enormous return barrage from Union artillery.

The artillery duel on this third day of the battle began as a low rumbling sound and became a deafening roar that shook the ground. A woman in Gettysburg said it sounded like "heaven and earth ... crashing together."[30] A newspaperman wrote that the varied projectiles "shrieked, whirled, moaned, and whistled and wrathfully fluttered over our ground. As many as six in a second, constantly two in a second, bursting and screaming."[31]

Trailing sparks from their fuses, explosive shells passed overhead to blow up ammunition wagons, dissolve trees in bursts of splinters, and smash into rocks in showers of steel and stone. Solid shot plowed grooves in the earth; Mesnard could see "a dozen at a time bounding along like footballs."[32] Sixteen horses tethered near Meade's headquarters neighed frantically, leaping and pulling at their tethers until all were killed. Clouds of smoke filled the valley between the two armies, until, about two hours after it had started, the artillery fire stopped and silence returned.

Then a westerly breeze drew away the smoke like a curtain, revealing fifteen thousand Confederate soldiers on a mile-wide front, marching perfectly with banners flying as if on dress parade, heading toward the center of the Union line. On Cemetery Ridge, blue-clad men waiting behind stone walls stared, fascinated. "I had not gazed upon so grand a sight as ... that beautiful mass of gray," a Union officer recalled.[33] Then Union artillery began savaging the beautifully aligned Confederate marchers, tearing great holes in their ranks. "Arms, heads, blankets, guns and knapsacks were thrown and tossed in the clear air," the 8th Ohio's Lt. Col. Franklin Sawyer recalled.[34] But the

Confederates closed the gaps in their ranks and kept coming.

This was what is popularly known as Pickett's Charge, although Pickett commanded only part of it. Having failed to crush the Union flanks, Lee now hoped to blast through the center, although Longstreet, his "Old Warhorse," advised against it. The Union center was held primarily by Maj. Gen. Winfield Scott Hancock's II Corps. Only one Ohio regiment was positioned here, but its role was an important one.

Assigned earlier to picket duty between the lines, the 8th Ohio had been left there, as if forgotten. It was still dangling several hundred yards in front of the main Union positions, concealed by vegetation, when the Confederate charge began on the third day at Gettysburg. As enemy ranks passed, the 8th was able to pour volleys into their unsuspecting flank. Rattled, the far left end of the Confederate line melted and its men turned to flee, throwing away their equipment as they ran.

"We dashed among them, taking prisoners in droves," Thomas F. Galwey of the 8th remembered. By day's end, the 8th Ohio had lost to death or wounds nearly half of the 216 men with which it had started the day, but it had captured more prisoners than it had losses.[35]

Among the 8th Ohio's wounded was Capt. Azor H. Nickerson, shot through one arm and his lungs. Carried behind the lines in a blanket, he had been left lying on Cemetery Ridge. Struggling to his feet, blood gushed from his mouth and he fainted. He awoke in a roughly bouncing ambulance that took him to a makeshift hospital in a barn. "I am not afraid to hear the worst; is there any hope for me, doctor?" Nickerson asked a surgeon. "No," the surgeon said, patting him gently on the forehead and looking away. "No, none whatsoever."[36] To Nickerson's amazement, he would not only survive after a long convalescence, but also return to Gettysburg months later.

Lee's attack on the Union's tough center achieved a brief breakthrough, the so-called "high-water mark of the Confederacy," but then the shattered Southerners had to retreat. The next day, July 4—the same day Grant was marching into Vicksburg—the two exhausted armies rested. Lee sent a long train of groaning wounded streaming southward. Like their Union counterparts, wounded men being transported in the horse-drawn ambulances of the day had to endure a ride, unsoftened by springs, over rough ground.

Long after the war, a Confederate general remembered the screams of the suffering ambulance passengers: "O God! Why can't I die?" and "My God! Will no one have mercy and kill me?"[37] That night, the rest of Lee's army headed toward Virginia, a gray river of defeated men. Lee's invasion of the

North—what one historian called the "Confederacy's supreme effort of the war"—had failed for overreaching, but his army escaped, though terribly damaged, and so the fighting and dying would go on for nearly two more years.[38]

The Army of the Potomac had proven it could win. The XI Corps had fought bravely at Gettysburg, but, sadly, that didn't seem to help its reputation. The wounded Sergeant Mesnard was riding a train away from the battlefield when he heard someone deriding the XI Corps. Leaping to his feet, Mesnard threatened the speaker with his good arm, exclaiming, "I belong to the XI Corps. Take that back." Other men came up "and would have mashed the fellow but for me."[39]

For veterans of the XI Corps, the battles of Chancellorsville and Gettysburg would never end. They would spend the rest of their lives defending their honor.

What Followed the Battle

Silhouetted against the sultry July sky, an expectant mother and an old man worked on the heights above Gettysburg, their spades rising and falling as they bent to their task. Probably the only sounds were their heavy breathing and the blades cleaving the earth. There was not much to say. They were digging graves.

They were Elizabeth Thorn, six months pregnant, and her elderly father. Her husband was the cemetery's caretaker, but he was with the Union army in Virginia. A few days after the battle had ended, Elizabeth, her children, and her elderly parents,\ returned to their home, the cemetery's two-story arched brick gatehouse. They found windows shattered and everything gone except for three blood-soaked and muddy mattresses. Fifteen Union soldiers had been buried in shallow graves near their back door and dead horses lay bloating among the cemetery's toppled monuments, torn-up turf, and trampled flowerbeds.

Home to only 2,400 people, Gettysburg had been overrun by 160,000 strangers, stripped of most of its food, and robbed of horses, clothing, and even some of its furniture. Bullets had pockmarked houses. Inside some, blood had soaked into carpets, cushions, and books that had been used as pillows for the wounded. Barns had been burned, fences torn down, and crops flattened. Lying everywhere were wrecked artillery pieces, broken rifles, torn clothing, soiled blankets, crumpled letters, and so many minié balls they were still being picked up a century later. Catholic nuns arriving to help found residents dazed, wandering aimlessly, and looking like "frightened ghosts."[40]

The family that lived in the cemetery gatehouse at Gettysburg returned to find it wrecked, with dead soldiers buried in shallow graves nearby.

The smell of decaying flesh smothered the town and crept into every home. The morbid stink caused retching and it poisoned sleep. Scattered across a twenty-five-mile-square area were at least seven thousand corpses, some hurriedly buried in shallow graves, others left to rot in the sun. There were thousands of carcasses of horses and mules, legs pointing to the sky as they swelled. Carrion birds had been frightened away by the noise of battle, but "every fence and bush was black with flies."[41]

The two armies' fifty-one thousand casualties (killed, wounded, missing or captured) made Gettysburg the costliest clash of the entire war and, in the American imagination, its iconic battle. By various estimates, 4,300 to 4,400 Ohioans had been in the fight and nearly one of every three (28.9 percent by one calculation) had been killed, wounded, or captured.[42]

Townspeople went to work burying the dead. By themselves, Thorn and her father dug 110 graves. In Gettysburg and around it, decomposing bodies lay hidden under bushes, in brooks, and in the crevasses of rocks. Some sat with their backs against trees, as if they had quietly waited to die; others had torn up the ground in their death agonies. Some of the corpses would not be found

At least seven thousand corpses were left behind at Gettysburg, with some in shallow graves and others left for townspeople to bury.

for months and remains were still being found early in the twentieth century.

Not long after the battle, Gettysburg lawyer David Wills, horrified that hogs were feeding on bodies, proposed an official resting place on Cemetery Hill where the hurriedly buried Union soldiers could be reburied together. Seventeen acres were purchased where bodies could be properly re-interred from dozens of makeshift burial sites around Gettysburg.

Ohio was among the states pledging its support to the cemetery. Many of the dead could not be identified, but eventually 131 of Ohio's known dead were buried in the state's section of the cemetery.[43] By November the soldiers' cemetery was ready for dedication by President Lincoln.

Capt. Azor Nickerson of the 8th Ohio, recuperating in Washington from wounds suffered at Gettysburg, slipped uninvited aboard a train of dignitaries headed to the dedication ceremony. Greeted as a hero, he was issued an impromptu invitation to the speakers' stand on Cemetery Ridge. That is why, on November 19, 1863, an Ohio volunteer officer of middling rank was on the platform with the nation's dignitaries, sitting so close to the president that he could see "every lineament in the sad, earnest face of Mr. Lincoln." Because Lincoln was scheduled to follow two hours of polished oratory from Edward Everett, "everyone felt sorry for him," Nickerson recalled.

Then Lincoln arose, "the tallest and most awkward man I had ever seen," and stood almost exactly over the spot where the wounded Nickerson had lain a few months before. As the Ohioan struggled with his emotions, the president, holding a bit of paper about the size of a visiting card but not consulting it, began his plain little speech: *Four score and seven years ago …*

It was, Nickerson later wrote, "the shortest, grandest, speech … to which I have ever listened."[44]

THE GREAT OHIO RAID

In the summer of 1863, Kentucky cavalier John Hunt Morgan, with nearly 2,500 men, his largest force yet, set off on an expedition authorized by Braxton Bragg to go raiding wherever he chose so long as he stayed in Kentucky. Bragg's orders be damned; Morgan had other ideas. With Federal cavalry in pursuit, Morgan crossed from Kentucky into Indiana in July 1863, using two commandeered steamboats. Then he began galloping eastward toward Ohio, where he hoped to cause enough panic to draw Union troops away from other fronts.

Once again, alarm bells rang all over the Buckeye state. Blustering about "bagging" Morgan, General Burnside declared martial law in Cincinnati. Governor Tod re-activated the Squirrel Hunters in thirty-seven counties. Women dropped silverware down wells; men rushed to hide their horses and cattle; some families moved north. One woman hid the family horse by taking it into her parlor, locking her doors, and latching the shutters.

After fighting his way eastward through southern Indiana, Morgan crossed into Ohio, just west of Cincinnati, on July 13. One Union cavalry force was hot on his heels while another was trying to intercept him. The hapless Burnside was still organizing his forces when Morgan raced by Cincinnati heading east and passing within sight of a mostly empty Camp Dennison.

Morgan kept his men in the saddle an average of twenty-one hours a day. Some fell asleep while riding, and some dropped out. Bushwhackers shot at them from hiding places and civilians burned bridges and felled trees to block roads. When they weren't fighting off Ohio soldiers and militia, the raiders roared into terrified towns to ransack stores, rip up railroad tracks, and capture horses to replace their own exhausted animals. Heading east across southern Ohio and having done all the damage he could, Morgan planned to escape across the Ohio River to reach friends waiting in West Virginia.[45]

On July 19 at Buffington Island, the worn-out Confederates found themselves caught between Union soldiers, militia, and two gunboats. (Two future Presidents—Col. Rutherford B. Hayes and 2nd Lt. William

McKinley, Jr., both of the 23rd Ohio, were present.) Only a handful of Union men were killed in the ensuing encounter, including sixty-five-year-old Maj. Dan McCook, father of General McCook. More than a third of the Confederates were killed, wounded, or captured in this, Ohio's only Civil War battle, but Morgan and hundreds of his men escaped.

Fifteen miles north of Buffington's Island, three hundred raiders crossed to West Virginia, but Morgan and his remnants kept fleeing northward along Ohio's eastern edge, battling Union infantry and militia units that swarmed like angry hornets. On July 26, thirteen days after invading Ohio, Morgan and more than three hundred men surrendered, trapped by Federals in a field in Columbiana County on Ohio's eastern border. It was the furthest point north reached by a regular Confederate fighting force during the Civil War.

For all its daring, Morgan's raid was a failure. It briefly kept some Union troops busy, but "it was of very little military importance," Maj. Gen. Jacob D. Cox later wrote, and for this, "a whole Confederate division of cavalry was sacrificed."[46] Instead of heartening opponents of the war, the raid infuriated most Ohioans, who saw Morgan's men more as thieves than soldiers. Perhaps because of this, Morgan and several of his officers were treated as criminals rather than prisoners of war and were taken to the Ohio State Penitentiary in Columbus.

Four months later, however, he and six fellow officers tunneled their way out of the "escape-proof" Ohio State Penitentiary and in little over a week Morgan was back in Tennessee. Angered by his failure to obey Bragg and confine his raiding to Kentucky, Confederate authorities did not greet him warmly. Finally, however, Morgan was returned to action, but he seemed unable to repeat his old successes. On September 1, 1864, he awoke in Greeneville, Tennessee, to find his headquarters surrounded by Federal troops. When Morgan tried to surrender, a Union soldier reportedly replied, "Surrender and be God damned—I know you," and fired. As Morgan died, the soldier shouted, "I've killed the damned horse thief."[47]

This is how the tale of a cavalier ends. Morgan left a young widow, a Southern belle called Mattie, newly pregnant. Months later, she gave birth to their only child to survive to adulthood, a daughter she named "Johnnie" in her late husband's honor. Mattie later remarried but died at forty-six. Johnnie died at twenty-three, leaving John Hunt Morgan with no descendents. The Kentucky cavalier and his family were separated even in death. Although Morgan had been buried in Kentucky, his wife and daughter were laid to rest in Tennessee.

Confederate John Hunt Morgan's cavalry raid on southern Ohio in July 1863 was a daring venture, but it ended in Morgan's capture.

After Morgan's death, Mattie had written a relative, "My poor husband gambled on life and he lost."[48]

THE RIVER OF DEATH

A river of whiskey flowed through nineteenth-century Ohio, a stream of aqua vitae that was guzzled as social lubricant, medicine, and balm against the jagged edges of daily life. It poured from hundreds of small distilleries throughout Ohio and some big ones in Cincinnati, the whiskey production and distribution center of the Midwest and a veritable geyser of brown goods.

So it was not taken amiss when James B. Steedman, commander of the 14th Ohio, packed some Old Kentucky Rye in his kit. On a rough Kentucky road early in 1862, however, Steedman's demijohn of whiskey had fallen from a wagon and shattered, liquor flowing into a mule track. Instantly, soldiers gathered on hands and knees to slurp up the precious fluid, some drinking enough "to make them feel rather happy." Discovering his loss later, "the old colonel … roared like distant thunder, and his long hair and large head shook worse than any caged lion" while his soldiers, lying low in their tents, snorted with amusement.[49]

Of all the untrained volunteers who helped lead Union armies to victory, Steedman was one of the most colorful. Large both in achievement and loutishness, Steedman was fat, loud, profane, and argumentative. But the Toledoan exuded a crude command presence. He had won a brigadier generalship scarcely a year after entering the war and his hard-charging brigade helped secure victory at Perryville. In August 1863 General Rosecrans gave Steedman command of a division of his Reserve Corps.

Rosecrans and Steedman were intelligent, energetic men whose soldiers called them, respectively, "Old Rosy" and "Old Steady." Both fancied a drink and both could swear prodigiously. But there were differences. Rosecrans had attended West Point and had a formal education in the theory and practice of warfare; Steedman, a school drop-out with almost no military know-how, was a rank amateur. Soon, all-out battle would test both Ohioans.

Generals Rosecrans and Bragg would play roles in the Battle of Chickamauga, Georgia, the bloodiest fight in the Western Theater, second only to Gettysburg as the war's costliest. Gettysburg had been a set-pierce battle unfolding with deliberation across a panoramic landscape. It was three days of bloody theater ending a strategic victory for the Union. And it could hardly have been avoided. Chickamauga, occurring two-and-a-half months later, was something else entirely—a bloody mess lasting for two terrible days, ending in another strategic victory—this time, for the Confederacy—that turned into a poison pill. And it need never have happened.

There was another difference: Only a sliver—less than five percent—of the Union forces that fought at Gettysburg came from Ohio. At Chickamauga, about half did. Some Ohio families had suffered losses at Gettysburg, but many more did at Chickamauga.

After Bragg's defeat at Stones River in January 1863, Rosecrans and Washington resumed dancing the *gavotte,* he demanding more of everything an army needs, the government demanding more of what an army is supposed to do. Finally, in the summer of 1863, Rosecrans got moving, launching two sets of maneuvers as brilliant as any the war would see. First he used strategy and guile to chase Bragg from middle Tennessee, a fertile land and Confederate breadbasket, and then he did it all over again by scaring Bragg out of Chattanooga in southeastern Tennessee. This was warfare according to classroom theory, for it cost Rosecrans few casualties while capturing territory important to the Confederacy. But it didn't destroy any armies, so Washington was underwhelmed.

After those successes, Rosecrans's ablest corps commander urged him to rest and refit in Chattanooga, but Rosecrans wouldn't listen. Flushed with victory and feeling unappreciated, Old Rosy cast off his usual caution and impetuously charged south into northwest Georgia in pursuit of Bragg. Visions of capturing Atlanta and perhaps ending the war may have danced in the Ohioan's head. But Bragg, though battered, did not feel beaten, and Richmond was sending him reinforcements (including Gen. James Longstreet, who had been a roommate of Rosecrans at West Point).[50] Rosecrans recklessly split up his army to advance on several fronts, presenting Bragg with the opportunity to chew up him piecemeal.

A few miles southeast of Chattanooga, on rolling land in the northwest corner of Georgia, was a dark and ancient forest. Shaded by a thick canopy of trees, its floor was clogged by patches of brush and tangles of vines, limiting vision to a few yards. Only a few narrow roads and an occasional clearing opened the land to the sky. Landmarks were scarce. This foreboding place was bordered on the east by a meandering creek the Cheyenne called the Chickamauga. The word means "River of Death."

It was here that Rosecrans, finally realizing he was in danger from Bragg, frantically reunited his army and reversed course, the pursuer turning into the pursued. By the night of September 18 Old Rosy was sidling northward, shuffling divisions this way and that in the dark. Moving on the army's left, George Thomas's XIV Corps marched up a smoky road eerily lit by burning fences. Capt. John Hartzell of the 105th Ohio, a farmer from Portage County, remembered a dry old pine tree flaming like a torch, "casting weird, uncanny shadows" as the men tramped by.[51] Danger seemed to lurk in the dark.

The next morning, a Saturday, the 14th Ohio was having breakfast when it was suddenly ordered into the woods. Trying to chew hardtack and drink coffee as they hurried over uneven ground ("ludicrous in the extreme," someone observed[52]), the men ran into dismounted Confederate cavalrymen and attacked.[53] Lt. Col. Henry D. Kingsbury, who had been sheriff of Lucas County, led the 14th on foot, pausing to fire his musket and shout encouragement until he was hoarse. "[S]uch slashing, slaying and killing of men as now took place—why, I never before saw or heard of," recalled Pvt. Augustus C. May of the 14th Ohio. "[A]ll that day, and the next, I believe we fought as never men fought before."[54]

The fight began with a staccato of scattered musket fire, but soon grew into "one continued roar ... as uninterrupted as the rattling of wagons on the pavements of Broadway in daylight," a Toledoan wrote.[55] As Federals and Confederates closed on each other, men fell—some without a word, others

Fighting in the tangled woods of Chickamauga was difficult for both sides, but Confederates slowly gained the upper hand.

crying, "O God!" A bullet hitting a body sounded like the thud of a fist hitting a pillow. Under the heavy gunfire, bits of bark flew off trees while leaves pinwheeled to the forest floor. Stray bullets kicked up dirt and caused the corpses of unlucky soldiers to twitch.

The fighting broadened into a battle, spreading like lava through the woods and into fields and clearings. Trees and brush limited visibility. Lost in bloody confusion, the two armies flailed at each other as smoke wreathed the trees. Seeing little, Rosecrans and Bragg fed troops into combat piecemeal, able only to tell commanders to "move toward the sound of battle." Messengers got lost; brigades headed the wrong way; enemies stumbled into each other.

The battle seesawed as patches of land were fought over, captured, lost, and recaptured. The 26th Ohio, veterans drawn mostly from central and southern Ohio, spent the afternoon on the land of a farmer named Viniard, attacking and losing nearly half the regiment, retreating, then attacking again, only to end the day about where it had started.[56] In the evening dusk, confused soldiers fired on friendly forces. Saturday was a stand-off, accomplishing nothing more than long casualty lists on both sides.

Darkness ended the day's fighting, but not the misery. Surgeons worked by firelight cutting off torn limbs. Soldiers trying to sleep could hear the forest ringing with the cries of the wounded left behind. On this unusually cold night, recalled Lt. Wilson Vance of the 21st Ohio, a dozen men huddled together for warmth, lying front to back like spoons.[57] Water was scarce. Ambrose Bierce wrote how, in the gloom, a farmer's land undulated with strange, silent, crawling shapes. They were wounded men on hands and knees, struggling foot by foot to reach a farm pond. Some used only their hands, dragging their legs behind them. Their motions were strange, unnatural, their arms rising and falling as if to pray. Here and there, a shape fell motionless; other men died as they drank, their heads disappearing below the surface. Streaked with gore, the site became known as "Bloody Pond."[58]

The fog blanketing Chickamauga next morning fit the mood in both headquarters. General Longstreet, whose reinforcements had arrived during the night, noticed a dismal air in Bragg's headquarters.[59] In the other army, a *Cincinnati Commercial* correspondent was filled with "indefinable dread" as he watched the usually talkative commander Rosecrans emerge from his quarters, uncharacteristically grim and silent, and ride away without a word.[60]

The early fighting on Sunday was as vicious and inconclusive as the day before. The Union left, at the northern end of Rosecrans's army, fared best, thanks to such hard-fighting units as a brigade of four regiments—two of them from Ohio—led by Col. Ferdinand Van Derveer, a former sheriff of Butler County. One of his regiments was the German-speaking 9th Ohio, a smart, proud outfit from Cincinnati that had developed a reputation for bayonet charges. It made one here in the face of a Confederate charge. The startled Confederates turned and ran.[61] *

Then Rosecrans made a fatal mistake. Rearranging his forces, he unwittingly opened a gap in his line of battle and, coincidentally, Longstreet struck at exactly that point. Confederates swarmed through the hole, flanking the Federals left and right. A soldier saw a stunned Rosecrans cross himself and thought to himself, "[W]e are in a desperate situation."[62] Soon, the Union right and center collapsed. Unable to rally their men and thinking the day was lost, Rosecrans and two of his corps commanders, McCook and Crittenden, joined their panicked soldiers and by mid-day were rushing toward Chattanooga. "We'll see you north of the Ohio," fleeing soldiers shouted to each other.[63]

A death mourned on both sides was that of Union Brig. Gen. William Haines Lytle, the "poet-soldier" from Cincinnati. Already hit in the spine, Lytle had been sitting on the ground in great pain when another bullet hit him, passing through his cheek and temple. His mouth filled with blood. Unable

* A historian of the 9th Ohio observed, "Our bayonets did not rust; they glittered in action so much they hurt the Rebels' eyes." [Grebner, 87]

Desperate, last-ditch fighting by Union forces swirled around the Snodgrass House at Chickamauga.

to speak, he embraced an officer around the knees, then fell back, dead.
The bullet came from a Mississippi regiment commanded by Patton Anderson,
a man with whom Lytle, before the war, had sworn eternal friendship. After the
Confederates had captured the field, a sorrowful Anderson and other officers
filed by Lytle's body paying their respects. [64]

Rosecrans was partway to Chattanooga before he realized not all his army
had fled. Maj. Gen. George Thomas stubbornly remained where the Union left
had been, "serene amidst the storm" as he directed left-behind fragments
of McCook's and Crittenden's corps together with his own XIV Corps.[65]
For standing firmly against the Confederate horde that afternoon, he would
forever be known as "The Rock of Chickamauga." (Brigadier General Garfield,
now serving on Rosecrans's staff as his adjutant, bravely rode back
to encourage Thomas, but arrived too late to make a difference.)

Thomas's patchwork force arranged itself on and around a series of four
knolls forming a ridge known by various names, including Snodgrass Hill and
Horseshoe Ridge. Here, the outnumbered Federals fought throughout Sunday
afternoon, beating back one furious Confederate assault after another. Among
the Ohio regiments taking part were the 21st Ohio and the 125th Ohio, two
units that fought with very different results.

The 125th Ohio was a northeastern Ohio outfit commanded by Col.
Emerson Opdycke. A volunteer from Warren, Opdycke was brave to the point
of recklessness, braving enemy sharpshooters to remain on his horse.[66] It was

a dangerous perch from which, he wrote, "I constantly kept myself informed."[67] Having fought its way through the Confederates to reinforce Thomas, Opdycke's regiment was greeted by a Union general shouting, "That was a glorious charge and if I live it shall ... go into history." The 125th, the general declared, had fought like tigers. From that day on, the 125th was referred to as "Opdycke's Tigers."[68] Having done their best, however, Opdycke's men departed the battlefield, bringing with them an enviable reputation. The 21st Ohio would not be so fortunate.

Recruited from farmers in northwest Ohio, the 21st Ohio had become a battle-hardened regiment distinguished by its Colt Repeating Rifles. Resembling a revolver fitted with a stock and longer barrel, a fully loaded Colt could be fired five times to every one shot of a muzzle-loader. Anchoring Thomas's right, the men of the 21st lay on the ground using their extraordinary firepower to stun the Confederates who attacked repeatedly. A Confederate

Ohio Gen. William Haines Lytle, known as the "poet-soldier," died at Chickamauga, mourned even by Confederates who were acquainted with him.

prisoner seeing the regiment's thin line of men up close exclaimed, "My God, we thought you had a division here!"[69]

By early afternoon, however, Union ammunition was almost depleted and runners were scrounging bullets from the dead and wounded. "The thunder, as of a thousand anvils, still goes on in our front," Brig. Gen. John Beatty observed. "Men fall around us like leaves in autumn."[70] Thomas was beginning to think his patchwork defense force would have to resort to their bayonets and bare hands.

Several miles away, however, Union reserve forces had been listening to the racket drifting up from the south. Hearing nothing from Rosecrans, the Reserve Corps commander, Maj. Gen. Gordon Granger, decided to join the fighting without orders. The Reserve Corps's Gen. Steedman, leading nearly four thousand men accompanied by new supplies of ammunition, arrived at Horseshoe Ridge to the grateful cheers of Thomas's men. Asked what he wanted done if he were wounded or killed, Steedman is said to have replied, "I don't know what you could do for me except, by Gawd, to see that those damned reporters spell my name with two *ees*." (Steedman pronounced his name as if it were *Stedman*.)[71]

Sizing up the situation, Steedman then attacked the Confederates in a furious rush that drove them back at the cost of hundreds of his own men. His horse was shot out from under him, but he mounted another charge. When his force finally was forced to go on defense, it threw back repeated Confederate attacks coming so close that an Ohioan was able to seize an Alabama battle flag. By the end of the day, Steedman's division had lost 1,732 men out of the 3,900 with which he had arrived.[72]

By standing firm, Thomas, Steedman, and their men shielded the fleeing portions of the main army from attack. Around 4 p.m., Rosecrans was finally heard from with a message ordering Thomas to withdraw. The retreat became another chaotic chapter in a chaotic battle. Some units, including Steedman's reserve division, Beatty's brigade, and Opdycke's 125th Ohio, were able to retreat in good orders; others panicked, and in the confusion some, including the 21st and 89th Ohio, unwittingly remained too long on the battlefield.

These two Ohio regiments, together with the 22nd Michigan, had lost contact with the army's command structure and were unaware of the order to withdraw. As they faced a hopeless situation, a staff officer who has never been identified came up to them and ordered them to remain and fight, although they were almost out of ammunition. After the three weary regiments made a last desperate charge, relying mainly on their bayonets, many of the

Long delayed, a monument commemorating the 21st Ohio's brave stand was finally erected on Chickamauga's Horseshoe Ridge.

men were captured. Some Ohioans were able to elude their captors, but 171 men of the 89th Ohio and 116 of the 21st Ohio, including its commander, Maj. Arnold McMahan, were caught and sent to Confederate prisons, where many would die.

The tragedy did not end there. After the battle, Brig. Gen. John M. Brannan, a regular army man from Indiana, accused the 21st and its commander of cravenly giving up to the enemy, snidely claiming "[t]he surrender of your command was accomplished so quietly as to escape the notice of all but the regiment on your immediate left."[73]

McMahan, whose regiment had fought to the last moment under impossible circumstances, was outraged after he returned from captivity and learned what Brannan had said. He spent the rest of his life writing letters, gathering testimonials, and struggling to redeem his regiment's reputation. Ironically, the ultimate rescuer of the 21st Ohio's honor was associated with the Confederate cause. In 1911, Archibald Gracie, son of one of the Confederate generals at Chickamauga, published *The Truth About Chickamauga*, an exhaustive study of almost every move made on both sides. Gracie mostly concerned himself with Chickamauga's primacy as a lost opportunity for the Confederacy, but he also examined—in minute detail—the Brannan-McMahan disagreement and the movements of General Granger of the Reserve Corps as well.

Gracie collected testimony from numerous eyewitnesses. He concluded the 21st Ohio, as well as the 22nd Michigan and 89th Ohio, did not quietly give up, as Brannan charged, but were "[a]bandoned to their Fate by General Brannan" himself, and, unaware that Brannan had departed, fought bravely to the last possible moment.[74] Gracie also dismissed General Granger's claims of valor in the battle's final hours on Snodgrass Hill and Horseshoe Ridge. Granger wasn't even there, Gracie argued. Instead, he was indulging his well-known fondness for directing artillery and was a half-mile away from his own troops. Steedman, not Granger, had led the attempted relief of Thomas.[75]

Brig. Gen. John Beatty, commander of one of Thomas's brigades, described Rosecrans' retreat to Chattanooga as "a melancholy one."[76] Wounded men who had managed to escape the battlefield now lay on the roadside, exhausted, waiting to die. Hoping friends would aid them, they called out names and regimental numbers as the columns passed by. A wounded soldier whose bowels were protruding cried out, "Jesus, have mercy on my soul!"[77] Many of the wounded lay by the roadside for days before they were rescued.

By Tuesday, September 22, most of Rosecrans's army was safe in Chattanooga and a dazed Rosecrans was in despair. In Washington, Stanton gnashed his teeth in fury as reports of the loss flowed in. Lincoln remarked that the badly rattled Rosecrans reminded him of a duck that had been hit on the head. There was no joy in Bragg's camp either, for his so-called "victory," followed by a slowness to pursue, had allowed the main body of the Union army to escape to a sanctuary.

Years after the war, one of Bragg's generals, Daniel H. Hill, wrote bitterly, "That 'barren victory' sealed the fate of the Southern Confederacy."[78] After the battle, both Bragg and Rosecrans, the professionally trained soldiers, were removed from command, while Steedman, the amateur, remained and was recommended for promotion.

A beast dwells within a few men, and it is almost impossible to predict in whom it will appear. It can be trained, but it cannot be created. The courtly Robert E. Lee, the prayerful Stonewall Jackson, the civilian failure Ulysses S. Grant, and the Falstaffian James B. Steedman all had the rare ability to lead thousands of men to their deaths in order to achieve the deaths of thousands more of the enemy.

Such men were energized by battle. Their thinking seemed to clarify as pressures rose. Grant's military secretary, Adam Badeau, said of him, "In battle, the sphinx awoke. The outward calm was even then not entirely broken; but the utterance was prompt, the ideas were rapid, the judgment was decisive, the words were those of command. The whole man became intense, as it were, with a white heat."[79]

There was a long list of professionally educated military men within whom the beast did not dwell: George B. McClellan, who knew how to train and inspire an army, but loved it too much; the braggarts John Pope and Joseph Hooker, who lost their nerve at critical moments; the bumbling Ambrose Burnside and the steady but unimaginative George Meade; the professionally trained Henry Halleck, Don Carlos Buell, and William S. Rosecrans, commanders who squandered their opportunities; the saturnine Braxton Bragg, whose greatest genius lay in making enemies.

The drive to fight furiously in the face of great odds was a life-long part of James B. Steedman, a boorish man of questionable ethics who was hard to like but impossible to suppress. In 1857, a Toledo newspaper called him "a devoted partisan—we might almost say an unscrupulous one [who has] pluck to the bone."[80] New York newsman William F. G. Shanks remarked on Steedman's "roughness, nonchalance, and impudence."[81] One of Steedman's officers, Col. John Mitchell, a lawyer from Columbus, said that, except for fighting, "no more worthless man ever commanded men than General Steedman. He had no idea of the needs of his men. ... His devotion to cards and whiskey and women filled the measure of his delight except when under fire and then he was a lion."[82]

Unscrupulous, impudent, and almost "worthless." That was Steedman. But, oh, how the man could fight.

Liberty Warner

He was a preacher's kid, with a face of blushing innocence, growing up on the farm his Methodist minister father worked to keep body and soul together, in a remote corner of Wood County. He had been taught that swearing and killing and quite a few other things were very, very bad, but he was nineteen years old and war fever had seized men and boys everywhere, so his father, the Rev. Henry Warner, and his mother, Jane Elizabeth Wright Warner, sadly saw young Liberty Warner off as the 21st Ohio Infantry departed Findlay in late September 1861, headed for where fighting was expected: Kentucky.

Army life was a revelation. At Camp Dennison, a wide-eyed Warner saw a one-legged man beat an intact one in a foot race, witnessed soldiers stealing pies and cakes from vendors, and watched "all sorts foot races, boxing, wrestling, etc." Within a few weeks, in camp in Kentucky, however, the preacher's kid was expressing dismay over his rough company: "This is a hard

Nineteen-year-old Liberty Warner, an Ohio preacher's son, went off to war with the 21st Ohio and died on Horseshoe Ridge in the last hours of the Battle of Chickamauga.

place," he wrote his parents. "I have become fully disgruntled with the profanity & vulgarity of the soldiery and do not fall in with it."

Nevertheless, young Liberty Warner was not a complainer by nature and his letters suggest that he withstood the hard life of an infantryman bravely and well. He was devoted to his comrades, who called him "Lib." The 21st occupied Bowling Green, Kentucky, then Huntsville, Alabama, and by the end of 1862 young Warner was a seasoned infantryman, fighting at Stones River and receiving his first red badge of courage, one of the regiment's 140 casualties. He spent the next two months in a military hospital in Indiana, devoting his abundance of time—unsuccessfully—to attempting to raise a mustache.

"It appears just as smooth there as when I was a yearling," he sadly reported.

By March 1863, he was back with the Army of the Ohio and in late summer took part in Rosecrans's skillful, if unappreciated, maneuvering of Bragg southward. That meant Liberty Warner would take part in the disastrous battle at Chickamauga. On the Lord's Day—Sunday, September 20—he and his comrades found themselves abandoned and besieged on Horseshoe Ridge, running low on ammunition as they faced a rising tide of Confederates.

On October 3, Warner's cousin William Barber, one of the few members of the 21st who had escaped from Chickamauga, wrote his uncle, Henry Warner: *It falls to me to write you the sad news of the death of your son Liberty. He was killed in the battle of Sunday on the 20th Sept. He was shot in the breast and died almost instantly. ... Such a battle I never saw as the battle on Sunday.* Barber added notes to Aunt Jane—*I tell you we miss him*—and to Liberty's siblings: *He was beloved by all the company and all who knew him.*

On December 7 William Barber wrote again, probably responding to Henry and Jane Warner's request for their son's personal effects: *About Liberty's things. He did not have any here except an overcoat, which the lieutenant sold and said he would send the money to you. His clothing fell into the hands of the enemy … I did not see Liberty after he was shot.*

What Barber meant was that Liberty's body, like many others, had been left behind on Horseshoe Ridge, abandoned to the Confederates: *I do not know whether he was buried or no*, Barber admitted. The unmentioned reality was that there had been no time to bury the dead after the 21st Ohio was broken up, with some men fleeing and others captured.[83]

After Grant arrived in Chattanooga, broke the siege, and drove the Confederates out of the region, the 9th Ohio crossed the old Horseshoe Ridge battleground on an intelligence mission and found, according to the regiment's historian, "a sickening sight. Putrefying corpses, detached arms and legs, and skeletons with dried skins clinging to their bones, lay scattered everywhere." The Confederates had disposed of some corpses by stuffing them down a well.[84]

Liberty Warner's remains were never found.

OHIO MAKES A DECISION

Exiled by Lincoln and delivered under flag of truce to Confederate General Bragg in May 1863, Clement Laird Vallandigham of Dayton was a prize the Confederates wished they hadn't won and a gift they did not intend to keep. Northerners might call Vallandigham a traitor for opposing the Union war effort, but Vallandigham had also opposed secession and then had proposed compromise and reunion between North and South. The South wanted none of it and had no use for the man.

Vallandigham had departed Cincinnati, under guard, on May 22, 1863, arriving two days later at the Tennessee headquarters of General Rosecrans, who relished the opportunity to lecture Vallandigham on loyalty. Accustomed to captive audiences, Rosecrans proved no match for the wily politician. The Ohio Democrat not only made a monkey of the general, but also made him like it, and they parted cordially. By May 29 Vallandigham had been transferred, under flag of truce, to the company of Confederate General Bragg, who, with no sense of irony whatsoever, welcomed him to a "land of liberty."[85]

Far from seeking citizenship in Dixie, Vallandigham curtly declared himself a "prisoner of war" and a loyal citizen of the United States and Ohio.[86] Flummoxed by this political leper thrust in their midst, the Confederates finally

In late May 1863, former Ohio Congressman Clement L. Vallandigham was turned over to the Confederates, exiled for his outspoken opposition to the war.

decided that someone who so outraged the North couldn't be all bad, so they extended Southern hospitality, though cautiously. Val reciprocated it with a twinkling radiance that disarmed Southern newsmen. They looked the smiling forty-two-year-old Ohioan up and down, noting his hooked nose and florid complexion, and made no snide remarks about the size of his mouth. They were impressed by his "pleasant manner," his eloquence, and an "honesty … which has won your regard and admiration before you know it."[87]

The Confederate government was not displeased when Vallandigham made it clear he wanted to move on. After twenty-four days in the Confederacy, the Ohio Democrat boarded a blockade runner for Bermuda. From there, he went to Canada, eventually making his way to Windsor (in what is now Ontario) by August 24. He rented a two-room suite in a hotel facing Detroit just across the river. A Union gunboat happened to have been moored there with one of its guns seeming to bear on his windows, a blunt reminder that he could not return to America.

Vallandigham drew comfort from the fact his wife, Louisa, and their ten-year-old son, Charlie, joined him in Windsor. A nervous, fragile woman, Louisa had been badly shaken by her husband's difficulties. Her condition worried him during his absence, but now she seemed restored to health. Vallandigham also had work to do: enraged by his treatment and the Lincoln administration's apparent threat to the civil liberties of Americans, Ohio's Democratic rank and file had nominated Vallandigham for governor, which meant he would have to campaign without being able to go on the campaign trail.

Even without Vallandigham's presence, the Ohio gubernatorial election campaign of 1863 turned into an all-out fight that makes modern American election campaigns look like tea parties. It pitted a stubborn idealist looking backward to peace and a restoration of the Union as it had been (Vallandigham for the "Peace Democrats") against a pragmatic, down-to-earth stump speaker who could appeal to patriotism and the future (fat, untidy, tobacco-chewing John Brough for the Union Party favored by "War Democrats" and Republicans).

Each side fired broadsides of insults, lies, and accusations at the other. Vallandigham was incessantly accused of disloyalty ("Hurrah for Brough and Abraham / And a rope to hang Vallandigham" ran one jingle), while Democrats exploited racial bias ("Protect us from Negro Equality" was the most popular banner). To all this, Vallandigham could only contribute letters for surrogates to read at rallies. George E. Pugh, the Democratic candidate for lieutenant governor, drove himself so mercilessly on behalf of the ticket that his voice gave out.

The third largest state in the Union and a bellwether then as now, Ohio was watched anxiously by the rest of the nation. Had the election taken place in June, when Union morale was low and resentment over the Emancipation Proclamation high, Vallandigham might have won. By election day on October 13, however, Union victories at Vicksburg and Gettysburg had made the Republican administration's reputation improve. The raid on southern Ohio by John Hunt Morgan had also soured Ohioans on the Confederacy.

In a huge turnout, Vallandigham won the largest number of votes ever cast in Ohio until then, but Brough won a hundred thousand more, a crushing repudiation of the Democrats and an endorsement of the war effort. Soon the Copperhead movement would begin to lose steam. An exultant Lincoln is said to have wired Governor Tod, "Glory to God in the highest; Ohio has saved the Union."[88]

OHIO'S BLACK SOLDIERS

Early in November 1863, a blizzard screamed across central Ohio and into the faces of one of the most unusual groups of people the state had ever seen.

Headed by Governor Tod, the party included state officials, congressmen, military brass, and soldiers, and they were trudging through the storm together as if they were fellow human beings. They were that, of course, but never before had so many important Ohioans walked in something like friendship with so many African Americans. The soldiers were black.

After tramping from a railway depot to Camp Delaware, the group conducted a ceremony during which nearly eight hundred newly trained black soldiers heard Ohio officials "boldly" endorse abolition and an end to discrimination against blacks. Governor Tod even began his address of "fatherly counsel" to the men by asking if he could call them "his boys," in a gesture of affection, not condescension. It drew a roar of approval.

Governor Tod promised to fight for equal treatment and pay for the men, who were getting second-class treatment from the federal government. "His boys" swelled with pride. It was a throat-catching moment and a reporter present wondered "who, three years ago" could have imagined it. "The world moves, verily," he concluded.[89]

For much of Ohio's history, African Americans had been regarded by many whites as almost subhuman, to be feared, despised, and marginalized, and it has been observed that the state's first black regiment was "gotten up on the cheap to save white Ohioans from the draft."[90] But it was also another step forward in black Americans' long journey toward equality, a step that black leader John Mercer Langston predicted would "challenge the respect and admiration of the world."[91]

Langston, a lawyer and a graduate of Oberlin College, was Ohio's most admired black leader. For months he had been recruiting Midwestern African Americans for two black Massachusetts regiments, the 54th and 55th Massachusetts. At first, Governor Tod opposed Langston's raising a black regiment for Ohio, but by mid-June 1863 Tod had an epiphany: black enlistees could help meet the state's draft quota just as well as whites. Would Langston raise a regiment for Ohio?

Langston would. With rhetoric that could hold an audience spellbound for hours, Langston raised almost three hundred volunteers in scarcely a week. It was an uphill fight after that. White hostility dogged him on his travels around the state. To appease voters who feared "black equality," Washington decreed net pay for black soldiers would be $7, compared to $13 for whites, and there would be no federal bounty. Recruits suffered other problems. Uniforms were slow in coming. The men had to train with "inferior, condemned arms." Medical supplies were lacking.

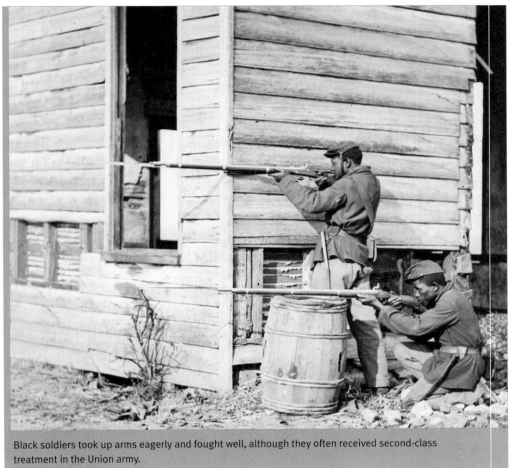

Black soldiers took up arms eagerly and fought well, although they often received second-class treatment in the Union army.

But Langston worked tirelessly, arguing that military service gave African Americans a chance to prove their "genius and power." He beseeched audiences throughout the state, "Pay or no pay, let us volunteer."[92] By early November, Langston had recruited nearly eight hundred men, two hundred more than the goal, for the 127th Ohio.

Accepted into Federal service and re-designated the 5th U.S. Colored Troops (5th USCT), the regiment was given white officers with progressive views. With Oberlin graduate and Latin tutor Giles W. Shurtleff as second in command (and eventual commander), the regiment shipped out to Norfolk, Virginia. It won praise for its performance in a number of engagements. Finally, in June 1864 Congress approved equal pay for black soldiers and early in 1865 made the first small gestures toward changing its all-white officer policy. By such small steps as these, the Day of Jubilo was coming closer.*

* In African-American tradition, Jubilo is the day on earth on which wrongs will be righted.

GRANT TO THE RESCUE

With no interesting battles in sight, Grant had languished for weeks at his Vicksburg headquarters after capturing the city. Suddenly, an electrifying telegram arrived. Grant seized Julia's hand and rushed east, ordered to a mysterious meeting in Nashville with an unidentified "officer of the War Department."[93] Reaching Indianapolis by October 17, Grant was about to continue on to Nashville when a special train arrived carrying the "officer of the War Department" who was determined to meet Grant even sooner than planned. It was the secretary of war himself, Edwin M. Stanton.

Grant had never met Stanton (although they had had "frequent conversations" by telegraph, their form of Instant Messenger). As Grant's train clacked its way to Nashville, Stanton aboard, the secretary of war gave Grant stunning news: Burnside's Department of the Ohio, Rosecrans's Department of the Cumberland, and Grant's own Department of the Tennessee—all together, most of the Western Theater—were being swept into one new "Military Division of the Mississippi," all of it to be under Grant's command immediately.

Stanton told Grant he could replace Rosecrans with Thomas, the "Rock of Chickamauga," if he so chose. Grant so chose.[94] Besieged in Chattanooga by Bragg, Rosecrans got news of his ouster by wire. Saying, "I cannot bear to meet my troops," he departed early the next morning for Cincinnati where he collapsed deeply anguished and racked by acute diarrhea.[95] On October 23, Grant's party arrived in Chattanooga at the little house that served Thomas for headquarters. They shared a warm meal, and then, as aides twitched in the background, Grant and Thomas sat stoically by the fire, smoking and saying nothing, two old soldiers in silent communion.

Next, Thomas and his officers described the situation in Chattanooga to Grant, who remained "immovable as a rock and silent as a sphinx." Then he fired questions at them. The next day, Grant went on an inspection tour of Union lines, the usual see-and-be-seen of new commanders. His reputation had outstripped the man, a member of Thomas's staff remarked: "Most of us were not a little surprised to find him a man of slim figure, five feet eight in height, slightly stooped, weighing only 135 pounds."[96] Grant could pass for a "slouchy little subaltern," another officer wrote.[97]

Having seen and heard all he needed, the unimpressive little leader of the new Department of the Mississippi returned to headquarters, sat down, and penned his first dispatches to his commanders, writing smoothly and without hesitation, pushing each finished page to the floor before beginning the next.

The orders went out in all directions and soon the Union's Western armies were shaking themselves awake. Sam Grant was in command now.

My Dear, *dear* Jamie

Until February 1863, James Garfield had been living in Washington, rooming with Secretary of the Treasury Chase, and awaiting a new assignment. Then Rosecrans appointed him his chief of staff. Despite strong religious differences—about which Rosecrans could not keep quiet—the two became close friends. Nonetheless, Garfield slowly became disillusioned with Rosecrans, peaking with the latter's failures at Chickamauga.

Two days after Rosecrans's army had retreated to Chattanooga, Garfield sent wife Lucretia two terse notes giving few details of what happened, but

Lucretia Garfield remained faithful to a husband who, in the early years of their marriage, was not faithful to her.

implying he was unharmed. He sent his love to mother and friends and "[k]isses to dear little Trot," now three, but neither to Crete. He unbent enough only to greet her as "Dearest Crete." (signing off with "Ever your own James.")[98]

Although Crete had felt coldness from James for much of 1862, she wrote back lovingly to "My Dear *dear* Jamie," telling him she longed to "draw your head close down to my heart and fondle and caress you as I would the trusting love-needing child."[99] It was Crete, of course, who needed expressions of tenderness and soon would need them even more.

On October 15, Rosecrans released Garfield from duty as his adjutant, as Garfield wished. On his way home to Hiram, he was questioned about Rosecrans by Secretary of War Stanton. Then Garfield went to Washington to deliver Rosecrans's official report—and, most likely, his own doubts about his former commander. He returned to Hiram when "Little Trot" took ill. She died on December 1 and five days later the bereaved father was back in Washington. In the aftershock of that loss, Garfield was gentler with Crete, even writing her [h]ow much I want you with me," not one of his more common sentiments.[100]

Having seen enough fighting and once again looking for Something Else, Garfield resigned his army commission December 6 to take the seat in Congress to which he had been elected the year before. He was glad to get back into politics. Soon enough, there would be another reason to enjoy his return east. Her name was Lucia Gilbert Calhoun.

To Learn More:

The deadly fields at Gettysburg—which saw the most famous though not the most important battle of the war—is a national military park (**www.nps.gov/gett/** or **717-334-1124, ext. 431**). Richard A. Baumgartner tells you all you could want to know about Ohio's role in *Buckeye Blood: Ohio at Gettysburg*.

Many Ohioans were lost in the Western Theater's one major defeat, Rosecrans' meltdown at Chickamauga in northwestern Georgia. Considerable information about the 21st Ohio, which was mauled at Chickamauga, can be found on the "Company C, 21st Ohio Volunteer Infantry Homepage (**http://hometown.aol.com/ dam1941/Coc21stovichickamauga.html**). Information for visitors to the national park encompassing the battlefields of both Chickamauga and Chattanooga can be found at **http://www.nps.gov/chch/** or **706-866-9241**).

It is still possible to visit the scene of the climactic battle of John Hunt Morgan's July 1863 raid through southern Ohio. The four-acre park at Buffington Island (which is not on an island) offers a monument, informative signs, a picnic ground, and an opportunity to reflect on a Southern cavalier who (as his widow put it) "gambled on life and ... lost."

African-American history and Oberlin's important role in it are celebrated by the Oberlin Heritage Center (**http://www.oberlinheritage.org/** or **440-774-1700**). One of its buildings is the Monroe House, a home of Giles W. Shurtleff, who commanded the first black regiment from Ohio. Nat Brandt wrote *The Town That Started the Civil War*, illustrating how central Oberlin and its people were to the struggle for black freedom and the Civil War.

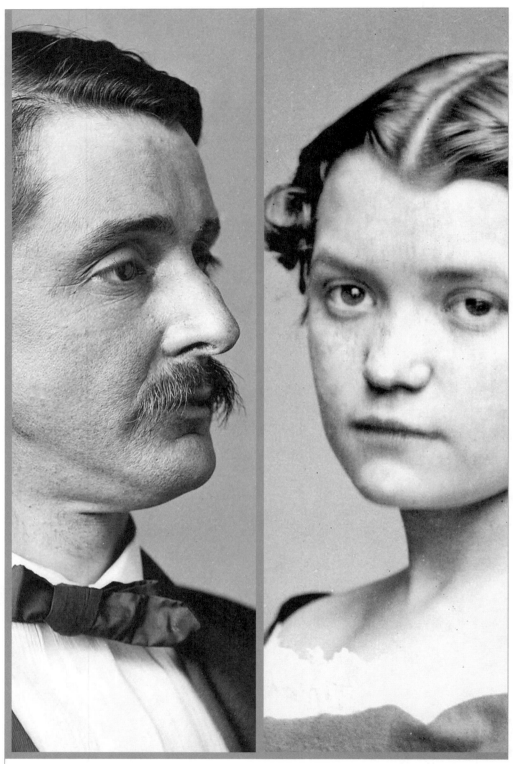

William Sprague was a wealthy Rhode Island politician. Ohioan Kate Chase was the belle of Washington society.

11

GRANT TAKES CHARGE

Late 1863 to August 1864

The wedding was all she could have ever wanted. The ceremony performed by a bishop. A reception for five hundred of Washington's royals: Cabinet members, Congressmen, diplomats, and those military big bugs not occupied elsewhere. President Lincoln at the reception for more than two hours. Guests dancing to music by the United States Marine Band and demanding encores of a march named in her honor.[1] The groom's gift to his bride a diamond-and-pearl tiara with matching bracelet and earrings adding a corona of glitter to her in her white velvet gown with its huge hoop skirt and train. Most of all, her dashing new partner in life, not only prominent in politics but rich, a man who could give her the caring, the intimacy, *the love*, that she had always craved.

Such was the wedding on November 12, 1863, of Catherine Jane "Kate" Chase and William Sprague. Eldest daughter of Secretary of the Treasury Salmon P. Chase, the swan-necked Kate had emerged from an Ohio childhood like a beautiful butterfly to instantly become Washington's reigning belle, capital society's virgin queen.

Statuesque, intelligent, and exquisitely poised, Kate was her widowed father's pilot navigating the perfumed waters of Washington society and, loyally and quietly, the tireless supporter of his quest for the presidency. The lucky man to marry all this was William Sprague, heir to a Rhode Island textile mill empire and known nationally as the "boy governor" because he had been elected to Rhode Island's highest office when he was barely thirty.

Kate and William had met in Cleveland in 1860. A few months later, William, in full military plumage topped with a yellow ostrich feather, led Rhode Island troops into Washington. Soon he was finding time to enjoy an "enhanced poetical sensation" with Kate.[2] The courtship continued with a barrage of cooing letters to "My darling Katie," and by late May 1863 Kate and William had agreed to marry that November.

The social event of the fall season, the Sprague-Chase nuptials set tongues a-flutter, inflating the value of Kate's tiara, bracelet, and earrings to $50,000. William's gift had cost only a fraction of that. It was not the only thing about this marriage that wasn't quite what it seemed.

After meeting William, presidential secretary John Hay pronounced the boy governor a "small, insignificant youth, who bought his place."[3] He wasn't the first to dislike William. Of indifferent intellect, untidy dress, and careless manners, young William was thought cloddish by Rhode Island's social elite, and probably caddish as well: in 1859 he had skipped out on the inconvenient pregnancy of a certain young woman in Providence.

Still, the highly cultivated Kate and the loutish William shared an odd kind of symmetry: both were prominent young scions, one motherless, the other fatherless. For those who could read the portents, however, a scene at their wedding would have seemed ominous.

Off-horse and out of uniform, the diminutive William in his plain black suit shrank into insignificance, left to dogpaddle in the wake of the dazzling Kate in full hoops. When the doors to the Chase rear parlor opened to present the newlyweds to reception guests, the effect was that of a horsefly hovering by a wedding cake.

The wedding spectacular flattened the secretary of treasury's purse, but Salmon Chase, who went to sleep every night dreaming of the presidency, probably saw it as an investment in public relations. In fact, all three principals had something to gain from this wedding. William, without a father since age thirteen, had grown up needing the respect of his peers and validation as a man. Playing soldier was one way he proved himself worthy; winning the hand of fair Kate, Washington's shiniest ornament, was another.

Kate needed loving intimacy. She had grown up motherless, much of her youth spent away from home in boarding school while her emotionally distant father was preoccupied with law and politics. Salmon was a nineteenth-century father-knows-best kind of man, not only aloof, but also afraid to risk too close an attachment to his daughter. After all, he had already lost three wives and four of six children to illness. What Salmon craved now, with an outsized sense of entitlement and a hunger that gnawed like a badger, was to be president of the United States.

These were three wounded and needy people. None would get what he or she wanted. One coveted the presidency and one yearned for respect. And then there was Kate. All she wanted was love.

THE BATTLES OF CHATTANOOGA

Civil War armies resting near each other sometimes softened around the edges, allowing unofficial truces and even fraternization to spring up. At first, Union and Confederate picket guards around Chattanooga popped away at each other to no great purpose until exasperated officers on both sides told them to knock it off. Soon enemy pickets were trading coffee, tobacco, and soldierly scuttlebutt. John Beatty watched a Confederate officer and a Union officer swap newspapers and then chat for a time. "There appears to be a perfect understanding that neither party shall fire unless an advance is made in force," the Ohioan remarked.[4]

Touring his new base, Grant rode along its edges, unburdened by pretense or armed escort. He waved off salutes from Union pickets, but from the enemy side of a narrow stream a sharp-eyed Confederate with a taste for the absurd called out, "Turn out the guard—General Grant!" Enemy pickets snapped smartly to attention and Grant politely lifted his hat in return.[5] Next, he struck up a conversation with a soldier before discovering he, too, was a Confederate. They chatted peaceably anyway.[6] Grant may have been grinning in his beard as he rode away, but he wanted fraternization to stop. And so, someone sighed, "malevolence prevailed once again." [7]

Grant's biggest problem at the moment was not fraternization, but a hungry army. After Rosecrans's ignominious retreat to Chattanooga, Bragg's Confederates had settled on Old Rosy's doorstep, determined to starve out the army they had failed to destroy at Chickamauga. Perched on the heights around the town, Confederates looked down on the Federal camps, which could receive only a trickle of supplies via one long, torturous wagon road.

Trapped in Chattanooga, Union soldiers on their hands and knees searched storerooms for crumbs and trailed forage wagons looking for kernels of corn. Horses and mules died by the hundreds. There was barely enough ammunition for one day's fighting.[8]

Rosecrans had gotten his army into quite a pickle, but the day after Grant arrived, "I issued orders for opening ... a *cracker* line, as the soldiers appropriately termed it"[9] ("Crackers" were hardtack, the military staple.)

During long intervals between battles, Confederate and Union soldiers sometimes declared unofficial truces to trade gossip, newspapers, coffee, and tobacco.

Implementing a plan developed but not yet executed under Rosecrans, the new Union commander ordered the capture of a strategic river crossing its route to a Union supply depot.

Confederates were taken by surprise. Their desperate night-time counterattack failed when they mistook stampeding Union mules for cavalry. The crossing fell to Union forces and the route was opened. Belying his sober appearance, Grant "laughed heartily" when he was petitioned to award the stampeding mules the "honorary rank of horses."[10] Scarcely a week after Grant's arrival, fresh supplies began arriving in Chattanooga, the hungry garrison cheering, "Full rations, boys! Three cheers for the Cracker Line"[11]

Long before Grant's arrival, Washington had dispatched reinforcements to Chattanooga. In September, Fighting Joe Hooker—still in service though in reduced command—had been ordered to take two corps from Meade's dormant Army of the Potomac and rush by rail to Rosencrans's aid. From the opposite direction, Sherman was marching overland from Mississippi. Arriving in November, Sherman "came bounding" into headquarters. Grant, more jocular with his friend Sherman than with other officers, offered him a cigar and "the chair of *honor*," a rocker. Sherman countered that it was Grant's by rights. He sat down when Grant quipped that he was only giving "proper respect to age" (Sherman was two years older.)[12]

To break out of his Chattanooga fishbowl, Grant had about sixty thousand men—seventeen thousand of them Ohio infantrymen, artillerists, and cavalrymen—and three seasoned commanders: Thomas, Hooker, and Sherman.[13] The ever-quarrelsome Bragg had forty-five thousand men perched on the heights around Chattanooga and his usual disaffected contingent of lieutenants.[14] Grant had the manpower, Bragg the position. Something had to give.

Knowing a fight was looming, Union men from general to private began a soldierly ritual: writing, without admitting it, what might be their last letters home, their sentiments carefully wrapped in banalities. Writing Julia in Louisville, Grant hoped she had visited her in-laws during a recent trip to Ohio, asked her to kiss son Jess—"the little rascal"— for him and closed, "Kisses for yourself dear Julia. Ulys."[15]

Hillory Shifflett, a forty-year-old private in a Dayton-area company of the 1st Ohio, wrote his wife, Jemima. "I hante no nuse [news] only we are looking for another fight ever minit," he scrawled. "I want you to git little Jonny a par of boots and all of the rest what tha neade and donte forgit yourself. So Mima … I will close these few lines so farwell my Dear wife untell Death."[16]

Military wisdom holds that no battle ever goes as planned, but almost everything about the Battles of Chattanooga was a surprise. The curtain-raiser went smoothly enough, when, on Monday, November 21, the Federals swept Confederate outposts from Orchard Knob, a hillock between the lines useful for command and control.

Grant and Thomas posted themselves there to watch the rest of the drama unfold. It did not follow the script.

Sherman had been given the biggest assignment: to attack the northern end of Missionary Ridge (known then as "Mission Ridge") and head down the ridge, rolling up the enemy as he went. From the southern end, Hooker was to push northward. Meanwhile, Thomas's Army of the Cumberland—which Grant assumed had been worn out by the horrors of Chickamauga—had the lightest duty, to watch the middle of the ridge and remain in reserve, stepping in only if needed.

That was the plan, but Sherman's attack the next day, Tuesday, was stalled by unexpectedly rough terrain and fierce resistance.[17] By contrast, Hooker put on a surprising show to the south, moving steadily through pockets of fog to sweep Confederates from their perches on supposedly impregnable Lookout Mountain.

As fascinated Union commanders on Orchard Knob watched through

Confederates who were besieging Chattanooga perched on steep Lookout Mountain until an attention-getting Union attack that had surprising results.

spyglasses, the tiny figures of Hooker's men could be seen pushing Confederates up Lookout Mountain's north slope, disappearing in woods or patches of fog only to emerge at higher points. When darkness fell, the musket flashes "resembled a line of fireflies intermitting their light," a spectator recalled.[18]

The outnumbered Confederates soon gave up Lookout Mountain, and the fight for it—really a series of skirmishes—became mythologized as the "Battle

Above the Clouds," an unexpected success to counter-balance Sherman's frustration a few miles north.

Bragg had lost Lookout Mountain but he had a better position on Mission Ridge on Chattanooga's east side. About five hundred feet high and several miles long, the ridge had a steep, brushy face scored by gullies and studded with outcroppings. To this the Confederates had added three lines of entrenchments: one along the base, another half-way up, and a third on the crest bolstered by artillery.

As Wednesday wore on, Sherman and Hooker were making little progress attacking Mission Ridge at its ends. Grant decided to take a chance and send Thomas's Army of the Cumberland head-on against the ridge's mid-section. Supposedly spent and demoralized by Chickamauga, they were ordered to attempt no more than the first line of entrenchments.

First, however, Thomas's soldiers would have to cross a field in full view of the enemy. Making the attack would be eighty-eight Union regiments, including thirty-two from Ohio, grouped in four divisions, each assigned a sector. Philip Sheridan commanded one of the divisions. Thomas's men had been waiting since dawn, staring at the ridge and watching the "Johnnies" at the top "waving their flags and guidons at us in defiance," Capt. John Hartzell of the 105th Ohio remembered.

Six Union cannon shots in mid-afternoon signaled the attack. "We all seemed to raise up and start at the time, the colors taking the lead and flanks hanging back, just as you see a flock of wild geese flying," according to Hartzell.[19] Time compressed for Col. Emerson Opdycke, now leading a small brigade in addition to his 125th Ohio. "Will I ever live to cross this plain?" he wondered.[20]

Union forces, including many Ohioans, attacked the base of Missionary Ridge as ordered, then kept on going.

Under "a terrible storm of shot and shell," the Union soldiers crossed the field and overran the line of rifle pits at the ridge's base, scattering their defenders. Here they were supposed to stop, but as Grant and Thomas on Orchard Knob watched in astonishment, the Federals kept going, clambering up the ridge's face in pursuit of fleeing Confederates. The attackers realized it was safer to scale the ridge, taking advantage of sheltering overhangs, than to remain crowded at the base exposed to enemy fire.

A member of the 105th Ohio remembered, "We had no orders and no distinct purpose. … [T]he enemy were fleeing up the slope and we were bound to follow them. We did not stop to think whether we could carry the crest or not—we did not think at all! ... The wave of men, drunk with the frenzy of battle, rolled and tumbled up the hill."[21]

Emerson Opdycke climbed the ridge's face on his horse, ranging back and forth on paths better suited to mountain goats, bending down to prick stragglers with his sword.[22] Although orders to halt reached some of the officers, Sheridan "could not bear to order the recall of troops now so gallantly climbing the hill step by step."[23] He told his brigade commanders "to go for the ridge."[24]

Scrambling up the ridge's face, the attackers split into six arrow-shaped columns heading for the top. Upset, Grant demanded, "Thomas, who ordered those men up the ridge?"[25] No one had, for this had turned into a "soldiers' battle"—one in which the men took the initiative away from senior commanders. As Grant and Thomas watched in mixed dismay and admiration, the soldiers kept scrambling up the steep face of the ridge until the six columns poured over the crest.

For the rest of their lives, the attackers of Mission Ridge would argue over who was first to reach the top. Brig. Gen. William B. Hazen devoted fifty pages of his memoirs to insisting it was one of his regiments—the 1st Ohio. Led up the slope by long-legged Lt. Col. E. Bassett Langdon, the Ohioans paused to catch their breath in a sheltered spot just three yards short of the top. Then—according to Hazen—they broke over the crest while other regiments were still climbing. Colonel Langdon was shot through the face after gaining the crest, but he remained in command.

His 1st Ohio paid a price for its aggressiveness: eighteen of its men were killed or mortally wounded. One of them was Hillory Shifflet, whose last letter to "Mima" had bid her "farewell my Dear wife untell Death." His left shoulder torn away by a cannonball, Shifflet died within an hour.

Some Confederates fled the crest as Federals scrambled onto it, but those defending Bragg's headquarters held fast, their artillery hurling a "storm of grape." Grapeshot "sweeping through the air around you causes the same vibrations that a flock of pigeons does, when darting close by you," Opdycke later explained to his wife.[26] But the Union men pressed on, capturing the

More than twelve thousand Union soldiers, including several of "Andrews' Raiders," are buried in the Chattanooga National Cemetery.

Rebel artillery, and Bragg himself barely escaped being taken prisoner. By the end of the day, the entire ridge belonged to Union forces. The Army of the Cumberland, battered veterans of Chickamauga, many of them Ohioans, had made the difference.

"Such a scene of wild exultation," John Hartzell recalled. For more than two months the men had thought capturing Mission Ridge "an impossibility," he said. "To attack and carry the fortified ridge had in no wise entered into our calculations; but here we were, and victory had sent our blood up. ... Well, we raged around there for a bit."[27] Men of the 105th Ohio walked about, clasping each others' hands and joining in repeated cheers.[28]

At the end of the day, the weary but happy soldiers lay down to sleep atop the ridge. "That night," an Ohioan observed, "our hardtack and coffee were better than a prince's feast, and our earthy bed was a couch for kings."[29] Then the men fell asleep, their feet to the fire. Hartzell awoke suddenly when his campfire got too close. He noticed the feet of the man lying next to him were ablaze. When Hartzell tried to rouse the man, he discovered he had been sleeping next to a dead Confederate.[30]

News of the victories reached Julia and the Grant children via the papers. "Hurrah! Hurrah! Bully for Grant!" son Jess shouted.[31] Lincoln wired his congratulations and in the House of Representatives Grant's old patron from

Illinois, Elihu Washburne, introduced a bill reinstating the rank of lieutenant general—the highest in the Union army—with Grant in mind.

In the South, morale plummeted among soldiers and civilians and the words "death knell of the Confederacy" were heard. Loss of the Mississippi River had split the Confederacy, much of it west of the Appalachians had been lost or isolated, and now, with Chattanooga gone, the Deep South was directly threatened.

On December 8, Gen. Robert E. Lee and CSA Pres. Jefferson Davis conferred in Richmond. Then Lee returned to his Army of Northern Virginia and Davis began working out whom he would appoint to replace the discredited Bragg. The Confederacy was becoming a walking corpse, but Lee and Davis had made up their minds: the bloodletting would go on.

CHANGE OF COMMAND

As Grant's star rose, so did Julia's anxiety about her *strabismus*—a muscle weakness that kept one eye from aligning with the other and caused her to allow photographs of herself only in profile. Pondering surgery, she told Ulys, "[Y]ou are getting to be such a great man, and I am such a plain little wife, I thought if my eyes were as others are I might not be so very, very plain." Embracing her, Grant replied, "Did I not see you and fall in love with you with those same eyes? I like them just as they are, and now, remember, you are not to interfere with them. They are mine."[32]

Treasuring the memory, Julia would write in her memoirs, "[M]y knight, my Lancelot!"[33] By early 1864, the North viewed Grant the same way. While Eastern armies, under Eastern eyes, had been tramping back and forth over the same bloody ground, seemingly to no avail, Grant had been achieving a string of victories and fracturing the Confederacy beyond the mountains and almost out of sight. But Washington was taking more and more notice.

Lincoln already was sold. By mid-1863 he had declared, "Grant is my man and I am his for the rest of the war."[34] Unlike his other constantly complaining generals, Grant "does the best he can with he has got," Lincoln gratefully noted.[35] Lincoln and Grant were plain men, kindred spirits from ordinary backgrounds, sons of the make-do, live-on-a-shoestring American Midwest.

Grant had rebuffed efforts in 1863 to bring him east to command strangers in a strange land. After his victory at Chattanooga, however, the quiet, self-effacing Westerner was the Union's man of the hour, even if he wished it otherwise. There was even talk of nominating him for the presidency, which he quickly dismissed.[36] With Grant in mind, Congress approved revival of the

Because of the misalignment of one of her eyes, Julia Grant allowed only pictures of herself in profile.

military grade of lieutenant general, the highest in the army.[37]

Duty called and Grant was forced to listen. In early March 1864 he went east to receive not only promotion to lieutenant general, the only one in the active forces, but also command of *all* Union armies, East and West.[38] Now Grant was the nation's general in chief and intended to act like one. Halleck, who had occupied the title but effectively relinquished its authority after Second Bull Run, would move into the background.

Grant met Lincoln for the first time at a White House reception, the rangy president beaming down on the stubby Grant like a proud father. Excited guests climbed on chairs and tables to get a better look at the general, obliging him to stand on a sofa. "The little, scared-looking man who stood on the crimson-covered sofa was the idol of the hour," a journalist observed.[39] "Really, it was very embarrassing," Grant told his wife later. "I heartily wished myself back in camp."[40]

In this imagined meeting of Lincoln and his generals, the president confers with three of his most important commanders: (l-r) Sherman, Sheridan, and Grant.

Formally commissioned lieutenant general the next day, Grant went upstairs in the White House for a private talk with the president. Lincoln and Grant came away from the meeting thoroughly pleased with each other. Next Grant paid a brief visit to the Army of the Potomac, where its commander, Meade, waited, fully expecting to be removed. Grant surprised Meade by retaining him.

A banquet was planned in Washington to honor to the new general in chief, but Grant declined, telling the president he had "had enough of this show business."[41] He hurried back to Nashville to close his Western headquarters and plan strategy.

Having suffered a succession of blowhards and failures in their own armies, Easterners liked everything they saw in the unpretentious and successful little Westerner. "We have found our hero," declared the *New York Herald*.[42]

THE WIDOW CALHOUN

Exactly who first said what and to whom we probably shall never know. Suffice it to say that in May 1864 Harmon Austin, an Ohio businessman and political ally of Garfield's, wrote the congressman in Washington and asked: *Are you having an affair?* and Garfield wrote back to say *No!*

But in June, Garfield suddenly appeared in Hiram. At first, he would only tell his wife, Lucretia, and their friend Almeda Booth he was so depressed that he was thinking of leaving Congress and returning to teaching. The same night, however, he burst out with a confession: he had fallen in love with a young New York widow named Lucretia Gilbert Calhoun. Calhoun is mostly a mystery woman. We only know she was quite young—twenty years old to James's thirty-two—and a writer for the *New York Tribune* and other periodicals. And, of course, for the perpetually restless Garfield, she was "Something Else."

Whether from genuine regret and regard for Crete or from awareness that public knowledge of the affair would scotch his political career, James promised to end the affair. Crete said, painfully, that she forgave him. Then he returned to Washington and an awkward exchange of letters with Crete followed. His first, dated June 12, was a mix of contrition (but not too much), defensiveness ("I still believe that I am worthy to be loved"), and the jarringly mundane ("I meant to say to you yesterday morning that I thought your garden could be improved a little in the way of hoeing.")[43] Hers to him—written the same day—expressed pain ("the sorrow you left in my heart"), hope ("is this not one of those struggles of the spirit by which a new life is gained?"), and enough anger to pass along the admittedly "cruel" remarks Garfield's old friend Almeda Booth had made soon after he left Hiram: "I feel as though a nightmare had gone away," Almeda said, and "[I]t is perfect childishness for him to feel so."[44]

Crete and James's letters during the summer of 1864 suggest he

A tall, handsome man with pale blue eyes, James A. Garfield was also a restless husband.

was finding it hard to break off the affair. But after his re-election that fall, the family was re-united. With the widow Calhoun out of the picture by now, Crete and their little son Harry joined Garfield in Washington until the following March. The Garfield marriage endured, without interruption, until the sudden end of James's life seventeen years later.

Uncle Billy Fancies Atlanta

On January 30, 1864, Pvt. Andrew Altman of the 68th Ohio had sat down with pen and paper near Vicksburg to send his father in Henry County some unwelcome news. "Father I did reinlist again," he wrote. That would earn him a $400 bounty and a furlough, he explained, and, "If I can make that money by laying in a tent it is all right, is it not." The anxious young soldier concluded, "Now father I do not want you to be angry with me, but wright to me. ... I am satisfied if you are and pleas tell me all about this in the next letter."[45]

There was nothing Altman's father could do about it, of course, and neither could Maj. Gen. William Tecumseh Sherman, who grumbled that re-enlistment furloughs like Altman's were stripping him of soldiers just when he needed them. While Altman had been working up his nerve to write home, Sherman, red-faced and impatient as usual, was swooping down on far-flung camps in the Mississippi Valley, rounding up his forces for the opening campaign of the 1864 fighting season.

By February 3, Sherman and twenty-one thousand men, including Altman's 68th Ohio, were heading east across Mississippi in two columns, one of them led by yet another Ohio general, James B. McPherson. They passed through Jackson, Mississippi's capital, which they had trashed the previous July after chasing away its defenders. Torching what remained, Sherman's men marched on, destroying towns in their path and provisioning themselves from the countryside.

Left behind was a trail of surreal images: a black boy fingering a piano lying by a curb, hogsheads of sugar spilling their contents in the street, Jefferson Davis's personal library trampled upon. Reaching the important rail junction of Meridian, the soldiers spent five days leveling the town and tearing up track, heating the rails and twisting them into knots called "Sherman's neckties." The job finished, Sherman reported, "Meridian with its depots, store-houses, arsenal, hospitals, offices, hotels, and cantonments no longer exists."[46]

Something ominous was happening to Sherman and his men. From psychological wreckage in the fall of 1861, Sherman had emerged a hardened man, his inner warrior freed by the confidence Halleck and Grant placed in him, his rage at the rebellious South inflamed by family tragedy. In the late summer of 1863, Ellen Sherman and their four children came for a long visit in the general's camp on Mississippi's Big Black River. It ended in grief.

In camp at Big Black River, nine-year-old Willy Sherman learned the manual of arms and was made an honorary sergeant by the 13th Regulars. But on October 3 Willy died of typhoid fever. Sherman was heartbroken over the son he called his "Alter Ego" and somehow the Rebel South was to blame.[47] He confided to his friend Grant that Willy was "the one I most prised on earth" and his death "had affected me more than any other misfortune could."[48] Some time later, the crusty general wrote Ellen from the field, "I cannot banish from my mind Poor Willy."[49]

Sherman's men had been annealed as well. Many had been in hostile territory for more than two years, separated from the niceties of ordinary society and leading lives that were dirty and dangerous. They had learned to shuck fodder from sullen civilians and drink water, clean or foul, where they could find it. When enemy troops polluted streams with animal carcasses, when guerillas gobbled up unwary pickets, and when Southern women spat on Union prisoners, the soldiers in blue vowed payback. They did not realize it, of course, but the swaths they had cut through Mississippi in their Jackson and Meridian campaigns were dress rehearsals. Sherman sensed what lay ahead. Looking toward civilian lands further east and sounding like the voice of an angry Jehovah, he warned, "[P]repare them for my coming."[50]

After his elevation to general in chief in March 1864, Grant chose Sherman to succeed him as commander of the Military District of the Mississippi. McPherson would take Sherman's place as head of the Army of the Tennessee. In the privacy of a room at Cincinnati's Burnett House, Grant and Sherman huddled to map strategy, the Union's top two commanders who had become close friends. As Sherman recalled years later, "He was to go for Lee and I was to go for Joe Johnston. That was the plan."[51]

About this time, Adam Badeau, a New York newsman who would become Grant's military secretary, compared and contrasted Grant and Sherman:

Sherman was tall, angular, and spare, as if his superabundant energy had consumed his flesh. His words were distinct, his ideas clear and rapid, coming, indeed, almost too fast for utterance. … Grant was calmer in

Maj. Gen. William Tecumseh Sherman—called "Uncle Billy"—was a restless commander with unusual ideas, as both his own troops and the Confederates learned.

manner a hundred fold. The habitual expression on his face was so quiet as to be almost incomprehensible. His manner [was] plain, placid, almost meek. ... In utterances he was slow and sometimes embarrassed, but the words were well-chosen.[52]

Hitherto, Union armies had been loosely coordinated, punching away here, there, and everywhere according to no particular system. Now Grant, commander of all the armies, intended to bring together all the Union's forces in unrelenting, *simultaneous* attacks pressing the Confederates on every front.

In early May, two huge armies led by Ohioans began closing like jaws on the Confederacy. One was the force, largely of Westerners, which would invade Georgia under Sherman, while the other, composed almost entirely of Easterners ostensibly under Meade but actually directed by Grant, was to carry the war to Lee in Virginia.

About a fourth of Sherman's force of one hundred thousand were Ohioans, among them seventy-eight infantry regiments, ten batteries, and a half dozen cavalry units. Many of the Ohio regiments had "veteranized"—that is, accepted bounties and furloughs for re-enlisting when their three-year terms expired. These were tough battle-tested units that had seen action on many of the war's killing grounds, in some cases having been worn down two-thirds or more by injuries and illness.

Unlike Grant's quietly affectionate letters home and Spiegel's effusive ones, Sherman's letters to Ellen had an air of formal obligation about them, and his last before the Georgia campaign was no exception. "My love to the children, & let what fate befall us, believe me always true to you & mindful of your true affection," he wrote, saying what had to be said without getting gushy about it.[53] (Ellen would write Cump a month later, "It never occurs to me that you may be anxious to hear from us."[54]) Grant had Julia as his rock; but for the twitchy Sherman, restless in his own skin and sometimes at odds with Ellen, Grant was the island of calm certitude to which he could anchor himself.

In Georgia, Sherman had a wily foe in Joe Johnston, a superb defensive commander who had replaced the unpopular Bragg soon after the latter's retreat from Chattanooga. Johnston was a military *eminence gris* with the suave elegance of a Southern aristocrat. In Sherman, Johnston faced a lanky, carelessly dressed, and stubbly-chinned Midwesterner of no elegance whatsoever. Sherman's deeply wrinkled face resembled an unmade bed and his small hard eyes and downturned mouth conveyed a warning that he expressed more than once: "*War is cruelty,* he would say. *There is no use trying to reform it; the crueler it is, the sooner it will be over.*"[55]

There was something paradoxical about Sherman. Seemingly an impulsive man, he so carefully planned logistics that his Western armies, long acquainted with hunger, could move through much of Georgia with their stomachs full. To advance on Atlanta, the manufacturing and transportation center of the Deep South, Sherman would follow the railroad from Chattanooga. The railroad stretched back to the huge Union supply depot at Nashville.[56] Sherman put Ohio's feisty Steedman in charge of guarding this lifeline and he warned Nashville's chief quartermaster, "[I]f you don't have my army supplied and keep it supplied we'll eat up your mules, sir—eat your mules up!"

Another paradox: despite his fierce talk, Sherman usually avoided bloody head-on assaults, pressuring Johnston by maneuver, sweeping around his side and threatening his rear so as to pry him out of position and force him back. For this, Sherman earned the gratitude of his soldiers, who called him "Uncle Billy" or "Old Billy." Veterans now, they had gotten over yearning for big exciting battles.

But "even if there was no great battle in the campaign from Dalton

Near Atlanta, Sherman's men relaxed in a captured gun emplacement.

to Atlanta," a veteran of the 105th Ohio recalled, "it presented, perhaps, more days of steady continuous fighting than any other campaign of the war."[57] It was mostly fire fights and sniping, but it was unrelenting.

Bobbing and weaving like boxers, Union and Confederate forces moved in a herky-jerky way across northern Georgia through the spring and summer of 1864, always in the direction of Atlanta. Sherman never shone at battlefield tactics, but in the Atlanta campaign he blossomed as a master of strategic maneuver.

Called "this great Anaconda" by an officer of the 14th Ohio, Sherman's Atlanta Campaign got under way May 7 and, undulating side to side, drove 170 miles to arrive at the outskirts of Atlanta in 71 days, where it settled down to a summer of slowly advancing trench warfare, a precursor of that common in World War I.[58]

It had experienced nasty skirmishes and engagements remembered by few other than the survivors: Rocky Face Ridge, Resaca, Dallas (or New Hope Church), Kennesaw Mountain, Chattahoochee River, and Peach Tree Creek among them, but if these fights failed to attain the status of major memorable battles in the popular imagination, there still was abundant suffering.

Sherman's Atlanta campaign was notable for its miseries. For most of June, rain had pelted the men's heads like soft bullets, the mud sucking at their feet as if it were trying to pull them into their graves. During July and August, the men suffered the heat of a Southern summer. Every time their drive paused, they had to build extensive earthworks, and then all too soon, abandon them to advance again, a process repeated endlessly. It was trench warfare on the move: unremitting labor, constant sniping and fire fights, rain, and heat.

Sherman's orders from Grant were "to move against Johnston's army, to break it up, and to get into the interior of the enemy's country as far as you can, inflicting all the damage you can against their war resources."[59] Usually, the soldiers were too busy fighting to ravage the countryside the way they would later during the famous March to the Sea, but plenty of damage was done nonetheless. Civilians who hadn't fled saw their foodstuffs taken and their crops trampled. Sometimes, to clear battle zones, whole families were rounded up, put in boxcars, and shipped to Nashville, forced into exile. Anything deemed of strategic value, such as a factory, was burned.

The Atlanta campaign had the usual assortment of low moments and high, the bizarre and the grim. When Confederate artillery zeroed in on a hilltop, a cluster of Union generals gathered there scattered—except for Sherman and Hooker. The two generals, who despised each other, strutted about in a test of wills until they found a way to depart simultaneously.[60]

The absurd was balanced by the unequivocally grim. One example occurred at the Battle of New Hope Church in late May. Soldiers fighting in the rain until dark endured savage Confederate artillery fire from sixteen cannons that found the range on five thousand men crammed into a small space called the "Hell Hole" and chewed them to bits, body parts flying and blood spattering.[61] After darkness fell, a veteran recalled, fires in forest openings revealed "men wounded, armless, legless and eyeless; some with heads bound up with cotton strips, some standing and walking nervously around, some sitting with bended forms, some prone on the earth."[62]

In late June, an impatient Sherman attempted a rare frontal attack, this at Kennesaw Mountain. It was repulsed with savage losses to the Federals, including two of their better officers. Brig. Gen. Charles G. Harker, a West Pointer whose Civil War career had begun with the colonelcy of the 65th Ohio, died on the field. Col. Daniel McCook of the "Fighting McCooks," commander of the 52nd Ohio, was so badly wounded at Kennesaw that he was sent home to Steubenville. Notified there of his promotion to brigadier general, McCook said, "The promotion is too late now. ... I decline the honor." He died the next day.[63]

Of Kennesaw, Sherman wrote Ellen, "It is enough to make the whole world start at the awful amount of death and destruction that now stalks abroad."[64] Victorious survivors of such fights had little strength left to cheer their success. A Confederate recalled, "I was as sick as a horse, and as wet with blood and sweat as I could be, and many of our men were vomiting with excessive fatigue, over-exhaustion, and sunstroke; our tongues were parched and cracked for water, and our faces blackened with powder and smoke, and our dead and wounded were piled indiscriminately in the trenches."[65]

And yet, the war's absurdities continued. Early in a scorching July, the 14th Ohio had a "lively skirmish" near the bank of the Chattahoochee River and its colonel was wounded. Despite that, the two sides agreed on a truce

Fires set by both Confederates and Sherman's men destroyed much of Atlanta and marked yet another turning point in the war.

and soon naked Federals and Confederates were swimming together and exchanging newspapers.[66] Even Sherman was said to have gone into the river naked.

By mid-July 1864, Sherman's army had arrived a few miles outside Atlanta, where it settled down for a siege. Artillery roared constantly and the musketry rattled on night and day. The two armies were so close that it was impossible to know from what direction danger might come. An Ohio soldier was sitting on the ground, peacefully grinding his coffee, when a sharpshooter's bullet struck him in the forehead, killing him instantly.[67] And yet, when called from the battle line to get their meat rations, several details from the same regiment passed unscathed through bullets "dropping upon the ground as thick as hail stones."[68]

By July 17, Confederate Pres. Jefferson Davis had run out of patience with Joe Johnston and his defensive strategy, which was preserving the bulk of his army but ceding territory. On July 17 Davis replaced Johnston with John Bell Hood, a proven though impetuous fighter. Hood, Robert E. Lee had remarked, was a lion, but not a fox.

For the rest of July and most of August, Hood launched attack after attack on Sherman, a strategy that gained him little but stunning numbers of casualties. Among the Union casualties was the death on July 22 of Maj. Gen. James B. McPherson, a West Pointer from Clyde, Ohio, and a favorite of both his men and the top command. Scouting his front, McPherson had unwittingly ridden into a Confederate regiment and been shot trying to escape.

Even as he was beating off Hood's attacks, Sherman was laying siege to Atlanta. Gradually he enveloped the city, breaking rail lines connecting it to the outside world. One of his first efforts, late in July, involved sending a cavalry expedition under Gen. George Stoneman to cut Confederate supply lines. At Stoneman's urging, the expedition was also charged with liberating Andersonville about 120 miles south of Atlanta.

Before Stoneman even got near the prison camp, however, he botched the expedition and briefly was captured himself. Unwilling to risk dividing his forces and lacking resources to care for inmates after their liberation, Sherman made no further effort to free Andersonville, where two hundred men a day were dying. War, as Sherman said, is cruelty.

Having enveloped Atlanta on the west and north, in late August Sherman began moving in from the south, severing the city's last rail connection. In the small hours of September 2, a sleepless Sherman was startled to see the night sky light up. Rumbling explosions could be heard from the city. Wondering about the cause, Sherman could only wait impatiently for morning. Then word came: Hood had abandoned Atlanta after setting huge quantities of stores and ammunition afire. The mayor officially surrendered the city and by noon, Union flags flew over city hall. Atlanta—close to Richmond in importance to the Confederacy—had fallen.

GRANT MEETS LEE

Ordinarily, Grant was deliberate in his movements, but the Union's new general in chief was a whirlwind in March 1864. After a flying visit to Meade's Army of the Potomac, he rushed back to Nashville to confer with his generals, huddled again with Sherman in Cincinnati, and then, with Julia, raced to Washington, pausing only in Philadelphia so she could replenish her wardrobe. They had been invited to a reception at the White House, but only Julia attended. Lincoln was "delighted" to learn Grant had chosen to go to the front instead.[69] After some meet-and-greet in Washington, Julia returned to St. Louis, leaving Ulysses to deal with business.

With Meade only nominally in charge, the Army of the Potomac would be Grant's weapon from now on. It was a well-groomed, friendly giant, in superb condition but used to long intermissions. Most of all, it was cautious. This army did not like to pick fights, although, if pressed, it would fiercely defend itself. It had learned from previous commanders that once the battle was over, it was time to rest and not pursue the matter. Time and again, after victory or defeat, the Army of the Potomac had simply dropped its fists and gone home.

The army had been in love once, the object of its affection being George B. McClellan. "Little Mac" had done a superb job of turning a rabble of youths into a snappy legion that looked good and felt good. But McClellan hated to put at risk what he had so lovingly created and, with the help of his successors, the army retained its aggression deficit. It had a habit of moving ponderously and losing offensive battles. One other thing: it still believed the war could be won if only the Confederacy's head was lopped off. Embedded in every soldier's mind was one thought: On to Richmond—someday.

Grant thought this Eastern army was very handsome but he knew it had to become a sledgehammer instead of a swagger stick. He started by converting hordes of rear-echelon personnel into combat troops, a move that delighted front-line soldiers. He also had a showdown with the always-pushy Stanton over who was really in charge of the army. Lincoln resolved the argument in Grant's favor, saying, "We have sent across the mountains for Mr. Grant, as Mrs. Grant calls him, to relieve us, and I think we had better leave him alone to do as he pleases."[70]

Doing as Grant pleased meant keeping things plain and simple, so the question for Easterners was how their elegant army would accept this rough-hewn stranger out of the West, set before them bark and all. Grant's new officers were unimpressed, one calling him "stumpy, unmilitary, slouchy, and western-looking; very ordinary, in fact."

Rank-and-file Eastern soldiers seemed to like Grant's down-to-earth ways, however. "He looks as if he means it," said one.[71] Southerners were dismissive, but Confederate Gen. James Longstreet, who was acquainted with Grant before the war, knew better. "[T]hat man will fight us every day and every hour till the end of this war," he warned.[72]

Before accepting his promotion to lieutenant general and general in chief, Grant had paused to write Sherman, graciously crediting him and McPherson "as the men, to whom, above all others, I feel indebted for whatever I have had of success."[73] Sherman thought this over, then declined the credit, giving Grant as fitting an encomium as any: in addition to his "common-sense," Sherman told him, "The chief characteristic of your nature is the simple faith in success you have always manifested."[74] To this, he added some advice: stay away from Washington or risk being tied down by politics, intrigue, and petty detail.

Grant had figured that out for himself and come up with a solution. He would make his headquarters in the field, traveling with Meade's army in Virginia while staying in touch with the capital by telegraph. Halleck would remain in Washington, no longer general in chief but Grant's chief of staff now, handling the details of daily management.

Meade would remain head—nominally—of the Army of the Potomac, but

Groping for each other in a confusing landscape, Grant and Lee clashed for the first time when the Army of the Potomac crossed into the Wilderness area of Virginia.

Grant would be looking over his shoulder, shaping the strategy. Grant "hasn't told me what his plans are," the president told one of his secretaries. "I'm glad to find a man who can go ahead without me."[75] Grant, said Lincoln, "is the first general I've had."[76]

On May 3, Union forces started moving around Lee's right, fording the Rapidan to launch Grant's Overland Campaign. Nearly four months of bloodletting would follow, with Lee's army being hammered with a relentlessness it had never known before. Grant began by attempting to move quickly through the dense thicket known as the Wilderness (scene of Hooker's debacle) to reach open ground beyond. There, he thought, he could wedge himself between Lee and the Confederate capital of Richmond and force the Confederates into battle in the open where Union numbers could prevail.

But on the morning of May 5, Lee's faster-moving forces attacked Grant's while they were still moving through the Wilderness's haunting landscape. Remarkably, Grant was unperturbed. If Lee wanted to fight in this miserable tangle of brush, "that is all right," he reassured his commanders.[77] He suggested to Meade they set up joint headquarters on a knoll. There Grant issued some quick orders, then sat down on a stump and began to whittle a stick while smoking one of the cigars he had stuffed in his pocket that morning.

The result was one of the costliest battles of the war, fought for two days in some of the Wilderness's clearings but mostly in thickets where visibility rarely exceeded twenty feet. The brush tore at men like claws, ripping their uniforms, breaking up formations, and canceling Grant's advantage in numbers.

The first day was a confusion of small battles, with errors and missed opportunities on both sides. That night, soldiers had to listen to the screams of wounded comrades as they were consumed by flames sweeping a no-man's-land of dry brush. Fighting resumed early the next day, but Grant's army answered his orders sluggishly. One of Meade's officers blamed the army's past commanders for "training it into a life of caution."[78] But even as fleeing soldiers rushed past his command post, Grant was unperturbed, rising calmly now and then from his stump to issue crisp orders. Unlike Hooker, Grant never lost his nerve, remaining the calm center around which the storm swirled.

Years later, Grant's aide, Horace Porter, remembered the horrors of the Wilderness:

Officers could rarely see their troops for any considerable distance, for smoke clouded the vision, and a heavy sky obscured the sun. ... It was a battle fought with the ear, and not the eye. ... At times the wind howled through the tree-tops, mingling its moans with the groans of the dying, and heavy branches were cut off by the fire of the artillery, and fell crashing upon the heads of the men, adding a new terror to battle. Forest fires raged; ammunition-trains exploded; the dead were roasted in the conflagration; the wounded, roused by its hot breath, dragged themselves along, with their torn and mangled limbs, in the mad energy of despair, to escape the ravages of the flames; and every bush seemed hung with shreds of blood-stained clothing.[79]

The experience of the brigade, which included the 4th and 8th Ohio regiments, was typical. It found itself surrounded by "Johnnies" and had to hurriedly retreat.[80] After struggling through the thorny brush, all that was left of the 8th Ohio was "broken little squads," Lt. Thomas F. Galwey remembered.[81]

Then the Federals got a lucky break. Confederate General Longstreet was wounded and much of the steam went out of the Rebel attack. The Battle of the Wilderness ended as a bloody draw. As in so many previous battles in Virginia, Grant and Lee had failed to destroy each other, but this time there was a difference: Union forces retained possession of the field.

Until now, the Army of the Potomac had always returned to camp to

Wounded men struggled frantically to escape fires caused by the fighting in the Wilderness.

heal and regain its confidence after its battles. A period of recuperation seems indicated here as well, for in the Wilderness the Union army had taken horrendous casualties—about 18,000 killed, wounded, or captured out of 102,000 engaged.[82] The army was not surprised, therefore, when, after dark on March 7, it was ordered to start moving—but something had changed.

As the soldiers marched, they realized the direction they were going and began to cheer. They were heading south instead of north. They weren't licked after all. In Washington, Lincoln received a message from Grant: "Whatever happens, there is to be no turning back." Lincoln put his arms around the bearer of the message and planted a kiss on his forehead.[83]

A great general gives his army a center of gravity, a sense of itself that sustains it in adversity. Under Grant, the men believed in the inevitability of their mission. "There is no fall back with U.S. Grant," one wrote.[84] That view fit with Sherman's observation of the steadfast, "simple faith in success" Grant possessed, and it was infectious. A New York newsman by the name of Cadwallader spent an evening in "pleasant chatty conversation" with Grant, the general's quiet confidence taking Cadwallader from "the slough of despond, to the solid bed-rock of unwavering faith."[85]

Abraham Lincoln unexpectedly showed up in Grant's camp for a few days of lounging about, inhaling the oxygen of calm steadfastness. The president returned to Washington, his spirits lifted. The visit "had done him good ... and strengthened him mentally," someone observed.[86]

After the Wilderness, Grant headed to Spotsylvania Court House. Once again, his army couldn't move quickly enough, so the Confederates took possession of the strategic crossroads, where they built an enormous fortified position called the "Mule Shoe." Once again, Grant showed how

Grant regretted his failed attack at Cold Harbor "more than any I have … ordered."

things were changing.

Before Grant, Eastern armies had never remained engaged with the enemy for more than a few days, but at Spotsylvania Grant kept up the pressure for two weeks, from May 8 to 21. Soon, Northern newspapers blossomed with a headline quoting Grant: "I propose to fight it out on this line if it takes all summer."[87]

In heavy rain, a force of twenty-five thousand Federals made their largest assault on May 12. For twenty hours some of the fiercest hand-to-hand combat of the war unfolded at a point dubbed "Bloody Angle." Federals and Confederates fought separated by only a few feet of earthworks, sometimes firing at each other through the chinks, sometimes flinging bayoneted rifles like harpoons.

"Nothing can describe the confusion, the savage bloodcurdling yells, the murderous faces, the awful curses … and the grisly horror of the melee!" Thomas F. Galwey of the 8th Ohio remembered.[88] Men jumped atop a battlement to fire down at the defenders, then leapt back if they survived their brief exposure. The trenches became mud pits, with the wounded and the dead trampled into the mire.

Horace Porter, one of Grant's aides, recalled:

Rank after rank was riddled by shot and shell and bayonet thrusts, and finally sank, a mass of torn and mutilated corpses … trees over a foot and a half in diameter were cut completely in two by the incessant musketry fire. … Skulls were crushed with clubbed muskets, and men stabbed to death with swords and bayonets thrust between the logs in the parapet which separated the combatants. Wild cheers, savage yells, and frantic shrieks rose above the sighing of the wind and the pattering of the rain.

After the fighting was over, Porter visited the "Bloody Angle," where he found dead bodies "piled upon each other in some places four layers deep. … Below the mass of fast decaying corpses, the convulsive twitching of limbs and writing of bodies showed that there were wounded men still alive and struggling to extricate themselves."[89]

Grant wrote Julia, "The world has never seen so bloody or so protracted a battle."[90] Under pressure, Lee withdrew a short distance to a new defensive line where he turned yet another attack by Grant into a costly failure. Union casualties totaled eleven thousand—but still Grant did not draw back.

Instead, he slid around Lee once more, although once again Lee beat him again to strategic ground. By June 2, the two armies were concentrated near a place called Cold Harbor (which was neither cold nor a harbor). Grant apparently had exhausted his deep well of patience, because on June 3 he simply flung his men against the deeply entrenched Confederates.

They responded to Grant's ill-advised attack with a "volcanic blast" of fire that cut down Union soldiers by the thousands. The Army of the Potomac suffered staggering losses and gained nothing. Confederate Gen. Evander M. Law declared, "It was not war, it was murder."[91] One historian wrote, "Grant made the biggest mistake of his military career," and Grant realized it.[92] That night, he said, "I regret this assault more than any I have ever ordered."[93]

After that, action around Cold Harbor settled down to trench warfare, the soldiers constructing elaborate earthworks while corpses rotted between the lines and flies plagued everyone. Union losses totaled twelve thousand.

The next day, Grant found some relief in writing a letter to daughter Ellen, whom he called "Nelly." He told her, "You do not know how happy it made me feel to see how well my little girl not yet nine years old could write … I think when I go home I will get a little buggy … so that you and Jess can ride about the country during vacation."[94]

Then Grant returned to business, and on June 12th finally outmaneuvered Lee. Slipping unnoticed from the trenches of Cold Harbor, Grant moved his huge army across the James River to Petersburg, putting him almost on Richmond's doorstep. Petersburg lay astride most of the road and rail lines connecting Richmond to the rest of the Confederacy.

Despite the brilliance of the move, Grant's army didn't act quickly enough to drive straight through to Richmond. Lee arrived to defend the city and Grant had to settle down to laying siege, using his advantage in numbers to lengthen his lines and stretch out Lee's ever-thinning ranks. At one point, Union miners burrowing under Confederate lines triggered an explosion that created a huge crater, momentarily stunning the Confederates. Once again, a slow-footed Union attack failed.

By late August, the Army of the Potomac had suffered sixteen thousand casualties around Petersburg and appeared stalled. And yet Lee's back was against the wall, his manpower dwindling, his lines of communication breaking down. Grant was relentless, undiscouraged when his predecessors would have been. Lee and his army were slowly being ground into dust.

All the while, Grant kept up with correspondence. His personal tent was furnished with a cot, washstand, two chairs, and a pine table where he could write. To the grieving grandmother of the late General McPherson, Grant wrote, "Your bereavement is great, but cannot exceed mine."[95] To his cavalry commander, Philip Sheridan, who he had sent to the Shenandoah Valley, he urged, "Give the enemy no rest."[96]

To his patron, Congressman Washburne of Illinois, Grant wrote that the Confederates, desperate for men, had "robbed the cradle and the grave equally to get their present force." Grant went on: "With the drain upon them the end is visible if we will but be true to ourselves. Their only hope now is in a divided North. I have no doubt but the enemy are exceedingly anxious to hold out until after the Presidential election."[97]

Gazette

Only weeks after the wedding of Kate Chase and William Sprague, the first warning signs of a marriage in trouble appeared. Claiming the press of business, William left Kate alone in Washington to go to Rhode Island, where he stayed without his wife through the 1863 Christmas and New Year's holidays.

Kate's pleading letters, written daily, drew only brusque responses. Finally, the two were reunited for the rest of the winter in Washington, but in the spring Kate—ostensibly for her health—spent weeks in upstate New York without her husband, then went to Newport after William got into a drunken brawl with some other men in Washington.

Meanwhile, Kate's father, Secretary of the Treasury Chase, had been getting crossways with the president. An unofficial committee pushing Chase's nomination for the presidency furtively released a circular scathingly critical of Lincoln. It didn't do the president much harm, and Chase's presidential hopes petered out for lack of broad support.

Lincoln was re-nominated on June 8, 1864, by a coalition of Republicans and War Democrats. Nonetheless, Chase had fatally wounded himself with his undying hunger for the presidency. When, in a pro forma way, he offered his resignation in June during an argument with Lincoln over patronage, the president surprised him by accepting it. Tossed overboard after one mistake too many, one of the most powerful men in Washington had to return

Salmon P. Chase was an effective secretary of the treasury, but had long felt he deserved the presidency. Chase's daughter Kate, widely admired for her grace and beauty, was her father's navigator through Washington society.

to private life. Life outside the capital spun out its narratives during the spring and summer of 1864. At Andersonville, Albert Mellor struggled to survive as his fellow captives from the 1st Ohio began to die. The first, in April, had died of wounds; then four more passed away in July, the life drained from them by chronic diarrhea.

In Cleveland, meanwhile, members of the governing committee of the Soldiers' Aid Society of North Ohio were working themselves into exhaustion. Believing the success of a fundraising event called a "Sanitary Fair" meant they were no longer needed and perhaps worn out themselves, volunteer workers no longer were coming to help the Soldiers' Aid Society. Elsewhere, Julia Grant (then in St. Louis) wondered if she could come east to spend the summer closer to her husband. Consumed by the bloody work of his Overland Campaign, Ulys replied that would be impractical adding, however, "How much I wish I could see you all."[98]

In Millerburg, Marcus Spiegel's widow, Caroline, was tormented by baseless rumors her husband was still alive. Some solace arrived on July 6, however, with the birth of a fifth child, a daughter, whom Caroline named Clara Marcus in her husband's honor.

In Georgia, while taking shelter at Big Shanty from incessant rain, Sherman learned on June 12 that Ellen had given birth the day before to a baby boy. He wrote to Ellen: "Of course, I am pleased to know the sex of the child, as he must succeed to the place left vacant by Willy."[99] Ellen named the child Charles after Cump's father.

Signs of fatigue were appearing in Sherman's army as it dug its way to Atlanta. Rationalizing the war to himself, Col. Emerson Opdycke wrote his wife "that lasting good to the human race *must* result from this terrible war. Such a sea of blood ought to regenerate any people."[100] Even Pvt. Andrew Altman of the 68th Ohio, who had begun the war as a great adventure and enjoyed most of it, was changing his tune. He wrote home, "I hope this cruel war will stop this fall some time but I am afriat it will not. I should like to come home and live in piece once more. It is no fun to fighte, let who say it who will."[101]

That, in a nutshell, was increasingly the feeling in the North. During the summer of 1864, war weariness had set in again. Although both Grant and Sherman were pushing the Confederate armies to the breaking point, the public was seeing stunning casualty lists and no dramatic victories. Lincoln was being pressured from the left by Peace Democrats to throttle back the war and from the right by Radical Republicans who thought the war could be ratcheted up. By August 23, Lincoln was so discouraged over public opinion that he had his Cabinet members sign a pledge to work with the next president:

> *This morning, as for some days past, it seems exceedingly probable that this Administration will not be re-elected. Then it will be my duty to so co-operate with the President elect, as to save the Union between the election and the Inauguration; as he will have secured his election on such ground that he can not possibly save it afterwards.*[102]

As happened so often in this war, the picture suddenly changed. On the same day Lincoln's Cabinet signed his memorandum, Union forces captured Fort Morgan near Mobile. Rear Adm. David G. Farragut had cleared Mobile Bay crying, "Damn the torpedoes!" Although the Democrats had nominated the popular former Gen. George B. McClellan, the party was split over its peace platform—which even McClellan himself repudiated. Then, on the evening of September 2, the War Department received word that Sherman's forces had occupied Atlanta, a powerfully symbolic victory. [103] Sherman had wired Washington, "Atlanta is ours, & fairly won."[104]

Now, a jubilant Lincoln realized, there was hope after all.

TO LEARN MORE:

Seeing the battlegrounds of Chattanooga requires an automobile and patience. The site of the opening battle, Orchard Knob, can be found, speckled with monuments, on Orchard Knob Avenue in a modest residential area of the city. Next, visit Lookout Mountain by following a steep, narrow road to the National Park Service visitor center at the top. Find directions on **http://www.nps.gov/ chch/** or call **423-821-7786**. After that, take Crest Road, the residential street along the crest of Missionary Ridge to see some markers and get a sense of the topography. Finally, visit the Chattanooga National Cemetery at 1200 Bailey Ave. (**http://www.cem.va.gov/CEM/cems/nchp/chattanooga.asp** or **423-855-6590**) where the Union dead lie by the thousand.

Ohio's beautiful Kate Chase's failure to find love after her storybook wedding marriage is recounted in Peg A. Lamphier's *Kate Chase and William Sprague: Politics and Gender in a Civil War Marriage*. Another troubled marriage is traced in *Crete and James: Personal Letters of Lucretia and James Garfield*, edited by John Shaw.

Maj. Gen. Jacob D. Cox provides an Ohio commander's thoughtful view of Sherman's first Georgia campaign. An interesting approach to Grant's campaign against Lee is found in William A. Frassanito's *Grant and Lee: The Virginia Campaigns, 1864-1865,* which matches historic photographs and modern views of the same scene, supplemented by concise commentary.

A man who dearly loved to fight—and was good at it—Philip H. Sheridan rose quickly to high command and fame.

12

WAR IS CRUELTY

September to December 1864

There was something about Philip Sheridan walking down the street that made men think about stepping aside, and it wasn't his size. Sheridan was a shrimpy five foot, five inches tall, shorter than Grant, and several inches shorter than the average soldier. But he was deep-chested and muscular and had one of those don't-tread-on-me, don't-even-think-about-it looks that said: I can take your head off and make the rest of you flee for the hills, and don't make me tell you twice.

Philip Sheridan was put on earth to fight, which he did exceedingly well, with a *joie de guerre* that diverted attention from certain lapses in decorum and veracity. "[O]n the 6th of March, 1831 … I was born, in Albany, N.Y., the third child" of Irish immigrants, he wrote in his memoirs, and that may or may not be true. It is more likely Sheridan was born in Ireland, an inconvenient fact that would have barred him from the presidency, should his nation have ever called him.[1] *

Around 1832 the Sheridans moved from New York to Somerset, a raw young town in the rolling countryside southeast of Columbus, Ohio, and their son grew up as an Ohioan. Young Philip played hooky from school "many a time" (he later admitted), went to work in local stores at age fourteen, and became known as a boy who knew how to fight and rather liked it.[2]

* For an unflattering but intriguing perspective on Sheridan, see Eric J. Wittenberg, *Little Phil: A Reassessment of the Civil War Leadership of Gen. Philip H. Sheridan* Washington: Brassey's, Inc., 2002.

A few months too young for West Point, Sheridan lied about his age and won appointment from a friendly politician. At West Point he was called "Little Phil." Angered early in his senior year by the "irritating" tone of an order from a cadet sergeant named Terrill, Sheridan remembered years later that he "made toward him [Terrill] with a lowered bayonet," stopping barely in time.[3] When Terrill reported the offense, Sheridan attacked him with his fists.

For attacking an officer, "Little Phil" was lucky to only be suspended for a year when he could well have been expelled. In 1853, he graduated to a military career in far-flung outposts with few prospects for promotion. Unmarried, Sheridan took what comfort he could from an Indian woman who shared his quarters in the Oregon Territory.

After the attack on Fort Sumter, Sheridan hovered on the edge of the army's consciousness for almost five months before being called to join the war. Even then, he was stuck in rear-echelon staff positions sullenly doing tedious work. He narrowly escaped court martial for disrespecting a superior. In May 1862, thanks to the army's desperate need for officers, young Captain Sheridan got a lucky break: a colonelcy and command of the 2nd Michigan cavalry.

The new colonel proved his mettle within weeks. Under attack and outnumbered at Booneville, Mississippi, he made a surprise counter-attack, routing the Confederates. "He is worth his weight in gold," his superiors were told, and Sheridan was quickly awarded a general's star.[4] In less than a year, he had gone from backwater captain to frontline brigadier general.

Stuck in neutral until now, Sheridan's career raced ahead. By September 1862 he commanded an infantry division of the Army of the Ohio. He fought well at Perryville in October and won a major general's star for his performance at Stones River at the end of the year. Although Major General Sheridan was caught up in the hurried retreat from Chickamauga in September 1863, he stood out at Missionary Ridge in Chattanooga. His division was said to be the only one that retained its cohesion during that attack and it came impressively close to capturing Confederate General Bragg.

Although Sherman disobeyed orders in leading his division to the top of Missionary Ridge instead of waiting for instructions, his courage and skill impressed Grant. After Grant became general in chief in 1864, he told Halleck he wanted "the very best man in the army" to take command of the Army of the Potomac's cavalry. Would Sheridan do? Halleck asked, and Grant answered, "The very man I want."[5]

Called to Washington, thirty-three-year-old Sheridan arrived on April 4,

After Grant told Sheridan in 1864 to "eat out the valley," new troops were sent into the Shenandoah region to take it away from the Confederates, once and for all.

1864, a youthful looking but desiccated 115 pounds. Someone said, "The officer you brought on from the West is rather a little fellow to handle your cavalry." Grant replied, "You'll find him big enough for the purpose before we get through."[6]

Eating Out the Valley

On Sunday, May 8, 1864, near Piney Branch Church in the Spotsylvania area of Virginia, a steaming cloud of profanity arose from the headquarters tent of George Meade. The commander of the Army of the Potomac had summoned his cavalry commander, Philip Sheridan, for a royal dressing down over alleged blunders in moving his horse soldiers. The highly excitable Meade was famous for his rages, but Sheridan, intimidated not in the least, replied with language that was, one of Grant's aides wonderingly recalled, "highly spiced and conspicuously italicized with expletives."[7]

At the heart of the argument were old versus new ideas on how cavalry should be used. Meade, a traditional infantry soldier, believed cavalry was best used for scouting and guarding supply trains. Sheridan wanted instead to "concentrate all the cavalry, move out in force against [Confederate cavalry commander J. E. B. "Jeb"] Stuart's command, and whip it."[8]

Red hot over Sheridan's impertinence, Meade rushed to Grant's tent

Rushing back to rally his beleaguered army, Sheridan showed what "one man could change the whole face of a battle."

to complain. When Grant learned what Sheridan wanted to do, he calmly told Meade: "Did Sheridan say that? Well, he generally knows what he is talking about. Let him start right out and do it."[9]

He did it. The next day, Sheridan launched his "Richmond Raid," plunging boldly into Confederate territory with ten thousand cavalrymen. Convinced of the superiority of Confederate cavalrymen, Stuart rushed to stop him and on May 11 the two forces collided in a swirling battle of horsemen at Yellow Tavern six miles from Richmond. Sheridan got the upper hand and Stuart was fatally wounded, depriving Lee of a superb cavalry commander.

With Stuart disposed of, Sheridan continued his daring raid, bypassing Richmond itself to cut railroad lines and destroy badly needed military stores. After completely circling Lee's army, Sheridan returned to Union lines on May 24, his first independent cavalry action a thumping success.

Sheridan, like Sherman, had come to believe in the concept of "total war." War was not just lines of soldiers confronting each other on a battlefield, Sheridan mused, and he did "not regret the system of living on the enemy's country. ... As war is a punishment, if we can, by reducing its advocates to poverty, end it quicker, we are on the side of humanity."[10] Total war. Grant liked that and he liked Sheridan's fighting spirit.

Energized by warfare, the younger man would come bounding into Grant's headquarters, an aide to Grant remembered, with "boundless enthusiasm, buoyant spirits, and cheery conversations [that] were always refreshing."[11] Like Grant, Sheridan had the Beast of War in him.

By late July, Grant had lost patience with Union Gen. David Hunter's efforts in the Shenandoah Valley. Jubal Early—a hard-drinking, cantankerous hater of all things Northern who Lee called "My Bad Old Man"—had brushed off every effort by Hunter to drive him out of the Shenandoah. "Old Jube" had shown he could dart from the Valley, threaten Washington (and, as Early put it, "scare Abe Lincoln like hell"), then skedaddle back.[12]

Looking for an end to his Shenandoah problem, Grant turned the Valley over to Sheridan, effective August 7. He was not only to drive out Early, but "[e]at out" the Valley "clear and clean … so that crows flying over it … will have to carry their provender with them."[13] It was to be total war.

At first, Sheridan and Early cautiously poked at each other. Although Union soldiers made themselves useful in the Valley by burning barns and mills and destroying crops, the Northern public wanted more. After five weeks of this, Grant showed up in Sheridan's camp on September 16, carrying a plan of action. A veteran stared at Grant and said, "When that old cuss is around there's sure to be a big fight on hand."[14] Grant never took the plan out of his pocket, because Sheridan revealed he already had a good one, and he was ready to attack. "Go in," Grant said approvingly, and left.

To fight Early, Sheridan had forty-eight thousand men (although many were tied down by guard duties). To create the Army of the Shenandoah, Grant had loaned Sheridan the Army of the Potomac's VI Corps and sent him the XIX Corps from the Gulf. Also joining Sheridan were two divisions from West Virginia led by thirty-six-year-old Maj. Gen. George Crook, another Ohioan and an old friend of Sheridan. The Army of West Virginia (also known as "Crook's Corps" or the Eighth Corps) emerged from the mountains, its soldiers Western men with rough edges hardened by years of scrambling up and down hills in guerilla warfare. They were tough and they were ready to fight.

Among the Midwestern units in Sheridan's Army of the Shenandoah were eleven from Ohio, seven of them in Crook's command. A quietly professional soldier known to his men as "Uncle George," Crook stood out in a hirsute army because of his whiskers. They flared out like two flying wings. Crook had been born on a farm near Dayton and educated at West Point. His officers included a fellow Ohioan, brigade commander Rutherford B. Hayes. The admiration that Hayes, the amateur soldier, had for Crook, the professional, knew no bounds.

As he had promised Grant, Sheridan attacked on September 19, hoping to catch Early off-guard near Winchester. His head-on assault was going badly until Crook's corps made a wide turn to its right, clambering over hills and through vales to burst out of the woods on the Confederate left flank.

Hayes, riding in the lead, shouted, "Come on, boys!" and, under fire, plunged into a daunting slough of muddy water. When his horse stuck in the mud, he crawled forward, as he told Lucy, "on all fours."[15] Hayes was the first to reach the other side and his brigade followed. Bolstered by cavalry, Crook's flank attack turned the tide and Early's panicked Confederates fled.

Galloping about, an ebullient Sheridan shouted, "Boys, it's just what I expected."[16] Early's forces had been sent "whirling through Winchester," as a staff officer put it. After fleeing twenty miles south, Old Jube pulled his shaken army together on Fisher's Hill, which a Union officer described as "an elevated, natural fort."[17]

An articulate lawyer who served as the quiet Crook's spokesman, Hayes proposed a plan for yet another surprise attack on the Confederate left. With the plan approved by Sheridan, Crook's Corps arose before sunrise on September 22, using their sinewy mountain legs to push through thickets and up hills and burst from the woods, scatter Early's left flank, and force him to flee yet again.

With Early twice beaten, Sheridan's men returned to burning barns, mills, and stacks of grain, a duty many disliked for its cruelty to civilians. "This valley will feed and forage no more Rebel armies," Hayes wrote Lucy. "It is completely and awfully devastated."[18] By early October, Sheridan decided to let his troops rest near Cedar Creek while he went to Washington. Hayes used the interlude to supervise absentee voting by the soldiers for the Congressional and gubernatorial elections. Hayes himself had been put up for an Ohio seat in Congress, which he won handily without campaigning. However, he refused to take his seat until the crisis was over.

Because they thought Early had been crushed, Union commanders arranged their camps carelessly. As their forces slept the night of October 18–19, gray-clad figures moved unnoticed through the fog. Between 4:30 and 5 a.m., Union soldiers were awakened by the rattle of musket fire and the boom of artillery coming from somewhere in the fog. The sounds grew louder, and then came triumphant Rebel yells.

Suddenly, the Union camps were engulfed. Hayes struggled to form a line of battle, but his panicked men fled. Thrown from his dying horse and briefly unconscious, Hayes awoke to face charging Confederates. He barely escaped

Union cavalrymen came to dominate Confederate horsemen, who had once prided themselves on their superiority.

into the woods and caught up with his men, who began reassembling after retreating two-and-a-half miles.

Here, elements of Sheridan's retreating army formed on a ridge, a good defensive position improved by sheltering stone walls. Their confidence rising, the Federals braced themselves for another Confederate attack—but for hours, none came. Not only had the attackers spent themselves for the moment, but, like other impoverished Confederates, they could not resist stopping to plunder the enemy camp. Moreover, Early uncharacteristically hesitated, unable to make up his mind what to do next.

As the Union soldiers waited, they could hear cheering from their rear. Then Sheridan, on his huge warhorse, Rienzi, galloped into view, waving his hat and shouting encouragement. He was trailed by hundreds of cheering soldiers shouting "Sheridan! Sheridan!" Little Phil had been returning from Washington when he realized what was happening.

Putting the spurs to Rienzi, Sheridan rushed eleven-and-a-half miles to the battlefield and rallied his forces, shouting, "Men, by God, we'll whip them yet! We'll sleep in our old tents tonight!"[19] Counter-attacking, he snatched victory from the jaws of defeat, ending Confederate domination of the Valley. In historian T. Harry Williams's view, it was "the most dramatic example in the war … of what one man could do to change the whole face of a battle."[20]

For Union troops in the trenches around Petersburg, an old army rule prevailed: Hurry up and wait.

In less than eleven weeks, Little Phil had achieved what others had failed to do in three years: rid the Valley of Confederates. Grant glowed with pride and the Northern public reveled in the discovery of a new hero. As it must to all great men of the era, some very bad poetry was dedicated to Sheridan. Within ten days, a onetime Ohioan named Thomas Buchanan Read unveiled an assault on rhyme and meter called "Sheridan's Ride," in which, it has been observed, the best lines went to the horse.[21]

Sheridan has often been included in the triptych of the Union's greatest generals, followed, inevitably, by revisionist thinking, most notably from Eric J. Wittenberg, a Columbus attorney and Civil War researcher. Wittenberg argues that "Little Phil" was not only overrated but also insubordinate, mendacious, and just plain mean when it served his purpose.[22]

Indeed, Sheridan tortured the truth on occasion (his reports of devastation wrought in the Valley were greatly exaggerated), handled some of his own people roughly, and didn't give a do-damn for rules and regulations. But he had that quality prized above all others in Civil War officers: *dash*, meaning courage garnished with style. And he did clear the Valley for the Union.

Generations of schoolchildren, obliged to memorize "Sheridan's Ride," drifted off to sleep to the thrumming of Rienzi's hooves and the image of that gallant little rider waving his very non-regulation porkpie hat over his head:

With foam and with dust the black charger was gray;
By the flash of his eye, and his red nostril's play;
He seemed to the whole great army to say:
"I have brought you Sheridan all the way
From Winchester down to save the day."
Hurrah! Hurrah! For Sheridan!
Hurrah! Hurrah! For horse and man![23]

GRANT AND THE SIEGE OF PETERSBURG

As the first hints of autumn began to soften the heat of late summer in Virginia, Grant's Army of the Potomac lay outside Petersburg, just south of Richmond, like an enormous panting beast. It was exhausted from nearly non-stop fighting since May. Thousands of its officers and men lay buried across Virginia and hospitals in Washington overflowed with its wounded. Draftees and new volunteers were arriving to fill the vacancies, but they needed seasoning. By late August, Grant—in ill health and feeling "languid and feeble," according to an aide—was ready to let the army rest.[24]

But late summer brought Grant his favorite tonic: a long visit from Julia and the Grant children: Frederick, 14; Ulysses, Jr., 12; Nellie, 9, and Jesse, 6. One morning, Grant aide Horace Porter entered a headquarters tent to find Grant on the floor, wrestling with his two oldest boys, all laughing merrily. Red in the face and nearly out of breath, a shirt-sleeved Grant disentangled himself and sheepishly told Porter, "Ah, you know my weaknesses—my children and my horses." Visitors sometimes found Grant's younger children hanging around his neck, jumbling his papers while he wrote. They were never scolded.[25]

Mrs. Grant quickly made friends with his staff officers, raising spirits with her cheerful conversation at mealtimes. In the evenings, Julia and Ulysses would sit hand in hand in a quiet corner, looking "as bashful as two young lovers," Porter wrote.[26] Julia habitually referred to her husband as "Mr. Grant" when speaking with others, Porter said, but addressed him as "Ulyss" and occasionally "Victor," a nickname she coined after the capture of Vicksburg. When Julia teased Ulysses for details of his next movement, he would respond with a droll recital of imaginary facts and figures. "No family could have been happier," Porter decided.[27]

The siege line around Petersburg was enlivened when Sherman captured Atlanta (Grant ordered a hundred-gun salute of live artillery fire aimed

During the long siege of Petersburg, Confederates dug long trenches and built many huts to shelter themselves. By late autumn, the Union's own siege line went on for thirty-two miles.

at Confederate lines) and when Sheridan licked Early at Winchester (another hundred-gun pasting of the Confederates). A low moment occurred when Wade Hampton led four thousand Confederate horsemen behind Union lines and drove a huge herd of cattle back to Lee's starving army. The animals had been grazing in the lush pastures Edmund Ruffin created with his soil science. After the "Beefsteak Raid," as it was called, someone asked Grant when he expected to starve out Lee. "Never, if our armies continue to supply him with beef-cattle," growled Grant.[28]

All the while, the Army of the Potomac was pushing its siege line westward, digging trenches and erecting battlements, forcing Lee's thinning ranks to do the same. On the night of September 28–29, Grant resumed hammer blows on both ends of Lee's Petersburg defenses, trading attacks with Lee for more than a week. The Union's greatest success was its bloody capture of Fort Harrison, a linchpin of Confederate defenses. Standing on one of the fort's parapets, Grant could even see Richmond's church spires.

On October 27, Grant ordered a two-pronged attack at the ends of the Confederate defenses. In a bitter fight at Hatcher's Run, Union Gen. Winfield Scott Hancock's troops were repulsed, but by now Confederate lines in defense of Petersburg had been stretched for thirty-five miles. Lee warned Jefferson Davis that unless his thin and hungry ranks were reinforced, "I fear a great calamity will befall us."[29] And yet Lee refused a desperately needed man-for-man exchange of prisoners with Grant that would have included black soldiers, because "Negroes belonging to our Citizens are not Considered Subjects of exchange."[30] It was a triumph of ideology over pragmatism.

With major offensives halted by approaching winter, the Union army concentrated on improving its entrenchments. By November 6, the Union's siege line stretched thirty-two miles, incorporating thirty-six forts and fifty artillery batteries. By now, both sides had erected defenses so formidable that it would have been madness to attack them head-on.

Trenches shored up with logs zigzagged across the Virginia countryside. Union and Confederate fortifications presented each other faces bristling like porcupines with abatis (felled trees, branches pointing outward) and chevaux-de-frise (rows of sharpened poles at breast height). "Bombproofs"—dank shelters constructed of planks, logs, and earth—dotted the works on both sides.

As the weather turned colder, the men built log shanties caulked with mud for their winter shelter. Their duties dwindled to serving on picket or working on fortifications and cutting firewood. They used leisure hours for reading, writing letters, and card-playing. Some went to prayer meetings.[31] The 126th Ohio enjoyed music from its own band.[32]

Life on the siege line was anything but pleasant, however. The duties were monotonous, the damp cold almost unbearable, the trenches filled with mud. Officers discouraged fraternization and sniping went on continually: to peek over a battlement was to invite death. Artillerymen pounded away daily. Hated most were mortars, which tossed bombshells high in the air where they would seem to hang for a moment, then drop, their fuses hissing "I'm a-coming, I'm a-coming" until their ear-splitting explosion announced, "I'm HERE!"[33]

For all their efforts to protect themselves, soldiers could still die in their own trenches from artillery fire, sharpshooters, and surprise attackers.

On November 17, Grant left for a short holiday in Burlington, New Jersey, where his children were attending school. Attempting to visit New York City and Philadelphia incognito, he was mobbed by eager citizens who recognized him in civilian clothes and wanted to shake his hand. He was relieved to return to winter camp, where he had replaced his well-worn tent with a small log hut, furnished plainly as usual.

Complaints were growing in the press about how long the siege was taking, but Grant was unperturbed. Noticing a dog that one of his generals had brought into camp, Grant asked, "Do you expect to take it into Richmond with you?" The man replied with mock seriousness, "I hope to; it is said to come from a long-lived breed." An aide recalled that Grant "joined heartily in the merriment."[34]

Grant could use the comic relief, for if there was little happening on the Petersburg front, there was plenty to worry about elsewhere. General Hood's Confederate army was threatening Nashville and George Thomas, the "Rock of Chickamauga," seemed rooted inside his fortifications, unwilling to take the offensive.

Sherman, meanwhile, had cut all communications and disappeared into eastern Georgia. "Sherman's army is now somewhat in the condition of a ground-mole when he disappears under a lawn," Grant mused one evening. "You can here and there trace his track, but you are not quite certain where he will come out till you see his head."[35] Soon, however, Grant would be ordering salutes to both generals.

LINCOLN'S RE-ELECTION

On the night of Thursday, June 14, 1864, five men crossed the Canadian border at Windsor, walked to a Detroit railroad station, and boarded a sleeping car in a train for Ohio. One of the men had disguised himself with false whiskers and a cape. His name was Clement L. Vallandigham, and he had decided to return—without permission—from the exile into which the Lincoln government had thrust him a year before.

Vallandigham and his escorts squirmed anxiously in their berths as their train clacked its way south, arriving in the southwestern Ohio city of Hamilton early Friday morning. Democrats were gathering there to elect two delegates to the Democratic National Convention from Ohio's Third Congressional District. When Vallandigham strode onto the platform—"an apparition from the clouds," as one witness put it—the crowd exploded with cheers.

Flummoxed authorities couldn't decide what to do about the exile's

Grant's tenacity—a quality lacking in his Eastern Theater predecessors—produced a caricature depicting him as the Union's "bulldog."

return, but Lincoln settled the matter by conspicuously ignoring it. Vallandigham's exile had become a civil-rights embarrassment to the administration. It seemed best to leave him alone. It was a presidential election year and Lincoln needed to avoid boiling any more pots than necessary.

Earlier in the year, Secretary of the Treasury Salmon P. Chase had maneuvered behind Lincoln's back for the Republican presidential nomination, but the effort failed abysmally. Even a Union-Republican caucus in Chase's home state of Ohio endorsed Lincoln. At an unusually quiet joint Union-Republican national convention in Baltimore in June, Lincoln was re-nominated on the first ballot by an almost unanimous vote (Missouri insisted on giving Ulysses Grant a symbolic nomination).

To broaden the ticket's appeal, Andrew Johnson, a War Democrat from Tennessee, was put up for vice president. Republican unity was threatened only by some party radicals who broke away to nominate John C. Frémont, the famed explorer, failed general, and Radical Republican.

At their presidential nominating convention, Democrats—panting hard and pushing—gave birth to a two-headed monstrosity. They picked Gen. George B. McClellan, the popular but unemployed soldier, to head the ticket. McClellan was favored by those Democrats who supported a continued war to reunite the country while leaving slavery alone. Confusingly, the Democratic ticket's candidate for vice president, their ticket's secondary head, was a peace-now, negotiate-later Democrat from Ohio, George Pendleton of Cincinnati.

The Democratic platform had a peace plank with delegate Vallandigham's fingerprints all over it, but shortly after the convention, McClellan— still a soldier loyal to the North—repudiated his party's own peace plank. The Democrats' quest for a horse had produced a camel. Democrats were looking loonier by the day, and then Republican unity was restored when Frémont withdrew his candidacy.

The 1864 presidential campaign was as vicious as any seen in the twenty-first century. Foreshadowing later generations of slash-and-burn partisans,

Former General McClellan was stingingly caricatured as two-faced when he ran against Lincoln in the 1864 election.

the *Cleveland Plain Dealer* called Lincoln "a miserable failure, a coarse filthy joker, a disgusting politician, a mean, cunning and cruel tyrant and the shame and disgrace of the nation." Another shrieker, the *Cincinnati Enquirer,* warned that Lincoln's re-election could extinguish "the experiment of free government."[36] In the end, these dire warnings made no difference.

When Sherman and Sheridan scored battlefield victories during the second half of 1864, public support for the Lincoln administration rebounded from its summer doldrums. In the October congressional elections, Republicans swept the majority of contests, taking seventeen out of nineteen congressional seats in Ohio alone. Ohio Congressman Samuel Cox, a Vallandigham ally, was voted out of office after four terms.[37]

In the presidential contest November 8, Lincoln crushed McClellan nationwide, carrying every state but three and winning his first clear majority nation-wide—fifty-five percent of the popular vote. Once again, he carried Ohio, which gave him nearly thirty-four thousand more votes than it did in 1860.

Writing in the *Cincinnati Gazette*, Whitelaw Reid neatly summed up the significance of Lincoln's re-election: "It wrought the death of something more important—SLAVERY! *That* is the true significance of our triumph....[Also,] the election decides another thing. This people...have decreed that at whatever further cost, the republic shall be undivided and indivisible!" [38]

DESPERATION

In three years, the dogs of war had chewed up so much of Confederate Gen. John Bell Hood that he had to be strapped into the saddle, but his lust for battle was diminished not a whit. A six-foot, two-inch giant from Kentucky,

Hood had graduated—just barely—from West Point in 1853 and was not regarded as one of the Academy's brighter lights.

Nonetheless, Hood's hell-for-leather style made him a peerless brigade and division commander in the cavalier mode so beloved by Southerners. Wounds at Gettysburg and Chickamauga crippled his left arm and reduced his right leg to a stump, but after Atlanta fell, Jefferson Davis rolled the dice and decided to send what was left of the mighty Hood with what was left of the Army of Tennessee on a desperate thrust north.

Hood began on September 29, 1864, by cutting Sherman's rail link to Chattanooga. That was supposed to lure Sherman's army away from Atlanta, so it could be destroyed on a field of Hood's choosing. Then Hood could turn north to reclaim Tennessee and perhaps Kentucky. It was a daring plan, and at first it seemed to work. The Confederates had a high old time tearing up railroad track and, sure enough, Sherman came galumphing after them. But Sherman repaired the railroad in short order and never obliged Hood by coming close enough to become a target for one of Hood's patented mad-bull attacks.

Hood gave up baiting Sherman who, for his part, decided he had better things to do as well. The two commanders turned their backs on each other in late October and headed in opposite directions. "Damn Hood!" Sherman said of his enemy's intentions. "Let him go North. My business is down South!"[39] Sherman returned to Atlanta to launch what he called "my big raid." Months earlier, someone had asked him for his ultimate destination. "Salt water. Salt water," he had replied.

Hood spent a few weeks in Alabama re-supplying himself from the Confederacy's skimpy larder. On the icy morning of November 21, the ragged soldiers of his Army of Tennessee, many barefoot, bent into a bitter snowy wind and trudged northward, crossing into middle Tennessee. Meanwhile Jefferson Davis was barnstorming the eastern Confederacy, telling worried civilians that "We ... must push the enemy back to the banks of the Ohio."[40] But a Confederate colonel had once observed that if Hood possessed a "lion's heart," he probably also had a "wooden head."[41] Events would soon demonstrate both.

To deal with Hood, Sherman sent Maj. Gen. George Thomas to Nashville and ordered substantial reinforcements for him. In addition, two Union army corps, numbering about thirty-two thousand men under Maj. Gen. John M. Schofield of New York, were sent to delay Hood south of Nashville until the city's defenses were complete. In Schofield's army, Ohioans David S. Stanley

Confederate General Hood's misguided campaign against Nashville ended his career and wrecked the Army of Tennessee.

and Jacob D. Cox commanded the IV and XXIII Corps respectively, with almost all their troops coming from the Midwest and more than a fourth from Ohio alone.

Hoping to divide and conquer, Hood began rushing north in an attempt to get ahead of Schofield and reach Nashville before it could be reinforced. Nashville was a prize worth striving for. Not only was it the capital of Tennessee, but also it was the hub of Union efforts in the Western Theater, a supply depot, hospital complex, and strategic center. It was a place the Union could ill afford to lose.[42]

Racing in Nashville's direction, the rival armies passed through a succession of small towns. On the afternoon of November 29, their advance forces clashed in a small battle at Spring Hill, Tennessee, the fighting halted by darkness. Come morning, Hood thought, he could surround and destroy the Federals. He should have thought harder.

In one of those flukes of war that are hard to believe, the Confederates left the road north unguarded during the night. Schofield's army was able to creep by the Confederates as they slept mere yards away. With the Union soldiers' canteens hitched tight and talking forbidden, the only sounds were the shuffling of feet as the seven-mile-long Union column tiptoed past Spring Hill. "It was the most remarkable incident in all our military experience," recalled Alexis Cope of the 15th Ohio.[43] When Hood awoke the next morning to find Schofield gone, he was "as wrathy as a rattlesnake," one of his staff officers recalled.[44]

By then, Schofield's army was hustling up the pike to Franklin, a short distance south of Nashville. By mid-afternoon, most of the Union soldiers had settled down there and protected themselves with trenches and breastworks, some bristling with thorny brush from Osage orange bushes. Left out in front of these defenses, however, were two brigades posted in vulnerable positions by Brig. Gen. George D. Wagner of Indiana.

The third of Wagner's three brigades was commanded by Col. Emerson Opdycke, and it had defiantly filed inside the main defense line, in spite of orders to the contrary. Opdycke—hardened by some of the war's fiercest battles—had refused Wagner's direct order to put his exhausted brigade in the same dangerous position as the other two, out in front of Union defenses. Wagner and Opdycke's bitter argument left Wagner sputtering in futility—but this act of insubordination would soon pay dividends.

At this point, Hood could have bypassed Schofield and headed for Nashville, but he had always triumphed by springing ahead like an angry bull, and the Spring Hill debacle had made him furious. Less professionalized than modern armed forces, the armies of the Civil War had room for sharply differing command styles on the battlefield. There were generals who were like broadswords in their fighting style, generals who were like scalpels, and there were tap-dancers. Hood was a very blunt instrument. A hammer. A *sledge*hammer.

Hood must have realized his chances for success in the current campaign were moving from slim in the direction of zero. But he was desperate and so, almost mindlessly, he did what he always did, employing the only strategy he knew: attack. At 4 o'clock on an Indian summer afternoon, Hood ordered a head-on charge on Schofield's lines at Franklin, even though part of Hood's army and most of his artillery hadn't arrived. His Confederates marched forward in neat ranks, flags flying, bands playing, as sheets of rifle and artillery fire tore into them, cutting them down like cornstalks.

The Union defenders had to hold their fire, however, when Wagner's two exposed brigades hightailed it back to Union lines. Fleet-footed Confederates followed so closely on Wagner's heels that they poured over the Federal defenses near the Fountain B. Carter farmhouse, forcing some of the Union soldiers to flee.

After defying Wagner's order, Opdycke's brigade had been posted in reserve only two hundred yards behind the Carter house. This turned out to be exactly where they were needed most. Shouting "First Brigade, forward to the works," Opdycke rushed to get out in front as his veterans spontaneously sprang ahead, bayonets lowered. The Carter garden became a swirling mass of Confederates and Federals firing rifles and pistols face to face, slashing and stabbing with bayonets, and clubbing each other with muskets.

Opdycke broke his empty revolver over a Confederate head then turned to swinging a musket like a truncheon. Crowded into ranks four or five deep, Federals in the rear loaded rifles and passed them forward to be fired. Thanks to Opdycke's brigade, the Confederate break-through was crushed within minutes.

Hood kept blindly attacking, with no success, until long after dark. Veterans called Franklin the most intense fight they had experienced. Opdycke said he had never seen enemy dead and wounded "so thickly piled one upon another; the carnage was awful."[45] "Our troops were killed by whole platoons," recalled a Confederate veteran, horrified by the corpses hanging on the thorns of the Osage orange barrier, the bodies ripped by "hundreds of minie balls and grape shot."[46] All Hood had achieved was a Confederate bloodbath—nearly 5,555 killed, wounded, or captured to Schofield's 1,222.[47]

There was one other Union casualty: General Wagner was sent home for his poor handling of troops. Opdycke proudly wrote his wife, Lucy, "Every one here says 'Col. Opdycke saved the day.'"[48] He had been insubordinate—but the decision was a fortunate one.

In Nashville, meanwhile, Thomas and his staff in Nashville savored news of Schofield's victory. Other Union reinforcements were filing into the city. Maj. Gen. A.J. Smith walked through the door of Thomas's headquarters to report his 10,461 men were arriving from St. Louis. Schofield's triumphant army arrived at the city's edge the next morning and Thomas put the thirty thousand weary men to work building additional defenses.

Maj. Gen. James B. Steedman showed up leading a detachment of 8,500 men composed largely of U.S. Colored Troops, plus a few white units. James H. Wilson's cavalry corps arrived as well. A hodgepodge of garrison troops, convalescents, and quartermaster's workers rounded out the defenders of Nashville. Altogether, Thomas had sixty-six thousand men, well-entrenched, for whatever Hood could throw at him.

Arriving outside Nashville on December 2, even Hood's one-track mind grasped that his badly diminished force—now twenty-three thousand men, hollow-eyed from hunger, wearing rags, many shoeless—could not storm the city's battlements. To have any chance of success, according to a Civil War maxim, an attacker needed three times as many soldiers as an entrenched defender. Here, the ratio was the exact reverse.

Hood had to face the facts. He decided to be patient for once, dig in, and let Thomas attack him, hoping a Confederate counter-attack would bring victory. For two weeks, the opposing armies eyed each other. Always deliberate, Thomas used the time to prepare for battle and wait for favorable weather, while back east the usually imperturbable Grant, not fully understanding the situation in Nashville, fired off telegram after telegram demanding that Thomas attack *now*. Thomas must have picked up some of the Western army's stubborn independence, because he ignored the telegrams.

His patience exhausted, Grant had already decided to replace the "Rock of Chickamauga" when, on the foggy morning of December 15, Thomas finally attacked. Aiming his heaviest blow at Hood's left, he ordered a lighter attack on Hood's right to distract him. Leading the thrust on Hood's right, Steedman and his African Americans fought bravely but were stopped by stronger resistance than expected. Confederates apparently took special delight in shooting the blacks.[49]

On the Confederate left, however, the Union's IV and XXIII Corps—with Emerson Opdycke in the thick of things—overran several enemy redoubts, driving back A.P. Stewart's corps about two miles. By the end of the day, Confederate officers could see their men were dispirited and demoralized.

Thomas wired Grant that night, "The whole action of today was splendidly successful." The general in chief, then in Washington on his way to Nashville, cancelled his plan to relieve Thomas and wired congratulations instead. "Push the enemy now, and give him no rest until he is entirely destroyed," he told Thomas. Then Grant returned to his headquarters near Petersburg.[50]

The next morning, Generals Steedman and Thomas J. Wood worked out a plan to attack the Confederate right on Overton Hill from two directions. A brigade composed mostly of white Ohioans, plus another brigade, would hit the north slope, while Steedman's U.S. Colored Troops—many of them only recently slaves—advanced from the east.

Encountering stiff resistance on Overton's slopes, the black and white Union forces converged, many falling together under enemy fire. The attack stalled. Seeing dead black and white soldiers lying side by side "removed from the mind and heart of at least one white soldier all prejudice against the Negro race," an officer of the 15th Ohio wrote of himself.[51]

At the opposite end of the Confederate line, a pulverizing Union artillery barrage followed by a tidal wave of infantry overwhelmed the Confederate defenders of Compton Hill. With that, the entire Confederate line fell like a house of cards, collapsing from west to east. At Overton Hill, the Union forces who had been stalled on the slopes were amazed to see the Confederate breastworks spontaneously empty as the defenders turned to flee.

Demoralized Confederate soldiers ignored Hood's demands they rally. Unable to stem the panic, officers joined the fleeing men. Everywhere there were running Confederate soldiers and riderless horses, regiments falling back, officers shouting orders to no avail. The final blow to Southern pride was to see black faces among their pursuers.

Nashville was one of the least costly Union victories. Thomas had 3,061 casualties, only 387 of whom were killed. Confederate figures were never reported, but Hood lost 4,462 men to capture alone and untold thousands more were killed or wounded.[52]

At the end of this terrible day, the retreating Hood made his headquarters in a home near Franklin. His soldiers were scattered and many were deserting. A private who happened into Hood's presence found him disconsolate. "He was much agitated and affected, pulling his hair with his hand, and crying like his heart would break," the soldier recalled.[53]

Vengeance is Mine

On the morning of September 20, 1864, Lt. Col. Horace Porter walked along an Atlanta street looking for the house where General Sherman had made his headquarters after capturing the city. A member of General Grant's staff, Porter was carrying a letter from the general in chief. Porter found the captor of Atlanta relaxing on a porch, tilted back in a large armchair and wearing worn carpet slippers, absorbed in a newspaper. Porter—who had never met Sherman—took in the forty-four-year-old general's "tall, gaunt form, restless hazel eyes, aquiline nose, bronzed face, and crisp beard" and thought to himself: this man was "the picture of 'grim-faced war.'"[54]

Porter sat quietly while the general perused the letter containing Grant's thoughts about Sherman's proposed next campaign. Then Sherman began talking about his plans. Vibrating with nervous energy, he rose from his chair and sat again, crumpling the newspaper in his hand and shoving his feet in and out of his slippers. The words burst from Sherman's lips "as rapidly as shots from a machine-gun." A fascinated Porter decided he was watching "one of the most dramatic and picturesque characters of the war."[55]

Porter returned to Grant carrying Sherman's latest thoughts on the biggest idea of his career, a daring plan as simple as it was extraordinary. His army would abandon its Atlanta base, cut its own communication and supply lines, and plunge eastward into Georgia, an isolated force living off the land until

The grim-faced William Tecumseh Sherman was, an aide to Grant wrote, "one of the most dramatic and picturesque characters of the war."

it reached the Atlantic coast and connected with Union forces there.

This bold stroke, Sherman argued, would demonstrate the futility of the Confederacy's cause, destroy many of its resources, and put Sherman in position to move north in support of Grant in Virginia. Despite his jerky mannerisms—and unlike Hood—Sherman was not impulsive. He had studied census data and maps and knew his army could live off the land. "I can make Georgia howl," he promised.[56]

By November 2 Sherman was confident that Hood was heading for Nashville and that George Thomas could handle him there. "It surely was a strange event—two hostile armies marching in opposite directions," Sherman admitted, but he had other fish to fry.[57] As he told Thomas, "I propose to demonstrate the vulnerability of the South, and make its inhabitants feel that war and individual ruin are synonymous terms."[58] He was going to wage "total war."

Sherman had given Atlantans a taste back in September. Declaring "Atlanta is no place for families or noncombatants," he had turned civilians out of their homes and evicted them from the city, arguing it would spare them the dangers of a war zone.[59] Sherman, a devoted Unionist, believed the Confederates had brought their miseries on themselves by causing the war. In his epigrammatic way, he told the city's protesting mayor, "War is cruelty, and you cannot refine it; and those who brought war into our Country deserve all the curses and maledictions a people can pour out. ... You might as well appeal against the thunder storm as against these terrible hardships of war."[60]

As soon as he was sure Hood was heading for Nashville, Sherman turned back to Atlanta, issuing orders as he went. His forces were to be stripped to the essentials, with those he called "the sick, the wounded and the worthless" sent back to Chattanooga, together with all unnecessary baggage.[61] There would be no general supply train. The army would "forage liberally on the country," and railroads, cotton gins, mills—anything that could serve the Confederate cause—would be destroyed.

So-called total war (actually, "hard war") had its limits in Sherman's orders. Soldiers must leave citizens sufficient food for their own maintenance. They were not to enter homes or destroy property in areas where there was no resistance. Where guerilla or other resistance arose, however, the army should impose "a devastation more or less relentless."[62] The men were to march fifteen miles a day, beginning at 7 a.m., their exact destination a mystery.

The last trains sped north to Chattanooga, the men aboard waving goodbye, and then Sherman's troops ripped up the track behind them. The telegraph line connecting Sherman to the rest of the nation was broken on November 12. After that, it seemed to the rest of the nation as if he and his army had disappeared into a black hole. For a month, Washington and the nation were reduced to trying to cipher out from the biased garble in Confederate newspapers where Sherman was and what he was doing.

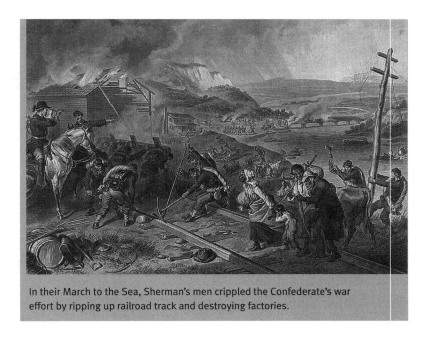

In their March to the Sea, Sherman's men crippled the Confederate's war effort by ripping up railroad track and destroying factories.

Before disappearing, soldiers had dispatched their "last letters." Sherman began his letters as usual with "Dearest Ellen," quickly drying up as he discussed mostly military affairs. Whenever his letters touched on their children he warmed to the subject, but this message was mostly as crisp and opaque as an autumn leaf, the husband drifting out of sight with "Yrs. Ever, W. T. Sherman."[63] He also wired Ellen about some last-minute loose ends: "We start today. My arm is quite well. The box of clothing came last night. I have all your letters too including Novr. 3. Write no more till you hear of me. Good Bye. W. T. Sherman."[64]

He had ordered Atlanta leveled, except for homes and churches. From the general's headquarters the evening of November 14, staff officer Maj. Henry Hitchcock saw "huge waves of fire roll up into the sky" against which "the skeletons of great warehouses stand out in relief." Sherman and his officers watched the fires move across the horizon in "angry waves" subsiding into a "fierce glow" and "a line of fire and smoke, lurid, angry, dreadful to look at."[65]

Sherman's famous March to the Sea began November 16, a sparkling day under the blue vault of heaven. The men were in high spirits, but Sherman worried if "this 'march' will be adjudged the wild adventure of a crazy fool."[66] From a hill he glanced back at Atlanta, black smoke "hanging like a pall over the ruined city."

A band struck up the "John Brown Song" and soon "Glory, glory, hallelujah" was rising from the ranks, the men moving rapidly, with a swinging pace. "Then we turned our horses' heads to the east," Sherman remembered. "Atlanta was soon lost behind the screen of trees and became a thing of the past."[67]

Sherman had sixty-two thousand men, about a fourth of them from Ohio, more than from any other state. His army was divided into two wings, a right wing composed of the XV and XVII Corps and a left of the XIV and XX Corps. A cavalry division operated separately. About half the soldiers in the XX Corps were highly disciplined, cautious Easterners who originally had been detached from the Army of the Potomac to assist Grant at Chattanooga.

Most of Sherman's soldiers were battle-hardened veterans from western states, long-haired, bewhiskered men, their faces leathery from a thousand suns. Careless about military etiquette and contemptuous of officious commanders, they marched with a confident stride. They were accustomed to victories.

There wasn't much they hadn't seen, and there wasn't much they hadn't done. More than one military expert has remarked that, for all its cocky insolence, this just may have been the best army in the world at the time. But these men carried with them harsh memories of deprivation and exhaustion; they could not forget the death and mutilation of comrades, and though they had professional respect for the Confederate fighting man, they had no respect for the traitorous cause for which he fought. Now, with almost no resistance in sight, the Southern land lay open before them.

Like a blue tsunami, Sherman's men fell upon the land, and Georgia howled. Near Covington, a wealthy widow and slave owner named Dolly Sumner Lunt cried out, in some detail, at the loss of her abundance:

> But like demons they rush in! My yards are full. To my smoke-house, my dairy, pantry, kitchen, and cellar, the famished wolves they come … The thousand pounds of meat in my smoke-house is gone in a twinkling, my flour, my meat, my lard, butter, eggs, pickles of various kinds—both in vinegar and brine—wine, jars and jugs are all gone. My eighteen fat turkeys, my hens, chickens, and fowls, my young pigs are shot down in my yard and hunted as if they were rebels themselves.

Confederate soldiers were going hungry and Union prisoners were starving while properties like Dolly Lunt's and the pristine Georgia countryside overflowed with bounty. Sherman's men felt no need to respect the wealth of people like Dolly Lunt.

By the laws of war, an army could take what it needed from the countryside and destroy the enemy's war resources, but even Sherman admitted that "many acts of pillage, robbery, and violence [to property], were committed."[68] Much of what Sherman's soldiers did broke the laws of warfare, but much did not. It was a mix. To take away the enemy's military supplies, the Union soldiers burned cotton gins and warehouses and tore up railroad track. However, they also plundered so much food they frequently left behind heaps to spoil and hunted for hidden valuables they didn't need. Bodily violence toward civilians was rare, however.

Few of the men shared a sense of guilt about all this. Sherman's soldiers were not criminals, but Midwestern farm boys, clerks, and cobblers who had been brought up on *McGuffey's Eclectic Reader* and the Bible. Their God was a stern God, not the avuncular model of the twenty-first century, and they had heard the Word: *Vengeance is mine, saith the Lord; I will repay.* Southerners had started a war to tear the nation apart. Now, someone must pay.

(Old attitudes linger to this day. Weary, apparently, of Southerners' persistent complaining about Sherman's march, author P. J. O'Rourke, a native of Toledo, recently told them to get over it: "People from Ohio *won* the Civil War. We still have our houses."[69])

Sherman's men spent nearly a month marching through eastern Georgia. To confuse the enemy, his four corps traveled on separate but parallel routes, spread across a front of about sixty miles, moving like a giant four-tined rake tearing into the hide of Georgia. Always the careful planner, Sherman had studied census data and knew Georgia's countryside, untouched by war, abounded with provisions. Each of his brigades regularly sent out foraging parties of about fifty men each to roam miles from the main column and take what they needed from farms and plantations.

Captain Robert W. Burt of the 76th Ohio commanded one of the forage parties. It was risky business, he recalled, but "the love of adventure, however, made it desirable" to the most daring soldiers. Small squads sent to distant farmhouses risked capture by guerrillas or Confederate cavalrymen who sometimes executed foragers. At the end of a good day, however, the foragers would be welcomed back to the main column laden with "bacon, sweet potatoes, chickens, turkeys, geese, etc."[70]

Well-fed and suffering few casualties, soldiers spent their evenings relaxing. A member of Sherman's staff never forgot the sweet languor of one Sunday night in camp after a long march. The commander and some of his officers relaxed in camp chairs, while others lay around, campfires burning in front of their tents. In every direction were the "sparkle drops of flame scattered all

During Sherman's March to the Sea, both his hungry foragers and a swarm of freebooters, criminals, and deserters from both sides came to be known as "Sherman's Bummers."

over the large open fields" where the huge army lay. Soon a band was heard and then the soldiers sang hymns, the first being, "Thus far the Lord hath led me on," the words rising into the night sky like sparks from the campfires.[71]

"The march was little more than a grand picnic," Gen. William B. Hazen remembered in a memoir.[72] It was not exactly that. The army's harrowing of the land attracted a cloud of lawless stragglers and deserters from both armies. There were Georgians with larceny on their minds and runaway slaves trailing their liberators. Army foragers and freebooting looters alike came to be known as "Sherman's bummers," and they were not easily restrained.

On one plantation, a soldier walked by Sherman carrying a ham on his musket, a jug of sorghum-molasses under his arm, and a honeycomb, which he was eating. Boldly catching Sherman's eye, he quoted the general's order: "Forage liberally on the country!"[73] Sherman scolded the man, reminding him foraging was limited to the assigned parties.

The damage from Sherman's march probably was more than the soldiers would later admit, but less than Georgians would later claim. Perhaps the most severe blow to the local economy was the departure of that pillar of the Confederacy's wealth: slaves. Giving lie to the Southern claim that slaves were contented, as many as five thousand escapees from captivity trailed Sherman on the march through Georgia.

Sherman shared in the racism of the time, but he was touched by how the runaways crowded around him. They were "simply frantic with joy," he wrote in his memoirs. "Whenever they heard my name, they clustered around my horse, shouted and prayed in their peculiar style, which had a natural eloquence that would have moved a stone. I have witnessed hundreds, if not thousands, of such scenes; and can now see a poor girl … hugging the banner of one of the regiments, and jumping, and jumping up to the 'feet of Jesus.'"[74]

On November 19, Georgia Gov. Joe Brown called for all civilian men to oppose Sherman, but he got few volunteers.[75] A frantic legislature at the then-capital of Milledgeville blustered angrily about Sherman, passed an act ordering most males (except themselves) into military service, and fled on a commandeered train. Governor Brown seized a train of his own to carry away the executive mansion's carpets, curtains, and furniture. Within four days, the Union forces occupied the capitol building. Sherman's officers entered the deserted legislative chambers, where they elected a "speaker" and held a mock session voting Georgia back into the Union.

On December 3, Sherman, accompanying the XVII Corps, arrived in Millen, site of a Confederate prison camp. The Union army arrived too late, because the prisoners had been spirited away only hours before. Infuriated by the foul conditions Sherman's soldiers found in the abandoned camp, they burned everything in sight. Their anger included slaveholders. On plantations they destroyed whipping posts and shot the bloodhounds used to hunt down runaways.

On December 10, 1864, Sherman reached the outskirts of Savannah, on the Atlantic coast, and the March to the Sea was over. In twenty-seven days Uncle Billy's army had marched three hundred miles, slashing through the Deep South with little effort, destroying huge amounts of supplies badly needed by the enemy, and showing the world that the Confederacy was less a "nation" than patches of territory where Union forces could roam at will. "I'm telling you, we had some high old times," an Ohio soldier wrote.[76]

Fighting along the way had been limited to a few cavalry engagements and one infantry encounter near Griswoldville, when an untrained Rebel militia attacked a Union rear guard composed of seasoned veterans armed with repeating rifles. After the outmatched Georgians were driven off, leaving the battlefield littered with Southern dead and wounded, the Union soldiers were shocked to find their opponents had been old men and teenaged military school cadets.

To defend Savannah, Confederate Gen. William Hardee had scrabbled together a defense force of ten thousand soldiers. Before attacking the city, however, Sherman needed to connect with a Union supply fleet lying outside the port. Blocking his way was Fort McAllister. On December 13th, he sent General Hazen to capture the fort.

As Sherman and his staff watched from a signal platform three miles away, smoke from the fort's cannons cleared long enough to reveal "the parapets were blue with our own men," many of them the members of the 30th, 47th, 54th, and 70th Ohio.[77] The fort fell into Union hands within hours.

Next, Sherman demanded Hardee avoid bloodshed by surrendering the city. Hardee's reply was defiant, but on the night of December 20th the Confederate commander evacuated his army and disappeared into South Carolina. Pvt. Andrew Altman of the 68th Ohio gloated in a letter home, "well father, Olde billey as we call him, played yankey a gain and down came Savannah and up went the stars and stripes proudly floating."[78]

Sherman's men marched into Savannah December 21st and were greeted with little overt hostility from its ten thousand residents. "Well, this is a nice city," Private Altman observed of the prosperous port.[79] On the 22nd, Sherman wired Lincoln, "I beg to present you as a Christmas gift the city of Savannah, with 150 heavy guns & plenty of ammunition & also about twenty-five thousand bales of cotton."[80]

Savoring his success, Sherman sat down on December 30 to read letters from his brother and in-laws. From them he learned of the December 4 death from croup of his baby son, Charles Celestine Sherman. His army's month-long disappearance had prevented word from reaching him sooner. With no way to inform her husband, Ellen had suffered through the infant's agonies as he coughed himself to death. Sherman had never seen the child who had been born when he was occupied with his Atlanta campaign. Now father and mother would have to do their mourning separately. *"War is cruelty,"* Sherman had said only three months before; *"you cannot refine it."*

Gazette

Discontent and hardship were widespread in the Confederacy during the winter of 1864–65 and yet there were those who continued to insist the Lord blessed Southerners, and hated Northerners. These true believers were still convinced they would win independence, thereby demonstrating yet again the heart's ability to delude itself.[81] With the destruction of Hood's Army of Tennessee, Lee's hungry, ragged Army of Northern Virginia was the Confederacy's sole

General Sherman and his wife, Ellen, endured a rocky relationship, but she rushed to his defense whenever he needed it.

remaining fighting force of consequence—and desertions were rising.

The Rebellion's contiguous heartland had been reduced to the Carolinas and part of Virginia. Across the Mississippi, Confederate military activity was limited to guerilla warfare. From inside the Confederate White House, Pres. Jefferson Davis's wife, Varina, confided to a friend, "Strictly between us, *things look* very anxious *here*." [82]

Smarting from their election defeats, some Northern Democrats blamed Vallandigham for stigmatizing the party. Unchastened, Vallandigham returned to the practice of law, while maintaining—from the sidelines—his interest in national affairs. In Washington, Lincoln relished his newly won political capital. Declaring the people united on the issue of national union, he asked Congress to make another effort to pass the Thirteenth Amendment abolishing slavery.

Meanwhile, in the federal city two prominent marital unions were under stress. Spending a rare few weeks together in the capital, James and Crete

Garfield were trying to recover from the pain caused by his illicit affair with the Widow Calhoun, revealed—and ended—a few months before.

Tensions were rising for another Washington couple. Separated by William's business activities in Rhode Island, William and Kate Chase Sprague had exchanged angry letters during the fall of 1864. At Christmas, William gave a disappointed (and now pregnant) Kate a mindless gift of money along with a lecture on how to use it.

Another member of the Chase family was in a better frame of mind. Demonstrating once more his ability to make peace with his rivals, Lincoln had nominated Salmon P. Chase to be chief justice of the Supreme Court. The Senate unanimously confirmed him, and Chase—who had long intrigued against Lincoln for the presidency—wrote him a grateful note of thanks.

In Cleveland, so many volunteers of the Northern Ohio Soldier's Aid Society had melted away, perhaps from burnout, that its officers were working themselves into exhaustion to meet the continuing needs of soldiers. Meanwhile, once-prominent names of certain Ohioans had faded from the headlines. After spending months fruitlessly awaiting orders in Indianapolis, Don Carlos Buell had resigned from the service in frustration.

Still in the service, but reduced to the fringes, were William S. Rosecrans, who now commanded the Department of the Missouri, and Irwin McDowell, sent over the horizon to command the Department of the Pacific. One Ohioan had returned to prominence, however: William Dennison, the state's first war governor, had been summoned east to become Lincoln's postmaster general.

In the Shenandoah Valley, a future president named McKinley, now a captain, distinguished himself under fire, for which he would be brevetted major before discharge the next year. General Crook had written that McKinley had "amidst the thickest of the fight cheered the men onward and encouraged them by example to do their whole duty."[83]

Grumbling on Christmas Day that there was "nothing to make it less dull & wearisome than any other Sunday," the old fire-eater Edmund Ruffin languished at his son's house in Virginia, hiding from Grant's soldiers ringing Richmond. Depressed by the succession of Union victories in the past few months, Ruffin told his diary the next day he had never "been so despondent & almost despairing."[84]

Grim war lay heavily on some Northerners as well. From one of the war's fringes, Capt. Oscar Ladley of the 75th Ohio wrote heavily, "Well this is Christmas and we have no way of putting in the day except just sitting still. ... A Merry Christmas and a Happy New Year to all."[85]

Philip Sheridan, the scourge of the Shenandoah Valley, asked Washington for permission to share his rations with the Valley's starving civilians. Displaying nothing of the Christmas spirit, Stanton replied that so long as the Valley's men were serving in the rebel ranks or bushwhacking, "our Government must decline to support their wives and children."[86]

Things were cheerier in Private Altman's camp near Savannah. "I hope next new years will finde me at home," he wrote shortly after New Year's. "The 4th Div. Of the 14th Corps was a shooting pretty near all nighte, shooting new years and hoping like Indians. ... Hoping you all a happy New years of 1865. [T]he last of this year there wont be a Secesh alive."[87]

To Learn More:

In *Sheridan: the Life and Wars of General Phil Sheridan*, Roy Morris, Jr. engagingly explains why the impetuous, cocky little commander from Ohio rose to fame so rapidly. In *Little Phil: A Reassessment of the Civil War Leadership of Gen. Philip H. Sheridan*, Ohioan Eric J. Wittenberg explains why he may not have deserved it. In the south-central Ohio town of Somerset, where Sheridan spent his youth, you can see his statue, erected in 1905 and rededicated in 2005. On his rearing steed—said to be the only equestrian statue in Ohio—Sheridan waves his hat as if to encourage us all.

One of the war's great partnerships was that of Julia and Ulysses Grant. Julia relates it in *The Personal Memoirs of Julia Dent Grant*, edited, with a useful introduction, by Grant scholar John Y. Simon. Widely regarded as one of America's finest autobiographies, Grant's *Memoirs* tells in his typically straightforward way the story of his war, including how he besieged Petersburg.

The siege lines, fought over by Grant and Lee for so many months, can be visited at the Petersburg National Battlefield (**http://www.nps.gov/pete/** or **804-732-3531**).

A first-hand and thoughtful account of Sherman's famous March to the Sea by one of his staff officers can be found in *Marching with Sherman: Passages from the Letters and Campaign Diaries of Henry Hitchcock*.

Like the Confederacy's Army of Tennessee and John Bell Hood himself, traces of Hood's disastrous invasion of Tennessee in late 1864 have largely been obliterated. Most of the battlefield at Franklin (except for the Carter house) and all of it at Nashville have been swallowed by development. However, the exploits of Col. Emerson Opdycke here and at Chickamauga are vividly captured in *To Battle for God and the Right: The Civil War Letterbooks of Emerson Opdycke*, edited by Glenn V. Longacre and John E. Hass.

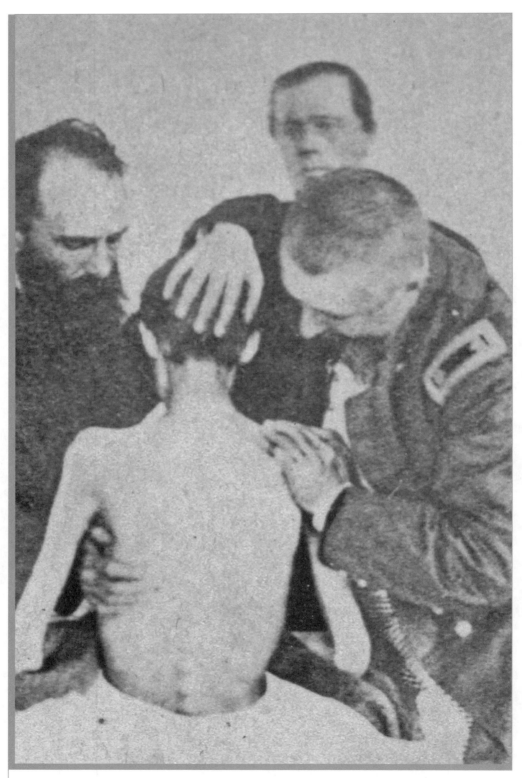

Gaunt prisoners released by the Confederates were examined by Union army doctors.

13

THE WARRIOR'S SONG

The War Years

For its time, it was a startling combination: the colonel from Maine with an Anglo-Saxon pedigree, about as white as a man could be, and his brigade of 2,300 new soldiers, very black and very eager to show what they could do in Grant's siege of Petersburg, Virginia. The blacks had been trained as well as any white regiment, the colonel thought, and they seemed better disciplined. "The regiments were entirely full and a colored deserter was a thing unknown," their Yankee commander, Col. Henry Goddard Thomas, said proudly.[1]

Progressive on matters of race, Thomas is thought to have been the first regular army officer to become a colonel of colored troops.[2] He had complete confidence in his men and, he recalled, "They believed us infallible."[3] Although Thomas was sure the black soldiers were the equal of whites, he noticed certain differences. For example, white soldiers eagerly discussed and debated official pronouncements, but the blacks greeted orders with a long silence.

The blacks would sit about in groups, silently "'studying,' as they called it," Thomas said. When "the spirit moved," one of the soldiers would raise his voice in a mighty and "wild sort of chant." To Thomas, it sounded like this:

> *We-e looks li-ke me-en a-a-marchin' on,*
> *We looks like men-er-war.*

If the singer got no response, he would alter the words or the music and try again, repeating the song until he was joined by a voice from the ranks.

The songs of the black soldiers seemed to rise unbidden from the ranks.

Others would follow, swelling into a chorus. The song had become "the song of command."[4]

In June 1864, Union soldiers who had been coal miners dug a tunnel under a Confederate earthwork outside Petersburg, planted four tons of black powder, and, in the small hours of June 30th, detonated it. It threw an enemy battery and most of a regiment into the air, caused an enormous crater about thirty feet deep, and momentarily stunned the Confederates.

Union troops, among them Thomas's black brigade, then attacked the Confederates by way of the crater, but the two brigadier generals supposedly in charge of things hid in a bomb shelter drinking rum instead of managing affairs.[5] The Confederates regained their poise and shot down black and white troops trapped in the crater. "Thus terminated in disaster what promised to be the most successful assault of the campaign," a disappointed Grant wrote in his report.[6]

Thomas's blacks had fought bravely, but had been repulsed with a loss of forty percent. To the skeptical, however, they had proven their courage. "Hundreds of heroes 'carved in ebony' fell," Thomas wrote. "These black men commanded the admiration and respect of every beholder."[7]

With the Emancipation Proclamation, in early 1863 the Union began recruiting African Americans in significant numbers. Belittled by doubters, black soldiers had to prove themselves over and over again. The first occasion occurred in the Western Theater in 1863 at Milliken's Bend, Louisiana. Several regiments of ex-slaves, with almost no training, suffered terrible losses but held back a swarm of Confederates. Because of that, Assistant Secretary of War Charles A. Dana, then with Grant in the West, told Stanton, "Prominent officers, who used to sneer in private at the idea [of using colored troops], are now heartily in favor of it."[8] But the event attracted little notice from the Eastern public.

Within weeks, however, the 54th Massachusetts, a black regiment that included a number of Ohioans recruited by John Mercer Langston, spearheaded a near-suicidal attack on Fort (or Battery) Wagner in Charleston harbor. Fighting fiercely, the black soldiers briefly gained a foothold, but were beaten back with terrible losses. One of the black soldiers from Xenia, Ohio, wrote his hometown paper, "[O]ur little Xenia band stood up like men and did not disgrace its name by cowardice [although] [t]he minie balls sang around us like bees."[9] This time, reports of the blacks' courage quickly seized the popular imagination. Aided by the movie "Glory," the 54th is today the most famous of all the black regiments.

In February 1864, the 54th participated in a losing Union effort at Olustee, Florida. After a white regiment from New Hampshire fell apart on receiving a wrong command, Confederate attention shifted to the 8th United States Colored Infantry, an untested unit organized only months before. The greenhorns of the 8th held their position for a while, but suffered heavy casualties and retreated when their colonel was killed. Stopping the Confederates fell to the 54th Massachusetts. Once again, it proved its courage by holding its ground long enough to allow the Union forces to withdraw.

One of the war's worst atrocities occurred in April at Fort Pillow, a Union position on the Mississippi, forty miles north of Memphis.[10] The fort was held by force of about five hundred, equally divided between whites and blacks.

In July 1863, black soldiers proved their bravery in a doomed attack on the Confederates' Fort Wagner in Charleston's harbor.

After an overwhelming attack by Confederates led by Nathan Bedford Forrest, a number of blacks who had been wounded or who had surrendered were shot or bayoneted to the cries of "Kill the damn niggers."[11]

Confederate sympathizers have long denied a massacre took place, but most historians agree one did. In his report of the action, Forrest (who would lead the Ku Klux Klan after the war) wrote he hoped the battle would "demonstrate to the Northern people that negro soldiers cannot cope with Southerners."[12] Instead of intimidating black soldiers, however, "Fort Pillow" became their rallying cry as they went into battle.

In September 1864, the 5th United States Colored Troops (which originated as the 127th Ohio) saw heavy fighting near Petersburg, Virginia. The Ohio regiment was understrength at the time, but after a rousing address by its colonel, Oberlin's Giles W. Shurtleff, it joined in the attack on New Market Heights and Fort Gilmer. More than half the men of the 5th were killed, wounded, or captured. When their white officers fell, four black sergeants—Powhatan Beatty, James Bronson, Robert Pinn, and Milton Holland—rallied their companies and pressed on. All four were awarded the Medal of Honor for their courage and leadership.[13]

Black men proved again and again that they could be as good soldiers as whites. Paid less than whites at first, they won equal pay by act of Congress in 1864. And, despite nearly insurmountable barriers to advancement, by the end of the war more than one hundred African Americans, on the basis of demonstrated merit alone, had been promoted to lieutenant, captain, or major.[14]

MAKING LINCOLN LAUGH

Noah Brooks, a newsman who had known Abraham Lincoln in Illinois before the war, had been "shocked" when the two men renewed their acquaintance in Washington late in 1862. "The change which a few years had made was simply appalling," Brooks recalled years later. The light was gone from Lincoln's eyes and "there was over his whole face an expression of sadness, and a far-away look in the eyes, which were utterly unlike the Lincoln of other days ... I was so pained that I could almost have shed tears."[15]

Political attacks coming from both left and right, the death in February 1862 of the Lincolns' playful and precocious ten-year-old son, Willie, and the stresses of war all weighed heavily on the president. He needed to laugh now and then. Among Lincoln's favorite humorists were two Ohioans: Charles Farrar Browne, creator of a character named Artemus Ward, and David Ross Locke, creator of Petroleum Vesuvius Nasby.

At a Cabinet meeting in the White House on September 22, 1862, President Lincoln is said to have read aloud a chapter of "Artemus Ward," finishing with a hearty laugh. While a stony-faced Cabinet sat in silence and Secretary of War Stanton seethed at the "buffoonery," Lincoln read another chapter. Finally, the

By 1865, Abraham Lincoln's face had been worn and saddened by four years of savage warfare and fierce politics.

President sighed and said, "Gentlemen, why don't you laugh? With the fearful strain that is upon night and day, if I did not laugh I should die, and you need this medicine as much as I do." [16]

Then Lincoln pulled from his pocket a draft of the Emancipation Proclamation. It declared that on January 1, 1863, all slaves in Confederate territory "shall be henceforth and forever free." Stanton, an ardent opponent of slavery, spoke up: "Mr. President, if reading chapters of Artemus Ward is a prelude to such a deed as this, the book should be filed among the archives of the nation and the author should be canonized." The Cabinet chorused, "Amen."[17]

Browne and Locke had been writers for the *Toledo Blade* and the

Cleveland Plain Dealer. Browne's Artemus Ward and Locke's Petroleum V. Nasby were rustic characters given to mangled spellings, outrageous puns, and wild understatements and overstatements. Both were precocious, entertaining bumpkins, for which their authors had very different agendas.

Browne was a political conservative who used Artemus Ward to satirize reformers and to ridicule anyone different from himself. He mocked abolitionists, Mormonism, feminism, Oberlin College for its pro-Negro and feminist ideas, and John Brown. In a typical piece, Browne had Ward greet the "Bunkumville Female Reformin and Wimin's Rite's Associashun" this way: "O woman, woman! [W]hen you desert your firesides, and with your heds full of wimin's rites noshuns go round like roarin lions ... when you undertake to play the man, you play the devil and air an emfatic noosance."[18]

While Browne's reactionary Artemus Ward considered any reformer "an emphatic noosance," Locke used Nasby to make conservatives look foolish. Nasby was depicted as a bigot living in the benighted backwater of Wingert's Corners. After South Carolina seceded, Locke had Nasby announce that "Wingert's Corners, ez trooly Dimecratic ez any uv em, hez follered soot" and seceded from Ohio. Among Nasby's imaginary adventures was his opening of a college for bigots that was celebrated with the ceremonial whipping to death of a Negro.[19]

Lincoln laughed at Ward, a political opposite, but had a special place in his heart for Nasby. He kept Nasby pamphlets in his desk, wrote Locke to thank him for his service to the war effort, and remarked that, "For the genius to write such stuff as that I would gladly give up my office."[20]

Nasby letters were said to be the last literature read by Lincoln on the day of his assassination. Convinced Locke's work had aided public opinion, George S. Boutwell, Lincoln's last secretary of the treasury, said, "Three forces—the army, the navy, and the Nasby letters—caused the downfall of the Confederacy."[21]

ANDERSONVILLE

Years later, Albert Mellor could muster a smidgen of humor in remembering one of the worst experiences of his life. "In the terrible battle of Chickamauga our army ... was forced to fall back into Chattanooga," he recalled. "Unfortunately for me. I was unable to fall back, falling forward rather into the hands of the enemy as prisoner of war."[22]

Mellor, from Steubenville, had been a corporal in the 1st Ohio. In the smoky gloom of Chickamauga's dark woods that day, another Ohioan

The Andersonville prison camp in Georgia packed thirty thousand men into twenty-six acres bisected by a filthy creek.

recalled, "nothing could be seen from the flash of the rebel guns ... I could not distinguish the blue from the gray."[23] Nearly forty members of Mellor's regiment were captured, some after stumbling into Confederate lines while searching for their haversacks.[24] Counting noses safely back in Chattanooga, the Army of the Cumberland learned that nearly five thousand of its fifty-eight thousand members were missing.[25] Some of the missing had died unnoticed in the confusion of battle and some had fled, but many had been taken prisoner.[26]

After the Chickamauga battle in September 1863, the Confederates packed their prisoners into boxcars and sent them to Atlanta, where women spat on them as they were marched through the streets. When prisoners spat back, the outraged women demanded—unsuccessfully—that the guards shoot their captives.[27]

From Atlanta, the prisoners were sent to Richmond, Virginia. Arriving at the Belle Isle stockade, Mellor recalled, "I shall never forget the feeling of utter desolation that came over me."[28] Lacking shelter or even blankets, groups of fifty or sixty men would huddle, spoon-fashion, for warmth as they slept on the cold ground.[29] Periodically, someone would call out, "Over, spoon," and the group would roll the opposite direction.

Early in 1864, the Confederacy transferred many prisoners to Georgia, where a log stockade had been hastily thrown up around sixteen and a half acres (later, twenty-six acres) of bare land bisected by a creek. Northerners would come to know it as Andersonville. The first sight greeting Mellor as he

Union soldiers held prisoner at Andersonville lay on the bare ground in tiny tents they fashioned to protect themselves from sun and rain.

stepped into the prison pen was of fourteen corpses lying at the entrance. By now, however, he was tougher, and he made a resolution: "I determined that whatever might befall me, I would not die of despondency, but would live if I could, to tell the story of a crime against prisoners of war."[30]

Mellor would need every bit of that resolve. Captivity at first had been Purgatory, but Andersonville was Hell. As the weeks passed, the stockade filled with skeleton-thin men covered with sores infested with worms and dressed in rags overrun with vermin, forced to burrow in the ground for shelter from the sun and rain. Drinking water came from a sluggish stream used as a sewer by the guards. Unceasing diarrhea drained the life from thousands.

Prisoners weakened by scurvy died of blood poisoning from no more than tiny scratches. Every morning a creaking wagon rolled through the stockade, collecting the previous day's dead. In the afternoon, the same filthy wagon returned, carrying the day's rations: typically, cornbread covered with dead flies, bean soup filled with bugs, and a small piece of rotten pork. Desperate for more, some men searched the feces of others for scraps of undigested food.

By the summer of 1864, Andersonville held thirty thousand men in a stockade that had been designed for ten thousand. Thousands were Midwesterners, among them thirty-six of the surviving members of the 1st Ohioans captured at Chickamauga. Struggling to stay alive himself, Mellor watched as others died.

A few escapees made their way to Sherman's army as it pushed into Georgia after the Union success at Chattanooga. They described the horrors of Andersonville, 120 miles south of Sherman's destination, Atlanta. The day would come when Sherman would have to make a decision: Should he try to liberate Andersonville and free its sufferers?

THE CLEVELAND LADIES

Women in nineteenth-century Ohio were butterflies, some of iron and others of silk, all caught in a web of male sovereignty. Men had their reasons for that, of course, and didn't hesitate to cite them. Women were too emotional and, like butterflies, too fragile for the hard mental and physical tasks—such as war—that were reserved for males. That was the thinking then.

But if it were not for women, the Union's men might have lost the war. Women did more than provide love and moral support. Quickly grasping that their government was unprepared for war, thousands volunteered to nurse the sick and wounded, gather medical supplies, and collect food and clothing. Because tattered, sick, and hungry Western forces often dangled at the end of the Union's supply line, Midwestern women could make the difference in an army's ability to fight.

Working in their own kitchens and church basements, women throughout Ohio rolled bandages, knitted socks, and packed food from kitchen gardens. Their production was sent to Cincinnati, Columbus, and Cleveland, where volunteer agencies working with the United States Sanitary Commission managed distribution to soldiers, mostly in the Western Theater. Women provided most of the labor, but in Cincinnati and Columbus, men were in charge.

Not in Cleveland. With the élan of a crack army, Cleveland women alone organized and ran one of the nation's most ambitious programs of war relief. They mapped relief strategies, flogged the countryside for contributions, and packed crates themselves. No butterflies they.

Much of the credit for that goes to a bespectacled whirlwind from New England named Rebecca Cromwell Rouse. In 1830, she and her husband had arrived in the frontier town of Cleveland, where she threw herself into women's groups distributing Bible tracts and battling the Demon Rum. When, thirty years later, Fort Sumter fell on Sunday, April 14, the indefatigable Rouse heard the trumpets as clearly as any young warrior. By the following Saturday, she had the Soldiers' Aid Society of Cleveland organized and ready to work. It was said to be the first such group in the nation.

Almost immediately, an appeal from nearby Camp Taylor sent the women scurrying through the city on a "blanket raid" to collect warm coverings for new soldiers. Next came a "clothing raid" for poorly dressed recruits, and then the women sat down to sew a thousand flannel army shirts. By May, Cleveland women were caring for sick soldiers in Camp Taylor's infirmary. Learning field hospitals were poorly supplied, they shipped to the field armies enough towels, reading matter, jellies, wines, lemons, and "a stock of dainties" for two regiments.

By summer, the Cleveland group was known as the Soldiers' Aid Society of Northern Ohio, affiliated with the United States Sanitary Commission. The Cleveland group became the mother ship to more than five hundred rural women's organizations throughout northeastern Ohio.

Reports of scurvy among western soldiers in 1863 prompted a "grand vegetable raid" on northern Ohio farms. By the winter of 1863–1864, the ladies of the Soldiers' Aid Society of Northeast Ohio had shipped the soldiers tons of jellies, dried fruits, eggs, pickles, vegetables, and wines. Their work had its hazards: on one occasion, defectively packed containers of chicken spoiled and exploded in the society's headquarters, producing an odor that forced the women to work with cologne-drenched handkerchiefs pressed to their noses.

To raise money to purchase more supplies, the group organized one of the nation's most successful "Sanitary Fairs." A combination exposition, bazaar, and entertainment event, Cleveland's Sanitary Fair was housed in a huge temporary wooden building that stood on Public Square from February 22 through March 10, 1864. It housed exhibits of manufactures, handcrafts, and produce; had an auditorium that could seat two thousand; and, because the Cleveland ladies understood male appetites, offered a dining hall staffed by "scores of pretty girls" dressed in a "coquettish" manner. The fair cleared $78,000, a huge sum at the time.

The women used the profits to buy still more foodstuffs and medical supplies for armies in the Western Theater. Also going out under their auspices were thousands of pairs of underwear, sets of bedding, mittens provided with trigger fingers, and hand-knitted socks. Sometimes the women would pin messages to garments, intended for any soldier:

> *Brave sentry, on your lonely beat,*
> *May these warm stockings warm your feet,*
> *And when from wars and camps you part,*
> *May some fair knitter warm your heart.*[31]

The hardworking women volunteers of the Cleveland branch of the Sanitary Commission created "Floral Hall" as part of their Sanitary Fair fundraiser.

THE COLONEL WHO LOVED TOO MUCH

On August 1, 1863, a train arrived at Millersburg, Ohio, and from it, lying on a cot, emerged Col. Marcus Spiegel of the 120th Ohio. Spiegel had been wounded by "friendly fire" near Jackson, Mississippi, when a defective shell from a Michigan battery exploded prematurely. Ordered to a long convalescence, Spiegel had returned home to his beloved wife, Caroline, and their four children.

Spiegel was a passionate man torn between two love affairs. One was romantic, with "Cary," his "dear dear and sweet wife!" The other, platonic, was with his regiment. His men idolized him. A grateful soldier wrote that Spiegel "is so kind and good to all the boys that they not only respect him as an officer, but reverence him as a father."[32] Success in warfare must have been intoxicating to Spiegel, a Jew who not only lived in an age of open anti-Semitism, but also had not achieved the business success he yearned for in civilian life.

The convalescing Spiegel could not resist the lure of the regiment for long. In mid-November, against doctor's orders and over Caroline's objections, he returned to the 120th Ohio, then in Louisiana. Using a crutch, he arrived in camp about 5 a.m., but even at that hour the regiment awoke to cheer him. Writing home to Cary, the colonel glowed: "It was a Scene long to be remembered; everybody felt good and I felt better. I truly feel proud of it."[33]

Col. Marcus Spiegel loved his "dear dear and sweet wife" and promised never to cause her "a sad feeling," but he never returned.

But he had left a wife struggling with fear, loneliness, strained finances, and the challenge of raising four children by herself. As much as he savored life with the regiment, that troubled Spiegel. "I somehow or other do not feel as well at home in the Army as I used to, many nights I lay & think of home," he wrote Caroline.

> *I frequently think I can hear you cry as you dit a certain night & say I know you don't care any thing about me, it startles me. Caroline my love, I want some positive assurance of you, that you are not mad at me any more and if I ever done or said any thing to injure your feelings forgive me, forgive me, for God knows I love you as no man loves his wife. Write me a long letter and say it is all right.*[34]

His plea brought a somewhat reassuring letter, although Spiegel could see "considerable of the 'blues' throughout it." He responded with the pledge of errant husbands throughout history: "I will make due and full reparation for the past" and "never never" would Caroline "have a sad feeling over any action of mine"[35] Relations between husband and wife improved after that, although he remarked wistfully on one occasion, "I think you are really proud of your Soldier man, only you do not like to let on."[36]

Edmund Kirby Smith—the same general who had scared the daylights out of Cincinnati in 1862—commanded thirty thousand Confederates marooned west of the Mississippi. Grant thought they could be left to twist in the wind, but Lincoln and Stanton wanted to recapture part of Texas as a precaution against a French threat to Mexico that might cross the border into the United States.

The result, from March 10 to May 22, 1864, was the disastrous Red River campaign, led by Nathaniel P. Banks, a Massachusetts politician with almost no tactical skills and a sorry record in the Shenandoah Valley to prove it. Banks's ineptitude asserted itself here as well and his Federals were mauled on April 8 at Sabine Cross Roads. The entire 48th Ohio, which had survived Shiloh almost exactly two years before, was taken prisoner.[37] With what was left of his army, Banks began a slow retreat.

Spiegel's regiment had not yet joined the Red River campaign. On April 27 Spiegel began a long letter to his wife, probably working on it over a period of days. Unable to leave a touchy subject alone, he enclosed pictures of some of his men, writing "they are truly good boys I love them and I believe the feeling is mutual."[38]

In his letter, Spiegel mentioned his 120th Ohio was being ordered up the Red River to reinforce Banks ("a good politician but not worth a pinch of snuff as a soldier.")[39] He and his regiment were only awaiting transportation, he wrote, and then he turned to mundane matters:

The weather here is very hot, as hot as it is in Ohio in July, everything is in full growth & we get beans new Potatoes & any kind of Vegetables or living is very good but not near as good as it was some time

The letter stopped in the middle of the page.

On April 30, letter unfinished, Spiegel and his regiment boarded the steamer *City Belle*. Spiegel was downcast, for he had just learned son Hamlin had lost a finger in an accident. "Ben, I am not doing justice to my family," he told one of his officers. "I ought to be at home but I cannot leave the boys [his soldiers]. I fear this regiment will be the death of me yet."[40]

On May 3, as Spiegel's steamboat chugged up the river, Confederates hidden on the riverbank opened "a torrent of shot and shell" on the unarmored vessel. Panicked soldiers jumped overboard as the boat drifted out of control. A bullet hit Spiegel in the abdomen and he, with many of his men, fell into the hands of the Confederates. Knowing abdominal wounds were usually fatal, he cried out, "This is the last of the husband and father, what will become of my poor family?"[41] Conscious almost to the end, Spiegel died the next day and was buried on the riverbank.

Searchers working some time later couldn't locate Spiegel's grave. Eventually the family concluded it had been washed away by the shifting of the river and that the remains of Cary's "soldier man" would never be found. Captives from Spiegel's regiment spent the rest of the war in a "miserable" prison camp in Texas. Those few who had escaped capture were merged with other decimated regiments and on November 27, 1864, the 120th Ohio officially passed out of existence. Within months, the colonel and the regiment who loved each other had disappeared forever.

Ohio's Unwilling Guests

Like heat lightning, rumors of plots, conspiracies, and subversions crackled along the neural pathways and lit up the ganglia of Ohioans during much of the war, tormenting most of all those living in the borderlands, including dwellers along the coastline forming Ohio's northern edge. Separated from Canada only by Lake Erie, north-coast Ohioans faced a nation that was officially neutral but served nonetheless as a convenient harbor for Confederate sympathizers, enemy agents, and the occasional wandering Rebel with irregular ideas about warfare.

Few places on Ohio's north coast seemed more at risk than the harbor town of Sandusky, midway between Toledo and Cleveland. Sandusky was important to both sides in the Civil War, for in the sheltering arms of its bay lay Johnson's Island, one of the Union's major camps for Confederate prisoners of war, most of them officers. As if in warning, a large Canadian island named Pelée just a few miles north pointed a finger-like peninsula directly at Sandusky.

War hysteria joined the occasional case of indigestion to roil the sleep of loyal Sanduskyites, proudly but painfully aware that some of Rebeldom's most able leaders, from lieutenants to a major general, were kept nearby. That made it a plum objective for Confederate agents who might be lurking just over the horizon. Why, therefore, Sandusky citizens didn't seem concerned about the mysterious stranger who appeared in their midst in August 1864 is only one of the unanswered questions in what came to be known as the Lake Erie Conspiracy.

The stranger gave his name as Charles H. Cole, which was true, and said he represented a Pennsylvania oil company, which was not. In reality, he filled

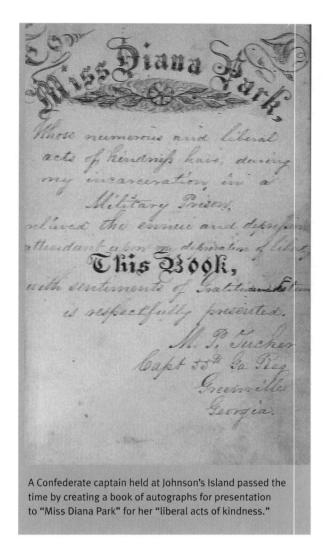

A Confederate captain held at Johnson's Island passed the time by creating a book of autographs for presentation to "Miss Diana Park" for her "liberal acts of kindness."

the dual roles of captain in the Confederate army and lieutenant in the Confederate navy. During August and September, Cole—sometimes accompanied by a woman he called his wife—stayed several times at Sandusky's West House.

Conveniently for Cole's purposes, the hotel offered views of Sandusky Bay, Johnson's Island, and the U.S.S. *Michigan,* anchored nearby and the lone Union warship on the Great Lakes. The convivial Cole slid smoothly into the social life of the hotel, where he especially enjoyed entertaining officers from the *Michigan* and the prison. It was a congenial time for all concerned.

The three hundred acres of Johnson's Island had been leased by the U.S. government in the fall of 1861 and a fifteen-acre stockade created. This would become the only Union prison exclusively for officers. The first prisoners arrived on April 10, 1862. By the following winter the camp held a capacity 2,600 men and—to the authorities' surprise—at least one woman, for a prisoner gave birth to a "bouncing boy."[42] Prisoners were sheltered in thirteen two-story wooden barracks equipped with stoves. As officers and gentlemen, they were given fresh bread and meat regularly, at least at first, and allowed some comforts and diversions.

Early Monday morning, September 19, 1864, a side-wheel steamer named the *Philo Parsons* sailed from Detroit heading for Sandusky. It carried forty passengers and picked up more along the way. As the vessel approached Sandusky in the late afternoon, some of the passengers revealed themselves to

Confederate prisoners, mostly enlisted men and a few civilians, were held in a fenced-in portion of Camp Chase in Columbus.

be Confederates, armed with weapons from an old trunk they had lugged aboard.

The Confederates locked the rest of the passengers and most of the crew in the hold and put them ashore on an isolated island. The *Philo Parsons* had been deftly turned into a weapon against the Union, commanded by Confederate Navy officer John Y. Beall, a Virginian. He was assisted by an adventurous Scot named Bennet G. Burley.

Next, the Confederates planned to work with Cole to overpower the *Michigan's* crew, then free the Johnson's Island prisoners. What their plans were after that is not clear, but it has been speculated the *Michigan* would have been used to shell Northern cities. Meanwhile, the freed Confederate officers would commandeer trains and race south to Columbus to release the enlisted men imprisoned at Camp Chase.

In this way, an enemy army would be born in the very heartland of the Union. If that was the scheme, it made about as much sense as John Brown's feckless attempt to free the slaves by attacking Harpers Ferry. Whatever the Confederate plan, it was undone, in part, by none other than John Brown Jr. A son of the abolitionist, he owned a vineyard near Sandusky.

Before the *Philo Parsons* had left Detroit, an informer alerted Federal authorities that piracy was in the wind. However, it took the younger Brown, noticing that the vessel's passengers were stranded on Middle Bass Island, to confirm the plot was unfolding. In Sandusky, Charles Cole, who was supposed to pave the way for the plot by somehow compromising the *Michigan* crew and prison officials, was quickly arrested. Fully aroused authorities there, on Johnson's Island, and on the *Michigan* were ready and waiting for the *Philo Parsons* as it approached Sandusky, but something spooked the pirate crew. They turned the vessel around and fled to Canada. The threat to Sandusky, Johnson's Island, and Camp Chase was over.

Weeks later, Captain Beall was arrested in Buffalo, charged with piracy and spying, and hanged on February 24, 1865. Cole was held until after the war but released in 1866, apparently on a technicality. His "wife," actually a prostitute from Buffalo, was never charged. And Burley, extradited from Canada and charged with armed robbery, escaped from the Ottawa County jail and fled to Europe. Changing his name to a more elegant "Burleigh," he joined a London newspaper and became one of the most famous foreign correspondents of his time.

In the course of the war, a total of nine thousand Confederate prisoners, mostly officers and the cream of Confederate society—including Robert E. Lee's second son, "Rooney" Lee—passed through Johnson's Island. At Columbus, one hundred miles to the south, was the much larger facility at Camp Chase, where a total of twenty-six thousand Confederates, mostly enlisted men, were held at various times. The first handful had arrived on July 5, 1861, and as a rising tide poured in from Union victories, the prison grew to 42 whitewashed wooden barracks holding as many as 9,400 men at one time.

Surrounded by a high board fence, the Camp Chase prison was tucked into ten acres in one corner of the 165-acre Union training camp four miles west of Columbus. A photograph of one of the prison's three compounds shows a row of drab, shed-like barracks and clusters of idling prisoners in the hodgepodge of baggy uniforms and homespun in which they had been captured. Standing, lying, and sitting casually along the compound's bleak main street, they gaze dolefully at the photographer, looking—and probably feeling—as if they were frozen in time.

When Camp Chase was new, however, incarceration was so gentlemanly that Confederate officers were permitted to keep their slave servants and visit the city in full uniform, wearing swords or sidearms. At Johnson's Island, one of the first inmates called it "the least disagreeable prison I saw or heard from … [I]t is a salubrious, pleasant place."[43] Early in the war, Confederates held in both prisons staged entertainments, whittled craft items, and bought little luxuries from a vendor known as the sutler. Food at Camp Chase was supposed to equal that of Union soldiers in the field, while at Johnson's Island inmates received fresh bread, meat, and milk daily. Prisoners could expect to be freed as part of an exchange system between North and South.

By July 1863, however, bitter disagreements over exchanges between the Union and Confederacy caused Secretary of War Stanton to end the exchange system. After that, prison populations soared on both sides. Union prisoners in the South suffered terribly from the shortages that afflicted the Confederacy's own soldiers—as well as, according to escaped prisoners, vindictiveness by those keepers afflicted by the phobic hatred of Yankees widespread in the South.[44] As harrowing reports of the prisoners' hardships reached Northern ears, reprisals occurred in Union prison camps, with food rations reduced and comforts such as blankets deliberately withheld from Confederate prisoners. Inmates grew gaunt and emaciated North and South. In both of Ohio's prisons, desperate prisoners were said to have hunted down rats for food.

A major reason the Union suspended prisoner exchanges was the Confederacy's refusal to recognize black soldiers as legitimate prisoners of war. (They not only were *our property,* Confederates argued, but they were "savages" and using them as soldiers was "a barbarity." When Confederates took them as prisoners of war, black soldiers were apt to be executed or re-enslaved.)[45] Thousands of unexchanged captives overwhelmed prison facilities. Sickness and privation caused enormous suffering in both Union and Confederate prisons, although nothing exceeded the horrors of the Confederate prison at Andersonville, Georgia. Miles from the battlefield, thousands of Americans North and South died, not from bullets, but from neglect.

STRONG WOMEN

A few days after the battle at Shiloh in April 1862, Julia Grant and her children were visiting her husband's family in Covington, Kentucky, when "a tall, handsome woman, clad in deepest mourning" entered the parlor. The tearful woman told Mrs. Grant she was the widow of Lt. Col. Herman Canfield of the 72nd Ohio. Canfield, who had been a prominent attorney in Medina, was mortally wounded on the first day of the battle.

Mrs. Canfield had tried to reach her husband's bedside at the temporary military hospital in Savannah, Tennessee. Refused admittance, she went a few miles up the river to Shiloh, where she rushed past a guard to collar General Grant as he was being helped off his horse. "Do, for God's sake, allow me to proceed," she begged. Grant listened, then said he would give her a pass and permission to ride back to the Savannah hospital on his dispatch boat.

Then he bid her goodbye, "all this," Mrs. Canfield told Mrs. Grant, "so kindly, so gently, so full of sympathy."

But Canfield arrived at her husband's cot to find his face covered with a blanket, his body still warm, blood clotted on his beard and breast. "I think he might have lived if I had been near," she told Mrs. Grant, adding that, because of her experience, "I have determined to devote my time to the wounded soldiers during the war. My husband only needed the services of a kind nurse."

Canfield went to Memphis after its surrender in June 1862. The city's churches and major buildings were turned into hospitals with beds for five thousand sick and wounded.[46] There, according to Julia Grant, Canfield "for three long, weary years devoted her entire time to the hospitals, nursing and caring for our wounded and sick soldiers."[47] She even used some of her own funds to set up a "colored orphans' asylum" in Memphis.[48]

At the end of the war, during the grand review of the triumphant Union forces in Washington, Mrs. Grant saw Mrs. Canfield once again, "her fair face and brow … furrowed and browned by care and exposure, her mourning robes … worn and faded.[49] She had spent the war working to save lives.

By such deeds, women of the Civil War redeemed their fallen warriors and saved wounded ones. In some ways, the conflict remained an "improvised war" to its end. Civilians near battlefields sheltered and nursed the wounded in their homes, burying those they could not save. Hometown volunteers gathered and shipped food, medical goods, and clothing to the starving, sick, and threadbare men dangling at the end of supply lines. Family members rushed to field hospitals to care for their kin.

On Friday, October 31, 1862, eight-year-old Maud Morrow and her mother, with five-month-old Mary in her arms, climbed onto a stagecoach in the Ohio River village of Aberdeen and went bouncing down the road, headed for a recent battleground in Mississippi. Two other Morrow children had been hurriedly left in the care of friends. Maud was allowed to come only after much begging and many promises to be helpful. After traveling five hundred miles by coach, steamboat, and railroad, Mrs. Morrow and her two children arrived in Corinth, Mississippi, within five days and rushed to the bedside of Dr. Coridon Morrow, Maud's father. He lay in a makeshift military hospital, and he was dangerously ill.

Dr. Morrow, a physician in Bainbridge, a town in south-central Ohio, had joined the 43rd Ohio in early September 1862 as assistant surgeon. Scarcely a month passed before he found himself at the hard-fought battle of Corinth

The primitive state of medical care in the American military created crowds of wounded who, for lack of shelter, often received care outdoors.

on October 3–4, 1862, the Confederates trying in vain to regain the rail junction they had given up a few months before. After patching up the wounded in the shelter of a railroad cut, Dr. Morrow had fallen ill, "owing to bad water and change of climate."[50] He sent his wife an urgent message "in an almost illegible scrawl," begging her to come to his aid.

For weeks, Mrs. Morrow looked after the needs of her husband and other soldiers in the Corinth hospital, cooking food that otherwise would have been poorly prepared. Maud roamed the hospital and battle-torn town, befriending soldiers. The wounded men, weary of war, homesick, and lonely, begged to see the infant Mary and a doctor remarked that it was "quite a treat to hear a baby cry." The surgeon in charge of the ward would laughingly call out, "Where is my Little Rosebud?" and carry little Mary around the hospital grounds.

Dr. Morrow recovered in a few weeks and his family was able to leave Corinth while he went back on duty. In 1901, Maude Morrow published a little book she called *Recollections of the Civil War: From a Child's Point of View.* In it she remembered the soldiers she had met and wondered what had happened to them. She knew what had happened to one: the surgeon who had carried the infant Mary in his arms had died of disease later in the war.

Some women were moved to act on behalf of kin while others, many of them social activists, volunteered from principle. Typical of the breed was Frances Dana Gage, who came from McConnelsville. Gage was a walking megaphone for human rights, the kind of social reformer who would be dismissed by Artemus Ward as "an emfatic noosance." She was also a woman who "had it all," before the phrase had been invented. She was a wife, the mother of eight, a prominent lecturer, and an author who, among other things, fit into her busy schedule a newspaper advice column she wrote as "Aunt Fanny."

Most of all, Frances Dana Gage was someone who fought for social change. Born in Ohio in 1808 as Frances Barker, she developed a social consciousness early on. Her father was a state legislator and a judge. As a child, Frances helped her mother and grandmother take food and clothing to fugitive slaves. At age twenty, she married James L. Gage, an attorney. He was, of course, an opponent of slavery.

In 1850 Mrs. Gage organized a women's rights convention in McConnelsville and circulated a petition asking that the words "white male" be excluded from the Ohio Constitution. In 1851, she served as president of a women's rights convention in Akron, famous for the "Ar'n't I a Woman" speech given there by former slave Sojourner Truth. When she wasn't going to conventions or writing articles, Gage went on the road to give rousing speeches for women's rights and against slavery and, for good measure, against liquor.

The Civil War caused a hiatus in women's rights activity as women worked instead for emancipation and an antislavery amendment to the Constitution. In 1862, Gage and one of her daughters went to South Carolina, where they worked as volunteers caring for freed slaves. Then Gage was given an official role as superintendent of the Fourth District of the Freedman's Bureau, serving five hundred former slaves. She returned North to raise money for her relief work and encourage support for emancipation.

In 1864 she went back to the South as an agent of the Western Sanitary Commission, helping freed slaves and wounded soldiers both white and black. Injuries suffered in a carriage accident in September 1864 forced her to limit her activities to writing. After the war she urged rights for both blacks and women, two causes that came into conflict with each other. Some suffragettes opposed granting the vote to blacks when women still could not vote. True to her belief in rights for all, however, Gage—now handicapped by a stroke— refused to join them. She died in 1884.[51]

GAZETTE

Lincoln's solid re-election victory in November 1864 gave him the political capital to revive a proposed Constitutional amendment to ban slavery entirely, completing the promise implied in the Emancipation Proclamation. The proposal had passed the Senate but been defeated in the House of Representatives eight months earlier.

In an age when many American supported slavery and many more considered blacks inferior beings, a determined minority demanded equality for all people.

In January 1865, fierce debate over the amendment broke out in the House of Representatives. Democrat Samuel S. Cox of Ohio opposed "compounding powers of the Federal Government" by passing the amendment, while Ohio Republican James A. Garfield argued for it. It squeaked by the House on January 31 and went to the states for ratification.

In February, the Ohio General Assembly ratified the Thirteenth Amendment and in celebration two hundred guns were fired on the grounds of the State House.[52] Ratified by every free state except New Jersey, the amendment went into effect December 18. It had taken three-quarters of a century, thousands of lives, and untold human misery, but the United States had finally reversed what William Lloyd Garrison called "a covenant with death and an agreement with Hell": the protection of slavery by the Constitution of the United States.[53]

In the course of the war, the Union raised 166 black regiments. By war's end, twelve percent of the Union army was African American. Persistent prejudice meant the African Americans performed more fatigue duty than whites and saw less fighting, but they still fought in 41 major battles and 449 smaller affairs. Sixteen blacks—at least four of whom probably were Ohioans—won the Medal of Honor. Of the 179,000 blacks who served, more than 80 percent came from the Confederate states and most had been slaves.

What Southerners had feared most before the war—the rising up against them of their slaves—had occurred. In fighting for their freedom, African

Americans showed they were not property but human beings; not things, but men:

> *We-e looks li-ke me-en a-a-marchin' on,*
> *We looks like men-er-war.*

To Learn More:

Most of one of the nation's largest training grounds and prisoner of war camps, Camp Chase in Columbus, has been replaced by private homes, but the burial ground of more than 2,000 Confederates, mostly enlisted men, remains at 2900 Sullivant Avenue. (**http://www.geocities.com/Pentagon/Quarters/5109/**). Confederate officers are buried at Johnson's Island, near Sandusky, where preservation and research are supported by the Friends and Descendants of Johnson's Island Civil War Prison (**http://www2.heidelberg.edu/johnsonsisland/about.html**).

Of war's horrors, few can touch the Confederate prison camp at Andersonville, Georgia, and few works of Civil War literature can surpass MacKinlay Kantor's compelling fact-based novel *Andersonville*. The Andersonville National Historic Site is in southwestern Georgia (**www.nps.gov/ande/** or **229-924-0343**). You can look up names of many of the Ohioans who died at Andersonville at **http://www.angelfire.com/ga3/Andersonvilleprison/index.html**.

One of the war's most touching stories is contained in the letters of Col. Marcus M. Spiegel, the Holmes County soldier "who loved too much" and paid with his life. His story unfolds in his own words in *A Jewish Colonel in the Civil War*, skillfully edited by Jean Powers Soman and Frank L. Byrne.

The Civil War's importance in advancing women's role in society is explained in *Bonnet Brigades* by Mary Elizabeth Massey, reissued, with an introduction by Jean V. Berlin, as *Women in the Civil War*.

Set afire by retreating Confederates, Grant's troops found much of the Confederate capital of Richmond reduced to rubble.

14

ENDINGS

January to June 1865

This is what happened to John Bell Hood.

A Confederate general, Hood called himself a Texan, but he had grown up in Kentucky, the rambunctious son of a prosperous physician. In the eyes of the planter aristocracy to the east, Kentuckians were Westerners — crude frontiersmen. Despite that, his daring leadership on the battlefield had, by 1863, turned "the Gallant Hood," as he was called, into a cavalier, the beau ideal of Southern manhood, a leading actor in the romantic myth the South spun for itself.

And that was his weakness. As a modern biographer has observed, "Hood's faults and virtues were those of the mid-nineteenth-century South."[1] Like the South, he was a romantic locked in combat with a relentless Northern reality, his crippled arm and amputated leg the badges of a furious courage. Early in 1864, Confederate President Jefferson Davis had promoted the thirty-two-year-old Hood to lieutenant general with responsibilities beyond his capacity. "Hood is a bold fighter," Robert E. Lee confided to Davis. "I am doubtful as to the other qualities necessary."[2] The same might be said of the South.

Recuperating from woundings at Gettysburg and Chickamauga, the lumbering Hood, his face sad as a bloodhound's, met Sally Buchanan Campbell Preston, a highly polished member of South Carolina's elite. Nicknamed "Buck," she was a hothouse magnolia—a fickle tease who scattered her favors like fairy dust, causing men to fall in love while never quite doing so herself.

Smitten, Hood launched a persistent courtship, confiding to a friend it was "the hardest battle he had ever fought."[3] When Buck accepted Hood's ring, an

John Bell Hood's sad face seems to reflect his personal and military misfortunes.

acquaintance observed, "Buck can't help it. … She must flirt. She does not care for the man. It is sympathy with the wounded soldier. Helpless Hood."[4]

Deeply in love, Hood returned to war. Then came his crushing losses at Atlanta, Franklin, and Nashville. His spirit crushed, he relinquished command of the Army of Tennessee and headed to Richmond and oblivion.[5] Stopping to see Buck, Hood appeared "maimed and helpless—with his face of the tortured in Hades," according to their mutual friend, Mary Boykin Chesnut.[6] Looking for solace from his fiancée, Hood found instead a wavering Buck, who "pretended to be in a rage" (she confessed to Chesnut) when he tried to hug and kiss her.[7]

Much had changed since Hood had last seen Buck. The Preston family had decided that Hood was beneath their class and Buck had lost her fascination with the wounded general. Even Chesnut called him "a rough Texan." Hood paid a last, sad visit to Buck on April 15 and by May 15 Chesnut was telling her diary that "Buck rides with Rawly Lowndes."[8] The engagement was over. Buck and Hood never saw each other again.

Three decades earlier, a love affair of another kind was born when a wide-eyed young tourist rushed home to France to write about democracy in America. The "privileges … of class have been abolished," Alexis de Tocqueville enthused. "[T]he idea of progress comes naturally into every man's mind; the desire to rise swells in every heart."[9]

Not quite.

Tocqueville had caught the spirit of the Northern states, where by 1861 the "idea of progress" could be heard in a rising din of steam whistles, immigrant tongues, city traffic, and the restlessness of feet itching to move on, move on, move on. It was quieter in the pastoral South, where fewer trains and factories disturbed a lulling landscape of farmland cultivated with mules, many driven by African Americans. The blacks had only a few more rights than the mules.

Both the mules and the blacks were the property of a self-styled aristocracy that sneered at the "greasy mechanics" and money-grubbers of the North. Instead of moving on, Southerners looked back to an imagined past of romance, chivalry, and honor ruled by a proud white elite.

The North looked ahead, the South the other way. On foundations of hubris and human bondage, the Confederacy and knights errant like Hood built castles in the air. They were all lost causes.

GRANT TAKES RICHMOND

As 1864 ended and 1865 began, the North celebrated its triumphs—in the Shenandoah Valley, at Nashville, and across Georgia—but around Petersburg, Virginia, soldiers in gray and blue huddled in cold, muddy trenches while artillery showered iron on them and sharpshooters' bullets took the lives of the careless. An immense apparatus of ships, warehouses, and military railroads served the Union soldiers, while shortages of food and clothing were turning Lee's men into scarecrows. Quoting Victor Hugo, the Rebels called themselves "Lee's Miserables."[10]

Rats roamed the trenches, feeding off abundance on the Union side only to risk becoming food themselves on the Confederate side. ("I saw a man catch a large rat and eat it," a North Carolina soldier wrote early in January.)[11] The effects of Sherman's laceration of Georgia could be seen in desertions as men, frantic over their families, slipped away from Lee's army. Lee warned President Davis that disaster loomed if he wasn't re-supplied and reinforced.

On January 1, 1865, Grant had sixty thousand men—mostly Easterners plus a few Western units—with which to threaten Lee's Petersburg defense line. Among his officers was Brig. Gen. J. Warren Keifer, a young lawyer from Springfield who led a brigade in the VI Corps. Meeting Grant the first time cleared up any reservations Keifer had about his commander. He told his wife he was "impressed with [Grant's] quiet & determined manner. He seems fully aware of the great responsibility that rests upon him."[12]

That month, Grant ordered an expeditionary force to capture Fort Fisher, which defended the port of Wilmington, North Carolina, a haven for the Confederacy's blockade runners. Naval guns pulverized the fort and a combined force of soldiers, sailors, and marines overran it. That shut down the last connection the Confederacy had with the outside world.[13]

During the long siege of Petersburg, Grant's headquarters was located at City Point, a spit of land on Virginia's James River. War had turned City Point into a clattering collection of rail lines, wharves, storehouses, military hospitals, workshops, and eateries. Grant's wooden cabin was an island of calm, the general quietly running the Union war machine without raising his voice, courteous even to the hero-worshipping hordes of visitors who came to see the great man.

Grant's calm belied an anxiety. "I was afraid, every morning, that I would awake from my sleep to hear that Lee was gone, and nothing was left but a picket line," he recalled.[14] Grant knew Lee couldn't hold Richmond much longer. That Lee might slip away, go south, and link up with Joe Johnston's army in the Carolinas, was Lee's only hope and Grant's biggest fear.

As the winter days drifted slowly by, Grant sat silently in his cabin, thinking as he gazed at the smoke rising from his cigar. His forces shivered and waited, their lives typified by the 110th Ohio, one of a handful of Midwestern units helping Eastern troops hold the siege line. Men from Clark, Darke, Greene, and Miami counties in west-central Ohio composed the 110th, who had been nicknamed the "Weary Boys" by an impatient Eastern general who thought they moved too slowly.

With a few other regiments, they garrisoned two forts and manned nearby trenches in the western part of the line.

When not on picket duty, the men of the 110th built and rebuilt their shanties and cut firewood, in one instance taking turns with Confederates hacking away at the same tree. Fraternization was forbidden, but sometimes pickets from the two sides would chat while nearby pickets were firing at each other.[15] Cpl. John Rhoades wrote his wife that Confederates had trained a dog to cross enemy lines carrying messages in its mouth.[16]

On February 5, the drowsy armies came awake when Grant launched his first offensive of the new season. His forces seized still more Virginia countryside to the west, stretching Lee's ever-thinning defenses to thirty-seven miles. Slowly, Grant's anaconda was enclosing Richmond.

In quiet moments assorted dignitaries and privileged civilians, like Julia Grant and Edwin Stanton's family, visited the Union lines. Soldiers would be rushed into line for review by the visitors. On one occasion, General Keifer had only 30 minutes notice to turn out his 3,300-man brigade.

Other diversions included a St. Patrick's Day celebration in which the men ran foot races and watched horse races.[17] On March 11, Keifer's brigade was ordered to stand at attention as a Pennsylvania private was shot for desertion.

Seriously weakened by months of siege warfare, Lee's army could not prevent the loss of Petersburg, gateway to the Confederate capital.

A few hours later, Keifer learned that President Lincoln had pardoned the man.[18]

Lee and his crumbling army had one punch left, and they launched it on March 25 with an unexpected attack on an earthwork named Fort Stedman. After overrunning the surprised defenders, however, the Confederates ran out of steam. By now, long deprivation had severely weakened the Southern soldiers. J. E. Henderson, a young corporal in the 60th Ohio, watched in amazement as a much smaller counter-charge by Union reinforcements pushed back the stumbling, disorganized Confederates and reclaimed the fort.[19] Lee's emaciated warriors had lost their ability to dominate a battlefield.

Sherman arrived at City Point for an impromptu visit with Grant. The generals greeted each other with the exuberance of schoolboys, joking and teasing Mrs. Grant. By chance, President Lincoln was nearby, aboard the steamboat *River Queen*, so the generals paid him a social call. Sherman entertained the president with tales from his recent marches, probably in what Grant's aide, Porter, called his "nervous, offhand, rattling manner."

Grant and Sherman returned to shore for tea with Julia.[20] "Well, you are a pretty pair!" she exclaimed when two generals, looking like embarrassed children, admitted they had forgotten to inquire after Mrs. Lincoln. A contrite Grant promised they would do better the next day (and did, although Mrs. Lincoln, pleading illness, did not come out to meet them.)[21]

The generals and President Lincoln spent their second day together discussing strategy and the war's aftermath. One more campaign was needed, the generals said. The president told them he was prepared to return full civil rights to Confederate citizens after the war.[22]

Bodies of a Confederate and a Union soldier lie near each other at Fort Mahone, Petersburg.

Grant introduced several of his Eastern generals to Sherman. One of Meade's aides recalled the tall, sinewy Sherman was "a very remarkable-looking man, … a very homely man, with a regular nest of wrinkles on his face … but his expression is pleasant and kindly. But he believes in hard war. I heard him say: 'Columbia!—pretty much all burned; and burned good!'"[23]

Then Sherman returned to North Carolina. Grant said goodbye to a pale and sorrowful Julia, kissing her over and over before climbing aboard a military train for the Petersburg front.[24] There he would launch his Appomattox Campaign, the final, decisive blow against Lee, while Julia waited at City Point.

Sheridan, who had been operating north of the James River, now joined Grant, and, "pacing up and down, he chafed like a hound in the leash," declaring "I'm ready to strike out tomorrow and go to smashing things."[25]

Meanwhile, Lee was scraping together supplies and waiting for passable roads. As Grant feared, he planned to slip around Union lines and move south to link up with Joe Johnston in North Carolina. To keep an escape route open, he sent Generals George Pickett and Fitzhugh Lee to Five Forks, a major road intersection, which they were ordered to hold "at all hazards."[26] But Sheridan's cavalry, bolstered by Warren's V Corps and Humphreys' II Corps, headed for Five Forks as well.

As they approached Five Forks on March 31, Sheridan's cavalry (including the 2nd, 6th, and 13th Ohio Cavalry) clashed with Confederates near Dinwiddie Court House. During the fight, Grant's aide Porter, came on one of Sheridan's bands playing "'Nellie Bly' as cheerfully as if furnishing music for a country picnic." Sheridan liked to mount his bands on gray horses and have them play their liveliest tunes at the front even as bullets ripped through their instruments and the concussion from exploding shells crushed their drums. The music was said to have an excellent effect on the fighting men, but this fight ended in a draw.[27]

The next day, Pickett and Fitzhugh Lee unwisely slipped away from their troops to attend a fish fry. During their absence, Sheridan attacked again, assaulting Five Forks with his usual pyrotechnic style, galloping about while shaking his fist and waving his battle flag, "encouraging, entreating, threatening, praying, swearing ... the very incarnation of battle," according to Porter.[28] Seeing a man drop after being struck in the neck, Sheridan shouted, "You're not hurt a bit! Pick up your gun, man, and move right to the front." The man rushed forward a dozen paces and fell dead.[29]

Sheridan told Porter, "I have never in my life taken a command into battle, and had the slightest desire to come out alive unless I won."[30] By day's end he had wrecked Lee's right wing and taken 4,500 prisoners, nearly half Pickett's force. Porter rushed to headquarters with the news, startling the phlegmatic Grant by clapping him on the back. At that, Grant—"with scarcely a word of comment"—walked to his tent, wrote several orders, and, "as coolly as if remarking on the state of the weather," announced, "I have ordered a general assault along the lines."[31]

To lay the way for the enormous infantry attack Grant had ordered the next morning, Keifer's brigade sent out men with axes to clear away the brush and pointed stakes the Confederates had planted as defenses. They were followed by a wave of infantrymen with unloaded rifles who plunged their bayonet-tipped weapons into the face of the steep Confederate earthworks to create improvised ladders.

The next wave of Union soldiers, carrying loaded rifles, climbed the improvised ladders and swept over the parapets. Demoralized and worn out, many Confederates gave up without a fight. Two men of the 110th Ohio— "weary boys" no longer—won Medals of Honor for capturing Confederate battle flags.

Now that Grant had breached Petersburg's fortifications, there was nothing for Lee to do but abandon the defensive line and try to escape. He notified President Jefferson Davis he was giving up his defense of the Confederate capital and would attempt to evade Grant. At that, Davis and his government abandoned Richmond and fled south.

The Federals marched into Petersburg unopposed and then into Richmond, where they found sullen whites, joyous blacks, and numerous fires set by retreating Confederates. On Tuesday, President Lincoln visited Richmond, where he sat in President Davis's chair.

By now, Grant was almost as concerned about Sherman as the Confederates. Sherman was barreling his way north through the Carolinas, raising the possibility he might join Grant in delivering the final blow to Lee. Grant told Lincoln that the Eastern armies needed to finish off Lee by themselves rather than wait for Sherman to arrive.

Rivalry between the Eastern and Western sections of the North were just too strong to ignore. Grant feared there could be political fall-out if it looked as if Western troops had to finish the job for the Easterners. Grant urged his forces onward, hoping to outstrip Sherman.

The last serious engagement between Grant and Lee occurred April 6 at Sailor's (or Sayler's) Creek when Brig. Gen. George A. Custer's horsemen cut off part of Lee's retreating column. Sheridan's cavalry included the 2nd, 6th and 13th Ohio, joined by the 4th Ohio Infantry Battalion. (The 4th Battalion was an amalgamation of the few remaining veterans of the 4th and 8th Ohio regiments.) The Federals poured into the area, setting the stage for the capture of several generals and eight thousand Confederates—a third of Lee's rapidly dwindling force.

No matter how any battle went, however, both sides were enveloped—as always—by the fog of war. General Keifer wandered into Confederate lines in the dusky woods, but wasn't recognized. Pretending to be their commander, the quick-witted Keifer issued orders to the Confederates before they realized what was happening. Then he spurred his horse and dashed back to Union lines.

On the evening of April 7 Grant stood on the front porch of a hotel in Farmville, informally reviewing his cheering troops as they rushed by. Bands played triumphantly while bonfires and torches illuminated the street. Spontaneously, one of the regiments burst into "John Brown's Body" and soon a whole division of thousands of men was shouting out the chorus.[32] *Glory, glory hallelujah* echoed off the walls of Farmville's shops and homes, loud enough to wake Old Brown himself.

Grant had begun sending Lee messages pointing out the "hopelessness of further resistance."[33] By his replies, Lee appeared to be stonewalling. On the evening of April 8, a frustrated Grant was suffering severe headaches from fatigue and anxiety. Reading Lee's latest response to his entreaties, Grant shook his head and said, "It looks as if he still means to fight." [34] Then he lay down again to try to sleep.

Sherman's "Quixotic Venture"

Founded in 1733 as Georgia's first city, Savannah had grown into a gracious pillar of Southern aristocracy, home to twenty-two thousand people by the Civil War. Here, in March 1861, Vice President of the Confederacy Alexander Stephens had proclaimed that the Confederacy's "cornerstone rests, upon the great truth that the negro is not equal to the white man; that slavery, subordination to the superior race, is his natural and moral condition."[35]

Savannah was a handsome place of boulevards and public squares shaded by majestic oaks dripping with Spanish moss. Its streets were lined with fine houses stocked with books, pictures, silver, and imported china. Behind the houses were alleys lined with the hovels of slaves and free blacks, an ugly reality behind the grandeur.[36]

War had ravaged the city's economy, so the grand old lady of Georgia was tatty around the edges when Sherman arrived, but she was a lady still and received the invaders with grace. "[G]ood social relations arose at once between [residents] and the army," wrote Sherman. It helped that he had promised not to destroy the city.[37]

Camped in and around Savannah, deep in the heart of the Cotton Kingdom, Sherman's men refreshed themselves. They had Christmas dinner, went to church on Sunday, and strolled the boulevards. A member of the 47th Ohio remembered a night "lively with bands playing and the boys singing, 'The Girl I Left Behind Me' and 'Rally Round the Flag' in all directions."[38] Sgt. Nixon B. Stewart of the 52nd Ohio recalled awakening every morning to flocks of robins singing "chir-up, cheer-up."[39]

Streams of African Americans sought out Sherman to shake his hand. "[T]hey flock to me old & young they pray & shout—and mix up my name with that of Moses & Simon," the conquering hero remarked.[40] Secretary of War Stanton came to investigate rumors that Sherman had mistreated blacks during the march. When black leaders told him that they "could not be in better hands," the secretary was satisfied, at least for the moment.[41] He returned to Washington after drafting an order for Sherman to announce. It offered black families "forty acres and a mule"—up to forty acres of abandoned plantation land, plus use of army mules.[42]

Sherman had written Ellen the day after he learned of baby Charles's death. He preferred facts to sentiment. Having never seen Charles, he admitted grieving more for Willy. War, he added, had made him "callous to death. It is so common." So far as Ellen's feelings were concerned, he observed, "You are stayed by the Religious faith of a better and higher life elsewhere."

Nevertheless, he continued to ignore entreaties to join her in Roman Catholicism. All business, he closed with a terse advisory: "It will not be long before I sally forth again on another dangerous & important Quixotic venture. Love to all. Yrs. Ever Sherman."[43]

Sherman intended to drill northward through the Carolinas in Grant's direction, a "quixotic venture" he thought would far exceed his March to the Sea. "My aim, ..." Sherman wrote in his memoirs, "was to whip the rebels, to humble their pride, to follow them to their innermost recesses, and make them fear and dread us."[44] He had the humbling of South Carolina in mind most of all.

South Carolina, the first state to secede, had been the noisy cockpit of rebellion and Sherman's men blamed it more than any other for the war. "[T]he whole army is burning with an insatiable desire to wreak vengeance upon South Carolina," he wrote Halleck. "I almost tremble at her fate, but feel that she deserves all that seems in store for her."[45]

By February 1, Sherman's sixty thousand soldiers, a fourth of them Ohioans, had crossed into South Carolina. To mislead the Confederates, Sherman again split his forces into two wings, to his right the XV and XVII Corps ("Army of the Tennessee") seeming to threaten symbolically important Charleston, while on his left the XIV and XX Corps ("Army of Georgia") menaced the manufacturing center at Augusta, South Carolina. The overawed Confederates (for which "I had a species of contempt," wrote Sherman) limited themselves to skirmishing, sniping, and felling trees and burning bridges.[46]

Confederate engineers had assumed that South Carolina's flooded swamps, meandering watercourses, and thicketed forests made it "absolutely impossible for an army to march across the lower portion of the state in winter," as one of them put it.[47] They were wrong. In the war's most remarkable triumph over nature, Sherman's grim-faced soldiers waded in icy water for miles, hacking through brushy forests, building bridges, and improving roads so quickly there was ample time left over to lay waste to the landscape.

In Georgia, Sherman's men had spared houses with occupants, but here they reduced whole towns—eighteen in two weeks by one count— to ashes. "[T]he demon of destruction seized possession of everybody," General Hazen wrote. "[E]ven the smallest drummer-boy seemed to [be] determined to get even."[48] Sergeant Stewart of the 52nd Ohio recalled, "Not a house or a fence was left standing, along our march."[49]

Sherman shuttled between his wings, chewing on a slim cigar, his small eyes twitching back and forth, missing nothing. He frequently rode alongside

Sherman said that South Carolina's capital of Columbia was "pretty much all burned, and burned good!"

his infantrymen. Uncle Billy's tough Westerners, undaunted by rank, kept up a good-natured running conversation with their commander. Sherman admired one soldier's well-developed legs and offered to trade. Sherman recalled, "He sized up my legs with his eye, and evidently considered them mere spindle-shanks compared with his, and then looked up at me and said: 'General, if it's all the same with you, I guess I'd rather not swap.'"[50]

By February 16, Sherman's XV Corps was on the bank of the Congaree River opposite South Carolina's capital of Columbia. Confederate defenders withdrew from the capital without a fight and Union soldiers walked in. They found stacks of cotton bales lining the streets and wind blowing loose cotton about, some of it catching in the trees and reminding them of snow. Soldiers wandered about, fraternizing with the citizens and getting drunk from the huge store of liquor that the Confederates had left.

Pvt. Charles Willison of the 76th Ohio, one of the earliest units to enter Columbia, believed the cotton had been set afire by retreating Confederates, but "I have no doubt our exasperated soldiers—some of them—may have had a hand in keeping it going."[51] By evening, flames had erupted in many places, and, aided by the wind, spread rapidly through the city.

Sherman rushed from bed to direct firefighting during the night, but as

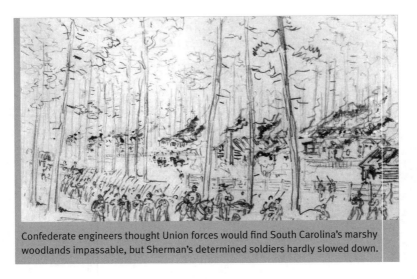
Confederate engineers thought Union forces would find South Carolina's marshy woodlands impassable, but Sherman's determined soldiers hardly slowed down.

some Union soldiers were putting out fires, others, drunk and vengeful, were setting them. By dawn, about half of Columbia, including its old Statehouse, had been turned into "ashes and smouldering heaps."[52] People who had lost their homes stood about with their small piles of furniture.[53]

Sherman blamed Confederate Wade Hampton for setting the first fires, but the Union commander also ordered the destruction of all machine shops, warehouses, and buildings of value to the enemy. The plant where Confederate money was printed was wrecked after the men had looted it, gambling away the nearly worthless currency in "the most lavish manner."[54] Departing the city, he left behind five hundred beef cattle to feed the citizens and one hundred rifles to help the mayor preserve order. To the east, meanwhile, Confederate General Hardee abandoned Charleston, fooled by Sherman's maneuvers into thinking the city of Fort Sumter was about to be attacked.

By February 20th, Sherman's right and left wings were on the move again, curving northeasterly now, splashing through soaking rains toward Cheraw near the North Carolina border. Joining Sherman from the east were the Union troops who had been victorious at Wilmington, North Carolina, including the 5th U.S. Colored Troops, which had begun life as the 127th Ohio. Coming from Nashville, Tennessee, to the west, were still more regiments from Ohio under Maj. Gen. Jacob D. Cox.

Meanwhile, an increasingly worried Confederate Congress was forcing changes on a reluctant Jefferson Davis. Lee—hitherto commander only of the Army of Northern Virginia—was at long last appointed general in chief of all Confederate forces, a role Davis hitherto had reserved for himself. In turn, Lee called Joe Johnston back from retirement to defend against Sherman in the Carolinas.

On March 3, Sherman's forces, nearing North Carolina, entered the South Carolina town of Cheraw. The town had been left burning by the rapidly retreating Confederates. Meanwhile, in Washington President Lincoln was delivering his second inaugural address: "With malice toward none; with charity for all; with firmness in the right, as God gives us to see the right, let us strive to finish the work we are in."[55] Out of Lincoln's sight there had been considerable malice, of course, but Sherman's men eased up on their destructive ways once they had crossed into North Carolina. Their officers reminded them that North Carolina had been the last state to secede and contained a substantial Unionist minority.

By March 11, Sherman's entire army had gathered at Fayetteville, where Sergeant Stewart of the 52nd Ohio noted, "The citizens were glad to see us and said, 'We are tired of this cruel war.'"[56] After long silence, Sherman re-opened communications with the outside world, firing off "ten letters of 4 pages each" to higher command and also to "Dearest Ellen." He told Stanton, "I have done all I proposed, and the fruits seem to me ample. ... Now no place in the Confederacy is safe against the armies of the West."[57] To Ellen, he wrote, "South Carolina has had a visit from the West that will cure her of her pride and boasting."[58]

By March 15 Sherman's army was on the move again. He had learned that Joe Johnston, "my special antagonist" from the Atlanta campaign, was back in command and patching together an army. Heading for Goldsboro, the Union general moved more carefully now, sending wagon trains out of reach of trouble and warning troops to stay alert in case of battle.[59] A clash at Averasborough (Averysboro) showed that Confederates still had some fight left in them, but it did them no good and they kept retreating.

By March 18, Sherman's concern about Johnston was easing and the wings of his army were approaching Goldsboro separately. Twenty miles west at Bentonville, however, Johnston's cobbled-together force of about twenty-one thousand attacked Sherman's unsuspecting left wing, hoping to crush it before Sherman could collect his wits—and the rest of his forces. Hazen's division from the right wing rushed to their comrades' aid, however, giving Sherman time to swing the rest of his army into position.

The fighting was the fiercest of Sherman's Carolinas' campaign. It went on for two days, some of it in a swamp darkened by a thick pine forest. The dank morass was left littered with "[g]uns and scabbards, dead horses, and the wrecks of ambulances," Sergeant Stewart recorded. "Bloody garments and bloody men strewed the ground."[60] He noticed a dead lieutenant grasping a bush "as if he died vainly feeling for a little hold upon earth and life."[61]

The battle ended in yet another failure for the Confederates. Outnumbered, Johnston retreated before dawn. Although Sherman could have pursued Johnston, he did not, which spared lives on both sides in the last days of the war.

By March 24, Sherman's entire army was encamped at Goldsboro, having journeyed 425 miles in fifty marching days from Savannah, Georgia, averaging almost 10 miles a day in often difficult country. South Carolina's railroads had been wrecked and its capital devastated. Three major arsenals had been wiped out and a vast amount of the food and forage that otherwise would have gone to the Confederate forces had been consumed or destroyed.

"Thus was concluded one of the longest and most important marches ever made by an organized army in a civilized country," Sherman boasted in his memoirs.[62] On March 31 he recounted the feat to "Dearest Ellen," repeating a favorite line, "I hardly have time nowadays to write letters," but advising that she could trace his whereabouts through the newspapers "and almost find out what I get for breakfast."[63]

Some of Sherman's men had arrived in Goldsboro ragged and shoeless after "having been shut up in hostile country for a little more than two months."[64] Nonetheless, "[t]he *morale* of this army is superb[,]" Henry Hitchcock wrote. "[T]heir confidence alike in Sherman and themselves ... is the confidence of veterans, familiar with danger, skillful and wary in encountering it, *not* of rash ignorance."[65]

When word was received April 12 that Lee had surrendered, "The whole army went crazy," Sergeant Stewart recalled of Sherman's armies. "Joy knew no bounds. Pandemonium had broken loose. 'Old Billy' was as crazy as any one, for in the height of his joy he shouted, "Glory to God and our glorious country!"[66]

On April 14, a Confederate messenger carrying a flag of truce arrived in Union lines with a message from General Johnston addressed to Sherman. Sherman opened the message and read, "I am ... induced to address you in this form the inquiry whether, to stop the further effusion of blood and devastation of property, you are willing to make a temporary suspension of active operation ... the object being to permit the civil authorities to enter into the needful arrangements to terminate the existing war."[67]

Sherman took pen in hand and began to write.

Capitulations and Humiliations

To call the gawky young men milling about a field in Marietta, Ohio, in September 1862 "The 116th Ohio Volunteer Infantry" was an act of charity, but they had been Governor Tod's choice to defend the state against a marauding Confederate general named Jenkins. Earlier that summer, Jenkins had staged a brief raid on Ohio, killed one civilian, and dashed back to the safety of West Virginia's mountains, leaving behind some badly rattled southeastern Ohioans screaming for protection.

Governor Tod knew the power of the political gesture. He cast about and found the 116th, forming but not yet mustered in. They would have to do. Still in their civilian clothes, the greenhorns of the 116th, armed with rusty and mostly unusable Belgian muskets and innocent of all military knowledge, were rushed across the Ohio River to West Virginia to deal with Jenkins, should he appear in their nearly useless sights. He didn't and the threat fizzled out. More than a month later, the 116th was properly mustered in, given its equipment, and shown how to drill. But they had done the job Tod needed, when he needed it.

The 116th spent the next couple of years toughening up and being blooded in West Virginia's low-level fire-fights. By the summer of 1864 it had become a well-weathered veteran regiment in Crook's Corps when it moved out of the mountain shadows to join Sheridan's Shenandoah Valley Campaign. After that, in December 1864, the 116th had joined the siege of Petersburg and by early April was taking part in the pursuit of Lee's dying army. What happened then apparently put it closer than any other Ohio regiment to the war's center stage.

On the morning of April 9, 1865, skirmishers from the 116th chased some Confederates to within sight of Lee's headquarters, in their enthusiasm getting ahead of their own forces. Lt. Ransom Griffin of the 116th ordered his men to take cover behind a rail fence and wait for the rest of the army to catch up. Then one of Griffin's men called out, "Do you see that flag?" Stooping to peer under some trees, Griffin could see a white flag fluttering at Lee's headquarters, about 250 yards away.

As Griffin and his skirmishers watched, they saw a Confederate horseman carrying another white flag appear and then still more white flags along Confederate lines. Hours passed. After mid-day, T. S. Smith, the regimental surgeon of the 116th, "saw the Generals come separately—Lee first—riding up to the appointed place of meeting."

The place chosen by Lee was the red brick home of Wilmer McLean at the west end of the village of Appomattox Court House and visible to the main body of the 116th. The Ohioans watched as Grant came riding up, "rather faster than usual," exchange greetings with Sheridan, and enter the house.

Grant had been suffering from a "sick headache" that morning, but "I was cured" on learning Lee had agreed to meet on the Union commander's terms."[68] When the dirt-plain Westerner walked into the McLean parlor where the aristocratic Southerner was waiting, the contrast was striking. Sixteen years older than Grant and taller by five inches, with hair and beard silver-gray, the ramrod-straight Lee was dressed in a new uniform and sash with a bejeweled presentation sword at his side.

Slightly stooped with nut-brown hair, Grant was in what he later called "rough garb": no sword, a dark blue flannel soldier's blouse with only his shoulder straps to denote rank, muddy trousers and boots.[69] It was a powerful symbolic contrast: the proud, elegant Confederate versus the plain, slouchy Midwesterner.

The two generals shook hands cordially and chatted briefly about their experiences in the Mexican War. Lee was impassive, his feelings entirely hidden, but Grant, who had been enjoying his triumph until that moment, now was "depressed." He remembered later that he "felt like anything rather than rejoicing at the downfall of a foe who had fought so long and valiantly," although the cause that he had fought for, Grant insisted, was "one of the worst for which a people ever fought."[70]

The generals quickly agreed on terms. The Confederates would turn over their arms and ammunition, be paroled, and allowed to return home

To encourage his men, Sheridan ordered a band to play even in the thick of the fighting.

For the surrender ceremony at Appomattox Court House, General Lee's fine uniform contrasted noticeably with General Grant's simple clothing and muddy boots.

undisturbed. In his usual unhesitating manner, Grant added that officers could keep their side arms, private horses, and baggage. It was an act of generosity, and it touched Lee. Verbally, Grant also agreed to let enlisted men who owned their own horses to take them home as well and he promised to send twenty-five thousand rations to Lee's starving men. Lee expressed appreciation.

After some more paperwork and conversation, Lee shook Grant's hand and left the house. Grant and his officers raised their hats to him in respect and Lee returned the gesture. Then the two commanders parted.

Having no interest in watching the conquered army give up its arms, Grant departed the next day for Washington to start winding down his military establishment. First, however, he hurried back to Julia, who had prepared a celebratory dinner.

On April 12, Confederate General Gordon led Lee's troops in surrendering their arms and battle flags as Union forces stood at attention. Grant had ordered that his men not cheer. The Federals were ordered to "carry arms," a gesture of respect returned by the Confederates, "honor answering honor."[71] Ohio troops in the area included the 2nd, 6th, and 13th Cavalry, the 4th Ohio Battalion (which included the remnants of the one-time rivals, the old 4th and 8th Ohio), and the 62nd, 67th, 116th, and 122nd Ohio infantry.

In North Carolina, meanwhile, Sherman was pushing on to Raleigh in pursuit of Johnston. To Johnston's message proposing an armistice, Sherman replied he was "fully empowered" to negotiate an end to hostilities and hoped "to save the people of North Carolina the damage they would sustain" if his army kept advancing.

On April 17, as Sherman was boarding a train to meet Johnston, he received a telegram reporting Lincoln's assassination. The two generals, who did not know each other, met in the bedroom of a small frame house. When Sherman showed Johnston the telegram, the Confederate general burst out, "'Great God! Terrible!'"

Admitting his cause was "gone," Johnston talked with Sherman for two days, joined on the second by the Confederate Secretary of War, Maj. Gen. John C. Breckinridge, who also was a lawyer and a skilled politician. Anxious to quickly arrange a surrender lest Johnston's army escape to the Carolina mountains, Sherman let himself be coaxed into unusually generous terms. The Union general Southerners thought was so cruel (and some still do), was in no mood to be harsh.

In his impulsive way, Sherman dashed off the proposed terms with no hesitation and that night sent his aide Hitchcock to Washington to submit them for approval. Thrilled, he wrote Ellen that government acceptance would mean "this cruel war will be over. I can hardly realize it, but I can see no slip."[72]

He couldn't have been more wrong. Dismayed by the generosity of Sherman's terms to Johnston, Grant quickly requested a Cabinet meeting that evening. All present agreed the terms were not acceptable: not only were they too generous militarily, but also they involved civil affairs over which Sherman had no authority.

Sherman had agreed that Confederate troops could keep their weapons until turning them in at their state capitals, that Confederate political leaders could resume their positions after taking an oath of allegiance to the federal Constitution, and the right to vote was returned to all Confederates. In effect, the agreement called for Washington to recognize existing Rebel governments. Even Ellen Sherman and Hitchcock were dismayed.

Now in Washington, Grant was ordered to go personally to Sherman, inform him the truce unacceptable, that warfare was to resume, and that he, Grant, was to take Sherman's place. Grant never mentioned the last to Sherman, who took the rejection of his terms matter-of-factly and notified Johnston a new effort was required. He even wrote Stanton a letter to "admit my folly."[73] But Stanton—who had never been one of Sherman's biggest fans—

was furious and not to be mollified, and he launched the equivalent of total war against Sherman. Stanton's fury may also have stemmed from his grief and anger over Lincoln's death.

Sherman learned that Stanton and Halleck were so violently denouncing Sherman's actions that something close to treason was being implied. Widely known for his abrasive manner, Stanton turned his full fury on Sherman, perhaps influenced by rumors that the highly popular general "was the coming man of the Copperheads" and looming as a presidential candidate in 1868.[74] There even were allegations Sherman let Jefferson Davis escape in return for a huge bribe. The denunciations were leaked to the press in a deliberate humiliation of a highly successful general.

Grant tried to tell Stanton that Sherman had been acting in good faith. Recalling his meeting with Lincoln on March 28 at City Point, Sherman had thought he was reflecting the late president's desire for a conciliatory peace. Stanton was not satisfied by the explanation. Now, in front of his generals, Sherman exploded in rage over Stanton's behavior, "pacing up and down the room like a caged lion," spouting "an eloquence of furious invective that made us all stare." Sherman wrote his old friend Grant, saying he expected his military career was at an end.

DEATH OF A PRESIDENT

Shortly after 10 p.m. on the evening of Good Friday, April 14, 1865, Secretary of War Stanton had been undressing for bed when he heard his wife, Ellen, shout from downstairs, "Mr. Seward is murdered!" Stanton, who had visited Secretary of State Seward scarcely an hour before, was skeptical, but he dressed quickly and hurried downstairs.

Stanton found a roomful of excited people, some saying Lincoln had been assassinated as well. Thoroughly aroused now, Stanton rushed out into the night, despite urgings to remain in the safety of his home, and raced by hackney cab to Seward's home a few blocks away.

There Stanton found his own bodyguard, Sgt. Louis Koerth, who gave him a garbled account of the attack on Lincoln. Stanton ordered Koerth to post guards around the homes of Cabinet members and the vice president. After quickly checking on Seward, who had been stabbed but was alive, Stanton rushed to the vicinity of Ford's Theater. Pushing through excited crowds, he entered the house where Lincoln had been taken. He found the president unconscious and breathing heavily, reminding Stanton of how his infant son sounded when he died in his arms years before.

The deaths of Stanton's first wife and infant son had given him such a horror of death that he had worried constantly that Lincoln would be attacked. The president had brushed aside many of Stanton's efforts to protect him and now Stanton had to cope with the consequences. As the room in which Lincoln was lying became more crowded, Stanton's take-charge nature asserted itself. He sent for Vice President Andrew Johnson, but knowing that Mary Lincoln did not like Johnson, advised him not to linger.

Ignoring the turmoil around him, Stanton continued making rapid-fire decisions. Even as Lincoln's grip on life weakened, Stanton launched the effort to capture the perpetrators. He told a shorthand clerk to take testimony from witnesses, put military forces in the capital's vicinity on alert, and ordered outbound trains stopped.

Still thinking clearly in the midst of chaos, he pieced together a medley of accounts and dictated a narrative of events for release to the nation's press. By 3 a.m. he had learned enough to order the arrest of John Wilkes Booth.

At 7:22 Saturday morning, April 15, Lincoln died. Secretary of War Stanton said, "Now he belongs to the ages" or words to that effect.[75] Then he wept openly, the one demonstration of emotion he allowed himself. As Stanton and Lincoln worked together in managing the war effort, the secretary of war's early disdain for Lincoln had turned into deep affection and respect. At 11 a.m. Andrew Johnson was sworn in as president. All the while, the indefatigable Stanton was pushing the search for the perpetrators and helping plan the funeral.

For the few hours between Lincoln's death and Johnson's swearing in, Stanton was, in effect, the nation's chief executive, guiding events with a firm hand. The attack on Seward, who would survive his wounds, suggested a plot against the entire government. It was later learned that Vice President Johnson had been targeted by a co-conspirator whose courage had failed him at the last minute.

General Grant may have been another target. The Grants had been invited to join the Lincoln party at Ford's Theater that evening, but had chosen instead to rejoin their children in Burlington, New Jersey. In the train station Mrs. Grant noticed a man acting suspiciously and the next day her husband received an anonymous letter stating, "[T]hank God that you [are] still live. It was your life that fell to my lot, and I followed you on the [train] cars. Your car door was locked, and thus you escaped me, thank God!"[76]

Newspapers throughout Ohio reported Lincoln's death on front pages darkened by "turned rules"—heavy black lines separating the columns.

Clusters of shocked Ohioans gathered on street corners. In armies still in the field, Union commanders rushed to head off reprisals against Southerners. In North Carolina, where Sherman's soldiers "stood around ... silent or talking in subdued but bitter tones ... many of them weeping like children," guards were quickly doubled to protect citizens against reprisals.[77]

In Virginia, General Keifer ordered out a fully armed company of the 110th Ohio for crowd control before he announced the assassination to his troops, urging them to use "moderation, conciliation, and magnanimity."[78] Privately, however, his fury spilled out in a letter to his wife pledging himself to "the complete annihilation of the Southern Slaveholding race."[79] (In fact, Keifer returned quietly to his Ohio law practice.)

On Tuesday, April 18, Lincoln lay in state in the crape-hung East Room of the White House, General Grant standing alone at the head of the catafalque. On Wednesday funeral services were held, with family, government officials, and diplomats in attendance. The body was moved to the Capitol and on Thursday a steady stream of thousands of mourning citizens passed the catafalque in the Rotunda.

Americans had developed a deep affection for President Lincoln and news of his death came as a personal blow. Lt. Holiday Ames, stationed with the 102nd Ohio in Alabama, wrote his wife in Ashland, "[I]t made me feel so bad that I went to bed and have not felt like getting up since. ... I tell you Lincoln was the idol of the army ... how can I feel any other way than like crying."[80] Even Lincoln's critics were disarmed. Clement Vallandigham had come to respect the president because of his moderate reconstruction policy, terming it "liberal and conciliatory." Lincoln's death, Vallandigham declared, was "the worst public calamity which could have befallen the country."[81]

On Friday, April 21, Lincoln's body was placed on a special train for a twelve-day, seventeen-hundred-mile journey to Springfield, Illinois, for burial on May 4. Ohio Governor Brough and state officials met the train at Wickcliffe after it entered Ohio on April 28. In Cleveland, a huge "General Committee of Arrangements" had been organized, with subcommittees for every detail. Six squads of honor guards were selected. A "Lincoln Pavilion" in Chinese pagoda style complete with gas lighting was quickly constructed in Public Square and shrouded in white and black for the reception of the coffin. Homes and public buildings were draped in black and white as well.

So many mourners arrived by train that Cleveland's hotels overflowed and hundreds slept on the floor. A salute of thirty-six guns was fired when the funeral train arrived on the morning of April 28. A slight rain, "dripping

On April 28, President Lincoln's body lay in state in a pagoda-style pavilion in Cleveland's Public Square.

like tears," fell on the coffin as it was taken along Euclid Street to the Lincoln Pavilion. The hearse, pulled by six white horses, was accompanied by an escort so big it was divided into six divisions of military units, civic organizations, and bands playing dirges. Somber crowds lined the streets. After a service led by the Episcopal bishop of Ohio, more than one hundred thousand mourners, in silent ranks of four, filed past the open coffin. The mournful boom of an artillery salute was heard every half hour.

At midnight, the funeral train departed for Columbus, moving at a stately pace as it passed crowds standing in the rainy dark. Bonfires and torches lit the night, church bells tolled, and flags stood at half staff. Approaching Columbus, the train passed an elderly woman, tears on her cheeks, hair disheveled, holding a black scarf in one hand and holding out a bouquet of wildflowers, "which she stretched imploringly toward the funeral car."[82]

Arrangements as elaborate as Cleveland's had been made in Columbus. Crowds speaking in whispers filled sidewalks, windows, and balconies as Lincoln's coffin was transported via High Street to the Statehouse rotunda in an enormous, specially constructed hearse. The western columns of the Statehouse had been wrapped with black crape in spiral turns. During six-and-a-half hours, more than fifty thousand mourners, walking in twos on either side of the catafalque, passed the open coffin in which Lincoln lay, head and upper body slightly raised. After the coffin's removal, the catafalque remained, with fresh flowers added every morning, until May 4.

At 8 p.m., the funeral train resumed its westward journey, passing crowds that had gathered around bonfires and were slowly waving handkerchiefs. Occasionally the train paused at stations where young ladies were allowed to board and place flowers on the coffin. Arriving at Piqua at twenty minutes past midnight, the train was met by ten thousand people, two bands, and a choir.

Early on the morning of April 30, the funeral train entered Indiana. It was four years, two months, and eighteen days since Lincoln had crossed into Ohio, heading the other direction, destined to lead the nation through a great civil war.

The *Sultana* Disaster

Of all the cruelties in a cruel war, few compare with what happened on the Mississippi River near Memphis in the rainy dark of April 27, 1865. At about 2 o'clock that morning, an explosion and fire destroyed the steamboat *Sultana,* killing fifteen to seventeen hundred passengers, many of them Ohioans.

In this worst maritime disaster in American history, most of the victims were newly freed prisoners of war, homeward bound after years of suffering in Confederate stockades at Andersonville, Georgia, and Cahaba, Alabama. As if to rebuke memory, the event was largely ignored by news media and the public, drowned out by the end of the war and the assassination of Lincoln, and it remains relatively unnoticed to this day.

The *Sultana* was a 1,719-ton steam-powered, coal-fired sidewheeler built in Cincinnati in January 1863 and designed to carry 376 passengers. In a

In Columbus, President Lincoln's body was transported from the railroad station to the Statehouse in a specially constructed hearse.

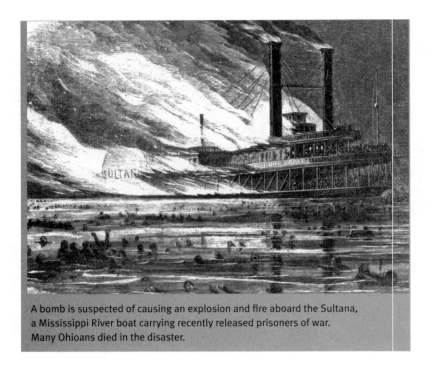

A bomb is suspected of causing an explosion and fire aboard the Sultana, a Mississippi River boat carrying recently released prisoners of war. Many Ohioans died in the disaster.

testament to greed and expediency, on this night she was carrying more than 2,200 persons, although poor record keeping prevents precision in numbers. Perhaps two thousand newly released Union prisoners of war were aboard, as well as two companies of infantry, and about 100 civilian passengers and crew. Some horses and mules had also been taken aboard.

Still weak from their experiences, the ex-prisoners were a "jolly crowd," buoyed by the expectation they'd be home soon. "A happier lot of men I think I never saw than those poor fellows," a survivor recalled.[83] From bow to stern, the sleeping men crammed every nook and cranny of the vessel, covering the decks and even filling the stairways.

About two hours into the morning of April 27 a great explosion shook the *Sultana,* throwing men in the air and the water. Some passengers were scalded and some had limbs blown off. Spears of timber impaled some men; others were crushed by the collapse of the vessel's upper structure and smokestacks. Holes opened in the decks and passengers fell through, landing on those below. As fire consumed the vessel, panicked groups of passengers, many of whom couldn't swim, leaped into the water. The night was filled with shouts, curses, and pleas for help, while the mules and horses shrieked with terror.

Help took two hours to arrive while survivors struggled to stay afloat in frigid water that shimmered in the fire's light. Those in the river fought over pieces of wood, the stronger pushing away the weaker. Survivors recalled that "the water seemed to be one solid mass of human beings" frantically grasping at each other only "to go down in squads."[84] Ultimately, five to seven hundred survivors were taken to Memphis hospitals, but more than two hundred of them died after being rescued.

Ex-prisoners from eight loyal states were aboard, with Ohio losing the largest number—by one estimate, 652 men.[85] Aboard the *Sultana* were Ohioans from sixty-six different infantry regiments, a dozen cavalry regiments, and one artillery battery, with especially large numbers from the 50th, 102th, and 115th Ohio Volunteer Infantry.

The *Sultana* had been a regular traveler between New Orleans and St. Louis. She had left New Orleans April 21, arriving at Vicksburg, where one of her boilers was repaired and where she took on the two thousand recently released prisoners. She arrived at Memphis on the evening of April 26, refueled, and at about 1 a.m. resumed her journey northward. Passing through a group of islands called "Old Hen and Chickens," one of the *Sultana's* boilers blew off its base, exposing a coal fire. Soon the dry wood of the boat's structure was ablaze. Because of flooding, the river was even wider at this point than its usual three miles, and the water was icy cold.

In the days and weeks after the disaster, three quick investigations by the army found that the unnecessary crowding resulted from careless decisions by a quartermaster named Hatch and an assistant adjutant general named Speed. They had allowed the steamboat's captain to overload the vessel so as to profit from the government fares. It could not be determined why the boiler had exploded. Improper repairs may have been the cause. Insufficient water in the boiler was another theory. Or there may be another explanation.

After the war broke out, a St. Louis painter named Robert Louden (or Loudon or Lowden) had thrown in his lot with the Confederates, smuggling mail from Rebel armies in the South to their families in Union territory. He also became involved with a gang of saboteurs who successfully burned a number of steamboats until he was arrested in September 1863. Sentenced to hang, he fled custody the following October and was still being sought at the end of the war. He died of yellow fever in 1867.

More than twenty years after the war, a St. Louis sign painter named William C. Streetor told a newspaper reporter a strange story. Streetor said that Louden, who had worked with him after the war, claimed to have planted a so-called "Courtenay Torpedo" to destroy the *Sultana*. The "torpedo"—in modern parlance, a bomb—was disguised as a lump of coal that Louden had surreptitiously placed in the Memphis coal supply from which the *Sultana* was refueled. It is true that Confederate authorities had financed saboteurs. Moreover, a specimen "Courtenay Torpedo" was found on the desk of Jefferson Davis when Unions troops occupied Richmond.[86]

If Louden had expressed regret about causing a huge loss of life after the war was over, Streetor didn't mention it. Whether Louden targeted the *Sultana* in particular or simply hoped to sabotage any civilian steamboat that refueled itself is not known, nor is it material. The result was the same: in April 1865, when peace was supposed to have returned to the land with malice toward none, America was blighted by the assassination of a president and the murder of innocents.

"THE GRANDEST REVIEW"

It was "the grandest review that was ever seen in the world," a giddy veteran of the 47th Ohio recalled of what took place in Washington in late May 1865.[87] It was also an opportunity for the armies of the Western Theater to prove themselves once again and it turned out to be powerfully symbolic.

With the war effectively over in April, Grant's and Sherman's armies were summoned to an unprecedented command performance—the "Grand Review"—in Washington on May 23 and 24. On the first day, immense crowds, cheering, waving handkerchiefs, and throwing bouquets, watched the Army of the Potomac march by. These were the soldiers best known to the Easterners, in effect hometown boys performing for a hometown crowd. Neatly attired, some of the Easterners had new uniforms and some wore white gloves; all wore jaunty kepi caps. Nearly one hundred thousand men marched smartly in ranks of sixty, a sea of blue that was drillmaster perfect.

The Eastern Theater's artillery trains rumbled along and platoons of cavalrymen pranced by with sabers drawn. Flags fluttered, bagpipes squealed, and the sun glinted off the polished steel of bayonets. Smoothly flowing by a reviewing stand where President Johnson, General Grant, and other dignitaries sat, senior officers in the march presented swords as drums ruffled and flags dipped. If he had been there, ex-General George B. McClellan, that brilliant organizer of armies, would have agreed with the *New York Times'* pronouncement that it was a "splendid spectacle."[88]

But on the second day, even bigger crowds turned out to watch the Western armies, which few Easterners had ever seen. "The enthusiasm of to-day far exceeded that of yesterday," the *New York Times* reported. What they saw was very different from the day before.

Never very concerned with spit-and-polish, Sherman's men had a "war-

Sherman's Western troops proudly marched down Washington's Pennsylvania Avenue in the Grand Review marking the end of the war.

worn" look to them, having marched thousands of miles and endured countless hardships.[89] Ragged and dirty, the Westerners' uniforms were "a cross between regulation blue and Confederate gray" and their weapons "were of all designs … which each man carried as he pleased."[90] Instead of snappy little kepis, many Westerners wore sensible wide-brimmed felt hats, the better to keep the sun off.

To entertain the crowd, the Western column included a moving sideshow: a crowd of black "contrabands"—among them, two large blacks riding small white mules—plus a pack train of mules being ridden by a half-dozen game cocks and "a sure-footed goat."[91]

According to one historian, some Western soldiers even lacked shoes.[92] Nonetheless, they were "the most superb material ever molded into soldiers," the *Times* reporter enthused. "The magnificent physique of the men at once elicits the admiration of all: tall, erect, broad-shouldered, stalwart men, the peasantry of the West."[93]

Leading them down Pennsylvania Avenue, General Sherman looked back and was relieved to see his rough-and-ready, mulish soldiery was doing itself proud, at least at first: "The column was compact, and the glittering muskets looked like a solid mass of steel, moving with the regularity of a pendulum," he wrote in his memoirs.[94]

"Many good people, up to that time, had looked upon our Western army as a sort of mob," Sherman wrote, "but the world then saw, and recognized the fact, that it was an army in the proper sense, well organized, well commanded and disciplined; and there was no wonder that it had swept through the South like a tornado."[95]

The Westerners carried their colors, in some cases so badly ripped by shot and shell that only bits of rag hung from bare poles. Bands played "Marching through Georgia" as crowds cheered, waved handkerchiefs, and showered

General Sherman was excoriated by Secretary of War Stanton's denunciation of a short-lived mistake in accepting a Confederate general's surrender.

the soldiers with flowers. After passing the reviewing stand, Sherman dismounted, marched into the stand, and passed along the row of dignitaries, shaking hands with all—except one. Sherman ignored Stanton's outstretched hand until the secretary dropped it finally ("and the fact was universally noted," Sherman noted with satisfaction in his memoirs years later.)[96]

Sherman's marchers could not hide their exuberance. The day before, Eastern troops had marched with precision, looking neither left nor right, but—as one of the Eastern officers remarked sourly—the Westerners "chatted, laughed and cheered, just as they pleased," both officers and men "bowing on all sides" to the cheering crowd.[97]

Nevertheless, "our boys fell into a long swinging step, evry man in perfect time," one of the Westerners recalled; "it seemed to me that the men had never marched so well before."[98] Marching as they pleased, with that lilt in their step, Sherman's army seemed to be saying, *We won this war.* And the awe-struck crowd, by its presence, seemed to whisper back, *We know.*

Gazette

Sherman had been in a white heat over Stanton and Halleck's public criticism of the original, tentative surrender terms he and Joe Johnston had agreed upon."[99] (Within a few days, Johnston and Sherman agreed on final surrender terms the same as Lee had accepted.) Ellen wrote her beleaguered husband that "however much I may differ from you I honor and respect you for the heart that could prompt such terms to men who have cost … the loss of Willy."[100]

Once again, Ellen and her family had come riding to Sherman's rescue. She and members of the Sherman-Ewing clan used all their political influence in an attempt to pressure Stanton into apologizing for the harshness of his criticism. The secretary, whose characteristic bearishness probably was aggravated by Lincoln's death, refused to back down.

Sherman even received a telegram from his old friend Halleck begging forgiveness, but Sherman refused the offer. On the way to Washington, Sherman had marched his troops through Richmond after warning Halleck to stay out of the city. In Washington, Sherman was greeted warmly by President Johnson; however, on May 22, Sherman testified before the Congressional Committee on the Conduct of the War, explaining his original peace proposals. By now, public opinion had swung back in Sherman's favor and Stanton, never a public favorite, was being excoriated for his harsh treatment of Sherman. During this brightening time, Ellen came east to view the Grand Review in Washington.

Then came Sherman's public snubbing of Stanton, "universally noted." Ellen the peacemaker was dismayed. The next morning, the doorbell rang at the Stanton home and the secretary's son Edwin answered. A bouquet of flowers had arrived from Mrs. Sherman as a "mute appeal for forgiveness." A few days later, Ellen paid a visit to Stanton at his home and passed a friendly half-hour. Once again, undoubtedly without his permission, Ellen had come to the general's aid.[101] But Stanton would not make a public retraction and Sherman would not forgive him.

Sherman's soldiers enjoyed a raucous night of celebration after the Grand Review. Then they settled down to eat, sight-see, and await mustering out.[102] For the tens of thousands of men camped in and around Washington, it was hurry-up-and-wait as usual. For example, it took the mustering officers until June 21 to reach Keifer's brigade of Ohioans and Eastern regiments.

The 6th Maryland was the first of Keifer's regiments to be mustered out. The happy new civilians celebrated their dismissal with farewell visits to their fellow units in the Third Division of VI Corps. That night, men of Keifer's brigade returned the salute by putting candles on their bayonets and marching to the Marylanders' camp. "[I]t mad[e] as grand a sight as I ever saw," Cpl. Charles H. Berry of the 110th Ohio thought. "We didn't get through until about 3 o'clock in the morning."[103]

Assembled by Stanton, the Union's huge arsenal was one of the factors in the Confederacy's defeat.

Four days later, the 110th Ohio's "Weary Boys" (unfairly nicknamed, for they had suffered more combat deaths and wounds than many other regiments) completed their paperwork, were mustered out, and sent back to Columbus by rail. At Camp Chase they received their final pay. By June 30 they were scattering to their homes in the state's western counties.

Kate Chase Sprague had sat out Washington's social scene in the winter of 1864–65, confined by her first pregnancy. Her husband was busy covering up his connection to a scheme to smuggle Southern cotton. If detected, it could have marked him as a traitor. What Kate knew or what role she played in the cover-up is unknown, but it could hardly have helped their marriage. In June 1865, Kate's unhappiness was masked by the birth of a son. Kate wanted to name the infant after her father, but both Salmon (who considered his name rather "fishy") and her husband objected, so the child was formally named William and informally called Willie. Finally, Kate had someone she could love unreservedly.[104]

After spending the winter of 1864–65 together in Washington, distance separated the Garfields once again. Crete and little Harry, born in 1863, returned to Hiram in April while James concentrated on his duties as a congressman in the nation's capital. The pain of infidelity lingered, however. Writing "My Darling Jamie," Crete mentioned a dream "that made me so unhappy that I awoke and could not sleep again for a long time."[105] Knowing full well what she meant, James promptly wrote back, "Your dream had no basis in reality," but he did not return home until July 4.[106]

On Saturday morning, June 17, 1865, Edmund Ruffin returned to his room at Redmoor, his son's plantation house in Virginia, and turned to his diary:

And now...with what will be near to my latest breath, I hereby repeat & would willingly proclaim my unmitigated hatred to Yankee rule— to all political, social, & business connections with Yankees, & to the perfidious, malignant, & vile Yankee race.

Then Ruffin took a rifle, placed the muzzle in his mouth, and, using a forked stick, pulled the trigger. Hearing the report, young Ruffin rushed upstairs to find his father's corpse sitting ramrod straight, defiant to the end, gun smoke and malevolence lingering in the air. [107]

To Learn More:

After a perceptive French aristocrat named Alexis de Tocqueville toured the United States in 1831 and 1832, he published his observations of the young nation in *Democracy in America*. See "American Journey" on **www.tocqueville.org** to learn about Tocqueville's visits to Ohio on July 21 and December 1-4, 1831.

For all the attention given Sherman's March to the Sea, his Carolinas campaign deserves equal attention. It receives it in John G. Barrett's *Sherman's March Through the Carolinas*.

Further north, lives of Ohio soldiers on the siege lines around Petersburg are vividly described in *The Weary Boys*, Thomas E. Pope's tribute to the 110th Volunteer Infantry and its commander, Col. J. Warren Keifer of Springfield.

The tragic story of the burning and sinking of the *Sultana*, crowded with newly released prisoners of war, many from Ohio, is told the survivors' own voices in *Loss of the Sultana and Reminiscences of Survivors.*, edited by Chester D. Berry.

The war's survivors came home scarred by the "intimate violence" they had experienced. Images of dead men were etched in their memories.

15

"WHERE IS YOU? WHERE IS YOU?"

From 1865 Until Now

Two-and-a-half years before the war ended, a tired and thirsty 105th Ohio lay down at mid-day to rest in a woods near Perryville in central Kentucky. It was October 8, 1862, and the young soldiers had been marching past the brown fields and fiery foliage of a drought-stricken land, the polished steel of their untested weapons glinting through clouds of dust. New to the business of war, they had no regimental flag and were so unpracticed that, until recently, one officer recalled, "[s]carcely ten men in our regiment knew how to 'right, face.'"[1]

Green or not, these northeastern Ohioans had been rushed with others to help Don Carlos Buell fend off two Confederate armies slashing northward through Kentucky. Buell's Army of the Ohio was the only large force the Union had in the region. It had to stop the gray armies before they regained Kentucky for the Confederacy or—even worse—invaded the American heartland north of the Ohio River. Cincinnati shivered at the possibility.

The regiment's rations had run out days before and a few of the men were gnawing on the tough meat of ducks they had found on an abandoned plantation. One of them was a newly minted second lieutenant, twenty-four-year-old John Calvin Hartzell, fresh off the farm and as richly ignorant of warfare as his men. Years later, Hartzell remembered that cannon fire from about a dozen enemy guns suddenly "came over us shrieking and howling: "Where is you? Where is you?'"[2] Spoiling for a fight, the greenhorns of Hartzell's Company H blustered defiance ("We'll show you where we is") until their grim captain, a forty-year-old veteran of the Mexican War, warned, "[Y]ou don't know what this means. I do."[3]

Moments later, the Ohioans were ordered forward on the double-quick, crashing through woods and brush, panting up hill and down, thrilled to be chasing the Johnnies at last. But when swarms of gray-clad reinforcements rose out of the dry grass ahead of them, the regiment's colonel shouted, "105th Ohio, retreat!" and the chasers became the chased.

Buzzing "like angry bees," Confederate bullets came searching for the hurriedly retreating Ohioans, dropping men here and there, catching several as they struggled over an old rail fence. The deadly reality of war came as a shock to the new soldiers, not one of whom had ever seen a young man like himself, full of bravado one moment, reduced to a bundle of rags the next. In time, they would develop an uneasy acceptance of this and learn the veteran soldier's term for a corpse, poignant in its studied casualness. There, they would say, lies "somebody's darlin'."

Hartzell and about twenty men tried to make a stand behind the fence, "but the bullets were coming like hail" and they were ordered back. Relentlessly pursuing the Ohioans, the Confederates swarmed over the fence, their arms wigwagging ominous semaphores each time they paused to reload and fire. Lungs burning, brush slapping their faces, weakened by hunger and thirst, the blue-clad survivors ran, all discipline gone, every man for himself. Some raced into a cornfield, bullets rattling the leaves and kicking up dirt around them. Thankfully, Wisconsin troops already positioned in the cornfield joined with nearby artillery to check the Confederates.

Safe for the moment, the Ohioans lay on the ground, panting and listening to the gunfire fade away. By nightfall there was only the occasional "surly bellow of a great gun ... [and] the moans and groans of the poor, luckless fellows we had left behind," Hartzell recalled. The young, inexperienced second lieutenant was now the ranking officer in his company. Their somber captain had been killed and the first lieutenant had fled before the battle. The searching bullets had found and killed or mortally wounded nine other members of the company. Two men were missing, perhaps captured. The rest of the company had been scattered to who-knew-where.

Hartzell and sixteen men, all that was left of Company H for the moment, huddled by a spring for the night. Finally, "dead tired, heartsick and homesick, hungry and discouraged," Hartzell fell asleep.[4]

Beginning in late spring 1865, streams of demobilized soldiers flowed into Ohio, the men scattering to joyous homecomings across the state.

Coming Home

Perryville had receded into memory, just another bloody milepost on the long road to Appomattox when, in the spring and summer of 1865, Ohio's lean, weather-beaten, and combat-hardened soldiers returned for demobilization in Cleveland, Columbus, and Cincinnati. Recalling raucous nights in 1861 when excited recruits had filled the capital, Columbus residents braced for a flood of tough, thirsty men with muster-out money burning holes in their pockets. They needn't have worried.

Wanting only to get home as quickly as possible, the veterans flowed quietly through the city, barely pausing to bid farewell to comrades in arms "[M]any were the tears that trickled down the bronzed cheeks of the veterans," a member of the 53rd Ohio remembered of the partings.[5] A lone exception to those rushing home was a man seen striding along High Street with the swinging gait of one who had marched many miles. The ex-soldier was "glorying in all the finery of a new rig [of civilian clothes], not excepting kid gloves"—and he was marching barefoot.[6]

The late spring and early summer of 1865 saw mustered-out soldiers and exchanged prisoners passing in and out of Camp Chase in Columbus in a steady stream. The outbound stream was swelled by Confederate prisoners released in early June after taking oaths of allegiance. Some ex-prisoners chose to stay in Ohio and seek work.

Returnees to Ohio were welcomed with banquets and speeches until the stream turned into a flood beyond the abilities of the welcomers. By the fall, the stream had diminished to one unit a week, among them the men of the 5th U.S. Colored Troops, who had been recruited in 1863 as the 127th Ohio. Finally, in July 1866 the 11th Ohio Volunteer Cavalry returned from the Far West where they had fought Indians, who were thought to have been incited by Confederates. The 11th Cavalry was the last force of Civil War-era volunteers from Ohio to return, and when it was demobilized, the fighting was finally over for the citizen-soldiers from the Buckeye state.

Unexpectedly quiet during the veterans' return during 1865, Columbus turned noisy on July 13 when shouting multitudes, artillery salutes, and showers of roses welcomed General Sherman. "I take pride in referring to Ohio as my home," the warrior hero told a crowd in front of the Statehouse— poppycock, since he had sworn never to live in his native state again.

Sherman had long refused to make his home in Ohio, defying Ellen's dogged efforts to persuade him otherwise. For Cump, Ohio probably held painful memories of parental abandonment as well as old feelings of inadequacy compared to his prominent foster father. But now Sherman the speaker soldiered on, paying homage to the state. "[F]rom Columbus to Portsmouth, from the Ohio River to the Lakes, you will find in every house and every hamlet a blue-coated boy who marched with Sherman," he declared grandly.[7] After that performance, the theater-loving Sherman rewarded himself by attending an opera that night. He departed for his residence in St. Louis the next morning.

On October 3, Ohio's greatest hero of all, General Grant, received a joyous welcome to Ohio's capital. The general in chief was honored with an assiduous tour of Columbus led by the proud city fathers, the itinerary not excluding the Asylum for the Insane. At every point the taciturn Grant graciously thanked his hosts but declined speech-making. Then he, too, departed to return to Washington, his peacetime headquarters.

REASONS WHY

Ohio's "blue-coated boys" brought home a new appreciation for life's pleasures: a warm body in bed beside them, fresh strawberries from the kitchen

In the course of the war, white soldiers began mingling with blacks in ways they never had before.

garden, the smell of good earth turning under the plow, and the comfort in knowing death wasn't lurking among nearby trees. Like most veterans, they didn't talk much about the war at first.

Gradually, however, their stories emerged as they struggled to find meaning and purpose in what they had done. John Hartzell of Company H, 105th Ohio, was typical of many when he sat down more than thirty years after the fact to record his memories. He had gone to war to save the Union, he said, and slavery had been the cause of the problem.[8]

Hartzell had it about right, in economy form, for if the causes contributing to the irrepressible conflict were many and complex, historians have settled what was at the irreducible core. If you need a one-word answer to what caused the Civil War, says Edward L. Ayers, a professor of history and dean at the University of Virginia, "go ahead and just say slavery."[9]

There's more to it than that, of course, but those bitter-enders who still argue the primacy of "states' rights" or that "the South just wanted to be left alone" to enjoy its "way of life" (meaning a white master race) or that, weirdly, the South was "right," are in denial. In a heavily researched book-length reply to such contrarians, Prof. Bruce Levine of the University of California, Santa Cruz, concludes, as professional historians everywhere have for decades, that "slavery *was* at the heart of the political struggles that culminated in civil war."[10]

The Confederates said so themselves. Voting in December 1860 to secede from the Union because Abraham Lincoln had been elected president, the South Carolina legislature issued a list of "immediate causes," almost all of which explicitly had to do with perceived threats to slavery.[11] Confederate Vice President Alexander Stephens famously confirmed it in his 1861 speech in Savannah in which he lauded the superiority of whites and the importance of slavery as the "cornerstone" of the Confederacy.[12]

Swept by hysteria since the John Brown raid, and terrified its captive blacks would turn on it, the South triggered a war in defense of its peculiar institution. It launched a preemptive strike against Fort Sumter. At first, prevailing sentiment in the North was simply to preserve the Union. Under Lincoln's leadership, however, that broadened into a moral crusade against slavery as the stubborn Confederacy dragged out the fighting. In the end, Levine wrote, the Confederacy's gamble on rebellion only "hastened the destruction of the antebellum South."[13]

Paying heavily for its war of choice, the South lost almost everything—its slaves, political clout, lives by the tens of thousand, and much of its economy—everything except, as the next hundred years would demonstrate, a firm belief in the superiority of the white race.

"THE ELECTRIC CORD"

More than two generations would pass before electricity became a common household servant, but it was understood widely enough for Abraham Lincoln to use it as a metaphor in 1858. America's immigrants, he said, could look at the Declaration of Independence and find the "electric cord ... that links the hearts of patriotic and liberty-loving men together." That energized connection would last, he said, "as long as the love of freedom exists in the minds of men throughout the world."[14]

The electric cord led directly to the Declaration's promise that "we hold these truths to be self-evident, that all men are created equal." Throughout Lincoln's career, the "equality promise," as culture-and-society critic Greil Marcus has called it, formed the cornerstone of his thinking. On the way to his first inauguration, Lincoln told an audience in Philadelphia's Independence

This Carolina satire demonstrated an outsider's view: a dissolute south underpinned by a corrupt institution.

Hall, "I have never had a feeling, politically, that did not spring from the sentiments embodied in the Declaration of Independence."[15]

Lincoln was mentioning the equality idea as early as 1837 when he praised the nation's "political edifice of liberty and equal rights."[16] He saw no exceptions, writing in 1854 that "equality in society alike beats inequality, whether the latter be of the British aristocratic sort or of the domestic slavery sort."[17]

Slavery was the greatest challenge to the equality promise in his time and Lincoln referred to it as "the double-refined curse of God upon his creatures." But the equality promise applied to everyone; slavery wasn't the only point at issue. Equality was the American hallmark, Lincoln told his Independence Hall audience. The great principle "that kept this [nation] so long together ... was not the mere matter of separation of the colonies from the motherland," he said, "but that sentiment in the Declaration of Independence which gave hope to all the world, for all future time ... that *all* [emphasis added] should have an equal chance."[18]

That was why confronting the Southern rebellion was about more than holding the nation together or even abolishing slavery. As Lincoln scholar Douglas L. Wilson has commented, Lincoln's "most basic argument for resisting the rebellion [was] that it would undermine and ultimately destroy

Belying Southern claims of "contented slaves," swarms of runaway blacks trailed Union armies as they sliced through conquered territory.

the American experiment, and with it, popular government itself."[19] President Lincoln told his secretary John Hay in May 1861, "I consider the central idea pervading this struggle is … of proving that popular government is not an absurdity. We must settle this question now, whether in a free government the minority have the right to break up the government whenever they choose. If we fail it will go far to prove the incapability of the people to govern themselves."[20]

The Confederacy's secession was not just a civil war: it was an attempted revolution or even counter-revolution. Historians Emory M. Thomas and Manisha Sinha have pointed that out in works separated by nearly thirty years. The "last Americans to engage in active revolution were Southern Confederates," Thomas wrote in 1971. Their Rebellion was about more than the preservation of slavery. The Confederacy was a "radical" attempt "to achieve conservative ends" of localism, agrarianism, "moonlight and magnolia" romanticism, and the perpetual aristocracy of the planter class of "men who enjoyed wealth and influence."[21]

It was even more than a revolution, argued Manisha Sinha, then on the history faculty of the University of South Carolina. The secession by the American South was actually a "counterrevolution," a repudiation of the Declaration's insistence that "all men are created equal." It was a denial of democracy and the assertion of oligarchical power by a few. In South Carolina, the white aristocracy's support of racial slavery, Sinha insisted, was "a direct challenge to 'the ideals of universal liberty, equality, and democracy that lay at the heart of the American experiment.'"[22] Quoting numerous examples,

Sinha said that secessionist leaders believed that "inequality, not equality, was the necessary condition of man."[23]

Although Carolineans had led the defense of slavery since the Constitutional Convention in 1786, it was Virginian George Fitzhugh who most eloquently expressed counter-revolutionary thinking. "The American Revolution was an exceedingly vulgar, commonplace affair," he angrily insisted, and the "bombastic absurdity" of its Declaration of Independence [was] "pompous," "mal-apropos," and "silly." Fitzhugh was far from alone in deriding the "equality promise." Other Southerners as well derided Jefferson's claim that "all men are born equal" as "nonsense" and "ridiculously absurd."[24] And, from then until now, any effort to reduce inequality in American life has been derided by opponents as "socialism."

That was why, for Lincoln, the Civil War was about more than reuniting the country, more than freeing the slaves. Fundamentally, the war was about preserving the twin ideals of liberty and equality of opportunity. Losing the war would prove that the promise of liberty and equality was not enough, that a democratic society could not preserve itself. Losing the war would allow a selfish few to return part of the country to the class-based society of England, with its calcified barriers between the privileged, on the one hand, and the mass of commoners on the other.

With that in mind, Lincoln set out in his Gettysburg Address to find the meaning in the soldiers' sacrifice and the continuing war. His first words in that memorable address reminded the audience that their forefathers had created

a new nation, conceived in liberty, and dedicated to the proposition that all men are created equal.

The Civil War, therefore, was a test of whether "any nation so conceived and so dedicated can long endure." The soldiers buried at Gettysburg "gave their lives" so that it would. That was the meaning of the struggle still under way. It was why the living must be dedicated to "the great task remaining before us ... that this nation shall have ... a new birth of freedom—and that government of the people, by the people, for the people, shall not perish from the earth."

The equality promise applied to everyone, even if slavery was the great issue of the moment. On August 22, 1864, Lincoln addressed the 166th Ohio, one of the hundred-day regiments, then on its way home. Never mentioning race, Lincoln said the struggle was "not merely for today, but for all time to come ... [to] perpetuate for our children's children that great and free government which we have enjoyed all our lives."

The president told the white soldiers that winning the war was necessary "in order that each of you may have, through this free government which we have enjoyed, an open field and a fair chance for your industry, enterprise, and intelligence; that you may all have equal privileges in the race of life, with all of its desirable human aspirations." Clearly, Lincoln meant equality *of opportunity*, not the "leveling" with which opponents have always charged the Equality Promise. Reaching once again for a metaphor, Lincoln concluded, "The nation is worth fighting for, to secure such an inestimable jewel."[25]

It was "an inestimable jewel" worth fighting for. Because the Civil War generation fought for it, we are still connected by Lincoln's "electric cord" to the Declaration of Independence in 1776. Lincoln was talking about the "American Dream"—that sense of possibility, of social mobility, of opportunity each of us has to invent, and re-invent, ourselves. As a literary critic once put it, "America is not about who you are, but who you want to be."

The American Dream. Opportunity. Fairness to all. That's why we debate Affirmative Action, the Equal Rights Amendment, gay rights, and Title IX. It's why we keeping asking ourselves, *What is equality?* and *How do we achieve it?* as we struggle to understand the "equality promise" and make it work. Perhaps you can feel the electricity.

THE FRUITS OF WAR

The 105th Ohio had returned to Cleveland in early June 1865, three long years after it saw the elephant at Perryville. "THE END OF THE WAR! TROOPS COMING HOME! ARRIVAL OF THE 105TH O.V.I.," the *Cleveland Daily Leader* happily shouted.[26] The northeastern Ohio regiment was no longer young, innocent, and looking for a fight. Of the 1,099 men who had served in it, scarcely a third—355 men—assembled for the last time on the Camp Cleveland parade ground. The war had crushed or scattered the rest.[27]

Two of every ten soldiers of the 105th had died from wounds or disease and been buried in lonely graves from Kentucky to Georgia.[28] Two or three more of every ten had been discharged during the war, so sick or badly injured they were useless as soldiers.[29] Others were absent at muster-out because they had been transferred to special duties (among them, John Hartzell) or to other units. Some remained in hospitals.

Perplexing families and authorities alike were the thirty-six men for whom there was no accounting. They had deserted, perhaps, vanishing into the restless American population, or were missing in action, their bodies left

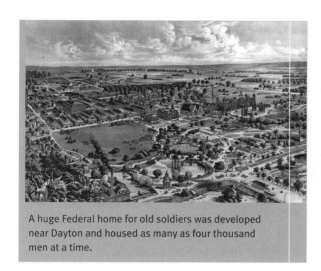

A huge Federal home for old soldiers was developed near Dayton and housed as many as four thousand men at a time.

to melt into southern soil, recognized only as somebody's darlin'. [30]

Among *Ohio* regiments, the 105th's fatality rate was not remarkable. Nearly forty other Ohio regiments had experienced more combat deaths.[31] All had suffered other miseries as well. Nearly a fourth of the men of the 105th had been wounded (some of whom recovered enough to return to duty). Sixteen percent had endured captivity under the Confederates.

No more than a fourth of the 105th Ohio's men had escaped death, wounds, or capture. Long after the war, many men would continue to suffer with wounds that had never healed properly, phantom pain from amputated limbs, chronic diseases, and stress.[32]*

For many veterans, the invisible injuries may have been the worst. Physical wounds were visible badges of honor and amputees were especially respected. Pyschological damage was another matter. Some of the symptoms of Post-Traumatic Stress Disorder (PTSD) were recognized at the time, if inconsistently, and called "nostalgia," "soldier's heart," or "irritable heart syndrome." However, such ailments were poorly understood and treated. Sometimes the victims were ridiculed or derided as cowards.

Now and then a veteran would kill himself or become so crazy as to be institutionalized, but for many sufferers little could be done. After the war, almost every town and village had its "odd ducks"—old soldiers who had become eccentric string-savers and hermits and porch-sitters, strangely silent men who stared into space as if they were listening to something far away.

For all its horse-and-musket quaintness, the American Civil War was a gruesomely efficient generator of death and injury. Fortunately, a grateful nation agreed that the war's damaged survivors deserved assistance. To help widows, dependent mothers, and handicapped Union veterans, Congress

* The mortality rate of the 105th exceeded the *national* average and so did its number of wounded. Information sources vary widely, but the percentage of Union soldiers who died from all causes is thought to range from 12.8 percent to 16.5 percent (22.6 percent of the men of the 105th died), with 9.8 percent to 12.7 percent, of all members, wounded (compared to 23.5 percent of the 105th).[33] [34]

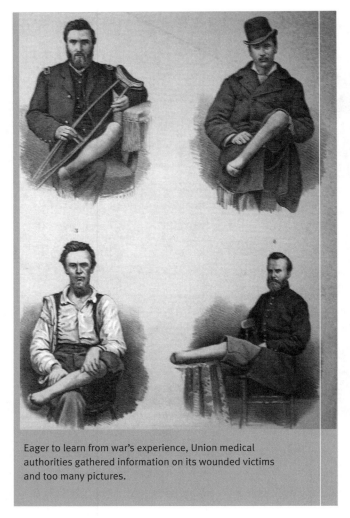

Eager to learn from war's experience, Union medical authorities gathered information on its wounded victims and too many pictures.

approved a pension system in 1862.

Pension applicants had to demonstrate their need to gimlet-eyed examiners and the benefits weren't large—by 1883, widows typically were receiving $8 a month and injured veterans, with occasional exceptions, $2 to $12—but this would grow into the largest social benefit program the nation had ever attempted. The Civil War pension system, the benefits of which were later improved by Congress several times, greatly expanded the federal government and foreshadowed Social Security.

In 1883, Ohio had twenty-five thousand federal pensioners, most from the Civil War, although there were a few aged veterans of the War of 1812. Every Ohio county had its pensioners and so did most towns and villages. Lancaster, for example, was home to 130 pensioners, nearly half of them widows or mothers who had depended on a son, now dead or handicapped from war injuries.

The pension rolls were catalogs of misery, tersely enumerated. Of Lancaster's seventy-four soldier pensioners, the cruelties that had changed their lives included: "loss r. leg," "chr. diarr.," "dis. of brain," "dis. of eyes," "chr. rheum.," "wd. thighs." The largest pension, $31.25 monthly, had been awarded on the grounds of "insanity."[35]

Not every pensioner had a home to which he could return. Some Ohio veterans were recent immigrants yet to put down roots, while others— muttering about town, constantly sick, and unable to work—soon proved they needed more care than families could provide. To house the war's human wreckage, the federal government built several soldiers' homes across the country, the largest near Dayton.

Within ten years the Dayton facility grew to a small city of 132 buildings, including a dining room that could serve four thousand men in two sittings and numerous residence halls called "barracks" (one of which was reserved for loud snorers).

The Dayton home's administration did its best to impose a quasi-military order on the place and the residents did their best to ignore it, now and then going on alcoholic toots. The grounds were tastefully landscaped with trees, ponds, and the occasional cannon. A funeral tunnel was built to discreetly send the deceased on their way to the home's own cemetery.

Even this enormous federal facility was not enough for all of Ohio's needy veterans, so in November 1888 the state opened its own Soldiers' and Sailors' Home near Sandusky. It remains there today, known as the Ohio Veterans Home. It was joined in 2003 by a second Ohio Veterans Home, located—as if to pay tribute to history—in Georgetown, Ulysses S. Grant's home town in southern Ohio. (From 1870 to 1997 the state also operated the Ohio Veterans' Children's Home in Xenia.)

Meanwhile, the National Soldiers Home near Dayton, where four of the original buildings remain, has grown into an ultra-modern, busy Veterans Administration Medical Center. America's supply of damaged soldiers never seems to run out.

Remembrance

War is a jealous god. It hates letting go of its victims. Thousands of Ohio soldiers received wounds that were permanently disfiguring, disabling, or endlessly painful. Maj. Ephraim C. Dawes of the 53rd Ohio received a disfiguring facial wound in Georgia. He had to grow a beard to cover it. Many years later, the regiment's historian wrote, "He once said that he had never known one waking moment free from pain."[36]

Perhaps Dawes was one of the lucky ones. Worn down by hard marching, poor food, and disease, some veterans returned home only to die within weeks or months. Lt. Col. E. Bassett Langdon, commander of the 1st Ohio, was shot in the face at Mission Ridge in 1863, the bullet passing out the back of his neck. Two years after the war, he slumped over the dinner table and was gone, age forty.

Ohio's soldiers came home only to discover they had left very little behind

In the Stones River National Cemetery, more than 6,100 Union soldiers are buried. The identities of more than a third are unknown.

in the war except their innocence. Modern researchers, poring over old records and feeding data into computers, are beginning to understand how combat can claw its way into the hearts and minds and guts of men long after a war is over. Among the evidence was that uncovered by three behavioral scientists at a California university who studied the military careers and pension records of 17,700 Civil War veterans nationwide to learn about post-traumatic stress disorders.

They learned that war-time traumas, such as being wounded or captured, were clearly "related to signs of disease and mortality" in veterans many years after the war. But so was witnessing the injury and death of comrades, an experience the researchers called "intimate violence." Long after the war, veterans who had had traumatizing war-time experiences like these were suffering elevated levels of cardiac, gastrointestinal, and nervous diseases— and early death.[37]

"Intimate violence" didn't end with the war, either. Civil War armies often enrolled clusters of men from the same area. Veterans restored to their own communities suffered quietly as nearby friends, neighbors, and relatives with whom they had served passed away, their deaths hastened, perhaps, by their wartime experiences. By 1890, about a fourth of the war's survivors had died and the typical veteran, by then in his late forties or early fifties, probably had lost several comrades.

For the traumatized veteran, sleep didn't bring rest. James K. Brady, a Marion County boy, had enrolled illegally at sixteen in the 64th Ohio. While still an adolescent, Brady was wounded twice, imprisoned at Andersonville weighing 154 pounds and freed weighing 96, then nearly drowned in the sinking of the *Sultana*.

A quarter-century later, Brady admitted moving restlessly from one occupation to another and "at the present time not doing much of anything." He could not forget the mass of struggling bodies on the night of the *Sultana*'s death. "I often see it in my sleep and wake with a start," Brady said.[38]

Old soldiers remembered songs they sang while they marched, proud and confident—"We are coming Father Abra'am" and "Rally Round the Cause Boys" and, most of all, the thundering cadence of "John Brown's Body" with its multitudinous verses ("We'll hang Jeff Davis on a sour apple tree/As we go marching on" was a favorite)—but they remembered sadder songs as well.[39] For Charles A. Willison, there was one that especially troubled him.

Willison's 76th Ohio had used the old hymn "How Firm a Foundation" as one of its funeral marches. Willison, who had been a private in the regiment, wrote forty years after the war, "I can never hear or join in it but it seems I can almost hear the muffled roll of drums and the plaintive accompaniment of the fife as some poor comrade was being borne to his long home in the South Land."[40]

For veterans, triggers to memory were everywhere: the staring eyes of a hunter's dead quarry, fallen branches that resembled bony hands reaching up from the earth, rotting offal in the open garbage dumps smelling like decaying human flesh. Thunder sounded like distant artillery. Carpenters hammering sounded like gunshots. One of the worst sounds was that of the winter wind. It came out of the southwest and, unimpeded by mountains, crossed Ohio heading east, ruffling the dried grass on Confederate graves at Camp Chase and blowing snow around the G.A.R. markers in country cemeteries. The wind spoke to the old soldiers as they turned uneasily in their beds. It moaned like men in pain and whistled like the searching bullets that asked, *Where is you? Where is you?*

John Calvin Hartzell remembered it all as he labored to explain the war to his family. Beginning January 1, 1896, he spent part of his winter downtime from farm chores writing his memories. In his fifties, he was responding to a "round robin" request from dozens of relatives and family members: *Dear Uncle Cal: We would like to read your boyhood and manhood recollections. ... Set about it at once and oblige your loving and curious and admiring family.*[41]

He began with a description of his youth, remembering the life of a farm youngster in northeastern Ohio in the 1830s and 1840s. Half his writing was devoted to a wistful remembrance of the first twenty-four and a half years of his life. "I should just like to roll up my trousers once more and wade into [a brook], feel the soft, cozy mud squash up between my toes, pull rushes, and get a big handful of skunk cabbage to run under [sister] Lucy's nose, and then see her run and tell 'Pap,'" he wrote.[42]

In 1862, the war drew him in, and he devoted the second half of the memoir to his three years of service. He began, "[O]ne hot, harvest day I hung my grain cradle on a little sugar tree in the wheat field as two young fellows came along the dusty road with fife and drum, jumped the fence, followed them to town and enlisted."[43]

Hartzell worked on his memoir on winter evenings for three years. Sometime between January 28 and April 22, 1898, he concluded, "I rejoice that I was permitted to bear ever so humble a part in securing the unity of our great country, and to share a little in the suffering of its noble sons. This great war … called into its ranks, on both sides, the best and noblest men, from priest to profligate, statesmen to philosophers, to school boys, and was a fight to the finish."

Having put down his "boyhood and manhood recollections" as requested, he dipped his pen one more time, and wrote, "and so I bid good-bye forever to my old comrades and this poor story."[44]

John Hartzell, farmer and family man, had done a soldier's duty.

MOCKINGBIRDS AND FIRE IN THE SKY

To the end of their days, the dwindling veterans of the Union and Confederate armies formed a mystic brotherhood of shared experience, holding secrets no civilian could understand. They had seen the elephant and learned unforgettable things about the fragility of life, the nearness of death, and the nobility and inhumanity of man. They had learned the romantic notions young men have of war, the Currier & Ives lithographs of smartly uniformed men in neat ranks, led by gallant generals on prancing white horses, were lies, and the reality of the battlefield was stink and noise and terror, every sense under assault.

And yet, in spite of its horrors, most of them had remained in service to their country, dedicated to high purpose, piling up a debt that we still owe them. Paradoxically, as if to hold on to their humanity, they could even find beauty in the midst of the terror and devastation. Pvt. Isaac Jackson of the 83rd

Ohio gathered "quite a nice bouquet" of roses while stationed at Milliken's Bend. Later, outside Vicksburg, he loved to listen to the mockingbirds. "They are plenty here and the prettiest singers I ever heard," he said. One bird used to sit in an old dead tree and sing while Jackson lay in his tent, gazing at him.[45] Other soldiers liked to lie on their backs in the warm Mississippi nights and watch as mortar shells, trailing sparks from their fuses, traced arcs high into the sky at a rate of one per minute before falling, screaming, to explode inside Confederate lines. The golden hue of wheat in the field, the green carpet of rolling landscapes, and the azure blue of a clear sky all drew notice from men whose business was death and destruction.

But most of the sights and sounds of war were ugly. Ordered to join the battle at Bull Run, a talented young Confederate cavalry officer named J. E. B. Stuart led his troopers by a field hospital at which, an aide recalled after the war, "[t]ables about breast high had been erected upon which screaming victims were having arms and legs cut off" by surgeons, who were stripped to the waist and spattered with blood. The screams, the flies, and the stench of this place were too much for the moving line of cavalrymen, who leaned over the pommels of their saddles and vomited as they trotted past.[46]

Young men who had known only the peace and quiet of rural life found themselves in a new world of sound, sight, and smell. The journalist Whitelaw Reid, on the battlefield at Gettysburg, remembered how the air was "alive with all mysterious sounds, and death in every one of them." There were "muffled howls" of projectiles that "seemed in rage because they had missed you." And then came still others that made the air distinct with menace, quickening it with "vivid alarm … long wails" and "fluttering screams."[47]

The sights of battlefield could be disorienting. Instead of the neat lines of soldiers depicted in romantic lithographs in which the sun always shone, soldiers frequently were enveloped in smoke and dust on the battlefield, sometimes forced to fire blindly in the direction the enemy was thought to be. Lines of battle rippled confusingly back and forth, sometimes wavering and then rushing ahead, sometimes dissolving. The acrid smell of black powder burned the nose and throat, combining with heat and fear to dehydrate soldiers. To the end of his days, a Gettysburg civilian remembered trying to sleep as a wounded Confederate soldier, forsaken and out of reach in a no-go zone, cried out through the night in his "soft Southern voice, 'Wahter! Wahter!'"[48]

A young officer, in the Army of the Ohio, remembered arriving on the muddy field at Shiloh early on the battle's second day:

A simple stone marks the Stones River grave of Pvt. Henry Fairchild. Company A, 174th Ohio Volunteer Infantry, who died January 28, 1865. Fairchild's unit was not in the Battle of Stones River, but saw later action in the area.

The first dead soldier we saw had fallen on the road; our artillery had crushed and mangled his limbs, and ground him into the mire. He lay a bloody, loathsome mass, the scraps of his blue uniform furnishing the only distinguishable evidence that a hero there had died. ... Near him lay a slender rebel boy—his face in the mud, his brown hair floating in a muddy pool.[49]

War and remembrance. Even as they celebrated their victories and what they had meant to the preservation of the nation and its promise, the veterans of the Civil War could never forget what—and who—they had left behind on the battlefields. Suffering the nightmares and the daytime memories that afflict trauma victims, the old soldiers slipped away with the years, joining their comrades at last, the arms of the dead reaching out to them, having learned Antigone's truth:

> It is the dead
> Not the living,
> Who make the longest demands.
> We die forever.

TO LEARN MORE:

Historians agree that slavery was at the heart of the war, but Lincoln believed the war was about something even larger: the Declaration of Independence's assertion that "all men are created equal." At the heart of the American Dream, the "Equality Promise" pledges each of us—despite our differences—an equal opportunity to get ahead, an equal voice in governance, and equal justice under the law. The psychic landscape of America is supposed to be a level playing field. Lincoln's own words on the subject appear in *The Words of Abraham Lincoln: Speeches, Letters, Proclamations, and Papers of our Most Eloquent President*, edited by Martin Lubin. To "meet" Lincoln and his family, visit Springfield, Illinois, and tour his home (**www.nps.gov/liho/** or **217-492-4241, ext. 266**) and other sites, most notably the spectacular new Abraham Lincoln Presidential Library and Museum "combining scholarship and showmanship" (**http://www.alplm.org/** or **800-610-2094**).

The historian James M. McPherson uncovers what ordinary soldiers believed they were fighting for in *For Cause and Comrades: Why Men Fought in the Civil War*.

A bronze sentinel, permanently on guard in Cincinnati's Spring Grove Cemetery, stands near a section where many Civil War soldiers are buried.

16

SOMEBODY'S DARLIN'

In February 1828, the steamboat *Criterion* came chugging up the Ohio River to Cincinnati, where it deposited an English lady of refinement named Frances Trollope. Endowed with no business sense whatsoever, Trollope was determined to open an exotic department store in the New World and redeem the tattered fortunes of her Old World family. She failed. Two years later, reduced to near-poverty, Trollope and her party departed Cincinnati in a raging snit, regretting "that we had ever entered it; for we had wasted health, time, and money there."[1]

Cincinnati, a hardworking river port and manufacturing city only recently a frontier town, had shunned Trollope's fripperies. The rejection turned out to be a gift in disguise. An aggressive, sarcastic woman, Trollope went home to England, dipped her pen in acid, and wrote a book, *Domestic Manners of the Americans*. It was an instant hit.

Domestic Manners of the Americans was the kind of tell-all screed we read on the beach and it made Trollope famous. Energized by its success, she turned into a whirlwind producer of novels and travel narratives. (A son, Anthony, also became a novelist, his work a mother lode of English costume dramas for American public television.)

In *Domestic Manners*, Trollope included some observations that were not unfavorable. She was impressed by Ohio thunderstorms, conceding English ones were weak beer by comparison. Mostly, however, she riveted audiences by dishing dirt. Cincinnati was "an uninteresting mass of buildings," Trollope wrote of the Midwest's greatest city.[2] "Unsavoury" hogs roamed Cincinnati's streets, slurping up rotten swill, while free-range cows made deposits in the

Long before the Civil War, Cincinnati had become a bustling port on the Ohio River, serving commerce between the North and South.

gutters.[3] Her proper English nose wrinkling furiously, Trollope summed up Cincinnati as "a place I cordially disliked."[4]

But it was the Americans themselves who roiled Trollope's sangfroid most of all. The men drawled, guzzled cheap whisky, and spat continually from "polluted" lips, she reported, while the women, though "handsome," were deficient in grace. In Trollope's view, Americans of both genders lacked that *sine qua non* of civilization: refinement.[5]

Trollope pinpointed an enduring feature of the national character. Americans, she said, believe "they are the first and best of the human race, that nothing is to be learnt, but what they are able to teach, and that nothing is worth having, that they do not possess."[6] In that regard, some would say, nothing has changed.*

Misunderstanding the War

The book flew off store shelves. Northeasterners smirked while Ohioans squirmed in anger. Trollope claimed to be writing about all Americans, but hadn't she spent most of her time in the "West" (the area we know today as the Midwest)? The Trollopian wigging of Ohioans confirmed Northeastern belief that not only were wealth and power in short supply on the sunset side of the Appalachians, so were culture and refinement.

To inhabitants of New York, Boston, and other hives of sophistication, Westerners were provincial clods, out of the loop and rightly so. Midwesterners

* The reference here is to "American exceptionalism," the long and widely held belief of Americans in "the supremacy of U.S. democratic ideals" and other national characteristics. See "The Paradoxes of American Nationalism" in *Foreign Policy* magazine, May/June 2003, pp. 31-37. Tocqueville noticed the same phenomenon a few years later and called it "irritable patriotism."

today will not find this a revelation. In 2006, a politician from a flyover state said her constituents "believe that people from the East Coast or the West Coast don't think that people in the heartland are smart."[7] In 2007, an Indianan living in New York City observed, "The Midwest for some New Yorkers is the other side of the world."[8]

Nineteenth-century Northeasterners gave Midwesterners, and dwellers still further west as well, credit for courage and industry, but thought them ignorant, boorish, and prone to violence. Typical was a New Englander who called them "a set of half savages, and in fact *a nation of drunkards.*"[9] For their part, Midwesterners saw themselves as "manly, politically astute, and egalitarian." They disdained Easterners—especially New Englanders—as snobbish weaklings and sharp dealers.[10]

The long-standing view from the West was summed up in a 1902 novel, *The Last Word,* published by a popular Ohio-born author named Alice MacGowan. "Throughout the novel," a modern reviewer has written, "the values represented by the West—democratic freedom, openness, tolerance, natural virtue—are contrasted with those of autocratic control, limitation, intolerance" residing in New York.[11]

Frances Trollope, caricatured in this nineteenth-century drawing, considered Americans "unrefined." Not surprisingly, Americans disagreed.

Soldiers of all ranks carried these attitudes into the Union's Eastern and Western armies. Col. Marcus Spiegel of the 120th Ohio complained that the "gentlemen soldiers from Massachusetts and Connecticut ... laugh at us rough looking Western men."[12] Gen. George G. Meade, a Pennsylvanian, airily dismissed Western troops as "armed rabble."[13]

In 1863, John Codman Ropes, a Massachusetts lawyer and military historian, hoped—despite the promise shown by Ulysses S. Grant—that "the Administration may be spared the humiliation ... of putting a western general like Grant over the Army of the Potomac."[14] John Chipman Gray, another Bostonian,

This well-equipped sergeant from New York resembled his shabbier Western counterparts in one way: a grim view of the Confederate cause.

said he had discovered in his travels that "the same lack of discipline exists in all" Western troops. He quoted Gen. George H. Gordon of Massachusetts as "very doubtful" it could be improved.[15]

For their part, Westerners like Colonel Spiegel called Easterners "bandbox soldiers" and were riled on discovering how well Eastern troops were outfitted.[16] Sizing up Pope's defeated troops after Second Bull Run, Rutherford Hayes pronounced them unable to fight as well as Westerners (for which he blamed poor generalship).[17]

When Sgt. Thomas F. Galwey's 8th Ohio moved into the Shenandoah Valley in 1862, he grumbled, "By now we look like a pack of thieving vagabonds—no crowns in our hats, no soles to our shoes, no seats to our pantaloons. We make a good foil to the sleek, well-fed soldiers of McDowell's corps."[18] Pvt. William Bakhaus of the 47th Ohio expressed a similar view late in the next year when Sherman's Westerners encountered "Fighting Joe" Hooker's Easterners during the relief of besieged Chattanooga: "[W]e were a very motley looking set of men. Many were hatless and shoeless, clothing tattered and torn. ... In striking contrast to our appearance were Hooker's men, all dressed up as if for parade, in short neat looking jackets and paper collars." Hooker's men and even Hooker himself taunted the Westerners, who turned on their handsome tormentors, laughing at them so much that "we actually came to blows." Whenever the Westerners spotted Hooker himself, according to Bakhaus, "there came from all quarters an unearthly yell of 'Hello, Joe!'... and he rightly remarked that we 'were the damndest, most undisciplined set of men he ever saw or heard of.'"[19]

Eastern hauteur and its Western reciprocal were rooted in a deeper sectionalism, for hostility between North and South formed only one of the national divides in antebellum America. There was tension between the Northeast and the lands west of the Appalachians, and it went both ways.

Western farmers and workingmen believed Eastern businessmen were crafty and untrustworthy, allied with Republicans against Western interests. Afraid that freed blacks would compete with them for jobs, a number of Westerners opposed Republican anti-slavery measures as well, and usually voted Democratic. Ohioan Clement L. Vallandigham became the Democrats' spokesman and he and his pitchfork army of disgruntled voters proved a continual trial to Lincoln's war effort.

When Easterners weren't scorning Westerners, they were ignoring them. Then as now, major media of news and commentary were clustered on the East Coast. Easterners were preoccupied with capturing Richmond, so war correspondents, photographers, and artists preferred to follow Eastern armies. East Coast journalists easily shuttled between their offices and nearby battlefields, but Western armies were scattered over a vast landscape and—in Eastern minds—doing less important things anyway. Out of sight, inelegant, and boorish, Westerners were, for self-absorbed Easterners, largely out of mind. So was their share of the war.

The insults never ended. After the war, apologists for a defeated Confederacy created a seductive fiction known as the Lost Cause. Its mythology has given us such enduring legends as the chivalrous Southern cavalier, the infallible Robert E. Lee, the villainy of Sherman's March to the Sea, "Grant the Butcher," and the overstated horrors of Reconstruction. This gauzy version of history focused on Virginia and nearby because that's where Confederate forces had had the most success. The Confederacy's many failures elsewhere—for much of the war, in the Western Theater—were brushed over.[20] Ironically, in the postwar propaganda wars, Southerners were often the victors.

Lost Cause legends, Eastern prejudices, and geography have all created a gigantic misunderstanding of the Civil War. In many minds today, the war was a long struggle to capture Richmond, with Gettysburg the war's turning point, and the Army of the Potomac the winning team. Americans crowd Eastern battlefield parks and consume vast amounts of literature about the struggles in Virginia and nearby. They are looking for history in the wrong places. Old prejudices linger. The Midwest is unappreciated. Trollope would not be surprised.

SEEING THE WAR FROM ANOTHER ANGLE

Dismissed as a sideshow then and now, the Western Theater was where the American Civil War was decided, and it was Midwesterners who decided it. The Eastern Theater was the real sideshow, bloody and nearly pointless until early 1864, when an Ohioan named Grant came east and took charge of things. After that, fighting in the Eastern Theater—meaning Virginia—was an anti-climax, the painful encore to a settled matter. For the last year or so of the war, the South was dead on its feet, its fate sealed, but too punch-drunk or stubborn to realize it.

Too many writers—including academics who should have known better—have been seduced by habits of thought, geography and Lost Cause mythology. "Until recently ... the sprawling expanse between the Appalachian Mountains and the Mississippi River ... was something of a poor relation in Civil War historiography," an Ohio State University history professor wrote in 1996.[21]

When the enemy attacked unexpectedly, a long drum roll by an army's young drummers summoned soldiers to action.

In 2002, an independent scholar named Richard A. McMurry said, bluntly, what had to be said. "Defeat for the Rebels came in the West," he wrote. Eastern battles simply postponed the inevitable: "The victories Lee won in Virginia—and only those victories—kept the Southern nation alive two or three years beyond the time it otherwise would have expired."[22] For that unnecessary bloodletting, both sides can take the blame.

The biggest mistake the Union made in the Eastern Theater—"the one gigantic Yankee blunder," as McMurry puts it—was its obsession with capturing the Confederate capital of Richmond.[23] Lop off the head and you kill the beast was the theory, a bit of received wisdom that turned into an ideology, a mantra in the minds of the public and many soldiers.

The North's blunder was matched by the myopia of Robert E. Lee and Jefferson Davis. Neither Confederate leader understood the war as a whole the way Grant and, eventually, Lincoln did. The remarkably skillful General Lee refused to look very far beyond the borders of his beloved Virginia. He would have served his cause better by applying his talents to a larger front, as Grant did. (The British military historian and analyst Maj. Gen. J. F. C. Fuller wrote that Grant "sees the war as a whole ... far more than Lee ever saw it" and "I believe that Grant was right when he said: Lee was not a highly imaginative man."[24]

The Confederates compounded their shortsightedness with another mistake. Fired by a warrior tradition, too many commanders sacrificed the natural advantage they would have enjoyed in fighting a purely defensive war. Rebel commanders repeatedly went on the attack against the hated Yankees, squandering scarce resources of manpower and running up casualty rates exceeding Grant's. Infected with that fighting spirit, rank-and-file soldiers

The Battle of Spotsylvania Court House saw some of the fiercest hand-to-hand combat of the war unfold as the "Bloody Angle."

attacked so recklessly the Yankees sometimes thought they were intoxicated.

Nonetheless, in the Eastern Theater (eastern Virginia, plus parts of nearby Maryland and Pennsylvania), the Confederate armies handed Union forces humiliating defeats for the first three years of the war. Lee was able to cross the Potomac twice and invade Northern territory: in Maryland in 1862, ending in the battle of Antietam, and in 1863, ending with the battle of Gettysburg. Both were Union victories—but they were hollow ones. Antietam and Gettysburg were purely defensive battles that gained no territory, were fought on Northern soil at great cost, and failed to destroy Lee's army. West of the Appalachians, by contrast, the Confederates were never able to cross the Ohio River for a major invasion of the Midwest.

On offense, all the Army of the Potomac seemed able to do until early 1864 was advance about fifty miles from Washington, halfway to the Confederate capital of Richmond. Grant recalled that he came east to take overall command early in 1864, "The opposing forces stood in substantially the same relations toward each other as three years before, or when the war began."[25]

Defending Washington and the North as well as tying up Confederate troops, were important to the Union, of course, but they didn't do much to advance the quest for victory. For three years, about all both sides did was maintain the status quo. It was as if the Army of the Potomac had been mired in mud.

Things changed early in 1864. As general in chief, Grant was able to coordinate the Union's many armies and press the Confederates on all fronts, simultaneously—for the North, an elusive concept until then. With one of the

Union's two largest armies, Sherman launched his Atlanta campaign on May 7, heading for the most important city in the Confederate southeast. In Virginia with the Union's other big army, Grant had begun his Overland Campaign on May 4. He would drive Lee backward with a tenacity the Army of the Potomac had never seen before, a relentlessness that would not end until Lee surrendered. Between Grant and Sherman, the Confederacy was caught in the jaws of a vice.

Sherman captured Atlanta on September 2, a victory that helped Lincoln win re-election. Sheridan handed Lincoln another success by driving the Confederates out of the Shenandoah Valley by autumn 1864. Meanwhile, Sherman marched through eastern Georgia with little opposition, and occupied Savannah, a Christmas present to Lincoln.

Early in 1865, Sherman began drilling north through the Carolinas, his "quixotic venture" still more proof the Confederacy was a near-empty shell, unable to defend itself, with almost no claim to nationhood. In Virginia, Lee's army slowly fell apart, ragged, hungry, demoralized, thoroughly worn out. Richmond fell at last—to Grant. In April, Robert E. Lee in Virginia and Joseph E. Johnston in North Carolina, both surrendered to Western generals, finally conceding what had been apparent for some time: the great Southern rebellion had been a costly failure.

And so, the "Confederate States of America" sputtered out of existence, its armies, economy, and vaunted "way of life" in shambles, its effort to break apart the nation to preserve a master race failed, its counterrevolution against the equality promise of the Declaration of Independence squashed. The Confederacy's cause was, Grant wrote, "one of the worst for which a people ever fought, and one for which there was the least excuse."[26]

"The Confederates lost the war because they lost the battles in the West," McMurry insists.[27] William W. Freehling is among the historians who agree: "[T]he huge early losses in the West ultimately swamped the Confederates," he says.[28] In McMurry's view, for much of the war Westerners were peeling away chunks of the Confederacy between the Appalachians to the Mississippi and south of Virginia, while the fighting back East boiled down to one thing: "a bloody strategic stalemate."[29]

As historic events recede into the past, the passage of time makes them seem inevitable. From our moment in time, the outcome of the Civil War seems destined to happen the way it did. It only seems that way. If Western forces hadn't triumphed in the Western Theater and Western generals hadn't come east to finish the war, there could have been another outcome.

Turning Points

"White Southerners emerged from the Civil War thoroughly beaten but largely unrepentant," a leading historian of the war has observed.[30] The smoke had hardly cleared from the battlefields when diehards began substituting white supremacy for slavery and displacing history with the heroic legends of the Lost Cause. Preservation of what historian Sean Wilentz calls "Master Race democracy"—a sense of white community built on the backs of blacks—was at stake.[31]

While turning Lee into the "Marble Man," Grant into a plodding brute, and slavery into anything but the cause of the war and not all that bad anyway, Lost Cause thinkers also defended the honor of their soldiers. Southern armies were dashing and skillfully commanded, they argued, and, rather than being outfought, the Confederates were overwhelmed by the sheer weight of a Northern colossus that was bound to win in the end.

In Lost Cause thinking, a noble effort was doomed to die beneath a behemoth's heel. It wasn't a fair fight. A cherished anecdote has it that a Union veteran told a Southern one, "Well, we whipped you," to which the "unreconstructed rebel" replied, "No, we just wore ourselves out whipping you."[32] To which McMurry and other historians probably would say, "Nonsense."

The image of a Southerner grieving for his lost comrades was typical of the sentimental art of the Civil war era.

Most historians reject Lost Cause claims, including those of today's neo-Confederates, as a combination of denial, defensiveness, and wishful thinking. At the same time, historians doubt the inevitability of the Confederacy's defeat. The Civil War was a far closer thing than we realize, they say, and its outcome was not predetermined. "Historians today

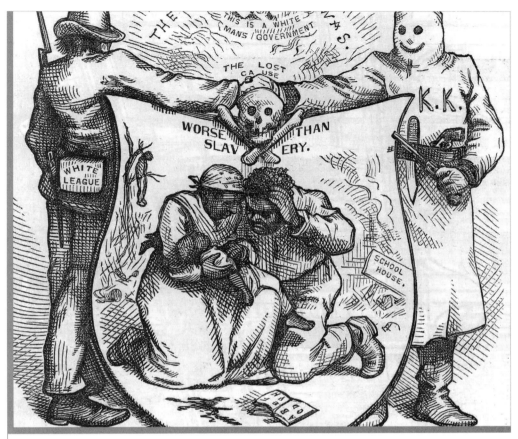

This bitter political cartoon argues post-war racial oppression by the South's "White League" and Ku Klux Klan was "worse than slavery."

generally believe that the South could have won the Civil War," says one of them, Gary W. Gallagher.[33] After all, these historians point out, history is full of examples of smaller powers defeating larger ones. (Our own American Revolution comes to mind.)

For example, the North's advantages in manpower and materials could have been countered by the South if it had stuck to fighting a defensive war. In time, a protracted Southern defense, fought without exception on the Confederacy's own ground, could have exhausted Northern patience (which, in fact, it nearly was in 1862 and 1864). That was an insight Southern leaders possessed at first, lost to a hunger for more aggressive and decisive action, then regained when it was too late. Moreover, because the Confederacy lacked the logistical genius of a Stanton, the resources it had were not fully utilized.

Between one thing and another, it is possible to see a rough parity between North and South. As a result, some historians have identified turning points when the war could have taken another direction. "For me at least," historian

Allen Guelzo has said, "nothing gives the subject [of the war] so sharp and chilling an edge as the realization it could very easily have gone the other way."[34] Several historians have come up with lists of reasons why the war could have taken another direction. Their conclusion about the war: "We could have lost it."

In 1966, historian James M. Rawley observed, "A quarter century of writing by a variety of historians appears to have sustained the idea of turning points during the Civil War." He filled a book by explaining his choice of seven, ranging from Antietam to Atlanta.[35] More recently, James McPherson came up with his own list of turning points (the Confederate failed counter-offensives in Maryland, Kentucky, and Mississippi in the latter half of 1862, for example) in his Pulitzer-Prize-winning history of the Civil War, *Battle Cry of Freedom* (which has been called "the preeminent single-volume history of the war"[36]).

In McPherson's view, not until all those pivotal times had passed—essentially, by late summer of 1864, with the capture of Atlanta and the destruction of Early's Confederates in the Shenandoah Valley—"did it become possible to speak of the inevitability of Union victory."[37]

The lists of turning points historians have made do not always agree with each other, but, collectively, they say this: the Civil War was a close thing made up of many close things. We can imagine other outcomes and remain within the realm of possibility. So why did the turning points turn the way they actually did?

We come now to the Ohioans.

HOW OHIOANS WON THE CIVIL WAR

It's not easy being flat, which a lot of Ohio is. Like being short, lack of altitude can cost you visibility and maybe *gravitas*. That could explain why Hollywood has decided Ohio is where characters in a movie should come from when they come from no place special. *Our name is Noone and we're from Erewhon,* those extraordinarily ordinary play-actors seem to be saying.

And yet Ohio was special indeed in the nineteenth century, not just one of the nation's younger states, but also one of its largest and most important, a major actor before, during, and after the Civil War. If history has turning points, the sheer size and vigor of nineteenth-century Ohio and its sons and daughters must have turned some, influencing *what* happened, or *when* or *where* it happened.

The idea of a turning point is an old one in the behavioral and physical sciences, sometimes called "the inflection point" at which "critical mass" is achieved. Critical mass doesn't have to be massive, either. In 2000, Malcolm Gladwell made that clear in *The Tipping Point: How Little Things Can Make a Big Difference*. It seems there are more tipping points in heaven and earth than we might dream.

Like snowballs, tipping points can start small and gather size and speed. Ohio had more than its share. There was what Southerners angrily referred to as "*that* book." From what Harriet Beecher Stowe saw of slavery's fleeing victims while she was living in Ohio came her powerful novel, *Uncle Tom's Cabin,* in 1852. With its iconic image of Eliza fleeing over the ice floes—*Ohio River* ice floes*,* in fact—the book aroused Northern sympathy for the slaves like nothing before—a turning point. Southerners resented the book. Also angering them—and increasingly energizing the North—were those who were conducting the Underground Railroad. Ohio's "system" for helping slaves escape was the largest west of the Appalachians.

Always fearful of a slave revolt and aggravated by *Uncle Tom's Cabin,* the Underground Railroad, and endless hectoring by abolitionists, some of the loudest of whom were Ohioans, Southerners were convinced by John Brown's raid in 1859 that Northerners hoped to cause an insurrection. Brown gave us another turning point. With Southerners in near-hysteria, it took only the election of Lincoln to trigger secession. Professor David S. Reynolds summed up the Ohio fanatic's influence in the title of his 2005 book, *John Brown, Abolitionist: The Man Who Killed Slavery, Sparked the Civil War, and Seeded Civil Rights.*[38]

Other Ohio influentials, among them the Western Anti-Slavery Society, Oberlin College, and outspoken religionists like Theodore Weld and John Rankin, rallied popular feeling against slavery in the pre-war years. Just when, how, and where, if ever, the Civil War would have broken out is unknowable, but this seems likely: Ohioans had a lot to do with when it did.

Like other Northern states, Ohio "won the war" through the courage, persistence, and sacrifice of its people, as has been described here. So many states affected the course of the struggle it is hard to imagine the same outcome absent any of them. All things considered, however, no state and its offpsring had more connections to the war's outcome than Ohio. No state and its progeny played a larger part in Union victory than the Buckeye state. That so many turning points in the war turned the way they did was affected by three things in particular: *the numbers of Ohio's people* participating, *the leadership of Ohioans*, and *the Western personalities* of both.

Some of Ohio's soldiers marching off to war were given a bounteous repast at Cincinnati's Fifth Street Market, a muster point for troops.

The Numbers

Ohio furnished an estimated three-hundred thousand soldiers, more than any other state in the Western Theater, the region where the outcome of the war was settled. Among *all* Union states, east and west, Ohio provided the third largest number of troops, second only to New York and Pennsylvania, the only two states with larger populations than Ohio at that time.*

Most of Ohio's infantry regiments, artillery batteries, and cavalry units operated in the Western Theater, although some fought in the Eastern Theater and other regions. While Ohioans were never a majority at any major battle, they so often formed a substantial minority—often the largest among the states represented—that it is hard to imagine many Union victories without them.

On the first day of battle at Shiloh, Grant's Army of the Tennessee was nearly pushed into the river, but held onto a sliver of battlefield long enough to receive reinforcements the next day and go on to victory. On that first day, about seventeen percent of Grant's infantry regiments were Ohioan, many of whom received Johnston's initial attack and slowed it down. Grant couldn't have survived without them.

Joined the next day by Lew Wallace's division and Buell's Army of the

* Civil War records count only enlistments, not individuals. Because some individuals enlisted more than once and because of other record-keeping issues, we cannot be sure how many men—as opposed to enlistments—Ohio provided. The author estimates the number of individuals to be about 300,000. The number of enlistments recorded was 319,659, according to Eicher and Eicher's *Civil War High Commands* (p. 53). These numbers, while not exact, are useful in comparisons with those of other states.

Ohio, Union forces beat the surprisingly stubborn Confederates into retreat, though not easily. With fewer troops, Union forces would have had a hard time prevailing when they did, if they prevailed at all. In Wallace's division, roughly half the infantry regiments were Ohioans, and in Buell's army, about thirty percent of the infantry regiments were Ohioan. Overall, about a fifth of the forces at Shiloh were from Ohio.[39]

The large numbers of Ohioans participating in battles later in 1862, at Perryville, Corinth, and Stones River—all close fights—suggest similar conclusions. In Grant's successful siege of Vicksburg in 1863, a truly pivotal victory that re-opened the Mississippi River to Western commerce, about eighteen percent of his infantry and thirty percent of his artillery were Ohioan.[40] While the Union victory at Gettysburg recovered no long-lost territory, Vicksburg did.

Bitter, last-ditch fighting on Chickamauga's Horseshoe Ridge by Thomas's command and Steedman's reserve division, both enrolling many Ohioans, allowed the greater part of Rosecrans's army to escape to the safety of Chattanooga. To that time, Chickamauga was the one major Union defeat in the Western Theater, compared to several in the Eastern Theater. In the battles of Chattanooga in November, a successful assault on Mission Ridge by Thomas's Army of the Cumberland, which included thirty-one Ohio regiments, finished the fight in the Union's favor.[41]

So it went for the rest of the war. About fourteen thousand Ohioans participated in Sherman's March to the Sea. About a fourth of the forces crushing Hood at Nashville were Ohio infantrymen and artillerymen.[42] By the end of the war, more troops from Ohio than any other state had spent time in western Virginia, protecting loyalists as they carved a free state of West Virginia out of the Old Dominion.

Ohioans participated, though in smaller numbers, in almost every Eastern Theater campaign, with several regiments in the thick of the fighting at Antietam and Gettysburg, and, later, Sheridan's Shenandoah Valley Campaign, as well as Grant's Overland, Petersburg, and Appomattox campaigns.

One other statistic speaks for itself. No other state *but one* lost as many men to death from wounds and disease. Of the three-hundred thousand lives Ohio sent into war, 35,475—one of every ten—never returned.[43]

THE LEADERS

On March 10, 1864, in a letter marked PRIVATE AND CONFIDENTIAL and probably written on the steamboat *Westmoreland* as it shuddered and shook its way up the Mississippi, heading for Memphis, Maj. Gen. William Tecumseh Sherman (born and raised in Lancaster, Ohio) wrote to his friend, Ulysses S. Grant (born in Point Pleasant and raised in Georgetown, Ohio). Grant was about to become the nation's general in chief, the job George Washington originated, and Sherman told him:

> I believe you are as brave, patriotic, and just, as the great prototype Washington; as unselfish, kind-hearted, and honest, as a man should be; but the chief characteristic of your nature is the simple faith in success you have always manifested, which I can liken to nothing else than the faith a Christian has in his Saviour.
>
> This faith gave you victory at Shiloh and Vicksburg. Also, when you have completed your best preparations, you go in to battle without hesitation, as at Chattanooga—no doubts, no reserve; and I tell you that it was this that made us act with confidence. I knew wherever I was that you thought of me, and if I got in a tight place you would come—if alive.
>
> My only points of doubt were as to your knowledge of grand strategy, and of books of science and history; but I confess your common-sense seems to have supplied all this.[44]

Nearly a century later, British Maj. Gen. J. F. C. Fuller published a study of Grant and Lee intended "to examine the influence of personality upon generalship."[45] "At base, seven-eighths of the history of war is psychological," Fuller asserted, and he quoted a European military authority: "The human heart is the starting point in all matters pertaining to war."[46] Grant, Fuller concluded, was a better general than Lee and for some of the same reasons cited by Sherman. Grant seemed to intuitively understand not only the battlefield, but also the larger war on all its fronts; unlike Lee, whose genius was at the battlefield level, he could move between theaters because they were all part of one big picture.

Despite years of Lost Cause burnishing of Lee's image, most professional historians consider Grant the war's greatest commander. Efforts by Southern detractors to paint Grant as a "butcher" for his 1864 Overland Campaign in Virginia fail under close examination. Historian Gordon C. Rhea, for example, found in that campaign that Grant "was losing soldiers at a lower percentage than his adversary [Lee]" and that "[n]o single day of Grant's pounding" of Lee saw as many casualties as the ever-cautious McClellan incurred at Antietam.[47] Taking the long view in 1890, former Confederate commander

General Grant's horsemanship was impressive, but his typical attire included a Western-style slouch hat, enlisted man's uniform, and muddy boots.

James Longstreet, Lee's "old warhorse," wrote of Grant, "He eclipses us all."[48]

In 2003, six historians had a panel discussion to settle on the Civil War's "Top Ten Generals" from both sides. They ranked Grant first of all, Lee second. Sherman ranked third among all generals, on average, and three panelists included Ohio's Philip Sheridan among their top ten. George Thomas, the loyal Virginian, was the only other Union commander mentioned more than once by the panelists.[49] (A survey by *The Atlantic* magazine, published in its December 2006 issue, reported the consensus opinion of "ten eminent historians" was that, of the hundred most influential Americans of all time, Grant ranked twelfth among them all, and among the generals, second only to Washington. Lincoln was rated the most influential American in history.)

Sherman considered himself the more cerebral of the Union's two leading generals, Grant the more intuitive. In rising to leadership himself, Sherman first had to find his center of gravity. Helping him do it were his old friend Halleck; his wife Ellen—always Cump's protector when he needed one—and Grant, who provided the kind of emotional anchor and safe harbor that Julia gave Ulysses. In Sherman's first battlefield success, his surefooted handling of his division at Shiloh, he proved to himself that he had the right stuff, and after that, combat only tempered him.

Union soldiers went into combat with leather bullet cases holding forty rounds of ammunition.

Sherman was not a great tactician, but a creative thinker who pondered Grant's all-fronts plan for ending the war and put his own spin on it. He, too, had a larger vision of the war. Grant wanted Sherman to concentrate on destroying Joe Johnston's army in Georgia. Without saying he wouldn't do it, Sherman had a better idea: slice southeastward through Georgia, maneuvering Johnston steadily backward while avoiding head-on battle as much as possible.

Sherman's objective: capture Atlanta, jewel of the Deep South, then continue eastward to the sea, laying waste to a wide swath of Georgia, living off the land, and showing the world in general and Southerners in particular that their so-called nation was a fiction, unable to even protect its heartland. After that, his troops could drive north through the Carolinas, falling like wolves on that cockpit of rebellion and fountain of insolence, South Carolina, and perhaps link up with Grant, leaving the Confederacy mentally and physically in shreds.

Sherman had lived in the South and liked it and its people while remaining agnostic on the issue of slavery, but he could not forgive Confederates for their disloyalty and the rebellion they caused. To those who (hypocritically, in Sherman's mind) protested his invasion of the Confederate heartland, Sherman had an answer:

> *If the people raise a howl against my barbarity and cruelty, I will answer that war is war, and not popularity-seeking. If they want peace, they and their relatives must stop the war.*[50]

It was in Sherman's sense that war cannot succeed without the support of its people and Grant's that it has to be pressed on all fronts simultaneously that Union success was built. Some generals fought only battles. Grant and Sherman fought a war.

Philip Sheridan was another important commander, born somewhere else (we're not quite sure where), but raised from infancy in Somerset, Ohio. Sheridan succeeded in warfare through sheer audacity on horseback and a ruthlessness that liked "to smash things," although he rose to prominence later than Grant and Sherman.

Other Ohioans made contributions as well. For example, William Rosecrans, born in Delaware County, Ohio, was an effective if willful commander who played a useful role until his meltdown at Chickamauga. Two dozen of the Union's major or brigadier generals were Ohioans educated at West Point. Less well-known but critical to the Union's success were the hundreds of colonels who braved shot and shell to command men on the front lines. These Ohioans left jobs as lawyers, bankers, and businessmen to study tactics in their tents by night and train their regiments by day. The Union could not have prevailed without the leadership of those largely self-taught citizen-soldiers, seven of whom rose to the rank of major general. Dozens more became brigadier generals, or generals by brevet (an honorary title). None had the benefit of professional military education.[51]

Less eye-catching than the warriors but just as critical to the war effort was the work of Secretary of War Edwin M. Stanton, born and raised in Steubenville. "The Confederacy's military problem was not inadequate southern resources but inadequate ability to marshal all resources," historian William W. Freehling insists. By contrast, Stanton far outstripped his Southern rivals in collecting soldiers and military supplies and getting them to where they were needed. If "[s]uperior marshaling of superior resources triumphs [in warfare]," as Freehling believes, then Stanton deserves the credit.[52]

Stanton did more than manage logistics. He became Lincoln's closest advisor, the president spending more time with him "than any other Cabinet officer," according to Stanton's biographers.[53] "Stanton and Lincoln virtually conducted the war together," they concluded. Though very different personalities, the two men not only developed a warm, intimate friendship, but also they complemented each other, so that Stanton and Lincoln can be described, respectively, as the "[h]ead and heart of the war."[54]

Two other civilians, adopted Ohioans who spent important parts of their lives in the state, were at the nexus of the Union war effort. Secretary of the

Treasury Salmon P. Chase (born in New Hampshire, but moved to Ohio as a young man) found the money needed to feed the hungry Union war machine, much of it from Philadelphia banker Jay Cooke, who had been born and raised in Sandusky, Ohio. Chase also pressed a cautious Lincoln to end slavery and improve civil rights. Another Ohioan prominent in the war was the combative Sen. Benjamin F. Wade, a Radical Republican bitterly opposed to slavery. He used his Joint Congressional Committee on the Conduct of the War to keep a close watch on the military and to relentlessly pressure Lincoln on behalf of abolition and the blacks.

At the outbreak of war, native Ohioans Grant, Sherman, and Stanton had addresses elsewhere. Nonetheless, by birth and nurture, these three Midwesterners are best described as Ohioans. Each spent more years of his life, including the formative years of childhood and youth, in Ohio than in any other single place. Galena, Illinois, where Grant lived for scarcely a year, unabashedly calls him "Our Citizen."* Ohioans can call him "Our Son."

THE WESTERN PERSONALITY

Rural aristocrats conserving the grand old values or pretentious layabouts brutalizing a helpless people. Well-mannered wealth-builders or crafty nutmeg peddlers. Honest, self-reliant men and women or violent louts. Those were some of the opposing images nineteenth-century Americans—Southerners, Northeasterners, and Westerners, respectively—had of each other.

The extent to which anyone can marshal brute facts to support or deny these perceptions doesn't matter, not that they will stop trying. What matters is that perceptions like these seemed true for many people of the nineteenth century, forming their realities and influencing their behavior.

The idea that reality is what people make of it was introduced to the social and behavioral sciences years ago by sociologists Peter L. Berger and Thomas Luckman, whose "Social Construction of Reality" explains how you and I think we "know" things. What we know depends on what's in our heads—a way, perhaps, of dealing with that pesky question about a tree falling in the forest. The answer, of course, if you can see and hear it *in your mind,* you are apt to believe it.

In nineteenth-century America, lots of people thought they heard trees falling, and that made a difference to how they behaved in matters small and large. Where it made the largest difference of all: how people behaved during

* The phrase "Our Citizen" appears on the base of Galena's larger-than-life statue of Grant.

the Civil War. The pioneering demonstration of this is Michael C. C. Adams's 1978 book *Our Masters the Rebels: A Speculation on Union Military Failure in the East 1861–1865*.[55] Echoing Berger and Luckman, he explained, "[M]en do not necessarily act on what is objectively true but on what they perceive as the truth."[56]

And these were the truths for South and North. Southerners told each other endlessly that one Confederate was worth three-to-ten Yankees in fighting ability. They believed that the citified, sissified Northerneasterners, corrupted by vulgar pursuit of the dollar, could not stand up to men raised outdoors and on horseback, imbued with Southerners' traditions of honor, military prowess, and civilian violence. With that as his reality, the screaming Confederate soldier charged the enemy with a recklessness and disregard for his own life that stunned Union men.

The Southern *joie de guerre* so stunned Northerners that early victories by Confederates in the Eastern Theater fatally sapped the confidence of Union soldiers there. Combined with the inadequacies Union generals brought to the field, it immobilized McClellan and Meade, panicked Hooker, and confused Burnside, McDowell, and Pope. Like a virus infecting the human body, their hesitations filtered through the Union army, sapping its confidence with the deadly virus of self-doubt.

The ironic result, according to Adams: "Those Union soldiers with the *least confidence* faced the rebels with the *most self-esteem*—in Virginia."[57] Perception meeting perception, to the advantage of the Confederates. Walt Whitman observed after First Bull Run, "Resolution, manliness, seem to have abandoned Washington."[58] One of Lincoln's Cabinet members said the Confederacy felt safe in defying the North "because we hurt nobody, we frighten nobody, and we do our utmost to offend nobody."[59] A well-educated European immigrant who joined the Union cause commented, "The rebels, our masters, [are] taking our leaders by the nose."[60] Grant wrote, "The Northern press, as a whole … always magnified rebel success and belittled ours."[61]

Northeastern troops and their commanders were so intimidated for so much of the war, Adams contends, that expectation became reality: they turned into the losers they feared they might become. It was different in the Western Theater, where the troops came largely from a galaxy of Midwestern states, of which Ohio was the largest in population.

Here, in the 1860s, far more families worked the land than those in the Northeast. All Ohioans of European descent were recent descendents of pioneers, if not pioneers themselves, the frontier lingering in the collective memory. There were still old-timers in Ohio in the 1860s who had arrived before statehood and could tell tales of when the region was a howling wilderness, the roads no more than muddy trails, the memories of dangerous Indians still fresh. It took courage and perseverance to be a pioneer, and pioneers tended to raise children who understood those qualities.

Pushing into the wilderness, carving farms out of a dark and ancient forest, and trying to make a living in the face of unpredictable weather toughened the men and women of this place. To survive in the developing Midwest, you had to be self-reliant, accustomed to deprivation, and prepared for hardships in which Eastern niceties were of little help. That tough-minded pragmatism, with disdain for the delicacies and refinements of urban life, were exactly the qualities needed for effective soldiering in this war, despite all the sniffing by Easterners at Westerners' ragged appearance, orneriness, and body odor.

The fighting in the Western Theater was done largely by Western troops, most of them farmers with calloused hands, from Ohio, Indiana, Illinois, and nearby. They were rough men used to dealing with all the setbacks and deprivations that trying to make a living from the soil can throw at people. They were scornful of army spit-and-polish and not afraid to show it. (When an officious general at Perryville tried to chastise some Indianans for showing him insufficient respect, they threatened to kill him and jabbed his horse with a bayonet, causing the animal—and its rider—to bolt.[62])

Inured to hardship and hard times, Western soldiers were endowed with a tremendous capacity to absorb punishment and dish it out with interest. Raised in a land not far removed from frontier conditions, used to working by the sweat of their brows, forced to cope with the merciless vagaries of weather and crops, and on a first-name basis with hardship, Western men were not easily discouraged. In the Eastern Theater, failure or hollow victory followed by retreat for refitting and recuperation was the norm until 1864, but troops in the Western Theater tramped thousands of miles with few comforts, persevering despite heat, cold, hunger, and a stubborn foe, to score victory after victory.

Ohioans shared their "Westernness" with the other Western states, of course. Combined with their numbers and their leaders, Ohioans provided enough force to turn enough turning points to win the war. But Ohio did more than send President Lincoln fighting men with staying power and commanders imbued with large vision. Supporting the men and keeping the state working were their families, who had to bear the fear, loneliness, and hardship while their men were away. The war's first big soldiers' aid society was established in Cleveland exclusively by women, and the ensuing network of Sanitary

Commission chapters, staffed primarily by volunteer women, supplied Western armies with huge amounts of medical supplies, food, and clothing. Ohio was a breadbasket and a warehouse for the Union.

With the most mileage of railroad track in the nation, the state was a crossroads for Union supply and troop trains. Night and day, trailing smoke and showering sparks from their bell-shaped smokestacks, high-wheeled locomotives raced across Ohio with reinforcements for the Union armies. The state offered other advantages to the Union cause. It boasted the nation's largest number of horses, a critical need for transportation and cavalry operations. Ohio's sheep, more than in any other state, supplied the wool that substituted for the South's cotton. Ohio was a manufacturer of uniforms, weapons, and wagons, and the state was an immense grower of wheat, corn, and other foodstuffs.

The prominence of Ohio in the nineteenth century, almost forgotten in the twenty-first, continued after the war. Ohio sent four men to the White House, joined by an Indianan who had been born in Ohio. Between them, Ulysses S. Grant, Rutherford B. Hayes, James A. Garfield, Benjamin Harrison (the Indianan), and William McKinley occupied the presidency for almost half the years between 1869 and 1901. All had served in the Civil War; all were Republicans endorsed by the Grand Army of the Republic, a powerful organization of Civil War veterans. Only with the assassination of William McKinley in 1901 can it be said that Ohio's prominence because of the Civil War had ended.

Geographically, Ohio was situated on the edge of the Civil War, but its role in supplying tough, confident soldiers supported by strong families and led by commanders with vision made the state pivotal to the war's outcome.

The Natural Man

The Founding Fathers asserted in the Declaration of Independence the idea that all men are created equal is a "self-evident" truth. In fact, you had to be a political liberal like Thomas Jefferson, not a Tory, to see anything self-evident about it. Nonetheless, it was a claim with a reasoned foundation.

A few decades before Jefferson and company wrote the Declaration, Scottish academics and deep thinkers in Edinburgh were threshing out the meaning of life, debating ideas like "natural law" and the "rights of man" as they strolled Middle Meadow Walk or drank Madeira late into the clammy Lowlands night.

These intellectual Bravehearts caused an intellectual ferment by challenging

In an age when generals preferred stiffly formal portraits, Grant (in this Matthew Brady picture) allowed himself to be photographed leaning against a tree.

established religion as well as all ossified authority, tradition, and superstition. They asserted that human beings were imbued with a sufficient sense of justice and power of reason to discover what laws *naturally* should govern mankind, instead of having it imposed on them by those claiming a private line to God or a divine right to govern. We know this source of reasoned, humanistic thinking as the Enlightenment, and it is the foundation of American democracy.

An element of Enlightenment thinking at the time was that "natural man," unspoiled by city living and uncomplicated by the Industrial Revolution, could best understand life and divine natural law. It was thought that the intuition or "common sense" of "natural man" would arise more effectively in lives unfettered by the hurly-burly of daily commerce and the gaudy sophistications of complex society. In one of the most striking coincidences in American history, Ulysses S. Grant emerged as a "natural man" in defense of "natural rights." As Sherman put it, "I confess your common-sense seems to have supplied all" that Grant needed to know to lead Union forces.[63] Grant's self-confident "simplicity," forthrightness, and honesty, together with his ability to scan a battlefield and see things as they really were, were characteristic of the "natural man" and impressed onlookers repeatedly.

Horace Porter, an aide at Grant's side throughout most of his Eastern campaigns, saw again and again that "while the most critical movements were taking place, General Grant manifested no perceptible anxiety ... but gave his orders, and sent and received communications, with a coolness and deliberation" that impressed everyone nearby. In "sudden emergencies … General Grant was always at his best. His sense of proportion never deserted him," Porter said.[64]

In the last analysis, the Civil War was fought to preserve the "electric cord," as Lincoln termed it, that connects living generations to the Equality Promise Jefferson found in the Enlightenment's concept of natural man. It was the Union's good fortune that the man who commanded the armies that won the war and preserved the electric cord was himself a "natural man."

SOMEBODY'S DARLIN'

The dead, the dead, the dead, Walt Whitman scribbled in his notebook, *somewhere they crawl'd to die, alone, in bushes, low gullies, or on the sides of hills—(there, in secluded spots, their skeletons, bleach'd bones, tufts of hair, buttons, fragments of clothing, are occasionally found yet)—our young men once so handsome and joyous.*[65]

The war notes of the Good Gray Poet were published in 1892, one of the plump years of the Gilded Age and the year he died. The United States was turning into the greatest industrial power on earth and feeling good about itself, certain of its rectitude despite plundering Robber Barons, the growing distance between the rich and poor, and "conspicuous consumption" by the minority who could afford it.[66]* Smokestacks were shooting up in Ohio cities, beautiful ladies were dancing Viennese waltzes in Cincinnati ballrooms, and Cleveland's Mark Hanna, plutocrat turned kingmaker, was grooming Ohio Gov. William McKinley for bigger things.

The Civil War was almost forgotten. Bleached bones still lay in a few secluded spots, but the time of anguished mourning for lost boys in blue had passed. Soon, boys from North and South alike would be fighting side by side in the Spanish-American War, an imperialist adventure that would yield new candidates for the nation's soldiers' homes.

Nearly a generation after Appomattox, the Civil War was turning into an historical curiosity for Americans, an artifact of other times and other people. Most veterans had rounded the bend of middle age and were beginning to sense how the road to the Last Encampment was shortening, their relevance to current affairs diminishing.

* The phrase "conspicuous consumption" comes from economist and sociologist Thorstein Veblen's book, *The Theory of the Leisure Class*, a study of the behavior of the nouveau riche. First published in 1899, the book is still in print.

After a battle, soldiers searched the field for comrades who had fallen in combat. Desperate men plundered corpses for food or ammunition.

Responding to time's threat to memory, the old soldiers had been mounting a whirlwind of effort since the 1880s to erect monuments and write the memoirs and regimental histories that would memorialize their deeds. Today, those efforts stand on library shelves and in cemeteries and parks throughout Ohio, waiting to speak to us.

Men who have fought in a war doubt that civilians can ever comprehend what they went through or how a soldier's past is never really past. Capt. John Hartzell, writing his memoirs in 1898, told his family:

> You never stood in line of battle and heard the quick command, "Commence firing," and you never heard the snappy crackle of a thousand triggers, as, with thumb on hammer, the men flung the butts of their muskets to shoulder—ominous music. Well, you can't understand what I'm trying to tell you very well. It is only the fellow who has heard that crackle as it ran through the firing line, and has staid until the curtain fell who can understand it. Once heard, it is not easy to forget, but I don't recommend the music.[67]

To tell their stories to those who could understand, to recreate the mystical brotherhood that can be forged only in war, and to hold off the demons, Civil War veterans formed a new army not long after leaving the old one. It was called the Grand Army of the Republic.

The G.A.R. was founded by a handful of Midwestern Union veterans on April 6, 1866, in Decatur, Illinois. By 1890, national membership reached a peak of 409,489 in more than 7,000 chapters.[68] Created for camaraderie, the organizations went on to perform charitable work, establish soldiers' and orphans' homes, press for veterans' benefits, and develop a voice that politicians took seriously. Through the late nineteenth century, no Republican could be nominated for president without the G.A.R.'s endorsement.[69]

The G.A.R, was a voluntary, democratic organization—members addressed each other as "comrade"—but it had military touches. It called its local chapters "posts" and its elected leaders "commanders." In 1868, at the request of Commander-in-Chief "Black Jack" Logan, it began decorating veterans' graves on May 30.

The G.A.R.'s most public rituals were the Memorial Day and Fourth of July parades in which old soldiers, wearing their best suits, tried to keep in step as they marched down Main Street. With upwards of seven hundred G.A.R. posts in Ohio alone, meetings of Civil War veterans were a regular feature of life in almost every town and hamlet. During the eighty-three years the G.A.R. held national encampments, Ohio hosted twelve, more than any other state.[70]

The national encampment in Columbus in 1888 attracted tens of thousands of "wrinkled and gray 'boys' of 1861," as one reporter put it.[71] The city had sought the honor of hosting the encampment, much as modern cities seek the Olympics, and had made elaborate preparations. No official count was taken, but the Columbus encampment was thought to be the largest assemblage of the men of the Civil War since the Grand Review in Washington in 1865. For all that, it was not the most newsworthy, for in 1913 something more remarkable happened.

Several years earlier, in a rare instance of enlightened forward-thinking by politicians, the Pennsylvania legislature realized that the fiftieth anniversary of the battle of Gettysburg would occur in 1913. The legislators voted to support a reunion at the battlefield open to all veterans of the Civil War, regardless of the side for which they had fought. Pennsylvania and the federal government appropriated substantial sums to fund the event. It turned out to be a landmark act of healing.

With half the Civil War's veterans dead by 1913, and those remaining mostly in their seventies, reunion organizers weren't expecting the massive response they got. Legions of elderly citizen-soldiers headed for Gettysburg as if they were hearing the long drum roll once again. Between 45,000 and 54,000 veterans from 41 states—at least 657 from Ohio, and probably many more—poured into the town, beginning on June 28, 1913. Veterans from North and South filled every hotel room as well as a sea of 5,000 tents that covered 280 acres of the battlefield.[72]

Fifty years before, Yankees and the Rebels came here to kill each other. In three terrible days they turned the little town into a charnel house that consumed the lives, health, or freedom of fifty-one thousand men, more than any other Civil War battle. This time, the men came to make peace. Bonded by their survival of something terrible, old adversaries greeted one another joyfully, shaking hands, pounding each other on the back, sharing tents, and exchanging whoops and shouts, the Yanks even cheering when they heard the "Rebel Yell."[73]

As it had in 1863, the battlefield simmered under a grueling sun, but the old soldiers climbed its ridges and rocky dens with astounding energy. Union and Confederate veterans pointed out landmarks to each other, recalling who got shot where. On July 3, precisely at 3 p.m., fifty years later to the hour, Pickett's Charge was recreated by six hundred of the men who had participated the first time.

Most of the men in "Pickett's Second Charge" wore the suits, neckties, and fedoras expected of gentlemen at the time, but some were in their old blue or gray uniforms. About three hundred old Confederates emerged from the woods and, waving their hats, pottered toward the stone wall that had formed the battle's famous "Bloody Angle."

Sitting on the wall this time instead of crouching behind it, three hundred elderly Union men waited. The ground rose sharply the last few feet to the wall, but smiling Federals reached down to pull up the Confederates, and suddenly Blue and Gray were mingling together, embracing, shaking hands, showing each other where they had been that day when they had first met. The old men did not leave until sundown, and then they departed slowly, together, down the Emmitsburg Road. "Pickett's Second Charge" ended with Billy Yank and Johnny Reb walking side by side.[74]

At noon the next day, July 4, the old soldiers stood silently as church bells tolled, Union and Confederate buglers sounded taps, and cannons boomed a final salute. Having eluded death for a few days and completed their mission, the veterans headed home, where they resumed dying at their usual rate.

Recognizing the fragility of their elderly guests and expecting hundreds of casualties, the hosts at Gettysburg had set up two field hospitals, three regimental hospitals, and twenty first aid stations staffed by a large force of army surgeons and Red Cross nurses.[75] They were scarcely needed. Astonishingly, only nine men died at the reunion, far below their ordinary mortality rate.

The old warriors had pulled themselves together for one last campaign, this time for friendship. Once home, their ranks kept thinning precipitously. Almost every year the G.A.R.'s membership dropped by five or ten thousand. At the

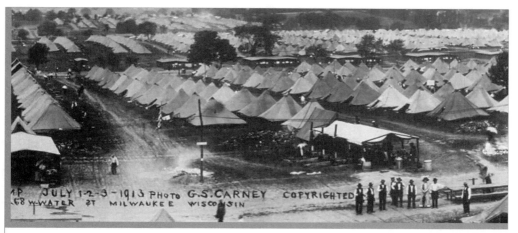

In 1913, fifty years after the carnage at the Battle of Gettysburg, tens of thousands of veterans from north and south returned for a friendly reunion.

75th anniversary reunion at Gettysburg in 1938, only 1,800 veterans appeared. By 1949, membership in the G.A.R. had dwindled to sixteen, only four more than the number who formed the first post.

In the tiny northeastern Ohio town of Atwater that year, John Henry Grate, a private in the 6th Ohio Volunteer Cavalry, had been planning a Memorial Weekend ceremony to close the books of the Ohio Department of the G.A.R. Grate, who had served under Sheridan, was the organization's national commander in chief and for fifteen years had commanded the Alliance, Ohio, post.

Now 103 years old, Private Grate conceded that he could no longer "carry on in the tradition of an active soldier." Before the closing ceremony could be held, however, Grate—cavalryman, private, and comrade—took ill and died at his home.[76]

Grate's death in 1949 left one Ohioan still living in the state he had served. In the northwest Ohio town of Wauseon, Daniel Clingaman was comfortably spinning out his days on the farm he had cleared in 1882, a few years after returning from service in the 195th Ohio. Clingaman had joined Union forces shortly after becoming old enough, but also shortly before the end of the war, so he saw only guard duty.

Viewing it as national news, the *New York Times* reported Clingaman's 104th birthday on September 25, 1950. Later, in a "Report from Wauseon" feature story, the *Times* included some of the details of Clingaman's life. The last of Ohio's three hundred thousand Civil War servicemen, "Uncle Dan" pepped up each day by smoking two cigars, one in the morning and one in the afternoon. On Saturdays he went to town "to be barbered."

Hundreds of Union soldiers—including Ohioans—who fell at Gettysburg are buried in the cemetery there.

The *Times* told how ex-Private Clingaman arose early every day, ate, and slept "like a farmer," appeared in parades and ceremonies whenever called upon, and offered "no theories about longevity."[77] Uncle Dan did not reach his 105th birthday, however, for he died on February 18, 1951.[78]

With ex-Private Daniel Clingaman's passing, the long blue line of Ohio's citizen-soldiers came to an end, gone but sturdily memorialized in parks, cemeteries, and public squares throughout the state. The memorials take various forms: tall columns topped by eagles, obelisks, plaques on stone blocks, and statues.

A few of the statues honor the famous: Ulysses S. Grant in Columbus, Philip Sheridan astride a horse in Somerset, William Tecumseh Sherman firmly (and unwillingly, if he had anything to say about it) anchored in Lancaster in front of the Chamber of Commerce. The most common statues, however, are the 120 figures of ordinary, anonymous soldiers standing in Ohio's cemeteries and parks.

Like the men they represent, they stand on guard night and day, hands on rifles, eyes fixed on distant tree lines, waiting for the long drum roll that summoned soldiers to action. Numbering only a few more than a regulation company, the figures represent the 300,000 Ohioans, most of them volunteers, who left their fields, schoolrooms, and law offices, saved the nation, and freed a people.

Hearts and minds nurtured in the Midwest, most of all in Ohio, supplied the leadership of Grant, Sherman, and Stanton. Those three, in addition to another Midwesterner named Lincoln, brought the Union a victory that was far less assured than we might think. The war, historians suggest, was a close thing with turning points that could have turned the other way.

With its huge outpouring of soldiers, the largest in the Western Theater, Ohio's manpower supplied the margin of victory in some of the most important battles in the Western Theater—where, in fact, the war was decided. And Ohioans and their allies not only preserved the Union and freed the slaves, but also, in Lincoln's eyes, saved the "electric cord" that connects Americans to the equality promise of the Declaration of Independence: *All men are created equal* ... entitled to equal opportunity to advance themselves, to voice in government, and to justice before the law.

The Ohioans had been both citizens and soldiers. Most of all, they were ordinary people who did extraordinary things. Some never came home and some came home to die before their time, but all lived their lives, short or long, knowing they had done something noble and true. They were not alone in that effort: unseen in the parks and cemeteries, but present in memory, are the neighbors, friends, and family who stood behind the soldiers—their sons, brothers, husbands, and fathers. Through the hard times of war, the soldiers were cherished not only for what they did, but also for who they were. Each and every one had been somebody's darlin'.

The battles of Chattanooga began at Orchard Knob, a low promontory that today bristles with memorials to the men who fought there.

To Learn More:

Richard M. McMurry's *The Fourth Battle of Winchester: Toward a New Civil War Paradigm* argues that the Civil War's outcome was settled in the Western Theater. The reasons for the greatness of Grant and Sherman's generalship are laid out by two esteemed British military historians: Maj. Gen. J.F.C. Fuller, in *Grant and Lee: A Study in Personality and Leadership*, and B.H. Liddell Hart in *Sherman: Soldier, Realist, American*.

For more information about Ohio's role in the Civil War, there are two excellent starting points: Whitelaw Reid's two-volume *Ohio in the War: Her Statesmen, Generals, and Soldiers*, found in many Ohio libraries, and an extremely useful bibliography of every Ohio unit that served in the war, "Ohio in the Civil War," maintained by Larry Stevens at **http://ohiocivilwar.com**.

Ohio's Civil War soldiers and leaders are buried throughout the state, in small cemeteries and large. In some places, cannon and statues commemorate the soldiers. In the nation's second largest cemetery, Cincinnati's Spring Grove Cemetery (**www.springgrove.org** or **513-681-7526**) 4521 Spring Grove Ave., Cincinnati, are buried more than forty Civil War generals (including "Fighting Joe" Hooker) and leaders (Salmon P. Chase among them), as well as many less well-known figures. Among other important burial grounds for veterans are Woodland Cemetery, 118 Woodland Ave., Dayton (**www.woodlandcemetery.org** or **937-228-3221**) where political opponents Robert C. Schenck and Clement L. Vallandigham both rest; Green Lawn Cemetery, 1000 Greenlawn Avenue, Columbus (**http://www.greenlawncolumbus.org/** or **614-444-1123**), the last resting place of Gov. William Dennison, and Glendale Cemetery, 150 Glendale Ave., Akron (**330-253-2317**).

17

THE REST OF THEIR STORIES

With the death of Abraham Lincoln, Ulysses S. Grant emerged as the nation's greatest living hero, rhapsodized by a Cleveland newspaper as "he of the magical name, the Captor of Armies, Generals and Strong Holds, the Slayer of the Dragon, the Savior of the Republic, and the Idol of all hearts."[1] After the war was over, Grant remained in prominence, continuing to serve as general in chief of the army. Congress also promoted him to four-star general, the nation's first.

Then, in 1868, Grant was unanimously acclaimed the Republican candidate for president. He hadn't harbored presidential ambitions, but once again, duty called and Grant felt obliged to serve. Elected to the nation's highest office, he was re-elected in 1872, both times by wide margins.

Master of warfare and a man of surpassing personal integrity, Grant presided calmly over one of the most corrupt administrations in American history, seemingly unaware of what was going on around him. James Garfield told his diary, "His imperturbability is amazing. I am in doubt whether to call it greatness or stupidity."[2] Grant, the man who missed nothing on the battlefield but turned into the oblivious president, puzzles us to this day.

After retiring from the presidency, Grant was reduced to near-poverty by a charlatan and forced to sell even his presentation swords and Congressional gold medal. To support his family he turned to writing his war memoirs. Soon he was being mentored by Mark Twain, who affectionately called the retired general "the most simple-hearted of all men," a man who was trusting to the point of gullibility.[3]

Their faces are solemn, but, surrounded by their children and joined by his mother in this picture circa 1882, Lucretia (left) and James Garfield had finally achieved marital happiness.

In the summer of 1884, Grant shuddered in pain as he ate a peach. Drinking water felt like "liquid fire." It was throat cancer, caused, perhaps, by years of smoking cigars. In constant pain, woozy from medication, Grant the author soldiered on through the spring and summer of 1885, producing 250,000 words in clean, muscular prose, the words—as they always had—streaming onto the page without hesitation. Exhausted, he finished his work by mid-July 1885. Four days later, as **Julia Grant** later wrote, "on the morning of July the twenty-third, he, my beloved, my all, passed away, and I was alone, alone."[4]

Grant had won his last battle, for the *Memoirs* sold handsomely. To this day, it is regarded as one of the finest American autobiographies and remains in print. In 1897, Julia attended the dedication of a magnificent mausoleum for Grant that had been erected, with contributions from around the world, on Riverside Drive in New York City. After her death in 1902, she was laid to rest beside her husband, closing the last chapter of the Civil War's greatest love story.

Col. Rutherford B. Hayes was elected to Congress in 1864, but, unlike Garfield, refused to leave military service until the fighting was over. He resigned his commission in June 1865 after being brevetted a major general of volunteers. A quiet, commonsensical kind of man with no pretenses, Hayes succeeded Grant to the presidency in 1877 after a disputed election resolved by a compromise—some called it a deal—with Democrats.[5] Hayes chose to serve only one term, his chief accomplishments the restoration of public confidence in the government's honesty and the end of Reconstruction with the withdrawal of Federal troops from the South. He also held the first Easter egg roll on the White House lawn.

In retirement, Hayes liked to tell soldiers' reunions, "As we grow older and the army stories grow larger, we thank God that we are enabled to believe them."[6] Hayes spent his last years at the family home, Spiegel Grove, in Fremont, now a house museum of the Gilded Age. Adjoining it is the nation's first presidential library. Lucy died in 1889, Hayes in 1893, and they are buried on the grounds of Spiegel Grove. Shortly after Hayes's death, William McKinley, then Ohio's governor, told a G.A.R. encampment in Sandusky, "I heard him once say that the Grand Army button he wore on his coat was the grandest decoration he ever had."[7]

During Hayes's service in the Civil War, his wife, **Lucy Webb Hayes**, had been called "Mother Lucy" by the men of the 23rd Ohio for her many kindnesses to them. A supporter of temperance, she banned liquor from the White House, earning another nickname: "Lemonade Lucy."

The wound to the marriage of **James and Lucretia Garfield** inflicted by his infidelity slowly healed, and in 1875 he was able to tell his diary, "If I could find the time and had the ability to write out the story of Crete's life and mine, the long and anxious questionings that preceded and attended the adjustment of our lives to each other, and the beautiful results we long ago reached and are now enjoying, it would be a more wonderful record than any I know in the realm of romance."[8]

After a long career in the House and a short one in the Senate, Garfield succeeded Hayes as president in 1881. A bit of a showboat, Garfield was a skilled politician with picture-perfect credentials. Born in a log cabin, he became a college president, was elected to the Ohio Senate, rose to major general of volunteers in the war, then served in Congress and the Senate. His skyrocketing career finished suddenly and shockingly, however, when his four-month-old presidency was ended by the bullet of (in the words of Garfield's biographer Allan Peskin) "an unhinged religious fanatic."[9]

After lingering in pain for eighty days, President Garfield died, his faithful wife **Lucretia Garfield** by his side to the end. For nearly thirty-seven years of widowhood, "Crete" devoted herself to preserving her husband's memory—including the correspondence that reflected their troubled early years of marriage and his infidelity.

In downtown Lancaster, a modern (2000) statue of William Tecumseh Sherman sternly watches the city where he grew up but to which he swore he would never return.

Chester A. Arthur and then Grover Cleveland—neither an Ohioan—held the presidency until 1889, when **Benjamin Harrison** came to office. Born in North Bend, Ohio, grandson of President William Henry Harrison, Benjamin Harrison graduated from Miami University. Admitted to the Cincinnati bar, he chose instead to establish a law career in Indianapolis. After leading an Indiana regiment in the war and serving in the U.S. Senate, he won the presidency in 1888. A fine public speaker but a cold case in person with an acute charisma deficiency, Harrison lost his re-election bid and returned to his lucrative corporate law practice in Indiana.

With Rutherford Hayes as his mentor, schoolteacher **William McKinley** rose from private to brevet major in the Civil War, returning to Ohio to become a prominent lawyer in Canton. Endowed with the likeability that Benjamin Harrison lacked, McKinley became an influential congressman and then governor of Ohio. In 1896 he conducted a successful campaign for the presidency from his front porch in Canton.

Having achieved the expanse of girth that signified peace and prosperity to nineteenth-century Americans, President McKinley radiated Republican good sense, declaring, "We cannot gamble with anything so sacred as money."[10] In 1898, he broke his campaign promise to avoid wars of expansion and endorsed war on Spain. Re-elected in 1900, he was assassinated in Buffalo in 1901 by an anarchist who, like McKinley, had made his home in northeast Ohio.

Repeatedly urged to run for the presidency, **William Tecumseh Sherman** wanted nothing to do with politics. He made his feelings abundantly and famously clear in a letter to the *New York Herald*: "I hereby state, and mean all that I say, that I HAVE NEVER BEEN AND NEVER WILL BE A CANDIDATE FOR PRESIDENT; THAT, IF NOMINATED BY EITHER PARTY, I SHOULD PEREMPTORILY DECLINE: AND EVEN IF UNANIMOUSLY ELECTED, I SHOULD DECLINE TO SERVE."[11]

Sherman advanced rapidly in the peacetime army. Assigned command of the region between the Mississippi and the Rockies, he set up headquarters in his adopted home town of St. Louis. Sherman's chief task was to protect the builders of the trans-continental railroad from disgruntled Indians, whom he addressed with his usual bluntness: "We build iron roads," he told the Cheyenne and the Sioux, "and you cannot stop the locomotive any more than you can stop the sun or moon, and you must submit, and do the best you can."[12]

After Grant was awarded four stars in 1866, Sherman was promoted to the vacated lieutenant generalship. On January 9, 1867, forty-two-year-old Ellen delighted Cump by giving birth to their fifth living and last child, Philemon Tecumseh. The child was also nicknamed "Cump" and his father became "his most obsequious slave," according to Ellen, who noted with amusement that Cump Sr. tried to alter his voice when secretly talking to the baby, "but he makes a horrible failure of it."[13]

On Grant's rise to the presidency in 1869, Sherman became general in chief and moved to Washington. He had made peace with Stanton, but never did with his old friend, Henry Halleck. Philip Sheridan visited the Shermans so often he was like a member of the family. Although he had been warned not to do so, little Cump couldn't help staring as the stubby Sheridan, perched on a chair, swung his legs. Amused, Sheridan called for a second chair so general and child could sit side by side, swinging their legs.[14]

Sherman had neither taste nor talent for Washington politics, so in 1874 he moved his office to St. Louis, tied to the capital by mail and the telegraph. He settled into a comfortable routine that included two glasses of bourbon and water daily (one called his "nooning"), voracious reading of matter ranging from poetry to military history, and the supervision of his careless wardrobe by stay-at-home daughter Lizzie.[15] Sherman's memoirs, published in 1875, were as blunt as the man and aroused his old rivals and enemies. Cump's response was, "Pooh upon such hypocrites!"[16] His memoirs and his wartime letters remain in print today.

In April 1876, Sherman decided to return to Washington while **Ellen**

Sherman remained in St. Louis, later moving to her beloved Lancaster. It was a time when husband and wife needed some distance from each other. Relations with Ellen had been strained by her never-ending campaign on behalf of what Cump called "that modern Moloch," the Catholic church.[17]

Son Tom's decision to give up a law career to join the Jesuits ("a vocation from Hell," in Cump's eyes) was the most crushing blow the father had experienced since the death of Willy. "I regard Tom as dead," Sherman wrote, declaring, "I can never have a home again."[18]

By May 1879, however, Cump had realized he could not live without Ellen, and so the family was reunited in Washington. Soon, old generals from both sides in the late war were paying social calls. By now, Cump's beard had turned white, his red hair dark brown, and he needed reading glasses. At a soldiers' reunion in Columbus in 1880, he remarked, "There is many a boy here to-day who looks on war as all glory, but boys, war is all hell." It was one of many times he made the famous "war is hell" remark.[19]

On November 1, 1883, General-in-Chief Sherman retired on full pay and Sheridan took his place, the third son of Ohio in succession to hold the nation's highest military office. The Shermans retired to New York City. They purchased a house on West Seventy-first Street, where Ellen's health confined her to the third floor, with a nurse in attendance. Sherman had a first-floor office where he liked to receive visitors or read.

On Thanksgiving Day 1888 Ellen's nurse called down to him that his wife was dying. Sherman rushed up two flights of stairs, calling, "Ellen, wait for me." But she was dead when he reached her side.[20] Ellen was buried in St. Louis's Calvary Cemetery and Sherman said he should be buried beside her, a union forever that accepted Catholicism in that small degree.

On his seventy-first birthday, February 8, 1891, Sherman folded down a page of Dickens's *Great Expectations*, which he had already read several times, and went to bed. He never returned to the book. Suffering asthma, he developed pneumonia. Asked during a period of wakefulness what he wanted on his monument, Sherman said, "Put 'Faithful & honorable; faithful & honorable."

Sherman had written, "Not only am I not a Catholic, but an enemy so bitter that written words can convey no meaning."[21] Almost from the moment he lost consciousness, however, he was enveloped in the Catholicism he had resisted throughout his life.

Lacking his consent, Sherman's children nonetheless agreed that a Catholic priest should administer the sacraments. He died on February 14 and was given

Philip Henry Sheridan, Grant's feisty little cavalry commander, remains permanently on the attack in this statue erected in 1908 in Washington, D.C.

Catholic funeral services in New York and St. Louis. Former Confederate Gen. Joe Johnston, who had become one of Sherman's closest friends after the war, served as a pallbearer. Refusing, out of respect to Sherman, to wear a hat, Johnston caught cold, struggled with pneumonia for weeks, and died the next month.

Philip H. Sheridan had been widely applauded for his rapid succession of victories in the Civil War's last year. In 1865 he was ordered to the Texas border with fifty thousand men to counterbalance Napoleon III's short-term seizure of Mexico. After that, Sheridan was assigned Reconstruction duties in Texas and Louisiana, which he carried out with a heavy hand. Later, he waged total warfare against the Indians and is credited with—or blamed for—saying, "The only good Indians I ever saw were dead."[22]

In 1875, when he was forty-four, Sheridan married Irene Rucker, a twenty-two-year-old army brat. The rough-hewn former bachelor settled into a blissful

In this memorial engraving, published shortly after his death in 1885, Ulysses and Julia are surrounded by the Grant children and grandchildren.

domesticity that soon included four children, on whom he doted. Sheridan succeeded Sherman as general in chief in 1884, but died of heart disease in 1888, only fifty-seven years old. He had finished reading the proofs of his memoirs the day before he died.[23]

After Lincoln's assassination and Vice President Andrew Johnson's ascendancy to the presidency, the grieving **Edwin M. Stanton** remained at his desk in the War Department. Bearish as always, he oversaw demobilization. He and Johnson increasingly moved apart as they disagreed over the president's Reconstruction policies. Working with a like-minded Grant, Stanton was able to influence Congress in ways that angered Johnson, who then tried to fire him. In turn, Congress impeached Johnson, but he was narrowly acquitted in the Senate.

Troubled by asthma since childhood and by a liver ailment as well, Stanton's hair was gray, and his face so haggard he appeared older than his early fifties. Stanton resigned May 26, 1868, exhausted and virtually impoverished by years of hard work at a relatively low salary. Even so, he campaigned for Grant's election, which left him a "wreck" of a man, according to a journalist.[24] He spent his last months a virtual invalid, his heart weakened by years of asthma. President Grant appointed him to the Supreme Court, but before Stanton could take his place, he died on Christmas morning, 1869. Only fifty-five, he had sacrificed his life and wealth to save the Union.

Stanton's widow, Ellen, and the children still at home were faced with poverty, but Congress voted her a year's salary of a Supreme Court justice and a private subscription drive raised more than $111,000 for the Stantons. The oldest son, Edwin Lamson Stanton, was, like his father, a brilliant lawyer seemingly on his way to greater things, but he died less than a decade after his father.

Salmon P. Chase would sooner have given up an arm than his presidential ambitions. Although he had achieved the exalted position of chief justice of the United States Supreme Court, he made a failed attempt to gain the Democratic nomination for president in 1868. He died in 1873 and is buried in Cincinnati's Spring Grove Cemetery. Ohio Sen. **Benjamin Wade** had once said, "Chase is a good man, but his theology is unsound. He thinks there is a fourth person in the Trinity."[25]

Wade, of course, had few doubts about himself or the rightness of his Radical Republicanism. All knew that he stood ready, as president pro tem of the Senate, to succeed President Andrew Johnson if Johnson's impeachment concluded with a conviction. When conviction failed by one vote in the Senate, it was clear that Wade's clout had run out of steam. He retired to Ohio, where he occupied himself with various reform movements, such as women's and workers' rights.[26]

Irvin McDowell, whose bad luck twice on the Bull Run battlefields made him, as he put it, "one of the *might-have-beens*," spent his post-war career administering military districts in the West and South, rising to major general before retiring to San Francisco.[27] Famed throughout the army as a prodigious eater, he died in 1885 from a digestive problem.[28]

William B. Hazen, a hard-driving fighter combative on the battlefield and off, remained in the regular army, rising to brigadier general despite an exceptional capacity for making enemies. Possessed of every talent except tact, Hazen was court-martialed for criticizing Secretary of War Robert Todd Lincoln (son of the late president), but public opinion supported Hazen and he escaped penalty. In 1887 he died in a diabetic coma, age fifty-six, unretired and unrepentant.

Other generals tested by the war realized they had no future in the military. After **"Fighting Joe" Hooker** quit Sherman's forces in Georgia in anger over assignments, he was put in charge of the military's Northern Department, with headquarters in Cincinnati. There he married Olivia Groesbeck, sister of a congressman. Hooker remained in the army only until 1868, retiring at age fifty-four. He died unexpectedly in 1879 and, as an adopted Ohioan, is buried in Cincinnati's Spring Grove Cemetery.

George B. McClellan, who had resigned his generalship to run against Lincoln for the presidency in 1863, turned to engineering after the war and then to politics. In the eyes of a modern commentator, McClellan was a "competent but undistinguished" governor of New Jersey.[29] As a general, he had been a remarkable combination of skills and flaws, aggressive in organizing an army, timid in leading it. "McClellan to me is one of the mysteries of the war," Grant wrote years after the war was over.[30] Late in life, McClellan took up the pen, writing his memoirs in defense of his military performance. He died in 1885 before his memoirs could be published.

Don Carlos Buell, who, like McClellan, had preferred waging limited war against the South, resigned his commission in 1864 after realizing he would be given no more assignments. He spent the rest of his life in the iron and coal industries in Kentucky, where he died in 1898.

William Rosecrans, who had succeeded Buell as commander of the Army of the Cumberland, was shunted off to the margins of the war after the disaster at Chickamauga, then spent two years without another assignment. He resigned his commission in 1867, served briefly as minister to Mexico, later was elected to two terms in Congress, and then was registrar of the U.S. Treasury from 1885–1893. He retired to his ranch in California and, like Buell, died in 1898.

Azor Nickerson, who survived a severe chest wound at Gettysburg but returned to share the platform with Lincoln as the president gave his famous address, came to grief several years after the war. He had joined the regular army, fought numerous battles with Indians, and rose to assistant adjutant general of the entire army. That all ended after he tried to trick his wife into a divorce because he had fallen in love with her dressmaker. He was dismissed for conduct unbecoming an officer and spent the rest of his life trying to have his name restored to the rolls of retired officers. That happened the week after his death in 1910.[31]

Most veterans simply went home to Ohio. **Capt. John Hartzell** of the 105th Ohio returned to Mahoning County in the northeastern part of the state to pick up his cradle scythe. Within three months he was married, and in the years to come would raise six children, as well as cattle and horses, some of which he imported from Europe. To the end of his days he remembered the war, its horrors, and its strange attraction. "I was a young fellow then," he wrote in 1898, "but the recollection of it kind of stiffens my gray hair and makes me hanker to see the like once more."[32] Hartzell died in 1918. The memoir he intended only for his family was published for a general audience in 2005.[33]

Pvt. **Andrew Altman** of the 68th Ohio married, fathered three children, and acquired the small farm in Henry County that he had yearned for. He died in 1903.

Corp. **John Rhoades** of the 115th Ohio returned to Sarah, Willie, and Rella and their farm in Miami County in west-central Ohio. Described in government records as "a stout hearty man" as a soldier, he suffered from rheumatism and heart trouble in his last years, and died in 1897, leaving Sarah a widow. Beginning January 21, 1898, she received a widow's pension of $8 a month.

Some veterans left Ohio. **Frances Marion Posegate** of the 48th Ohio, one of the first regiments to feel the shock of Rebel attack at Shiloh, returned to Missouri, where he had been raised. He served as mayor of St. Joseph and ran a printing company, said to be "the largest and most modern … between St. Louis and California."[34]

Despite his wartime achievements as commander of "Opdycke's Tigers," **Col. Emerson Opdycke** of the 125th Ohio was unable to obtain a postwar command with a satisfactory rank in the regular army. Feeling slighted, he resigned on January 1, 1866. He moved to New York City and entered the dry goods business. Opdycke remained active in veterans' affairs, but, like many other retired commanders, engaged in endless feuds and arguments over wartime achievements. Late in April 1884 he was cleaning his service revolver when it accidentally discharged, wounding him in the abdomen. He died on April 25, age fifty-four. In 2003 his wartime letters were published as a book.[35]

The Opdyckes's only child, Leonard, became a prosperous lawyer in New York, but retired when his health began to fail. On September 3, 1914, in a garden shed behind his home, he put the muzzle of a revolver in his mouth and pulled the trigger. He was only a year older than his father when he died.

Oscar D. Ladley, the dry goods clerk from Yellow Springs, joined the army days after Lincoln's first call for volunteers and, except for a brief interval of civilian life after the war, never left. Joining the regular army in 1867, he served a number of dusty frontier posts until he died in Colorado of a respiratory illness in 1880. He left a wife, a daughter, and an estate of less than one hundred dollars.

After the war, **Lt. Thomas F. Galwey** of the 8th Ohio earned bachelor's, master's, and doctoral degrees, mastered ten languages, and worked as a lawyer, college professor, and editor. He moved to Harlem in New York City, where he became known to many as "Captain Brevet," the honorary rank bestowed on him after the war. He offered to serve in the Spanish-American

War, but was declined because of deafness incurred during the Civil War. "Captain Brevet" died in 1913, honored for his many literary, academic, and legal accomplishments. His diary was published in 1961.[36]

Brig. Gen. John Beatty had resigned from the army in January 1864 after three years' service and returned to managing the family bank in Cardington. He was elected to Congress and twice re-elected. Later, he wrote three novels, articles on history, and popular books on political economy. He died in 1914. His wartime memoirs, which he doubted would be of great interest to anyone, were first published in 1879 and republished in 1946.[37]

Of Ohio's three war-time governors, the first, **William Dennison**, resigned as postmaster general at the end of Andrew Johnson's first term as president. Returning to Ohio, he remained active in Republican politics and business, dying in 1882 not only wealthy, but also respected—belatedly—for his achievements in organizing the state for war. Ohio's second war governor, Democrat **David Tod**, returned to business after serving one term, turning down Lincoln's offer to succeed Salmon P. Chase as secretary of the treasury. He remained active in politics, becoming a Republican after the war, but died in 1868. Ohio's third war governor was **John Brough**, an efficient but sometimes abrasive executive. Living barely long enough to see the Union victorious, he died August 29, 1865, four months before expiration of his term.

Jacob Dolson Cox, the Ohio state senator who rose to major general of volunteers, was elected governor on the Republican ticket in 1865, supported by Radical Republicans and others whose sympathies lay with blacks. But Cox stunned his allies by opposing black suffrage, arguing that he now believed blacks were not ready for equal rights. Cox's term, a contentious one, achieved little and he was denied renomination. He ended his career as president of the University of Cincinnati and author of several authoritative war histories.

The women that war's cruelty had left behind struggled to make lives for themselves. The widow of **Lt. Col. Herman Canfield** of the 72nd Ohio, killed at Shiloh, spent the next three years of the war as a volunteer nurse for sick and wounded soldiers. Still dressed in mourning clothes, she watched the Grand Review in 1865, worked as a clerk in the U.S. Bureau of Education during the Grant administration, and faded into anonymity.[38]

Caroline Spiegel, widow of **Col. Marcus Spiegel** of the 120th Ohio, killed on the Red River in 1864, gave birth to their fifth child two months later. The little girl was named Clara Marcus in her father's honor. In 1865, Caroline and the children moved to Chicago and later to Akron, where she ran small boarding houses. Marcus's brother Joseph returned safely from the war and opened the small dry goods store he and Marcus had often discussed. The little store grew into the Spiegel Catalogue Company, for many years one of the nation's largest mail-order retailers. Marcus Spiegel's letters to his wife were published in book form in 1995.[39]

Maj. Gen. James B. McPherson, the native of Clyde, was not only was loved by his troops, but also esteemed by Grant and Sherman. Killed during Sherman's Atlanta campaign, he was the highest-ranking Union officer to die in combat. He had been engaged to marry Emily Hoffman of Baltimore, who remained in her room for a year after his death. She finally emerged from mourning, but led a secluded life and never married.[40]

The death of **John Brown** and two of his sons in the failed raid on Harpers Ferry left his family in upstate New York not only stunned and financially bereft, but also the object of persistent public curiosity, not all of it friendly. Surviving the old man were wife, Mary, and children ranging in age from five to thirty-eight. Death pursued the family: Martha, wife of Oliver Brown, who had been killed in the raid, died after giving birth to their child, who also died.

Supporters sent funds and words of encouragement to John's widow and the Alcotts hosted her at their home in Concord, Massachusetts. Crowds, some of whom were sympathizers and some only curiosity seekers, dogged the Browns. Soon, son Salmon headed west, followed by Mary and the smallest children. The Browns were pursued part of the way by murderous Confederate sympathizers. In California, the family finally found safety. Nonetheless, Salmon recalled, "The passing years did not heal the horrible wounds made by the country father had tried so hard to help to a plane of higher living."[41]

David Ross Locke, the writer whose loutish Copperhead "Petroleum V. Nasby" so amused President Lincoln, later edited the *Toledo Daily Blade*, wrote novels and plays, and became a popular lecturer. Weary of his most famous creation, he complained, "I wish to God that I had never heard of the Nasby stuff."[42] **Charles Farrar Browne**, creator of "Artemus Ward," contracted tuberculosis and died in 1867 in London, where his humorous columns in *Punch* had achieved popularity.

Unabashed by the war's outcome, **Clement L. Vallandigham** continued to be a lightning rod for controversy, insisting the Southern states should be returned to the Union with full rights and without punishment. Accepting the reality of Emancipation, he nonetheless remained a diehard racist, arguing against political and social rights for blacks. He won no offices in post-war politics, but in his law practice enjoyed considerable success in defending those accused of crimes.

In June 1871, Vallandigham picked up a loaded weapon to show some fellow lawyers how he would use it as an exhibit and accidentally shot himself. He died the following morning following twelve hours of suffering.[43] Thousands of admirers, joined by some of the state's most prominent politicians, attended his funeral. Workingmen throughout the area took the day off "to honor a man they regarded as their champion."[44]

After **Robert C. Schenck** was wounded at Second Bull Run, he retired from the military in December 1863 to campaign against Vallandigham, then gave full time to his newly elected position as congressman from Ohio's Third District. Schenck was not re-elected in 1870, but President Grant appointed him ambassador to England. While there, he was drawn into a scandal over an alleged fraud involving a mine in the American West. Although Schenck was acquitted of all charges, he never returned to public life and died in Washington in 1890. Schenck was such a skillful player of draw poker that he published a book on the subject.

At the end of the war, **Maj. Gen. James B. Steedman** was appointed military commander of Georgia, where he served until the summer of 1866. President Johnson appointed him collector of internal revenue at New Orleans. In 1869 he returned to Toledo, where he edited a Democratic newspaper. Always attracted to where the action was, he was thrown in a dungeon in Cuba where he had gone to meddle in Spanish affairs. Only intervention by the United States government saved him from execution.

Safely back in Ohio, Steedman was elected to the Ohio Senate in 1877. In 1878 he married his third wife when she was seventeen and he was sixty-two. The union produced three children. One of his grandchildren, Mary Ann Wanatick, became a schoolteacher and in 1988 told his story in a master's thesis. Elected chief of police in Toledo in 1882, Steedman died of pneumonia on October 18, 1883.

John Mercer Langston, who had done so much to recruit blacks to the Union forces, organized the Law Department at Howard University after the war and for a time served as Howard's acting president. For eight years he was consul general in Haiti, returning in 1885 to become the president of Virginia Normal and Collegiate Institute. He represented Virginia for six months in the House of Representatives, the first African American elected to Congress from the state. He died in 1897 after a long career of fighting for black rights. Langston University, Oklahoma's only historically black university, is named in his honor.

The seventeen **"Fighting McCooks,"** the sons of Dan and John McCook,

Drums, like this one in the American Civil War Museum in Bowling Green, were an important means of communication during the Civil War.

stamped their name on Civil War history in a big way. Seven achieved the rank of general, while five others served as officers, surgeons, or chaplains. The highest ranking member, Alexander McDowell McCook, was a West Pointer and professional soldier. One of those charged with blame for the Chickamauga debacle, he was cleared, remained in service after the war, and retired a major general. Four McCooks died during the war, three of wounds. From the surviving McCooks there emerged, postwar, two prominent theologians, a lawyer, a legislator, and the twice-governor of the Colorado Territory.

Kate Chase Sprague gave birth to two daughters after son Willie. In 1881, she petitioned the Rhode Island Supreme Court for a divorce from William who, she charged, "has committed adultery with divers women at divers places" since their marriage."[45] He counter-sued, arguing she, too, had been unfaithful (with prominent politician Roscoe Conkling), and "persisted in reckless, extravagant, lavish, and foolish expenditure of money and style of living … many times absented herself from [William's] home … [and] persisted in a course of slanderous and abusive language … rendering his life miserable."[46]

The divorce was granted to Kate, but she received no alimony or other settlement. She was forced to live off the sale of her jewelry, dresses, china, and works of art. The one-time belle of Washington never remarried. Exhausted by a life of unhappiness, hard work, and, finally, poverty, she developed kidney problems, congestive heart failure, and high blood pressure, and died in 1899 after suffering days of convulsions. She died in obscurity, a beautiful woman who had spent her life hoping for love and finding little of it. In 1868, as the life went out of her marriage, she had written on a scrap of paper,

I dwell so constantly upon the absence from my life of a ... kinder, devoted love ... One by one hopes fade away. ... Vigor & youth remain as yet & when they too, as time speeds on, fade away, God help me![47]

Ex-husband William died in Paris, outliving Kate by sixteen years. His body was returned to Providence, Rhode Island, where he was laid to rest with a seventeen-gun salute and the playing of taps. His wife had been buried in Columbus with little ceremony.

The after-stories of another failed romance —that of Confederate **Gen. John Bell Hood** and **Sally Buchanan "Buck" Preston**—do not end happily. Three years after rejecting Hood, Buck married Rawlins "Rawly" Lowndes, scion of an old South Carolina family. After giving birth to three children— two of whom would die young—Buck died at age thirty-eight. She had been married only twelve years. Meanwhile, ex-fiancé Hood moved to New Orleans, where he married the daughter of a prominent Catholic family and struggled to make a success in various businesses. In ten years Mrs. Hood gave birth to eleven children, including three sets of twins. In 1879, in the aftermath of a yellow fever epidemic, Mrs. Hood, one of her children, and Hood himself all died in one week. The ten Hood orphans were divided among seven adopting families. Coincidentally, the separate marriages of Buck and Hood occurred only a month apart and their untimely deaths within sixteen months of each other.

Contemplating the Civil War's legion of memorable individuals, one wonders how they are resting. The body of **John Brown**, whose murderous fanaticism had a great deal to do with triggering the war, lies a-mouldering on his farm in North Elba, New York, a state historic site. Brown was buried at the edge of a huge boulder, which is probably what it took to hold him down during the generations of racial injustice that followed the Civil War.

Brown's counterpart in the South, **Edmund Ruffin**, the quarrelsome defender of slavery and hater of all things Northern, lies under a simple headstone on his Marlbourne, Virginia, estate, defeated and gone, but hardly forgotten. On the Web site findagrave.com, a number of condolence messages have been posted, some from unreconstructed Rebels who like to add a Confederate flag and cry "Deo Vindice"(the Confederacy's official motto, meaning "God will vindicate" or "God will defend"). Among the messages that Ruffin—always hungry for public approval—would appreciate: "May your spirit lead us in a new beginning," "Rest Well Great Patriot," "God bless you, Sir," and "You were a great man."

In Calvary Cemetery in St. Louis lies **William Tecumseh Sherman**. As requested, his monument bears the words "Faithful and Honorable" and, as requested, Cump lies next to **Ellen** in a Roman Catholic cemetery. Whether the restless, ever twitchy Sherman is resting in peace among so many Catholics is an open question, but he is where he asked to be—united for all time with Ellen, she his protector, he hers.

In New York City, the impressive structure built to honor **Ulysses S. Grant** suffered some vandalism in recent years but it has been restored to its original appearance. Inside Grant's Tomb, in unadorned marble sarcophagi bearing only their names, lie the quiet warrior Ulysses and his beloved **Julia**. *Ulys and Dearest Julia together forever; kisses to all.*

To Learn More:

James M. Perry's *Touched by Fire* tells the stories of "five presidents and the battles that made them." All five were born in Ohio. In addition to Grant's birthplace in Point Pleasant and Sherman's in Lancaster, Ohio offers three major sites preserving the memory of Civil War leaders: the Rutherford B. Hayes Presidential Center in Fremont, encompassing the Hayes home, a museum, and a history and genealogy research library (**http://www.rbhayes.org** or **419-332-2081**); the William McKinley Presidential Library and Museum in Canton (http:// **www.mckinleymuseum.org** or **330-455-7043**), and "Lawnfield," in Mentor, which James A. Garfield purchased in 1876 and where his widow, Crete, lived for many years after his assassination. You can use long sets of steps, as Grant did just before the war, to climb the explore the hilly town of Galena, Illinois. Then you can tour the house Galena gave the Grants in 1865 (**http://www.granthome.com/** or **815-777-3310**).

Among the finest overall treatments of the war are James McPherson's Pulitzer-Prize-winning *Battle Cry of Freedom*, which discussed what led to the war as well as what shaped the outcome; David J. Eicher's *The Longest Night*, which concentrates on the war's military aspects, and Eicher's *Dixie Betrayed: the South Really Lost the Civil War*, which argues that the Confederacy doomed itself from the beginning.

David Herbert Donald's *Lincoln* is regarded as a classic, while Doris Kearns Goodwin's *Team of Rivals* tells the remarkable story of how a canny Lincoln assembled a Cabinet of opponents and political in-fighters and made it work. Finally, Bruce Catton's *The Civil War*, published in 1960, endures as the more readable account of a civil war that was, in reality, a rebellion against the promises of liberty and equality made by the nation's forefathers.

The state's newest museum is the American Civil War Museum of Ohio, 123 East Court St., Bowling Green, with exhibits illustrating soldier life, Civil War medicine, and the life of prisoners of war, all with an Ohio emphasis (**http://www. acwmo.org/** or **410-352-0209**).

❧ ACKNOWLEDGEMENTS

Writers like to say they work in solitude and that theirs is a lonely craft, but we emerge now and then for food, oxygen, and love—but also because writing requires it. We need information from which to tell our stories and sometimes we need direction and occasionally we need a good smack upside the head.

Among those who have made this book possible are my good-natured publisher, Marcy Hawley, and editorial director, John Baskin, whose patience and support are greatly appreciated. A tip of my Western campaigner's slouch hat to them both, and to all at Orange Frazer Press, especially proofreader Amber Stephens.

I am grateful to readers of my work in progress: Professors Ronald Partin and Andrew Schocket, the very knowledgeable Stephen Simms, and my always-perceptive son, Andrew Bissland. All contributed thoughts and suggestions that helped greatly.

The following have been especially generous with their assistance: Marilyn Levinson, curator of manuscripts, and the staff of the Bowling Green State University Center for Archival Collections; and Nan Card, curator of manuscripts at Rutherford B. Hayes Presidential Center. Both archives are marvelous resources for historians, with troves of information about the Civil War. The State Library of Ohio, Columbus, also has fine resources.

The staff members of the research library of the Ohio Historical Society—Ohio's treasure-filled "attic"—have always been courteous and helpful. Unfortunately, reduced state funding has limited library hours and raised picture usage fees beyond the reach of authors and small publishers, denying readers some of the benefits of the OHS collection.

Thanks also go to Park Ranger Jim Lewis, Stones River National Battlefield; Chief Park Ranger Stacy Allen, Shiloh National Military Park; Renée Klish, curator of art at the U.S. Army Center of Military History; Jean Powers Soman, who supplied pictures of Col. Marcus Spiegel, and Jill Spiegel of "The Jill Spiegel Show," Minneapolis, who helped; Carolyn J. Burns, genealogist, Dayton Veterans Administration; Lee Edwards, curator, Ripley (Ohio) Museum; Steve Repp, a master of the history of Galena, Illinois; the always helpful Kausalya A. Padmaraj of BGSU's Jerome Library; and Kathleen Jones, the energetic president of the Greater Toledo Civil War Roundtable.

Anyone working on Ohio's role in the Civil War owes a debt of gratitude to the extraordinary efforts of Larry Stevens in assembling "Ohio in the Civil War" (*http://ohiocivilwar.com*), a comprehensive on-line list of sources of information for every Ohio unit. The site contains many other useful tools.

Most of all, my appreciation goes to my beloved Joan, who makes all things possible and all things worthwhile.

Of course, no one but myself is responsible for any errors that may appear in this work, and the opinions expressed and points of view I have taken are solely my own.

☙ ILLUSTRATION CREDITS

American Civil War Museum, Bowling Green, Ohio: 405, 484, 513.

Army Art Collection, United States Army Center of Military History, Washington, D.C., Renée Klish, Army art curator: Cover (top portion), 258.

Author: 13, 44, 50, 51, 153, 246, 258, 262, 310, 312, 335, 460, 464, 466, 497, 502.

Battles and Leaders of the Civil War, ed. Robert Underwood Johnson and Clarence Clough Buel (New York: The Century Company, 1887-88). Four vols.: 75, 109, 139, 140, 141, 143, 163, 165, 178, 182, 184, 186, 200, 210, 214, 217, 237, 245, 257, 265, 275, 294, 297, 308, 311, 365, 384, 392, 430, 473, 474, 483, 492.

Bowling Green State University Center for Archival Collections: 316.

Dayton Veterans Administration Medical Center, Carolyn J. Burns, genealogist: 457.

Frank Leslie's Illustrated Famous Leaders and Battle Scenes of the Civil War, (New York: Mrs. Frank Leslie, Publisher: 1896): 82, 98, 104, 194.

Harper's Pictorial History of the Great Rebellion, by Alfred H. Guernsey and Henry M. Alden (Chicago: McDonnell Bros., 1866, 1888). Part First: 25, 29,129.

History of the Fifty-Third Regiment, Ohio Volunteer Infantry During the War of the Rebellion, by John K. Duke (Portsmouth, Ohio: The Blade Printing Company, 1900): 192.

Howe's Historical Collections of Ohio, by Henry Howe (Cincinnati: Henry Howe, 1851): 199, 468.

Library of Congress: Front cover (below title), frontispiece (all), xvi, 10, 12 , 15, 18, 20, 22, 24, 32, 36, 43, 52, 54, 59, 60, 62, 66, 71, 84, 88, 89, 110, 114, 116, 120. 122, 124, 125, 126, 144, 147, 150, 154, 158, 174, 189, 195, 205, 216, 218, 222, 224, 229, 230, 234, 235, 242, 243, 248, 251, 271, 274, 277, 280, 283, 287, 296, 301, 302, 318, 321, 323, 326, 332, 333, 337, 338, 342, 344, 346, 349, 351, 352, 361, 362, 366, 368, 369, 371, 372, 374, 379, 382, 390, 393, 395 397, 398, 410, 412, 414, 419, 420, 425, 426, 431, 436, 437, 438, 441, 442, 444, 446, 451, 454, 469, 470, 475, 477, 495, 496, 500, 505, 506.

National Archives: 87, 198, 238, 266, 339, 355 (both), 358, 416, 490.

Ohio in the War: Her Statesmen, Generals and Soldiers, by Whitelaw Reid. (Two vols. Moore, Wilstach & Baldwin, 1868. Columbus, Ohio: Eclectic Publishing Co., 1893) 77, 241, 303, 480.

Our Acre and Its Harvest: Historical Sketch of the Soldiers' Aid Society of Northern Ohio, by Mary Clark Brayton and Ellen E. Terry (Cleveland: Fairbanks, Benedict & Co., 1869): 401.

Pictorial Book of Anecdotes of the Great Rebellion, by Frazar Kirkland (St. Louis: W.E. Allen, Publishers, 1887): 160.

Jean Powers Soman: 402.

The Story of Camp Chase, by William H. Knauss (Nashville : Publishing House of the Methodist Episcopal Church, South: 1906): 406.

The Truth About Chickamauga, by Archibald Gracie (Boston: Houghton, Mifflin, 1911): 95, 131, 132, 133.

University of Notre Dame Archives, Elizabeth Hogan, archivist, photographs: 387.

Notes for the Foreword

1   Martin Lubin, ed. *The Words of Abraham Lincoln.* (New York: Tess Press, 2005), 282.

Notes for the Introduction

1   Ulysses S. Grant, *Ulysses S. Grant: Memoirs and Selected Letters* (New York: Library of America, 1990), 152.
2   Jean Edward Smith, *Grant* (New York: Simon & Schuster, 2001), 87.
3   Grant, *Grant: Memoirs and Selected Letters.* 141.
4   Hamlin Garland, *Ulysses S. Grant: His Life and Character* (New York: Macmillan, 1920), 153.
5   William Tecumseh Sherman, *Memoirs of General W. T. Sherman* (New York: Penguin Books, 2000), 157.
6   Benjamin P. Thomas and Harold M. Hyman, *Stanton: The Life and Times of Lincoln's Secretary of War* (New York: Alfred A. Knopf, 1962), 120.
7   Ibid. 41.
8   Ibid. 55.
9   David Herbert Donald, *Lincoln* (New York: Simon & Schuster Paperbacks, 1995), 237
10 "Lincoln's Illinois Heritage: A Supplement to American Heritage Magazine," (New York: American Heritage, 2005).
11 Allan Gurganus, "The Rebellion Continues, at Least in the Southern Short Story," *Oxford American*, Winter 2006,146.
12 John H. Eicher and David J. Eicher, *Civil War High Commands* (Stanford, California: Stanford University Press, 2001), 53.
13 Jill Lepore, "The Sharpened Quill," *The New Yorker*, October 16, 2006, 168.
14 Greil Marcus, *The American Dream,* (http://www.salon.com/opinion/feature/2006/07/04/american_dream).

Notes for Chapter 1

1   Robert Leslie Jones, *History of Agriculture in Ohio to 1880* (Kent, Ohio: Kent State University Press, 1983), *Passim.* George W Knepper, *Ohio and Its People,* paperback ed. (Kent, Ohio: Kent State University Press, 1989), 227. U.S. Civil War Centennial Commission, *The United States on the Eve of the Civil War as Described in the 1860 Census* (U.S. Civil War Centennial Commission, 1963), *Passim.*
2   David S. Reynolds, *John Brown, Abolitionist* (New York: Alfred A. Knopf, 2005), 395–6. Murat Halstead, "The Execution of John Brown," *Ohio Archaeological and Historical Publications [now Ohio History]* XXX (1921): 295–6.
3   Halstead, "Execution," 295. *Life, Trial and Execution of Captain John Brown; 1859* (Robert M. De Witt, 1859), 100.
4   *Life, Trial and Execution of Captain John Brown; 1859.* Halstead, "Execution," 100.
5   Edmund Ruffin, *The Diary of Edmund Ruffin,* ed. William Kauffman Scarborough, 3 vols., vol. I (Baton Rouge: Louisiana State University Press, 1972), 369.
6   Donald W. Curl, "Murat Halstead," in *For the Union: Ohio Leaders in the Civil War*, ed. Kenneth W. Wheeler (Columbus: Ohio State University Press, 1968): 321. Donald Walter Curl, "Murat Halstead, Editor and Politician" (Dissertation, Ohio State University, 1964), *Passim.*
7   Halstead, "Execution," 292.
8   Ibid, 292, 294. Ruffin, *Ruffin Diary.* I, 369.
9   Ibid. Halstead, "Execution." Maud E. Morrow, *Recollections of the Civil War: From a Child's Point of View* (Lockland, Ohio: 1901).
10 Reynolds, *John Brown, Abolitionist,* 398.

11   National Park Service, *John Brown's Raid, National Park Service History Series*
     (Washington, D.C.: Office of Publications, National Park Service, U.S. Department of the
     Interior, 1974), 56.
12   Ibid, 49.
13   Reynolds, *John Brown, Abolitionist*, 388.
14   Halstead, "Execution," 295–6. Stephen B. Oates, *To Purge This Land with Blood*, 2nd ed.
     (Amherst: University of Massachusetts Press, 1984), 331–2.
15   Halstead, "Execution," 296.
16   Oates, *To Purge This Land with Blood*, 352. Rev. William Henry Griffis, "Refutation
     of Several Romances About the Execution of John Brown," *Southern Historical* 13 (1885):
     341.
17   Halstead, "Execution," 295.
18   Betty L. Mitchell, *Edmund Ruffin: A Biography* (Bloomington: Indiana University Press,
     1981), 148.
19   Eric H. Walther, *The Fire-Eaters* (Baton Rouge: Louisiana State University Press, 1992).,
     258–259.
20   Halstead, "Execution," 296.
21   Oates, *To Purge This Land with Blood*, Ruffin. *Ruffin Diary*. I, 370.
22   Curl, "Murat Halstead, Editor and Politician".
23   Oates, *To Purge This Land with Blood*, 352. Walther, *Fire-Eaters*, 259.
24   Michael W. Kauffman, *American Brutus* (New York: Random House, 2004). 103.
25   Ruffin, *Ruffin Diary* 371.
26   Oates, *To Purge This Land with Blood*, 353.
27   Ibid. Kauffman, *American Brutus*, 106.
28   Quoted in Doris Kearns Goodwin, *Team of Rivals: The Political Genius of Abraham
     Lincoln* (New York: Simon & Schuster, 2005), 228.
29   Oates, *To Purge This Land with Blood*, 354.
30   "The War Begun!!," *Ohio State Journal*, April 13, 1861.
31   "An Incident of the Day," *Daily Toledo Blade*, December 3, 1859.
32   "The War Begun!!! Fort Sumter Attacked Yesterday Morning!," *Cleveland Morning Leader*,
     April 13, 1861.
33   Frank L. Klement, *The Limits of Dissent* (Lexington: University Press of Kentucky, 1970),
     23.
34   Eugene H. Roseboom and Francis P. Weisenburger, *A History of Ohio* (Columbus, Ohio:
     Ohio Historical Society, 1953), 179.
35   Ruffin, *Ruffin Diary*.
36   James M. McPherson, *Battle Cry of Freedom: The Civil War Era*, paperback ed. (Oxford,
     England, and New York: Oxford University Press, 1988), 212–3.
37   Oliver Crenshaw, "The Psychological Background of the Election of 1860 in the South,"
     The North Carolina Historical Review XIX, no. 3 (1942), *Passim*.
38   Murat Halstead, *Three Against Lincoln: Murat Halstead Reports the Caucuses of 1860*, ed.
     William B. Hessltine (Baton Rouge: Louisiana State University Press, 1960), 12–18.
39   Ibid, 13.
40   Walther, *Fire-Eaters*, 48.
41   Edward J. Renehan Jr., *The Secret Six* (New York: Crown Publishers, Inc., 1995).
42   Klement, *The Limits of Dissent*, 33–4.
43   Halstead and Hesseltine, *Three Against Lincoln*, 67.
44   Ibid, 211.
45   McPherson, *Battle Cry of Freedom*, 221–2.
46   Ibid. 216.
47   Halstead and Hesseltine, *Three Against Lincoln*, 165.
48   McPherson, *Battle Cry of Freedom*, 223.
49   "Presidential Elections: 1860," (http://www.multied.com/elections/1860.html:
     HistoryCentral.Com, 2004).
50   "The Beginning of the End," *Daily Toledo Blade*, November 13, 1860.
51   "The Jubilee," *Daily Toledo Blade*, November 14, 1860.
52   Abner Doubleday, "Abner Doubleday Defends Fort Sumter," in *The Civil War Archive*, ed.
     Henry Steele Commager and Erik Bruun (New York: Tess Press, 2000), 69.

53, 54 ———, *Reminiscences of Forts Sumter and Moultrie in 1860–'61* (New York: Harper &
     Brothers, 1876), 143–4, 153–4.

55 Mary Chesnut, "Mrs. Chesnut Watches the Attack on Fort Sumter," in *The Civil War Archive*, ed. Henry Steele Commager and Erik Bruun (New York: Tess Press, 2000), 68.

56 E.B. Long, with Barbara Long, *The Civil War Day by Day: An Almanac 1861–1865* (Garden City, New York: Doubleday, 1971; reprint, by Da Capo, n.p., n.d.), 3–4.

57 "First Gallant South Carolina Nobly Made the Stand," in *The Civil War Archive*, ed. Henry Steele Commager and Erik Bruun (New York: Tess Press, 2000), 42–3.

58 "The News," *Daily Toledo Blade*, April 10, 1861.

59 Nicolay, *Outbreak of the Rebellion.*

60 Jacob D. Cox, "War Preparations in the North," in *Battles and Leaders of the Civil War*, ed. Robert Underwood Johnson and Clarence Clough Buel (New York: The Century Co.), I, 85.

61 Alfred E. Lee, *The History of the City of Columbus*, 2 vols., vol. II (Columbus, Ohio: Franklin County Genealogical and Historical Society, 2000), 88.

62 H. Wayne Morgan, *William McKinley and His America* (Syracuse, New York: Syracuse University Press, 1963), 15.

63 "The Reception of the News from Charleston in This City," *Cincinnati Commercial*, April 13, 1861.

64 "The War Begun!!" *Ohio State Journal*, April 13, 1861.

65 "THE ISSUE IS MADE UP!" *Daily Toledo Blade*, April 13, 1861.

66 "The War Has Begun!!! Fort Sumter Attacked Yesterday Morning!" *Cleveland Morning Leader*, April 13, 1861.

67 "Latest News," *Cleveland Morning Leader*, April 18, 1861.

68 "The Great Pulsation," *Cleveland Morning Leader*, April 13, 1861.

69 "The Feeling," *Toledo Daily Herald and News*, April 16, 1861.

70 "Local and Miscellaneous," *Daily Toledo Blade*, April 15, 1861.

71 Kathleen Jones, "Toledo Answers the Call, Part II," (http://www.angelfire.com/oh4/civwar/14thohio/toledo2.html).

72 "The War Spirit in Cincinnati," *Cincinnati Daily Commercial*, April 15, 1861.

73 "The War News," *Cleveland Morning Leader*, April 13, 1861.

74 "Town and Country," *Toledo Daily Herald and Times*, April 17, 1861.

75 Lee, *The History of the City of Columbus*, II, 89.

76 "The Feeling," *Toledo Daily Herald and News*, April 16, 1861.

77 "A Special Request," *Cincinnati Daily Commercial*, April 15, 1861.

78 "Local and Miscellaneous," *Daily Toledo Blade*, April 13, 1861.

79 "The Feeling."

80 Ibid.

81 "War Spirit in Elyria," *Elyria Independent Democrat*, April 17, 1861.

82 "Town and Country," *Toledo Daily Herald and Times*, April 16, 1861.

83 "The Flag of Our Union Forever," *Daily Toledo Blade*, April 16, 1861.

84 "Union Meeting, Held in the Union Depot Last Evening—Immense Enthusiasm—3000 Present," *Toledo Daily Herald and Times*, April 16, 1861.

85 "Meeting at Springfield, Ohio," *Cincinnati Daily Commercial*, April 17, 1861.

86 "Grand Union Demonstration," *Cincinnati Daily Commercial*, April 16, 1861.

87 "Great Impromptu Meeting of the People," *Cincinnati Daily Commercial*, April 18, 1861.

88 "Stop Up the Mouths of Traitors," *Sandusky Daily Commercial Register*, April 16, 1861.

89 "Well Said!" *Sandusky Daily Commercial Register*, April 16, 1861.

90 "Significant," *Daily Toledo Blade*, April 19, 1861.

Notes for Chapter 2

1 Betty L. Mitchell, *Edmund Ruffin: A Biography* (Bloomington: Indiana University Press, 1981), 13–15.

2 W. M. Mathew, "Edmund Ruffin and the Demise of the *Farmers' Register*," *The Virginia Magazine* 94, no. 1 (1986): 4–5.

3 Mitchell, *Edmund Ruffin*, 110.

4 Edmund Ruffin, *The Diary of Edmund Ruffin*, ed. William Kauffman Scarborough, 3 vols., vol. I (Baton Rouge: Louisiana State University Press, 1972), 80.

5 Ibid, 468.

6 Alexis de Tocqueville and J. P. Mayer, ed., *Journey to America* (New Haven: Yale University

Press, 1959), 263–4.

7   Ruffin, *Ruffin Diary*,I, 468.

8   Stephen B. Oates, *To Purge This Land with Blood*, 2nd ed. (Amherst: University of Massachusetts Press, 1984), 8.

9   Ibid, 14.

10 Ibid, 70.

11 Ibid, 129.

12 David S. Heidler and Jeanne T. Heidler, eds., *Encyclopedia of the American Civil War* (New York: W. W. Norton & Company, 2000), 293.

13 *Life, Trial and Execution of Captain John Brown; 1859* (Robert M. De Witt, 1859), 8.

14 Oates, *Purge This Land*, 271.

15 David S. Reynolds, *John Brown, Abolitionist* (New York: Alfred A. Knopf, 2005). 299.

16 Ruffin, *Ruffin Diary*, I, 349.

17 Oates, *Purge This Land*, 289–90. National Park Service, *John Brown's Raid*, *National Park Service History Series* (Washington, D.C.: Office of Publications, National Park Service, U.S. Department of the Interior, 1974), 25–7.

18 Oates, *Purge This Land*, 274–89.

19 Ibid, 291.

20 Ibid, 294.

21 Ibid, 276.

22 Ibid, 294.

23 Service, *John Brown's Raid* 48.

24 Oates, *Purge This Land*, 303.

25 Ibid, 306.

26 Ibid, 327.

27 Reynolds, *John Brown, Abolitionist*, 427.

28 Thomas C. Mulligan, "Lest the Rebels Come to Power: The Life of William Dennison, 1815–1882, Early Ohio Republican" (Dissertation, Ohio State University, 1994), 112.

29 Reynolds, *John Brown, Abolitionist*, 340–343, 429–430.

30 Gregory Toledo, *The Hanging of Old Brown* (Westport, Connecticut: Praeger, 2002), 223.

31 Oliver Crenshaw, "The Psychological Background of the Election of 1860 in the South," *The North Carolina Historical Review* XIX, no. 3 (1942): 275.

32 Ibid, 269.

33 Ibid, 264.

34 Murat Halstead, "The Execution of John Brown," *Ohio Archaeological and Historical Publications [Ohio History]* XXX (1921): 293.

35 Reynolds, *John Brown, Abolitionist*, 398–399.

36 Ibid, 427.

37 Ruffin, *Ruffin Diary*, 371.

38 Eric H. Walther, *The Fire-Eaters* (Baton Rouge: Louisiana State University Press, 1992), 228–69.

39 Toledo, *The Hanging of Old Brown*, 245. F. B. Sanborn, "The Virginia Campaign of John Brown, II," *The Atlantic Monthly*, February 1875: 721.

40 Henry Bibb, *The Life and Adventures of Henry Bibb, an American Slave* (Madison: University of Wisconsin Press, 2000), 54.

41 Ibid, 55.

42 Ibid, xi–xiii.

43 Ibid, 13.

44 Ibid, 16.

45 J. Blaine Hudson, *Fugitive Slaves and the Underground Railroad in the Kentucky Borderland* (Jefferson, North Carolina: McFarland & Company, Inc., 2002), 7.

46 Wilbur H. Siebert, *The Underground Railroad from Slavery to Freedom* (Gloucester, Massachusetts: Peter Smith, 1968), viii–ix.

47 Byron D. Fruehling and Robert H. Smith, "Subterranean Hideaways of the Underground Railroad in Ohio: An Architectural, Archaeological and Historical Critique of Local Traditions," *Ohio History* 102 (1993): 98–117.

48 Larry Gara, "The Underground Railroad: Legend of Reality?," *Proceedings of the American Philosophical Society* 105, no. 3 (1961): 334–9.

49 Hudson, *Fugitive Slaves*, 119.

50 Rev. John Rankin and Alison Gibson, eds., *Life of Rev. John Rankin, Written by Himself in His 80th Year, Circa 1872* (Ripley, Ohio: Rankin House National Historic Landmark, owned by the Ohio Historical Society and operated by Ripley Heritage, Inc., n.d.), 35–6.

51 Hudson, *Fugitive Slaves*, 153.

52 Ibid, 130.

53 George W. Knepper, *Ohio and Its People*, paperback ed. (Kent, Ohio: Kent State University Press, 1989), 217.

54 John P. Parker, *His Promised Land* (New York: W. W. Norton & Company, 1996), 25.

55 Hudson, *Fugitive Slaves*, 152–3.

56 Parker, *His Promised Land*, 93–6.

57 Ibid, 107–16.

58 Ibid, 87.

59 Catherine Drinker Bowen, *Miracle at Philadelphia: The Story of the Constitutional Convention, May to September 1787* (Boston: Little, Brown & Co., 1966). Carol Berkin, *A Brilliant Solution* (New York: Harcourt, Inc., 2002).

60 Berkin, *A Brilliant Solution*, 113. Sean Wilentz, *The Rise of American Democracy: Jefferson to Lincoln* (New York: W. W. Norton & Company, 2005), 34.

61 Wilentz, *The Rise of American Democracy*, 34.

62 Francis Fukuyama, "After the 'End of History'," in *Open Democracy* (2006): 6.

63 Knepper, *Ohio and Its People*, 206.

64 Ibid, 209.

65 Frederick J. Blue, "Salmon Portland Chase," in *Encyclopedia of the American Civil War*, ed. David S. Heidler and Jeanne T Heidler (New York: W. W. Norton & Company, 2000), 408.

66 Keith P. Griffler, *Front Line of Freedom* (Lexington: University Press of Kentucky, 2004), 112.

67 Nat Brandt, *The Town That Started the Civil War* (Syracuse, New York: Syracuse University Press, 1990), 213.

68 Kenneth N. Owens, *Galena, Grant, and the Fortunes of War* (Northern Illinois University, in cooperation with the Galena Historical Society, 1963), 35.

69 Brooks D. Simpson, *Ulysses S. Grant: Triumph over Adversity, 1822–1865* (Boston: Houghton Mifflin Company, 2000), 77.

70 Ulysses S. Grant, *Ulysses S. Grant: Memoirs and Selected Letters* (New York: Library of America, 1990), 152–3.

71 William T. Sherman, *Sherman's Civil War: Selected Correspondence of William T. Sherman, 1860–65*. ed. Brooks D. Simpson and Jean V. Berlin (Chapel Hill: University of North Carolina Press, 1999), 71.

72 Ibid, 70.

73 H. Wayne Morgan, *William McKinley and His America* (Syracuse, New York: Syracuse University Press, 1963), 16.

74 Benjamin P. Thomas and Harold M. Hyman, *Stanton: The Life and Times of Lincoln's Secretary of War* (New York: Alfred A. Knopf, 1962), 121.

75 Ibid, 122.

NOTES FOR CHAPTER 3

1 George W. Knepper, *Ohio and Its People*, paperback ed. (Kent, Ohio: Kent State University Press, 1989), 57.

2 Conrad Richter, *The Trees* (New York: Alfred A. Knopf, 1940), 8.

3 Andrew R. L. Cayton, "The Significance of Ohio in the Early American Republic," in *The Center of a Great Empire*, ed. Andrew R. L. Cayton and Stuart D. Hobbs (Athens, Ohio: Ohio University Press, 2005), 1.

4 Knepper, *Ohio and Its People*, 95.

5 Carl M. Becker, "Miles Greenwood," in *For the Union: Ohio Leaders in the Civil War*, ed. Kenneth M. Wheeler (Columbus: Ohio State University Press, 1968), 259.

6 Robert Leslie Jones, *History of Agriculture in Ohio to 1880* (Kent, Ohio: Kent State University Press, 1983), 182.

7 Ibid, 50–1.

8 James Dalzell, *Private Dalzell: His Autobiography, Poems and Comic War Papers* (Cincinnati: Robert Clark & Co., 1888), 15–6.

9 Jacob Dolson Cox, "Military Reminiscences of the Civil War," (http://www.sonofthesouth.net/leefoundation/cw1.htm: Robert E. Lee Historical Preservation Initiative, 1900), Chapter 1.

10 Whitelaw Reid, *Ohio in the War: Her Statesmen, Generals and Soldiers*, 1895 ed., vol. 1, *The History of Ohio During the War and the Lives of Her Generals* (Cincinnati: The Robert Clarke Company, 1895), 931.

11 Robert H. Jones, "Whitelaw Reid," in *For the Union: Ohio Leaders in the Civil War*, ed. Kenneth W. Wheeler (Columbus, Ohio: Ohio State University Press, 1968), 121–3.

12 Reid, *Ohio in the War*, 932.

13 Thomas C. Mulligan, "Lest the Rebels Come to Power: The Life of William Dennison, 1815–1882, Early Ohio Republican" (Dissertation, Ohio State University, 1994), 123–6.

14 David J. Eicher, *The Longest Night: A Military History of the Civil War* (New York: Simon & Schuster, 2001), 58.

15 "Henry Beebee Carrington," http://www.virtualogy.com/henrybeebeecarington/.

16 Harry Comer, "Letter No. 4, from Company A," *Lancaster Gazette & Democrat*, June 6, 1861.

17 "Letter from Columbus April 16th, 1861," *Cincinnati Daily Commercial*, April 17, 1861.

18 Mulligan, "Lest the Rebels Come to Power," 146.

19 "Aid and Comfort to Company a, Capt. Stafford," *Lancaster Gazette*, June 27, 1861.

20 Jones, "For the Union," 123.

21 Reid, *Ohio in the War*, I, 42.

22 Ibid, I, 43.

23 Ibid, I, 29.

24 Alfred E. Lee, *The History of the City of Columbus*, 2 vols., vol. II (Columbus, Ohio: Franklin County Genealogical and Historical Society, 2000), 89.

25 Reid, *Ohio in the War*, I, 27.

26 Mulligan, "Lest the Rebels Come to Power," 366–80.

27 Jacob D. Cox, "War Preparations in the North," in *Battles and Leaders of the Civil War*, ed. Robert Underwood Johnson and Clarence Clough Buel (New York: The Century Co.), I, 87.

28 Ibid, I, 86–7.

29 Ibid, I, 89.

30 Ernest B. Furgurson, *Freedom Rising: Washington in the Civil War* (New York: Alfred A. Knopf, 2004).

31 Cox, "Battles and Leaders," I, 90.

32 Harry Comer, "Letter No. 1 from Company A, April 21, 1861," *Lancaster Gazette & Democrat*, April 25, 1861.

33 Cox, "Military Reminiscences."

34 Milton McCoy, "First Bull Run: Experiences of an Ohio Three Months' Man," *National Tribune*, October 23, 1884.

35 E.B. Long with Barbara Long, *The Civil War Day by Day: An Almanac 1861–1865* (Garden City, New York: Doubleday, 1971; reprint, by Da Capo, n.p., n.d.), 62.

36 Harry Comer, "Harrisburg Encampment, Pa.," *The Ohio Eagle*, April 25, 1861.

37 Julia Ward Howe, "Reminiscences of Julia Ward Howe," *The Atlantic Monthly*, May 1899.

38 Harry Comer, "Camp Dennison, Lancaster, Pa," *The Ohio Eagle*, May 2, 1861.

39 Comer, "Letter No. 1 from Company A, April 21, 1861."

40 Albert Kern, *History of the First Regiment Ohio Volunteer Infantry in the Civil War 1861–1865* (Dayton: 1918; reprint, n.d., Curt Dalton, Dayton, Ohio), 5.

41 Comer, "Letter No. 1 from Company A, April 21, 1861."
42 McCoy, "First Bull Run: Experiences of an Ohio Three Months' Man," *National Tribune*, October 23, 1884.
43 Ibid.
44 Sharon Roberts, "Sanitary Commission Quilt Stories," (http://www.shasta.com/suesgoodco/ newcivilians/articles/roberts1.htm: 2004).
45 Reid, *Ohio in the War*, I, 257.
46 Eicher, *The Longest Night*.
47 Henry Howe, *Historical Collections of Ohio*, 2 vols., vol. II (Norwalk: State of Ohio, The Laning Printing Co., Public Printers, 1896).
48 Lee, *The History of the City of Columbus*, 95.
49 "Local Matters," *Cincinnati Daily Commercial*, April 19, 1861.
50 "Concert," *Lancaster Gazette*, May 2, 1861.
51 Mary Ann Steedman Wanatick, "Major General James Blair Steedman" (Thesis, University of Toledo, 1988).
52 Roberts, "Sanitary Commission."
53 Louis Leonard Tucker, *Cincinnati During the Civil War, Publications of the Ohio Civil War Centennial Commission* (Columbus, Ohio: Ohio State University Press, 1962), 25.
54 Joseph Hinson, "The Baltimore Passage," *National Tribune*, February 21, 1884.
55 Milton McCoy, "First Bull Run: Experiences of an Ohio Three Months' Man," *National Tribune*, October 23, 1884.
56 Donald W. Curl, "Murat Halstead," in *For the Union: Ohio Leaders in the Civil War*, ed. Kenneth W. Wheeler (Columbus: Ohio State University Press, 1968), 338–9.
57 Comer, "Letter No. 4, from Company A."
58 Reid, *Ohio in the War*, I, 738.
59 Ibid, I, 727.
60 Albert A. Woldman, "Book Review: Lincoln and His Generals," *Ohio History* 61, no. 3 (1952): 317.
61 Reid, *Ohio in the War*, I, 658.
62 Julia Dent Grant and John Y. Simon eds., *The Personal Memoirs of Julia Dent Grant* (New York: G. P. Putnam's Sons, 1975), 92.
63 Stephen W. Sears, *George B. McClellan, the Young Napoleon* (New York: Ticknor & Fields, 1988), 72.
64 Reid, *Ohio in the War*, I, 33.
65 Sears, *George B. McClellan*, 72.
66 Benjamin P. Thomas and Harold M. Hyman, *Stanton: The Life and Times of Lincoln's Secretary of War* (New York: Alfred A. Knopf, 1962), 124.
67 Betty L. Mitchell, *Edmund Ruffin: A Biography* (Bloomington: Indiana University Press, 1981), 183–190.

NOTES FOR CHAPTER 4

1 Harry Comer, "Letter No. 4, from Company A," *Lancaster Gazette & Democrat*, June 6, 1861.
2 Peg A. Lamphier, *Kate Chase and William Sprague: Politics and Gender in a Civil War Marriage* (Lincoln: University of Nebraska Press, 2003), 24.
3 Ernest B. Furgurson, *Freedom Rising: Washington in the Civil War* (New York: Alfred A. Knopf, 2004),12–15.
4 Murat Halstead, "The City Dusty, and Hackmen as Usual," *Cincinnati Daily Commercial*, June 4, 1861.
5 Warren Lee Goss, "Going to the Front," in *Battles and Leaders of the Civil War*, ed. Robert Underwood Johnson and Clarence Clough Buel (New York: The Century Co., 1887), 157.
6 Halstead, "The City Dusty, and Hackmen as Usual."
7 William D. Bickham, "Our Army in West Virginia," *Cincinnati Daily Commercial*, July 19, 1861.

8   John G. Nicolay, *The Outbreak of the Rebellion* (New York: Da Capo Press, 1995).

9   Keith P. Griffler, *Front Line of Freedom: African-Americans and the Forging of the Underground Railroad in the Ohio Valley* (Lexington, Kentucky: University Press of Kentucky, 2004).

10   Whitelaw Reid, *Ohio in the War: Her Statesmen, Generals and Soldiers*, 1895 ed., vol. 1., *The History of Ohio During the War and the Lives of Her Generals* (Cincinnati: The Robert Clarke Company, 1895), 46.

11   Ibid, I, 47.

12   Ibid, I, 47–8.

13   W. C. Daniels, "From the Regiment," (http://www.angelfire.com/oh4/civwar/14thohio/daniels.html: 1861).

14   Ibid.

15   Ambrose Bierce, *Phantoms of a Blood-Stained Period: The Complete Civil War Writings of Ambrose Bierce* Russell Duncan and David J. Klooster, eds.,(Amherst: University of Massachusetts Press, 2002), 37.

16   Thomas Francis Galwey, *The Valiant Hours* (Harrisburg, Pennsylvania: The Stackpole Company, 1961), 2.

17   Robert O. Curry, "McClellan's Western Virginia Campaign of 1861," *Ohio History* 71, no. 2 (1962): 91.

18   David S. Heidler and Jeanne T. Heidler, eds., *Encyclopedia of the American Civil War* (New York: W. W. Norton & Company, 2000), 1,677.

19   W. Hunter Lesser, *Rebels at the Gate* (Naperville, Illinois: Sourcebooks, Inc., 2004), 98.

20   Constantin Grebner, *We Were the Ninth: A History of the Ninth Regiment, Ohio Volunteer Infantry, April 17, 1861, to June 7, 1864*, trans. Frederic Trautmann (Kent, Ohio: Kent State University Press, 1987), 47.

21   Lesser, *Rebels at the Gate*, 103.

22   John Beatty, *Memoirs of a Volunteer 1861–1863* (New York: W. W. Norton & Company, 1946), 27.

23   Galwey, *The Valiant Hours*, 5.

24   Jacob D. Cox, "McClellan in West Virginia," in *Battles and Leaders of the Civil War* (New York: The Century Co., 1887), I, 135.

25   Lesser, *Rebels at the Gate*. William D. Bickham, "Our Army in West Virginia," *Cincinnati Daily Commercial*, July 19, 1861.

26   T. Harry Williams, *Hayes of the Twenty-Third: The Civil War Volunteer Officer* (New York: Alfred A. Knopf, 1965), 45.

27   Ibid, 10.

28   Ibid, 48.

29   George M. Finch, "The Boys of '61," in *G. A. R. War Papers*, ed. E. R. Monfort, H. B. Furness, and Fred. H. Alms (Cincinnati: Fred C. Jones Post, No. 401, 1891), 245.

30   Ibid, 250–251.

31   Ibid, 248–9.

32   Ibid, 249–50.

33   Eugene C. Tidball, *"No Disgrace to My Country"* (Kent, Ohio: Kent State University Press, 2002), 5.

34   *The War of the Rebellion: A Compilation of the Official Records of the Union and Confederate Armies*, 70 vols. (Washington, DC: 1880–1901). Series I, Vol. 2, Chapter IX, (Serial # 2), No. 3.

35   Reid, *Ohio in the War*, I, 694.

36   Edwin C. Bearss, *Fields of Honor: Pivotal Battles of the Civil War* (Washington, D.C.: National Geographic, 2006), 40.

37   JoAnna M. McDonald, *We Shall Meet Again: The First Battle of Bull Run (Manassas)* (n.p.: Oxford University Press, 1999), 9.

38   Bearss, *Fields of Honor*, xv.

39   T. Harry Williams, *Lincoln and His Generals* (New York: Alfred A. Knopf, 1952). 21.

40   McDonald, *We Shall Meet Again*, 191–196.

41 Tidball, *"No Disgrace to My Country,"* 204.

42 McDonald, *We Shall Meet Again*, 23.

43 Finch, "Boys of '61," 255.

44 Ibid, 257.

45 McDonald, *We Shall Meet Again*, 52.

46 David J. Eicher, *The Longest Night: A Military History of the Civil War* (New York: Simon & Schuster, 2001), 96.

47 McDonald, *We Shall Meet Again*, 135.

48 Ethan Rafuse, *A Single Grand Victory: The First Campaign and Battle of Manassas*, ed. Steven E. Woodworth, *Books on the Civil War Era* (Wilmington, Delaware: Scholarly Resources Inc., 2002), 175–6.

49 William T. Sherman, *Sherman's Civil War: Selected Correspondence of William T. Sherman, 1860–1865*, ed. Brooks D. Simpson and Jean V. Berlin (Chapel Hill: The University of North Carolina Press, 1999), 124.

50 McDonald, *We Shall Meet Again*, 136–7.

51 Ibid, 113.

52 Ibid, 99.

53 Ibid, 135.

54 Ibid, 140.

55 *The War of the Rebellion: A Compilation of the Official Records of the Union and Confederate Armies*, (1899).

56 Sherman, Simpson, and Berlin, *Sherman's Civil War*, 124.

57 *Official Records, Armies*. Series I, Vol. II, Chapter IX (Serial # 2), No. 19.

58 Tidball, *"No Disgrace to My Country,"* 213.

59 McDonald, *We Shall Meet Again*, 167.

60 Betty L. Mitchell, *Edmund Ruffin: A Biography* (Bloomington: Indiana University Press, 1981), 196.

61 Alfred E. Lee, *The History of the City of Columbus*, 2 vols., vol. II (Columbus, Ohio: Franklin County Genealogical and Historical Society, 2000), 101.

62 Howard Carroll, *Twelve Americans: Their Lives and Times, Essex Index Reprint Series* (Freeport, New York: Books for Libraries Press, 1971), 248.

63 McDonald, *We Shall Meet Again*, 191.

64 Milton McCoy, "First Bull Run: Experiences of an Ohio Three Months' Man," *National Tribune*, October 23, 1884.

65 Quoted in Eicher, *The Longest Night*, 101.

66 Williams, *Lincoln and His Generals*, 23.

67 John Y. Simon, ed., *The Papers of Ulysses S. Grant*, vol. 4 (Carbondale, Illinois: Southern Illinois University Press, 1972), *Passim*.

68 Jean Edward Smith, *Grant* (New York: Simon & Schuster, 2001), 23.

69 Hamlin Garland, *Ulysses S. Grant: His Life and Character* (New York: Macmillan, 1920), 43.

70 Julia Dent Grant, *The Personal Memoirs of Julia Dent Grant,* ed. John Y. Simon (New York: G. P. Putnam's Sons, 1975), 49.

71 Ibid. 50.

72 William S. McFeely, *Grant: A Biography* (New York: W. W. Norton & Company, 1981), 46–47.

73 Ibid, 27.

74 Smith, *Grant*, 85.

75 Grant and Simon ed., *The Personal Memoirs of Julia Dent Grant*, 89.

76 Smith, *Grant*, 108–9.

77 Ulysses S. Grant, *Ulysses S. Grant: Memoirs and Selected Letters* (New York: Library of America, 1990), 164.

78 Jacob Dolson Cox, "Military Reminiscences of the Civil War," (http://www.sonofthesouth.net/leefoundation/cw1.htm: Robert E. Lee Historical Preservation Initiative, 1900). Chapter 5.

79 Ibid, Chapter 4.

80 Ibid.

81 H. Wayne Morgan, *William McKinley and His America* (Syracuse, New York: Syracuse University Press, 1963), 21–2.

82 Cox, "McClellan in West Virginia," 148.

83 Reid, *Ohio in the War*, I, 38.

84 Thomas C. Mulligan, "Lest the Rebels Come to Power: The Life of William Dennison, 1815–1882, Early Ohio Republican" (Dissertation, Ohio State University, 1994). 213–6.

85 Whitelaw Reid, *Ohio in the War: Her Statesmen, Generals, and Soldiers*, 1895 ed., vol. 1, *The History of Ohio During the War and the Lives of Her Generals* (New York: Moore, Wilstach & Baldwin, 1868), I, 57.

86 Joseph E. Johnston, "Responsibilities of the First Bull Run," in *Battles and Leaders of the Civil War*, ed. Robert Underwood Johnson and Clarence Clough Buel (New York: The Century Company, 1887), I, 252.

NOTES FOR CHAPTER 5

1   Ron Chernow, *Titan: The Life of John D. Rockefeller, Sr.* (New York: Random House, 1998), 48.

2   Ibid, *Passim*.

3   Julia Ward Howe, "Reminiscences of Julia Ward Howe," *The Atlantic Monthly*, May 1899: 704.

4   George Kimball, "Origin of the John Brown Song," *The New England Magazine*, December 1889: 372.

5   Julia Ward Howe, "The Battle Hymn of the Republic," (http://www.law.ou.edu/hist/ bathymn.html: University of Oklahoma Law Center, 1862).

6   Allan Peskin, *Garfield* (Kent, Ohio: Kent State University Press, 1978), 26.

7   James and Lucretia Garfield, *Crete and James: Personal Letters of Lucretia and James Garfield,* ed. John Shaw (East Lansing, Michigan: Michigan State University Press, 1994), xii.

8   Ibid, 103.

9   Peskin, *Garfield*, 70.

10 Garfield and Shaw, *Crete and James*, 103.

11 Ibid, 104.

12 Ibid, 113.

13 Peskin, *Garfield*, 97.

14 Robert L. Kimberly and Ephraim S. Holloway, *The Forty-First Ohio Veteran Volunteer Infantry in the War of the Rebellion, 1861–1865* (Cleveland: W. R. Smellie, 1897), 9.

15 W. B. Hazen, *A Narrative of Military Service* (Huntington, West Virginia: Blue Acorn Press, 1993, 3–7.

16 Ibid, 7.

17 W. Hunter Lesser, *Rebels at the Gate* (Naperville, Illinois: Sourcebooks, Inc., 2004), 247.

18 Ibid. 244.

19 T. Harry Williams, *Hayes of the Twenty-Third: The Civil War Volunteer Officer* (New York: Alfred A. Knopf, 1965), 97.

20 Thomas Francis Galwey, *The Valiant Hours* (Harrisburg, Pennsylvania: The Stackpole Company, 1961), 18.

21 Oscar D. Ladley, *Hearth and Knapsack: The Ladley Letters, 1857–1880*, ed. Carl M. Becke and Ritchie Thomas (Athens, Ohio: Ohio University Press, 1988), 24.

22 Lesser, *Rebels at the Gate*, 241–2.

23 Ladley, Becker, and Thomas, *Hearth and Knapsack*, 23.

24 Stephen W. Sears, *George B. McClellan, the Young Napoleon* (New York: Ticknor & Fields, 1988), 103, 128, 132. James M. McPherson, *Battle Cry of Freedom: The Civil War Era*, paperback ed. (Oxford, England, and New York: Oxford University Press, 1988), 348–50.

25 McPherson, *Battle Cry of Freedom*, 360.

26 Alfred E. Lee, *The History of the City of Columbus*, 2 vols., vol. II (Columbus, Ohio: Franklin County Genealogical and Historical Society, 2000), 95.

27 John H. Eicher and David J. Eicher, *Civil War High Commands* (Stanford, California: Stanford University Press, 2001), 47.

28 Andrew Altman, "Andrew Altman Papers, 1861–1937," in *Bowling Green State University*

Center for Archival Collections. "January the 25, 1862".

29 Ibid, "Febuary the 5 1862".

30 Ibid, "Febuary the 8 1862".

31 Gilbert F. Dodds, *Camp Chase: The Story of a Civil War Post* (Columbus, Ohio: Franklin County Historical Society, n.d.), 3.

32 Altman, "Altman Papers." "January the 25 1862".

33 Jacob Bruner, "Bruner, Jacob, Letters, 1861–1863," (http://dbs.ohiohistory.org/africanam/msa/mss994.cfrr: Ohio Historical Society, 1861–3).

34 Marcus M. Spiegel, *A Jewish Colonel in the Civil War, ed.* Jean Powers Soman and Frank L. Byrne (Lincoln: University of Nebraska Press, 1995), 20.

35 Ibid, 21.

36 Lee, *The History of the City of Columbus*, 97.

37 John E. Richardson, "The Civil War Letters of John E. Richardson: October 1861–February 1862, Camp Dennison," (http://www.48ovvi.org/oh48jer1.htm: 1861–2).

38 John A. Bering and Thomas Montgomery, "History of the Forty-Eighth Ohio Vet. Vol. Inf.," (http://www.48ovvi.org/oh48hist.htm: 1880).

39 Richardson, "Richardson Letters."

40 Bering and Montgomery, "The Forty-Eighth Ohio."

41 Richardson, "Richardson Letters."

42 Hans L. Trefousse, "The Motivation of a Radical Republican," *Ohio History* 73: 64.

43 Mary Land, "'Bluff' Ben Wade's New England Background," *New England Quarterly* 27, no. 4 (1954): 484.

44 Ibid, 485.

45 Ibid, 486.

46 Ibid, 487.

47 Julia Dent Grant, *The Personal Memoirs of Julia Dent Grant*, ed. John Y. Simon (New York: G. P. Putnam's Sons, 1975), 93.

48 Ulysses S. Grant, *Ulysses S. Grant: Memoirs and Selected Letters* (New York: Library of America, 1990), 184.

49 Jean Edward Smith, *Grant* (New York: Simon & Schuster, 2001), 109.

50 Ibid, 117.

51 Grant, *Grant: Memoirs and Selected Letters*, 190.

52 John Y. Simon, ed., *The Papers of Ulysses S. Grant*, vol. 4 (Carbondale, Illinois: Southern Illinois University Press, 1972), 162.

53 David J. Eicher, *The Longest Night: A Military History of the Civil War* (New York: Simon & Schuster, 2001), 172.

54 Smith, *Grant*, 155.

55 Grant, *Grant: Memoirs and Selected Letters*, 206.

56 Altman, "Altman Papers." "Febuary the 22 1862".

57 Smith, 160.

58 Grant, *Grant: Memoirs and Selected Letters*, 208.

59 Ibid, 208.

60 Smith, *Grant*, 147.

61 Lee Kennett, *Sherman: A Soldier's Life* (New York: HarperCollins, 2001), 7.

62 John F. Marszalek, "General and Mrs. William T. Sherman, a Contentious Union," in *Intimate Strategies of the Civil War*, ed. Carol K. Bleser and Lesley J. Gordon (New York: Oxford University Press, 2001), 139–41.

63 Kennett, *Sherman*, 82.

64 Ibid, 114.

65 William T. Sherman, *Sherman's Civil War: Selected Correspondence of William T. Sherman, 1860–1865*, ed. Brooks D. Simpson and Jean V. Berlin (Chapel Hill: The University of North Carolina Press, 1999), 121–2.

66 Kennett, *Sherman*, 128.

67 Ibid, 139.

68 "William Tecumseh Sherman," (http://en.wikiquote.org/wiki/William_Tecumseh_Sherman:

Wikiquote, 1862).

69   Sherman, Simpson, and Berlin, *Sherman's Civil War*, 154.
70   Stanley P. Hirshson, *The White Tecumseh: A Biography of General William T. Sherman* (New York: John Wiley & Sons, Inc., 1997), 101.
71   William T. Sherman, *Sherman's Civil War: Selected Correspondence of William T. Sherman, 1860–1865*, ed. Brooks D. Simpson and Jean V. Berlin (Chapel Hill: The University of North Carolina Press, 1999), 156.
72   Marszalek, "Intimate Strategies," 148.
73   Kennett, *Sherman*, 145.
74   O. Edward Cunningham, "Shiloh and the Western Campaign of 1862" (Dissertation, Louisiana State University, 1966), 158.
75   Brooks D. Simpson and Jean V. Berlin, eds., *Sherman's Civil War*, Civil War America (Chapel Hill: University of North Carolina, 1999), 198.

Notes for Chapter 6

1   Jean Edward Smith, *Grant* (New York: Simon & Schuster, 2001), 123.
2   "Andrew Altman Papers, 1861–1937," in *Bowling Green State University Center for Archival Collections, Passim*.
3   Joseph Orville Jackson, ed., *"Some of the Boys ..." The Civil War Letters of Isaac Jackson, 1862–1865* (Carbondale, Illinois: Southern Illinois University, 1960), 14.
4   James A. Garfield, *The Wild Life of the Army: Civil War Letters of James A. Garfield* (East Lansing, Michigan: Michigan State University Press, 1964), 91.
5   Sarah Rhoades, "Corporal John R. Rhoades Papers, 1858–1865," in *Hayes Presidential Center* (Fremont, Ohio: 1862). "November Friday 21st at home 1862."
6   Stephen F. Williams, "The Buckeye from Missouri," (http://www.48ovvi.org/oh48buckeye.htm).
7   Margaret E. Wagner, Gary W. Gallagher, and Paul Finkelman, eds., *The Library of Congress Civil War Desk Reference* (New York: Simon & Schuster, 2002), 254.
8   Ulysses S. Grant, *Ulysses S. Grant: Memoirs and Selected Letters* (New York: Library of America, 1990), 246.
9   David J. Eicher, *The Longest Night: A Military History of the Civil War* (New York: Simon & Schuster, 2001), 160–1.
10   Whitelaw Reid, *Ohio in the War: Her Statesmen, Generals, and Soldiers*, vol. 2., *The History of Her Regiments and Other Military Organizations* (Cincinnati: The Robert Clarke Company, 1895), 105.
11   O. Edward Cunningham, "Shiloh and the Western Campaign of 1862" (Dissertation, Louisiana State University, 1966).
12   John K. Duke, *History of the Fifty-Third Regiment, Ohio Volunteer Infantry, During the War of the Rebellion...* (Portsmouth, Ohio: The Blade Printing Company, 1900), 14.
13   Larry J. Daniel, *Shiloh: The Battle That Changed the Civil War* (New York: A Touchstone book, published by Simon & Schuster, 1998), 135.
14   Ibid, 135.
15   Duke, *History of the Fifty-Third Regiment*, 1.
16   Ibid, 1–2.
17   Ibid, 3.
18   Ibid, 5–6.
19   Ibid, 7–8.
20   Ibid, 41.
21   Ibid, 14.
22   Eicher, *The Longest Night*, 223.
23   Ibid, 223.
24   Duke, *History of the Fifty-Third Regiment*, 13.
25   Ibid, 43.
26   Ibid, 44.

27 Ibid, 44.

28 Ibid, 44–45.

29 Nan Card, "Experience of Death in the Civil War: Sandusky County, Ohio" (Thesis, Bowling Green State University, 2001), 35.

30 Duke, *History of the Fifty-Third Regiment*, 45.

31 Ibid, 46–47.

32 Ibid, 47–48.

33 Ibid, 39.

34 *The War of the Rebellion: A Compilation of the Official Records of the Union and Confederate Armies*, 70 vols. (Washington, DC: 1880–1901). Series I, Vol. X, Chapter IX, Part I (Series #10), No. 206.

35 William T. Sherman, *Sherman's Civil War: Selected Correspondence of William T. Sherman, 1860–1865*, ed. Brooks D. Simpson and Jean V. Berlin (Chapel Hill: The University of North Carolina Press, 1999), 201.

36 Grant, *Grant: Memoirs and Selected Letters*, 227.

37 Capt. F. M. Posegate, 48th OVI, "The Sunday Battle at Shiloh," (http://www.48ovvi.org/oh48shilohsun.htm).

38 Ibid.

39 Grant, *Grant: Memoirs and Selected Letters*, 228.

40 Daniel, *Shiloh*, 227.

41 Ibid, 250.

42 Eicher, *The Longest Night*, 229.

43 Grant, *Grant: Memoirs and Selected Letters*, 234–235.

44 Garfield, *Wild Life of the Army*, 67.

45 Ambrose Bierce, *Phantoms of a Blood-Stained Period: The Complete Civil War Writings of Ambrose Bierce,* ed. Russell Duncan and David J. Klooster, (Amherst: University of Massachusetts Press, 2002). 93–4.

46 Ibid, 99.

47 Andrew Altman, "Andrew Altman Papers, 1861–1937," in *Bowling Green State University Center for Archival Collections.* "April the 13 1862."

48 Posegate, "Posegate."

49 William Caldwell, "Caldwell Family Papers," in *Hayes Presidential Center* (Fremont, Ohio).

50 Bierce, Duncan, and Klooster, *Phantoms of a Blood-Stained Period*, 103–104.

51 Daniel, *Shiloh*, 272.

52 Reid, *Ohio in the War: Her Statesmen, Generals, and Soldiers*, II, 837.

53 Emerson Opdycke, *To Battle for God and the Right: The Civil War Letterbooks of Emerson Opdycke,* ed. Glenn V. Longacre and John E. Hass (Urbana, Illinois: University of Illinois Press, 2003), 28, 30, 31.

54 James and Lucretia Garfield, *Crete and James: Personal Letters of Lucretia and James Garfield,* ed. and John Shaw (East Lansing, Michigan: Michigan State University Press, 1994), 132, 134.

55 James M. McPherson, *Battle Cry of Freedom: The Civil War Era*, paperback ed. (Oxford, England, and New York: Oxford University Press, 1988), 413.

56 Daniel, *Shiloh*, 304.

57 Julia Dent Grant, *The Personal Memoirs of Julia Dent Grant,* ed. John Y. Simon (New York: G. P. Putnam's Sons, 1975), 99.

58 Lee Kennett, *Sherman: A Soldier's Life*, softcover ed. (New York: Perennial/HarperCollins, 2001), 170.

59 Sherman, Simpson, and Berlin, *Sherman's Civil War*, 201–202.

60 Ibid, 202.

61 William T. Sherman and Ellen Ewing Sherman, "William T. Sherman Family Papers," (http://archives.nd.edu/findaids/ead/index/SHR001.htm: April 19, 1862), University of Notre Dame.

62 Daniel, *Shiloh*, 309.

63 Ibid, 308.

64 Opdycke, Longacre, and Hass, *To Battle for God and the Right*, 27.
65 Whitelaw Reid, *Ohio in the War: Her Statesmen, Generals and Soldiers*, 1895 ed., vol. 1., *The History of Ohio During the War and the Lives of Her Generals* (Cincinnati: The Robert Clarke Company, 1895), 377.
66 Ibid, 614; William Pittenger, *Daring and Suffering* (New York: War Pub. Co., 1887), passim.
67 Grant, *Grant: Memoirs and Selected Letters*, 251.
68 Brooks D. Simpson, *Ulysses S. Grant: Triumph over Adversity, 1822–1865* (Boston: Houghton Mifflin Company, 2000), 141.
69 William Tecumseh Sherman, *Memoirs of General W. T. Sherman* (New York: Penguin Books, 2000), 236.
70 Ibid, 236.
71 Simpson, *Ulysses S. Grant*, 139.
72 Lisa Tendrich Frank, "Women," in *Encyclopedia of the American Civil War*, ed. David S. Heidler and Jeanne T. Heidler (New York: W. W. Norton & Company, 2000).
73 Smith, *Grant*, 216.
74 Reid, *Ohio in the War*, I, 375–8.

NOTES FOR CHAPTER 7

1   David S. Heidler and Jeanne T Heidler, "Medicine" in *Encyclopedia of the American Civil War*, ed. David S. Heidler and Jeanne T Heidler (New York: W.W. Norton, 2000), 1,303.
2   United States Civil War Center [Louisiana State University], "Statistical Summary [of] America's Major Wars," (http://www.cwc.lsu.edu/cwc/other/stats/warcost.htm).
3   Frederick H. Dyer, *A Compendium of the War of the Rebellion*, Three vols., (New York: Thomas Yoseloff, 1959). I, 11–18. See also "Statistical Summary, America's Major Wars" on the Louisiana State University's "United States Civil War Center" Web site, http://www.cwc.lsu.edu/other/stats/warcost.com.htm(consulted by author on March 27, 2007.)
4   Nan Card, "Experience of Death in the Civil War: Sandusky County, Ohio" (Thesis, Bowling Green State University, 2001), 1–2.
5   Gary Laderman, *The Sacred Remains: American Attitudes toward Death, 1799–1883* (New Haven: Yale University Press, 1996), 96–116.
6   Quoted in Jane E. Schultz, "The Inhospitable Hospital: Gender and Professionalism in Civil War Medicine," *Journal of Women in Culture and Society* 17, no. 2 (1992). 387.
7   Card, "Experience of Death," 124.
8   Ibid, 71.
9   Ibid, 72.
10 Ibid, 71.
11 Ibid, 73.
12 Henry L. Dawes, "Recollections of Stanton under Lincoln," *Atlantic Monthly*, February 1894: 169.
13 Benjamin P. Thomas and Harold M. Hyman, *Stanton: The Life and Times of Lincoln's Secretary of War* (New York: Alfred A. Knopf, 1962), 30.
14 Ibid, 40–1.
15 Ibid, 55.
16 Ibid, 59.
17 Ibid, 66.
18 Michael Burlingame and John R. Turner Ettlinger, eds., *Inside Lincoln's White House: The Complete Civil War Diary of John Hay* (Carbondale, Illinois: Southern Illinois University Press, 1997), 37.
19 Thomas and Hyman, *Stanton*, Opposite 124.
20 David J. Eicher, *The Longest Night: A Military History of the Civil War* (New York: Simon & Schuster, 2001), 101.
21 Dawes, "Recollections of Stanton," 163.
22 Eicher, *The Longest Night*, 163.

23 "Good News from Washington," *Plain Dealer*, January 14, 1862. "A New Order of
   Things," *Plain Dealer*, January 20, 1862.
24 Thomas and Hyman, *Stanton*, 147.
25 Eric L. McKitrick, "Stanton: The Life and Times of Lincoln's Secretary of War [Review],"
   Journal of Southern History 28, no. 3: 369.
26 Dawes, "Recollections of Stanton," 164.
27 Charles F. Benjamin, "Recollections of Secretary Stanton," *The Century*, March 1887: 767.
28 Peter Cozzens, *General John Pope: A Life for the Nation* (Urbana, Illinois: University of
   Illinois Press, 2000), 75.
29 Thomas and Hyman, *Stanton*, 173.
30 Eugene C. Tidball, "Duty, Honor, Country, and Skullduggery: Lincoln's Secretary of War
   Meddles at West Point.," *Civil War History* 45, no. 1: 24.
31 Thomas and Hyman, *Stanton*, 361–2.
32 David S. Heidler and Jeanne T. Heidler, eds., *Encyclopedia of the American Civil War* (New
   York: W. W. Norton & Company, 2000), 1,059–60.
33 Eicher, *The Longest Night*, 208.
34 Brian McGinty, "John Charles Fremont," in *Historical Times Illustrated Encyclopedia of the
   Civil War*, ed. Patricia L. Faust (New York: Harper & Row, 1986), 291.
35 Thomas Francis Galwey, *The Valiant Hours* (Harrisburg, Pennsylvania: The Stackpole
   Company, 1961), 19–20.
36 Oscar D. Ladley, *Hearth and Knapsack: The Ladley Letters, 1857–1880*, ed. Carl M.
   Becker and Ritchie Thomas (Athens, Ohio: Ohio University Press, 1988). 35.
37 Galwey, *The Valiant Hours*, 22.
38 Ladley, Becker, and Thomas, *Hearth and Knapsack*, 35.
39 Stephen W. Sears, *George B. McClellan, the Young Napoleon* (New York: Ticknor &
   Fields, 1988), 95.
40 Eicher, *The Longest Night*, 217.
41 John Pope, "The Second Battle of Bull Run," (http://www.civilwarhome.com/
   popemanassas.htm).
42 Cozzens, *General John Pope*, 73.
43 Mark Mayo Boatner III, *The Civil War Dictionary*, rev. ed. (New York: Vintage Books,
   1991), 659.
44 Ibid, 859.
45 David T. Thackery, *A Light and Uncertain Hold: A History of the Sixty-Sixth Ohio
   Volunteer Infantry* (Kent, Ohio: Kent State University Press, 1999), 88–94.
46 Cozzens, *General John Pope*, 103–104.
47 Eicher, *The Longest Night*, 322.
48 John J. Hennessy, *Return to Bull Run: The Campaign and Battle of Second Manassas* (New
   York: Simon & Schuster, 1993), 127.
49 Ibid, 196.
50 Ibid, 357.
51 Cozzens, *General John Pope*, 161.
52 Hennessy, *Return to Bull Run*, 391.
53 Jacob Dolson Cox, "Military Reminiscences of the Civil War," (http://www.sonofthesouth.
   net/leefoundation/cw1.htm: Robert E. Lee Historical Preservation Initiative, 1900).
   Chapter 12, p. 3.
54 Judith E. Harper, *Women During the Civil War: An Encyclopedia* (New York: Routledge,
   2004), 34.
55 Ibid, 34.
56 Nina Brown Baker, *Cyclone in Calico: The Story of Mary Ann Bickerdyke* (Boston: Little,
   Brown and Company, 1952), 83.
57 Rick Sowash, *Heroes of Ohio: 23 True Tales of Courage and Character* (Bowling Green,
   Ohio: Gabriel's Horn Publishing Company, 1998), 49.
58 Ibid, 50. Baker, *Cyclone in Calico*, 160.
59 Edmund Ruffin, *The Diary of Edmund Ruffin*, 3 vols., vol. 2 (Baton Rouge: Louisiana State

University Press, 1976), 291.

NOTES FOR CHAPTER 8

1   "Women," in *The Library of Congress Civil War Desk Reference,* ed. Margaret E. Warner et al. (New York: Simon & Schuster, 2002), 701–10.

2   Sarah Wilson Rice, "Letters to Dr. John B. Rice," (Fremont, Ohio: Hayes Presidential Center, 1863–64). "Home March 5th, 1863."

3   Ibid, July 2, 1863.

4   Dale L. Walker, *Mary Edwards Walker: Above and Beyond* (New York: Forge: Tom Doherty Associates, 2005), 115.

5   Rev. Nixon B. Stewart, *Dan McCook's Regiment, 52nd O.V.I. A History of the Regiment, Its Campaigns, and Battles* (n.p.: Author, 1900; reprint, 1999, Huntington, West Virginia: Blue Acorn Press), 91–2.

6   American Association of University Women St. Lawrence County (New York) Branch, "Mary Edwards Walker: Civil War Doctor," (http://www.northnet.org/stlawrenceaauw/ walker.htm: 2005).

7   Jane E. Schultz, "The Inhospitable Hospital: Gender and Professionalism in Civil War Medicine," *Journal of Women in Culture and Society* 17, no. 2 (1992): 363.

8   Lisa Tendrich Frank, "Women," in *Encyclopedia of the American Civil War,* ed. David S. Heidler and Jeanne T. Heidler (New York: W. W. Norton & Company, 2000), 2,142.

9   James and Lucretia Garfield, *Crete and James: Personal Letters of Lucretia and James Garfield,* ed. John Shaw, (East Lansing, Michigan: Michigan State University Press, 1994), x.

10 James M. McPherson, *Battle Cry of Freedom: The Civil War Era,* paperback ed. (Oxford, England, and New York: Oxford University Press, 1988), 537.

11 T. Harry Williams, *Hayes of the Twenty-Third: The Civil War Volunteer Officer* (New York: Alfred A. Knopf, 1965), 138.

12 Jacob Dolson Cox, "Military Reminiscences of the Civil War," (http://www.sonofthesouth. net/leefoundation/cw1.htm: Robert E. Lee Historical Preservation Initiative, 1900).

13 David J. Eicher, *The Longest Night: A Military History of the Civil War* (New York: Simon & Schuster, 2001), 347.

14 Stephen W. Sears, *Landscape Turned Red: The Battle of Antietam* (Boston: Houghton Mifflin, 1983), 211.

15 David T. Thackery, *A Light and Uncertain Hold: A History of the Sixty-Sixth Ohio Volunteer Infantry* (Kent, Ohio: Kent State University Press, 1999), 105.

16 *The War of the Rebellion: A Compilation of the Official Records of the Union and Confederate Armies,* 70 vols. (Washington, DC: 1880–1901). Series I, Vol. XIX, Part I (Serial # 27), No. 184.

17 Thackery, *A Light and Uncertain Hold,* 106.

18 Thomas Francis Galwey, *The Valiant Hours* (Harrisburg, Pennsylvania: The Stackpole Company, 1961), 40–41.

19 Ibid, 41.

20 Ibid, 42–43.

21 Ibid, 44.

22 Ibid, 45.

23 Ethan S. Rafuse, "William Mc Kinley," in *Encyclopedia of the Civil War,* ed. David S. Heidler and Jeanne T Heidler (New York: W. W. Norton & Company, 2000), 1,289.

24 Thackery, *A Light and Uncertain Hold,* 108–109.

25 Ibid, 108.

26 Stephen W. Sears, *George B. McClellan, the Young Napoleon* (New York: Ticknor & Fields, 1988), 341.

27 Benjamin P. Thomas and Harold M. Hyman, *Stanton: The Life and Times of Lincoln's Secretary of War* (New York: Alfred A. Knopf, 1962), 225.

28 Timothy H. Donovan Jr. et al., *The American Civil War,* ed. Thomas E. Griess, *West Point Military History Series* (Garden City Park, New York: Square One Publishers, 2002),

123.

29 *Official Records, Armies*. Series I, Vol. XXI (Serial # 31), No. 93.

30 Galwey, *The Valiant Hours*, 61.

31 William Kepler, *History of the Three Months' and Three Years' Service from April 16ᵗʰ, 1861, to June 22ᵈ, 1864, ... Of the Fourth Infantry Regiment Ohio Volunteer Infantry* (Cleveland: Leader Printing Company, 1886), 95–96.

32 Galwey, *The Valiant Hours*, 65.

33 Ibid, 65.

34 Ibid, 65–66.

35 Louis Leonard Tucker, *Cincinnati During the Civil War, Publications of the Ohio Civil War Centennial Commission* (Columbus: Ohio State University Press, 1962), 27. Whitelaw Reid, *Ohio in the War: Her Statesmen, Generals and Soldiers*, 1895 ed., vol. 1, *The History of Ohio During the War and the Lives of Her Generals* (Cincinnati: The Robert Clarke Company, 1895), 87.

36 Charles H. Wesley, *Ohio Negroes in the Civil War, Publications of the Ohio Civil War Commission* (Columbus: Ohio State University Press for the Ohio Historical Society, 1962), 18.

37 Robert S. Harper, *Ohio Handbook of the Civil War* (Columbus, Ohio: Ohio Historical Society for the Ohio Civil War Centennial Commission, 1961), 25.

38 Tucker, *Cincinnati During the Civil War*, 30.

39 Ibid, 33.

40 Harper, *Ohio Handbook of the Civil War*, 25–6. Tucker, *Cincinnati During the Civil War*, 34.

41 Telephone interview with Shiloh National Military Park Chief Ranger Stacy Allen, January 25, 2007.

42 Oscar L. Jackson, *The Colonel's Diary* (Sharon, Pennsylvania: 1922), 71.

43 Ibid, 76.

44 Kenneth W. Noe, *Perryville: This Grand Havoc of Battle* (Lexington: University Press of Kentucky, 2001), 144–5.

45 Lowell H. Harrison, "Kentucky," in *Encyclopedia of the American Civil War*, ed. David S. Heidler and Jeanne T Heidler (New York: W. W. Norton & Company, 2000), 1,116.

46 Donovan Jr. et al., *The American Civil War*, 67–68.

47 Kenneth W. Noe, *This Grand Havoc of Battle* (Lexington: University Press of Kentucky, 2001), *Passim*.

48 John H. Eicher and David J. Eicher, *Civil War High Commands* (Stanford, California: Stanford University Press, 2001), 524.

49 Roy Morris, Jr., *Sheridan: The Life and Wars of General Phil Sheridan* (New York: Vintage Books, 1993), 93.

50 John Beatty, *Memoirs of a Volunteer 1861–1863* (New York: W. W. Norton & Company, 1946), 137.

51 Ibid, 138.

52 Ibid, 139.

53 Ibid, 135.

54 Ibid, 138.

55 Noe, *Perryville, This Grand Havoc of Battle*, 305.

56 Mark Mayo Boatner III, *The Civil War Dictionary*, rev. ed. (New York: Vintage Books, 1991), 643–644.

57 Noe, *Perryville, This Grand Havoc of Battle*, 308.

58 "History of the Battle of Perryville," (http://www.perryville.net/history.html: Perryville Enhancement Project).

59 Kenneth W. Noe, "Remembering Perryville: History and Memory at a Civil War Battlefield," in *Popular Culture Association and American Culture Association Conference* (Philadelphia: 2001): 2.

60 Ammi Williams, "Ammi Williams Letters to Henry Williams," in *Hayes Presidential Center*

Civil War Collection LH-Misc. Mss. (Fremont, Ohio: 1862), *Passim.*

61 Edmund Ruffin, *The Diary of Edmund Ruffin*, 3 vols., vol. 2 (Baton Rouge: Louisiana State University Press, 1976), 456.

62 Ibid, 450.

NOTES FOR CHAPTER 9

1   "Battle of Fredricksburg," *Wikipedia* (2007), http://wikipedia.com.

2   Frederick J. Blue, "Friends of Freedom: Lincoln, Chase, and Wartime Racial Policy," *Ohio History* 102 (1993).

3   Benjamin P. Thomas and Harold M. Hyman, *Stanton: The Life and Times of Lincoln's Secretary of War* (New York: Alfred A. Knopf, 1962), 233.

4   "The New Year Day," *Ohio State Journal*, January 2, 1863.

5   Eugene H. Roseboom, *The Civil War Era*, ed. Carl Wittke, vol. 4, *The History of the State of Ohio* (Columbus, Ohio: Ohio State Archaeological and Historical Society, 1944), 402.

6   Ibid. 156.

7   H. Lee Cheek Jr., "Alexander Hamilton Stephens" in *Encyclopedia of the American Civil War*, ed. David S. Heidler and Jeanne T. Heidler (New York: W. W. Norton & Company, 2000).

8   Oscar D. Ladley, *Hearth and Knapsack: The Ladley Letters, 1857–1880,* ed. Carl M. Becker, and Ritchie Thomas, ed., (Athens, Ohio: Ohio University Press, 1988), 53.

9   William F. G. Shanks, *Personal Recollections of Distinguished Generals* (New York: Harper & Brothers, Publishers, 1866), 261.

10 James Lee Mc Donough, *Stones River—Bloody Winter in Tennessee* (Knoxville: University of Tennessee Press, 1980), 65.

11 John Beatty, *Memoirs of a Volunteer 1861–1863* (New York: W. W. Norton & Company, 1946), 176–7.

12 Shanks, *Personal Recollections of Distinguished Generals*, 144.

13 Ibid, 160.

14 Edward T. Downer, *Ohio Troops in the Field, Ohio Civil War Centennial Commission Publications* (Columbus, Ohio: Ohio State University Press for the Ohio Historical Society, n.d.).

15 Peter Cozzens, *No Better Place to Die: The Battle of Stones River* (Urbana, Illinois: University of Illinois Press, 1990), 87.

16 Robert L. Kimberly and Ephraim S. Holloway, *The Forty-First Ohio Veteran Volunteer Infantry in the War of the Rebellion, 1861–1865* (Cleveland: W. R. Smellie, 1897), 42.

17 James M. McPherson, *Battle Cry of Freedom: The Civil War Era*, paperback ed. (Oxford, England, and New York: Oxford University Press, 1988), 582.

18 Beatty, *Memoirs of a Volunteer*, 159.

19 *The War of the Rebellion: A Compilation of the Official Records of the Union and Confederate Armies*, 70 vols. (Washington, DC: 1880–1901). Series I, Vol. XXV, Chapter 37, Part I (Serial # 39), No. 284.

20 Ladley, Becker, and Thomas, *Hearth and Knapsack*. 131.

21 David Herbert Donald, *Lincoln* (New York: Simon & Schuster Paperbacks, 1995), 411–412.

22 James Meredith, "Joseph Hooker," in *Encyclopedia of the American Civil War: A Political, Social, and Military History*, ed. David S. Heidler and Jeanne T. Heidler (New York: W.W. Norton & Company, 2000), 1,001.

23 Ernest B. Furgurson, *Chancellorsville 1863: The Souls of the Brave* (New York: Vintage Books, 1993), 56.

24 David J. Eicher, *The Longest Night: A Military History of the Civil War* (New York: Simon & Schuster, 2001), 477.

25 Darius N. Couch, "The Chancellorsville Campaign," in *Battles and Leaders of the Civil War*, ed. Robert Underwood Johnson and Clarence Clough Buel (New York: The

Century Co., 1888), 161.

26 E. R. Monfort, "The First Division, Eleventh Corps, at Chancellorsville," in *G. A. R. War Papers*, ed. E. R. Monfort, H. B. Furness, and Fred H. Alms (Cincinnati: Fred C. Jones Post, No. 401, n.d.), 64.

27 Hartwell Osborn and others, *Trials and Triumphs, the Record of the 55th Ohio Volunteer Infantry* (Chicago: A. C. McClurg & Co., 1904), 72–3.

28 J. H. Peabody, "Battle of Chancellorsville," in *G.A.R. War Papers*, ed. E. R. Monfort, H. B. Furness, and Fred H. Alms (Cincinnati: Fred C. Jones Post, No. 401, n.d.), 53.

29 John E. Collins, "When Stonewall Jackson Turned Our Right," in *Battles and Leaders of the Civil War*, ed. Robert Underwood Johnson and Clarence Clough Buel (New York: The Century Co., 1888), 184.

30 Peabody, "Battle of Chancellorsville," 53.

31 William Kepler, *History of the Three Months' and Three Years' Service from April 16th, 1861, to June 22d, 1864, ... of the Fourth Infantry Regiment Ohio Volunteer Infantry* (Cleveland: Leader Printing Company, 1886), 111.

32 Ibid. 113.

33 Couch, "The Chancellorsville Campaign," 164.

34 Ladley, Becker, and Thomas, *Hearth and Knapsack*, 121–2.

35 Edward C. Culp, *The 25th Ohio Vet. Vol. Infantry in the War for the Union* (Topeka, Kansas: Geo. W. Crane & Co., 1885).

36 Osborn and others, *Trials and Triumphs*, 81.

37 Julia Dent Grant, *The Personal Memoirs of Julia Dent Grant*, ed. John Y. Simon (New York: G. P. Putnam's Sons, 1975), 111.

38 Jean Edward Smith, *Grant* (New York: Simon & Schuster, 2001), 230.

39 Ibid, 231.

40 Ibid, 231.

41 A. Wilson Greene, "From Chancellorsville to Cemetery Hill: O. O. Howard and the Eleventh Corps Leadership," in *The First Day at Gettysburg: Essays on Confederate and Union Leadership*, ed. Gary W. Gallagher (Kent, Ohio: Kent State University Press, 1992).

42 Duane Schultz, *The Most Glorious Fourth: Vicksburg and Gettysburg, July 4th, 1863* (New York: W. W. Norton & Company, 2002), 88.

43 McPherson, *Battle Cry of Freedom*, 631.

44 Smith, *Grant*, 232–3.

45 Marcus M. Spiegel, *A Jewish Colonel in the Civil War*, ed. Jean Powers Soman and Frank L. Byrne (Lincoln: University of Nebraska Press, 1995), 284.

46 Schultz, *The Most Glorious Fourth*, 112.

47 Richard W. Burt, "Siege of Vicksburg, Sunday, May 30th, 1863," (http://my.ohio.voyager.net/~lstevens/burt/may30.html).

48 Charles A. Willison, *Reminiscences of a Boy's Service with the 76th Ohio* (1908; repr. Huntington, West Virginia: Blue Acorn Press, 1995; reprint, 1908), 57.

49 Schultz, *The Most Glorious Fourth*, 120.

50 Manning F. Force, "Personal Recollections of the Vicksburg Campaign," in *Sketches of War History 1861–1865 [Ohio Commandery of MOLLUS]* (Wilmington, North Carolina: Broadfoot Publishing Company, 1888), 37.

51 Andrew Altman, "Andrew Altman Papers, 1861–1937," in *Bowling Green State University Center for Archival Collections*. "May the 26th 1863 Camp near camp in sight of vixburg."

52 Joseph Orville Jackson, ed., *"Some of the Boys ..." The Civil War Letters of Isaac Jackson, 1862–1865* (Carbondale, Illinois: Southern Illinois University, 1960), 99.

53 Ibid, 97.

54 Force, "Personal Recollections of the Vicksburg Campaign," 308.

55 Charles A. Willison, *Reminiscences of a Boy's Service with the 76th Ohio* (1908; repr. Huntington, West Virginia: Blue Acorn Press, 1995; reprint, 1908), 61.

56 Willison, *Reminiscences of a Boy's Service*, 59.

57 Jackson, *"Some of the Boys ..."* 112–4.

58 Ibid, 112–3.

59 Ibid, 110.

60 Smith, *Grant*, 258.

61 Ibid, 257.

62 Spiegel, Soman, and Byrne, *A Jewish Colonel*, 300.

63 Edward J. Renehan Jr., *The Secret Six* (New York: Crown Publishers, Inc., 1995).

64 Frank L. Klement, *The Limits of Dissent* (Lexington: University Press of Kentucky, 1970), 125.

65 Ibid, 149.

66 Ibid, 166.

67 Ibid, 171.

68 William Cheek and Aimee Lee Cheek, *John Mercer Langston and the Fight for Black Freedom* (Urbana, Illinois: University of Illinois Press, 1989), 359.

69 Ibid, 392.

70 Altman, "Altman Papers." "April the 9th 1863 Camp Bristle Landing [Louisiana]."

71 Richard Lowe, "Battle on the Levee: The Fight at Milliken's Bend," in *Black Soldiers in Blue*, ed. John David Smith (Chapel Hill: University of North Carolina Press, 2002), 120.

72 Jacob Bruner, "Bruner, Jacob, Letters, 1861–1863," (http://dbs.ohiohistory.org/africanam/msa/mss994.cfrr: Ohio Historical Society, 1861–3).

Notes for Chapter 10

1 Kenneth H. Wheeler, "Local Autonomy and Civil War Draft Resistance: Holmes County, Ohio," *Civil War History* 40, no. 2 (1999): 152.

2 Marcus M. Spiegel, *A Jewish Colonel in the Civil War*, ed. Jean Powers Soman and Frank L. Byrne (Lincoln: University of Nebraska Press, 1995), 295.

3 Oscar D. Ladley, *Hearth and Knapsack: The Ladley Letters, 1857–1880*, ed. Carl M. Becker, and Ritchie Thomas (Athens, Ohio: Ohio University Press, 1988), 150.

4 Eugene C. Murdock, *One Million Men: The Civil War Draft in the North* (Westport, Connecticut: Greenwood Press Publishers, 1980).

5 ———, *Ohio's Bounty System in the Civil War*, Publications of the Ohio Civil War Centennial Commission (Columbus, Ohio: Ohio State University Press for the Ohio Historical Society, 1963), 53.

6 A. Wilson Greene, "From Chancellorsville to Cemetery Hill: O. O. Howard and the Eleventh Corps Leadership," in *The First Day at Gettysburg: Essays on Confederate and Union Leadership*, ed. Gary W. Gallagher (Kent, Ohio: Kent State University Press, 1992), 57.

7 Franklin Sawyer, *A Military History of the 8th Regiment Ohio Vol. Inf'y: Its Battles, Marches and Army Movements* (Huntington, West Virginia: Blue Acorn Press, 1994), 120.

8 David T. Thackery, *A Light and Uncertain Hold: A History of the Sixty-Sixth Ohio Volunteer Infantry* (Kent, Ohio: Kent State University Press, 1999), 143.

9 Richard Wheeler, *Witness to Gettysburg* (New York: Harper & Row, 1987), 141.

10 Bradley M. Gottfried, *Brigades of Gettysburg: The Union and Confederate Brigades at the Battle of Gettysburg* (n.p.: Da Capo Press, 2002), 301–47.

11 Wheeler, *Witness to Gettysburg*, 154.

12 Greene, "From Chancellorsville to Cemetery Hill," 79.

13 Ibid, 83.

14 Wheeler, *Witness to Gettysburg*, 144–5.

15 Gottfried, *Brigades of Gettysburg*, 339–40.

16 Wheeler, *Witness to Gettysburg*, 174.

17 John W. Busey and David G. Martin, *Regimental Strengths and Losses at Gettysburg* (Hightstown, Maryland: Longstreet House, 1994), 81–6.

18 Greene, "From Chancellorsville to Cemetery Hill," 88.

19 Luther B. Mesnard, "Excerpts from the Diary of Luther B. Mesnard Regarding His Actions During the Battle of Gettysburg," (http://www.forttejon.org/oh55/mesnard/%20diary%20gburg.html).

20 Wheeler, *Witness to Gettysburg*, 175.

21 Ibid, 196.

22 Thomas Francis Galwey, *The Valiant Hours* (Harrisburg, Pennsylvania: The Stackpole Company, 1961), 109–10.

23 Mesnard, "Excerpts from the Diary of Luther B. Mesnard."

24 Galwey, *The Valiant Hours*, 110–11.

25 Thackery, *A Light and Uncertain Hold*, 152.

26 Ladley, Becker, and Thomas, *Hearth and Knapsack*, 142–3.

27 Gottfried, *Brigades of Gettysburg*, 165.

28 Ibid, 165.

29 Thackery, *A Light and Uncertain Hold*, 147.

30 Margaret S. Creighton, *The Colors of Courage: Gettysburg's Forgotten History* (New York: Basic Books, 2005), 140.

31 Whitelaw Reid and James G. Smart, ed., *A Radical View: The "Agate" Dispatches of Whitelaw Reid 1861–1865*, 2 vols., vol. 2 (Memphis: Memphis State University Press, 1976), 65.

32 Mesnard, "Excerpts from the Diary of Luther B. Mesnard."

33 Galwey, *The Valiant Hours*, 115.

34 Sawyer, *A Military History of the 8th Regiment Ohio*.

35 Galwey, *The Valiant Hours*, 119.

36 A. H. Nickerson, "Personal Recollections of Two Visits to Gettysburg," *Scribner's Magazine*, July 1893: 21.

37 John D. Imboden, "The Confederate Retreat from Gettysburg," in *Battles and Leaders of the Civil War*, ed. Robert Underwood Johnson and Clarence Clough Buel (New York: The Century Co., 1888), 424.

38 Edward J. Stackpole, *They Met at Gettysburg* (Harrisburg, Pennsylvania: Stackpole Books, 1986; reprint, 1986), 321.

39 Mesnard, "Excerpts from the Diary of Luther B. Mesnard."

40 Gerard Patterson, *Debris of Battle*, Electronic (NetLibrary) ed. (Mechanicsburg, Pennsylvania: Stackpole Books, 1997), 1–2.

41 Gregory A. Coco, *A Strange and Blighted Land, Gettysburg: The Aftermath of Battle* (Gettysburg, Pennsylvania: Thomas Publications, 1995), 84.

42 Frank L. Klement, *The Gettysburg Soldiers' Cemetery and Lincoln's Address: Aspects and Angles* (Shippensburg, Pennsylvania: White Mane Publishing Company, Inc., 1993), 54. Busey and Martin, *Regimental Strengths and Losses at Gettysburg*, 275.

43 Klement, *The Gettysburg Soldiers' Cemetery*, 54, 63.

44 Nickerson, "Personal Recollections of Two Visits to Gettysburg," 27–8.

45 Mark Mayo Boatner III, *The Civil War Dictionary*, rev. ed. (New York: Vintage Books, 1991), 569.

46 Jacob Dolson Cox, *Military Reminiscenses of the Civil War* (http://www.sonofthesouth.net/leefoundation/cw1.htm).

47 Edison H. Thomas, *John Hunt Morgan and His Raiders* (Lexington: University Press of Kentucky, 1975), 110.

48 Lester V. Horwitz, *The Longest Raid of the Civil War: Little-Known and Untold Stories of Morgan's Raid into Kentucky, Indiana & Ohio* (Cincinnati: Farmcourt Publishing, Inc., 1999), 374.

49 J. A. Chase, *History of the Fourteenth Ohio Regiment, O.V.V.I.* (Toledo, Ohio: St. John Printing House, 1881), 39–41.

50 Hillory Shifflet, "Hillory Shifflet Letters, Compiled by Kate Forster," (http://www.geocities.com/~jcrosswell/War/CW/hillory.htm).

51 Captain John Calvin Hartzell and Charles I. Switzer, ed., *Ohio Volunteer: The Childhood and Civil War Memoirs of Captain John Calvin Hartzell* (Athens: Ohio University Press,

2005). 124.

52 Peter Cozzens, *This Terrible Sound* (Urbana: University of Illinois Press, 1992). 125.

53 Chase, *History of the Fourteenth Ohio Regiment, O.V.V.I.* 47–8.

54 Augustus C. May, "Letter Written by Pvt. Augustus C. May: The Fourteenth at Chickamauga," (http://www.angelfire.com/oh4/civwar/14thohio/acmay.htm).

55 "N", "Account of the Battle of Chickamauga Written By "N"," (http://www.angelfire.com/oh4/civwar/14thphio/chick_n.htm: 1863).

56 William A. Frassanito, *Early Photography at Gettysburg* (Gettysburg, Pennsylvania: Thomas Publications, 1995).

57 Cozzens, *This Terrible Sound*, 280.

58 Ambrose Bierce, *Phantoms of a Blood-Stained Period: The Complete Civil War Writings of Ambrose Bierce,* ed. Russell Duncan and David J. Klooster, (Amherst: University of Massachusetts Press, 2002), 191.

59 Glenn Tucker, *The Battle of Chickamauga* (n.p.: Eastern Acorn Press, 1969), 26.

60 Cozzens, *This Terrible Sound*, 310.

61 Steven E. Woodworth, *Six Armies in Tennessee: The Chickamauga and Chattanooga Campaigns* (Lincoln: University of Nebraska Press, 1998), 110. Constantin Grebner, *We Were the Ninth: A History of the Ninth Regiment, Ohio Volunteer Infantry, April 17, 1861, to June 7, 1864*, trans. Frederic Trautmann (Kent, Ohio: Kent State University Press, 1987), 143, 150.

62 Woodworth, *Six Armies in Tennessee*, 118.

63 Tucker, *Battle of Chickamauga*, 34.

64 Cozzens, *This Terrible Sound*, 386–9.

65 Emerson Opdycke, *To Battle for God and the Right: The Civil War Letterbooks of Emerson Opdycke.* ed. Glenn V. Longacre and John E. Hass, (Urbana, Illinois: University of Illinois Press, 2003), 101.

66 Cozzens, *This Terrible Sound*, 431.

67 Opdycke, Longacre, and Hass, *To Battle for God and the Right*, 101.

68 Cozzens, *This Terrible Sound*, 410.

69 Virginia Kepler, "Buckeyes Make a Stand," (http://www.historynet.com/cwti/blbuckeyes/index.html).

70 John Beatty, *Memoirs of a Volunteer 1861–1863* (New York: W. W. Norton & Company, 1946), 251.

71 Mary Ann Steedman Wanatick, "Major General James Blair Steedman" (Master's, University of Toledo, 1988), 20.

72 John H. Morgan, "Old Steady: The Role of General James Blair Steedman at the Battle of Chickamauga," *Northwest Ohio Quarterly* XXII, no. 2 (1950), 90–1.

73 Archibald Gracie, *The Truth About Chickamauga* (Boston: Houghton Mifflin Company, 1911), 206.

74 Ibid, 227.

75 Ibid, 132–159.

76 Beatty, *Memoirs of a Volunteer*, 252.

77 Ibid, 252–3.

78 Cozzens, *This Terrible Sound*, 536.

79 Jean Edward Smith, *Grant* (New York: Simon & Schuster, 2001), 295.

80 Wanatick, "Steedman," 8.

81 William F. G. Shanks, *Personal Recollections of Distinguished Generals* (New York: Harper & Brothers, Publishers, 1866), 322.

82 Cozzens, *This Terrible Sound*, 440.

83 Liberty Warner and William Barber, "Liberty Warner Papers," in *Center for Archival Collections* (Bowling Green, Ohio: Bowling Green State University, 1871–3).

84 Grebner, *We Were the Ninth: A History of the Ninth Regiment, Ohio Volunteer Infantry, April 17, 1861, to June 7, 1864*, 167–8.

85 Frank L. Klement, *The Limits of Dissent* (Lexington: University Press of Kentucky, 1970), 194–5.

86 Ibid, 202–3, 205.
87 Ibid, 207.
88 Ibid, 252.
89 William Cheek and Aimee Lee Cheek, *John Mercer Langston and the Fight for Black Freedom* (Urbana: University of Illinois Press, 1989), 407–8.
90 Ibid, 406.
91 Ibid, 399.
92 Ibid, 399.
93 Julia Dent Grant *The Personal Memoirs of Julia Dent Grant,* ed. John Y. Simon (New York: G. P. Putnam's Sons, 1975), 123.
94 Smith, *Grant,* 264–5.
95 Cozzens, *This Terrible Sound.* Larry J. Daniel, *Days of Glory: The Army of the Cumberland 1861–1865* (Baton Rouge: Louisiana State University Press, 2004), 355.
96 Smith, *Grant,* 269.
97 Ibid, 269.
98 James and Lucretia Garfield, *Crete and James: Personal Letters of Lucretia and James Garfield,* ed.John Shaw (East Lansing, Michigan: Michigan State University Press, 1994). 189–190.
99 Ibid, 191.
100 Ibid, 193.

NOTES FOR CHAPTER 11

1 Ernest B. Furgurson, *Freedom Rising: Washington in the Civil War* (New York: Alfred A. Knopf, 2004), 270.
2 Peg A. Lamphier, *Kate Chase and William Sprague: Politics and Gender in a Civil War Marriage* (Lincoln: University of Nebraska Press, 2003), 43.
3 John Hay, *Inside Lincoln's White House: The Complete Civil War Diary of John Hay,* ed. Michael Burlingame and John R. Turner Ettlinger Turner (Carbondale: Southern Illinois University Press, 1997), 12.
4 John Beatty, *Memoirs of a Volunteer 1861–1863* (New York: W. W. Norton & Company, 1946), 258.
5 Horace Porter, *Campaigning with Grant* (Lincoln: University of Nebraska Press, 2000), 11.
6 Ulysses S. Grant, *Personal Memoirs of U. S. Grant,* 2 vols., vol. 1 (New York: The Century Co., 1917), 509–510.
7 Constantin Grebner, *We Were the Ninth: A History of the Ninth Regiment, Ohio Volunteer Infantry, April 17, 1861, to June 7, 1864,* trans. Frederic Trautmann (Kent, Ohio: Kent State University Press, 1987), 160.
8 Porter, *Campaigning with Grant,* 5.
9 Grant, *Personal Memoirs of U. S. Grant,* 501.
10 Jean Edward Smith, *Grant* (New York: Simon & Schuster, 2001), 268. Porter, *Campaigning with Grant,* 10.
11 Mark Mayo Boatner III, *The Civil War Dictionary,* rev. (New York: Vintage Books, 1991), 143. Carolyn V. Platt, "Three Cheers for the Cracker Line!" *Timeline,* April–June 2005: 47.
12 Stanley P. Hirshson, *The White Tecumseh: A Biography of General William T. Sherman* (New York: John Wiley & Sons, Inc., 1997), 169.
13 Edward T. Downer, *Ohio Troops in the Field, Ohio Civil War Centennial Commission Publications* (Columbus, Ohio: Ohio State University Press for the Ohio Historical Society, n.d.), 24.
14 Thomas L. Livermore, *Numbers & Losses in the Civil War in America: 1861–65, Civil War Centennial Series* (Bloomington: Indiana University Press, 1957), 106–7.
15 Ulysses S. Grant, *Ulysses S. Grant: Memoirs and Selected Letters* (New York: Library of America, 1990), 1,038.
16 Hillory Shifflet, "Hillory Shifflet Letters, Compiled by Kate Forster," (http://www.geocities.

com/~jcrosswell/War/CW/hillory.htm).

17 Boatner III, *Civil War Dictionary*, 158–9.

18 W. B. Hazen, *A Narrative of Military Service* (____; reprint, Huntington, West Virginia: Blue Acorn Press, 1993), 172.

19 Captain John Calvin Hartzell and Charles I. Switzer, ed., *Ohio Volunteer: The Childhood and Civil War Memoirs of Captain John Calvin Hartzell* (Athens: Ohio University Press, 2005), 149.

20 Emerson Opdycke, *To Battle for God and the Right: The Civil War Letterbooks of Emerson Opdycke,* ed. Glenn V. Longacre and John E. Hass(Urbana: University of Illinois Press, 2003), 135.

21 Albion W. Tourgee, *The Story of a Thousand: Being a History of the Service of the 105th Ohio Volunteer Infantry ...* (Buffalo, New York: S. McGerald & Son, 1896), 286–7.

22 Opdycke, Longacre, and Hass, *To Battle for God and the Right*, 135–6.

23 Philip H. Sheridan, *Personal Memoirs of P. H. Sheridan, General United States Army*, 2 vols., vol. I (New York: Charles L. Webster & Company, 1888), 311.

24 Ibid, 310.

25 James M. McPherson, *Battle Cry of Freedom: The Civil War Era*, paperback ed. (Oxford, England, and New York: Oxford University Press, 1988), 680.

26 Opdycke, Longacre, and Hass, *To Battle for God and the Right*, 140.

27 Hartzell and Switzer, *Ohio Volunteer*, 150.

28 Tourgee, *The Story of a Thousand*, 288.

29 Hirshson, *The White Tecumseh*, 174.

30 Hartzell and Switzer, *Ohio Volunteer*, 153.

31 Julia Dent Grant, *The Personal Memoirs of Julia Dent Grant,* ed. John Y. Simon (New York: G. P. Putnam's Sons, 1975), 124.

32 Ibid, 126–127.

33 Ibid, 127.

34 Smith, *Grant*, 259.

35 Ibid, 259.

36 Ibid, 285.

37 Ibid, 284–285.

38 Furgurson, *Freedom Rising*, 285.

39 Smith, *Grant*, 290.

40 Grant and Simon, *The Personal Memoirs of Julia Dent Grant*, 128. Furgurson, *Freedom Rising*, 286.

41 Smith, *Grant*, 294.

42 Ibid, 204.

43 James and Lucretia Garfield, *Crete and James: Personal Letters of Lucretia and James Garfield*, ed. John Shaw (East Lansing, Michigan: Michigan State University Press, 1994), 210–211.

44 Ibid. 211–212.

45 Andrew Altman, "Andrew Altman Papers, 1861–1937," in *Bowling Green State University Center for Archival Collections*. "January the 30th 1864 Vicksburg, Miss."

46 Hirshson, *The White Tecumseh*, 184.

47 Ibid, 166.

48 William T. Sherman, *Sherman's Civil War: Selected Correspondence of William T. Sherman, 1860–1865*, ed. Brooks D. Simpson and Jean V. Berlin (Chapel Hill: The University of North Carolina Press, 1999), 498.

49 Hirshson, *The White Tecumseh*, 168.

50 Ibid, 179.

51 Smith, *Grant*, 296.

52 Ibid, 295.

53 Hirshson, *The White Tecumseh*, 190.

54 Sherman, Simpson, and Berlin, *Sherman's Civil War*, 657.

55 Hirshson, *The White Tecumseh*, 181.

56 Nick Overby, "Supplying Hell: The Campaign for Atlanta," (http://www.qmfound.com/

supplying_hell_the_campaign_for_atlanta.htm).

57 Tourgee, *The Story of a Thousand*, 362.
58 J. A. Chase, *History of the Fourteenth Ohio Regiment, O.V.V.I.* (Toledo, Ohio: St. John Printing House, 1881), 63.
59 Boatner III, *Civil War Dictionary*, 30.
60 Hirshson, *The White Tecumseh*, 211.
61 Ibid, 215. Albert Castel, *Decision in the West: The Atlanta Campaign of 1864* (Lawrence: University Press of Kansas, 1992), 225.
62 David J. Eicher, *The Longest Night: A Military History of the Civil War* (New York: Simon & Schuster, 2001), 701.
63 Hirshson, *The White Tecumseh*, 224.
64 Quoted in Eicher, *The Longest Night*, 703.
65 Quoted in McPherson, *Battle Cry of Freedom*, 749.
66 Chase, *History of the Fourteenth Ohio Regiment, O.V.V.I.*, 61.
67 Ibid, 65.
68 Ibid, 68.
69 Grant and Simon, *The Personal Memoirs of Julia Dent Grant*, 129.
70 Smith, *Grant*, 297.
71 Ibid, 306.
72 Ibid, 301.
73 Ibid, 287.
74 Ibid, 288.
75 Ibid, 307.
76 Ibid, 307.
77 Ibid, 320.
78 Ibid, 322.
79 Porter, *Campaigning with Grant*, 72–3.
80 William Kepler, *History of the Three Months' and Three Years' Service from April 16th, 1861, to June 22d, 1864, ... Of the Fourth Infantry Regiment Ohio Volunteer Infantry* (Cleveland: Leader Printing Company, 1886), 165.
81 Thomas Francis Galwey, *The Valiant Hours* (Harrisburg, Pennsylvania: The Stackpole Company, 1961), 199.
82 Livermore, *Numbers & Losses*, 110.
83 Smith, *Grant*, 334–5.
84 Ibid, 366.
85 Ibid, 336.
86 Ibid, 376–7.
87 Ibid, 349.
88 Galwey, *The Valiant Hours*, 210.
89 Henry Steele Commager and Erik Bruun, eds., *The Civil War Archive: The History of the Civil War in Documents* (New York: Tess Press, 2000), 736–737.
90 Smith, *Grant*, 355.
91 Gary W. Gallagher, Stephen D. Engle, Robert K. Krick, and Joseph Glatthaar, et. al., *The American Civil War: This Mighty Scourge of War* (London: Osprey Publishing, 2003), 199.
92 Richard D. Loosbrock, "Battle of Cold Harbor," in *Encyclopedia of the American Civil War*, ed. David S. Heidler and Jeanne T. Heidler (New York: W. W. Norton & Company, 2000), 463.
93 Smith, *Grant*, 364.
94 Grant, *Grant: Memoirs and Selected Letters*, 1,056.
95 Ibid, 1,064.
96 Ibid, 1,067.
97 Ibid, 1,064–5.
98 Ibid, 1,059–60.
99 Hirshson, *The White Tecumseh*, 217.
100 Opdycke, Longacre, and Hass, *To Battle for God and the Right*, 217.

101 Altman, "Altman Papers." "Camp near Atlanta, Geo, August the 11ᵗʰ, 64"
102 E.B. Long with Barbara Long, *The Civil War Day by Day: An Almanac 1861–1865* (Garden City, New York: Doubleday, 1971; reprint, by Da Capo, n.p., n.d.), 559.
103 Furgurson, *Freedom Rising*, 322–3.
104 Hirshson, *The White Tecumseh*, 240.

NOTES FOR CHAPTER 12

1 Philip H. Sheridan, *Personal Memoirs of P. H. Sheridan, General United States Army*, 2 vols., vol. I (New York: Charles L. Webster & Company, 1888), 2.
2 Ibid, 4.
3 Ibid, 11.
4 Ibid, 73.
5 Ulysses S. Grant, *Personal Memoirs of U.S. Grant*, 2 vols., vol. 2 (New York: The Century Co., 1917), 60.
6 Horace Porter, *Campaigning with Grant* (Lincoln: University of Nebraska Press, 2000), 24.
7 Ibid, 84.
8 Ibid, 84.
9 Ibid, 84.
10 Roy Morris Jr., *Sheridan: The Life and Wars of General Phil Sheridan* (New York: Crown Publishers, Inc., 1992), 179.
11 Porter, *Campaigning with Grant*, 228.
12 Morris Jr., *Sheridan*, 180.
13 Jean Edward Smith, *Grant* (New York: Simon & Schuster, 2001), 380.
14 Ibid, 385.
15 T. Harry Williams, *Hayes of the Twenty-Third: The Civil War Volunteer Officer* (New York: Alfred A. Knopf, 1965), 260.
16 Ibid, 256–63.
17 Jonathan A. Noyalas, "False Gibralter at Fisher's Hill," *America's Civil War*, March 2006: 36.
18 Williams, *Hayes of the Twenty-Third*, 283.
19 Morris Jr., *Sheridan*, 214.
20 Williams, *Hayes of the Twenty-Third*, 308.
21 Morris Jr., *Sheridan*, 220.
22 Eric J. Wittenberg, *Little Phil: A Reassessment of the Civil War Leadership of Gen. Philip H. Sheridan* (Washington, D.C.: Brassey's, Inc., 2002), *Passim*.
23 Ibid, vii–viii.
24 Noah Andre Trudeau, *The Last Citadel: Petersburg, Virginia, June 1864–April 1865* (Boston: Little, Brown and Company, 1991), 190.
25 Porter, *Campaigning with Grant*, 283–4.
26 Ibid 284.
27 Ibid, 285.
28 Trudeau, *The Last Citadel*, 201.
29 Smith, *Grant*, 387.
30 Ibid, 387.
31 Thomas E. Pope, *The Weary Boys: Colonel J. Warren Keifer and the 110ᵗʰ Ohio Volunteer Infantry* (Kent, Ohio: Kent State University Press, 2002), 96.
32 J. H. Gilson, *Concise History of the One Hundred and Twenty-Sixth Regiment, Ohio Volunteer Infantry ... New ed.* (Huntington, West Virginia: Blue Acorn Press, 2000), 107.
33 Trudeau, *The Last Citadel*, 291.
34 Porter, *Campaigning with Grant*, 331.
35 Ibid, 332–3.
36 Eugene H. Roseboom, *The Civil War Era*, ed. Carl Wittke, vol. 4, *The History of the State of Ohio* (Columbus: Ohio State Archaeological and Historical Society, 1944), 434–5.

37 Ibid, 435.

38 Whitelaw Reid, *A Radical View: The "Agate" Dispatches of Whitelaw Reid 1861–1865*, ed. James G. Smart, vol. 2 (Memphis: Memphis State University Press, 1976), 186–7.

39 Stanley P. Hirshson, *The White Tecumseh: A Biography of General William T. Sherman* (New York: John Wiley & Sons, Inc., 1997), 246.

40 Wiley Sword, *The Confederacy's Last Hurrah: Spring Hill, Franklin, and Nashville*, paperback ed. (n.p.: University Press of Kansas, 1993), 4.

41 Ibid, 32.

42 Patrick Brennan, "Last Stand in the Heartland," *North & South*, May 2005: 23.

43 Alexis Cope, *The Fifteenth Ohio Volunteers and Its Campaigns* (Columbus, Ohio: Alexis Cope, 1916), 605.

44 Sword, *The Confederacy's Last Hurrah*, 156.

45 Emerson Opdycke, *To Battle for God and the Right: The Civil War Letterbooks of Emerson Opdycke,* ed. Glenn V. Longacre and John E. Hass (Urbana, Illinois: University of Illinois Press, 2003), 250.

46 John M. Copley, "A Sketch of the Battle of Franklin, Tenn.; with Reminiscences of Camp Douglas," (http://docsouth.unc.edu/copley/copley.html).

47 Thomas L. Livermore, *Numbers & Losses in the Civil War in America: 1861–65*, Civil War Centennial Series (Bloomington: Indiana University Press, 1957), 131–2.

48 Opdycke, Longacre, and Hass, *To Battle for God and the Right*, 250.

49 Brennan, "Last Stand in the Heartland," 34.

50 Cope, *The Fifteenth Ohio Volunteers*, 645.

51 Ibid, 651.

52 Livermore, *Numbers & Losses*, 133.

53 Sword, *The Confederacy's Last Hurrah*, 391.

54 Porter, *Campaigning with Grant*, 289–90.

55 Ibid, 290.

56 Lee B. Kennett, "'Hell' or 'High Old Times',", *America's Civil War*, January 2005: 48.

57 William T. Sherman, *From Atlanta to the Sea, ed.* B. H. Liddell Hart (London: The Folio Society, 1961). 157.

58 B. H. Liddell Hart, *Sherman: Soldier, Realist, American* (n.p.: Da Capo Press, 1993). 323–4.

59 William T. Sherman, *Sherman's Civil War: Selected Correspondence of William T. Sherman, 1860–1865*, ed. Brooks D. Simpson and Jean V. Berlin (Chapel Hill: The University of North Carolina Press, 1999), 704.

60 Ibid, 708.

61 Kennett, "'Hell' or 'High Old Times'," 48.

62 David J. Eicher, *The Longest Night: A Military History of the Civil War* (New York: Simon & Schuster, 2001), 763.

63 Sherman, Simpson, and Berlin, *Sherman's Civil War*, 741–4.

64 Ibid, 758.

65 Henry Hitchcock, *Marching with Sherman: Passages from the Letters and Campaign Diaries of Henry Hitchcock, Major and Assistant Adjutant General of Volunteers, November 1864–May 1865*, ed. M. A. DeWolfe Howe (New Haven: Yale University Press, 1927), 57.

66 William Tecumseh Sherman, *Memoirs of General W. T. Sherman* (New York: Penguin Books, 2000), 544.

67 Sherman and Liddell Hart, *From Atlanta to the Sea*, 163.

68 Ibid, 167.

69 P. J. O'Rourke, "Why It's Good to Come from Nowhere," in *Good Roots: Writers Reflect on Growing up in Ohio*, ed. Lisa Watts (Athens, Ohio: Ohio University Press, 2007), 43.

70 Richard W. Burt, "Foraging for Sherman's Army: Often Dangerous and Exciting Work Done by Fearless Men," in *National Tribune* (Washington, D.C.: 1898).

71 Hitchcock and Howe, *Marching with Sherman*, 141.

72 W. B. Hazen, *A Narrative of Military Service* (___; repr. Huntington, West Virginia: Blue Acorn Press, 1993), 313.

73 Sherman and Liddell Hart, *From Atlanta to the Sea*, 165.

74 Ibid, 164.

75 E.B. Long with Barbara Long, *The Civil War Day by Day: An Almanac 1861–1865* (Garden City, New York: Doubleday, 1971; reprint, by Da Capo, n.p., n.d.), 598.

76 Kennett, "'Hell' or 'High Old Times," 52.

77 Sherman and Liddell Hart, *From Atlanta to the Sea*, 180. Hazen, *A Narrative of Military Service*, 321–2.

78 Andrew Altman, "Andrew Altman Papers, 1861–1937," in *Bowling Green State University Center for Archival Collections*. "January the 14 1865 Camp Near Savannah, Ga."

79 Ibid, "Camp in Savannah, Ga. Dec the 24th, 1864."

80 Sherman, Simpson, and Berlin, *Sherman's Civil War*, 772.

81 Herman Hattaway and Richard E. Beringer, *Jefferson Davis, Confederate President* (Lawrence, Kansas: University Press of Kansas, 2002), 336.

82 Ibid. 343.

83 H. Wayne Morgan, *William McKinley and His America* (Syracuse, New York: Syracuse University Press, 1963), 30.

84 Edmund Ruffin, *The Diary of Edmund Ruffin: Volume III, a Dream Shattered: June, 1863– June, 1865*, ed. William Kauffman Scarborough, 3 vols., vol. 3 (Baton Rouge: Louisiana State University Press, 1989). 688–9.

85 Oscar D. Ladley, *Hearth and Knapsack: The Ladley Letters, 1857–1880*, ed. Carl M. Becker and Ritchie Thomas (Athens, Ohio: Ohio University Press, 1988), 183.

86 Morris Jr., *Sheridan*, 235.

87 Altman, "Altman Papers." January 14, 1865.

Notes for Chapter 13

1 Henry Goddard Thomas, "The Colored Troops at Petersburg," in *Battles and Leaders of the Civil War*, ed. Robert Underwood Johnson and Clarence Clough Buel (New York: The Century Company, 1888), 563.

2 Mark Mayo Boatner III, *The Civil War Dictionary*, rev. ed. (New York: Vintage Books, 1991), 836.

3 Thomas, "The Colored Troops at Petersburg," 563.

4 Ibid, 563.

5 David J. Eicher, *The Longest Night: A Military History of the Civil War* (New York: Simon & Schuster, 2001), 721.

6 Dorothy L. Drinkard, "Battle of the Crater," in *Encyclopedia of the American Civil War*, ed. David S Heidler and Jeanne T. Heidler (New York: W.W. Norton, 2000), 515–7.

7 Thomas, "The Colored Troops at Petersburg," 564.

8 Richard Lowe, "Battle on the Levee: The Fight at Milliken's Bend," in *Black Soldiers in Blue*, ed. John David Smith (Chapel Hill: University of North Carolina Press, 2002), 127.

9 Charles H. Wesley, *Ohio Negroes in the Civil War, Publications of the Ohio Civil War Commission* (Columbus, Ohio: Ohio State University Press for the Ohio Historical Society, 1962), 30.

10 Ibid, 31.

11 Bruce Tap, "Fort Pillow Massacre," in *Encyclopedia of the American Civil War*, ed. David S. Heidler and Jeanne T. Heidler (New York: W.W. Norton, 2000), 747.

12 Joseph T. Glatthaar, *Forged in Battle: The Civil War Alliance of Black Soldiers and White Officers* (New York: The Free Press, 1990), 157.

13 Versalle F. Washington, *Eagles on Their Buttons: A Black Infantry Regiment in the Civil War*, ed. Herman Hattaway and Jon Wakelyn, *Shades of Blue and Gray Series* (Columbia: University of Missouri Press, 1999), 56.

14 Glatthaar, *Forged in Battle: The Civil War Alliance of Black Soldiers and White Officers*, 279–80.

15 Noah Brooks, "Personal Reminiscences of Lincoln," *Scribners Monthly*, February 1878: 563.

16 Harvey Wish, "Artemus Ward and Petroleum Nasby," in *For the Union: Ohio Leaders in the Civil War*, ed. Kenneth W. Wheeler (Columbus, Ohio: Ohio State University Press, 1968), 439–40.

17 Don C. Seitz, *Artemus Ward (Charles Farrar Browne): A Biography and Bibliography* (New York: Harper & Brothers, 1919), 114.

18 Wish, "Artemus Ward and Petroleum Nasby," 447.

19 Ibid, 456–9.

20 Ibid, 460.

21 Ibid, 461.

22 Albert Mellor, "Experiences in Southern Military Prisons," in *G.A.R. War Papers: Papers Read before Fred C. Jones Post, No. 401, Department of Ohio, G.A.R.*, ed. E. R. Monfort, H. B. Furness, and Fred H. Alms (Cincinnati: Fred C. Jones Post, No. 401, G.A.R., 1891?), 266.

23 James Cozzens, *This Terrible Sound* (Urbana, Illinois: University of Illinois Press, 1992), 270.

24 Albert Kern, *History of the First Regiment Ohio Volunteer Infantry in the Civil War 1861–1865* (Dayton: 1918; reprint, n.d., Curt Dalton, Dayton, Ohio), 18.

25 Cozzens, *This Terrible Sound*, 534.

26 Thomas L. Livermore, *Numbers & Losses in the Civil War in America: 1861–65*, Civil War Centennial Series (Bloomington, Indiana: Indiana University Press, 1957), 105.

27 Thomas N. Way, *In the Jaws of Death, or Eighteen Months a Prisoner of War in Southern Prisons* (Salem, Ohio: Journal Steam Print, 1872), 1st text page.

28 Mellor, "G.A.R. War Papers," 268.

29 Way, *In the Jaws of Death*, 1.

30 Mellor, "G.A.R. War Papers," 275.

31 Mary Clark Brayton and Ellen F. Terry, *Our Acre and Its Harvest: Historical Sketch of the Soldiers' Aid Society of Northern Ohio* (Cleveland: Fairbanks, Benedict & Co., 1869), 62.

32 Marcus M. Spiegel, *A Jewish Colonel in the Civil War*, ed. Jean Powers Soman and Frank L. Byrne (Lincoln: University of Nebraska Press, 1995), 309.

33 Ibid, 308.

34 Ibid, 309.

35 Ibid, 310–311.

36 Ibid, 322.

37 Boatner III, *Civil War Dictionary*, 685–688.

38 Spiegel, Soman, and Byrne, *A Jewish Colonel*, 333.

39 Ibid, 334.

40 Ibid, 335.

41 Ibid, 336.

42 Charles E. Frohman, *Rebels on Lake Erie* (Columbus, Ohio: The Ohio Historical Society, 1965; reprint, 1997), 13.

43 Ibid, 8.

44 William B. Hesseltine, *Civil War Prisons: A Study in War Psychology* (Columbus: Ohio State University Press, 1930), 173–7.

45 James M. McPherson, *Battle Cry of Freedom: The Civil War Era*, paperback ed. (Oxford, England, and New York: Oxford University Press, 1988), 792.

46 Frank R. Freemon, *Microbes and Minie Balls: An Annotated Bibliography of Civil War Medicine* (Rutherford, New Jersey: Associated University Presses, 1993), 199.

47 Julia Dent Grant, *The Personal Memoirs of Julia Dent Grant*, ed. John Y. Simon (New York: G. P. Putnam's Sons, 1975), 100.

48 Ibid, 116.

49 Ibid, 101.

50 Maud E. Morrow, *Recollections of the Civil War: From a Child's Point of View* (Lockland, Ohio: 1901), *Passim*.

51 Barbara A. Terzian, "Frances Dana Gage and Northern Women's Reform Activities in the

Nineteenth Century," in *Builders of Ohio: A Biographical History*, ed. Warren Van Tine and Michael Pierce (Columbus, Ohio: Ohio State University Press, 2003), 108–20.

52   Eugene H. Roseboom, *The Civil War Era*, ed. Carl Wittke, Six vols., vol. IV, *The History of the State of Ohio* (Columbus: Ohio State Archaeological and Historical Society, 1944), 435.

53   Edward R. Crowther, "Thirteenth Amendment," in *Encyclopedia of the American Civil War*, ed. David S. Heidler and Jeanne T. Heidler (New York: W.W. Norton, 2000), 1940.

Notes for Chapter 14

1   Richard M. McMurry, *John Bell Hood and the War for Southern Independence* (Lexington: The University Press of Kentucky, 1982), 190.

2   Margaret E. Wagner, Gary W. Gallagher, and Paul Finkelman, eds., *The Library of Congress Civil War Desk Reference* (New York: Simon & Schuster, 2002), 413.

3   McMurry, *John Bell Hood*. 83.

4   Mary Boykin Chesnut, *Mary Chesnut's Civil War*, ed. C. Vann Woodward (New Haven: Yale University Press, 1981), 505.

5   McMurry, *John Bell Hood*, 182.

6   Chesnut and Woodward, *Mary Chesnut's Civil War*, 709.

7   Ibid, 804.

8   Ibid, 813.

9   Doris Kearns Goodwin, *Team of Rivals: The Political Genius of Abraham Lincoln* (New York: Simon & Schuster, 2005), 28.

10 J. Tracy Power, *Lee's Miserables: Life in the Army of Northern Virginia from the Wilderness to Appomattox*, ed. Gary W. Gallagher, *Civil War America* (Chapel Hill: University of North Carolina Press, 1998), iii.

11 Henry Steele Commager and Erik Bruun, eds., *The Civil War Archive: The History of the Civil War in Documents* (New York: Tess Press, 2000), 756.

12 Thomas E. Pope, *The Weary Boys: Colonel J. Warren Keifer and the 110th Ohio Volunteer Infantry* (Kent, Ohio: Kent State University Press, 2002), 95.

13 David J. Eicher, *The Longest Night: A Military History of the Civil War* (New York: Simon & Schuster, 2001), 796–7.

14 Ulysses S. Grant, *Ulysses S. Grant: Memoirs and Selected Letters* (New York: Library of America, 1990), 687.

15 Pope, *The Weary Boys*, 97.

16 Ibid, 98.

17 Ibid, 99.

18 Ibid, 98–9.

19 J. E. Henderson, "60th Ohio Memoirs: Gen. Gordon's View," (http://freepages.genealogy.rootsweb.com/~volker/history.civilwar/).

20 Horace Porter, *Campaigning with Grant* (Lincoln: University of Nebraska Press, 2000), 418.

21 Ibid, 420.

22 William Tecumseh Sherman, *Memoirs of General W. T. Sherman* (New York: Penguin Books, 2000), 682.

23 Stanley P. Hirshson, *The White Tecumseh: A Biography of General William T. Sherman* (New York: John Wiley & Sons, Inc., 1997), 301.

24 Porter, *Campaigning with Grant*, 425.

25 Ibid, 429.

26 E.B. Long with Barbara Long, *The Civil War Day by Day: An Almanac 1861–1865* (Garden City, New York: Doubleday, 1971; reprint, by Da Capo, n.p., n.d.), 661.

27 Porter, *Campaigning with Grant*, 431.

28 Ibid, 439.

29 Ibid, 437.

30 Ibid, 441.

31 Ibid, 442–3.

32 Ibid, 459.

33 Ibid, 459.

34 Ibid, 463.

35 Commager and Bruun, eds., *The Civil War Archive*, 600.

36 Hirshson, *The White Tecumseh*, 266.

37 William T. Sherman, *From Atlanta to the Sea*, ed. B. H. Liddell Hart (London: The Folio Society, 1961).

38 Joseph A. Saunier, ed., *A History of the Forty-Seventh Regiment Ohio Veteran Volunteer Infantry* (Hillsboro, Ohio: Lyle Printing Company, 1903), 383.

39 Rev. Nixon B. Stewart, *Dan McCook's Regiment, 52nd O.V.I. A History of the Regiment, Its Campaigns, and Battles* (n.p.: Author, 1900; reprint, Huntington, West Virginia: Blue Acorn Press, 1999), 150.

40 Brooks D. Simpson and Jean V. Berlin, eds., *Sherman's Civil War, Civil War America* (Chapel Hill: University of North Carolina, 1999), 778.

41 Sherman and Liddell Hart, *From Atlanta to the Sea*, 219.

42 Hirshson, *The White Tecumseh*, 273.

43 William T. Sherman, *Sherman's Civil War: Selected Correspondence of William T. Sherman, 1860–1865*, ed. Brooks D. Simpson and Jean V. Berlin (Chapel Hill: The University of North Carolina Press, 1999), 785.

44 William Tecumseh Sherman, *Memoirs of General W. T. Sherman*, two volumes in one vol., *The Library of America* (New York: Literary Classics of the United States, 1990), 729.

45 Sherman and Liddell Hart, *From Atlanta to the Sea*, 203.

46 Sherman, *Memoirs of General W. T. Sherman*, 752.

47 Hirshson, *The White Tecumseh*, 277.

48 W. B. Hazen, *A Narrative of Military Service* (Boston: Ticknor and Company, 1885), 336.

49 Stewart, *Dan McCook's Regiment, 52nd O.V.I*, 154.

50 Porter, *Campaigning with Grant*, 418.

51 Charles A. Willison, *Reminiscences of a Boy's Service with the 76th Ohio* (1908; repr., Huntington, West Virginia: Blue Acorn Press, 1995), 115–6.

52 Sherman and Liddell Hart, *From Atlanta to the Sea*, 248.

53 Sherman, *Memoirs of General W. T. Sherman*, 767.

54 Ibid, 768.

55 Martin Lubin ed., *The Words of Abraham Lincoln: Speeches, Letters, Proclamations, and Papers of Our Most Eloquent President* (New York: Tess Press, 2005), 525.

56 Stewart, *Dan McCook's Regiment, 52nd O.V.I*, 158.

57 Sherman, *Memoirs of General W. T. Sherman*, 778.

58 Sherman, Simpson, and Berlin, *Sherman's Civil War*. 823–4.

59 Sherman, *Memoirs of General W. T. Sherman*, 781.

60 Stewart, *Dan Mc Cook's Regiment, 52nd O.V.I.*, 162.

61 Ibid, 163.

62 Sherman, *Memoirs of General W. T. Sherman*, 661.

63 Sherman, Simpson, and Berlin, *Sherman's Civil War*, 817.

64 Stewart, *Dan Mc Cook's Regiment, 52nd O.V.I.*, 167.

65 Henry Hitchcock and M. A. DeWolfe Howe, eds., *Marching with Sherman: Passages from the Letters and Campaign Diaries of Henry Hitchcock, Major and Assistant Adjutant General of Volunteers, November 1864–May 1865* (New Haven: Yale University Press, 1927), 282.

66 Stewart, *Dan Mc Cook's Regiment, 52nd O.V.I.*, 168–9.

67 Sherman, *Memoirs of General W. T. Sherman*, 703.

68 Grant, *Grant: Memoirs and Selected Letters*, 731.

69 Ibid, 735.

70 Ibid, 735.

71 Long, *The Civil War Day by Day: An Almanac 1861–1865*, 674.

72 Hirshson, *The White Tecumseh*, 306.

73 Ibid, 308.

74 Ibid, 309–10.

75 Benjamin P. Thomas and Harold M. Hyman, *Stanton: The Life and Times of Lincoln's Secretary of War* (New York: Alfred A. Knopf, 1962), 396–401.

76 Julia Dent Grant, *The Personal Memoirs of Julia Dent Grant,* ed. John Y. Simon (New York: G. P. Putnam's Sons, 1975), 156–7.

77 Hitchcock and Howe, *Marching with Sherman*, 307.

78 Pope, *The Weary Boys*, 108.

79 Ibid, 108.

80 Holiday Ames "Waiting for the War's End: The Letter of an Ohio Soldier in Alabama," ed. Louis Filler, *Ohio History* 74 (1998): 56–7.

81 Frank L. Klement, *The Limits of Dissent* (Lexington: University Press of Kentucky, 1970), 295.

82 Daniel J. Ryan, *Lincoln and Ohio* (Columbus, Ohio: Ohio State Archaeological and Historical Society, 1923), 249.

83 Chester D. Berry, ed., *Loss of the Sultana and Reminiscences of Survivors* (Knoxville: University of Tennessee Press, 2005), 48.

84 Ibid, xviii.

85 Ibid, xxiii.

86 D. H. Rule, "Sultana: The Case for Sabotage," *North & South*, December 2001: 76–87.

87 Saunier, ed., *History of the Forty-Seventh Regiment*, 456.

88 "Review of the Armies: Propitious Weather and a Splendid Spectacle," *New York Times*, May 24, 1865.

89 "Review of the Armies: The Second and Last Day of the Great Pageant," *New York Times*, May 25, 1865.

90 Stuart McConnell, *Glorious Contentment: The Grand Army of the Republic, 1865–1900* (Chapel Hill: University of North Carolina Press, 1992), 6.

91 "Review of the Armies: The Second and Last Day of the Great Pageant."

92 Margaret Leech, *Reveille in Washington 1860–1865*, Time Reading Program, Special Edition ed. (New York: Time Incorporated, 1962), 513.

93 "Review of the Armies: The Second and Last Day of the Great Pageant."

94 Sherman, *Memoirs of General W. T. Sherman*, 731.

95 Sherman, *Memoirs of General W. T. Sherman*, 731–2.

96 Ibid, 731.

97 McConnell, *Glorious Contentment*, 7.

98 Ibid, 7.

99 Hirshson, *The White Tecumseh*, 312.

100 Ibid, 313.

101 Thomas and Hyman, *Stanton*, 417.

102 Saunier, ed., *History of the Forty-Seventh Regiment*, 456.

103 Pope, *The Weary Boys*, 110.

104 Peg A. Lamphier, *Kate Chase and William Sprague: Politics and Gender in a Civil War Marriage* (Lincoln: University of Nebraska Press, 2003), 80.

105 James and Lucretia Garfield, *Crete and James: Personal Letters of Lucretia and James Garfield,* ed. John Shaw (East Lansing, Michigan: Michigan State University Press, 1994), 217.

106 Ibid, 218.

107 Betty L. Mitchell, *Edmund Ruffin: A Biography* (Bloomington, Indiana: Indiana University Press, 1981), 255–6.

NOTES FOR CHAPTER 15

1   Captain John Calvin Hartzell, *Ohio Volunteer: The Childhood and Civil War Memoirs of Captain John Calvin Hartzell,* ed. Charles I. Switzer (Athens, Ohio: Ohio University Press, 2005), 92.

2   Ibid, 94.

3   Ibid, 94.
4   Ibid, 97.
5   John K. Duke, *History of the Fifty-Third Regiment, Ohio Volunteer Infantry, During the War of the Rebellion* ... (Portsmouth, Ohio: The Blade Printing Company, 1900), 200.
6   Alfred E. Lee, *The History of the City of Columbus*, 2 vols., vol. II (Columbus, Ohio: Franklin County Genealogical and Historical Society, 2000), 160–1.
7   Ibid, 164–5.
8   Hartzell and Switzer, *Ohio Volunteer*, xxiii, 129, 193–4.
9   Edward L. Ayers, "What Caused the Civil War?," *North & South*, September 2005: 17.
10 Bruce Levine, *Half Slave and Half Free: The Roots of Civil War*, rev. ed. (New York: Hill and Wang, 2005), x.
11 Margaret E. Wagner, Gary W. Gallagher, and Paul Finkelman, editors, *The Library of Congress Civil War Desk Reference* (New York: Simon & Schuster, 2002). 66–7.
12 H. Lee Cheek Jr., "Alexander Hamilton Stephens" in *Encyclopedia of the American Civil War*, ed. David S. Heidler and Jeanne T. Heidler (New York: W. W. Norton & Company, 2000), 1,859.
13 Levine, *Half Slave and Half Free*, 226.
14 Martin Lubin ed., *The Words of Abraham Lincoln: Speeches, Letters, Proclamations, and Papers of Our Most Eloquent President* (New York: Tess Press: Black Dog & Leventhal Publishers, Inc., 2005), 67–8.
15 Ibid, 269.
16 Ibid, 10.
17 Ibid, 269.
18 Ibid, 269.
19 Douglas L. Wilson, *Lincoln's Sword: The Presidency and the Power of Words* (New York: Alfred A. Knopf, 2006), 202.
20 Doris Kearns Goodwin, *Team of Rivals: The Political Genius of Abraham Lincoln* (New York: Simon & Schuster, 2005), 256.
21 Emory M. Thomas, *The Confederacy as a Revolutionary Experience* (Englewood Cliffs, New Jersey: Prentice-Hall, Inc., 1971), 1–22.
22 Susan-Mary Grant, "The Problem of Slavery in the Age of Counterrevolution," *Reviews in American History* 30, no. 1 (2002), 36.
23 Manisha Sinha, *The Counterrevolution of Slavery: Politics and Ideology in Antebellum South Carolina* (Chapel Hill: University of North Carolina Press, 2000), 255.
24 Ibid, 89.
25 Lubin ed., *Words of Abraham Lincoln*, 487–8.
26 "The End of the War!," *Cleveland Daily Leader*, June 6 1865: 4.
27 Albion W. Tourgee, *The Story of a Thousand: Being a History of the Service of the 105th Ohio Volunteer Infantry* ... (Buffalo: S. McGerald & Son, 1896), 383.
28 Ibid, 383.
29 Ibid, 383, lxiv. (Table XI).
30 Ibid, lxiv. (Table XI).
31 Frederick H. Dyer, *A Compendium of the War of the Rebellion*, Three vols., vol. I (New York: Thomas Yoseloff, 1959), 43–4.
32 Tourgee, *The Story of a Thousand*, 384.
33 Susan B. Carter, et al., eds., *Historical Statistics of the United States*, 5 vols., vol. 5 (Cambridge: Cambridge University Press, 2006), 350.
34 "Statistical Summary [of] America's Major Wars," (http://www.cwc.lsu.edu/cwc/other/stats/warcost.htm: United States Civil War Center [Louisiana State University]).
35 W. Louis Phillips, C.G., *Index to Ohio Pensioners of 1883* (Bowie, Maryland: Heritage Books, Inc., 1987). *List of Pensioners on the Roll January 1, 1883*, vol. III (Baltimore: Genealogical Publishing Company, 1970), 89–91.
36 Duke, *History of the Fifty-Third Regiment*, 251.
37 Judith Pizarro, Roxane Cohen Silver, and JoAnn Prause, "Physical and Mental Health Costs of Traumatic War Experiences among Civil War Veterans," *Archives of General*

Psychiatry 63 (2006): 193–200.

38 Chester D. Berry, ed., *Loss of the Sultana and Reminiscences of Survivors* (Knoxville: University of Tennessee Press, 2005), 64.

39 Steven H. Cornelius, *Music of the Civil War Era*, ed. David J. Brinkman, *American History through Music* (Westport, Connecticut: Greenwood Press, 2004), 28, 51, 72.

40 Charles A. Willison, *Reminiscences of a Boy's Service with the 76th Ohio* (1908; repr., Huntington, West Virginia: Blue Acorn Press, 1995), 9.

41 Hartzell and Switzer, *Ohio Volunteer*. xxx.

42 Ibid, 15.

43 Ibid, 90.

44 Ibid, 193–5.

45 Joseph Orville Jackson, ed., *"Some of the Boys ..." The Civil War Letters of Isaac Jackson, 1862–1865* (Carbondale, Illinois: Southern Illinois University, 1960), 109.

46 Ethan Rafuse, *A Single Grand Victory: The First Campaign and Battle of Manassas*, ed. Steven E. Woodworth, *Books on the Civil War Era* (Wilmington, Delaware: Scholarly Resources Inc., 2002), 164.

47 Whitelaw Reid and James G. Smart, eds., *A Radical View: The "Agate" Dispatches of Whitelaw Reid 1861–1865*, 2 vols., vol. 2 (Memphis: Memphis State University Press, 1976), 55.

48 Richard Wheeler, *Witness to Gettysburg* (New York: Harper & Row, 1987). 166.

49 Earl J. Hess, *The Union Soldier in Battle: Enduring the Ordeal of Combat* (Lawrence: University Press of Kansas, 1997), 8.

Notes for Chapter 16

1 Frances Trollope and Donald Smalley, ed., *Domestic Manners of the Americans* (New York: Alfred A. Knopf, 1949), 181.

2 Ibid, xx.

3 Ibid, 39, 62.

4 Ibid, 157.

5 Ibid, 340, 413.

6 Ibid, 408.

7 Jeffrey Goldberg, "Letter from Washington: Central Casting," *The New Yorker*, May 29 2006: 65.

8 Nick Carrabine, "Jim Gaffigan's Double Life," *Toledo Blade*, February 8 2007.

9 Nicole Etcheson, *The Emerging Midwest: Upland Southerners and the Political Culture of the Old Northwest, 1787–1861*, ed. James H. Madison and Thomas J. Schlereth, *Midwestern History and Culture* (Bloomington: Indiana University Press, 1998), 9.

10 Ibid, 10.

11 Charles I. Switzer, ed., "The Mac Gowan Sisters: Early-Twentieth-Century Popular Writers," *Journal of Popular Culture* 34, no. Summer (2000): 97.

12 Marcus M. Spiegel, *A Jewish Colonel in the Civil War,* ed. Jean Powers Soman and Frank L. Byrne, ed., (Lincoln: University of Nebraska Press, 1995), 87.

13 Stanley P. Hirshson, *The White Tecumseh: A Biography of General William T. Sherman* (New York: John Wiley & Sons, Inc., 1997), 213.

14 John Chipman Gray and John Codman Ropes, *War Letters 1862–1865 of John Chipman Gray and John Codman Ropes* (Boston: Houghton Mifflin Company, 1927), 127.

15 John Chipman Gray, "John Chipman Gray Views the Western Soldier," in *The Civil War Archive: The History of the Civil War in Documents*, ed. Henry Steele Commager and Erik Bruun (New York: Tess Press, 2000), 302.

16 Spiegel, Soman, and Byrne, *A Jewish Colonel,* 87.

17 T. Harry Williams, *Hayes of the Twenty-Third: The Civil War Volunteer Officer* (New York: Alfred A. Knopf, 1965), 132.

18 Thomas Francis Galwey, *The Valiant Hours* (Harrisburg, Pennsylvania: The Stackpole Company, 1961), 20.

19 "East Meets West: A Study in Soldierly Contrasts, Autumn 1863," (Huntington, West Virginia: Blue Acorn Press, 2005).

20 Gary W. Gallagher ed. and Alan T. Nolan ed., *The Myth of the Lost Cause and Civil War History* (Bloomington, Indiana: Indiana University Press, 2000), *Passim.*

21 Mark Grimsley, "Western Theater," in *The American Civil War: A Handbook of Literature and Research*, ed. Steven E. Woodworth (Westport, Connecticut: Greenwood Press, 1996), 270.

22 Richard M. McMurry, *The Fourth Battle of Winchester: Toward a New Civil War Paradigm* (Kent, Ohio: Kent State University Press, 2002), 143–4. William W. Freehling et al., "Could the Confederacy Have Won the Civil War?," *North & South*, May 2006: 12–25.

23 Freehling et al., "Could the Confederacy Have Won the Civil War?" 16.

24 J. F. C. Fuller, *Grant and Lee: A Study in Personality and Generalship* (Bloomington: Indiana University Press, 1982), 244.

25 Michael C. C. Adams, *Our Masters the Rebels: A Speculation on Union Military Failure in the East 1861–1865* (Cambridge, Massachusetts: Harvard University Press, 1978), 159.

26 Ulysses S. Grant, *Ulysses S. Grant: Memoirs and Selected Letters* (New York: Library of America, 1990), 735.

27 Freehling et al., "Could the Confederacy Have Won the Civil War?" 22.

28 Ibid, 23.

29 McMurry, *Fourth Battle of Winchester*, 52.

30 Gallagher and Nolan eds., *The Myth of the Lost Cause and Civil War History*, 1.

31 For a further discussion of "Master Race democracy," see Sean Wilentz, *The Rise of American Democracy: Jefferson to Lincoln* (New York: W. W. Norton & Company, 2005), *Passim.*

32 Grady McWhiney, "Who Whipped Whom? Confederate Defeat Reexamined," in *Battles Won and Lost: Essays from Civil War History*, ed. John T. Hubbell (Westport, Connecticut, Greenwood Press, 1975), 261.

33 Gallagher and Nolan eds., *The Myth of the Lost Cause and Civil War History*, 22.

34 Freehling et al., "Could the Confederacy Have Won the Civil War?" 24.

35 James A. Rawley, *Turning Points of the Civil War* (Lincoln: University of Nebraska Press, 1966), xv.

36 David J. Eicher, *The Civil War in Books: An Analytical Bibliography* (Urbana, Illinois: University of Illinois Press, 1997), 261.

37 James M. McPherson, *Battle Cry of Freedom: The Civil War Era*, paperback ed. (Oxford, England, and New York: Oxford University Press, 1988), 858.

38 David S. Reynolds, *John Brown, Abolitionist* (New York: Alfred A. Knopf, 2005), ix.

39 Robert S. Harper, *Ohio Handbook of the Civil War* (Columbus, Ohio: Ohio Historical Society for the Ohio Civil War Centennial Commission, 1961), 51.

40 Ibid, 51.

41 Ibid, 52.

42 Ibid, 51–2.

43 John H. Eicher and David J. Eicher, *Civil War High Commands* (Stanford, California: Stanford University Press, 2001), 62.

44 William Tecumseh Sherman, *Memoirs of General W. T. Sherman* (New York: Penguin Books, 2000), 369–70.

45 Fuller, *Grant & Lee*, 7.

46 Ibid, 7, 6.

47 Gordon C. Rhea, "'Butcher Grant' And the Overland Campaign," *North & South*, November 2000, 55.

48 Jean Edward Smith, *Grant* (New York: Simon & Schuster, 2001), 15.

49 Steven E. Woodworth, et al., "Who Were the Top Ten Generals?," *North & South*, May 2003: 12–22.

50 Sherman, *Memoirs of General W. T. Sherman*, 479.

51 Harper, *Ohio Handbook of the Civil War*, 53–7.

52 Freehling et al., "Could the Confederacy Have Won the Civil War?" 14.

53 Benjamin P. Thomas and Harold M. Hyman, *Stanton: The Life and Times of Lincoln's Secretary of War* (New York: Alfred A. Knopf, 1962), 385.

54 Ibid, 386.

55 Adams, *Our Masters the Rebels: A Speculation on Union Military Failure in the East 1861–1865.*

56 Ibid, vii.

57 Ibid, ix. [Emphasis added.]

58 Ibid, 73.

59 Ibid, 66.

60 Ibid, xiii.

61 Grant, *Grant: Memoirs and Selected Letters,* 476.

62 Kenneth W. Noe, *Perryville: This Grand Havoc of Battle* (Lexington: University Press of Kentucky, 2001), 123.

63 Sherman, *Memoirs of General W. T. Sherman,* 369–70.

64 Fuller, *Grant & Lee,* 76–7.

65 Walt Whitman, "Specimen Days 100. The Million Dead, Too, Summ'd Up," (http://www.bartleby.com/229/1100.html: 1892).

66 John M. Murrin et al., *Liberty, Equality, Power: A History of the American People [since 1863],* 2 vols., vol. 2 (Forth Wort: Harcourt Brace College Publishers, 1999). 637–640.

67 Captain John Calvin Hartzell, *Ohio Volunteer: The Childhood and Civil War Memoirs of Captain John Calvin Hartzell,* ed. Charles I. Switzer (Athens, Ohio: Ohio University Press, 2005), 180.

68 "The Grand Army of the Republic and Kindred Societies: National Encampments: Bibliography," (http://www.loc.gov/rr/main/gar/national/natlist.html: Library of Congress).

69 Gladys B. Knight, "Sons of Union Veterans of the Civil War: Brief History of the Grand Army of the Republic," (http://suvcw.org/gar.htm).

70 "Grand Army of the Republic and Kindred Societies."

71 "Grand Army Encampment: Thousands of Veterans on the Ground and More Coming," *New York Times,* September 11, 1888.

72 "Veteran Vanguard Now in Gettysburg," *New York Times,* June 29, 1913.

73 "Old Soldiers Defy Gettysburg Heat," *New York Times,* July 2, 1913.

74 "Pickett's Charge Fifty Years After," *New York Times,* July 4, 1913.

75 "Veteran Vanguard."

76 "John H. Grate, 103, Civil War Veteran," *New York Times,* June 8, 1949.

77 "Civil War Veteran Turns 104," *New York Times,* September 26, 1950. Frederic Fox, "Report from Wauseon—Fall, 1950," *New York Times,* November 5, 1950.

78 "G.A.R. Veteran, 104, Dies," *New York Times,* February 19, 1951.

Notes for Chapter 17

1 "Lieut.-General Grant in Cleveland," *Cleveland Daily Leader,* June 10, 1865.

2 Jean Edward Smith, *Grant* (New York: Simon & Schuster, 2001), 595.

3 Ibid, 623.

4 Julia Dent Grant, *The Personal Memoirs of Julia Dent Grant,* ed. John Y. Simon (New York: G. P. Putnam's Sons, 1975), 331.

5 Samuel Eliot Morison, *The Oxford History of the American People* (New York: Oxford University Press, 1965), 733–4.

6 T. Harry Williams, *Hayes of the Twenty-Third: The Civil War Volunteer Officer* (New York: Alfred A. Knopf, 1965), ix.

7 Ibid, 7.

8 Margaret Leech and Harry J. Brown, *The Garfield Orbit* (New York: Harper & Row, 1978), 194.

9 Allan Peskin, "James A. Garfield," in *The Reader's Companion to American History,* ed. Eric Foner and John A. Garraty (Boston: Houghton Mifflin, 1991), 439.

10 Damaine Vonada, ed., *The Ohio Almanac*, 1992/93 ed. (Wilmington, Ohio: Orange Frazer Press, 1992), 33.

11 Stanley P. Hirshson, *The White Tecumseh: A Biography of General William T. Sherman* (New York: John Wiley & Sons, Inc., 1997), 346.

12 Ibid, 332.

13 Lee Kennett, *Sherman: A Soldier's Life*, softcover ed. (New York: Perennial/HarperCollins, 2001), 291.

14 Hirshson, *The White Tecumseh*, 342.

15 Ibid, 354.

16 Ibid, 357.

17 Ibid, 382.

18 Ibid, 367.

19 Ibid, 372.

20 Kennett, *Sherman*, 334–5.

21 Hirshson, *The White Tecumseh*, 365–6.

22 David S. Heidler and Jeanne T. Heidler, eds., *Encyclopedia of the American Civil War* (New York: W. W. Norton & Company, 2000), 1,762.

23 Roy Morris Jr., *Sheridan: The Life and Wars of General Phil Sheridan* (New York: Crown Publishers, Inc., 1992), 355–6, 391.

24 Benjamin P. Thomas and Harold M. Hyman, *Stanton: The Life and Times of Lincoln's Secretary of War* (New York: Alfred A. Knopf, 1962), 631.

25 Heidler and Heidler, eds., *Encyclopedia of the American Civil War*, 410.

26 Ibid, 2,043.

27 Whitelaw Reid, *Ohio in the War: Her Statesmen, Generals, and Soldiers*, 1895 ed., vol. 1, *The History of Ohio During the War and the Lives of Her Generals* (New York: Moore, Wilstach & Baldwin, 1868), 694.

28 "Gen. M'dowell Dying," *New York Times*, May 1, 1885.

29 Russell Roberts, "Governor McClellan: Deja Vu All over Again?" *Civil War Times*, May 2006.

30 James M. McPherson, *Battle Cry of Freedom: The Civil War Era*, paperback ed. (Oxford, England, and New York: Oxford University Press, 1988), 358.

31 Tim Wood, "The Tarnished Soldier: New Book Details Heroism, Scandal of Nickerson Ancestor," *Cape Cod Chronicle*, January 23, 2003.

32 Captain John Calvin Hartzell, *Ohio Volunteer: The Childhood and Civil War Memoirs of Captain John Calvin Hartzell*, ed. Charles I. Switzer (Athens, Ohio: Ohio University Press, 2005), 178.

33 Ibid, xxi, 199.

34 Stephen F. Williams, "The Buckeye from Missouri," (http://www.48ovvi.org/oh48buckeye. htm).

35 Emerson Opdycke, *To Battle for God and the Right: The Civil War Letterbooks of Emerson Opdycke, ed.* Glenn V. Longacre and John E. Hass (Urbana, Illinois: University of Illinois Press, 2003).

36 Thomas Francis Galwey, *The Valiant Hours* (Harrisburg, Pennsylvania: The Stackpole Company, 1961).

37 John Beatty, *Memoirs of a Volunteer 1861–1863* (New York: W. W. Norton & Company, 1946).

38 Grant and Simon, *The Personal Memoirs of Julia Dent Grant*, 116.

39 Marcus M. Spiegel, *A Jewish Colonel in the Civil War, ed.* Jean Powers Soman and Frank L. Byrne (Lincoln: University of Nebraska Press, 1995).

40 Hirshson, *The White Tecumseh*, 231.

41 Sandra Weber, "Living Legacies of Harpers Ferry," *Civil War Times*, February 2005: 44.

42 Peter Corodimas, "John M. Harrison, the Man Who Made Nasby, David Ross Locke," *American Quarterly* 22, no. 2, Part 2 (1970): 282.

43 Frank L. Klement, *The Limits of Dissent* (Lexington: University Press of Kentucky, 1970), 310.

44 Ibid, 312.

45 Peg A. Lamphier, *Kate Chase and William Sprague: Politics and Gender in a Civil War Marriage* (Lincoln: University of Nebraska Press, 2003), 253.

46 Ibid, 258.
47 Ibid, 242.

❧ SOURCES CONSULTED

NEWSPAPERS

Cincinnati Daily Commercial, Cleveland Daily Leader, Cleveland Morning Leader, Cleveland Plain Dealer, Daily Toledo Blade, Elyria Independent Democrat, Lancaster Eagle, Lancaster Gazette, National Tribune, New York Times, Ohio State Journal, Sandusky Daily Commercial Register, Toledo Daily Herald and News.

PRIMARY SOURCES

"Aid and Comfort to Company A, Capt. Stafford." *Lancaster Gazette*, June 27, 1861.

Altman, Andrew. "Andrew Altman Papers, 1861–1937." In *Bowling Green State University Center for Archival Collections.*

Ames, Holiday, and Louis Filler, ed. "Waiting for the War's End: The Letter of an Ohio Soldier in Alabama." *Ohio History* 74 (1998): 55–62.

"A New Order of Things." *Cleveland Plain Dealer*, January 20, 1862.

"An Incident of the Day." *Daily Toledo Blade*, December 3, 1859.

Beatty, John. *Memoirs of a Volunteer 1861–1863.* New York: W. W. Norton & Company, 1946.

Benjamin, Charles F. "Recollections of Secretary Stanton." *The Century*, March 1887, 758–68.

Bering, John A., and Thomas Montgomery. "History of the Forty-Eighth Ohio Vet. Vol. Inf." http://www.48ovvi.org/oh48hist.htm, 1880.

Bibb, Henry. *The Life and Adventures of Henry Bibb, an American Slave.* Madison, Wisconsin: University of Wisconsin Press, 2000.

Bickham, William D. "Our Army in West Virginia." *Cincinnati Daily Commercial*, July 19, 1861.

Bierce, Ambrose, *Phantoms of a Blood-Stained Period: The Complete Civil War Writings of Ambrose Bierce.* Edited by Russell Duncan and David J. Klooster. Amherst, Massachusetts: University of Massachusetts Press, 2002.

Brayton, Mary Clark, and Ellen F. Terry. *Our Acre and Its Harvest: Historical Sketch of the Soldiers' Aid Society of Northern Ohio.* Cleveland: Fairbanks, Benedict & Co., 1869.

Brooks, Noah. "Personal Reminiscences of Lincoln." *Scribners Monthly*, February 1878: 561–69.

Bruner, Jacob. "Bruner, Jacob, Letters, 1861–1863." http://dbs.ohiohistory.org/africanam/msa/mss994.cfrr: Ohio Historical Society, 1861–3.

Burt, Richard W. "Foraging for Sherman's Army: Often Dangerous and Exciting Work Done by Fearless Men." In *National Tribune.* Washington, D.C., 1898.

Burt, Richard W. "Siege of Vicksburg, Sunday, May 30th, 1863." http://my.ohio.voyager.net/~lstevens/burt/may30.html.

Caldwell, William. "Caldwell Family Papers." In *Hayes Presidential Center.* Fremont, Ohio.

Chase, J. A. *History of the Fourteenth Ohio Regiment, O.V.V.I.* Toledo, Ohio: St. John Printing House, 1881.

Chesnut, Mary Boykin. *Mary Chesnut's Civil War*, Edited by C. Vann Woodward. New Haven: Yale University Press, 1981.

Chesnut, Mary. "Mrs. Chesnut Watches the Attack on Fort Sumter." In *The Civil War Archive*, edited by Henry Steele Commager and Erik Bruun, 65–69. New York: Tess Press, 2000.

"Civil War Veteran Turns 104." *New York Times*, September 26, 1950: 28.

Collins, John E. "When Stonewall Jackson Turned Our Right." In *Battles and Leaders of the Civil War*, edited by Robert Underwood Johnson and Clarence Clough Buel, 183–85. New York: The Century Co., 1888.

Comer, Harry. "Camp Dennison, Lancaster, Pa." *The Ohio Eagle*, May 2, 1861.

_____. "Letter No. 1 from Company A, April 21, 1861." *Lancaster Gazette & Democrat*, April 25, 1861.

———. "Harrisburg Encampment, Pa." *The Ohio Eagle*, April 25, 1861.

———. "Letter No. 4, from Company A." *Lancaster Gazette & Democrat*, June 6, 1861.

"Concert." *Lancaster Gazette*, May 2, 1861.

Cope, Alexis. *The Fifteenth Ohio Volunteers and Its Campaigns*. Columbus, Ohio: Alexis Cope, 1916.

Copley, John M. "A Sketch of the Battle of Franklin, Tenn.; with Reminiscences of Camp Douglas." http://docsouth.unc.edu/copley/copley.html.

Couch, Darius N. "The Chancellorsville Campaign." In *Battles and Leaders of the Civil War*, edited by Robert Underwood Johnson and Clarence Clough Buel, 154–71. New York: The Century Co., 1888.

Cox, Jacob D. "McClellan in West Virginia." In *Battles and Leaders of the Civil War*, vol. I, 126–48. New York: The Century Co., 1887.

_____. "Military Reminiscences of the Civil War." (1900). http://www.sonofthesouth.net/leefoundation/cw1.htm: Robert E. Lee Historical Preservation Initiative.

_____. "War Preparations in the North." In *Battles and Leaders of the Civil War*, edited by Robert Underwood Johnson and Clarence Clough Buel vol. I, 84–98. New York: The Century Co., 1887.

Culp, Edward C. *The 25th Ohio Vet. Vol. Infantry in the War for the Union*. Topeka, Kansas: Geo. W. Crane & Co., 1885.

Dalzell, James. *Private Dalzell: His Autobiography, Poems and Comic War Papers*. Cincinnati: Robert Clark & Co., 1888.

Daniels, W. C. "From the Regiment." http://www.angelfire.com/oh4/civwar/14thohio/daniels.html, 1861.

Dawes, Henry L. "Recollections of Stanton under Lincoln." *Atlantic Monthly*, February 1894: 162–69.

Doubleday, Abner. "Abner Doubleday Defends Fort Sumter." In *The Civil War Archive*, edited by Henry Steele Commager and Erik Bruun, 69–72. New York: Tess Press, 2000.

———. *Reminiscences of Forts Sumter and Moultrie in 1860–'61*. New York: Harper & Brothers, 1876.

Duke, John K. *History of the Fifty-Third Regiment, Ohio Volunteer Infantry, During the War of the Rebellion ...* Portsmouth, Ohio: The Blade Printing Company, 1900.

Finch, George M. "The Boys of '61." In *G. A. R. War Papers*, edited by E. R. Monfort, H. B. Furness and Fred. H. Alms, 237–63. Cincinnati: Fred C. Jones Post, No. 401, 1891.

"First Gallant South Carolina Nobly Made the Stand." In *The Civil War Archive*, edited by Henry Steele Commager and Erik Bruun, 42–4. New York: Tess Press, 2000.

Force, Manning F. "Personal Recollections of the Vicksburg Campaign." In *Sketches of War History 1861–1865 [Ohio Commandery of MOLLUS]*, 293–309. Wilmington, North Carolina: Broadfoot Publishing Company, 1888.

Fox, Frederic. "Report from Wauseon—Fall, 1950." *New York Times*, November 5, 1950.

"G.A.R. Veteran, 104, Dies." *New York Times*, February 19, 1951.

Galwey, Thomas Francis. *The Valiant Hours*. Harrisburg, Pennsylvania: The Stackpole

Company, 1961.

Garfield, James A. *The Wild Life of the Army: Civil War Letters of James A. Garfield*. East Lansing, Michigan: Michigan State University Press, 1964.

Garfield, James and Lucretia. *Crete and James: Personal Letters of Lucretia and James Garfield*. Edited by John Shaw. East Lansing, Michigan: Michigan State University Press, 1994.

Garland, Hamlin. *Ulysses S. Grant: His Life and Character*. New York: Macmillan, 1920.

"Gen. M'dowell Dying." *New York Times*, May 1, 1885.

Gilson, J. H. *Concise History of the One Hundred and Twenty-Sixth Regiment, Ohio Volunteer Infantry* ... Huntington, West Virginia: Blue Acorn Press, 2000.

"Good News from Washington." *Cleveland Plain Dealer*, January 14, 1862: 2.

Goss, Warren Lee. "Going to the Front." In *Battles and Leaders of the Civil War*, edited by Robert Underwood Johnson and Clarence Clough Buel, 149–59. New York: The Century Co., 1887.

"Grand Army Encampment: Thousands of Veterans on the Ground and More Coming." *New York Times*, September 11, 1888.

Grant, Julia Dent. *The Personal Memoirs of Julia Dent Grant*. Edited by John Y. Simon. New York: G. P. Putnam's Sons, 1975.

Grant, Ulysses S. *Ulysses S. Grant: Memoirs and Selected Letters*. New York: Library of America, 1990.

Gray, John Chipman, and John Codman Ropes. *War Letters 1862–1865 of John Chipman Gray and John Codman Ropes*. Boston: Houghton Mifflin Company, 1927.

Gray, John Chipman. "John Chipman Gray Views the Western Soldier." In *The Civil War Archive: The History of the Civil War in Documents*, edited by Henry Steele Commager and Erik Bruun, 301–02. New York: Tess Press, 2000.

Grebner, Constantin. *We Were the Ninth: A History of the Ninth Regiment, Ohio Volunteer Infantry, April 17, 1861, to June 7, 1864*. Translated by Frederic Trautmann. Kent, Ohio: Kent State University Press, 1987.

Griffis, Rev. William Henry. "Refutation of Several Romances About the Execution of John Brown." *Southern Historical* 13 (1885): 336–42.

Halstead, Murat. *Three against Lincoln: Murat Halstead Reports the Caucuses of 1860*. Edited by William B. Hesseltine. Baton Rouge: Louisiana State University Press, 1960.

Halstead, Murat. "The Execution of John Brown." *Ohio Archaeological and Historical Quarterly* [now *Ohio History*] XXX (1921): 290–99.

Hartzell, Captain John Calvin, and Charles I. Switzer, ed. *Ohio Volunteer: The Childhood and Civil War Memoirs of Captain John Calvin Hartzell*. Athens, Ohio: Ohio University Press, 2005.

Hay, John, *Inside Lincoln's White House: The Complete Civil War Diary of John Hay*. Edited by Michael Burlingame and John R. Turner Ettlinger Turner. Carbondale, Illinois: Southern Illinois University Press, 1997.

Hazen, W. B. *A Narrative of Military Service*. Boston: Ticknor and Company, 1885.

"Henry Beebee Carrington." http://www.virtualogy.com/henrybeebeecarington/.

Hinson, Joseph. "The Baltimore Passage." *National Tribune*, February 21, 1884.

"History of the Battle of Perryville." http://www.perryville.net/history.html: Perryville Enhancement Project.

Hitchcock, Henry. *Marching with Sherman: Passages from the Letters and Campaign Diaries of Henry Hitchcock, Major and Assistant Adjutant General of Volunteers, November 1864–May 1865*. Edited by M. A. DeWolfe Howe. New Haven: Yale University Press, 1927.

Howe, Julia Ward. "Reminiscences of Julia Ward Howe." *The Atlantic Monthly*, May 1899, 701–12.

Imboden, John D. "The Confederate Retreat from Gettysburg." In *Battles and Leaders of the*

Civil War, edited by Robert Underwood Johnson and Clarence Clough Buel, 420–29. New York: The Century Co., 1888.

Jackson, Joseph Orville, ed. *"Some of the Boys ..." The Civil War Letters of Isaac Jackson, 1862–1865*. Carbondale, Illinois: Southern Illinois University, 1960.

Jackson, Oscar L. *The Colonel's Diary*. Sharon, Pennsylvania, 1922.

"John H. Grate, 103, Civil War Veteran." *New York Times*, June 8, 1949.

Johnston, Joseph E. "Responsibilities of the First Bull Run." In *Battles and Leaders of the Civil War*, edited by Robert Underwood Johnson and Clarence Clough Buel, vol. I, 240–61. New York: The Century Company, 1887.

Kepler, William. *History of the Three Months' and Three Years' Service from April 16th, 1861, to June 22d, 1864, ... Of the Fourth Infantry Regiment Ohio Volunteer Infantry*. Cleveland: Leader Printing Company, 1886.

Kern, Albert. *History of the First Regiment Ohio Volunteer Infantry in the Civil War 1861–1865*. Dayton, 1918. Reprint, n.d., Curt Dalton, Dayton, Ohio.

Kimberly, Robert L., and Ephraim S. Holloway. *The Forty-First Ohio Veteran Volunteer Infantry in the War of the Rebellion, 1861–1865*. Cleveland: W. R. Smellie, 1897.

Ladley, Oscar D. *Hearth and Knapsack: The Ladley Letters, 1857–1880*. Edited by Carl M. Becker and Ritchie Thomas. Athens, Ohio: Ohio University Press, 1988.

"Latest News." *Cleveland Morning Leader*, April 18, 1861.

"Letter from Columbus April 16th, 1861." *Cincinnati Daily Commercial*, April 17, 1861.

"Letter from Columbus April 17, 1861." *Cincinnati Daily Commercial*, April 18, 1861.

"Lieut.-General Grant in Cleveland." *Cleveland Daily Leader*, June 10, 1865.

Life, Trial and Execution of Captain John Brown; 1859. Robert M. De Witt, 1859.

List of Pensioners on the Roll January 1, 1883. Vol. III. Baltimore: Genealogical Publishing Company, 1970.

"'Local and Miscellaneous'." *Daily Toledo Blade*, April 13, 1861.

"Local Matters." *Cincinnati Daily Commercial*, April 17, 1861.

"Local Matters." *Cincinnati Daily Commercial*, April 19, 1861

Lubin, Martin, ed. *The Words of Abraham Lincoln: Speeches, Letters, Proclamations, and Papers of Our Most Eloquent President*. New York: Tess Press, 2005.

May, Augustus C. "Letter Written by Pvt. Augustus C. May: The Fourteenth at Chickamauga." http://www.angelfire.com/oh4/civwar/14thohio/acmay.htm.

McCoy, Milton. "First Bull Run: Experiences of an Ohio Three Months' Man." *National Tribune*, October 23, 1884.

Mellor, Albert. "Experiences in Southern Military Prisons." In *G.A.R. War Papers: Papers Read before Fred C. Jones Post, No. 401, Department of Ohio, G.A.R.*, edited by E. R. Monfort, H. B. Furness and Fred H. Alms, 264–83. Cincinnati: Fred C. Jones Post, No. 401, G.A.R., 1891?

Mesnard, Luther B. "Excerpts from the Diary of Luther B. Mesnard Regarding His Actions During the Battle of Gettysburg." http://www.forttejon.org/oh55/mesnard/%20diary%20gburg.html.

Monfort, E. R. "The First Division, Eleventh Corps, at Chancellorsville." In *G.A.R. War Papers*, edited by E. R. Monfort, H. B. Furness and Fred H. Alms, 60–75. Cincinnati: Fred C. Jones Post, No. 401, n.d.

Morrow, Maud E. *Recollections of the Civil War: From a Child's Point of View*. Lockland, Ohio, 1901.

"N". "Account of the Battle of Chickamauga Written By 'N.'" http://www.angelfire.com/oh4/civwar/14thphio/chick_n.htm, 1863.

"News From Columbus, April 19, 1861." *Cincinnati Daily Commercial*, April 19, 1861

Nickerson, A. H. "Personal Recollections of Two Visits to Gettysburg." *Scribner's Magazine*,

July 1893: 19–28.

Nicolay, John G. *The Outbreak of the Rebellion*. New York: Da Capo Press, 1995.

"Old Soldiers Defy Gettysburg Heat." *New York Times*, July 2, 1913.

Opdycke, Emerson. *To Battle for God and the Right: The Civil War Letterbooks of Emerson Opdycke*. Edited by Glenn V. Longacre and John E. Hass. Urbana, Illinois: University of Illinois Press, 2003.

Osborn, Hartwell, and others. *Trials and Triumphs, the Record of the 55th Ohio Volunteer Infantry*. Chicago: A. C. McClurg & Co., 1904.

Parker, John P. *His Promised Land*. New York: W. W. Norton & Company, 1996.

Phillips, W. Louis, C.G. *Index to Ohio Pensioners of 1883*. Bowie, Maryland: Heritage Books, Inc., 1987.

"Pickett's Charge Fifty Years After." *New York Times*, July 4, 1913.

Pittenger, William. *Daring and Suffering: A History of the Andrews Railroad Raid*. New York: War Publishing Company, 1887.

Pope, John. "The Second Battle of Bull Run." http://www.civilwarhome.com/popemanassas.htm.

Porter, Horace. *Campaigning with Grant*. Lincoln: University of Nebraska Press, 2000.

Posegate, Capt. F. M., 48th OVI. "The Sunday Battle at Shiloh." http://www.48ovvi.org/oh48shilohsun.htm.

"Presidential Elections: 1860." http://www.multied.com/elections/1860.html: HistoryCentral. Com, 2004.

Rankin, Rev. John. *Life of Rev. John Rankin, Written by Himself in His 80th Year, Circa 1872*. Edited by Alison Gibson. Ripley, Ohio: Rankin House National Historic Landmark, owned by the Ohio Historical Society and operated by Ripley Heritage, Inc., n.d.

Reid, Whitelaw. *A Radical View: The "Agate" Dispatches of Whitelaw Reid 1861–1865*. 2 vols. Edited by James G. Smart. Memphis: Memphis State University Press, 1976.

Reid, Whitelaw. *Ohio in the War: Her Statesmen, Generals and Soldiers*. 1895 ed. 2 vols. Vol. 1. *The History of Ohio During the War and the Lives of Her Generals*. Cincinnati: The Robert Clarke Company, 1895.

———. *Ohio in the War: Her Statesmen, Generals, and Soldiers*. 2 vols. Vol. 2. *The History of Her Regiments and Other Military Organizations*. Cincinnati: The Robert Clarke Company, 1895.

"Review of the Armies: Propitious Weather and a Splendid Spectacle." *New York Times*, May 24, 1865.

"Review of the Armies: The Second and Last Day of the Great Pageant." *New York Times*, May 25, 1865.

Rhoades, Sarah. "Corporal John R. Rhoades Papers, 1858–1865." In Hayes Presidential Center. Fremont, Ohio, 1862.

Rice, Sarah Wilson. "Letters to Dr. John B. Rice." Fremont, Ohio: Hayes Presidential Center, 1863–64.

Richardson, John E. "The Civil War Letters of John E. Richardson: October 1861—February 1862, Camp Dennison." http://www.48ovvi.org/oh48jer1.htm, 1861–2.

Ruffin, Edmund. *The Diary of Edmund Ruffin*. 3 vols. Edited by William Kauffman Scarborough Baton Rouge: Louisiana State University Press, 1976–1989.

Saunier, Joseph A., ed. *A History of the Forty-Seventh Regiment Ohio Veteran Volunteer Infantry*. Hillsboro, Ohio: Lyle Printing Company, 1903.

Sawyer, Franklin. *A Military History of the 8th Regiment Ohio Vol. Inf'y: Its Battles, Marches and Army Movements*. Huntington, West Virginia: Blue Acorn Press, 1994.

Sherman, William T. *From Atlanta to the Sea*. Edited by B. H. Liddell Hart. London: The Folio Society, 1961.

Sherman, William T., and Ellen Ewing Sherman. "William T. Sherman Family Papers." http://

archives.nd.edu/findaids/ead/index/SHR001.htm: University of Notre Dame.

Sherman, William T. *Sherman's Selected Correspondence of Civil War*. Edited by Brooks D. Simpson and Jean V. Berlin. Chapel Hill: University of North Carolina Press, 1999.

Sherman, William Tecumseh. *Memoirs of General W. T. Sherman*. New York: Penguin Books, 2000.

Shifflet, Hillory. "Hillory Shifflet Letters, Compiled by Kate Forster." http://www.geocities.com/~jcrosswell/War/CW/hillory.htm.

"Significant." *Daily Toledo Blade*, April 19, 1861.

Simon, John Y., ed. *The Papers of Ulysses S. Grant*. Vol. 4. Carbondale, Illinois: Southern Illinois University Press, 1972.

Spiegel, Marcus M. *A Jewish Colonel in the Civil War*. Edited by Jean Powers Soman and Frank L. Byrne. Lincoln: University of Nebraska Press, 1995.

Stewart, Rev. Nixon B. *Dan McCook's Regiment, 52nd O.V.I. A History of the Regiment, Its Campaigns, and Battles*. n.p.: Author, 1900. Reprint, 1999, Blue Acorn Press.

The War of the Rebellion: A Compilation of the Official Records of the Union and Confederate Armies. [The "Official Records" or "O.R."] 70 vols. Washington, DC, 1880–1901.

"The Beginning of the End." *Daily Toledo Blade*, November 13, 1860.

"The City—the Enthusiasm—the Work." *Cincinnati Daily Commercial*, April 20, 1861.

"The End of the War!" *Cleveland Daily Leader*, June 6 1865.

"The Feeling." *Toledo Daily Herald and News*, April 16, 1861.

"The Flag of Our Union Forever." *Daily Toledo Blade*, April 16, 1861.

"The Grand Army of the Republic and Kindred Societies: National Encampments: Bibliography." http://www.loc.gov/rr/main/gar/national/natlist.html: Library of Congress.

"The Great Pulsation." *Cleveland Morning Leader*, April 13, 1861.

"The Issue Is Made Up!" *Daily Toledo Blade*, April 13, 1861.

"The New Year Day." *Ohio State Journal*, January 2, 1863.

"The Sacrifice to the God of Slavery." *Sandusky Daily Commercial Register*, December 2, 1859.

"The War Begun!!! Fort Sumter Attacked Yesterday Morning!" *Cleveland Morning Leader*, April 13, 1861.

"The War Begun!!" *Ohio State Journal*, April 13, 1861.

"The War News." *Cleveland Morning Leader*, April 13, 1861.

Thomas, Henry Goddard. "The Colored Troops at Petersburg." In *Battles and Leaders of the Civil War*, edited by Robert Underwood Johnson and Clarence Clough Buel, 563–7. New York: The Century Company, 1888.

Tocqueville, Alexis de. *Journey to America*. Edited by J. P. Mayer. New Haven: Yale University Press, 1959.

Tourgee, Albion W. *The Story of a Thousand: Being a History of the Service of the 105th Ohio Volunteer Infantry ...* Buffalo: S. McGerald & Son, 1896.

"Town and Country." *Toledo Daily Herald and Times*, April 16, 1861.

"Town and Country." *Toledo Daily Herald and Times*, April 17, 1861

Trollope, Frances. *Domestic Manners of the Americans*. Edited by Donald Smalley. New York: Alfred A. Knopf, 1949.

"Union Meeting, Held in the Union Depot Last Evening—Immense Enthusiasm—3000 Present." *Toledo Daily Herald and Times*, April 16, 1861.

"Veteran Vanguard Now in Gettysburg." *New York Times*, June 29, 1913.

"War Spirit in Elyria." *Elyria Independent Democrat*, April 17, 1861.

"Well Said!" *Sandusky Daily Commercial Register*, April 16, 1861.

"William Tecumseh Sherman." http://en.wikiquote.org/wiki/William_Tecumseh_Sherman: Wikiquote.

Williams, Ammi. "Ammi Williams Letters to Henry Williams." In *Hayes Presidential Center Civil War Collection, LH-Misc. Mss.* Fremont, Ohio, 1862.

Williams, Stephen F. "The Buckeye from Missouri." http://www.48ovvi.org/oh48buckeye.htm.

Willison, Charles A. *Reminiscences of a Boy's Service with the 76th Ohio.* Huntington, West Virginia: Blue Acorn Press, 1995.

SECONDARY SOURCES

Adams, Michael C. C. *Our Masters the Rebels: A Speculation on Union Military Failure in the East 1861–1865.* Cambridge, Massachusetts: Harvard University Press, 1978.

Allen, Stacy. Chief Ranger, Shiloh National Military Park. Telephone interview January 25, 2007.

American Association of University Women, St. Lawrence County (New York) Branch. "Mary Edwards Walker: Civil War Doctor." http://www.northnet.org/stlawrenceaauw/walker.htm, 2005.

Ayers, Edward L. "What Caused the Civil War?" *North & South* [magazine], September 2005: 12–18.

Baker, Nina Brown. *Cyclone in Calico: The Story of Mary Ann Bickerdyke.* Boston: Little, Brown and Company, 1952.

Baringer, William. *Lincoln's Rise to Power.* St. Clair Shores, Michigan: Scholarly Press, 1979.

"Battle of Fredricksburg." *Wikipedia* (2007), http://wikipedia.com.

Bearss, Edwin C. *Fields of Honor: Pivotal Battle of the Civil War.* Washington, DC: National Geographic, 1966.

Becker, Carl M. "Miles Greenwood." In *For the Union: Ohio Leaders in the Civil War*, edited by Kenneth M. Wheeler, 259–319. Columbus, Ohio: Ohio State University Press, 1968.

Berkin, Carol. *A Brilliant Solution.* New York: Harcourt, Inc., 2002.

Berry, Chester D., ed. *Loss of the Sultana and Reminiscences of Survivors.* Knoxville: University of Tennessee Press, 2005.

Blue, Frederick J. "Friends of Freedom: Lincoln, Chase, and Wartime Racial Policy." *Ohio History* [journal] 102 (1993): 85–97.

Blue, Frederick J. "Salmon Portland Chase." In *Encyclopedia of the American Civil War*, edited by David S. Heidler and Jeanne T. Heidler, 408–10. New York: W. W. Norton & Company, 2000.

Boatner III, Mark Mayo. *The Civil War Dictionary.* rev. ed. New York: Vintage Books, 1991.

Bowen, Catherine Drinker. *Miracle at Philadelphia: The Story of the Constitutional Convention, May to September 1787.* Boston: Little, Brown & Co., 1966.

Brandt, Nat. *The Town That Started the Civil War.* Syracuse, New York: Syracuse University Press, 1990.

Brennan, Patrick. "Last Stand in the Heartland." *North & South* [magazine], May 2005: 20–45.

Burlingame, Michael, and John R. Turner Ettlinger, eds. *Inside Lincoln's White House: The Complete Civil War Diary of John Hay.* Carbondale, Illinois: Southern Illinois University Press, 1997.

Busey, John W., and David G. Martin. *Regimental Strengths and Losses at Gettysburg.* Hightstown, Maryland: Longstreet House, 1994.

Card, Nan. "Experience of Death in the Civil War: Sandusky County, Ohio." Thesis, Bowling Green State University, 2001.

Carrabine, Nick. "Jim Gaffigan's Double Life." *Toledo Blade*, February 8, 2007.

Carroll, Howard. *Twelve Americans: Their Lives and Times*, Essex Index Reprint Series.

Freeport, New York: Books for Libraries Press, 1971.

Carter, Susan B., et al., eds. *Historical Statistics of the United States*. 5 vols. Vol. 5. Cambridge: Cambridge University Press, 2006.

Castel, Albert. *Decision in the West: The Atlanta Campaign of 1864*. Lawrence, Kansas: University Press of Kansas, 1992.

Cayton, Andrew R. L. "The Significance of Ohio in the Early American Republic." In *The Center of a Great Empire*. Edited by Andrew R. L. Cayton and Stuart D. Hobbs, 1–9. Athens, Ohio: Ohio University Press, 2005.

Cheek, William, and Aimee Lee Cheek. *John Mercer Langston and the Fight for Black Freedom* Urbana, Illinois: University of Illinois Press, 1989.

Chernow, Ron. *Titan: The Life of John D. Rockefeller, Sr.* New York: Random House, 1998.

Coco, Gregory A. *A Strange and Blighted Land, Gettysburg: The Aftermath of Battle*. Gettysburg, Pennsylvania: Thomas Publications, 1995.

Commager, Henry Steele, and Erik Bruun, eds. *The Civil War Archive: The History of the Civil War in Documents*. New York: Tess Press, 2000.

Cornelius, Steven H. *Music of the Civil War Era*. Edited by David J. Brinkman. American History through Music series. Westport, Connecticut: Greenwood Press, 2004.

Corodimas, Peter. "John M. Harrison, the Man Who Made Nasby, David Ross Locke." *American Quarterly* 22, no. 2, Part 2 (1970): 282–3.

Cozzens, James. *This Terrible Sound*. Urbana, Illinois: University of Illinois Press, 1992.

Cozzens, Peter. *General John Pope: A Life for the Nation*. Urbana, Illinois: University of Illinois Press, 2000.

——————. *No Better Place to Die: The Battle of Stones River*. Urbana: University of Illinois Press, 1990.

Creighton, Margaret S. *The Colors of Courage: Gettysburg's Forgotten History*. New York: Basic Books, 2005.

Crenshaw, Oliver. "The Psychological Background of the Election of 1860 in the South." *The North Carolina Historical Review* XIX, no. 3 (1942): 260–79.

Crowther, Edward R. "Thirteenth Amendment." In *Encyclopedia of the American Civil War*. Edited by David S. Heidler and Jeanne T. Heidler, 1939–40. New York: W.W. Norton, 2000.

Cunningham, O. Edward. "Shiloh and the Western Campaign of 1862." Dissertation, Louisiana State University, 1966.

Curl, Donald W. "Murat Halstead, Editor and Politician." Dissertation, Ohio State University, 1964.

Curl, Donald W. "Murat Halstead." In *For the Union: Ohio Leaders in the Civil War*. Edited by Kenneth W. Wheeler, 321–75. Columbus, Ohio: Ohio State University Press, 1968.

Curry, Robert O. "McClellan's Western Virginia Campaign of 1861." *Ohio History* [journal] 71, no. 2 (1962): 83–96.

Daniel, Larry J. *Days of Glory: The Army of the Cumberland 1861–1865*. Baton Rouge: Louisiana State University Press, 2004.

Daniel, Larry J. *Shiloh: The Battle That Changed the Civil War*. New York: A Touchstone book, published by Simon & Schuster, 1998.

Dodds, Gilbert F. *Camp Chase; the Story of a Civil War Post*. Columbus, Ohio: Franklin County Historical Society, n.d.

Donald, David Herbert. *Lincoln*. New York: Simon & Schuster Paperbacks, 1995.

Donovan Jr., Timothy H, Roy K. Flint, Arthur V. Grant Jr., and Gerald P. Stadler. *The American Civil War*. Edited by Thomas E. Griess, *West Point Military History Series*. Garden City Park, New York: Square One Publishers, 2002.

Downer, Edward T. *Ohio Troops in the Field*, Ohio Civil War Centennial Commission Publications. Columbus: Ohio State University Press for the Ohio Historical Society, n.d.

Drinkard, Dorothy L. "Battle of the Crater." In *Encyclopedia of the American Civil War*, edited by David S. Heidler and Jeanne T. Heidler. New York: W.W. Norton, 2000.

Dyer, Frederick H. *A Compendium of the War of the Rebellion*. Three vols. New York: Thomas Yoseloff, 1959.

Eicher, David J. *The Civil War in Books: An Analytical Bibliography*. Urbana, Illinois: University of Illinois Press, 1997.

Eicher, David J. *The Longest Night: A Military History of the Civil War*. New York: Simon & Schuster, 2001.

Eicher, John H., and David J. Eicher. *Civil War High Commands*. Stanford, California: Stanford University Press, 2001.

Etcheson, Nicole. *The Emerging Midwest: Upland Southerners and the Political Culture of the Old Northwest, 1787–1861*. Edited by James H. Madison and Thomas J. Schlereth, *Midwestern History and Culture*. Bloomington, Indiana: Indiana University Press, 1998.

Frank, Lisa Tendrich. "Women." In *Encyclopedia of the American Civil War*. Edited by David S. Heidler and Jeanne T. Heidler, 2,142–5. New York: W. W. Norton & Company, 2000.

Frassanito, William A. *Early Photography at Gettysburg*. Gettysburg, Pennsylvania: Thomas Publications, 1995.

Freehling, William W., Allen C. Guelzo, Bruce Levine, Richard M. McMurry, James M. McPherson, and Stephen W. Sears. "Could the Confederacy Have Won the Civil War?" *North & South* [magazine], May 2006: 12–25.

Freemon, Frank R. *Microbes and Minie Balls: An Annotated Bibliography of Civil War Medicine*. Rutherford, New Jersey: Associated University Presses, 1993.

Frohman, Charles E. *Rebels on Lake Erie*. Columbus, Ohio: The Ohio Historical Society, 1965. Reprint, 1997.

Fruehling, Byron D., and Robert H. Smith. "Subterranean Hideaways of the Underground Railroad in Ohio: An Architectural, Archaeological and Historical Critique of Local Traditions." *Ohio History* [journal] 102 (1993): 98–117.

Fukuyama, Francis. "After the 'End of History'." In *Open Democracy* [online journal], http://www.opendemocracy.net. posted February 5, 2006.

Fuller, J. F. C. *Grant and Lee: A Study in Personality and Generalship*. Bloomington, Indiana: Indiana University Press, 1982.

Furgurson, Ernest B. *Chancellorsville 1863: The Souls of the Brave*. New York: Vintage Books, 1993.

Furgurson, Ernest B. *Freedom Rising: Washington in the Civil War*. New York: Alfred A. Knopf, 2004.

Gallagher, Gary W. and Alan T. Nolan eds. *The Myth of the Lost Cause and Civil War History*. Bloomington, Indiana: Indiana University Press, 2000.

Gallagher, Gary W., Stephen D. Engle, Robert K. Krick, and Joseph T. Glatthaar. *The American Civil War: This Mighty Scourge of War*. London: Osprey Publishing, 2003.

Garland, Hamlin. *Ulysses S. Grant: His Life and Character*. New York: Macmillan, 1920.

Glatthaar, Joseph T. *Forged in Battle: The Civil War Alliance of Black Soldiers and White Officers*. New York: The Free Press, 1990.

Goldberg, Jeffrey. "Letter from Washington: Central Casting." *The New Yorker*, May 29, 2006, 62–71.

Goodwin, Doris Kearns. *Team of Rivals: The Political Genius of Abraham Lincoln*. New York: Simon & Schuster, 2005.

Gottfried, Bradley M. *Brigades of Gettysburg: The Union and Confederate Brigades at the Battle of Gettysburg*. n.p.: Da Capo Press, 2002.

Gracie, Archibald. *The Truth About Chickamauga*. Boston: Houghton Mifflin Company, 1911.

Grant, Susan-Mary. "The Problem of Slavery in the Age of Counterrevolution." *Reviews in*

American History 30, no. 1 (2002): 31–38.

Greene, A. Wilson. "From Chancellorsville to Cemetery Hill: O. O. Howard and the Eleventh Corps Leadership." In *The First Day at Gettysburg: Essays on Confederate and Union Leadership*. Edited by Gary W. Gallagher, 57–91. Kent, Ohio: Kent State University Press, 1992.

Grimsley, Mark. "Western Theater." In *The American Civil War: A Handbook of Literature and Research*. Edited by Steven E. Woodworth, 270–86. Westport, Connecticut: Greenwood Press, 1996.

Gurganus, Allan. "The Rebellion Continues, at Least in the Southern Short Story." *Oxford American* [magazine], Winter 2006, 40–146.

Harper, Judith E. *Women During the Civil War: An Encyclopedia*. New York: Routledge, 2004.

Harper, Robert S. *Ohio Handbook of the Civil War*. Columbus, Ohio: Ohio Historical Society for the Ohio Civil War Centennial Commission, 1961.

Harrison, Lowell H. "Kentucky." In *Encyclopedia of the American Civil War*. Edited by David S. Heidler and Jeanne T. Heidler, 1,116–7. New York: W. W. Norton & Company, 2000.

Hattaway, Herman, and Richard E. Beringer. *Jefferson Davis, Confederate President*. Lawrence: University Press of Kansas, 2002.

Heidler, David S., and Jeanne T. Heidler, eds. *Encyclopedia of the American Civil War*. New York: W. W. Norton & Company, 2000.

Henderson, J. E. "60th Ohio Memoirs: Gen. Gordon's View." http://freepages.genealogy rootsweb.com/~volker/history.civilwar/.

Hennessy, John J. *Return to Bull Run: The Campaign and Battle of Second Manassas*. New York: Simon & Schuster, 1993.

Hess, Earl J. *The Union Soldier in Battle: Enduring the Ordeal of Combat*. Lawrence: University Press of Kansas, 1997.

Hesseltine, William B. *Civil War Prisons: A Study in War Psychology*. Columbus, Ohio: Ohio State University Press, 1930.

Hirshson, Stanley P. *The White Tecumseh: A Biography of General William T. Sherman*. New York: John Wiley & Sons, Inc., 1997.

Jones, Robert Leslie. *History of Agriculture in Ohio to 1880*. Kent, Ohio: Kent State University Press, 1983.

Kauffman, Michael W. *American Brutus*. New York: Random House, 2004.

Kennett, Lee B. "'Hell' or 'High Old Times'." *America's Civil War* [magazine], January 2005, 46–52.

Kennett, Lee. *Sherman: A Soldier's Life*. softcover ed. New York: Perennial/HarperCollins, 2001.

Kepler, Virginia. "Buckeyes Make a Stand." http://www.historynet.com/cwti/blbuckeyes/index.html.

Kern, Albert. *History of the First Regiment Ohio Volunteer Infantry in the Civil War 1861–1865*. Dayton, 1918. Reprint, n.d., Curt Dalton, Dayton, Ohio.

Kimball, George. "Origin of the John Brown Song." *The New England Magazine*, December 1889, 371–77.

Klement, Frank L. *The Gettysburg Soldiers' Cemetery and Lincoln's Address: Aspects and Angles*. Shippensburg, Pennsylvania: White Mane Publishing Company, Inc., 1993.

Klement, Frank L. *The Limits of Dissent*. Lexington: University Press of Kentucky, 1970.

Knepper, George W. *Ohio and Its People*. paperback ed. Kent, Ohio: Kent State University Press, 1989.

Knight, Gladys B. "Sons of Union Veterans of the Civil War: Brief History of the Grand Army of the Republic." http://suvcw.org/gar.htm.

Laderman, Gary. *The Sacred Remains: American Attitudes toward Death, 1799–1883*. New Haven: Yale University Press, 1996.

Lamphier, Peg A. *Kate Chase and William Sprague: Politics and Gender in a Civil War Marriage.* Lincoln: University of Nebraska Press, 2003.

Land, Mary. "'Bluff' Ben Wade's New England Background." *New England Quarterly* 27, no. 4 (1954): 484–509.

Lee, Alfred E. *The History of the City of Columbus.* 2 vols. Vol. II. Columbus, Ohio: Franklin County Genealogical and Historical Society, 2000.

Leech, Margaret, and Harry J. Brown. *The Garfield Orbit.* New York: Harper & Row, 1978.

Leech, Margaret. *Reveille in Washington 1860–1865.* Time Reading Program, Special Edition ed. New York: Time Incorporated, 1962.

Lepore, Jill. "The Sharpened Quill." *The New Yorker*, October 16, 2006, 168–75.

Lesser, W. Hunter. *Rebels at the Gate.* Naperville, Illinois: Sourcebooks, Inc., 2004.

Levine, Bruce. *Half Slave and Half Free: The Roots of Civil War.* Revised ed. New York: Hill and Wang, 2005.

Liddell Hart, B. H. *Sherman: Soldier, Realist, American.* n.p.: Da Capo Press, 1993.

"Lincoln's Illinois Heritage: A Supplement to *American Heritage* Magazine." New York: American Heritage, 2005.

Livermore, Thomas L. *Numbers & Losses in the Civil War in America: 1861–65, Civil War Centennial Series.* Bloomington, Indiana: Indiana University Press, 1957.

Long, E.B., with Barbara Long. *The Civil War Day by Day: An Almanac 1861–1865.* Garden City, New York: Doubleday, 1971. Reprint, by Da Capo, n.p., n.d.

Loosbrock, Richard D. "Battle of Cold Harbor." In *Encyclopedia of the American Civil War.* edited by David S. Heidler and Jeanne T Heidler. New York: W. W. Norton & Company, 2000.

Lowe, Richard. "Battle on the Levee: The Fight at Milliken's Bend." In *Black Soldiers in Blue.* Edited by John David Smith, 107–35. Chapel Hill: University of North Carolina Press, 2002.

Marcus, Greil. 2006. "The American Dream." In http://www.salon.com/opinion/feature/2006/07/04/american_dream/p... (accessed.

Marszalek, John F. "General and Mrs. William T. Sherman, a Contentious Union." In *Intimate Strategies of the Civil War.* Edited by Carol K. Bleser and Lesley J. Gordon, 138–56. New York: Oxford University Press, 2001.

Mathew, W. M. "Edmund Ruffin and the Demise of the *Farmers' Register.*" *The Virginia Magazine* 94, no. 1 (1986): 5–24.

Mathias, Frank F. "John Randolph's Freedmen: The Thwarting of a Will." *Journal of Southern History* 39, no. 2 (May) (1973): 263–72.

McConnell, Stuart. *Glorious Contentment: The Grand Army of the Republic, 1865–1900.* Chapel Hill: University of North Carolina Press, 1992.

McDonald, JoAnna M. *We Shall Meet Again: The First Battle of Bull Run (Manassas).* n.p.: Oxford University Press, 1999.

McDonough, James Lee. *Stones River—Bloody Winter in Tennessee.* Knoxville: University of Tennessee Press, 1980.

McFeely, William S. *Grant: A Biography.* New York: W. W. Norton & Company, 1981.

McGinty, Brian. "John Charles Fremont." In *Historical Times Illustrated Encyclopedia of the Civil War.* Edited by Patricia L. Faust, 291. New York: Harper & Row, 1986.

McKitrick, Eric L. "Stanton: The Life and Times of Lincoln's Secretary of War [Review]." *Journal of Southern History* 28, no. 3: 368–70.

McMurry, Richard M. *John Bell Hood and the War for Southern Independence.* Lexington: The University Press of Kentucky, 1982.

McMurry, Richard M. *The Fourth Battle of Winchester: Toward a New Civil War Paradigm.* Kent, Ohio: Kent State University Press, 2002.

McPherson, James M. *Battle Cry of Freedom: The Civil War Era*. paperback ed. Oxford, England, and New York: Oxford University Press, 1988.

McWhiney, Grady. "Who Whipped Whom? Confederate Defeat Reexamined." In *Battles Won and Lost: Essays from Civil War History*. Edited by John T. Hubbell, 261–82. Westport, Connecticut,

Meredith, James. "Joseph Hooker." In *Encyclopedia of the American Civil War: A Political, Social, and Military History*. Edited by David S. Heidler and Jeanne T. Heidler, 999–1002. New York: W.W. Norton & Company, 2000.

Mitchell, Betty L. *Edmund Ruffin: A Biography*. Bloomington, Indiana: Indiana University Press, 1981.

Morgan, H. Wayne. *William McKinley and His America*. Syracuse, New York: Syracuse University Press, 1963.

Morgan, John H. "Old Steady: The Role of General James Blair Steedman at the Battle of Chickamauga." *Northwest Ohio Quarterly* XXII, no. 2 (1950): 73–94.

Morison, Samuel Eliot. *The Oxford History of the American People*. New York: Oxford University Press, 1965.

Morris Jr., Roy. *Sheridan: The Life and Wars of General Phil Sheridan*. New York: Crown Publishers, Inc., 1992.

Morrow, Maud E. *Recollections of the Civil War: From a Child's Point of View*. Lockland, Ohio, 1901.

Mulligan, Thomas C. "Lest the Rebels Come to Power: The Life of William Dennison, 1815–1882, Early Ohio Republican." Dissertation, Ohio State University, 1994.

Murdock, Eugene C. *Ohio's Bounty System in the Civil War*, Publications of the Ohio Civil War Centennial Commission. Columbus, Ohio: Ohio State University Press for the Ohio Historical Society, 1963.

———. *One Million Men: The Civil War Draft in the North*. Westport, Connecticut: Greenwood Press Publishers, 1980.

Murrin, John M., Paul E. Johnson, James M. McPherson, Gary Gerstle, Emily S. Rosenberg, and Norman L. Rosenberg. *Liberty, Equality, Power: A History of the American People* [since 1863]. 2 vols. Vol. 2. Fort Worth: Harcourt Brace College Publishers, 1999.

National Park Service. *John Brown's Raid*, National Park Service History Series. Washington, DC: Office of Publications, National Park Service, U.S. Department of the Interior, 1974.

Noe, Kenneth W. *Perryville: This Grand Havoc of Battle*. Lexington: University Press of Kentucky, 2001.

———. "Remembering Perryville: History and Memory at a Civil War Battlefield." In *Popular Culture Association and American Culture Association Conference*. Philadelphia, 2001.

Noyalas, Jonathan A. "False Gibralter at Fisher's Hill." *America's Civil War*, March 2006, 34–40.

Oates, Stephen B. *To Purge This Land with Blood*. 2nd ed. Amherst, Massachusetts: University of Massachusetts Press, 1984.

O'Rourke, P. J. "Why It's Good to Come from Nowhere." In *Good Roots: Writers Reflect on Growing up in Ohio*. Edited by Lisa Watts, 37–45. Athens, Ohio: Ohio University Press, 2007.

Overby, Nick. "Supplying Hell: The Campaign for Atlanta." http://www.qmfound.com/supplying_hell_the_campaign_for_atlanta.htm.

Owens, Kenneth N. *Galena, Grant, and the Fortunes of War*. Dekalb, Illinois: Northern Illinois University, in cooperation with the Galena Historical Society, 1963.

Patterson, Gerard. *Debris of Battle*. Electronic (NetLibrary) ed. Mechanicsburg, Pennsylvania: Stackpole Books, 1997.

Peabody, J. H. "Battle of Chancellorsville." In *G.A.R. War Papers*. Edited by E. R. Monfort, H.

B. Furness and Fred H. Alms. Cincinnati: Fred C. Jones Post, No. 401, n.d.

Peskin, Allan. "James A. Garfield." In *The Reader's Companion to American History*. Edited by Eric Foner and John A. Garraty, 438–39. Boston: Houghton Mifflin, 1991.

Peskin, Allan. *Garfield*. Kent, Ohio: Kent State University Press, 1978.

Pizarro, Judith, Roxane Cohen Silver, and JoAnn Prause. "Physical and Mental Health Costs of Traumatic War Experiences among Civil War Veterans." *Archives of General Psychiatry* 63 (2006): 193–200.

Platt, Carolyn V. ""Three Cheers for the Cracker Line!"" *Timeline*, April–June 2005: 36–49.

Pope, Thomas E. *The Weary Boys: Colonel J. Warren Keifer and the 110th Ohio Volunteer Infantry*. Kent, Ohio: Kent State University Press, 2002.

Power, J. Tracy. *Lee's Miserables: Life in the Army of Northern Virginia from the Wilderness to Appomattox*. Edited by Gary W. Gallagher, *Civil War America*. Chapel Hill: University of North Carolina Press, 1998.

Rafuse, Ethan S. "William McKinley." In *Encyclopedia of the Civil War*. Edited by David S. Heidler and Jeanne T. Heidler, 1,288–9. New York: W. W. Norton & Company, 2000.

Rafuse, Ethan. *A Single Grand Victory: The First Campaign and Battle of Manassas*. Edited by Steven E. Woodworth, *Books on the Civil War Era*. Wilmington, Delaware: Scholarly Resources Inc., 2002.

Rawley, James A. *Turning Points of the Civil War*. Lincoln: University of Nebraska Press, 1966.

Renehan Jr., Edward J. *The Secret Six*. New York: Crown Publishers, Inc., 1995.

Reynolds, David S. *John Brown, Abolitionist*. New York: Alfred A. Knopf, 2005.

Rhea, Gordon C. "'Butcher Grant'" And the Overland Campaign." *North & South*, November 2000: 44–55.

Richter, Conrad. *The Trees*. New York: Alfred A. Knopf, 1940.

Roberts, Russell. "Governor McClellan: Deja Vu All over Again?" *Civil War Times*, May 2006: 44–50.

Roberts, Sharon. "Sanitary Commission Quilt Stories." http://www.shasta.com/suesgoodco/newcivilians/articles/roberts1.htm, 2004.

Roseboom, Eugene H. *The Civil War Era*. Edited by Carl Wittke. 6 vols. Vol. 4, *The History of the State of Ohio*. Columbus, Ohio: Ohio State Archaeological and Historical Society, 1944.

Roseboom, Eugene H., and Francis P. Weisenburger. *A History of Ohio*. Columbus, Ohio: Ohio Historical Society, 1953.

Rule, D. H. "Sultana: The Case for Sabotage." *North & South*. December 2001: 76–87.

Ryan, Daniel J. *Lincoln and Ohio*. Columbus, Ohio: Ohio State Archaeological and Historical Society, 1923.

Sanborn, F. B. "The Virginia Campaign of John Brown, II." *The Atlantic Monthly*, February 1875: 704–21.

Schultz, Duane. *The Most Glorious Fourth: Vicksburg and Gettysburg, July 4th, 1863*. New York: W. W. Norton & Company, 2002.

Schultz, Jane E. "The Inhospitable Hospital: Gender and Professionalism in Civil War Medicine." *Journal of Women in Culture and Society* 17, no. 2 (1992): 363–92.

Sears, Stephen W. *George B. McClellan, the Young Napoleon*. New York: Ticknor & Fields, 1988.

———. *Landscape Turned Red: The Battle of Antietam*. Boston: Houghton Mifflin, 1983.

Seitz, Don C. *Artemus Ward (Charles Farrar Browne): A Biography and Bibliography*. New York: Harper & Brothers, 1919.

Shanks, William F. G. *Personal Recollections of Distinguished Generals*. New York: Harper & Brothers Publishers, 1866.

Sheridan, Philip H. *Personal Memoirs of P. H. Sheridan, General United States Army*. 2 vols.

Vol. I. New York: Charles L. Webster & Company, 1888.

Siebert, Wilbur H. *The Underground Railroad from Slavery to Freedom*. Gloucester, Massachusetts: Peter Smith, 1968.

Siebert, Wilbur Henry. *The Mysteries of Ohio's Underground Railroads*. Columbus, Ohio: Long's College Book Company, 1951.

Simpson, Brooks D. *Ulysses S. Grant: Triumph over Adversity, 1822–1865*. Boston: Houghton Mifflin Company, 2000.

Sinha, Manisha. *The Counterrevolution of Slavery: Politics and Ideology in Antebellum South Carolina*. Chapel Hill: University of North Carolina Press, 2000.

Smith, Jean Edward. *Grant*. New York: Simon & Schuster, 2001.

Sowash, Rick. *Heroes of Ohio: 23 True Tales of Courage and Character*. Bowling Green, Ohio: Gabriel's Horn Publishing Company, 1998.

Stackpole, Edward J. *They Met at Gettysburg*. Harrisburg, Pennsylvania: Stackpole Books, 1986. Reprint, 1986.

"Statistical Summary [of] America's Major Wars." http://www.cwc.lsu.edu/cwc/other/stats/warcost.htm: United States Civil War Center [Louisiana State University].

Switzer, Charles I., ed. "The MacGowan Sisters: Early-Twentieth-Century Popular Writers." *Journal of Popular Culture* 34, no. Summer (2000): 85–103.

Sword, Wiley. *The Confederacy's Last Hurrah: Spring Hill, Franklin, and Nashville*. paperback ed. n.p.: University Press of Kansas, 1993.

Tap, Bruce. "Fort Pillow Massacre." In *Encyclopedia of the American Civil War*. Edited by David S. Heidler and Jeanne T. Heidler, 746–8. New York: W.W. Norton, 2000.

Terzian, Barbara A. "Frances Dana Gage and Northern Women's Reform Activities in the Nineteenth Century." In *Builders of Ohio: A Biographical History*. Edited by Warren Van Tine and Michael Pierce, 108–20. Columbus, Ohio: Ohio State University Press, 2003.

Thackery, David T. *A Light and Uncertain Hold: A History of the Sixty-Sixth Ohio Volunteer Infantry*. Kent, Ohio: Kent State University Press, 1999.

Thomas, Emory M. *The Confederacy as a Revolutionary Experience*. Englewood Cliffs, New Jersey: Prentice-Hall, Inc., 1971.

Tidball, Eugene C. "Duty, Honor, Country, and Skullduggery: Lincoln's Secretary of War Meddles at West Point." *Civil War History* 45, no. 1.

Tidball, Eugene C. *"No Disgrace to My Country."* Kent, Ohio: Kent State University Press, 2002.

Toledo, Gregory. *The Hanging of Old Brown*. Westport, Connecticut: Praeger, 2002.

Trefousse, Hans L. "The Motivation of a Radical Republican." *Ohio History* 73: 63–74.

Trudeau, Noah Andre. *The Last Citadel: Petersburg, Virginia, June 1864—April 1865*. Boston: Little, Brown and Company, 1991.

Tucker, Glenn. *The Battle of Chickamauga*. n.p.: Eastern Acorn Press, 1969.

Tucker, Louis Leonard. *Cincinnati During the Civil War*, Publications of the Ohio Civil War Centennial Commission. Columbus, Ohio: Ohio State University Press, 1962.

United States Civil War Centennial Commission. *The United States on the Eve of the Civil War as Described in the 1860 Census*: U.S. Civil War Centennial Commission, 1963.

United States Civil War Center [Louisiana State University]. "Statistical Summary [of] America's Major Wars." http://www.cwc.lsu.edu/cwc/other/stats/warcost.htm.

Vonada, Damaine, ed. *The Ohio Almanac*. 1992/93 ed. Wilmington, Ohio: Orange Frazer Press, 1992.

Wagner, Margaret E., Gary W. Gallagher, and Paul Finkelman, eds. *The Library of Congress Civil War Desk Reference*. New York: Simon & Schuster, 2002.

Walker, Dale L. *Mary Edwards Walker: Above and Beyond*. New York: Forge: Tom Doherty

Associates, 2005.

Walther, Eric H. *The Fire-Eaters*. Baton Rouge: Louisiana State University Press, 1992.

Wanatick, Mary Ann Steedman. "Major General James Blair Steedman." Thesis, University of Toledo, 1988.

Warner, Liberty, and William Barber. "Liberty Warner Papers." In *Center for Archival Collections*. Bowling Green, Ohio: Bowling Green State University, 1871–3.

Washington, Versalle F. *Eagles on Their Buttons: A Black Infantry Regiment in the Civil War*. Edited by Herman Hattaway and Jon Wakelyn, *Shades of Blue and Gray Series*. Columbia: University of Missouri Press, 1999.

Way, Thomas N. *In the Jaws of Death, or Eighteen Months a Prisoner of War in Southern Prisons*. Salem, Ohio: Journal Steam Print, 1872.

Weber, Sandra. "Living Legacies of Harpers Ferry." *Civil War Times*. February 2005: 42–8.

Wesley, Charles H. *Ohio Negroes in the Civil War, Publications of the Ohio Civil War Commission*. Columbus, Ohio: Ohio State University Press for the Ohio Historical Society, 1962.

Wheeler, Kenneth H. "Local Autonomy and Civil War Draft Resistance: Holmes County, Ohio." *Civil War History* 40, no. 2 (1999): 147–59.

Wheeler, Richard. *Witness to Gettysburg*. New York: Harper & Row, 1987.

Whitman, Walt. "Specimen Days 100. The Million Dead, Too, Summ'd Up." http://www.bartleby.com/229/1100.html, 1892.

Wilentz, Sean. *The Rise of American Democracy: Jefferson to Lincoln*. New York: W. W. Norton & Company, 2005.

Williams, Ammi. "Ammi Williams Letters to Henry Williams." In *Hayes Presidential Center Civil War Collection LH-Misc. Mss.* Fremont, Ohio, 1862.

Williams, Stephen F. "The Buckeye from Missouri." http://www.48ovvi.org/oh48buckeye.htm.

Williams, T. Harry. *Hayes of the Twenty-Third: The Civil War Volunteer Officer*. New York: Alfred A. Knopf, 1965.

———. *Lincoln and His Generals*. New York: Alfred A. Knopf, 1952.

Wilson, Douglas L. *Lincoln's Sword: The Presidency and the Power of Words*. New York: Alfred A. Knopf, 2006.

Wish, Harvey. "Artemus Ward and Petroleum Nasby." In *For the Union: Ohio Leaders in the Civil War*. Edited by Kenneth W. Wheeler. Columbus, Ohio: Ohio State University Press, 1968.

Wittenberg, Eric J. *Little Phil: A Reassessment of the Civil War Leadership of Gen. Philip H. Sheridan*. Washington, DC: Brassey's, Inc., 2002.

Woldman, Albert A. "Book Review: Lincoln and His Generals." *Ohio History* 61, no. 3 (1952): 317–19.

Wood, Tim. "The Tarnished Soldier: New Book Details Heroism, Scandal of Nickerson Ancestor." *Cape Cod Chronicle*, January 23, 2003.

Woodworth, Steven E. *Six Armies in Tennessee: The Chickamauga and Chattanooga Campaigns*. Lincoln: University of Nebraska Press, 1998.

Woodworth, Steven E., et al., "Who Were the Top Ten Generals?" *North & South* [magazine], May 2003: 12–22.

TO LEARN MORE

You may want to read more about the Civil War and its fascinating people, visit places described in this book, correct or challenge the author, or share something you know. For up-to-date help with any of these, go to the author's Web site. You'll also find information on buying the book or having the author speak to your group. I'm looking forward to hearing from you.

—*James Bissland*

For more information or to contact the author, go to:
www.BloodTearsandGlory.com
Or: *www.orangefrazer.com/btg*
Or: *www.orangefrazer.com*

James H. Bissland, a New Englander who has lived in Ohio since 1976, has spent most of a lifetime reading and researching American history. He earned a bachelor's degree in history from Cornell University and master's in American history from the University of Massachusetts. He received a Ph.D. in mass communication studies from the University of Iowa after course work there and at Brown University that included work in history. He is the author, co-author, or editor of several books, including *Bountiful Ohio: Good Food and Stories from Where the Heartland Begins* and *Long River Winding: Life, Love, and Death Along the Connecticut.*